Expectations and Aspirations

A New Framework for Education in the Middle East and North Africa

Safaa El Tayeb El-Kogali
and Caroline Krafft
Editors

© 2020 International Bank for Reconstruction and Development / The World Bank
1818 H Street NW, Washington, DC 20433
Telephone: 202-473-1000; Internet: www.worldbank.org

Some rights reserved
1 2 3 4   22 21 20 19

This work is a product of the staff of The World Bank with external contributions. The findings, interpretations, and conclusions expressed in this work do not necessarily reflect the views of The World Bank, its Board of Executive Directors, or the governments they represent. The World Bank does not guarantee the accuracy of the data included in this work. The boundaries, colors, denominations, and other information shown on any map in this work do not imply any judgment on the part of The World Bank concerning the legal status of any territory or the endorsement or acceptance of such boundaries.

Nothing herein shall constitute or be considered to be a limitation upon or waiver of the privileges and immunities of The World Bank, all of which are specifically reserved.

Rights and Permissions

This work is available under the Creative Commons Attribution 3.0 IGO license (CC BY 3.0 IGO) http://creativecommons.org/licenses/by/3.0/igo. Under the Creative Commons Attribution license, you are free to copy, distribute, transmit, and adapt this work, including for commercial purposes, under the following conditions:

Attribution—Please cite the work as follows: El-Kogali, Safaa El Tayeb, and Caroline Krafft, eds. 2020. *Expectations and Aspirations: A New Framework for Education in the Middle East and North Africa*. Washington, DC: World Bank. doi:10.1596/978-1-4648-1234-7. License: Creative Commons Attribution CC BY 3.0 IGO

Translations—If you create a translation of this work, please add the following disclaimer along with the attribution: *This translation was not created by The World Bank and should not be considered an official World Bank translation. The World Bank shall not be liable for any content or error in this translation.*

Adaptations—If you create an adaptation of this work, please add the following disclaimer along with the attribution: *This is an adaptation of an original work by The World Bank. Views and opinions expressed in the adaptation are the sole responsibility of the author or authors of the adaptation and are not endorsed by The World Bank.*

Third-party content—The World Bank does not necessarily own each component of the content contained within the work. The World Bank therefore does not warrant that the use of any third-party-owned individual component or part contained in the work will not infringe on the rights of those third parties. The risk of claims resulting from such infringement rests solely with you. If you wish to re-use a component of the work, it is your responsibility to determine whether permission is needed for that re-use and to obtain permission from the copyright owner. Examples of components can include, but are not limited to, tables, figures, or images.

All queries on rights and licenses should be addressed to World Bank Publications, The World Bank Group, 1818 H Street NW, Washington, DC 20433, USA; e-mail: pubrights@worldbank.org.

ISBN (paper): 978-1-4648-1234-7
ISBN (electronic): 978-1-4648-1235-4
DOI: 10.1596/978-1-4648-1234-7

Cover design: Concept by Safaa El Tayeb El-Kogali; calligraphy by Aya Krisht. The design consists of three words in Arabic: "Knowledge, education, learning." Background image by Kjpargeter/Freepik.com. Used with permission; further permission required for reuse.

Interior image credits: The following images are by individual artists from thenounproject.com: Figure O.1/Figure 2.1: "Rope" by Pedro Baños Cancer. Figure O.2/Figure 2.2: "Diploma" by Ben Davis; "Brain" by Max Hancock. Figure O.7/Figure 4.1: "Handshake" by Gregor Cresnar; "Climbing" by IYIKON; "Man Pushing Big Ball" by Gan Khoon Lay; "Pull" by Pavel, N. Figure O.17/Figure 4.2: "Brain" by Max Hancock. Figure O.21/Figure 4.4: "Handshake" by Gregor Cresnar; "People" by Anastasia Latysheva; "Idea" by Ben Markoch. Figure 3.1: "Immigration" by Yosef. Figure 3.4: "Manual Barrier" by ProSymbols, US; "Teacher" by Arif Fajar Yulianto; "Resilience" by Attilio Baghino; "Student" by Doub.co.

Library of Congress Cataloging-in-Publication Data has been requested.

Contents

Editors' Note . . . . *xiii*

Acknowledgments . . . . *xv*

About the Editors and Authors . . . . *xvii*

Abbreviations . . . . *xix*

Overview 1
  Safaa El Tayeb El-Kogali

  Education has large untapped potential for the Middle East and North Africa 1
  Much has changed in MENA—and the world—but education in MENA remains stuck 2
  Four tensions are holding back education in MENA 4
  A new framework is needed to realize education's potential in MENA 12
  Push for learning 13
  Pull for skills 37
  Recognize that context matters for learning and skills 42
  A new education pact 46
  Unleashing the potential of education is attainable 52
  Notes 53
  References 53

1. A New Lens on Education in MENA 67
  Igor Kheyfets, Elisabeth Sedmik, Mohammed Audah, Laura Gregory, and Caroline Krafft

  MENA's economic and social challenges require a renewed focus on human
    capital development 67
  Learning and skills are essential to build human capital 73
  Notes 81
  References 82

2. **Behaviors, Norms, and the Political Economy of Education in MENA** 85
   Safaa El Tayeb El-Kogali

   Education is an inherently political and social process 85
   Four tensions are holding back education in MENA...............................86
   Recognizing and addressing these constraints are critical for education in MENA 93
   Notes 93
   References 93

3. **Securing Learning for Children in Conflict and Crisis**.........................97
   Noah Yarrow and Maja Capek

   Remove barriers to education access 98
   Improve the learning experience of displaced children 107
   Strengthen resilience at the systems level 108
   Rethink external funding mechanisms for education sectors in crisis..............111
   Notes 112
   References 113

4. **Adopting a New Framework for Education in MENA** 121
   Safaa El Tayeb El-Kogali and Caroline Krafft

   Push for learning: Focus on learning, not just on schooling 121
   Pull for skills: Complementary reforms are needed for education to achieve its potential....122
   A new education pact: Create a unified vision for education.....................125
   Note 129
   References 129

5. **Establishing a Foundation for Lifelong Learning** 131
   Igor Kheyfets and Samira Nikaein Towfighian

   Intervene early for biggest impact 131
   Universalize preschool education...132
   Build strong foundational skills in the early years..............................138
   Notes 141
   References 141

6. **Ensuring Inclusive and Equitable Learning** 143
   Laura Gregory and May Bend

   Remove barriers to access 143
   Recognize and address learning gaps by supporting the lowest-performing
     students and schools 146
   Improve the quality of boys' education and address MENA's gender paradox 148
   Increase resources for special needs to reduce inequality.......................151
   Notes 153
   References 153

Spotlight 1: Choosing a Language of Instruction.................................155
   May Bend and Laura Gregory

   Modern standard Arabic 155
   Multiple local languages 156
   Instruction in a foreign language...156

    Begin in the child's mother tongue...157
    Increase research into Arabic-language learning...................................158
    Improve foreign language instruction at all levels..................................158
    References...159

7. Modernizing Curricula, Instruction, and Assessment to Improve Learning......161
Laura Gregory and May Bend

    Modernize curricula to meet students' needs......................................161
    Encourage instructional practices that maximize children's potential.............168
    Provide classroom environments conducive to learning...........................173
    Use assessment methods to adapt instruction and promote higher-order skills.....176
    Notes...178
    References..179

Spotlight 2: Measuring Learning..183
Laura Gregory and Elisabeth Sedmik

    National and international large-scale student assessments monitor education
        system progress...183
    Public examinations can catalyze reform but also can create perverse incentives.....186
    Noncognitive and socioemotional skills should be assessed alongside cognitive skills.....190
    Notes..190
    References..190

8. Leveraging Education Technology..193
Mariam Nusrat Adil, Venkatesh Sundararaman, and May Bend

    Digital technology is altering all facets of life in MENA............................194
    Innovations in EdTech are disrupting the education sector......................195
    Providing access to technology is not enough....................................198
    Blended learning approaches have yielded promising results....................199
    Online courses have grown rapidly in popularity..................................199
    Technology-based "nudges" can promote behavioral change in education.....201
    Online textbooks can facilitate access to information.............................201
    Smart classrooms are the classrooms of the future...............................202
    Navigating the technological landscape can be tricky............................203
    Notes..203
    References..204

9. Empowering Teachers to Lead the Way to Better Student Learning...........207
Lianqin Wang, Bob Prouty, Manal Bakur N Quota, and Angela Demas

    Recruit the best and prepare them to be effective teachers......................207
    Strengthen continuous professional support to teachers........................211
    Use teacher assessment to strengthen support and accountability...............217
    Provide meaningful incentives to motivate and reward teachers................218
    Notes..220
    References..221

10. Developing Effective School Leadership...225
Lianqin Wang, Angela Demas, Manal Bakur N Quota, and Bob Prouty

    Transform the role of the school principal from administrator to instructional leader.....225

Modernize criteria and processes to select new school leaders 228
Empower school leaders with professional development and rewarding career pathways 229
Provide school leaders with more authority to support teaching and learning 231
References 232

11. Prioritizing Investments to Promote Learning and Skills 235
Igor Kheyfets and Mohammed Audah

Invest sufficient public resources in education 235
Allocate resources toward learning 239
Manage the teacher workforce efficiently 243
Notes 248
References 249

Spotlight 3: Linking Budget Management to Learning 251
Igor Kheyfets

Link budgets to strategic national and education priorities 251
Budget for education with an explicit focus on learning 251
Improve budget execution rates to smooth service delivery 252
Notes 253
References 253

12. Strengthening Skills by Linking Education to the Labor Market 255
Almedina Music and Caroline Krafft

Workplace training can provide students with job-relevant skills 255
Companies in MENA report difficulties in finding an adequately skilled workforce 258
Improving labor market information flows can help both students and employers 259
Notes 260
References 261

13. Rethinking Tertiary Education: High-Level Skills and Research 263
Jamil Salmi

Tertiary education needs to confer skills relevant to the labor market and to focus
  on high-quality research 263
Attracting the best, investing adequate resources, and operating under enabling
  governance systems are key determinants of university performance 264
Rethinking tertiary education: The way forward 265
Notes 269
References 269

14. Strengthening Accountability for Better Learning Outcomes 271
Lianqin Wang, Manal Bakur N Quota, Angela Demas, and Bob Prouty

Establish accountability mechanisms within education systems 271
Involve communities and parents in accountability systems 278
Use media and technology to support accountability systems 282
Notes 283
References 283

15. Conclusion 287
Safaa El Tayeb El-Kogali and Caroline Krafft

Offering lessons for effective education reform 287
Unleashing the potential of education 290
References 290

Appendix: Overview of MENA Policy Recommendations 293

Boxes

O.1	Conflict has taken a large toll on education in MENA 4
O.2	*World Development Report 2018: Learning to Realize Education's Promise* 13
O.3	Prioritizing early childhood education in the United Arab Emirates 18
O.4	Attracting the best students to teaching depends on the right policies and programs 20
O.5	School principals also must act as instructional leaders 22
O.6	Teaching at the right level benefits students 25
O.7	Improving foreign language instruction is important 27
O.8	Conflict in MENA is depriving many children of education 30
O.9	MENA's gender paradox presents a dual challenge for human capital 33
O.10	EdTech offers opportunities to leapfrog learning 36
O.11	Signaling in education is communicating about skills 38
O.12	Reforming vocational education 42
O.13	Finland and the Republic of Korea rely on different successful education models ... 43
O.14	In Rwanda, education has played a role in building peace 46
O.15	Peru has found success in aligning interests 48
O.16	Egypt's education sector uses technology to ensure accountability 50
1.1	Migration affects education systems in MENA through three key channels 71
1.2	Technological change is driving the shift in labor market demand for skills ... 72
1.3	Income mobility lags behind educational mobility in MENA 77
3.1	Displaced within their countries' borders: IDPs' struggle to access education ... 100
3.2	Informing the global response to forced displacement: The need for better data ... 101
3.3	Great expectations, limited impact: EdTech for refugees 103
3.4	Learning from international experience: The European Qualifications Passport for Refugees 106
3.5	Sharing responsibility for the forcibly displaced: The Global Compact on Refugees ... 110
4.1	Signaling in education is communicating about skills 124
4.2	Peru has found success in aligning interests 127
5.1	Universalizing access to preprimary education in Argentina and Algeria 135
5.2	Prioritizing early childhood education in the United Arab Emirates 135
5.3	Combatting inequality through ECE: An example from Boston 137
5.4	Unifying ECE curriculum in the national core curriculum of New Zealand and Finland 139
5.5	Screening for literacy and numeracy development in England 140
6.1	Early grade literacy and numeracy interventions in Jordan have had different impacts on girls and boys 150

6.2	Negative attitudes toward disability and special education exist in MENA	152
7.1	Competency-based learning	162
7.2	Balancing repetition and high-level problem solving	165
7.3	Relevance in vocational education	167
7.4	Moving from poor to fair: The role of scripted lessons in structured pedagogy	172
7.5	Using peer instruction to assess, challenge, and engage in science, technology, engineering, and mathematics lessons	177
S2.1	Malaysia faced various challenges in introducing task-based assessment	189
8.1	Introducing disruptive technology in the classroom: From the blackboard to ICTs	194
9.1	Selection of initial teacher education candidates in Finland	208
9.2	Teacher licensing in the United States	210
9.3	Teaching-research groups in Shanghai	216
9.4	Professional development experiences in MENA	217
10.1	Distributed and collaborative school leadership in Singapore	227
10.2	Training school principals to become effective instructional leaders in New Zealand	228
10.3	School principals' career ladders in Shanghai	231
11.1	Public spending and expansion of access to education in Saudi Arabia	236
11.2	Growing public investment in early learning: The cases of Finland and Sweden	241
11.3	Capital budgeting in education: The use of national infrastructure plans	242
11.4	Class size policies across the OECD	245
13.1	The MENA University Governance Screening Card	269
14.1	Systems Approach for Better Education Results	272
14.2	Jordan's education reform: Evidence-supported accountability	274
14.3	Boston Public Schools' support systems	276
14.4	Social and behavior change communications	279
14.5	Using school report cards to promote transparency and accountability	280
14.6	Using technology in Egypt's education sector to ensure accountability	282
15.1	Finland and the Republic of Korea rely on different successful education models	288

Figures

O.1	Four tensions are holding back education in MENA	5
O.2	MENA is stuck in a credentialist equilibrium	6
O.3	MENA students are more likely to be asked to memorize	7
O.4	Obedience plays a central role in children's education in MENA	8
O.5	Teachers in MENA have less autonomy than teachers in OECD countries	10
O.6	Substantial time is devoted to religious education in MENA	11
O.7	"Push, pull, and pact" offers a new framework for education in MENA	12
O.8	What matters for growth is skills	13
O.9	When adjusted for learning, the number of years of effective schooling in MENA drops substantially	14
O.10	Preprimary enrollments are lower in MENA than in many other regions	17
O.11	Large differences in preprimary enrollment ratios are found across MENA	17
O.12	The required working hours for teachers in MENA are well below those in top-performing countries	23
O.13	Teacher absenteeism is prevalent throughout MENA	24
O.14	MENA has the biggest gaps in student achievement between top and bottom performers	31
O.15	MENA has the largest gender gaps in test scores	32

O.16	Computers are available in MENA's schools, although coverage varies considerably	35
O.17	MENA needs a skills equilibrium	37
O.18	A personal connection is critical to securing work in MENA	39
O.19	School principals in MENA have less authority than those in OECD countries	40
O.20	Tolerance is associated with education, but intolerance is high even among the educated in MENA	45
O.21	Learning is a collective responsibility, and everyone is accountable	49
BO.16.1	Technology can shape accountability relationships	50
1.1	Youth unemployment rates are higher than overall unemployment rates across MENA	68
1.2	Youth unemployment is highest among the most educated in many MENA economies	69
1.3	Rates of return to education are lower in MENA than in other regions	71
1.4	Rates of return to education in MENA are below the global average	73
1.5	Rapid population growth in MENA has been accompanied by large increases in school enrollment	75
1.6	What matters for growth is skills	76
1.7	When adjusted for learning, the number of years of effective schooling in MENA drops substantially	78
1.8	MENA countries have some of the lowest results on international student assessments	79
1.9	Achievement gaps in MENA tend to be greater for primary school than for secondary school	81
1.10	Many children in MENA have not reached basic proficiency by age 15	81
2.1	Four tensions are holding back education in MENA	86
2.2	MENA is stuck in a credentialist equilibrium	87
2.3	MENA students are more likely to be asked to memorize	89
2.4	Obedience plays a central role in children's education in MENA	90
3.1	A large share of the world's IDPs and refugees live in MENA	98
3.2	Syrian refugees' enrollment in education differs across MENA	99
3.3	Refugees' enrollment drops with age	100
3.4	Policy approaches to deliver on displaced children's right to education	112
4.1	"Push, pull, and pact" offers a new framework for education in MENA	122
4.2	MENA needs a skills equilibrium	123
4.3	A personal connection is critical to securing work in MENA	125
4.4	Learning is a collective responsibility, and everyone is accountable	128
5.1	Before they start school, many children are not developmentally on track	133
5.2	Preprimary enrollments are lower in MENA than in many other regions	134
5.3	Large differences in preprimary enrollment ratios are found across MENA	134
5.4	In West Bank and Gaza, opportunities for early childhood education are more likely for those from advantaged backgrounds	136
B5.3.1	Low-income children benefit relatively more than do middle- and high-income children from early childhood education	137
5.5	Many children in MENA cannot read a single word after two or three years of schooling	140
6.1	In MENA, household wealth disparities translate into large enrollment gaps	144
6.2	In MENA, socioeconomic differences translate into persistent learning gaps	146
6.3	MENA has the biggest gaps in student achievement between top and bottom performers	147
6.4	Gender gaps in MENA start early	149
6.5	MENA has the largest gender gaps in test scores	149

6.6	Female labor force participation is low in MENA	151
7.1	Learning is a complex process that involves multiple actors and factors	162
7.2	MENA students are more likely to be asked to memorize	163
7.3	Several MENA countries do not consistently challenge students beyond the instruction	164
7.4	Substantial time is devoted to religious education in MENA	165
7.5	Rote memorization and teacher-centered practices prevail in most MENA countries	169
7.6	Some MENA countries rely heavily on textbooks	172
7.7	Inadequacy of mathematics or science materials affects instruction for many students across MENA	176
8.1	Computers are available in MENA schools, although coverage varies considerably	197
8.2	Students in MENA rarely use computers in math or science classes	197
8.3	Public support for EdTech reform is strong in MENA	198
8.4	Most people in MENA approve of ICT use in the classroom	198
9.1	Some MENA countries provide insufficient professional development opportunities for teachers	212
9.2	In MENA, the number of teachers with appropriate subject knowledge may be insufficient	213
9.3	Teachers in MENA often employ traditional teaching methods	214
9.4	Teachers in MENA have less autonomy than teachers in OECD countries	220
10.1	Schools in MENA that emphasize academic success have better student learning	226
10.2	On average, school principals in MENA have lower education levels than principals elsewhere	229
10.3	School principals in MENA have less authority than those in OECD countries	232
B11.1.1	Saudi Arabia rapidly expanded school enrollments	236
11.1	Public spending on education in MENA grew steadily to 2000, then declined	237
11.2	Large variations exist in public spending on education across MENA	238
11.3	High private spending on education is common in MENA	239
11.4	Public investments in education in MENA disproportionately focus on tertiary education	239
11.5	Large differences in preprimary enrollment ratios are found across MENA	240
11.6	Large capital budgets reflect the demographic needs of many MENA economies	241
11.7	A wage bill's high share can crowd out other important education spending in MENA	242
11.8	Class size varies across MENA, with the Arab Republic of Egypt and Morocco having among the largest classes	243
11.9	Student-teacher ratios vary widely across MENA	244
11.10	Students across MENA face shortages of qualified mathematics and science teachers	246
11.11	The required working hours for teachers in MENA are well below those in top-performing countries	246
11.12	Teacher absenteeism is prevalent throughout MENA	247
12.1	Only a quarter of workers in Egypt and Tunisia acquired their technical skills through regular schooling	257
12.2	Firms in MENA vary in whether they face an inadequately educated workforce	258
12.3	Firms in MENA have below-average rates of formal training	259
13.1	Four steps can be taken toward successful tertiary education reform in MENA	265
14.1	Many MENA countries have developed school monitoring mechanisms	273
14.2	Few children in MENA benefit from sufficient literacy activities at home	282

Tables

O.1	MENA countries have some of the lowest results on international student assessments	15
O.2	Participation in national and international student assessments has surged in MENA since 2007	28
O.3	MENA's student achievement gaps have both narrowed and widened	32
1.1	Among regions, MENA has the lowest share of human capital as a percentage of total wealth	73
1.2	Most MENA economies have shares of human capital that are below the world average	74
1.3	MENA countries have some of the lowest results on international student assessments	80
3.1	Total population, IDPs, and refugees in the world and in MENA	99
6.1	MENA's student achievement gaps have both narrowed and widened	148
S2.1	Participation in national and international student assessments has surged in MENA since 2007	185
9.1	MENA countries are implementing a variety of collaborative approaches in teacher professional development	216
9.2	Many MENA economies have systems in place to monitor teacher performance	218
11.1	Teacher absenteeism affects teaching time in Morocco	247
11.2	A lack of key educational inputs affects many students in Morocco	248
S3.1	United Arab Emirates Vision 2021 lays out national key performance indicators for the education sector	252
14.1	Most decisions on education policy and inputs are made at the central level in MENA	277
A.1	Overview of MENA policy recommendations	293

Editors' Note

For decades, the Middle East and North Africa (MENA) region has made large investments in education and achieved impressive growth in enrollment rates and gender parity at almost all education levels. Despite these investments, the quality of education across the region has remained low. This begs a series of questions: Why has MENA not been able to realize the potential of education? How has the region, whose educational excellence over five centuries drove innovation in science and social development, become one of the worst performers in educational outcomes today? And why has the region not been able to improve despite substantial investments and reforms over the last five decades? These questions guided our research. Beyond the diagnosis of MENA's challenges, we focused on looking for solutions to emerge from this impasse and how MENA countries can unleash the potential of their human capital to create prosperous and peaceful societies.

The last such in-depth study of education in MENA was undertaken in 2008 (World Bank 2008). The region has experienced substantial economic and political challenges since then and created new opportunities for education to transform. The global research on what works in education has expanded vastly and been updated as well, particularly regarding what works to ensure learning—not simply schooling. This new base of knowledge provides MENA countries with an opportunity to learn from each other's experiences and other global examples.

To answer these questions, the research team studied the current socioeconomic context of the region and analyzed numerous data sets at the country and regional levels. In addition to the usual economic and technical analysis, we introduced a political economy lens that defined a set of tensions that are holding back the potential of education in MENA. Using regional and international experience and examples, the study proposes a new framework to unleash this potential. The research was conducted alongside the *World Development Report 2018: Learning to Realize Education's Promise* (World Bank 2018). Our regional findings and recommendations are aligned with the global report: calling for a concerted push for learning (not just schooling), a stronger pull for skills (from the labor market), and a new pact for education where actors align their interests to make the education system work for learners.

Government officials are the primary audience for this book because they have to make challenging decisions about how best to invest to ensure effective, lifelong learning. These officials are not only in the education sector but also in other, related sectors, such as finance and social protection. We hope that this book also will serve as a helpful reference for all development practitioners who are working in MENA and on education issues in the region and elsewhere in the world. Researchers can use the framework to dig deeper into the various tensions holding back education and apply it to other regional contexts to understand the political economy dimensions of education.

—*Safaa El Tayeb El-Kogali and Caroline Krafft, editors*

References

World Bank. 2008. *The Road Not Traveled: Education Reform in the Middle East and North Africa.* Washington, DC: World Bank.

———. 2018. *World Development Report 2018: Learning to Realize Education's Promise.* Washington, DC: World Bank.

Acknowledgments

The book is a compilation of chapters written by us and a team of experts composed of Mariam Nusrat Adil, Mohammed Audah, May Bend, Maja Capek, Angela Demas, Laura Gregory, Igor Kheyfets, Almedina Music, Samira Nikaein Towfighian, Bob Prouty, Manal Bakur N Quota, Jamil Salmi, Elisabeth Sedmik, Venkatesh Sundararaman, Lianqin Wang, and Noah Yarrow. We appreciate the guidance provided by World Bank management: Ferid Belhaj (regional vice president); Hafez Ghanem (regional vice president); Shantayanan Devarajan (former senior director); Jaime Saavedra (global director); Rabah Arezki (chief economist); Daniel Lederman (deputy chief economist); Luis Benveniste (regional director); Keiko Miwa (regional director); and Andreas Blom (education global practice manager).

We also acknowledge the contributions made by World Bank colleagues and consultants, including Husein Abdul-Hamid, Fadila Caillaud, Michael Drabble, Jiayue Fan, Kasra Farivari, Katherina Hruskovec Gonzalez, Samira Halabi, Yue-Yi Hwa, Pierre Kamano, Thomas Michael Kaye, Amira Kazem, Lisa Lahalih, Jee Yoon Lee, Juan Manuel Moreno, Harriet Nannyonjo, Shahram Paksima, Karine Pezzani, Samia Sekkarie, Sylvia Solf, Jee Peng Tan, Johanna Tatlow, Simon Thacker, Ayesha Vawda, and Mohamed Yassine. We also appreciate the contributions from St. Catherine University research assistants Kapono Asuncion, Zea Branson, Taylor Flak, Lyndsay Kast, Caitlyn Keo, and Johanna Tatlow.

Various drafts benefited from excellent comments and suggestions by Ragui Assaad, Benu Bidan, Kamel Braham, Michael Crawford, Luis Crouch, Amit Dar, Sameh El-Saharty, Mourad Ezzine, Tazeen Fasih, Deon Filmer, Poonam Gupta, Amer Hasan, Raja Bentaouet Kattan, Xiaoyan Liang, Lili Mottaghi, Halsey Rogers, and Sajjad Shah. We are also grateful for the comments from the World Bank MENA Regional Management Team.

The analysis and framework benefited greatly from feedback received during regional and in-country consultations. We would like to thank H. E. Dr. Omar Razzaz (prime minister and former minister of education of Jordan); H. E. Dr. Tarek Shawki (minister of education of the Arab Republic of Egypt); and H. E. Fadi Yarak (secretary general, Ministry of Education, Lebanon); as well as representatives from governments, academia, nongovernmental organizations, civil society organizations, and international development organizations from across MENA for their valuable feedback.

Our special thanks go to everyone who supported the preparation, publication, dissemination, and communication efforts. They include Elizabeth Forsyth, who edited the report, and Aziz Gokdemir, Jewel McFadden, and Stephen Pazdan, who coordinated the publication process in collaboration with Maja Capek, Emma Etori, and Elisabeth Sedmik from the MENA Education Unit. Aya Krisht developed the cover design. Maha Abdelilah Mahmoud El-Swais, Isabelle Poupaert, and William Stebbins provided guidance and support on communications and dissemination. Elisabeth Mekonnen provided overall administrative support.

The chapters draw on literature and documents by researchers and specialists from across the world and on the authors' own experiences and interactions with many dedicated educators, administrators, policy makers, and students in MENA.

About the Editors and Authors

Editors

Safaa El Tayeb El-Kogali is the Education Manager for Eastern and Southern Africa at the World Bank. Ms. El-Kogali was the Education Manager for the Middle East and North Africa between 2015 and 2019. She is a leading international development expert with more than 20 years of experience in public policy, strategic leadership, management, and research. In addition to holding numerous senior positions at the World Bank, she also served as regional director of the Population Council. Ms. El-Kogali has published and presented widely on human development, education, and poverty. She has an MPhil in development studies from the University of Sussex and a BA in economics from the University of Pennsylvania.

Caroline Krafft is an Assistant Professor of Economics at St. Catherine University, St. Paul, Minnesota. Her research examines issues in development economics, primarily labor, education, health, and inequality in the Middle East and North Africa. Current projects include work on refugees, labor market dynamics, life course transitions, human capital accumulation, and fertility. She received her MA in public policy from the University of Minnesota's Humphrey School of Public Affairs and her PhD from the Department of Applied Economics at the University of Minnesota.

Authors

Mariam Nusrat Adil, Education Specialist, World Bank
Mohammed Audah, Economist, World Bank
May Bend, Consultant, World Bank
Maja Capek, Analyst, World Bank
Angela Demas, Senior Education Specialist, World Bank
Safaa El Tayeb El-Kogali, Education Manager, Eastern and Southern Africa, World Bank
Laura Gregory, Senior Education Specialist, World Bank
Igor Kheyfets, Senior Economist, World Bank
Caroline Krafft, Assistant Professor of Economics, St. Catherine University, St. Paul, MN
Almedina Music, Economist, World Bank
Samira Nikaein Towfighian, Education Specialist, World Bank
Bob Prouty, Consultant Lead Education Specialist, World Bank
Manal Bakur N Quota, Education Specialist, World Bank
Jamil Salmi, Professor of Higher Education Policy, Diego Portales University, Santiago, Chile
Elisabeth Sedmik, Analyst, World Bank
Venkatesh Sundararaman, Lead Economist, World Bank
Lianqin Wang, Lead Education Specialist, World Bank
Noah Yarrow, Senior Education Specialist, World Bank

Abbreviations

ALMP	active labor market policy
ALP	accelerated learning program
CAL	computer-assisted learning
CCT	conditional cash transfer
CLA+	Collegiate Learning Assessment
COCs	conventional online courses
CRRF	Comprehensive Refugee Response Framework
DSAC	district and school assistance center
E4C	Education for Competitiveness
ECCE	early childhood care and education
ECD	early childhood development
ECE	early childhood education
EdTech	education technology
EDUCO	Community Managed Schools Program (El Salvador)
EGMA	Early Grade Mathematics Assessment
EGRA	Early Grade Reading Assessment
EMIS	education management information system
ESCS	economic, social, and cultural status
ESP	education sector plan
GCC	Gulf Cooperation Council
GDP	gross domestic product
GER	gross enrollment ratio
HEART	Healing and Education through the Arts for Children
HLO	harmonized learning outcome

IAEP	International Assessment of Educational Progress
ICT	information and communication technology
IDA	International Development Association
IDP	internally displaced person
IGM	intergenerational mobility
ILO	International Labour Organization
ISCED	International Standard Classification of Education
KPI	key performance indicator
LaNA	Literacy and Numeracy Assessment
LOI	language of instruction
M&E	monitoring and evaluation
MCL	multiclassroom leader
MELQO	Measuring Early Learning Quality and Outcomes
MENA	Middle East and North Africa
MICS	Multiple Indicator Cluster Survey
MOE	Ministry of Education
MOOC	massive open online course
MSA	modern standard Arabic
NCHRD	National Center for Human Resources Development
NDP	national development plan
NEAs	national education accounts
NGO	nongovernmental organization
NIP	national infrastructure plan
OECD	Organisation for Economic Co-operation and Development
PADILEIA	Partnership for Digital Learning and Increased Access
PBB	performance-based budgeting
PIRLS	Progress in International Reading Literacy Study
PISA	Programme for International Student Assessment
pre-K	prekindergarten
SABER	Systems Approach for Better Education Results
SAR	special administrative region
SBCC	social and behavior change communications
SDG	Sustainable Development Goal
SMART	specific, measurable, achievable, relevant, and time-bound
SMC	school management committee
STEM	science, technology, engineering, and mathematics
STR	student-teacher ratio
TALIS	Teaching and Learning International Survey
TIMSS	Trends in International Mathematics and Science Study

TVET	technical and vocational education and training
UGSC	University Governance Screening Card
UIS	UNESCO Institute for Statistics
UN	United Nations
UNESCO	United Nations Educational, Scientific, and Cultural Organization
UNHCR	United Nations High Commissioner for Refugees
UNICEF	United Nations Children's Fund
UNRWA	United Nations Relief and Works Agency
USAID	U.S. Agency for International Development

Overview

Safaa El Tayeb El-Kogali

ان رصيد أي امة متقدمة هو أبناؤها المتعلمون وان تقدم الشعوب والأمم انما يقاس بمستوى التعليم وانتشاره – شيخ زايد ال نهيان

The credit of any developed nation is its educated children, and the advancement of people and nations is measured by the status and reach of their education.

—Shaykh Zayed Alnahyan

Education has large untapped potential for the Middle East and North Africa

Young people in the Middle East and North Africa region (MENA)[1] today have more educational opportunities and have attained higher educational levels than their parents. Among the world's regions, MENA ranks highest in terms of absolute intergenerational education mobility (Narayan et al. 2018). However, its high levels of educational attainment have not translated into greater income opportunities. Intergenerational income mobility in MENA is low. Educational attainment and income mobility are strongly correlated in most other regions and within the world's high-income countries, but not in MENA (Narayan et al. 2018). Families and individuals invest in education in the hopes of benefiting from good work opportunities in the labor market, but in MENA the private returns to education in the labor market are among the lowest in the world (Patrinos 2016). Beyond the labor market, education in MENA is only weakly associated with social outcomes such as civic engagement and participation in community issues, unlike in other regions (Diwan 2016).

MENA also has the lowest share of human capital in total wealth globally (Lange, Wodon, and Carey 2018). The contribution of education to human capital, economic growth, and social outcomes is well documented (Becker 1962; Lochner and Moretti 2004; Milligan, Moretti, and Oreopoulos 2004; Mincer 1974; OECD 2014; Sala-i-Martin, Doppelhofer, and Miller 2004). Education has a large, untapped potential to contribute to the human capital, well-being, and wealth of MENA (Lange, Wodon, and Carey 2018). It has been at the heart of the region's history and civilizations for centuries. In the 20th century, education was central to countries' struggles for independence, to building modern states and economies, and to defining national identities.

MENA has made large investments in education over the last 50 years and has achieved impressive growth in enrollment rates and gender parity at almost all education levels. And yet all MENA countries—regardless of their geography, demography, economy, or society—have not been able to reap the full personal, social, and economic benefits of education. During these same 50 years, the Republic of Korea also invested in its human capital and succeeded in moving from a low-income country in the early 1960s to one of the top 20 economies in the world today. Korea established a world-class education system, and its students consistently rank among the top in international learning assessments. By contrast, MENA students have consistently ranked among the lowest on such assessments.

When asked in a 2017 World Bank MENA Facebook poll whether they thought education improves their chances in the job market in their country, 92 percent of respondents said "No," and one respondent said, "A thousand 'no's."[2] "What is taught in schools and universities has no relationship with work life or reality—time wasted in a failed system," wrote one respondent. "Education in our country is just to get a credential, and one ends up on a couch or in cafes with no work and a lost future for all students," wrote another. Thousands more expressed similar dissatisfaction with education in their countries. The frustration expressed by the Facebook poll respondents is not merely a perception; it is the reality facing millions of young people in MENA today. This can and should change.

Why has MENA not been able to realize the potential of education? How did the region whose educational excellence over five centuries drove innovation in science and social development and the region that catalyzed the European Renaissance and scientific revolution (Overbye 2001) become one of the worst performers in educational outcomes today? And why has the region not been able to improve despite substantial investments over the last five decades? More important, what can MENA countries do to emerge from this impasse and retake their position as leaders in education and innovation? How can they unleash the potential of their human capital to create prosperous and peaceful societies?

MENA countries have an opportunity to realize the untapped potential of education and fulfill the expectations and aspirations of their young citizens and future generations. But some hurdles must be overcome. This report identifies four sets of tensions that are holding back MENA's education potential: (1) credentials and skills; (2) discipline and inquiry; (3) control and autonomy; and (4) tradition and modernity. These tensions are found within countries, societies, communities, and households and are manifested and reinforced in schools and classrooms. Unless they are addressed, no amount of investment in education can reap the full benefits. The report proposes a new framework that calls for a concerted push for learning, a stronger pull for skills, and a new pact for education. Despite challenging regional geopolitics, socioeconomic pressures, and global trends, MENA has the capacity and resources to create education systems that will build its human capital.

Much has changed in MENA— and the world—but education in MENA remains stuck

Today, the 443 million residents of MENA are enduring a period of pronounced hardship. Ongoing threats to peace and economic stability are contributing to challenges across many sectors. Economic growth has remained persistently low in the aftermath of the Arab Spring (World Bank 2015b); youth unemployment rates have risen; and the quality of public services has deteriorated (Brixi, Lust, and Woolcock 2015; World Bank 2013a). Even in relatively stable countries, labor market outcomes for the educated have worsened (El-Araby 2013; Krafft 2017; Rizk 2016; Salehi-Isfahani, Tunali, and

Assaad 2009; Tzannatos, Diwan, and Ahad 2016). Exacerbating these challenges is the substantial downturn in the global oil market, which has placed more pressure on resource-rich countries (IMF 2017) and has created an even more urgent need to push for human capital development across MENA.

Although MENA countries vary substantially in their economic development, as well as in the nature of the social and political issues they face, they share many characteristics and challenges. The Arab countries that form the larger part of MENA share a common language and much of their history and culture. Many countries in the region have parallel education histories, which include some of the earliest universities in the world and substantial historical contributions to human knowledge and development (Abi-Mershed 2010; Rugh 2002). More recently, as a result of similar postindependence trajectories, there has been a substantial overlap in pedagogical methods and labor market issues. And throughout the region, education quality and learning outcomes have faced many of the same challenges.

A decade ago, the World Bank addressed the crisis in education quality in MENA in *The Road Not Traveled: Education Reform in the Middle East and North Africa* (World Bank 2008). It noted that MENA countries had succeeded in engineering an education system focused mainly on inputs, such as building schools, but they had done little to change the incentives and behavior of educators. The report proposed a new road toward education systems built on improving incentives and public accountability, on the one hand, and achieving an equilibrium in the labor market between the supply of educated individuals and labor demand, on the other. MENA countries have indeed embarked on numerous reforms in their education sectors, but with little or no success. In some instances, the reforms have been piecemeal or uncoordinated or have failed to tackle the fundamental issues. In others, they have not been sufficiently funded or communicated to stakeholders. Meanwhile, too often education reforms have paid insufficient attention to how the education sector interacts with other sectors, broader socioeconomic and political trends, and the behavioral norms and interests of various groups.

In the 10 years since *The Road Not Traveled*, much has changed in the region and the world, but MENA's education systems remain stuck, "engineering" to meet the high demand of a large and growing school-age population with the same delivery mechanisms of previous decades. During this decade, MENA countries have spent an average of 4.5 percent of their national income on education, and more than 15 million additional boys and girls have enrolled in schooling at all levels.[3] At the same time, the political economy landscape has changed drastically. From the 2011 Arab Spring arose a public outcry for better basic services and equal opportunities that changed long-standing dictatorships in the Arab Republic of Egypt, Libya, and Tunisia; amended constitutions in Jordan and Morocco; and altered the status quo in almost every county in the region. The Syrian Arab Republic and the Republic of Yemen continue to struggle with civil war (see box O.1), which has generated one of the worst refugee crises of all time. It has inflicted great suffering on millions of refugees across the region and the world and imposed serious constraints on host communities (Brussels Conference 2019; UNHCR 2019a).

The past 10 years have also been marked by remarkable technological advances. At the time of *The Road Not Traveled* report, the iPhone was one year old, Twitter was just taking off, and Facebook users numbered around 145 million globally (Guardian 2014). By 2016, there were 107 mobile subscriptions per 100 persons in MENA countries,[4] and by 2017 there were almost 100 million active social media users (Radcliffe and Lam 2018). Of the 2.1 billion current Facebook users, more than 100 million are in MENA. The social network WhatsApp, which was launched in 2009, has 1.5 billion users globally. Today, more than two-thirds of young Arabs use Facebook and WhatsApp. Furthermore, YouTube, which was three years

Box O.1   **Conflict has taken a large toll on education in MENA**

MENA has been rattled by violent conflict and protracted crises for years, forcing millions of people to leave their homes in search of safety and security. Although MENA is home to just 6 percent of the world's population, it hosts more than a third of the world's refugees and about a quarter of the world's conflict-related internally displaced persons (IDPs).[a] This situation has put great pressure on the host countries' education systems. For example, in 2018–19 Lebanon absorbed almost 213,000 non-Lebanese students in public schools, the majority of whom were accommodated by opening second shifts in 346 public schools across the country (Ministry of Education and Higher Education, Lebanon 2019). Jordan also operates 209 public double-shift schools and provides nonformal education services run jointly by international organizations and the Ministry of Education (Government of Jordan 2018). In addition to schools, host countries face other challenges in providing suitable education services for IDPs. For example, host countries often lack information about the education systems in refugees' countries of origin. Refugees also may not have the requisite documentation, or the receiving countries may not be able to verify the authenticity of their documents (ESU 2017).

At the tertiary level, only about 5 percent of Syrian refugees ages 18–24 in host countries across MENA are enrolled in higher education (European Commission 2018). Because tertiary education is not a priority in emergency assistance programs, funding remains a major roadblock (European Commission 2017; Nakweya 2017).

The education infrastructure and services in conflict countries have been heavily affected. For example, in the 16 cities that suffered heavy fighting during the war in Iraq, only 38 percent of the total school infrastructure remains intact, and 18 percent (190 facilities) was destroyed (World Bank 2018b). Two-thirds of schools in the Republic of Yemen need repairs (UNICEF 2018). In Syria, about one-third of school buildings have been damaged or destroyed, are occupied by parties to the conflict, or are being used to shelter IDPs (Brussels Conference 2017).

a. See IDMC (2019); UNHCR (2019a, 2019b); UNRWA (2019); World Bank, World Development Indicators database.

old in 2008, currently has 1.5 billion users globally, and Saudi Arabia is its biggest market in per capita consumption. Young Saudi Arabians ages 15–24 spend on average 72 minutes a day watching online videos (Radcliffe and Lam 2018). At the same time, the world and the region have seen a sharp increase in EdTech—information and communication technology (ICT) applications aimed at improving education—investments, which reached a record US$9.5 billion in 2017 (Shulman 2018). Khan Academy, which opened its doors in 2008, uses YouTube to provide lessons to millions.

Meanwhile, technological advances, automation, and innovation are increasingly shaping new jobs and changing the nature of work. Although manual manufacturing jobs are being automated, technology has the potential to create new jobs and increase productivity (World Bank 2019). The role of technology as a demand shaper for the future of work is certain, but its role as a delivery catalyst is an opportunity that needs to be leveraged. That will require investment in human capital, education, and new skill sets in MENA.

Although much has changed politically, economically, and socially in MENA over the last decade, their education systems to a large extent have remained the same. Education has the potential to fuel important economic and social contributions, but its power to create change depends not only on its quality but also on complementary economic and social environments and the ability to leverage technology smartly.

Four tensions are holding back education in MENA

The education process consists of a complex set of factors and actors at multiple levels. Factors outside the education system—political, economic, and social—formally and informally interact with the education system and shape its outcomes. Behavioral norms and ideological polarization among governments, interest groups, and citizens can hold countries back from delivering public goods (World Bank 2016b). In MENA, education has been held back by these complex interactions, behavioral norms, and ideological polarization, which can be captured in four sets of tensions: credentials and skills, discipline and inquiry, control and autonomy, and tradition and modernity (see figure O.1).

These tensions are deeply embedded in the region's history, culture, and political economy. They are reflected to varying degrees in all countries in the region, and to a large extent they define social and political relations. They have informed and shaped education policy in MENA countries since independence, and they are at the heart of current national discourses on education reforms. These tensions have held back education systems from evolving and delivering the skills that prepare students for their future. Schools and classrooms are the platforms where these tensions are exercised through curricula, pedagogy, and the norms that define interactions among principals, teachers, parents, and students. These tensions ultimately shape the education outcomes of young people in MENA and affect their lives, as well as the economies and societies in which they live. In an increasingly connected world, the effects of these tensions can reach beyond the region's borders. Unless these tensions are addressed, MENA will not be able to reap the full benefits of education, no matter how much money is invested.

Four features of these tensions are noteworthy. First, they are not mutually exclusive, and they coexist along a continuum. The challenge for countries is to determine where they want to be on the continuum and what balance would be optimal to deliver the desired outcomes. Second, the four tensions overlap in some areas and can reinforce each other. For example, notions of control and autonomy could also be associated with discipline and inquiry or tradition

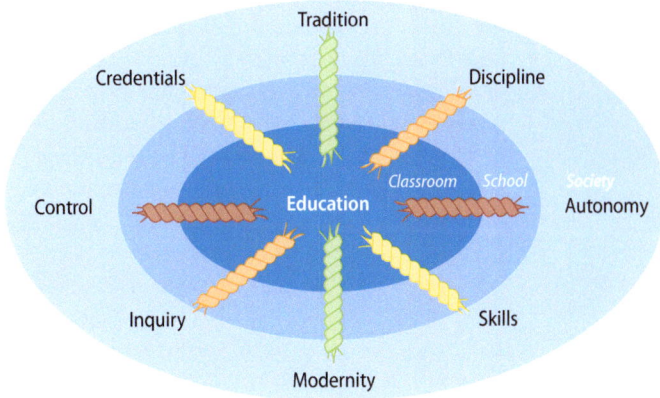

FIGURE O.1 Four tensions are holding back education in MENA

Source: World Bank.

and modernity. Third, the tensions are neither unique to MENA nor time-specific. Throughout history, countries across the world have struggled with these tensions in defining their goals and policies. Fourth, no one position applies to every country or region. Each country, based on its national development goals and vision, needs to decide where it wants to place its education system within these tensions.

Credentials and skills

The tension between credentials and skills has been a source of debate for almost 50 years. Since the 1970s, economists and sociologists have argued about the links between education, skills, and the labor market, using numerous theories and models, such as Becker's human capital theory (Becker 1962), Collins's credentialist theory (Collins 1979), and Spence's signaling model (Spence 1973). A credential in the form of a degree, diploma, or certificate is usually associated with the acquisition of a specific set of skills or knowledge. In the labor market, credentials signal productivity, based on the assumption that more years of education are associated with higher productivity (Page 2010). Credentials also bestow a certain status in society, where a higher degree is associated with higher status and figures in matters such as marriage.

The history of education as a tool to generate bureaucrats for the public sector shaped the current structure of the education system and labor market in MENA. Public sector employment was typically guaranteed for anyone who had a sufficient education credential—diploma or degree. The requirement was more for the credential—the diploma or certificate—than for the skills. As a result, MENA countries have become societies in which there is little or no link between education credentials and skills (Assaad, Krafft, and Salehi-Isfahani 2018). In the meantime, little pressure has been placed on education institutions to ensure that credentials mean that the graduate possesses the relevant skills.

Although the size of the public sector as an employer has declined in many MENA countries, its legacy continues in the form of a "credentialist equilibrium" (Salehi-Isfahani 2012). In such an equilibrium, public sector employers communicate a strong demand for credentials, and the private sector's signals for skills are weak. Responding to market signals, students and families focus more on the credential (degree or diploma) and less on the skills and competencies that these credentials would ideally represent (see figure O.2).

The credentialist equilibrium in MENA countries has been created in part by imbalances in the labor market, where the large public sector is the preferred employer (Barsoum 2015; World Bank 2013a). In addition to higher wages, the desire for public employment is motivated by greater prestige, more generous benefits, and a better work environment, particularly for women (Barsoum 2015). Expectations of the public sector are also high because employment opportunities are often treated as a right, further disconnecting these opportunities from education. Several regional constitutions include the "right to work," engendering a common attitude that employment should be provided by the government and not by the private sector (Barsoum 2015). That attitude is a legacy of the government employment guarantees that were part of the region's social contract (Assaad 1997, 2014). The high wages and outsized role of government employment in MENA crowd out the private sector (Behar and Mok 2013; Nabli 2007), and government strategies to increase high-quality private sector employment have largely failed, resulting in poor or limited opportunities for new graduates (Dahi 2012; Salehi-Isfahani 2012; Springborg 2011) and reducing the demand for skills.

The notion of reducing public sector employment, a key aspect of a new Arab social contract, has gained little traction in the region (Devarajan and Ianchovichina 2018). Since the Arab Spring, calls for a new social contract have not yielded meaningful change in the role of the public sector. In fact, Egypt, Jordan, and Tunisia have all raised public salaries to stem further protests (Capital Economics 2017). While placating social discontent and temporarily supporting the economy, this approach also reinforces the notion that public sector employment is the only path to high salaries, career growth, and status within society—and so it will keep the region stuck in a credentialist equilibrium.

Discipline and inquiry

The terms *discipline* and *inquiry* have multiple meanings and uses. Here, *discipline* is defined as "the practice of training people to obey rules or a code of behavior" (*Oxford*) or "training that corrects, molds, or perfects the mental faculties or moral character" (*Merriam-Webster's*). *Inquiry* is defined as

FIGURE O.2 **MENA is stuck in a credentialist equilibrium**

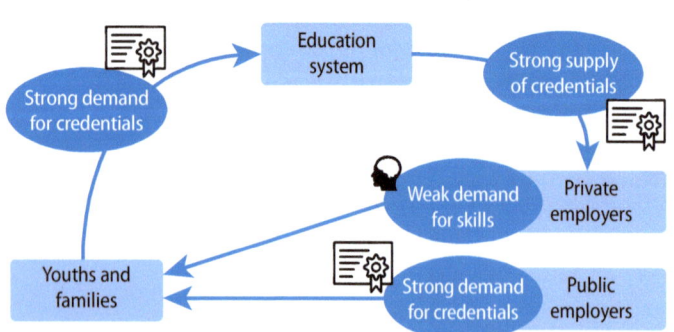

Source: Adapted from Assaad, Krafft, and Salehi-Isfahani 2018.

"an examination into facts or principles" (*Merriam-Webster's*). In societies with strong social norms, discipline is a key factor in ensuring adherence to norms. Although discipline in respect and self-restraint is important, too much restraint may constrict students' ability to learn, think, explore ideas, or question concepts. Inquiry, by contrast, allows students to understand their surroundings or contextualize concepts through questions and experimentation.

Some degree of discipline is important and necessary, but violent discipline[5] negatively affects children's physical, psychological, and social development and hampers their learning and school performance, ultimately reducing human capital development (El-Kogali and Krafft 2015; UNICEF 2010). Violent child discipline is widespread in MENA. In a study of 50 countries, UNICEF (2013) found that MENA has the highest percentage of children ages 2–14 years who are violently disciplined, ranging from 79 to 95 percent in Algeria, Egypt, Iraq, Morocco, Syria (pre-conflict), Tunisia, West Bank and Gaza, and the Republic of Yemen (El-Kogali and Krafft 2015).

Concepts of discipline and inquiry are closely linked to pedagogy and curricula, as well as to the day-to-day interactions of students with teachers; the emphasis on discipline leads to passive learning and memorization. Across MENA, curricula focus heavily on rote memorization, leaving little time for the development of critical thinking skills. According to teachers, the share of grade 8 students required to memorize mathematics and science rules, procedures, and facts for all or most lessons in many MENA countries is almost twice the international average (see figure O.3). The share exceeds 50 percent in Egypt, the Islamic Republic of Iran, Jordan, Lebanon, Oman, and Saudi Arabia, which is far above that in many high-performing countries. For example, only 10 percent of grade 8 students in Canada and New Zealand are required to memorize during most mathematics lessons, 11 percent in Sweden and the United States, and 14 percent in Ireland and

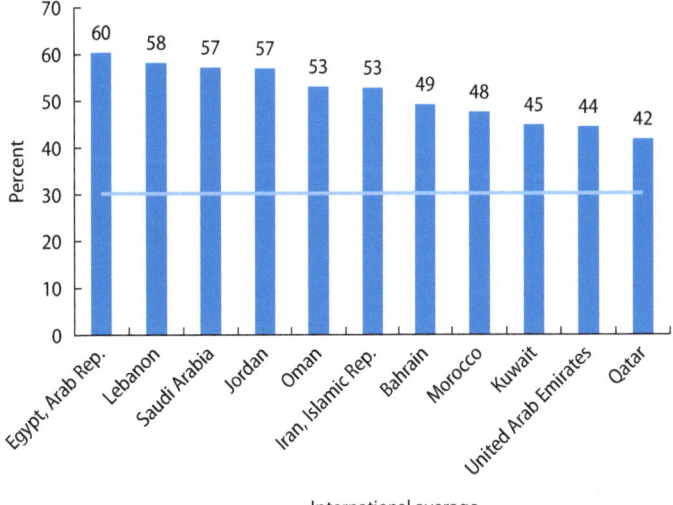

FIGURE O.3 MENA students are more likely to be asked to memorize

Percentage of grade 8 students asked to memorize science facts and principles for every lesson or almost every lesson, 2015

Source: Martin et al. 2016.

Singapore. Because of the emphasis on memorizing rules, procedures, facts, and principles, students are unable to show a basic understanding of everyday applications. In the 2015 Trends in International Mathematics and Science Study (TIMSS), fewer than half of Morocco's grade 4 students could read a basic graph. And only about 55 percent of Egypt's and Saudi Arabia's grade 8 students could interpret a basic pictogram (Mullis et al. 2016).

The overemphasis on memorization of facts, principles, rules, and procedures does not negate the fact that some knowledge needs to be retained. Rather, it is a question of the degree of emphasis and the overall experience of the child in the classroom. Cognitive science provides information that allows a more nuanced understanding of the balance between rote memorization and higher-level processes such as discovery learning. The capacity to solve problems and to think critically about new material depends on background knowledge retained in one's memory (Kirschner, Sweller, and Clark 2006). Repeated reflective practice is fundamental to building flexible knowledge and skills. In addition, students need guidance from teachers to develop the knowledge and skills that can facilitate independent, complex cognitive work. Therefore, ideally there is a balance between rote memorization and high-level problem-solving, and, depending on the task and level, it is a matter of striking the appropriate balance.

The tension between discipline and inquiry also reverberates in higher education, where it may hamper the push for solution-focused, multidisciplinary, high-impact research (World Bank 2017a). Effective postsecondary education programs emphasize practical training instead of theoretical knowledge. Mounting evidence provided by the cognitive and learning sciences indicates that interactive approaches facilitate an effective learning experience (Barkley, Cross, and Major 2005; Prince 2004). This combination allows future graduates to broaden their perspectives and equips them with the skills to enter the labor market. But postsecondary education programs in MENA are skewed toward theory over practice; they tend to have outdated curricula focused on theory and memorization, as opposed to practical knowledge and analytical reasoning (El Hassan 2013).

The tension between discipline and inquiry also applies to relationships such as those between teachers and principals and between parents and their children. In many MENA countries, obedience is viewed as an especially important quality that children should be encouraged to learn at home. Inquiry-driven qualities, such as imagination and self-expression, are emphasized less often (see figure O.4). Moreover, the tension between discipline and inquiry is also found in societies with strong social norms for class, gender, or hierarchy. For example, a recent comprehensive household survey of men and women ages 18–59 revealed that 90 percent of men and 58 percent of women in Egypt agree with the statement "A man should have the final word about decisions in the home" (UN Women

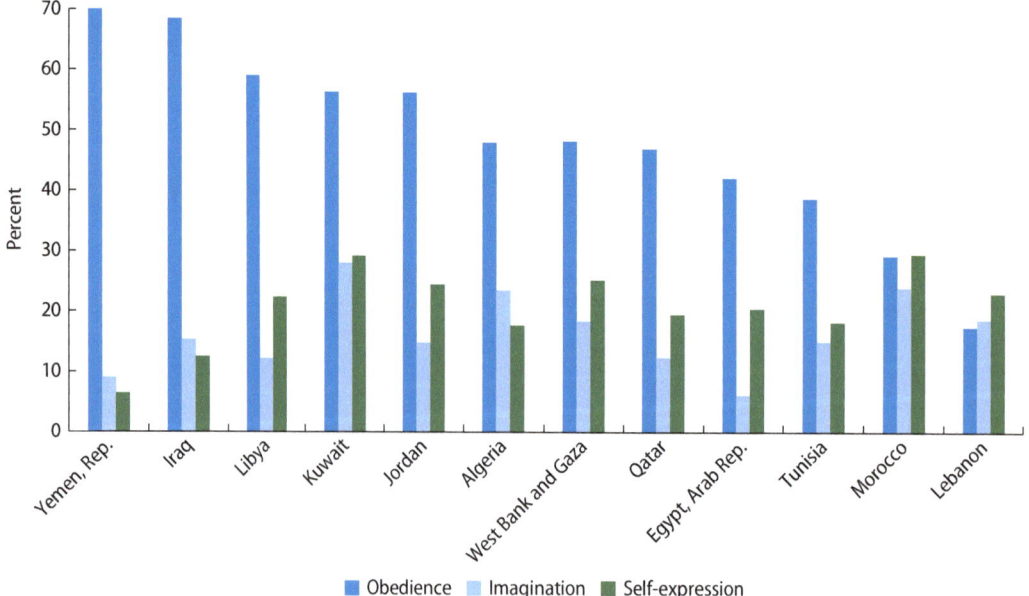

FIGURE O.4 **Obedience plays a central role in children's education in MENA**

Percentage of survey respondents who mentioned obedience, imagination, or self-expression as especially important qualities that children can be encouraged to learn at home

Source: World Values Survey, Wave 6 (2010–14), from Inglehart et al. 2014.
Note: These results are drawn from the following question: "Here is a list of qualities that children can be encouraged to learn at home. Which, if any, do you consider to be especially important? Please choose up to five." Potential answers included independence, hard work, feeling of responsibility, imagination, tolerance and respect for other people, thrift/saving money and things, determination/perseverance, religious faith, unselfishness, obedience, and self-expression.

and Promundo 2017). Results were similar in West Bank and Gaza (80 percent of men and 48 percent of women) and Morocco (71 percent of men and 47 percent of women). These social norms may negatively affect the attitudes of girls and women toward inquiry and their right to ask questions both at home and in other settings such as school, university, or work.

Control and autonomy

The tension between control and autonomy is usually associated with the debate on decentralization of services and the balance of power between central ministries, regional offices, and schools. The goal of decentralization is typically to improve governance by fostering autonomy, accountability, and responsiveness to local conditions and needs. These attributes can improve student learning. Over the last few decades, several MENA countries experimented with some aspects of decentralization, deconcentration, and devolution of authority from the central to the regional and school levels, but their education systems remain highly centralized. The success of attempted decentralization has varied. In some instances, the decision-making power was authorized but was not supported by the resources needed to implement decisions. For example, decentralization in Egypt in 2002–07 was not supported by sufficient financial resources (Ginsburg et al. 2010). Decentralization in Saudi Arabia in the 2000s appears to have been adequately funded, but the tasks and duties transferred to the local level were more administrative than geared toward the development of local schools (Almannie 2015). In other instances, a decentralized model was rolled out in a policy without putting in place the capacity to carry out the decentralized functions at the regional or school level. For example, Morocco's regional academies for education and training (académies régionales d'éducation et de formation) were only granted autonomy to manage some logistical and financial decisions based on guidelines provided by the central government (World Bank 2015d).

There is no magic formula for balancing centralized control and autonomy in education. It must be determined within the country context, with size, geography, and population distribution playing important roles in the decision. What is important is finding the balance in defining the roles and responsibilities of institutional actors (for example, the central government, local government, and communities) and defining the locus of control of the education processes and mechanisms used to steer the system (World Bank 2005). In other words, the balance between central control and autonomy should reflect the roles and responsibilities of central versus local governance and political versus professional power and accountability.

Limited autonomy at the school and classroom levels can constrain efforts by principals and teachers to be proactive in the learning process and prevent them from taking responsibility for student learning outcomes if they consider themselves as merely implementing a centralized approach (Karami Akkary 2014). Teachers in MENA have far less decision-making responsibility than those in member countries of the Organisation for Economic Co-operation and Development (OECD) (see figure O.5). Studies in the Islamic Republic of Iran, Jordan, and Kuwait have found that central authorities maintain strict control of curricular content and teaching practices, leaving little autonomy for teachers (Afshar and Doosti 2016; Al-Yaseen and Al-Musaileem 2015; Namaghi 2009; World Bank 2015a).

Limited autonomy among teachers compromises job satisfaction and the development of student skills, in part because it impedes the ability of teachers to teach to the right level for their students, a critical element of effective teaching (Evans and Popova 2015). Limited autonomy at the regional, provincial, and school levels for the hiring and deployment of teachers also limits the ability to match teacher characteristics better with teaching needs.

Greater autonomy in higher education institutions tends to be associated with better

FIGURE 0.5 Teachers in MENA have less autonomy than teachers in OECD countries

Percentage of 15-year-old students attending schools in which teachers have considerable responsibility for instructional decisions, PISA 2015

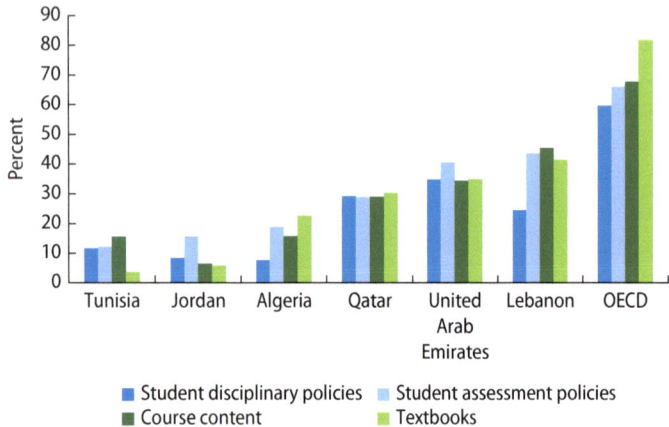

Source: OECD 2016a.
Note: OECD = Organisation for Economic Co-operation and Development; PISA = Programme for International Student Assessment.

performance (Aghion et al. 2009; World Bank 2011). However, most universities in MENA have very limited autonomy over academic, staffing, and financial matters. In 2012 the World Bank benchmarked the governance practices of 100 universities in Algeria, Egypt, Iraq, Lebanon, Morocco, Tunisia, and West Bank and Gaza (World Bank 2013c). Institutional autonomy was very low among public universities, with the local or central government making decisions about matters such as the academic program, hiring teaching faculty, and fundraising. Private universities, by contrast, enjoyed much greater autonomy across all seven MENA economies surveyed (World Bank 2013c). In a follow-up survey in 2016, autonomy did not seem to have changed much for both public and private universities (World Bank 2017b).[6] A comparison of self-assessment and actual scores revealed that public institutions perceive their autonomy to be higher than the autonomy score in the external evaluation, whereas private universities have a more accurate perception of their autonomy (World Bank 2017b).

Greater autonomy at a decentralized level requires capacity, resources, and accountability mechanisms. When autonomy and accountability are combined well, they tend to be associated with better student performance (OECD 2011b). Schools with more autonomy over teaching content, student assessment, and resource allocation tend to perform better than those with less autonomy. Ultimately, MENA school systems must find the balance between control and autonomy that will best support learning and provide schools with the resources and flexibility to establish and achieve ambitious goals for student learning.

Tradition and modernity

According to some scholars, the greatest challenge MENA countries face is aligning the development needs of a modern world and the moral imperatives of a religious society, resulting in tension between modernity and tradition (Cook 2000). The focus on tradition versus modernity, or the forces of change, can result in conflicts within education processes (Massialas and Jarrar 1987). This tension can be captured in the definition and purpose of education. In Arabic, *taaleem* (education) comes from the root word *ilm* (knowledge). The plural of *ilm* is *uloom*, which also means science or sciences. *Taaleem* encompasses both learning and teaching—the acquisition and provision of knowledge or science. Education in Arabic is also *tarbiya*, which refers to education in the sense of growing or rearing. Its root word, *rabba*, means raising or bringing up. *Taaleem* and *tarbiya* have meanings similar to those of the Latin words *educere*—to lead forth and to train—and *educare*—to rear and to educate (Bass and Good 2004; Cook 1999).

At the center of the debate on tradition and modernity is the extent to which education should focus on the acquisition of knowledge or science (*taaleem*) versus the acquisition of values (*tarbiya*). This question is reflected in the evolution of the names given to ministries of education in MENA countries. Names have shifted between ministries of *tarbiya* and ministries of *taaleem*, with some countries settling on both names as ministries of *tarbiya* and *taaleem*.[7] When education ministries were established in the middle of the 20th century after independence in most MENA countries, they were called ministries of *maarif*—plural of *maarifa* (knowledge). Egypt, for example, began with the Ministry of *Maarif* and then shifted to the Ministry of *Taaleem*. Currently, it is the Ministry of *Tarbiya* and *Taaleem*. The change was a deliberate decision made during the tenure of President Jamal Abdel Nasser, who regarded education as the process required to form the complete person and to shape the Egyptian identity (Ahramonline 2015).

The values and principles reflected in education in MENA are shaped by national discourses usually dominated by elites and powerful groups. Classrooms and curricula become the platforms on which the struggle between modernity and tradition are played out. The tension between tradition and modernity in defining the purpose of education is prevalent not only in MENA. Throughout history, countries worldwide have struggled to modernize while maintaining their cultural norms, values, and traditions, with education as the mechanism. In Japan, when the Meiji government (1868–1912) implemented reforms based on Western models of education, Japanese feared their identity and values would be lost. These fears led to the release of the Imperial Rescript of Education in 1890, emphasizing Japanese values and Confucian virtues. Since then, Japanese education policy has maintained a balance between retaining traditional Japanese values while adapting aspects of the world's best education systems (OECD 2011a). Ernst Friedrich Schumacher, a British economist in the 1970s, argued that the purpose of education is to transmit the values "through which we look at, interpret, and experience the world" and that science "cannot produce ideas by which we could live ... and is completely inapplicable to the conduct of our lives or the interpretation of the world" (Schumacher 1973). He believed that education was of no value if it did not transmit fundamental convictions. In other words, the purpose of education could be better understood not as *taaleem* but essentially as *tarbiya*.

The traditional values and fundamental convictions of MENA countries were established in Islam, which represents the foundation of national identity.[8] These values and convictions are at the heart of education. The proportion of instructional time devoted to religious education in most MENA countries is well above the average time that OECD countries spend on religious, ethics, and moral education (see figure O.6). For example,

FIGURE O.6 **Substantial time is devoted to religious education in MENA**

Percentage of instructional time allocated to religious education in grade 1 of primary school

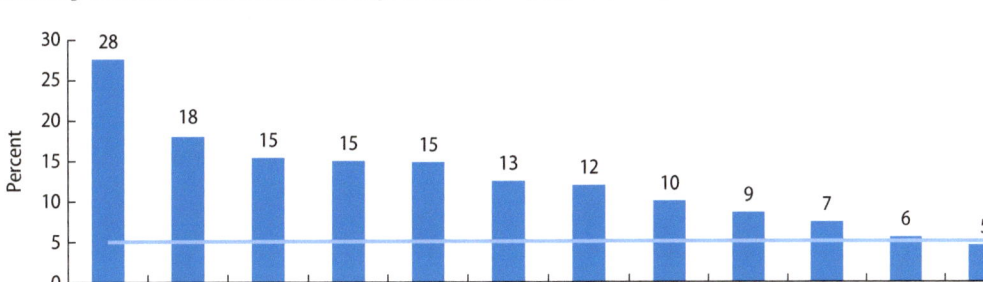

Sources: OECD 2017a for OECD average (refers to all grades of primary school); UNESCO 2011 for Algeria (2004), Bahrain (2004), Djibouti (2008), Iraq (2011), Kuwait (2004), Oman (2004), Tunisia (2008), and the Republic of Yemen (2004); World Bank calculations using various online sources for the Arab Republic of Egypt (2014), Morocco (2016), Saudi Arabia (2017), and the United Arab Emirates (2016).
Note: OECD = Organisation for Economic Co-operation and Development.

based on the most recent comparable information available, grade 1 students in Bahrain, Iraq, Kuwait, Morocco, Oman, Saudi Arabia, the United Arab Emirates, and the Republic of Yemen spend more than double the OECD average of 5 percent. Religious education also reflects traditional teaching practices that focus on memorization. The foundations of rote learning in MENA can be linked to the oral tradition among Arabs that predates Islam, which has also been used to preserve and spread Islamic teachings.

It it is up to countries to determine the values they want to bestow on their citizens. However, it is important to recognize the trade-offs in terms of the time distribution between subjects; more time on religious studies reduces the time allocated to other subjects such as math and science. It is also important to recognize the impact of traditional modes of teaching on learning. In many countries, attempts to reform the education system have been opposed as an attempt to change the national character. In Jordan, for example, the introduction of curriculum reforms sparked public outrage, mainly by conservative religious groups whose members characterized the reforms as an attempt to undermine the kingdom's Islamic values and character (Kirdar 2017). Similarly, in Kuwait various groups have protested ongoing curriculum reforms as the imposition of imported concepts.

Modernity does not mean importing a specific model. In many MENA countries, modernity is associated with foreign models and approaches and is used by both the proponents and opponents of change. Modernization is a process by which social norms evolve and are renewed; modernity can take multiple forms. The issue is not replacing tradition with one form of modernity. Rather, it is allowing review of the traditional practices and norms that are holding back the potential of education and engaging in a process of renewal. Modernity is inevitable as the world changes. MENA countries need to prepare their students with the knowledge, skills, and values to engage with, adapt to, and succeed in a changing world.

A new framework is needed to realize education's potential in MENA

To realize the potential of education, MENA countries need to tackle the four tensions and establish an education system that prepares all students for a productive and successful future. Such a system would be modern and flexible and would nurture a culture of excellence and creativity in learning. It also would leverage disruptive technologies and adopt modern approaches so it can offer young people the skills they need to define their trajectories in life and adapt to local, national, and global changes. Finally, it would be based on a shared national vision and would connect with the overall development goals of the country. All of society would be responsible for ensuring its success. To establish such a system, MENA countries need to adopt a new framework for education—one that includes a concerted *push* for learning, a wide-reaching *pull* for skills, and a new *pact* for education (see figure O.7). The remainder of this chapter describes the actions needed to implement this framework.

Related to this effort, the World Bank's *World Development Report 2018* highlights the global learning crisis (World Bank 2018e). It sheds light on the dimensions of the crisis and proposes a way forward that is well aligned with the push, pull, and pact framework described here. It further reinforces the importance of all stakeholders working together to promote a focus on learning and skills (see box O.2).

FIGURE O.7 **"Push, pull, and pact" offers a new framework for education in MENA**

Source: World Bank.

Box O.2 *World Development Report 2018: Learning to Realize Education's Promise*

There is nothing inevitable about low learning in low- and middle-income countries. When improving learning is a priority, great progress is possible, as evidenced by success stories such as Korea. To do better, a nation must (1) assess learning, to make it a serious goal; (2) act on evidence, to make schools work for all learners; and (3) align actors, to make the whole system work for learning. Together, these three policy actions can deliver a system in which the elements cohere and everything aligns with learning. The payoff to these efforts is education that delivers for growth and development. Countries have already made a start by getting so many children and youths into school. Now is the time to realize education's promise by accelerating learning for all.

Source: World Bank 2018e.

Push for learning

Focus on learning, not just on schooling

The potential of education is achieved only when it confers the skills and knowledge that constitute human capital. In fact, the skills conferred through learning—not the years of schooling—are what determine education's contribution to economic growth (see figure O.8) (Barro and Lee 2013; Hanushek and Woessmann 2008; World Bank 2018e).

MENA has succeeded in providing schooling; now it needs to achieve learning. The number of actual years of schooling has increased across MENA, with several countries reaching an average that is close to a full cycle of primary and secondary education. However, when the number of actual years of schooling is adjusted for learning, the number of effective years of schooling in MENA is on average 2.9 less than the number of actual years of schooling. In other words, the poor quality of education in MENA is equivalent to approximately three lost years of education. For example, in 2010 young adults in Jordan had on average 11 years of schooling, the same as Kazakhstan and New Zealand (see figure O.9). After adjusting for learning,

FIGURE O.8 What matters for growth is skills

Annual average per capita growth in GDP, 1970–2015, conditional on test scores, years of schooling completed, and initial GDP per capita, selected countries

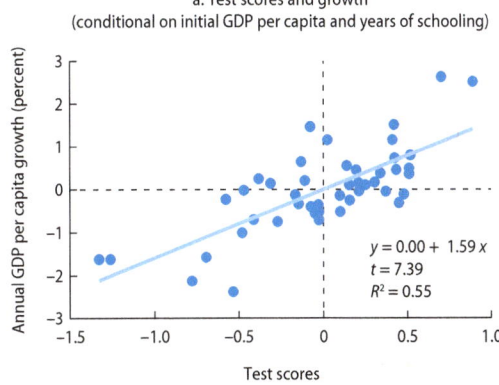
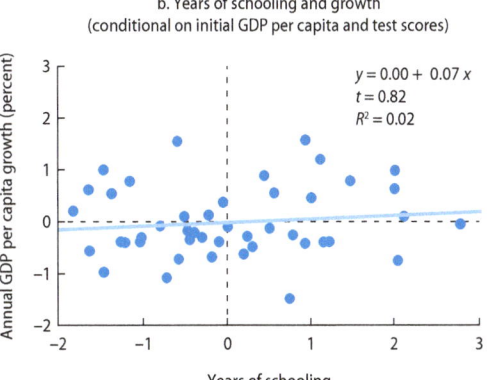

Source: World Bank 2018e, fig. 1.5.

FIGURE O.9 When adjusted for learning, the number of years of effective schooling in MENA drops substantially

Actual years and learning-adjusted years of schooling of young people, ages 25–29

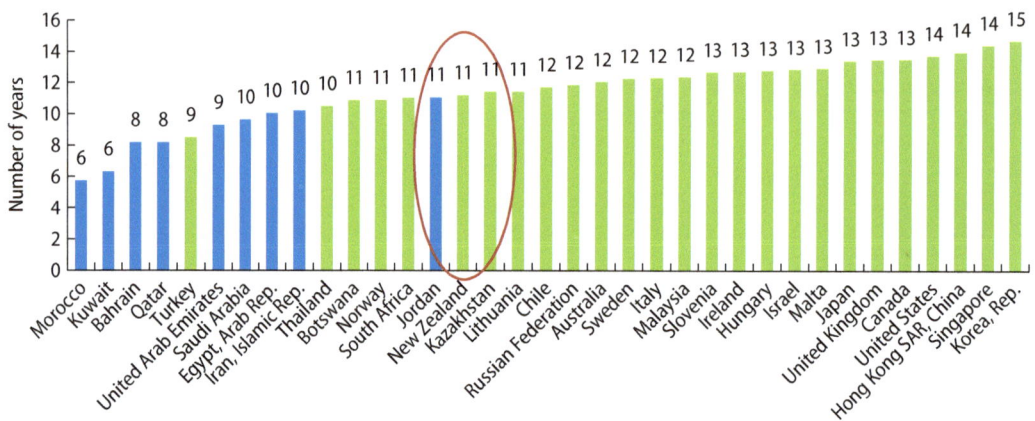

a. Actual years of schooling

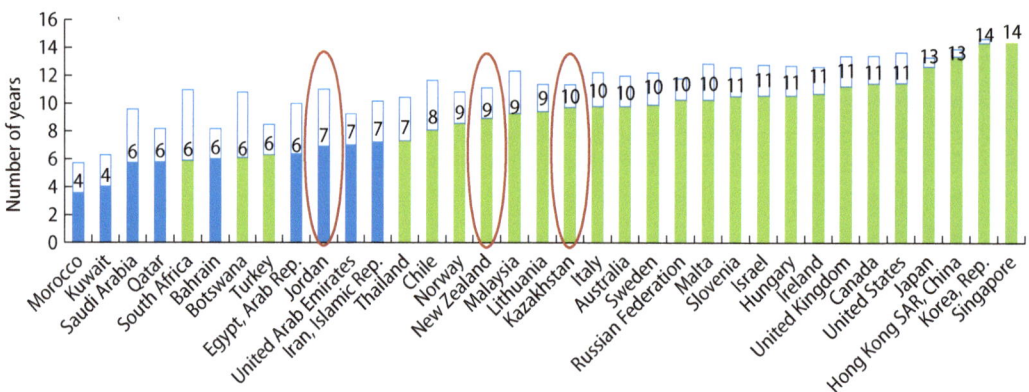

b. Learning-adjusted years of schooling

Sources: World Bank 2018e, based on 2010 data from Barro and Lee 2013 and TIMSS 2015 (Mullis et al. 2016).
Note: For the purposes of this illustration, years of schooling are adjusted using the grade 8 mathematics results from the 2015 Trends in International Mathematics and Science Study (TIMSS). Results are compared with those of Singapore (highest-scoring economy). The figure highlights, as an example, that Jordan has actual years of schooling similar to those of Kazakhstan and New Zealand (around 11 years in each country), but students in Jordan attain 2 to 3 fewer years of learning in these 11 years than students in the two other countries.

Jordan had two to three years less learning than New Zealand and Kazakhstan.

MENA's learning crisis is apparent across primary and secondary grades and across different subject areas. No MENA country came close to the international medians for the percentage of students reaching the low international benchmarks of the recent TIMSS and Progress in International Reading Literacy Study (PIRLS)—see table O.1. Only 42 percent of grade 8 students in Egypt had a basic understanding of science (Martin et al. 2016). In Morocco, only 36 percent of grade 4 students reached minimum levels of reading literacy. According to the results of the 2015 Programme for International Student Assessment (PISA), students age 15 in Algeria, Jordan, Lebanon, Qatar, Tunisia, and the United Arab Emirates are on average

TABLE O.1 MENA countries have some of the lowest results on international student assessments
Percentage of students reaching low international benchmarks of performance on TIMSS 2011 and 2015 and PIRLS 2011 and 2016

Mathematics (TIMSS)					
Grade 4			Grade 8		
Country	2011	2015	Country	2011	2015
International median	90	93	International median	75	84
Bahrain[a]	67	72	Bahrain[a]	53	75
United Arab Emirates[a]	64	68	United Arab Emirates	73	73
Iran, Islamic Rep.	64	65	Lebanon	73	71
Qatar[a]	55	65	Iran, Islamic Rep.[a]	55	63
Oman[a]	46	60	Qatar[a]	54	63
Saudi Arabia[b]	55	43	Oman[a]	39	52
Morocco[a]	26	41	Egypt, Arab Rep.	n.a.	47
Kuwait[b]	30	23	Jordan[b]	55	45
			Morocco[a]	36	41
			Kuwait	n.a.	37
			Saudi Arabia[b]	47	34

Science (TIMSS)					
Grade 4			Grade 8		
Country	2011	2015	Country	2011	2015
International median	92	95	International median	79	84
Bahrain	70	72	United Arab Emirates	75	76
United Arab Emirates[a]	61	67	Bahrain[a]	70	73
Qatar[a]	50	64	Iran, Islamic Rep.[b]	79	73
Iran, Islamic Rep.[b]	72	61	Oman[a]	59	72
Oman[a]	45	61	Qatar[a]	58	70
Saudi Arabia[b]	63	48	Jordan[b]	72	63
Morocco[a]	16	35	Lebanon	54	50
Kuwait[b]	37	25	Kuwait	n.a.	49
			Saudi Arabia[b]	68	49
			Morocco[a]	39	47
			Egypt, Arab Rep.	n.a.	42

Reading (PIRLS)		
Grade 4		
Country	2011	2016
International median	95	96
United Arab Emirates[a]	64	68
Qatar[a]	60	66
Iran, Islamic Rep.[b]	76	65
Saudi Arabia	65	63
Oman[a]	47	59
Morocco[a]	21	36

Sources: Mullis et al. 2016, 2017.
Note: The international medians for 2011 and 2016 cannot be compared because the set of countries in each year is not the same. PIRLS = Progress in International Reading Literacy Study; TIMSS = Trends in International Mathematics and Science Study; n.a. = not applicable (the Arab Republic of Egypt and Kuwait did not participate in TIMSS for grade 8 in 2011).
a. Statistically significant increase between 2011 and 2015/2016.
b. Statistically significant decrease between 2011 and 2015/2016.

two to four years of schooling behind the member countries of the OECD in applying their knowledge and competencies in reading, mathematics, and science to real-world situations. Algeria and Lebanon, both participating in PISA for the first time in 2015, found that more than two-thirds of their students did not meet a basic proficiency level in science, reading, and mathematics.

Low learning outcomes in MENA countries call for a push across several aspects of the educational process. To undertake a push for learning, countries need to focus on seven key areas:

1. Building the foundational skills—from early childhood development through the early grades of school—needed for future learning and success.
2. Ensuring that teachers and school leaders, who are the most important inputs to the learning process, are qualified, well selected, effectively utilized, and incentivized to continue to develop professionally.
3. Modernizing pedagogy and instructional practices to promote inquiry, creativity, and innovation.
4. Addressing the language of instruction challenge given the gap between spoken Arabic and modern standard Arabic. The close connection among language, religion, and national identity makes it difficult to make a regional recommendation. Even though this phenomenon is a regional one, it manifests itself in many different ways in different countries. Hence, it needs to be addressed with a very specific formula in each country.
5. Applying learning assessments that regularly monitor student progress to ensure that students are learning.
6. Giving all children, regardless of background or ability, an opportunity to learn—a requirement for raising learning outcomes at the national level.
7. Leveraging technology to enhance the delivery of education and promote learning among students and educators and preparing students for an increasingly digital world.

Prioritize the early years to build the foundations for learning

Start from early childhood

The period from before birth to approximately 6 years of age, when the brain undergoes its greatest development, is critical to children's development (Berlinski and Schady 2015; Heckman 2006; Leseman 2002). In these years, more than 1 million new neural connections are formed every second. It is also during this period that the building blocks of the brain are formed and the child's environment stimulates brain development (Center on the Developing Child 2009; Shonkoff and Garner 2012). Children's early environments and experiences, particularly the parenting they experience, are major contributors to their early cognitive development (Paxson and Schady 2007). Parenting and developmental interventions, especially those targeting disadvantaged children, can have large (arguably the largest) impacts on human capital (Hamadani et al. 2006; Heckman 2006; Temple and Reynolds 2007). Early childhood development (ECD) programs—including in-home programs, centers, and preprimary (kindergarten) education—can play an important role in human capital accumulation prior to primary school. However, the impact of ECD programs depends on their quality and may be greater for disadvantaged children (Berlinski, Galiani, and Gertler 2009; Berlinski, Galiani, and Manacorda 2008; Bouguen et al. 2013; Hazarika and Viren 2013; Jung and Hasan 2014; Temple and Reynolds 2007; Vegas and Santibáñez 2010).

Because of the importance of early development, the largest and most cost-effective impacts of public investment in education can be realized in the early stages of life. Investments made during the early years yield the highest return in terms of future productivity by laying the foundation for cognitive and socioemotional skills (World Bank 2018a). By contrast, if developmental growth is not supported from an early age, children may arrive at school well behind their peers. The opportunity costs of making up lost ground in later years through remedial education can be high. To take full advantage of the high returns to ECD, governments need to expand access to high-quality ECD programs, which include prenatal and neonatal nutrition, health, and parenting interventions as well as socioemotional and cognitive stimulation in the early years.

MENA has not invested sufficiently in ECD. As a result, most children begin school unprepared to learn. Gross enrollment ratios in preprimary education are just 31 percent, lower than in many other regions and with wide differences between countries (see figures O.10 and O.11). Moreover, MENA also has the lowest public provision of

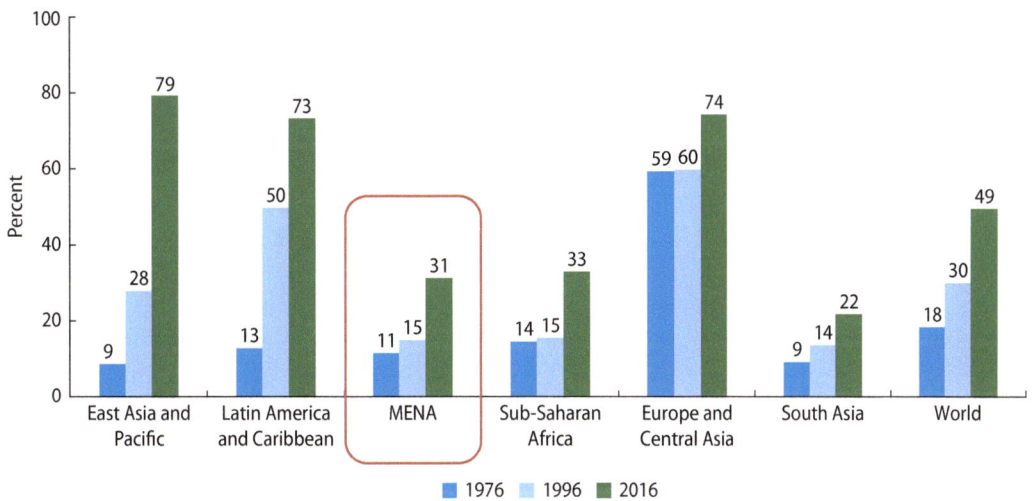

FIGURE O.10 Preprimary enrollments are lower in MENA than in many other regions

Preprimary gross enrollment ratios, 1976, 1996, and 2016

Source: World Bank EdStats database (http://datatopics.worldbank.org/education/), based on data from the UNESCO Institute for Statistics.

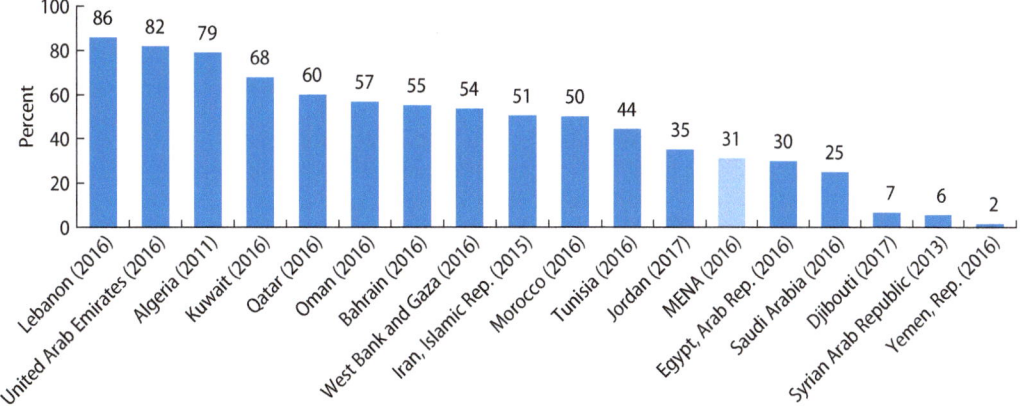

FIGURE O.11 Large differences in preprimary enrollment ratios are found across MENA

Preprimary gross enrollment ratio

Sources: For all except Jordan, World Bank EdStats database (http://datatopics.worldbank.org/education/), based on data from the UNESCO Institute for Statistics. For Jordan, Queen Rania Center at the Jordan Ministry of Education, provided in August 2018.
Note: Data are for the latest available year between 2011 and 2017.

preprimary education, with only 29 percent of preprimary enrollment in public programs, compared with 71 percent in private preschools and nurseries (El-Kogali and Krafft 2015).

Expanding ECD coverage is not enough; quality matters. High-quality ECD programs can boost children's intellectual and social development, preparing them to enter primary school ready to learn (Heckman 2006). Ample evidence shows that quality preschool education programs geared especially toward disadvantaged children have a positive impact on beneficiaries' earnings and even reduce crime (Elango et al. 2015; Schweinhart et al. 2005). These programs are also more cost-effective than other education interventions, such as reductions in class size, and help to close performance gaps in socioeconomic status, ethnicity, and geographic origin (Glewwe 2013; Heckman 2006).

MENA countries should accelerate the expansion of access to high-quality preprimary education. Because few data are available on early childhood education (ECE) programs implemented in MENA countries, it is difficult to determine whether the existing services are of high quality. Governments should focus on measuring child development outcomes and early learning environments to identify drivers of ECE quality in their respective contexts. Building on rigorous evidence, they can make informed decisions on the piloting and scaling up of early learning programs.

The expansion of compulsory preprimary education in Argentina in the 1990s is a good example of how a country can successfully raise student learning outcomes in the early years (by grade 3). A study revealed that adding one year of preprimary school in Argentina increased the average grade 3 test scores by 8 percent of the mean (Berlinski, Galiani, and Gertler 2009). Examples of excellence in expanding quality ECE provision can also be found in MENA countries. For example, in the United Arab Emirates universalization of preschool education is among the top key performance indicators of its ambitious Vision 2021 national agenda. The country is on pace to reach a goal of enrolling 95 percent of its children in preschool by 2021, an increase of more than 30 percentage points since the 1990s (see box O.3).

Children also develop their socioemotional skills and behaviors during the early preschool years. Their attitudes are shaped by their environment at home and school and by their interactions with parents, siblings, and teachers. Children develop cognitively, socially, and emotionally by engaging in development activities with their families. Reading, playing, looking at picture books, singing songs, and other activities all help children grow and learn and have been shown to have a positive link to cognitive test scores

---

Box O.3　Prioritizing early childhood education in the United Arab Emirates

Embedded in its national goal of developing a first-rate education system, the United Arab Emirates is expanding access to preschool so that all children receive a solid foundation for learning from an early age. As part of its ambitious Vision 2021 national agenda, the country has set a target for 2021 of 95 percent enrollment in preschools for the country's children, and it is well on track to reach that target. As of 2016, the gross preprimary enrollment ratio in the United Arab Emirates was at 82 percent. The United Arab Emirates is therefore at the top of MENA in terms of preschool enrollment and shows a vast improvement from enrollment rates of less than 30 percent in the 1970s and 60 percent in the 1990s.

Sources: United Arab Emirates National Agenda and Vision 2021, presentation, http://www.rwadubai.com/media/2578/uae-national-agenda.pdf; World Bank, Education Statistics (EdStats) database.

in young children and to promote school readiness (El-Kogali and Krafft 2015). Various interventions have proven to be effective and scalable in helping parents to engage with their children and promote their development. Jordan's Better Parenting project engaged parents and communities—including imams—to raise awareness of better parenting. In Turkey, a program targeting mothers addressed parent-child interactions and provided lessons on positive discipline. In Brazil, workshops involving mothers and home visits showed positive results. Outreach through different media—such as radio, television, and print—to communicate about ECD can help to reduce violent discipline and promote children's development (Eickmann et al. 2003; Kagitcibasi, Sunar, and Bekman 2001; Naudeau et al. 2011, cited in El-Kogali and Krafft 2015).

Build foundational skills in the first three grades of school

Because many children in MENA have a poor start to their formal education by not being developmentally on track in prereading skills, it is vital that the early grades of school emphasize these important foundational skills. Basic reading, writing, numeracy, and socioemotional skills lay the foundation for learning throughout a child's life and into adulthood. Children lacking these skills are at risk of falling behind, becoming disengaged from school, and not acquiring the more advanced skills increasingly demanded in today's labor market. Ultimately, if children lack the foundational skills that should be developed in the early grades of school, they cannot take advantage of the benefits that their education could provide.

Many children in MENA remain illiterate and innumerate after two or three years of schooling. The Early Grade Reading Assessment (EGRA) revealed that more than one in three grade 2 children in Iraq, Morocco, and the Republic of Yemen could not read a single word of connected text. By grade 3, this proportion had dropped, but still more than one in six children could not read a single word of connected text after more than two full years of school (USAID 2018). In Kuwait, Morocco, and Saudi Arabia, less than 50 percent of grade 4 students in 2015 had basic mathematical knowledge as measured by TIMSS, while across all participating countries 93 percent of grade 4 students had mastered these basic mathematical skills (Martin et al. 2016; Mullis et al. 2016, 2017).

Early grade reading interventions can make a substantial difference. A review of 18 early grade reading programs found that almost all were effective, and many were highly cost-effective (Graham and Kelly 2018). Several countries in MENA have made concerted efforts to address literacy during the early grades. Piloting early childhood and early grade interventions to identify which successfully boost children's foundational skills is an effective strategy to maximize the use of scarce resources. Measuring early childhood development outcomes using early grade literacy and numeracy assessments can shed further light on the key drivers of early learning and help to identify gaps in the development of key foundational skills from a young age.

To enhance children's readiness to learn, education policies in MENA could aim to align preprimary schooling with primary education to ensure a smooth transition for young children. Entering primary classrooms where a different educational philosophy (or language of instruction) is practiced can be a difficult transition for young children. Moving from play-based, collaborative, child-centered learning—often conducted in a child's mother tongue—to traditional teacher-centered instruction—often in modern standard Arabic (MSA)—can undermine the positive impacts of even the most successful ECE programs. Therefore, aligning preschool and primary grade instructional styles is important, with both focusing on developmentally appropriate teaching and learning techniques. For example, the United Arab Emirates is in the process of aligning grades 1 and 2 of primary school with preprimary education, which consists of two years of kindergarten, to create a holistic ECE cycle covering all children from ages 0 to 8. Finland, New Zealand, and various other OECD countries have undertaken similar efforts to align early childhood education with learning in the early grades (OECD 2012b, 2017c).

Select, prepare, support, empower, and motivate effective teachers and school leaders

Effective teachers and school leaders have a profound impact on students' learning and their educational and career aspirations. Effective teachers are those who are knowledgeable in both pedagogy and their subject areas, who adapt and innovate their teaching practices to facilitate students' critical thinking, and who support learning for students with different learning styles (Hightower et al. 2011; Metzler and Woessmann 2012; OECD 2012a). School leaders have an indirect but powerful effect on student achievement through their interactions with teachers and their role in shaping school culture (Pont, Nusche, and Moorman 2008; Witziers, Bosker, and Kruger 2003). Evidence shows that teacher effectiveness is the most important school-related factor influencing student achievement (Darling-Hammond 2000; Hanushek 2005; Mourshed, Chijioke, and Barber 2010), and among school factors school leadership is second only to classroom teaching in its impact on student learning (Jensen, Downing, and Clark 2017a; Leithwood, Harris, and Hopkins 2008; Leithwood and Mascall 2008).

Select and support the best teachers and school leaders

It is paramount that education systems recruit, train, and support those men and women who have the greatest potential to be effective teachers and school leaders. These systems must also provide for ongoing career development and upskilling to ensure that the best teachers remain in the classrooms and that classrooms and schools are providing the most up-to-date and effective teaching practices and learning environments.

Attracting and selecting highly qualified candidates to enter initial teacher education programs are the first step in the long-term process of building an effective teaching force (see box O.4). International experience points to the importance of establishing high standards to ensure that the best candidates are selected for initial teacher education programs and that these candidates have a reasonable opportunity to be hired after graduation (Barber and Mourshed 2007; Bruns and Luque 2015). In most MENA countries, the screening process for initial teacher education

---

Box O.4 Attracting the best students to teaching depends on the right policies and programs

Attracting and retaining the best students into the teaching profession depends on policies and programs such as scholarships and tuition support, opportunities to progress and grow in the teaching career, competitive salaries, and other benefits such as housing assistance (World Bank 2013d). Moreover, it is critical to attract the candidates who want to make teaching a profession rather than use it as a ticket for a public sector job.

In some MENA countries, teachers are offered competitive starting packages, but the increase in salaries over time is relatively modest. After 15 years, teachers can expect to earn only between 1.2 and 1.5 times their initial salaries (World Bank 2015e). Such compressed salary scales within the teaching career in MENA may negatively affect how appealing the teaching profession is to talented candidates. In such instances, policies that address wage compression could be fundamental to improving the quality of teaching. Recognizing this link, Jordan has embarked on a reform to decompress the salary scales for teachers (World Bank 2016a).

is dependent on test scores from secondary school graduation examinations (World Bank 2015c). However, the scores needed to accept students in the education field are lower than those in other fields. In Egypt, for example, the required secondary school passing grade on the national examination for admission into education and literature majors is 75–85, whereas it is 80–88 for science and mathematics majors and 96–98 for medical school (World Bank 2010). Although test scores are necessary, they are not a sufficient basis for selection. Other criteria—such as creativity, engagement with education issues, and ability to work well with others—are important traits to consider.

Many MENA countries are raising the qualifications to enter the teaching profession by requiring a bachelor's degree, with some raising the required level to a master's degree. However, most MENA countries do not apply hiring criteria and processes that look beyond academic degrees to assess candidates' subject knowledge and pedagogical and other skills. A teaching credential should signify strong knowledge of subject-matter content *and* the teaching skills to deliver this content effectively while addressing specific learning challenges (Loughran, Berry, and Mulhall 2012; Shulman and Shulman 2004; Thames and Ball 2010). Only 4 of the 10 MENA countries that participated in TIMSS 2015 required teacher candidates to pass qualifying examinations for selection to teaching posts (Mullis et al. 2016).

Developing effective school leadership starts with the selection and preparation of skilled, well-equipped new principals. Most MENA countries employ a variety of criteria for selecting principals, and, as in teacher selection, a strong emphasis is often placed on academic qualifications and teaching experience (Mullis et al. 2016).[9] In Oman, for example, school principals are chosen according to seniority and experience in teaching and classroom management. Potential school principals in Bahrain are required to have experience as a teacher, adviser, or education specialist. Some principals in Oman and Saudi Arabia have degrees in educational leadership in addition to teaching qualifications. In Lebanon, leadership training programs are the main preparation route to becoming a principal. Principals must pass an interview and a yearlong training program in leadership and supervision. Egypt has rigorous professional requirements: all school principals must have a minimum of 15 years of teaching experience and a minimum of five years of administrative experience. Candidates for the position of principal must hold a tertiary education degree and are required to complete specific training. They also must pass a written test, successfully complete a supervised internship, and participate in an induction and mentoring program (Mullis et al. 2016).

Where credentials do not appropriately capture skills—one of the four tensions in MENA—the risk of not selecting the most qualified teachers and school leaders is high. This disconnect could jeopardize student learning. In many developed education systems, rigorous processes are in place for selecting the best-performing graduates of initial teacher education programs for teaching positions, often requiring them to hold certificates or licenses. Some of the oldest and most established licensing systems are in the United States, where state teaching licenses ensure a consistent set of standards with a certain level of teaching proficiency recognized by all schools. Several MENA countries are beginning to explore the introduction of licensing and certification requirements for teachers as a mechanism to raise and maintain standards.

Because technology, research, and labor market needs are changing rapidly, teachers and school leaders must be able to update their knowledge and skills regularly. Intensive, content-focused professional development programs can improve teachers' subject matter knowledge and their ability to use this knowledge in their teaching (NCEE 2016). Professional development programs for teachers should focus on content and on improving teaching skills so that teachers can effectively deliver content to all types of students (Loughran, Berry, and Mulhall 2012; Shulman and Shulman 2004; Thames and Ball 2010). Training programs that teach

> **Box O.5** **School principals also must act as instructional leaders**
>
> School principals also serve as instructional leaders who can lead, guide, and monitor instructional practices related to pedagogy and curriculum (Jensen, Downing, and Clark 2017a; OECD 2016a, 2016b). Instructional leadership fosters a school environment that focuses more on academic success, which in turn enhances student learning. For example, higher average mathematics achievement is associated with principals' reports of a greater school emphasis on academic success (Mullis et al. 2016). Because of the degree and importance of skills transfers between principals and teachers, investing in the transformation of all principals into instructional leaders is one of the most effective steps a country can take to improve student learning. In MENA countries, such a change for school principals could improve teaching practice and student learning. Successful change depends on how principals are appropriately selected, supported, and given the needed blend of autonomy and accountability to perform.

pedagogy specific to subject areas—such as how to teach a mathematics class effectively, with follow-up visits in which trainers observe and support teachers in the classroom—are highly effective (Darling-Hammond et al. 2009). Some MENA countries have put in place promising professional development programs for teachers.

Professional development is most effective in changing classroom practice when teachers work collaboratively (Brown, Smith, and Stein 1995; Darling-Hammond et al. 2017; Evans and Popova 2015; Yoon et al. 2007). Collaboration allows teachers to benefit from one another's knowledge and skills and creates opportunities for best practice sharing and mentoring (Angrist and Lavy 2001; Borko 2004; Darling-Hammond et al. 2017). High-performing countries in East Asia and elsewhere have practiced collaborative approaches in professional development for decades, with positive results (Evans and Popova 2015; World Bank 2018a; Yoon et al. 2007). Technology and social media can be powerful tools in promoting peer-to-peer learning and collaboration between teachers. Many teachers in MENA are using groups on Facebook or WhatsApp to exchange information. Moreover, lessons on platforms such as Nafham, the Arabic version of the Khan Academy, not only help students to learn but can also help teachers to learn how to conduct a lesson effectively.

Professional development is equally important for principals who have been in the position for a long time because a principal's role and the demands of schooling change over time (Jensen, Downing, and Clark 2017a; OECD 2012a). Although professional development for principals needs to be tailored to the local context and needs, a few core elements are shared by many high-performing systems (Jensen, Downing, and Clark 2017a; World Bank 2018e). These elements include structuring leadership development around a vision for the school, whereby the school leader manages and oversees implementation of this vision. Other elements include linking leadership development to practical problems by means of action learning in a real school environment that is supported by mentors. Furthermore, school leadership programs should develop leaders' resilience, critical thinking skills, and ability to adapt practices to new situations. In high-performing systems, principals are often instructional leaders (see box O.5). Finally, leadership development programs should continue over the course of a leader's career through a systematic and comprehensive approach that is career-long and systemwide.

Assign the best teachers to where they are most needed
Decisions on teacher recruitment in most high-performing systems are made at the

school level (Barber and Mourshed 2007; Bruns and Luque 2015), which allows a better match between teacher characteristics and teaching needs, as identified by the school. In MENA countries, however, teacher hiring and assignment in the public system generally take place at the central level and usually by a civil service ministry. This arrangement has been a key challenge in enhancing performance because schools do not have the autonomy to hire good teachers or fire poorly performing ones. Managing performance then becomes a long bureaucratic process, which ultimately limits student learning as well as teacher motivation. As noted earlier, decentralized decision making requires capacity, resources, and accountability mechanisms. Ultimately, MENA school systems must find the balance between autonomy and accountability that will best support learning and provide schools with the resources and flexibility to establish and achieve ambitious goals for student learning.

Having an adequate number of qualified teachers in the classroom is a basic prerequisite for learning. However, students in some MENA countries are in classes so large that effective instruction can be difficult. Egypt, Jordan, and Morocco have some of the largest classes among TIMSS participants, while class sizes in Gulf Cooperation Council (GCC) countries are generally in line with the international average of TIMSS participants and those found in East Asia—though still higher than in countries such as Australia and Sweden (Mullis et al. 2016).

Even in countries in which teachers are recruited and assigned in adequate numbers, they are often not used efficiently. In MENA, low teacher working hours are common (see figure O.12). Only half of the MENA economies in 2010 required working hours for teachers that were comparable

FIGURE O.12 **The required working hours for teachers in MENA are well below those in top-performing countries**

Statutory teaching and working time required for teachers in primary education in selected MENA (2010) and OECD (2007) economies

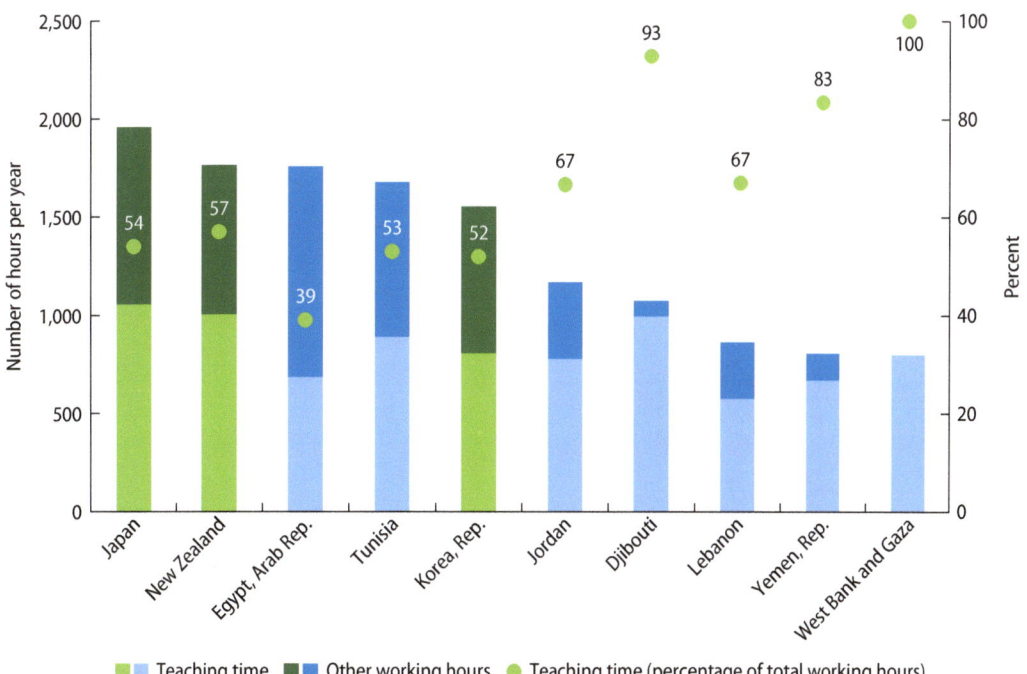

Source: World Bank 2015c.
Note: OECD = Organisation for Economic Co-operation and Development.

to those of the top-performing countries (World Bank 2015c). Egypt and Tunisia were within the range of top-performing countries such as Japan, Korea, and New Zealand. Others—such as Djibouti, Jordan, West Bank and Gaza, and the Republic of Yemen—were all well below the threshold of 1,200 working hours a year for teachers in primary education. In Lebanon, the working hours required of primary and secondary education teachers were less than half of those observed in top-performing countries.

Teacher absenteeism is a chronic problem plaguing MENA school systems. Among MENA countries participating in TIMSS 2015, an average of 16 percent of students in grade 8 were enrolled in schools whose principals reported teacher absenteeism to be a "serious problem" (see figure O.13). The problem is most acute in Morocco (affecting 28 percent of students), followed by Saudi Arabia, Oman, and Egypt. By comparison, only 4 percent of grade 8 students in OECD member countries were enrolled in schools with serious problems with teacher absenteeism. Similarly, low levels were observed in the Islamic Republic of Iran (2 percent) and the United Arab Emirates (7 percent).

Encourage instructional practices that maximize children's potential

Teaching and learning are multifaceted and complex. Children arrive at school with diverse backgrounds, life experiences, and individual characteristics. Teachers interact with children in a multitude of ways because they have a variety of backgrounds, life experiences, and teaching styles. The experience of students in the classroom rests on decisions teachers make about delivering the curriculum. How teachers prepare and engage with students of various abilities has an impact on their students' learning. Teaching at the right level, or adaptive instruction, is important to support student learning (Evans and Popova 2015)—see box O.6. Between 2013 and 2015, at least six systematic meta-analyses examined interventions that improve learning outcomes in low- and middle-income countries (Conn 2014; Glewwe et al. 2013; Kremer, Brannen, and Glennerster 2013; Krishnaratne, White, and Carpenter 2013; McEwan 2015; Murnane and Ganimian 2014). Across the reviews, pedagogical interventions (including computer-assisted learning) that tailor teaching to student skill levels ranked among the most

FIGURE O.13 **Teacher absenteeism is prevalent throughout MENA**

Percentage of grade 8 students attending schools whose principal reports that teacher absenteeism is a "serious problem," TIMSS 2015

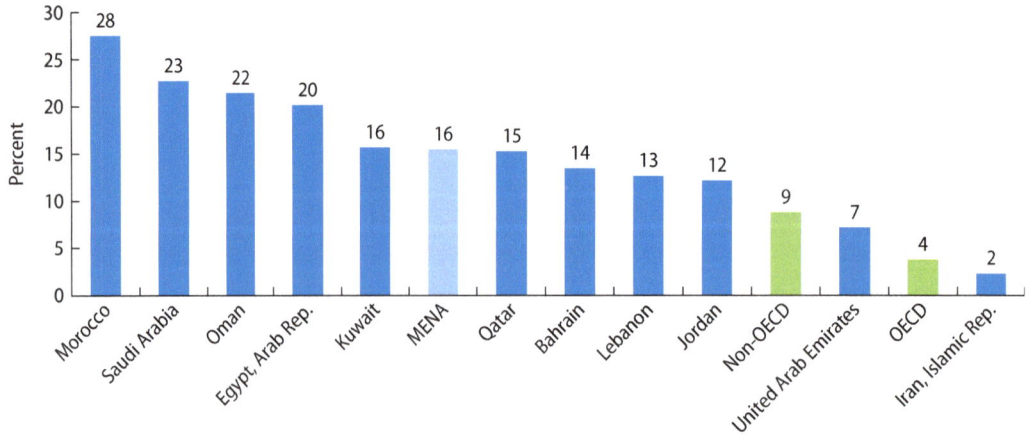

Source: IEA Trends in International Mathematics and Science Study—TIMSS 2015.
Note: OECD = Organisation for Economic Co-operation and Development; TIMSS = Trends in International Mathematics and Science Study.

> **Box O.6** **Teaching at the right level benefits students**
>
> Various models for instruction take into account the different abilities of students, ranging from grouping students by ability in the classroom for part of the school day or after school (Banerjee 2012) to giving screening tests to students at the beginning of the school year to identify student abilities and target support accordingly (OECD 2011c). In Canada and Finland, extensive personalized support is available to any student who is struggling with the expected levels of learning, especially during the formative years of primary school (World Bank 2018e). Evidence suggests that such targeted interventions and remedial lessons are more effective than other models of level-appropriate instruction, such as grade repetition and between-class ability grouping. Grade repetition, which is practiced in some MENA countries, requires students who do not pass the year-end examinations to repeat the prior school year rather than moving into the next grade with their peers (OECD 2016a). Between-class ability grouping entails grouping students in the same grade into classes based on prior achievement, so that classes are homogeneous in learning levels. A meta-analysis of 100 years of research on ability grouping found that such between-class grouping did not, in fact, benefit students (Steenbergen-Hu, Makel, and Olszewski-Kubilius 2016).

effective means of improving student learning in low- and middle-income countries.

Where the instructional capacity of teachers is low, structured pedagogy programs can be effective. Such programs typically include training courses for teachers and learning resources for both teachers and students. In addition to improving instructional quality on a topic, structured pedagogy programs can change existing classroom practice because they incorporate learning activities and pedagogical training. A review of 420 scholarly analyses of educational interventions in low- and middle-income countries found that structured pedagogy interventions had the largest and most consistently positive effects on student learning outcomes. Although none of the structured pedagogy interventions reviewed had taken place in MENA countries, some of the interventions were in countries performing at similar levels on TIMSS and PISA, such as Chile, Costa Rica, and South Africa (Snilstveit et al. 2015). A variety of scripted lessons and teacher coaching can help to overcome deficits in teacher skills in low-performing education systems (Mourshed, Chijioke, and Barber 2010). This can be an important short- to medium-term intervention until teachers' professional skills are further developed.

Address the language of instruction challenge

A key area that affects learning is the language of instruction (LOI). The LOI is normally shaped by culture, history, and current economic and political trends. For decades, choosing the language to use for instruction has posed a major challenge for MENA, with tension between tradition and modernity arising in several ways. The first tension is the question of whether to use modern standard Arabic—also referred to as classical Arabic—as the language of instruction. MSA differs from the language spoken daily in all Arabic-speaking MENA countries. Because MSA is the language by which the Quran was revealed and written, it has been kept sacred and has not changed with time, whereas the day-to-day language of societies has evolved, creating a large gap between everyday language and MSA. As a result, when children start school and encounter classical Arabic, they must learn it almost as a new language. They then struggle to acquire basic literacy skills and may feel substantial linguistic insecurity because of their lack of familiarity with MSA (Maamouri 1998). Research has shown that students in MENA may be considered at a linguistic disadvantage because they learn

MSA as if it were a second language (Bouhlila 2011; Ibrahim and Aharon-Peretz 2005; Salmi 1987).

Before students can learn in a language of instruction, they need to have learned enough of it. In every language, a vocabulary threshold must be met to understand simple text. For example, to understand English text, students must know at least 5,000 words in English. Typically, children come to school knowing 4,000–6,000 words in their mother tongue. On average, children can learn four vocabulary words per hour of second-language instruction. Thus 1,000 or more schooling hours are needed to build enough vocabulary to begin learning in a second language (van Ginkel 2014). If students fail to achieve both oral and written comprehension of MSA in early primary school, their future studies will be limited to memorizing and regurgitating information without achieving a synthesis of the information. Where teachers are themselves not comfortable operating in MSA, the problem is likely to be exacerbated.

Some MENA countries have addressed the MSA/dual-language challenge by designing curricular materials and providing additional support in the early grades. For example, a program introduced by the U.S. Agency for International Development (USAID) and the Ministry of Education in Egypt showed promise and is being scaled up. The program included eight days of teacher training in addition to curriculum inputs. Grade 2 students who received six months of intervention improved their performance by an entire grade level (Gove, Brombacher, and Ward-Brent 2017). In Jordan, the intervention included allotting daily time for low-performing students to practice foundational skills in reading and mathematics. Beyond an enhanced curricular emphasis on foundational skills, the intervention provided teachers with 10 days of training and additional in-school coaching on how to target remedial support where needed. As a result, not only did the number of low-performing students decrease, but schools also noted an increase in high-performing students (Gove, Brombacher, and Ward-Brent 2017).

The second tension in the LOI relates to the multiple languages used in some MENA countries. For example, in Algeria and Morocco a substantial proportion of the population speaks Tamazight; in Iraq and Syria there are Kurdish communities; and in Djibouti some communities speak Afar and Somali. Which language to use often becomes a political issue more than a technical one because language is closely associated with people's culture and identity. Because many of the MENA countries identify with Islam, they support the use of classical Arabic—the language of the Quran—as the language of instruction, even where large minorities are non-Arabic speakers, such as in Algeria, Iraq, and Morocco. However, there is substantial pressure from non-Arabic-speaking communities to use their language as the mode of instruction for their children.

The third tension occurs when opportunities for social and economic advancement are higher in a language that is not a student's mother tongue. Using a foreign language for instruction has been a topic of debate in MENA countries, with major implications for learning (see box O.7). Equity implications are a factor as well. In the 1980s, the movement of Algerian and Tunisian public education away from instruction in French and toward MSA resulted in greater inequality in education (elites pulled their children into private French-speaking schools) instead of the intended increase in classical Arabic skills. Furthermore, students who did not learn French were at a disadvantage in seeking future economic opportunities because higher-income positions continued to require French fluency (Benrabah 2007; Lefevre 2015). Addressing the language of instruction challenge is critical given the gap between spoken Arabic and modern standard Arabic. The close connection among language, religion, and national identity makes it difficult to make a regional recommendation. Even though this phenomenon is a regional one, it manifests itself in many different ways in different countries. Hence, it needs to be addressed with a very specific formula in each country.

Box O.7 Improving foreign language instruction is important

In Algeria, Morocco, and Tunisia, science and mathematics are taught in French at the secondary level. However, only 30 percent of Tunisians, most of whom live near the capital, are fluent in written and spoken French. In Algeria, urban populations are fluent in French, but only 55 percent of rural populations are fluent. A similar dynamic occurs in Morocco. Students in areas without French fluency have less access to education and less achievement (Lefevre 2015). In TIMSS 2007 and 2015, students being tested in their mother tongue performed better than those being tested in a language not used at home. If mathematics (or any other subject) is to be taught in a second language, adequate support for learning this language must be incorporated.

The language of instruction (LOI) has also been contentious and problematic at the tertiary education level, pointing to the need for improvement in foreign language instruction at all levels. Most Arab countries use either English or French as the LOI for mathematics, engineering, the medical sciences, and other sciences. Qatar's rapid expansion of higher education institutions in English generated resistance (MacLeod and Abou-El-Kheir 2016). Tunisia's system continues to embrace two languages, with Arabic used for all social sciences and French used for STEM (science, technology, engineering, and mathematics) studies. Recently, the Ministry of Higher Education in the Kurdistan Region of Iraq commissioned a study of its 13 state universities to assess the impact of English-medium instruction. The study found that 63 percent of instructors were satisfied with their own level of English, and, despite English being the official language of instruction, only 30 percent spoke English all the time or almost all the time in lectures. English was used for written materials and homework, but instructors widely stated that their students' language level was insufficient for English-medium studies, despite their 12 years of English-language instruction during their earlier schooling (Borg 2015). At any education level, employing an LOI that is not the students' mother tongue requires training teachers, providing adequate curriculum and classroom resources, and ensuring increased support for students.

Use assessments for learning, not credentials

Large-scale national and international assessments can catalyze education reform at the policy level. They are often used to measure and monitor student learning by tracking within-country trends in student learning, measuring what they have learned against learning targets, and providing points of comparison with other countries. MENA countries are increasingly participating in international large-scale student assessments (see table O.2). In addition, these countries are also conducting more national assessments, which have the benefit of being able to capture learning progress directly related to aspects of national education goals, the national curriculum, and national education policies (see table O.2).

Public examinations can generate powerful incentives for change at the school, teacher, and student levels. However, if used inappropriately, they can reinforce shallow forms of learning, and classroom assessments can consume valuable lesson time without enhancing student learning. In many MENA countries, students receive one of the only measures of their learning through high-stakes year-end examinations. These examinations are then typically used to determine whether students move to the next level. More regular feedback on their learning progress could be helpful to students and teachers. In addition, high-stakes assessments often lead to perverse incentives that negatively affect the behavior of teachers, students, and parents and limit learning outcomes.

Meanwhile, in MENA high-stakes examinations reinforce the focus on acquiring credentials rather than skills. As the sole determinant of whether a student moves on to higher education, passing high-stakes

TABLE O.2 Participation in national and international student assessments has surged in MENA since 2007

MENA economies undertaking national and international student assessments, 1995–2019

Economy	1995	1996	1997	1998	1999	2000	2001	2002	2003	2004	2005	2006	2007	2008	2009	2010	2011	2012	2013	2014	2015	2016	2017	2018	2019
Algeria													○●								□				
Bahrain													●			◇	○○◇	◇	◇	◇	○●	◀			○●
Djibouti																			×					+	◇
Egypt, Arab Rep.									●			◇	◇	●	×◇	◇	×		×	×	●	◀			○●
Iran, Islamic Rep.	○●			●		●			○●			◀	○●	●		◇	○●				○●	◀			◇
Iraq																		×+							
Jordan				●					●			□	●	◇	□		●	□×+		×+	○● □	◀		□	○●
Kuwait	○●					●						◀	○●				○				●				○●
Lebanon									●				●	◆			●				● ◆	×	◇	×□	●
Libya																									
Morocco			●			●			○●			◀	○●	◇			○●◀×+				○●	◇◀		□	○●
Oman											◇		●				○●◀				○●	◀			○●
Qatar												□◀	○●		□		○●◀	□			○●□	◀		□	○●
Saudi Arabia									●				●				○●◀				○●◇	◇◀		◇□	○●×◇
Syrian Arab Republic													●				●								
Tunisia			●							□		□	○●		□		●	□			□				
United Arab Emirates									○●○						□ᵃ		○●◀			×	○●□	◀		□	○●
West Bank and Gaza									●		◇						●							×	
Yemen, Rep.							◇		○		◇		○				○×								

| + EGMA | × EGRA | ◇ National or other assessment | ▲ PIRLS grade 4 | □ PISA | ○ TIMSS grade 4 | ● TIMSS grade 8 | ◆ TIMSS Advancedᵇ |

Source: Compiled by the World Bank, based on information from country task teams and international assessment organizations.

Note: Includes participating countries for which results were not reported because of sampling or other issues. EGMA = Early Grade Mathematics Assessment; EGRA = Early Grade Reading Assessment; PIRLS = Progress in International Reading Literacy Study; PISA = Programme for International Student Assessment; TIMSS = Trends in International Mathematics and Science Study.

a. The 2009 PISA scores pertain to the PISA 2009+ reported score for the United Arab Emirates (Dubai participated in 2009, and the remaining emirates participated in 2010).
b. TIMSS Advanced assesses the advanced mathematics and physics knowledge and skills of students in their final year of secondary school who have taken courses in advanced mathematics and physics. TIMSS Advanced was administered in 1995, 2008, and 2015.

examinations is the object of learning, especially in the last years of secondary education, rather than acquiring broader skills and learning to learn. Moreover, secondary-level high-stakes examinations usually emphasize straightforward recall and procedural applications, leading to cramming, private tutoring, and rote memorization. In Egypt, 53 percent of students resort to private tutoring, and a further 10 percent join paid study groups (Assaad and Krafft 2015).

Even in the lower grades, year-end school examinations affect opportunities for children to progress through grades, which can negatively influence teaching practices. Lebanon's students are tested monthly in class, take two examinations a year, and sit for national examinations at the end of grades 9 and 12. In the Islamic Republic of Iran and Jordan, students may pass on to the next level provided they do not fail more than three subjects in their year-end examinations. These examinations, or summative assessments, are intended to measure whether students have mastered the necessary content. They also channel students into educational tracks. However, their high-stakes nature often results in teachers emphasizing memorization for examinations over problem-solving skills (Akar 2016; Shuayb 2012). Morocco's system of examinations at each level is intended to channel students into educational and vocational tracks, and so it poses the risk of teachers using didactic rather than dialogic teaching methods (Akar 2016; IEA 2015; Shuayb 2012).

Recognizing the inherent risks, several MENA countries have reduced the emphasis on high-stakes examinations, especially in the lower grades. Jordan, Kuwait, and Lebanon have abolished high-stakes examinations that ration progression between grades 1 and 3. Kuwait's education officials noted that this change represented a substantial reduction in the dependence on examinations. Their example may guide further reforms aimed at ensuring that high-stakes examinations are rationed, do not create perverse incentives for teachers and students, and test higher-order thinking skills in other MENA countries.

Recently, East Asian countries with historically high scores on the PISA and TIMSS assessments have tried to reduce high-stakes testing at the upper-secondary level by introducing more process-oriented and student-centered assessment measures. For example, in an effort to eliminate teaching to the test and support curricular reforms aimed at learning to learn, in 2014 Japan proposed the Prospective University Entrant Scholastic Abilities Evaluation Test, which is an alternative examination to be implemented from 2019 onward. The examination will deemphasize rote memorization while giving priority to students' thinking ability, expression, and reasoning skills. The new test format includes a written questionnaire (Kimura and Tatsuno 2017).

In a similar effort to promote student learning, Korea implemented an exam-free semester nationwide in 2016 after pilot testing it for two years (Cheng 2017). So that lower-secondary school students can discover their dreams and talents free from the pressure of midterm and final exams, Korea allows teachers to make flexible use of the curriculum for one semester. This arrangement encourages student participation through discussion and practice and enables various activities such as career exploration.

There is compelling evidence that formative classroom assessments—the types of assessment procedures teachers use during the learning process to modify their activities and approaches in response to student learning—can raise learning outcomes by giving students timely feedback on how to improve (Black and Wiliam 2010; Hattie and Timperley 2007; Roediger, Putnam, and Smith 2011). Classroom assessment techniques can include verbal questioning and feedback, written quizzes, students holding up response cards or miniature whiteboards to give the teacher a real-time snapshot of classwide understanding, or activities requiring students to retrieve and apply newly acquired knowledge.

Although teachers in MENA regularly assess students, these classroom assessments are rarely aligned with student learning outcomes or used to adapt instruction to students' learning needs. Over 70 percent of students in MENA who participated in TIMSS 2015 had teachers who reported placing a major emphasis on monitoring students' progress in mathematics through students' ongoing work or classroom tests (Mullis et al. 2016). Yet across MENA countries, classroom assessments are rarely used to adapt instruction or provide students with meaningful feedback. For example, only one in four teachers in Jordan reported using classroom assessments to inform lesson planning (Rabie et al. 2017). Failure to do so limits the potential of classroom assessments to improve student learning.

Give all children a fair chance to learn

Countries reap the benefits of education when all children learn and develop their human capital. MENA countries have made impressive efforts to expand education, but millions of children are still out of school. In the 2014–15 academic year, 14 million children across the region were not in school. Among the unenrolled, 3.5 million were children of lower-secondary school age, 5.2 million of primary school age, and 5.3 million of preprimary age (UNICEF n.d.). A wide range of factors are associated with educational exclusion in MENA. These include disability, child labor, low maternal education, exposure to conflict (see box O.8), child marriage, migrant status, living in a rural or isolated area, and belonging to a nomadic group or a group that prevents children from attending school for cultural or religious reasons (UIS and UNICEF 2014).

Policies of inclusion mean that students with physical disabilities, learning difficulties, and other special educational needs are increasingly in school alongside their peers. An estimated 53 million persons with disabilities live in MENA, yet most countries in the region still have a limited supply of special education services (Alkhateeb and Hadidi 2015). This shortfall arises from limited funding, inadequate facilities, unqualified teachers, or negative attitudes toward disability and special education. Several MENA countries, such as Jordan, Kuwait, Qatar, Saudi Arabia, and the United Arab Emirates, have developed regulations and policies to create barrier-free accessible environments for students with

---

Box O.8 Conflict in MENA is depriving many children of education

MENA is host to about a quarter of the world's internally displaced persons (IDPs). As of May 2018, about 2 million people were internally displaced in the Republic of Yemen, 2 million in Iraq, and 0.2 million in Libya (IOM 2018; UNHCR 2018; UN OCHA 2018). Although there are few reliable data on school enrollment rates for this group, IDPs typically face high hurdles to access education services. Rough estimates place IDPs' school enrollment at just 28 percent in the Republic of Yemen and about 52 percent in Iraq (Ministry of Education, Republic of Yemen 2017; UNICEF 2017). Enrollment rates are often not disaggregated by level of education, but enrollment in upper-secondary and tertiary education is expected to be much lower than in basic education, similar to the enrollment patterns of refugees. In Syria and host countries, 7.7 million school-age Syrian children face great obstacles in accessing education services. Among Syrian refugee children, 46 percent are out of school (formal and nonformal) in Lebanon, 36 percent in Jordan, and 37 percent in Turkey (Brussels Conference 2019).

Beyond finding a political solution to the conflicts in Syria and the Republic of Yemen, more needs to be done to ensure that the generation of young refugees and displaced children is not left behind in education. This includes international support for countries that are hosting refugees, countries that are in conflict, and postconflict countries to help expand school infrastructure and provide the necessary inputs for teaching and learning. It is also important to help create safe learning environments and provide financial relief to displaced and refugee families. At the tertiary level, it is important to offer programs that enable refugee students to access higher education.

disabilities. However, inadequate school facilities and shortages of support personnel such as school psychologists, sign-language interpreters, speech and language pathologists, and physical and occupational therapists are a challenge (Alkhateeb and Hadidi 2015).

Mind the learning gaps and support the lowest performers

Although the average levels of student performance on international assessments have been low in MENA, there is a wide range of student performance within each country. Unlike in many advanced countries—such as Canada, Estonia, Finland, and Japan—where the link between test scores and socioeconomic status is generally weak, in MENA the learning gaps are substantial between students by socioeconomic level (OECD 2016a). Among 15-year-olds, the economic, social, and cultural status of their household correlates with substantial differences in student performance, as shown by the PISA 2015 results. In Lebanon, the gap is equivalent to a difference of more than two full years of schooling. Moreover, all nine MENA countries that participated in the 2015 grade 4 TIMSS mathematics assessment were among the 13 countries with the widest gaps between the top and bottom quartiles of performance (see figure O.14). Improving performance among those at the bottom would provide the most rapid improvement in overall levels of learning.

FIGURE O.14 MENA has the biggest gaps in student achievement between top and bottom performers

Difference in scale score between the 75th and 25th percentiles of grade 4 mathematics achievement, TIMSS 2015

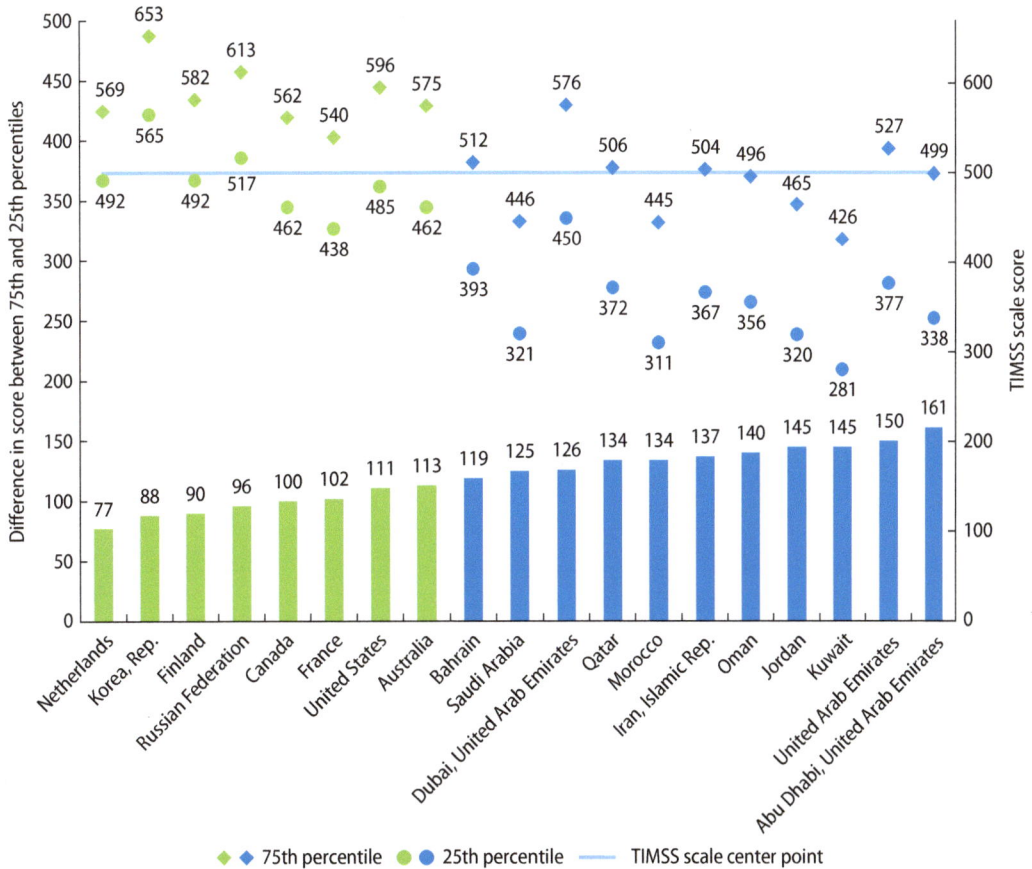

Source: Mullis et al. 2016.
Note: Includes all participating MENA countries (blue) and a selection of other countries. The diamonds represent the 75th percentile scores, and the circles represent the 25th percentile scores in the selected comparison countries. The horizontal blue line represents the TIMSS scale centerpoint, which is the mean of the overall achievement distribution in 1995 (kept constant over the years). TIMSS = Trends in International Mathematics and Science Study.

TABLE O.3 MENA's student achievement gaps have both narrowed and widened
Change in grade 8 TIMSS average achievement, 10th and 90th percentiles, 2011 and 2015

Country	Average score 2011	Average score 2015	Change in Average score	Change in 10th percentile	Change in 90th percentile
Mathematics					
Bahrain	409	454	45	72	19
Oman	366	403	37	54	22
Qatar	410	437	27	40	20
Iran, Islamic Rep.	415	436	21	20	23
Morocco	371	384	13	20	8
United Arab Emirates	456	465	9	−4	23
Lebanon	449	442	−7	−7	−7
Jordan	406	386	−20	−8	−22
Saudi Arabia	394	368	−26	−13	−35
Science					
Qatar	419	457	38	52	19
Oman	420	455	35	54	19
Morocco	376	393	17	18	16
Bahrain	452	466	14	12	18
United Arab Emirates	465	477	12	−3	22
Lebanon	406	398	−8	−13	−2
Iran, Islamic Rep.	474	456	−18	−16	−19
Jordan	449	426	−23	−15	−21
Saudi Arabia	436	396	−40	−59	−20

Source: Mullis et al. 2016, 72.
Note: TIMSS = Trends in International Mathematics and Science Study.

FIGURE O.15 MENA has the largest gender gaps in test scores
Highest score point difference in science (girls − boys), TIMSS grade 4, 2015

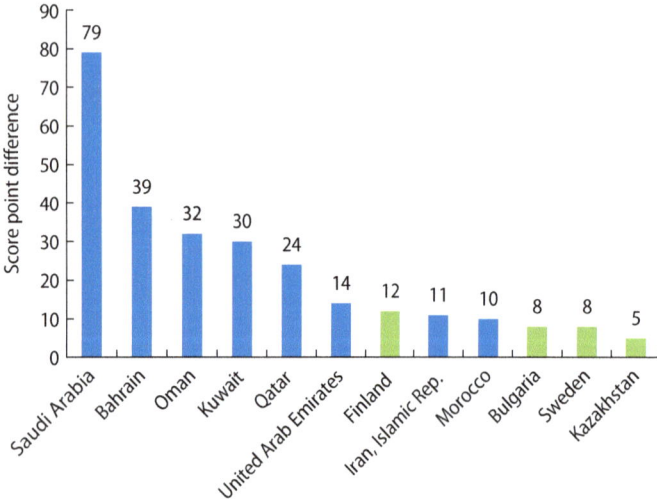

Source: Martin et al. 2016.
Note: The difference between girls and boys in the Islamic Republic of Iran is not statistically significant. TIMSS = Trends in International Mathematics and Science Study.

Some MENA countries are closing the achievement gap between their best and poorest performers, while others appear to have a widening gap (see table O.3). A notable case among all participating TIMSS countries is the United Arab Emirates, where the top students are performing better than in previous years, but the poorer performers are faring worse. Increasing retention through targeted programs can help bottom performers at risk of dropping out to stay in school.

Pay attention to the boys because they are falling far behind girls in learning outcomes

MENA has the largest gender disparities in student achievement, and they are consistently in favor of girls. Eight out of the 10 countries with the largest gender gaps in TIMSS are in MENA. Saudi Arabia has the largest gap, with boys significantly underperforming compared with girls (see figure O.15). Because the

Box O.9 MENA's gender paradox presents a dual challenge for human capital

The underperformance of MENA's boys is a phenomenon on a scale not seen elsewhere in the world. Education systems in MENA are clearly not meeting the learning needs of boys. And yet although girls are outperforming boys in education, MENA has the lowest female labor force participation rates among all regions in the world, according to the World Bank's World Development Indicators database. On average, across all MENA countries only 20 percent of women ages 15 and older participate in the labor force (World Bank, World Development Indicators database).

The inefficiencies and costs associated with the loss of learning among boys are substantial, economically and socially. Moreover, the underrepresentation of women in the labor market, despite the fact that women considerably outperform men in learning from the early years all the way to adulthood, represents a substantial underutilization of human capital.

---

learning outcomes for all MENA students are low, the pervasive gender gap amounts to a learning crisis for boys in the region. Gender gaps in learning appear early; by the second grade, girls are outperforming boys in reading. For example, in West Bank and Gaza there was a 10 percentage point gap between girls (17 percent) and boys (27 percent) who could not read a single word of connected text. Across the 18 countries that participated in the EGRA between 2010 and 2015, the gender gap is the most pronounced for MENA countries (USAID 2018). The early manifestation of gender gaps in foundational skills such as literacy and numeracy points to the need to address the specific learning needs of boys in the early grades. Indeed, interventions that are not targeting boys and students in need of additional support may exacerbate the gender gap (see box O.9).

Dedicate more resources to children from the poorest households

Inequality of opportunity[10] starts early in life. Therefore, efforts to address it must also start early. Children born into circumstances not conducive to their well-being are likely to fall behind in their health, nutrition, and physical, cognitive, social, and emotional development—all precursors to success in school. For example, at just 18 months of age, a child's vocabulary reflects the socioeconomic status of his or her parents (Center on the Developing Child 2009). By age 3, the vocabulary of a child whose parents have a college degree can be as much as three times larger than the vocabulary of a child whose parents have not completed high school (Center on the Developing Child 2009).

Access to early childhood education in MENA is highly unequal within countries. For example, in Djibouti and Egypt a child from the wealthiest quintile of households is six times more likely to attend an early childhood care and education (ECCE) program as a child from the poorest quintile (El-Kogali and Krafft 2015). In Iraq, Libya, and Tunisia, children from the most advantaged backgrounds are more than 17 times more likely to attend an ECCE program than children from the least advantaged backgrounds. What are the short- and long-term implications of inequalities in early childhood development, care, and education? When children start primary school, they are already set on different trajectories. Some children will have all they need for success in school and in adult life. Others will start their school life at a disadvantage, which will have subsequent effects throughout their years of schooling and beyond.

Finally, large enrollment gaps exist in MENA, particularly between the richest and the poorest children. For example, in Morocco more than half of lower-secondary school-age children in the poorest quintile of households are out of school, compared with

6 percent in the richest quintile. Gaps in rates of out-of-school children also occur by gender and location (urban versus rural).

Leverage technology toward a stronger push for learning

The rapid penetration of technology and the myriad opportunities it presents entice citizens and policy makers to invest in digital technologies. Across MENA, three underlying factors will keep access to technology at the forefront: (1) governments' desire to diversify away from an oil-dependent economy; (2) efforts by businesses to remain globally competitive by extending their reach on digital technologies; and (3) the opportunity offered by digital technology to support learning for all. A technology-driven future will require children to be technologically savvy, and education systems must support them in becoming so. Although many other sectors have already borne the brunt of technological disruption, the education sector has not changed substantially in its principal mode of delivery over the last 150 years—globally and in MENA. Technology offers a unique opportunity to deliver high-quality education in a more efficient and effective manner. If leveraged smartly, technology can help MENA countries to advance their education systems and support learning.

EdTech solutions hold promise to boost learning
EdTech—information and communication technology (ICT) applications aimed at improving education—have been growing fast globally. In 2017 revenue from the global EdTech market was estimated at US$17.7 billion (Business Wire 2018).[11] Several factors have fueled this growth: recognition of the importance of education to economic growth; a flattening or even decline in public financing of education, thereby creating space for private sector participation; and—perhaps most important—efforts to disrupt this sector through technology in the hope of increasing student learning and moving rapidly ahead in international education rankings.

Several conditions in MENA today support greater adoption of EdTech, including a young, dynamic, and tech-savvy population; an education market valued at about US$100 billion (Al Masah Capital 2012); and a region in which countries on average allocate about a fifth of their budget to education (Trade Arabia News Service 2013; World Bank 2008). All of this points to an environment conducive to EdTech and its growth.

Many online platforms in MENA are providing Arabic learning content. Some of the English-language content from Khan Academy and others has been translated into Arabic. MENA-based content providers such as Nafham have followed the Khan Academy format with original content that uses curricula from several countries in the region, along with crowdsourcing to upload lessons. Others—such as Bibliotheca Alexandrina in Egypt, the Education Media Company in Morocco, and Talal Abu-Ghazaleh International University in Lebanon—have created digital content in different languages.

Some initiatives allow qualified refugees to access online courses. For example, the German distance-learning university Fernuniversität Hagen allows qualified refugees to access all online courses and provides language training. Kiron University has partnered with massive open online course (MOOC) providers in the United States to organize a two-year online course for refugees, with the possibility of completing their studies at a host university in Germany (Unangst 2017). In the United Kingdom, the Department for International Development's Partnership for Digital Learning and Increased Access (PADILEIA) aims to address the higher education needs of young people displaced in Jordan and Lebanon by the Syrian crisis through blended academic programs, including MOOCs, targeted online learning, and classroom-based learning for displaced students (SPHEIR 2017).

Leverage the strong public support for education technology in MENA
Families, students, and the broader community in MENA countries strongly support further

integration of digital technology in classrooms to change the nature of education and training systems. In a survey on social media and education reform across 13 MENA countries, most respondents supported ICT in the classroom (ASMR 2013). Of those surveyed, 84 percent felt universal Internet access should be a norm and that children in schools should be able to access the Internet on personal devices. More than three-quarters felt that social media should be part of the school curriculum; indeed, 61 percent believed students should be allowed to use social networking media in class. Responding to a question on whether students should be allowed to engage in a range of computer-related activities, almost 80 percent noted they would be happy to have their children use "collaborative web tools" in classwork. Nevertheless, those surveyed also recognized that some aspects of access to technology could have detrimental effects on student learning.

Expand ICT infrastructure for wider reach of EdTech solutions

Accessing EdTech solutions and platforms requires ICT infrastructure. MENA countries have made substantial investments in school ICT infrastructure (Lightfoot 2011). ICT is available in most MENA schools, averaging about 2.7 computers for every 10 grade 8 students (see figure O.16). However, the international average is 4 computers for every 10 grade 8 students. Cross-country variability is quite wide, with 10.5 computers for every 10 students in Qatar, and only 1.0 computer for every 50 students in the Islamic Republic of Iran (Mullis et al. 2016).

EdTech is necessary but not sufficient to improve student learning outcomes

The evidence is mixed on the impact of technology on education. A recent study by the Massachusetts Institute of Technology's Abdul Latif Jameel Poverty Action Lab (J-PAL) evaluated more than 100 EdTech interventions and reveals important insights on the use of technology in education (Escueta et al. 2017). The study notes that online connectivity is a necessary but not sufficient condition for improving student learning outcomes aided by EdTech's most promising solutions. Teachers must be capable of guiding students on how to search online resources

FIGURE O.16 Computers are available in MENA's schools, although coverage varies considerably

Number of computers (including tablets) available for student use in school for every 10 grade 8 students, 2015

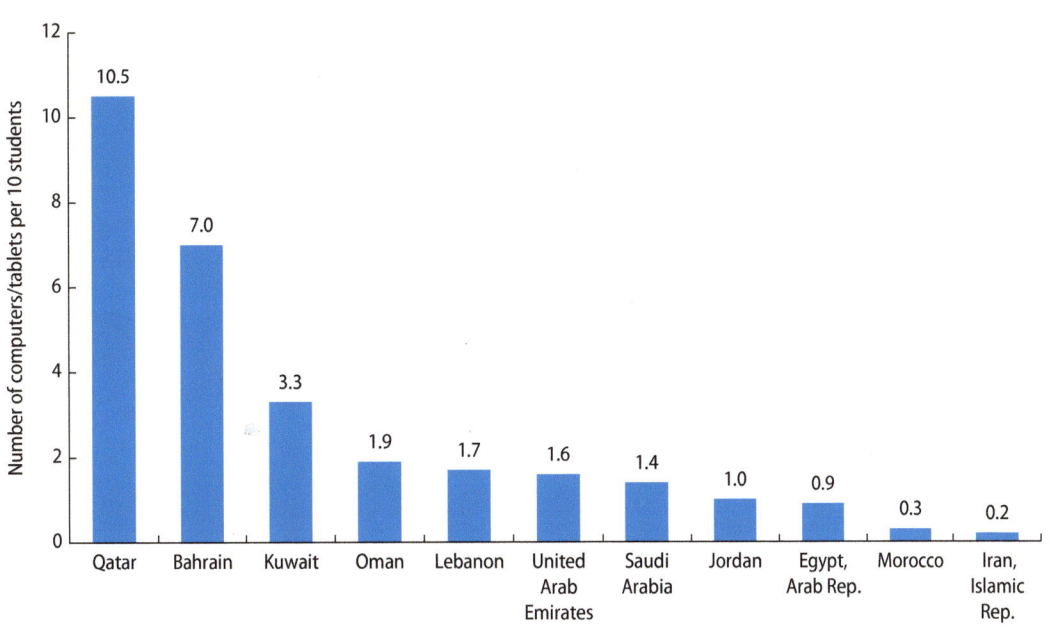

Source: Mullis et al. 2016.

> **Box O.10** **EdTech offers opportunities to leapfrog learning**
>
> *Computer-assisted learning (CAL) programs* pair face-to-face classroom learning with online curriculum components. These programs work well when delivered to students through structured online and in-class settings in which teachers are trained to facilitate this interaction. CAL occurs any time a student learns through a combination of supervised school experiences away from home and online content delivery, with some element of student control over time, place, path, or pace (Horn and Staker 2011). With blended learning, classroom and online experiences are tailored to reinforce one another (Horn and Staker 2012).
>
> *Technology-based behavioral interventions (nudging)* draw on insights from behavioral economics. These interventions are proving effective in a wide variety of education settings (Escueta et al. 2017). Nudging presents beneficiaries with choices without changing the costs of these choices in any real way. Typically, nudges reach users by text message, reminding parents to register children for early childhood development programs or review their children's secondary report card, or alerting university students that it is time to submit student loan materials (Economist 2017; Escueta et al. 2017; Pugatch and Wilson 2018).
>
> *Digital textbooks* are interactive and allow unique learning experiences for students. At one end of the spectrum in MENA are mobile apps that provide online interactive libraries, such as Rawy Kids in Egypt or the Kitabi Book Reader in Lebanon. At the other end are those that use entertainment and games to encourage learning, such as Sho'lah and Loujee, a "smart" Arabic toy aimed at learning-through-play (Arab News 2016). Recently, two smartphone app–based games were shown to improve early grade reading in conflict-ridden Syria: Antura and the Letters and Feed the Monster, both of which showed positive learning results on initial impact evaluations and won awards at the 2017 EduApp4Syria competition (Comings 2018).

and supporting the growth of critical thinkers who can organize, prioritize, and synthesize along the way. The study also offers some options that could be applied in MENA countries (see box O.10).

A recent analysis of PISA results for MENA countries confirms these findings. Access to technology alone cannot solve problems related to student outcomes (McKinsey 2017). The association with adding one more computer to a classroom is small, whereas supplying teachers with computers has a larger positive association; adding a computer for the teacher in each classroom is associated with a sixfold increase in student PISA scores versus giving a student a computer.[12] Although increasing access to computers and the Internet may not on its own measurably improve academic achievement, it has been successful in increasing the ease of technology use and the time spent learning to use digital devices. In this sense, online connectivity in the classroom could be a necessary but not sufficient condition for improving student learning outcomes aided by EdTech solutions.

To ensure learning for all, special attention should be paid to digital literacy skills. In many countries, youths from both advantaged and disadvantaged backgrounds spend roughly the same time online each week. However, there are important differences in the way they use the Internet. Even in high-income countries, where access to the Internet is almost equal for children from different socioeconomic backgrounds, students from disadvantaged backgrounds are more likely to chat or play video games than their richer peers, who use the Internet more to search for information or read the news (World Economic Forum 2016). To turn "opportunities into real opportunities" (OECD 2016d, 3) for everyone and reduce (digital) inequalities, schools must teach literacy skills while actively promoting technology as a means of improving skills and knowledge, including learning about potential job markets.

Pull for skills

Complementary reforms are needed for education to achieve its potential

For education to reach its full potential, it must provide students with skills that satisfy the economic and social needs of each country. A push for learning would move education closer to fulfilling its potential, but it would be a second-best approach that would leave most of that potential untapped (Rodrik 2008).

A first-best approach involves multisystem reforms that align a push for learning with a pull for skills. It includes economic reforms to match the skills required in the labor market with those conferred by education and sought by parents and students. Multisystem reform would seek to address distortions in the education sector and beyond. For example, it would address signals and incentives from the labor market as well as implement reforms within the education sector. Without a realignment of the labor market that increases the demand for skills, the education sector's contribution to goals such as economic diversification will not be fully realized. Moreover, without civil service reforms that support hiring, motivating, and empowering the best teachers, the teaching profession would remain undervalued and learning would be compromised. It is therefore important to understand how the education sector interacts with the economic, social, and political environment to achieve expected outcomes and to implement policies that address both the education system and labor market challenges.

Improve signaling for skills

Distortions in the labor market in MENA countries have led to an emphasis on credentials rather than skills. To break out of the current credentialist equilibrium in MENA and move toward a skills equilibrium, employers need to send youths and families strong signals of the kinds of skills needed. For their part, these youths and families need to in turn demand the relevant skills from the education system.

FIGURE O.17 MENA needs a skills equilibrium

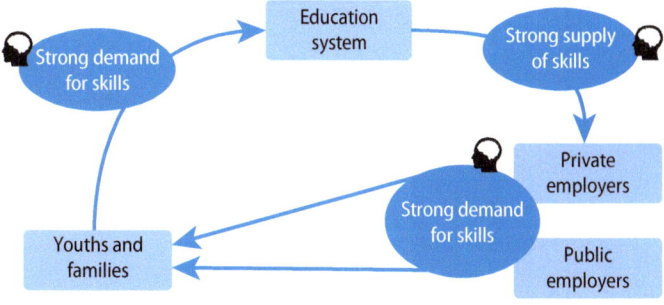

Source: Adapted from Assaad, Krafft, and Salehi-Isfahani 2018.

The education system needs to then respond by supplying the set of skills needed and signaling the skills acquired (see figure O.17).

However, employers in MENA are not effectively communicating (signaling) to the education system or students and parents what skills they need. This weak signaling is exacerbated by the fact that in most countries, private sector firms are disproportionately microenterprises, and these businesses lack the ability to send signals effectively to the region's education systems (Assaad, Krafft, and Salehi-Isfahani 2018). Nor are these firms well positioned to receive signals from the education system. Currently, the signals are essentially for credentials (see box O.11).

Address rigid labor policies

MENA's rigid labor policies also constrain the pull for skills. For example, labor laws make it extremely difficult for employers to fire employees (World Bank 2013a). This factor creates a disincentive for the private sector, and employers are therefore less likely to hire on a trial basis to learn about a candidate's skills, as is common practice in other parts of the world. That disincentive, coupled with the absence of information on the quality or productivity of graduates, means that firms tend to hire based on social networks.

Personal connections, not skills, drive labor market outcomes in MENA, further dampening the demand for skills. A Gallup

Box O.11 Signaling in education is communicating about skills

Countries across MENA are not in a skills equilibrium. The Gulf Cooperation Council is experiencing gaps between nationals and immigrant workers in terms of skills, labor prices, and labor mobility. There, policy makers are discussing the need for a fundamental reform of the skills system. For example, of the 23,000 annual new job seekers in Kuwait, some 10,000 would be unable to find suitable jobs. Placements for these job seekers would require the demand for labor to increase (employers wanting more of the kinds of workers currently produced by the education system) or education reforms to match skills more closely with the labor market (Sleiman-Haidar 2016).

Signaling is the process through which one party reveals some information about itself to another. For example, in the labor market employers do not immediately know the productive capabilities of their new hires. One prominent way in which applicants signal their abilities is through education (Arcidiacono, Bayer, and Hizmo 2010; Spence 1973). In the United States, the résumés of college graduates include information on grades, majors, and test scores. This information acts as a signal of ability and increases the likelihood that college graduates will be paid in line with their abilities.

Most high school graduates have fewer ways in which to signal their abilities, although the financial returns to ability increase steeply with experience (Arcidiacono, Bayer, and Hizmo 2010).

In MENA, test scores do not currently appear to provide adequate information about ability (Assaad, Krafft, and Salehi-Isfahani 2018). In addition to making test scores more meaningful (by measuring skills more effectively), changes in labor policy could provide employers with the information and flexibility they need by, for example, encouraging trial periods of employment prior to long-term contracts. Together, these practices would send employers a more accurate signal of graduates' skills.

Signals from employers to students and educational institutions are important as well. National employer surveys, with widely publicized reports and results, could be one route to signaling the skills that employers need. Career academies or other models of employer-school partnerships can give students information on the jobs available and the skills required. Partnerships that facilitate internships, mentoring, and other informational experiences may be effective (Lerman 2013).

Poll conducted in 16 MENA economies found that, on average, 70 percent of respondents agreed that a personal connection is critical to securing a job (see figure O.18). Families and students also lack incentives to focus on skills; in the labor market, measurable skills from education are rewarded much less than, if at all, social background or credentials (Assaad, Krafft, and Salehi-Isfahani 2018; Krafft and Assaad 2016; Krishnan et al. 2016).

Effective reforms, such as those in China, address both rigid labor policies and the education-specific challenges that contribute to low skills and poor signals. Previously in China, strict regulations, a lack of competition, and an inability to fire unproductive workers resulted in low productivity (Morrison 2011). Within the command economy, workers were guaranteed lifetime employment and assigned a job from which their employer was unable to terminate their appointment, with wages determined by seniority and education level (Meng, Shen, and Xue 2013). In the late 1970s, China successfully implemented multiple economic reforms, including giving more wage flexibility to firms and introducing a labor contracting system that moved away from lifetime tenure and gave state-owned enterprises the right to lay off workers. Following China's first national work conference in 1980, enterprises were granted more autonomy in hiring, and job seekers were given more autonomy to find jobs, including in the private sector (Brooks and Tao 2003). Wage flexibility, including instituting bonuses, has been gradually increased, and the share of bonuses in total wages for all enterprises increased from 2 percent of the wage bill in 1978

FIGURE O.18 A personal connection (*wasta*) is critical to securing work in MENA

Percentage responding to the statement that a personal connection is critical to securing work

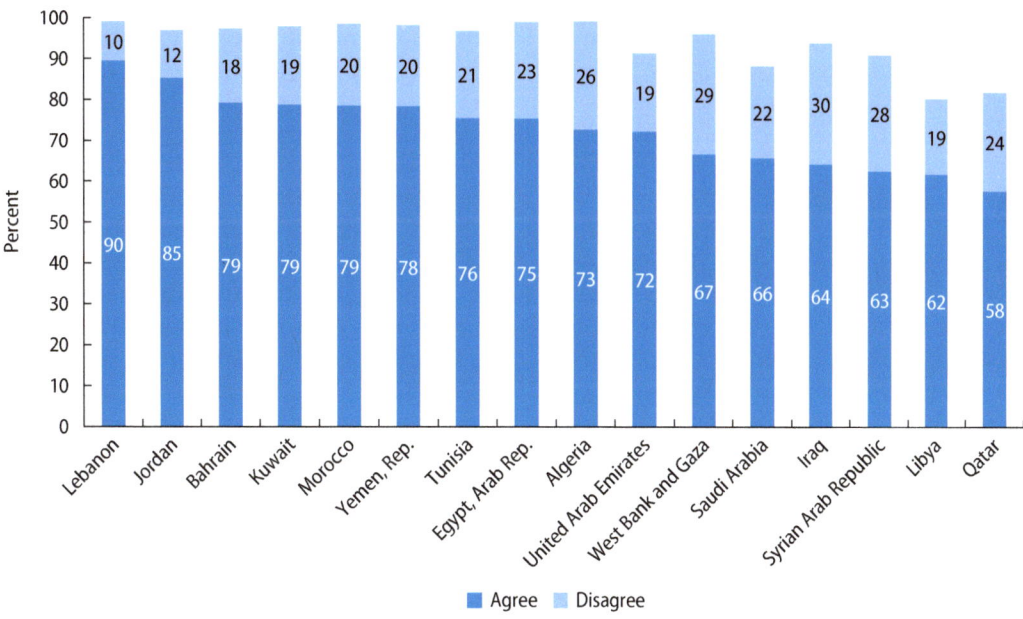

Source: Gallup Poll 2013.
Note: Percentages do not add up to 100 because respondents could also select "Don't Know" or refused to reply.

to 16 percent in 1997, effectively giving employees the incentive to perform well (Brooks and Tao 2003). Since 1997, earnings have almost doubled (Meng, Shen, and Xue 2013). Meanwhile, the reforms have led to higher returns to schooling (Zhang et al. 2005). Students have greater incentives to learn skills that will allow them to earn higher wages based on their skill set and productivity instead of their education credentials.

Reform civil service to attract the best educators

A pull for skills requires civil service reforms to recruit, retain, and empower the best educators. No education system will be successful unless it provides meaningful incentives (financial or professional) for teacher effort (World Bank 2018e). Although the evidence is mixed on the effects of financial incentives on teachers, professional incentives appear to hold the potential for better student learning outcomes. Merit pay systems may be warranted in some contexts, but the international evidence is clear that well-chosen professional incentives have even greater potential. Changes to career ladders and other forms of recognition for teachers have had substantial motivational effects in several high-performing countries. These systems use appraisal processes to identify talent and accomplishment (Darling-Hammond et al. 2017; Liang, Kidwai, and Zhang 2016).

In most MENA countries, teachers' career advancement pathways depend mainly on years of service, not performance (World Bank 2012). Greater efforts are needed to reform teacher incentive systems to promote good teaching and learning and to provide rewarding career pathways. These types of initiatives may require reforming civil service rules and regulations to support incentive and accountability systems. For example, in Shanghai teachers can advance professionally through a five-level ranking system (Liang, Kidwai, and Zhang 2016; World Bank 2018a). Australia, Canada, and Singapore have similar career ladders or pathways that reward teachers' knowledge, skills, and contributions (NCEE 2016).

Useful examples of rewarding and flexible pathways for school principals can be found around the world. For example, in Flemish Belgium a former principal can serve as director of a community of schools that collaborates on issues such as career guidance for students, course provision, and special needs education (Pont, Nusche, and Moorman 2008). England has created a Leadership Development Framework that provides a pathway of programs and standards that extend across a school leader's career, including opportunities for experienced school leaders to support other principals (Pont, Nusche, and Moorman 2008). In Shanghai, the career ladder of school principals has four levels that are aligned with job performance (Jensen, Downing, and Clark 2017b; Liang, Kidwai, and Zhang 2016; NCEE 2016).

In MENA, a school principal's authority to determine resource needs, budgeting, and personnel management is relatively low (World Bank 2015c). Most principals in MENA's public schools do not have the authority to select teachers for their schools or to fire underperforming or chronically absent teachers. By contrast, many OECD countries (Denmark, Ireland, the Netherlands, New Zealand, Slovenia, Switzerland, the United Kingdom, and the United States) give the school principal a substantial role in hiring and firing teachers (see figure O.19). Of the six MENA countries participating in PISA 2015, the three with the highest mathematics scores (Lebanon, Qatar, and the United Arab Emirates) grant a level of responsibility to principals for school governance that is similar to that in OECD countries, although more studies are needed to demonstrate whether the correlation between school governance and student performance is causal.

Efforts are under way to improve school leadership in some MENA countries, although it has been a slow process. Tunisia's primary school directors have

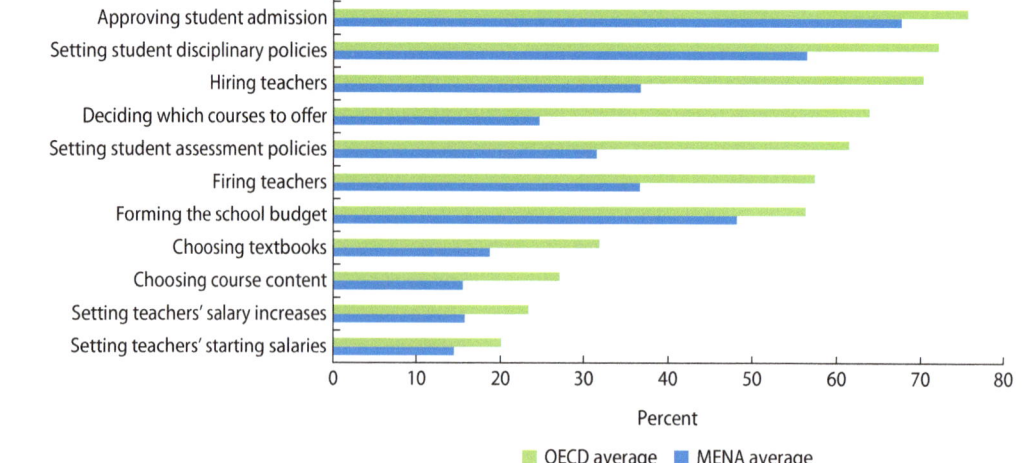

FIGURE O.19 **School principals in MENA have less authority than those in OECD countries**

Percentage of students in schools in which the principal has considerable responsibility for ...

Source: OECD 2016a.
Note: OECD = Organisation for Economic Co-operation and Development.

little access to financial resources. Although they are explicitly required by law to provide guidance to teachers on curriculum and teaching-related tasks, in practice these tasks are often left to pedagogical counselors and inspectors who make periodic visits. Tunisia's school directors also do not have the authority to select or remove teachers in their schools. Likewise, they do not have the authority to reward strong performance. Recognizing these governance issues in primary education, Tunisia has designed a project aimed at empowering school leaders and strengthening school management that will be implemented in the coming years (World Bank 2018c).

Align curricula with the skills demanded

Official curricula determine what education systems intend their students to learn. Ideally, those curricula should reflect the skills that prepare students for social and economic life, and any reforms should be aimed at ensuring that what students learn aligns with the skills they need. In fact, curricula are the nexus where the multiple spheres of society, the labor market, and the education system should meet. The shift from a credentialist equilibrium to a skills equilibrium can be observed through curricula. Systems are aligned when official curricula reflect the skills demanded by society and the labor market. Conversely, when official curricula are outdated and disconnected from practical, real-life content, the result is a mismatch between what students acquire and what society and employers require.

Across the world, curricular reforms are moving toward expressing outcomes in terms of skills and away from defining curricular content only as subject material to be taught (UNESCO 2017b). This shift represents a greater pull for skills as the focus moves from the acquisition of facts and toward what students are able to do with their learning—that is, the skills students have acquired as a result of the education process.

Curricula in education systems across MENA reflect the belief that education should provide academic content, workforce preparation, and social and civic development. Recent reforms over the last few decades have added, for example, life skills, foreign languages, problem-solving approaches, and more science, mathematics, and information technology to curricula (Alayan, Rohde, and Dhouib 2012). The legislative rhetoric in MENA countries on what skills students should acquire in school aligns with 21st-century skills. Most emphasize mastery of Arabic and foreign languages, awareness of human rights, desire for international cooperation, awareness of environmental and conservation issues, critical thinking, and research skills. For example, Saudi Arabia's education legislation states that students should have the skills and knowledge to contribute to society economically and culturally and to build up their communities. The United Arab Emirates' curriculum document states that its education system trains students for physical, intellectual, and emotional development and prepares them for their future. Morocco's goals focus on language acquisition, developing appropriate social skills, understanding civic matters, and preparing students for future careers (UNESCO 2011).

Yet even though the legislative rhetoric may reflect a modern approach to education, the material studied, and the pedagogical approaches used, many MENA classrooms remain traditional and disconnected from students' everyday lives (Bouhlila 2011). Material is presented as a set of facts and processes to be memorized and in a manner that does not encourage independent learning and investigation. Connections between theory and practice are left unexplored, as are links between past and present (Alrebh and Al-Mabuk 2016). In addition to the

> **Box O.12** **Reforming vocational education**
>
> In some MENA countries, the vocational education tracks are growing and include religious, technical, industrial, agricultural, and commercial education. Algeria has recently seen increased enrollment in vocational education. The nation has partnered with public and private companies to create programs in construction, public works, electricity, agriculture, and tourism (Oxford Business Group 2015). Bahrain began to introduce apprenticeships in 2007–08. After the 2011 revolution, the Tunisian Ministry of Education began to develop a reform plan that will include restructuring its vocational education tracks (Oxford Business Group 2017), and there is interest in other countries across the region in making vocational education work better for students and for the labor market.
>
> Vocational education works best when schools collaborate with employers. In Egypt, vocational schools lack appropriate facilities and hands-on learning opportunities (Krafft 2017). Vocational education has also failed to adapt appropriately to the available jobs, and it may be too rigid in its structure, failing to provide students with a broad enough foundation for employment.

poor learning that results, a lack of relevance to real life makes students less interested and less prepared for the world beyond school. Relevance is particularly important in programs that are intended to relate closely to the workplace (see box O.12).

Internationally, economies take a variety of approaches to creating and implementing skills- or competency-based curricula. In U.S. public schools, competency-based systems use state learning standards to determine academic expectations and define "proficiency" in a given course, subject area, or grade level (although other sets of standards may also be used, including standards developed by districts and schools or by subject-area organizations). Several high-scoring East Asian education systems (Hong Kong SAR, China; Japan; Korea; and Singapore) have begun to legislate and implement competency-based curricula to help students develop 21st-century skills by reducing the relative weight of subject-centered education. Among these economies, some, such as Korea, prefer greater control and prescribe the curriculum. Others, such as Japan, set general guidelines and grant greater autonomy to schools and teachers to develop their curricula (Asia Society and OECD 2018; Cheng 2017; Moon 2007).

A few MENA economies have recently begun to explore competency-based learning. Through its Integrated Education Reform Program, Kuwait is transforming its curricula and instructional and assessment methods. This approach focuses on the student, emphasizes applied knowledge, and caters to different learning abilities. A national curriculum framework has been developed by local education professionals, along with curricular standards for all subjects and grades. Competency-based textbooks are being developed in line with the new standards, as well as a national assessment to gauge progress at the national, school, and student levels.

Recognize that context matters for learning and skills

Implementing education reforms in MENA through a push for learning and a pull for skills will not achieve the same results across all contexts. There are multiple models for transforming education. Finland and Korea were both top scorers in PISA 2015, a signal of strong learning. Yet the two education systems producing this learning are quite different (see box O.13).

> **Box O.13** **Finland and the Republic of Korea rely on different successful education models**
>
> Both Finland and Korea have successful, high-performing education systems, and yet these systems differ greatly. Korea is known for its rigorous, test-driven system, whereas Finland has a more accommodating, flexible system with no mandated standardized tests, except for college entrance exams (Darling-Hammond, Wei, and Andree 2010). A high school student in Korea spends on average 10 hours a day at school and is under immense pressure from his or her family to do well (Ellinger and Beckham 1997). By contrast, Finland allows students to take courses at their own pace in their final years of schooling, enabling them to learn the material better with less stress and on their own time (Morgan 2014). There is no clearly "right" education system—both of these high-performing systems promote learning.
>
> And yet despite their different environments, these systems have a few distinct similarities. Both countries are committed to providing students with equal learning opportunities. In Korea, teachers rotate to different schools every five to seven years, creating more chances for exceptional teachers to interact with disadvantaged students (Morgan 2016). PISA revealed that the opportunities to learn in Finland are essentially the same throughout the country (Morgan 2016). Finnish schools offer welfare services and free early academic support for students who have needs in reading, writing, or math (Morgan 2014, 2016), which helps to diminish preexisting inequalities among students, enabling them to learn.
>
> In addition, both countries invest in and develop accomplished teachers. In Finland, teaching is a highly respected profession that is often perceived to be more important than medicine or law. Finland admits only the top 10 percent of students to the teacher education program. Teachers come out of the five-year intensive program well prepared, allowing them to have more autonomy to teach the way they feel is most effective (Morgan 2014). The program involves a wide variety of training, including observing teachers in the classroom, practicing teaching lessons with students, as well as preparing students to become researchers and practitioners. In Korea, teachers are required to take 90 hours of professional development courses every three years to enhance their teaching. One Korean professional development program offers an advanced certificate, which often leads to an increase in salary and sometimes to a promotion (Darling-Hammond, Wei, and Andree 2010).

MENA countries need to roll out reform efforts based on what is feasible in education, economic, or social reform. Successful reforms will depend on understanding the existing constraints (Rodrik 2008). For example, countries such as Jordan and Lebanon face a large influx of refugees from the civil war in Syria, so any reforms of their education systems must consider the need to accommodate refugee children in the system and the associated constraints. Another example is when coordination between the education sector and labor market is not feasible, and the information needed to provide specific in-demand job skills is not available. In this case, the education system could, in the interim, focus on important foundational skills in schools. When coordination between the education sector and labor market is feasible, the education system can emphasize the development of more targeted job skills because educators will know what skills employers need. Conditions that enable or hinder program success are a crucial aspect of successful reforms.

How reforms are designed, introduced, approved, and implemented within a specific country also determines their success. For example, in Mexico reforms were introduced after substantial negotiations with teachers' unions, which resulted in their successful implementation. In Tunisia, the reform process became confrontational and was ultimately blocked (Grindle 2004; Kingdon et al. 2014; World Bank 2018c).

The effectiveness of different policy options often depends on whether complementary conditions are in place. For example, school-based decision making can be effective in improving learning outcomes, but it may be less effective in disadvantaged contexts in which parents are less able to participate (Carr-Hill, Rolleston, and Schendel 2016). Meanwhile, early childhood development programs have enormous potential to improve learning outcomes, but they are ineffective when program quality is low (Bouguen et al. 2013; Jung and Hasan 2014; Temple and Reynolds 2007) or when they are not available for the highest-risk populations (Karoly 2017).

Sufficient resources and a sustained approach that stays the course to the end while continuously monitoring results are also important. In Morocco, a lack of adequate funding was a big obstacle to achieving the goals of education reform between 2005 and 2009 (European Commission 2010). High turnover among the top leadership of ministries of education and senior administrators also stalls reform efforts. Between 2010 and 2017, Jordan had six ministers of higher education, Egypt had seven, and Lebanon had four—all of whom were in office for less than three years.[13] Recent high turnover in ministers of education has also been noted in Kuwait, Morocco, and Saudi Arabia.

Tackle social norms that hold back education

To make any substantial changes in education, countries must tackle the inefficient social norms that inhibit reform. Changing social norms is not easy, but it can be done. Raising awareness about the costs or inefficiencies of certain norms or the benefits that would accrue to society from reforms can influence a shift in the social mind-set. However, such an effort would have to be based on credible evidence not connected to any ideological or political rhetoric and would have to focus on real, substantial reforms and not minor changes in policies (Khemani 2017). Changing laws can also lead to a shift in norms. For example, laws on wearing seat belts in cars led to a shift in the social norm for driving safety. However, it is not enough just to enact laws; they must be strictly implemented and encouraged. Meanwhile, a behavioral response to incentives in the short run can lead to longer-term shifts in behavior and social norms (World Bank 2015e). An example is nudging via text message to encourage parents to register their children for ECD programs (Escueta et al. 2017; Pugatch and Wilson 2018).

Another approach to influencing norms is to identify champions or norm entrepreneurs within social groups who could lead or demonstrate the change, thereby leveraging social influence to change behavior (World Bank 2015e). A good example is the Teachers First initiative in Egypt, which has developed a professional development program building on the UNESCO Competency Framework for Teachers. As of 2018, it had enrolled 10,000 teachers across eight governorates (Teachers First 2018). It trains school-based innovation teams to support teachers in adopting modern pedagogy in the classroom. Teachers First also aims to transform the teacher assessment system to capture changes in behavior over time, with the learner becoming more active in learning and assessment processes (Teachers First 2018).

Promote tolerance through education

The prospects for peace and stability in MENA will be shaped by its citizens' ability to coexist with people of different nationalities, ethnicities, and religions. Education is one of the principal means of building a culture of peace (UNESCO 1999). It can help to promote tolerance by enhancing knowledge and reasoning skills and reducing prejudices (Coenders and Scheepers 2003).

In MENA, higher levels of education are generally associated with higher levels of tolerance for people with different backgrounds (see figure O.20). In Algeria, Iraq, Jordan, Lebanon, Morocco, Tunisia, and West Bank and Gaza, higher levels of

FIGURE O.20 **Tolerance is associated with education, but intolerance is high even among the educated in MENA**

Percentage of respondents who would not like to have "people of a different religion" as neighbors, by highest education level attained

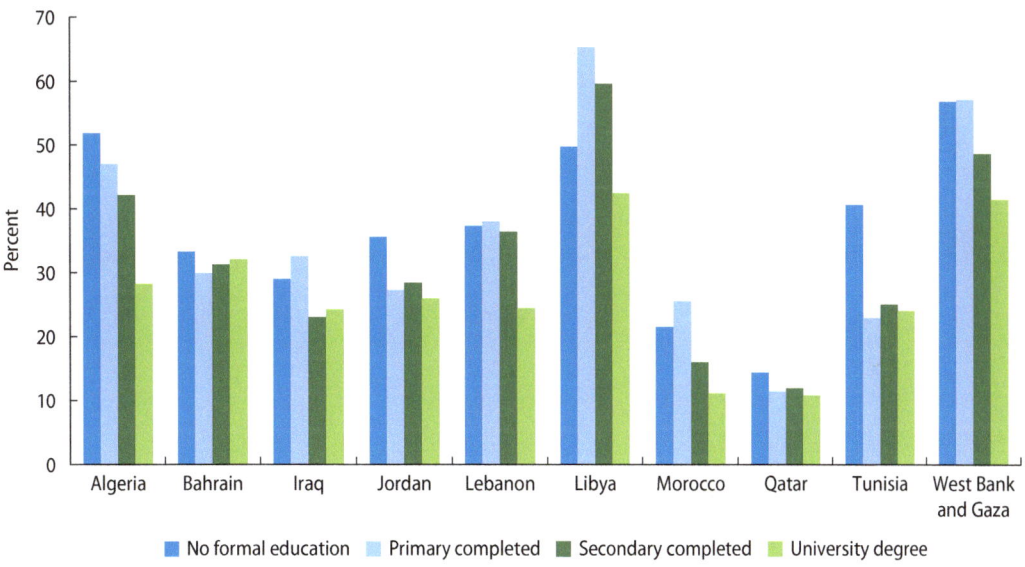

Source: Inglehart et al. 2014.

education correspond to more tolerance for people of a different religion. However, the association between level of education and social values in MENA is weaker than in the rest of the world (Diwan 2016).

Even the most educated in MENA have levels of intolerance at or above the rates of other regions in the world. For example, 34 percent of MENA respondents to the 2014 World Values Survey said they disliked having neighbors who were immigrants or foreign workers (Inglehart et al. 2014). This rate of dislike is three times higher than that observed in high-income countries (12 percent). Furthermore, 32 percent of respondents in the region disliked having neighbors of a different religion. This rate is the highest across all regions and almost eight times higher than that of high-income countries.

Thus, although education may contribute to greater tolerance, its effect may largely depend on what is taught and how it is taught in the classroom, as well as political orientation, social interactions, historical experiences, and labor market dynamics. Modern curricula that promote noncognitive or "soft skills" (as well as cognitive skills) and instructional practices that promote inquiry, discussion, reasoning, and teamwork can promote greater tolerance. Conversely, traditional curricula that are heavy in outdated content and narrowly defined concepts and emphasize knowledge recall, control, and discipline can lead to closed minds. In Rwanda, education has been an important part of a holistic, systemic approach to bringing about changes in attitudes leading to more tolerance and less violence (see box O.14).

In view of the conflicts MENA has been facing for almost a decade, there is an important role for education in the promotion of peace and social stability. However, education cannot do it alone. Improving political and economic conditions is also critical for the peace and stability of the region. This effort requires multisystem alignment as well as a wider social and political commitment.

> **Box O.14   In Rwanda, education has played a role in building peace**
>
> Education can be a crucial entry point for addressing the drivers of conflict. In Rwanda, education was recognized as the "vehicle for positive social transformation to reduce the likelihood of returning to violence." Schools became the common ground where parents could meet, rebuild trust, and seek a common goal. To develop education policies that explicitly addressed social cohesion and to contribute to national reconciliation, curricula were modified to emphasize "a culture of peace" and promote positive national values, justice, tolerance, respect, solidarity, and democracy. Curricular reform and the removal of social barriers took patience and time because they required agreements on language, values, girls' access to education, and attention to children with special needs. To improve their impact, education leaders sought support from complementary health and social programs that enhanced the educational experience for children. In short, the implementation of these agreements required communal ownership, trust, and time to develop. Greater authority over implementation at the school and district levels was granted, accompanied by greater accountability and operational efficiency, more responsive and efficient management, and continued capacity building.
>
> *Source:* World Bank 2013b.

A new education pact

Stakeholders' goals for education reflect the myriad roles that education can play in an economy and society. Many stakeholders have a shared sense of purpose around basic goals such as literacy; however, beyond these goals, groups have different views of the purpose of education. The dissonance across stakeholders' goals for education is a substantial obstacle. Education becomes a "battlefield" (Purpel and Shapiro 1995, 60) where the different stakeholders fight in pursuit of ideological hegemony.

In all countries, education is the subject of an ongoing national dialogue. In MENA, this national dialogue needs to be channeled toward a unified vision that takes into account the four tensions holding back education, the social norms that define them, and the local context. A shared vision also needs to take into account countries' development priorities, their economic opportunities, and their realities and resources so that the goals set are realistic and attainable.

To realize this unified vision, political will is critical. Moreover, the interests of a wide variety of stakeholders—including teachers, principals, inspectors, politicians, communities, employers, and students—need to be aligned through a powerful alliance. This effort would require strong leadership and shared accountability. It also would require bringing investments and resources in line with the vision's priorities. High-performing education systems—such as those of Japan, Korea, and Singapore—are champions of strong education pacts that underscore the role of a unified vision for education across stakeholders. That vision includes *consistent* and *coherent* reforms to achieve human capital–driven economic growth (Wong 2017).

National leaders must lead the change

Political will and leadership are critical to rallying MENA around a new pact for education. Political leadership can initiate shifts in behavioral norms to push for education reform (Acemoglu and Jackson 2015). The national leaders of Japan, Korea, and Singapore, in championing education reforms, made education a national priority with a vision and clear goals and cultivated a consensus among stakeholders (World Bank 2018e). Policies were built on the realization that the full potential of education can be achieved only through cross-sectoral policy alignment. The leaders succeeded in promoting a shared vision for education to which parents can aspire for their children's future (World Bank 2018e) and a shared responsibility among all stakeholders for assuming their role in educational outcomes (Wong 2017).

MENA has produced many great leaders whose charisma and vision have led to remarkable progress. For example, Egyptian educator Taha Hussein, who became blind as a young child, went on to become one of the preeminent thinkers of his time, leaving his mark on an entire nation (Cachia 2014). Serving as minister of education in the early 1950s, he worked to massively expand public education and to abolish school fees. Considering education essential to human existence, Hussein famously said, "Education is like water and air" (Cook and El-Refaee 2017).

Reconcile interests in a unified vision for education

A new pact and shared vision require aligning political will and multiple interests in society. Perverse behavioral norms and ideological polarization can hold countries back from delivering public goods (World Bank 2016b). Moreover, human sociality, whereby people associate and behave as members of a group and establish norms and patterns of cooperation, can also block reforms (Khemani 2017; World Bank 2015e). Some groups impede reforms that they perceive would reduce their power or ability to extract benefits (Khemani 2017; Kingdon et al. 2014). One example might be the teachers who are benefiting from the industry of private tutoring. This group could try to obstruct any reforms in assessment systems that would jeopardize the additional income they receive for holding private classes for students preparing for national examinations. This could also be true of teachers' unions that do not want to see reforms that would require teachers to work additional hours or to change their practice substantially. Resistance to reform may be driven not only by self-interest but also by peer pressure to comply with the norms and expectations of a group such as a teachers' union (Khemani 2017; World Bank 2015e).

Experience has shown that reforms can succeed if there is strong political will to implement them. This means that politicians and interest groups would have to refrain from using education as a tool to support their political views. An important step toward aligning political will and stakeholders' interests in education reform would be to reduce the number of policy makers who have the power to veto policy reforms for political interests and bring them in line with other stakeholders through a narrative of shared values (Acosta and Haddad 2014)—see box O.15 for an example of a successful use of this approach in Peru.

To rally support for education reform in 2008, Australia's deputy prime minister developed clear outreach strategies that engaged the news media. She personally briefed the media on new proposals in advance, using stories about schools and students to humanize the narrative around reform. She also communicated with the business community through "boardroom lunches," highlighting the business case for reforms (Bruns and Schneider 2016). The minister of education of Ontario, Canada, regularly visited schools and school boards across the province when he was shadow minister, meeting with about 6,000 people in an effort to spend time with teachers, students, and parents to engage them in policy dialogue and establish trust (OECD 2011c).

Recently, the president of Egypt has also been using the media and conferences to build support for education reforms. He has been advocating and supporting major reforms overhauling the education system, shifting from the traditional rote learning, high-stakes examination system that focuses on credentials to a modern system that focuses on learning and skills. He held several youth and education conferences to rally public support for the reforms, reassuring parents and students about the benefits of these reforms for them individually and for society and the economy as a whole. He announced that 2019 would be the year of education (Egyptian Gazette 2018).

> **Box O.15** **Peru has found success in aligning interests**
>
> Through political will and alignment of stakeholders' interests, Peru succeeded in reducing the rate of stunted growth among children under age 5 in only six years. This was achieved by reducing the number of policy makers with veto power. These "veto players" were brought in line with other stakeholders through a shared set of values. Stakeholders were unified under a common policy platform and advocacy coalition, the Children's Malnutrition Initiative. This coalition was established to convene both government and nongovernment stakeholders to consolidate a single objective of making children's malnutrition central to the government's fight against poverty. During the 2006 presidential campaign, all candidates pledged to reduce malnutrition by 5 percentage points for children under 5 years of age within 5 years (5×5×5). Once elected, the president of Peru renewed his public commitment and set a target reduction of 9 percentage points and secured support from the prime minister, the minister for women and social development, and regional governors. Between 2005 and 2011, Peru reduced stunting by 10 percentage points.
>
> *Source:* Acosta and Haddad 2014.

Share accountability to deliver results

Accountability is critical to improving learning. However, identifying who is accountable for learning outcomes is extremely difficult because different actors within and outside the education system interact to produce learning outcomes. Usually, educators, especially teachers, are the focus of accountability for student outcomes. Although teachers play a crucial role in student learning because they interact directly with students in the learning process, policy makers, school leaders, and parents, among others, also have an important role in shaping education outcomes. Therefore, accountability in education cannot be limited to any one individual or group (UNESCO 2017a; World Bank 2004).

In a new education pact for MENA, accountability needs to go beyond the education system. There would be multiple accountability mechanisms, whereby citizens hold governments accountable, policy makers hold schools accountable, and principals hold teachers accountable. However, if the system as a whole is not aligned, conflicts and distortions will arise between the stakeholders at various levels (Burns, Köster, and Fuster 2016). System alignment toward greater accountability means that all stakeholders work collectively within a common vision for education and share responsibility for learning. These stakeholders (policy makers, school leaders, teachers, parents, employers, and students) must first hold themselves accountable to ensure learning while demanding accountability from others. For MENA countries to reap the full benefits of education, responsibility and accountability have to be shared collectively (see figure O.21).

For accountability systems to be effective, the roles and responsibilities of the various stakeholders have to be clearly defined and understood. For example, a lack of understanding of the new roles for school administrators in Sweden resulted in varying approaches and structures, which made it difficult to evaluate and compare learning across municipalities (Burns, Köster, and Fuster 2016). Moreover, when accountability lines are not clear, blame could be shifted among service providers, and citizens would not be able to determine who is responsible (UNESCO 2017a). Without clearly defined roles and responsibilities, even well-designed accountability mechanisms can fail. On the one hand, parental monitoring in school can

FIGURE O.21 Learning is a collective responsibility, and everyone is accountable

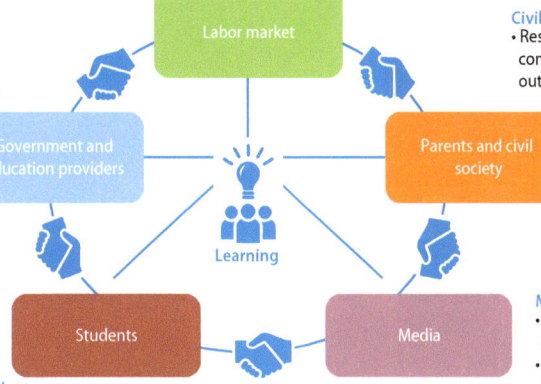

Policy makers
- Accountable for providing vision, leadership, and strategy for the education system to promote learning and skills
- Responsible for providing curricula, standards, and assessments development and effective and efficient management of resources (physical, financial, human, and information sharing)

School leaders
- Accountable for creating a school environment conducive to learning (safe, well-equipped, well connected)
- Responsible for monitoring, supporting, and empowering teachers to deliver learning and hold them accountable

Teachers
- Accountable for student learning progress in their classroom
- Responsible for monitoring student progress
- Responsible for undertaking continuous professional development and holding policy makers and school leaders accountable
- Responsible for sharing information on student progress with parents

Employers
- Responsible for sending the right signals to the education system and parents on skills required
- Accountable for rewarding skills not credentials

Students
- Responsible for being active and curious learners
- Responsible for demanding accountability and skills from schools, teachers, and policy makers
- Responsible for using technology and social media to exchange knowledge and learning and organize in a constructive manner

Parents
- Accountable for children going to and completing school
- Responsible for providing enabling learning environments at home, engaging in school activities, and seeking out feedback on student learning
- Responsible for holding policy makers, schools, and teachers accountable for learning by demanding qualified teachers, relevant curricula, and safe school environments

Civil society
- Responsible for demanding transparent communication of education inputs and outcomes

Media
- Accountable for reporting factual information and for correcting false claims
- Responsible for offering a platform for policy makers and other stakeholders to share information and promote greater transparency on education policies and other educational information
- Responsible for delivering news responsibly based on evidence and data

Source: World Bank.

be counterproductive if parental involvement becomes too invasive and schools do not grant the teacher sufficient autonomy (World Bank 2008). On the other hand, if schools do not understand and recognize parents' role in the education system, they may be unresponsive to legitimate parental initiatives and suggestions.

At the level of the education provider, teachers are responsible for monitoring and assessing their students' progress and for giving parents regular feedback. Teachers also should pursue ongoing professional development. School leaders are responsible for creating a school environment conducive to learning and ensuring that teachers are delivering on learning by monitoring and empowering them. Policy makers have the overall responsibility for providing vision and strategy and developing, leading, and supporting the implementation of education policies, developing curricula and standards, introducing national information systems that effectively monitor learning, and allocating resources at the national and regional levels (human, physical, and financial).

Parents are responsible for their children's education and for creating a supportive home environment. They are also responsible for engaging in school activities and monitoring their children's learning individually and collectively through parents' associations. Parents should also hold the education system (policy makers, schools, and teachers) accountable for their children's learning and demand qualified teachers, relevant curricula, and safe learning environments. Employers also have a responsibility in the learning process. They need to signal to parents, students, and the education system what skills are needed in the

Box O.16 Egypt's education sector uses technology to ensure accountability

The Arab Republic of Egypt has embarked on ambitious accountability reforms in the education sector using modern technology. It is enhancing accountability through the following channels:

- Increasing the amount of data and information available to policy makers and the public, thereby improving accountability for resource allocation and service delivery
- Enhancing transparency around student assessments and citizens' trust of assessment results
- Strengthening accountability across key stakeholders, giving the community and parents a greater voice in policy making
- Creating a better compact between the Ministry of Education and Technical Education and schools by improving district-level management.

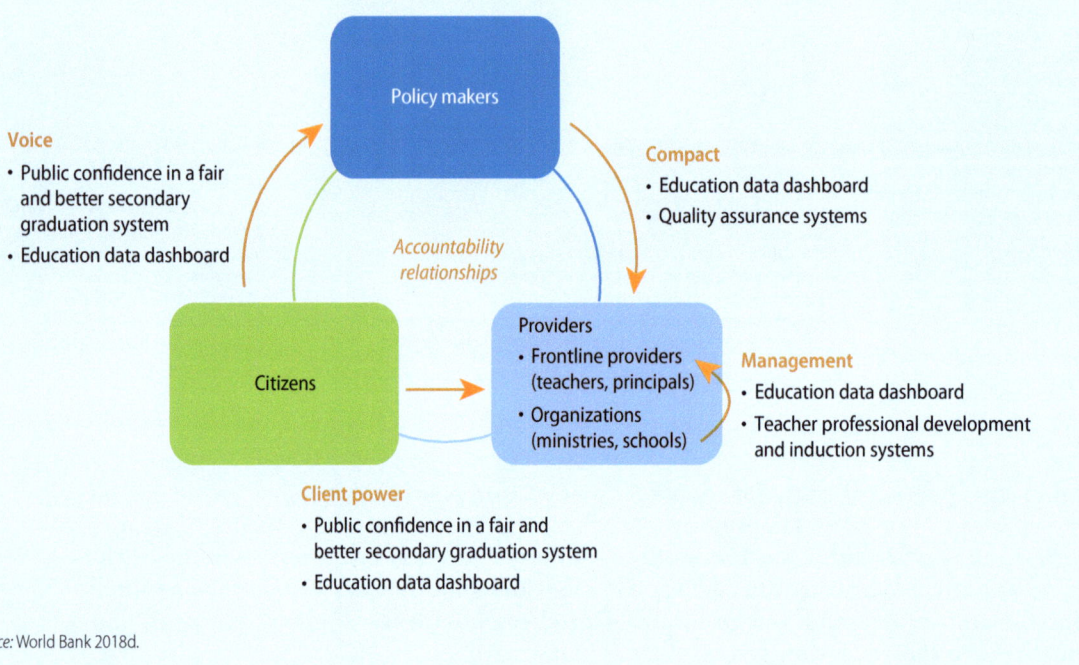

FIGURE BO.16.1 Technology can shape accountability relationships

Source: World Bank 2018d.

---

labor market. Finally, students are also responsible for their learning; they must not be passive recipients. With their growing access to social media, students have access to massive amounts of learning resources. In many instances, they may have more access to information than their parents on global skills and knowledge and can demand these skills from the education system. Students can also organize themselves to support their schools and hold service providers and educators to account.

The media play an important role in holding stakeholders accountable and in explaining complex issues. Social media are a growing major source of information in the world and in MENA countries, especially for youths, and they can serve as a platform for policy makers wishing to share information and promote greater transparency on education policy reforms. Social media also provide citizens with a mechanism to hold policy makers and educators accountable. And yet social media can also be exploited by interest groups to block important reforms and spread misinformation. In MENA countries such as Egypt, Jordan, and Kuwait, opponents of education reforms have launched strong social media campaigns against those reforms. Open channels for communication and debate are important to creating a pact around learning. Policy makers should engage with stakeholders through various channels to address concerns, correct information using evidence, and rally collective support for education reforms.

Beyond social media, technology can also be leveraged to establish accountability systems. Several countries are implementing education dashboards to facilitate open data and a move toward evidence-based policy making. The government of Egypt has effectively leveraged modern technology to promote accountability (see box O.16).

For its part, civil society is responsible for demanding transparent communication of education inputs and outcomes.

Prioritize investments to promote learning and skills

A new pact for education must include agreement on how and where resources are used. For decades, MENA countries have spent substantial shares of their income on education to meet the demand of growing populations over the last half-century. In fact, most MENA countries allocate far more to education than many wealthy countries. For example, Tunisia spends 20.6 percent of its national budget on education, which is nearly twice the OECD country average of 11.3 percent. Although the share of spending on education in MENA is relatively high, it has been declining since its peak at the turn of the century, from a median level of 20.6 percent in 2000 (and 5.9 percent of GDP) to 13 percent in 2016 (4 percent of GDP).[14] Spending adequate amounts on education is necessary but not sufficient for success. How resources are used is just as, if not more, important.

Spending needs to align with learning. MENA countries spend large shares of their education budgets on staff salaries—often more than 90 percent of all recurrent education spending. In doing so, they crowd out investment in other important inputs that contribute to learning, such as teaching and learning materials, professional development, and school rehabilitation and maintenance.

Countries everywhere are facing trade-offs when deciding whether to spend scarce resources on hiring additional teachers or financing other educational inputs. Investing in the professional development, working conditions, and salaries of current and future teachers often proves to be more effective for increasing student learning than employing more teachers. The same is true for greater investment in technology or the use of teaching assistants in the classroom (OECD 2017b). Investments in hiring additional teachers to reduce class sizes may have an impact on learning, but teachers should be targeted to areas in which class sizes are particularly large and act as a constraint on learning. A synthesis of more than 800 meta-analyses related to student achievement concluded that the value for money in raising performance is better achieved through interventions other than reducing class size (Hattie 2009). This conclusion is supported by research that finds that increasing teacher effectiveness has a greater value for money than reducing class sizes and suggests assigning the most effective teachers to the largest classes to maximize the potential benefit (Hanushek 2011; Rivkin, Hanushek, and Kain 2005).

Sufficient investment in early childhood education and in the early grades of schooling is also needed to ensure that students build foundational skills that enable them to learn effectively in the later stages of education. However, ECE has been the level that has received the least investment in MENA countries, resulting in enrollment rates that are closer to those in Sub-Saharan Africa and low-income countries, as indicated by the little international data available. No MENA country spends more than 0.4 percent of its GDP on ECE from the public budget. Most spend far less (well below 0.2 percent). By comparison, the average OECD country invests 0.7–0.8 percent of its GDP on ECE, and some countries—such as Sweden—invest as much as 1.3 percent of GDP. Because the region's young and growing populations consistently exhibit low levels of foundational skills, public investment in high-quality early learning programs for all children should be a policy priority.

Even though MENA countries have been spending large shares of their national budgets on education, it is important that spending on education be sustained and in some countries increased. Equally important, the spending must target learning. This requires concentrating on outcomes and not just inputs and outputs. Results-based or performance-based budgeting (PBB) seeks to introduce explicit measures of performance or results directly into the budgeting process with specific indicators that can be used to measure the effectiveness of budget implementation. Ministries of education that receive budgets under a results-based budgeting system would receive allocations to achieve certain sectoral outputs (for example, increasing preprimary enrollment) rather than to finance certain amounts of inputs (such as salaries or capital costs).

In Jordan, Morocco, and Tunisia, the ministries of education have been early adopters of those countries' performance-based budgeting systems (Beschel and Ahern 2012). In Western Europe and other member countries of the OECD, PBB approaches have been employed for some time. The Netherlands, for example, introduced proto-PBB approaches as far back as the 1970s and moved its entire public sector to program and performance budgeting in 1999. Such a move shifts the focus of ministries so that their activities coalesce around the achievement of their strategic sectoral policy agendas.

Unleashing the potential of education is attainable

MENA countries can enjoy the full benefits of education only when a push for learning is coupled with a pull for skills and a social pact for education. Specifically, MENA will realize the potential of education when (1) it gives priority to learning; (2) it focuses on the early years of schooling and opportunities are equally distributed, including for those affected by conflict; (3) curricula are modernized and educators are empowered; (4) employers demand skills and communicate them; (5) all stakeholders agree on a common vision for education and jointly take responsibility for its outcomes and are held accountable for their roles, which are clearly defined; and (6) resources are aligned with priorities. These changes will require a joint effort to address the four tensions holding education back in the MENA countries.

Improving education is not the responsibility of educators alone; it also involves all members of society—politicians, businesspeople, and community and religious leaders, as well as parents, teachers, school principals, and students themselves. By far the most difficult task is dealing with varying and often opposing views, strongly held convictions, and divergent interests. But it is not impossible. Countries with high-performing education systems have succeeded in rallying support around a common vision and shared responsibility.

The role of technology as a demand shaper in the future of work is certain, but its role as a delivery catalyst holds great potential that the region has not yet tapped. Indeed, technology is changing how today's students are prepared to enter the future workforce—that is, it is influencing not only the ends of education but also the means. Technology presents a unique opportunity to help to deliver high-quality education in a more efficient and effective manner. If leveraged smartly, technology can offer an opportunity for MENA countries to advance their education systems quickly and to support learning.

MENA has the history, culture, and resources to leap into a future founded on a learned society and a knowledge economy. The region has great expectations and aspirations. Unleashing the potential of education is attainable, but it will take a new pact to elevate education not only as a national priority but also as a national emergency. The question is: Are its leaders ready and do they have the will and grit to see through the implementation of policy reforms?

Notes

1. The World Bank defines MENA as including these countries and economies: Algeria, Bahrain, Djibouti, Arab Republic of Egypt, Islamic Republic of Iran, Iraq, Jordan, Kuwait, Lebanon, Libya, Malta, Morocco, Oman, Qatar, Saudi Arabia, Syrian Arab Republic, Tunisia, the United Arab Emirates, West Bank and Gaza, and the Republic of Yemen. This report excludes Malta from the analysis as it has little in common with the rest of the region.
2. The World Bank's Facebook poll (in both Arabic and English) asked residents of MENA about the state of education in their country. The question received 42,235 responses.
3. World Bank, Education Statistics (EdStats) database. Based on authors' calculations using data for 2007 (or closest) and 2016 (or latest).
4. World Bank, World Development Indicators database.
5. The definition of violent child discipline as used in the UNICEF Multiple Indicator Cluster Survey (MICS) is based on discipline by anyone in the household within the last month, and includes psychological aggression (shouted, yelled, or screamed at the child; called the child dumb, lazy, or another name like that); physical punishment (shook the child; spanked, hit, or slapped the child on the bottom with a bare hand; hit the child on the bottom or elsewhere on the body with something like a belt, hairbrush, stick, or other hard object; hit or slapped the child on the hand, arm, or leg); and severe physical punishment (hit or slapped the child on the face, head, or ears; beat the child with an implement—hit over and over as hard as one could).
6. In fact, the level of autonomy may have decreased; the overall score declined from 3.1 to 2.9 on a 5-point scale, with 5 representing the highest level of autonomy. A factor contributing to the lower overall autonomy score, however, may be that the sample of universities participating in the 2012 and 2016 assessments did not remain the same (more public institutions from centralized tertiary education systems took part in the survey), making it difficult to assess trends over time.
7. Seven economies use *tarbiya* in the official name of their ministry of education (Algeria, Iraq, Kuwait, Lebanon, Syria, Tunisia, West Bank and Gaza); three use *taaleem* (Libya, Qatar, and Saudi Arabia); and seven use both *tarbiya* and *taaleem* (Bahrain, Egypt, Jordan, Morocco, Oman, the United Arab Emirates, and the Republic of Yemen).
8. Malta is the exception; it is classified as part of the Middle East and North Africa in the World Bank's regional classifications.
9. The information in this paragraph is extracted from TIMSS 2015 Curriculum Questionnaire Exhibits.
10. Inequality of opportunity exists where unequal outcomes are attributable to factors beyond an individual's control.
11. Estimates of global EdTech revenues vary considerably, depending on the source of this information.
12. The analysis also found that computers have a greater association with scores in countries in which ICT penetration is low. Providing a teacher with a computer in the North African countries that participate in PISA (Algeria and Tunisia) was associated with higher PISA scores by 24.5 points. Doing the same in the two GCC countries (Qatar and the United Arab Emirates), where classroom technology is more common, was associated with an increase of just 1.1 PISA point.
13. These tenures for ministers of education were compiled from a variety of online sources, including the official websites of the Ministries of Education, news media, and World Bank events pages.
14. World Bank, Education Statistics (EdStats) database. MENA's regional median is computed as the median of all national data points available in a given year using the EdStats database.

References

Abi-Mershed, Osama, ed. 2010. *Trajectories of Education in the Arab World: Legacies and Challenges*. London: Routledge.

Acemoglu, Daron, and Matthew O. Jackson. 2015. "History, Expectations, and Leadership in the Evolution of Social Norms." *Review of Economic Studies* 82 (1): 1–34.

Acosta, Andrés Mejía, and Lawrence Haddad. 2014. "The Politics of Success in the Fight against Malnutrition in Peru." *Food Policy* 44: 26–35.

Afshar, Hassan Soodmand, and Mehdi Doosti. 2016. "An Investigation into Factors Contributing to Iranian Secondary School English Teachers' Job Satisfaction and Dissatisfaction." *Research Papers in Education* 31 (3): 274–98.

Aghion, Philippe, Mathias Dewatripont, Caroline M. Hoxby, Andreu Mas-Colell, and André Sapir. 2009. "The Governance and Performance of Research Universities: Evidence from Europe and the U.S." NBER Working Paper 14851, National Bureau of Economic Research, Cambridge, MA.

Ahramonline. 2015. Ahramonline. http://www.ahram.org.eg/News/131704/4/448902/-قضايا وآراء/فلسفة-مجانية-التعليم-في-عهد-عبد-الناصر.aspx.

Akar, Bassel. 2016. "Dialogic Pedagogies in Educational Settings for Active Citizenship, Social Cohesion, and Peacebuilding in Lebanon." *Education, Citizenship, and Social Justice* 11 (1): 44–62. doi:10.1177/1746197915626081.

Alayan, Samira, Achim Rohde, and Sarhan Dhouib, eds. 2012. *The Politics of Education Reform in the Middle East—Self and Other in Textbooks and Curricula*. New York: Berghahn Books.

Alkhateeb, Jamal, and Muna Hadidi. 2015. "Special Education in Arab Countries: Current Challenges." *International Journal of Disability Development and Education* 62 (5): 518–30.

Almannie, Mohamed A. 2015. "Leadership Role of School Superintendents in Saudi Arabia." *International Journal of Social Science Studies* 3 (3): 169–75.

Al Masah Capital. 2012. "MENA Education Report." Dubai, United Arab Emirates. http://www.almasahcapital.com/images/reports/report_89.pdf.

Alrebh, Abdullah F., and Radhi Al-Mabuk. 2016. "Teaching for Democracy in Post-Arab Spring." In *Education and the Arab Spring*, edited by Eid Mohamed, Hannah R. Gerber, and Slimane Aboulkacem. Rotterdam: SensePublishers.

Al-Yaseen, Wafaa Salem, and Mohammad Yousef Al-Musaileem. 2015. "Teacher Empowerment as an Important Component of Job Satisfaction: A Comparative Study of Teachers' Perspectives in Al-Farwaniya District, Kuwait." *Journal of Comparative and International Education* 45 (6): 863–85.

Angrist, Joshua, and Victor Lavy. 2001. "Does Teacher Training Affect Pupil Learning? Evidence from Matched Comparisons in Jerusalem Public Schools." *Journal of Labor Economics* 19 (2): 343–69.

Arab News. 2016. "8 Educational Apps from MENA That Are Changing Classrooms and Education." *Arab News*, April 25. Jeddah, Saudi Arabia.

Arcidiacono, Peter, Patrick Bayer, and Aurel Hizmo. 2010. "Beyond Signaling and Human Capital: Education and the Revelation of Ability." *American Economic Journal: Applied Economics* 2 (4): 76–104.

Asia Society and OECD (Organisation for Economic Co-operation and Development). 2018. *Teaching for Global Competence in a Rapidly Changing World*. New York: Asia Society; Paris: OECD. https://asiasociety.org/sites/default/files/inline-files/teaching-for-global-competence-in-a-rapidly-changing-world-edu.pdf.

ASMR (Arab Social Media Report). 2013. "Transforming Education in the Arab World: Breaking Barriers in the Age of Social Learning." Arab Social Media Report, Dubai School of Government, June. http://www.arabsocialmediareport.com/UserManagement/PDF/ASMR_5_Report_Final.pdf.

Assaad, Ragui. 1997. "The Effects of Public Sector Hiring and Compensation Policies on the Egyptian Labor Market." *World Bank Economic Review* 11 (1): 85–118.

———. 2014. "Making Sense of Arab Labor Markets: The Enduring Legacy of Dualism." *IZA Journal of Labor and Development* 3 (1): 1–25.

Assaad, Ragui, and Caroline Krafft. 2015. "The Evolution of Labor Supply and Unemployment in the Egyptian Economy: 1988–2012." In *The Egyptian Labor Market in an Era of Revolution*, edited by Ragui Assaad and Caroline Krafft, 1–26. Oxford: Oxford University Press.

Assaad, Ragui, Caroline Krafft, and Djavad Salehi-Isfahani. 2018. "Does the Type of Higher Education Affect Labor Market Outcomes? Evidence from Egypt and Jordan." *Higher Education* 75 (6): 945–95.

Banerjee, Abhijit. 2012. "Teaching at the Right Level." Presentation, Delhi, India, July 26. https://www.povertyactionlab.org/sites/default/files/documents/Session%201%20-%20Teaching%20to%20the%20Level.pdf.

Barber Michael, and Mona Mourshed. 2007. "How the Best-Performing School Systems

Come Out on Top." Consultant report, McKinsey and Company, Washington, DC.

Barkley, Elizabeth F., Patricia Cross, and Claire H. Major. 2005. *Collaborative Learning Techniques: A Handbook for College Faculty.* San Francisco: Jossey-Bass.

Barro, Robert J., and Jong Wha Lee. 2013. "A New Data Set of Educational Attainment in the World, 1950–2010." *Journal of Development Economics* 104: 184–98.

Barsoum, Ghada. 2015. "Young People's Job Aspirations in Egypt and the Continued Preference for a Government Job." In *The Egyptian Labor Market in an Era of Revolution*, edited by Ragui Assaad and Caroline Krafft, 108–26. Oxford: Oxford University Press.

Bass, Randall V., and J. W. Good. 2004. "Educare and Educere: Is a Balance Possible in the Educational System?" *Educational Forum* 68 (2): 161–68.

Becker, Gary S. 1962. "Investment in Human Capital: A Theoretical Analysis." *Journal of Political Economy* 70 (5): 9–49.

Behar, Alberto, and Junghwan Mok. 2013. "Does Public-Sector Employment Fully Crowd Out Private-Sector Employment?" IMF Working Paper WP/13/146, International Monetary Fund, Washington, DC.

Benrabah, Mohamed. 2007. "The Language Planning Situation in Algeria." *Current Issues in Language Planning* 6 (4): 379–502.

Berlinski, Samuel, Sebastian Galiani, and Paul Gertler. 2009. "The Effect of Pre-Primary Education on Primary School Performance." *Journal of Public Economics* 93 (1–2): 219–34.

Berlinski, Samuel, Sebastian Galiani, and Marco Manacorda. 2008. "Giving Children a Better Start: Preschool Attendance and School-Age Profiles." *Journal of Public Economics* 92 (5–6): 1416–40.

Berlinski, Samuel, and Norbert Schady. 2015. *The Early Years: Child Well-Being and the Role of Public Policy.* Washington, DC: Inter-American Development Bank.

Beschel, Robert P. Jr., and Mark Ahern. 2012. *Public Financial Management Reform in the Middle East and North Africa: An Overview of Regional Experience.* Washington, DC: World Bank. https://openknowledge.worldbank.org/handle/10986/9368.

Black, Paul, and Dylan Wiliam. 2010. "Inside the Black Box: Raising Standards through Classroom Assessment." *Phi Delta Kappan* 92 (1): 81–90. doi: https://doi.org/10.1177/003172171009200119.

Borg, Simon. 2015. "Researching Language Teacher Education." In *The Continuum Companion to Research Methods in Applied Linguistics*, edited by Brian Paltridge and Aek Phakiti, 541–60. London: Bloomsbury Academic.

Borko, Hilda. 2004. "Professional Development and Teacher Learning: Mapping the Terrain." *Educational Researcher* 33 (8): 3–15.

Bouguen, Adrien, Deon Filmer, Karen Macours, and Sophie Naudeau. 2013. "Impact Evaluation of Three Types of Early Childhood Development Interventions in Cambodia." Policy Research Working Paper 6540, World Bank, Washington, DC.

Bouhlila, Donia S. 2011. "The Quality of Secondary Education in the Middle East and North Africa: What Can We Learn from TIMSS' Results?" *Compare* 41 (3): 327–52.

Brixi, Hana, Ellen Lust, and Michael Woolcock. 2015. *Trust, Voice, and Incentives: Learning from Local Success Stories in Service Delivery in the Middle East and North Africa.* Washington, DC: World Bank.

Brooks, Ray, and Ran Tao. 2003. "China's Labor Market Performance and Challenges." IMF Working Paper WP/03/210, International Monetary Fund, Washington, DC. https://ssrn.com/abstract=880877. https://www.imf.org/external/pubs/ft/wp/2003/wp03210.pdf.

Brown, C. A., M. S. Smith, and M. K. Stein. 1995. "Linking Teacher Support to Enhanced Classroom Instruction." Paper presented at annual meeting of American Educational Research, New York.

Bruns, Barbara, and Javier Luque. 2015. *Great Teachers: How to Raise Student Learning in Latin America and the Caribbean.* Washington, DC: World Bank.

Bruns, Barbara, and Ben Ross Schneider. 2016. "Managing the Politics of Quality Reforms in Education: Policy Lessons from Global Experience." Paper commissioned for International Commission on Financing Educational Opportunity, New York.

Brussels Conference. 2017. "Preparing for the Future of Children and Youth in Syria and the Region through Education: London One Year On." Brussels Syria Conference, April 5.

———. 2019. "Investing in the Future: Protection and Learning for All Syrian Children and Youth." Brussels III Conference, March 12–14.

Burns, Tracey, Florian Köster, and Marc Fuster. 2016. *Education Governance in Action: Lessons from Case Studies.* Paris: Organisation for Economic Co-operation and Development.

Business Wire. 2018. "Growth Opportunities in the Education Technology Market—Forecast to 2022." Business Wire, January 11. https://www.businesswire.com/news/home/20180111006109/en/Growth-Opportunities-Global-Education-Technology-Market-2017.

Cachia, Pierre. 2014. "Introduction." In *The Days: His Autobiography in Three Parts*, by Taha Hussein, 2–6. Cairo: American University in Cairo Press.

Capital Economics. 2017. "Middle East Economics Focus." Singapore.

Carr-Hill, Roy, Caine Rolleston, and Rebecca Schendel. 2016. "The Effects of School-Based Decision Making on Educational Outcomes in Low- and Middle-Income Contexts: A Systematic Review." *Campbell Systematic Review* 2016 (9).

Center on the Developing Child. 2009. "Five Numbers to Remember about Early Childhood Development." Harvard University, Cambridge, MA. https://developingchild.harvard.edu/resources/five-numbers-to-remember-about-early-childhood-development/.

Cheng, Kai-ming. 2017. "Advancing 21st Century Competencies in East Asian Education Systems." Center for Global Education, Asia Society New York.

Coenders, Marcel, and Peer Scheepers. 2003. "The Effect of Education on Nationalism and Ethnic Exclusionism: An International Comparison." *Political Psychology* 24 (2): 313–43.

Collins, Randall. 1979. *The Credential Society: A Historical Sociology of Education and Stratification*. New York: Academic Press.

Comings, John. 2018. "Assessing the Impact of Literacy Learning Games for Syrian Refugee Children: An Executive Overview of Antura and the Letters and Feed the Monster Impact Evaluations." World Vision, Washington, DC; Foundation for Information Technology Education and Development, Quezon, Philippines.

Conn, Katharine. 2014. "Identifying Effective Education Interventions in Sub-Saharan Africa: A Meta-Analysis of Rigorous Impact Evaluations." Unpublished manuscript, Columbia University, New York.

Cook, Bradley. 1999. "Islamic versus Western Conceptions of Education: Reflections on Egypt." *International Review of Education* 45 (3): 339–58.

———. 2000. "Egypt's National Education Debate." *Comparative Education* 36 (4): 477–90.

Cook, Bradley, and Engy El-Refaee. 2017. "Egypt: A Perpetual Reform Agenda." In *Education in the Arab World*, edited by Serra Kirdar, 285–305. London: Bloomsbury Academic.

Dahi, Omar S. 2012. "The Political Economy of the Egyptian and Arab Revolt." *IDS Bulletin* 43 (1): 47–53. doi:10.1111/j.1759-5436.2012.00289.x.

Darling-Hammond, Linda. 2000. "Teacher Quality and Student Achievement: A Review of State Policy Evidence." *Education Policy Analysis Archives* 8 (1): 1–44.

Darling-Hammond, Linda, Dion Burns, Carol Campbell, A. Lin Goodwin, and Karen Hammerness. 2017. *Empower Educators: How High-Performing Systems Shape Teaching Quality around the World*. Hoboken, NJ: Jossey-Bass.

Darling-Hammond, Linda, Ruth Chung Wei, and Alethea Andree. 2010. "How High-Achieving Countries Develop Great Teachers." Research Brief, Stanford University, Stanford, CA.

Darling-Hammond, Linda, Ruth Chung Wei, Alethea Andree, Nikole Richardson, and Stelios Orphanos. 2009. *Professional Learning in the Learning Profession: A Status Report on Teacher Development in the United States and Abroad*. Dallas: National Staff Development Council.

Devarajan, Shantayanan, and Elena Ianchovichina. 2018. "A Broken Social Contract, Not High Inequality, Led to the Arab Spring." *Review of Income and Wealth* 64 (s1): s5–s25.

Diwan, Ishac. 2016. "Low Social and Political Returns to Education in the Arab World." ERF Policy Brief 19, Economic Research Forum, Giza, Egypt.

Economist. 2017. "Technology Is Transforming What Happens When a Child Goes to School." *Economist*, July 22. https://www.economist.com/briefing/2017/07/22/technology-is-transforming-what-happens-when-a-child-goes-to-school.

Egyptian Gazette. 2018. "Sisi Declares 2019 Year of Education." http://www.egyptiangazette.net.eg/egypt-news/7407-sisi-declares-2019-year-of-education.html.

Eickmann, Sophie H., Ana C. V. Lima, Miriam Q. Guerra, Marilia C. Lima, Pedro I. C. Lira, Sharon R. A. Huttly, and Ann Ashworth. 2003. "Improved Cognitive and Motor Development in a Community-Based Intervention of Psychosocial Stimulation in Northeast Brazil." *Developmental Medicine and Child Neurology* 45 (8): 536–41.

Elango, Sneha, Jorge Luis Garcia, James Heckman, and Andrés Hojman. 2015. "Early Childhood Education." NBER Working Paper 21766, National Bureau of Economic Research, Cambridge, MA. http://www.nber.org/papers/w21766.

El-Araby, Ashraf. 2013. "Economics of Egypt's Tertiary Education—Public versus Private and Fairness and Efficiency Considerations." In *Is There Equality of Opportunity under Free Higher Education in Egypt?* (in Arabic), edited by Asmaa Elbadawy, 135–62. New York: Population Council.

El Hassan, Karma. 2013. "Quality Assurance in Higher Education in Arab Region." *Higher Education and Management Policy* 24 (2): 73–84.

El-Kogali, Safaa, and Caroline Krafft. 2015. *Expanding Opportunities for the Next Generation: Early Childhood Development in the Middle East and North Africa*. Washington, DC: World Bank. https://openknowledge.worldbank.org/handle/10986/21287.

Ellinger, Thomas R., and Garry M. Beckham. 1997. "South Korea: Placing Education on Top of the Family Agenda." *Phi Delta Kappan* 78 (8): 624–25.

Escueta, Maya, Vincent Quan, Andre J. Nickow, and Philip Oreopoulos. 2017. "Education Technology: An Evidence-Based Review." NBER Working Paper 23744, National Bureau of Economic Research, Cambridge, MA. http://www.nber.org/papers/w23744.

ESU (European Students' Union). 2017. "Refugees Welcome? Recognition of Qualifications Held by Refugees and Their Access to Higher Education in Europe—Country Analyses." Brussels. https://www.esu-online.org/wp-content/uploads/2017/05/ESU-Are-Refugees-Welcome_-WEBSITE-1.compressed-1.pdf.

European Commission. 2010. "Document de travail des services de la commission accompagnant la communication de la Commission au Parlement Européen et au Conseil—Dresser le bilan de la politique européenne de voisinage—Rapport de suibi Maroc." Brussels. http://library.euneighbours.eu/sites/default/files/sec10_521_fr.pdf.

———. 2017. "Conference on Higher Education and Refugees in the Mediterranean Region—Report." Brussels. http://ec.europa.eu/education/sites/education/files/hopes-conference-report_en.pdf.

———. 2018. "Action Document for Vocational Education and Training and Higher Education Programme for Vulnerable Syrian Youth."

Evans, David, and Anna Popova. 2015. "What Really Works to Improve Learning in Developing Countries? An Analysis of Divergent Findings in Systematic Reviews." Policy Research Working Paper 7203, World Bank, Washington DC.

Gallup Poll. 2013. Gallup World Poll Survey 2013. Washington, DC.

Ginsburg, Mark, Nagwa Megahed, Mohammed Elmeski, and Nobuyuki Tanaka. 2010. "Reforming Educational Governance and Management in Egypt: National and International Actors and Dynamics." *Education Policy Analysis Archives* 18 (5): 1–54.

Glewwe, Paul. 2013. *Education Policy in Developing Countries*. Chicago: University of Chicago Press.

Glewwe, Paul, Eric A. Hanushek, Sarah Humpage, and Renato Ravina. 2013. "School Resources and Educational Outcomes in Developing Countries: A Review of the Literature from 1990 to 2010." In *Education Policy in Developing Countries*, edited by Paul Glewwe, 13–64. Chicago: University of Chicago Press.

Gove, Amber, Aarnout Brombacher, and Michelle Ward-Brent. 2017. "Sparking a Reading Revolution: Results of Early Literacy Interventions in Egypt and Jordan." *New Directions for Child and Adolescent Development* 155: 97–115.

Government of Jordan. 2018. "Jordan Response Plan for the Syria Crisis 2018–2020." Amman.

Graham, Jimmy, and Sean Kelly. 2018. "How Effective Are Early Grade Reading Interventions? A Review of the Evidence." Policy Research Working Paper 8292, World Bank, Washington, DC. http://documents.worldbank.org/curated/en/289341514995676575/How-effective-are-early-grade-reading-interventions-a-review-of-the-evidence.

Grindle, Merilee S. 2004. "Good Enough Governance: Poverty Reduction and Reform in Developing Countries." *Governance—An International Journal of Policy, Administration, and Institutions* 17 (4): 525–48.

Guardian. 2014. "Facebook: 10 Years of Social Networking, in Numbers." *Guardian*, February 4. https://www.theguardian.com/news/datablog/2014/feb/04/facebook-in-numbers-statistics.

Hamadani, Jena D., Syed N. Huda, Fahmida Khatun, and Sally M. Grantham-McGregor

2006. "Psychosocial Stimulation Improves the Development of Undernourished Children in Rural Bangladesh." *Journal of Nutrition* 136 (10): 2645–52. https://doi.org/10.1093/jn/136.10.2645.

Hanushek, Eric A. 2005. "Why Quality Matters in Education." *Finance and Development* 42 (2): 15–19.

———. 2011. "The Economic Value of Higher Teacher Quality." *Economics of Education Review* 30 (3): 466–79. http://hanushek.stanford.edu/publications/economic-value-higher-teacher-quality.

Hanushek, Eric A., and Ludger Woessmann. 2008. "The Role of Cognitive Skills in Economic Development." *Journal of Economic Literature* 46 (3): 607–68.

Hattie, John. 2009. *Visible Learning: A Synthesis of Over 800 Meta-Analyses Relating to Achievement*. London: Routledge.

Hattie, John, and Helen Timperley. 2007. "The Power of Feedback." *Review of Educational Research* 77 (1): 81–112. https://doi.org/10.3102/003465430298487.

Hazarika, Gautam, and Vejoya Viren. 2013. "The Effect of Early Childhood Developmental Program Attendance on Future School Enrollment in Rural North India." *Economics of Education Review* 34 (C): 146–61.

Heckman, James J. 2006. "Skill Formation and the Economics of Investing in Disadvantaged Children." *Science* 312 (5782): 1900–02.

Hightower, Amy M., Rachael C. Delgado, Sterling C. Lloyd, Rebecca Wittenstein, Kacy Sellers, and Christopher B. Swanson. 2011. "Improving Student Learning by Supporting Quality Teaching: Key Issues, Effective Strategies." Editorial Projects in Education, Bethesda, MD.

Horn, Michael, and Heather Staker. 2011. *The Rise of K-12 Blended Learning*. Lexington, MA: Innosight Institute.

———. 2012. *Classifying K-12 Blended Learning*. Lexington, MA: Innosight Institute.

Ibrahim, Rafique, and Judith Aharon-Peretz. 2005. "Is Literary Arabic a Second Language for Native Arab Speakers? Evidence from Semantic Priming Study." *Journal of Psycholinguistic Research* 34 (1): 51–70.

IDMC (Internal Displacement Monitoring Centre). 2019. *Global Report on Internal Displacement 2019*. Nijmegen: IDMC. http://www.internal-displacement.org/sites/default/files/publications/documents/2019-IDMC-GRID.pdf.

IEA (International Association for the Evaluation of Educational Achievement). 2015. "TIMSS 2015 Assessment Frameworks." TIMSS and PIRLS International Study Center, Lynch School of Education, Boston College, Chestnut Hill, MA. https://timssandpirls.bc.edu/timss2015/international-database/.

IMF (International Monetary Fund). 2017. "Regional Economic Outlook—Middle East and Central Asia." IMF, Washington, DC.

Inglehart, R., C. Haerpfer, A. Moreno, C. Welzel, K. Kizilova, J. Diez-Medrano, M. Lagos, P. Norris, E. Ponarin, and B. Puranen, eds. 2014. World Values Survey: Round Six—Country-Pooled Datafile Version. Madrid: JD Systems Institute. http://www.worldvaluessurvey.org/WVSDocumentationWV6.jsp.

IOM (International Organization for Migration). 2018. "Libya IDP & Returnee Report, Displacement Tracking Matrix, Round 19, March–April 2018." Geneva. https://www.iom.int/sites/default/files/dtm/libya_dtm_201804-05.pdf.

Jensen, Ben, Phoebe Downing, and Anna Clark. 2017a. *Preparing to Lead: Lessons in Principal Development from High-Performing Education Systems*. Washington, DC: National Center on Education and the Economy. http://ncee.org/wp-content/uploads/2017/10/PreparingtoLeadFINAL101817.pdf.

———. 2017b. *Preparing to Lead: Shanghai Continuing Professional Development. Case Studies for School Leadership Development Programs in High-Performing Education Systems*. Washington, DC: National Center on Education and the Economy.

Jung, Haeil, and Amer Hasan. 2014. "The Impact of Early Childhood Education on Early Achievement Gaps: Evidence from the Indonesia Early Childhood Education and Development (ECED) Project." Policy Research Working Paper 6794, World Bank, Washington, DC.

Karami Akkary, Rima. 2014. "Facing the Challenges of Educational Reform in the Arab World." *Journal of Educational Change* 15 (2): 179–202.

Kagitcibasi, Cigdem, Diane Sunar, and Sevda Bekman. 2001. "Long-Term Effects of Early Intervention: Turkish Low-Income Mothers and Children." *Journal of Applied Developmental Psychology* 22 (4): 333–61.

Karoly, Lynn A. 2017. *Investing in the Early Years: The Costs and Benefits of Investing in Early Childhood in New Hampshire*. RR-1890-E.

Santa Monica, CA: RAND Corporation. https://www.rand.org/pubs/research_reports/RR1890.html.

Khemani, Stuti. 2017. "Political Economy of Reform." Policy Research Working Paper 8224, World Bank, Washington, DC.

Kimura, Daisuke, and Madoka Tatsuno. 2017. "Advancing 21st Century Competencies in Japan." Center for Global Education, Asia Society, New York.

Kingdon, Geeta Gandhi, Angela Little, Monazza Aslam, Shenila Rawal, Terry Moe, Harry Patrinos, Tara Beteille, Rukmini Banerji, Brent Parton, and Shailendra K. Sharma. 2014. *A Rigorous Review of the Political Economy of Education Systems in Developing Countries*. Education Rigorous Literature Review. London: Department for International Development.

Kirdar, Serra. 2017. *Education in the Arab World*. London: Bloomsbury Academic.

Kirschner, Paul A., John Sweller, and Richard E. Clark. 2006. "Why Minimal Guidance during Instruction Does Not Work: An Analysis of the Failure of Constructivist, Discovery, Problem-Based, Experiential, and Inquiry-Based Teaching." *Educational Psychologist* 41 (2): 75–86. https://doi.org/10.1207/s15326985ep4102_1.

Krafft, Caroline. 2017. "Is School the Best Route to Skills? Returns to Vocational School and Vocational Skills in Egypt." *Journal of Development Studies* 54 (7): 1–21.

Krafft, Caroline, and Ragui Assaad. 2016. "Inequality of Opportunity in the Labor Market for Higher Education Graduates in Egypt and Jordan." In *The Middle East Economies in Times of Transition,* edited by Ishac Diwan and Ahmed Galal. New York: Palgrave Macmillan.

Kremer, Michael, Conner Brannen, and Rachel Glennerster. 2013. "The Challenge of Education and Learning in the Developing World." *Science* 340 (6130): 297–300.

Krishnan, Nandini, Gabriel Lara Ibarra, Ambar Narayan, Sailesh Tiwari, and Tara Vishwanath. 2016. *Uneven Odds, Unequal Outcomes: Inequality of Opportunity in the Middle East and North Africa*. Directions in Development. Washington, DC: World Bank.

Krishnaratne, Shari, Howard White, and Ella Carpenter. 2013. "Quality Education for All Children? What Works in Education in Developing Countries." 3ie Working Paper 20, International Initiative for Impact Evaluation, London.

Lange, Glenn-Marie, Quentin Wodon, and Kevin Carey. 2018. *The Changing Wealth of Nations 2018: Building a Sustainable Future*. Washington, DC: World Bank.

Lefevre, Raphael. 2015. "The Coming of North Africa's 'Language Wars.'" *Journal of North African Studies* 20 (4): 499–502.

Leithwood, Kenneth, Alma Harris, and David Hopkins. 2008. "Seven Strong Claims about Successful School Leadership." *School Leadership and Management* 28 (1): 27–42. https://doi.org/10.1080/13632430701800060.

Leithwood, Kenneth, and Blair Mascall. 2008. "Collective Leadership Effects on Student Achievement." *Educational Administration Quarterly* 44 (4): 529–61.

Lerman, Robert I. 2013. "Are Employability Skills Learned in U.S. Youth Education and Training Programs?" *IZA Journal of Labor Policy* 2 (1): 6.

Leseman, Paul. 2002. "Early Childhood Education and Care for Children from Low-Income or Minority Backgrounds." Paper for discussion at the OECD, Oslo Workshop, June 6–7.

Liang, Xiaoyan, Huma Kidwai, and Minxuan Zhang. 2016. *How Shanghai Does It—Insights and Lessons from the Highest-Ranking Education System in the World*. Washington, DC: World Bank.

Lightfoot, Michael. 2011. "Promoting the Knowledge Economy in the Arab World." Sage Open, 1–8. http://journals.sagepub.com/doi/abs/10.1177/2158244011417457.

Lochner, Lance, and Enrico Moretti. 2004. "The Effect of Education on Crime: Evidence from Prison Inmates, Arrests, and Self-Reports." *American Economic Review* 94 (1): 155–89.

Loughran, John, Amanda Berry, and Pamela Mulhall. 2012. *Understanding and Developing Science Teachers' Pedagogical Content Knowledge*. 2d ed. Rotterdam: Sense Publishers.

Maamouri, Mohamed. 1998. "Language Education and Human Development: Arabic Diglossia and Its Impact on the Quality of Education in the Arab Region." Mediterranean Development Forum, World Bank, Washington, DC.

MacLeod, Paul, and Amir Abou-El-Kheir. 2016. "English Education Policy in Bahrain: A Review of K–12 and Higher Education Language Policy in Bahrain." In *English Language Education Policy in the Middle East and North Africa*, edited by Robert Kirkpatrick, 9–32. New York: Springer.

Martin, Michael O., Ina V. S. Mullis, Pierre Foy, and M. Hooper. 2016. "TIMSS 2015 International Results in Science." TIMSS and PIRLS International Study Center, Boston College, Chestnut Hill, MA. http://timssandpirls.bc.edu/timss2015/international-results/.

Massialas, Byron G., and Samir A. Jarrar. 1987. "Conflicts in Education in the Arab World: The Present Challenge." *Arab Studies Quarterly* 9 (1): 35–52.

McEwan, Patrick J. 2015. "Improving Learning in Primary Schools of Developing Countries: A Meta-Analysis of Randomized Experiments." *Review of Educational Research* 85 (3): 353–94.

McKinsey. 2017. "Drivers of Student Performance: Insights from the Middle East and North Africa." McKinsey and Company, Washington, DC. https://www.mckinsey.com/industries/social-sector/our-insights/drivers-of-student-performance-insights-from-the-middle-east-and-north-africa.

Meng, Xin, Kailing Shen, and Sen Xue. 2013. "Economic Reform, Education Expansion, and Earnings Inequality for Urban Males in China, 1988–2009." *Journal of Comparative Economics* 41 (1): 227–44.

Metzler, Johannes, and Ludger Woessmann. 2012. "The Impact of Teacher Subject Knowledge on Student Achievement: Evidence from Within-Teacher Within-Student Variation." *Journal of Development Economics* 99 (2): 486–96.

Milligan, Kevin, Enrico Moretti, and Philip Oreopoulos. 2004. "Does Education Improve Citizenship? Evidence from the United States and the United Kingdom." *Journal of Public Economics* 88 (9–10): 1667–95.

Mincer, Jacob. 1974. *Schooling, Experience, and Earnings*. Cambridge, MA: National Bureau of Economic Research.

Ministry of Education, Republic of Yemen. 2017. "2015–2016 Educational Survey." Sana'a.

Ministry of Education and Higher Education, Lebanon. 2019. "RACE 2 Fact Sheet—March 2019." Beirut. http://racepmulebanon.com/images/fact-sheet-march-2019.pdf.

Moon, Yong-Lin. 2007. "Education Reform and Competency-Based Education." *Asia Pacific Education Review* 8 (2): 337–41.

Morgan, Hani. 2014. "The Education System in Finland: A Success Story Other Countries Can Emulate." *Childhood Education* 90 (6): 453–57.

———. 2016. "Lessons from the World's Most Successful Nations in International Testing." *Multicultural Education* 24 (1): 56–60.

Morrison, Wayne M. 2011. "China's Economic Conditions." Congressional Research Service, Washington, DC.

Mourshed, Mona, Chinezi Chijioke, and Michael Barber. 2010. *How the World's Most Improved School Systems Keep Getting Better*. London: McKinsey and Company.

Mullis, Ina V. S., Michael O. Martin, Pierre Foy, and M. Hooper. 2016. "TIMSS 2015 International Results in Mathematics." TIMSS and PIRLS International Study Center, Boston College, Chestnut Hill, MA. http://timssandpirls.bc.edu/timss2015/international-results/.

———. 2017. "PIRLS 2016 International Results in Reading." TIMSS and PIRLS International Study Center, Boston College, Chestnut Hill, MA. http://timssandpirls.bc.edu/pirls2016/international-results/.

Murnane, Richard J., and Alejandro J. Ganimian. 2014. "Improving Educational Outcomes in Developing Countries: Lessons from Rigorous Evaluations." Working Paper 180186, Harvard University, Cambridge, MA.

Nabli, Mustapha. 2007. "Breaking the Barriers to Higher Economic Growth: Better Governance and Deeper Reforms in the Middle East and North Africa." World Bank, Washington, DC.

Nakweya, Gilbert. 2017. "Mobile Learning—Empowering Refugees 'Where They Are.'" *University World News*, April 28. http://www.universityworldnews.com/article.php?story=20170427082935218/.

Namaghi, Seyyed Ali Ostovar. 2009. "A Data-Driven Conceptualization of Language Teacher Identity in the Context of Public High Schools in Iran." *Teacher Education Quarterly* 36 (2): 111–24.

Narayan, Ambar, Roy Van der Weide, Alexandru Cojocaru, Christoph Lakner, Silvia Redaelli, Daniel Gerszon Mahler, Rakesh Gupta N. Ramasubbaiah, and Stefan Thewissen. 2018. *Fair Progress? Economic Mobility across Generations around the World*. Equity and Development. Washington, DC: World Bank. https://openknowledge.worldbank.org/handle/10986/28428.

Naudeau, Sophie, Naoko Kataoka, Alexandria Valerio, Michelle J. Neuman, and Leslie K. Elder. 2011. *Investing in Young Children: An Early Childhood Development Guide for Policy Dialogue and Project Preparation*. Washington, DC: World Bank.

NCEE (National Center on Education and the Economy). 2016. "Developing High-Quality Teaching." Empowered Educators: How High-Performing Systems Shape Teaching Quality around the World Country Brief, National Center on Education and the Economy, Washington, DC.

OECD (Organisation for Economic Co-operation and Development). 2011a. "Japan: A Story of Sustained Excellence." In *Strong Performers and Successful Reformers in Education: Lessons from PISA for the United States*, 137–76. Paris: OECD.

———. 2011b. "School Autonomy and Accountability: Are They Related to Student Performance?" PISA in Focus 9, OECD, Paris.

———. 2011c. *Strong Performers and Successful Reformers in Education: Lessons from PISA for the United States*. Paris: OECD. http://www.oecd.org/pisa/46623978.pdf.

———. 2012a. *Preparing Teachers and Developing School Leaders for the 21st Century: Lessons from around the World*. Paris: OECD.

———. 2012b. *Starting Strong III: A Quality Toolbox for Early Childhood Education and Care*. Paris: OECD. http://dx.doi.org/10.1787/9789264123564-en.

———. 2014. "What Are the Social Benefits of Education?" Education Indicators in Focus 10, OECD, Paris.

———. 2016a. *PISA 2015 Results. Vol. 2: Policies and Practices for Successful Schools*. Paris: OECD Publishing. http://dx.doi.org/10.1787/9789264267510-en.

———. 2016b. "School Leadership for Developing Professional Learning Communities." Teaching in Focus 15, OECD, Paris.

———. 2016c. "School Leadership for Learning: Insights from TALIS 2013." OECD, Paris. http://dx.doi.org/10.1787/9789264258341-en.

———. 2016d. "Are There Differences in How Advantaged and Disadvantaged Students Use the Internet?" PISA in Focus 64, OECD, Paris. https://doi.org/10.1787/5jlv8zq6hw43-en.

———. 2017a. *Education at a Glance 2017: OECD Indicators*. Paris: OECD Publishing. https://doi.org/10.1787/eag-2017-en.

———. 2017b. *The Funding of School Education: Connecting Resources and Learning*. Paris: OECD. http://dx.doi.org/10.1787/978926oecd20174276147-en.

———. 2017c. *Starting Strong V: Transitions from Early Childhood Education and Care to Primary Education*. Paris: OECD. http://dx.doi.org/10.1787/9789264276253-en.

Overbye, Dennis. 2001. "How Islam Won, and Lost, the Lead in Science." *New York Times,* October 30. http://www.nytimes.com/2001/10/30/science/how-islam-won-and-lost-the-lead-in-science.html.

Oxford Business Group. 2015. *The Report: Algeria*. London. https://oxfordbusinessgroup.com/algeria-2015.

———. 2017. *The Report: Tunisia 2017*. London. https://oxfordbusinessgroup.com/overview/track-series-reforms-are-set-overhaul-sector.

Page, M. E. 2010. "Signaling in the Labor Market." In *Economics of Education,* edited by Dominic J. Brewer and Patrick J. McEwan, 33–36. Oxford: Elsevier.

Patrinos, Harry. 2016. "Estimating the Return to Schooling Using the Mincer Equation." IZA World of Labor 2016, July 7.

Paxson, Christina, and Norbert Schady. 2007. "Does Money Matter? The Effects of Cash Transfers on Child Health and Development in Rural Ecuador." Policy Research Working Paper 4226, World Bank, Washington, DC. https://openknowledge.worldbank.org/handle/10986/7076.

Pont, Beatriz, Deborah Nusche, and Hunter Moorman. 2008. *Improving School Leadership*. Vol. 1. Paris: OECD. http://www.oecd.org/education/school/44374889.pdf.

Prince, Michael. 2004. "Does Active Learning Work? A Review of the Research." *Journal of Engineering Education* 93 (3): 223–31.

Pugatch, Todd, and Nicholas Wilson. 2018. "Nudging Study Habits: A Field Experiment on Peer Tutoring in Higher Education." *Economics of Education Review* 62: 151–61. https://doi.org/10.1016/j.econedurev.2017.11.003.

Purpel, David E., and Svi Shapiro. 1995. *Beyond Liberation and Excellence: Reconstructing the Public Discourse on Education*. Westport, CT: Bergin and Garvey.

Rabie, Tamer Samah, Samira Nikaein Towfighian, Cari Clark, and Melani Cammett. 2017. *The Last Mile to Quality Service Delivery in Jordan*. Directions in Development—Human Development. Washington, DC: World Bank. https://openknowledge.worldbank.org/handle/10986/26577 License: CC BY 3.0 IGO.

Radcliffe, Damian, and Amanda Lam. 2018. "Social Media in the Middle East: The Story of 2017." University of Oregon. https://ssrn.com/abstract=3124077 or http://dx.doi.org/10.2139/ssrn.3124077.

Rivkin, Steven, Eric A. Hanushek, and John F. Kain. 2005. "Teachers, Schools, and Academic Achievement." *Econometrica* 73 (2): 417–58.

Rizk, Reham. 2016. "Returns to Education: An Updated Comparison from Arab Countries." ERF Working Paper 986, Economic Research Forum, Giza, Egypt.

Rodrik, Dani. 2008. "Second-Best Institutions." *American Economic Review* 98 (2): 100–04.

Roediger, H. L. III, A. L. Putnam, and M. A. Smith. 2011. "Ten Benefits of Testing and Their Applications to Educational Practice." In *The Psychology of Learning and Motivation.* Vol. 55: *The Psychology of Learning and Motivation: Cognition in Education,* edited by Jose P. Mestre and Brian H. Ross, 1–36. San Diego: Elsevier Academic Press.

Rugh, William A. 2002. "Arab Education: Tradition, Growth, and Reform." *Middle East Journal* 56 (3): 396–414.

Sala-i-Martin, Xavier, Gernot Doppelhofer, and Ronald I. Miller. 2004. "Determinants of Long-Term Growth: A Bayesian Averaging of Classical Estimates (BACE) Approach." *American Economic Review* 94 (4): 813–35.

Salehi-Isfahani, Djavad 2012. "Education, Jobs, and Equity in the Middle East and North Africa." *Comparative Economic Studies* 54 (4): 843–61.

Salehi-Isfahani, Djavad, Insan Tunali, and Ragui Assaad. 2009. "A Comparative Study of Returns to Education of Urban Men in Egypt, Iran, and Turkey." *Middle East Development Journal* 1 (2): 145–87.

Salmi, Jamil. 1987. "Language and Schooling in Morocco." *International Journal of Educational Development* 7 (1): 21–31.

Schumacher, Ernst F. 1973. *Small Is Beautiful: A Study of Economics as If People Mattered.* London: Blond and Briggs.

Schweinhart, Lawrence, Jeanne Montie, Zongping Xiang, W. Steven Bernett, Clive R. Belfield, and Milagros Nores. 2005. *Lifetime Effects: The High/Scope Perry Preschool Study through Age 40.* Ypsilanti, MI: High/Scope Press.

Shonkoff, Jack P., and Andrew S. Garner. 2012. "The Lifelong Effects of Early Childhood Adversity and Toxic Stress." *Pediatrics* 129 (1): 232–46.

Shuayb, Maha. 2012. "Social Cohesion in Secondary Schools in Lebanon." In *Rethinking Education for Social Cohesion: International Case Studies,* edited by Maha Shuay, 137–53. London: Palgrave Macmillan.

Shulman, Lee S., and Judith H. Shulman. 2004. "How and What Teachers Learn: A Shifting Perspective." *Journal of Curriculum Studies* 36 (2): 257–71.

Shulman, Robyn D. 2018. "EdTech Investments Rise to a Historical $9.5 Billion: What Your Startup Needs to Know." *Forbes,* January 26. https://www.forbes.com/sites/robynshulman/2018/01/26/EdTech-investments-rise-to-a-historical-9-5-billion-what-your-startup-needs-to-know/.

Sleiman-Haidar, Ribale, ed. 2016. "The Political Economy of Labour Markets and Migration in the Gulf: Workshop Proceedings." London School of Economics and Political Science, LSE Kuwait Programme, London.

Snilstveit, Birte, Jennifer Stevenson, Daniel Phillips, Martina Vojtkova, Emma Gallagher, Tanja Schmidt, Hannah Jobse, Maisie Geelen, Maria Grazia Pastorello, and John Eyers. 2015. *Interventions for Improving Learning Outcomes and Access to Education in Low- and Middle-Income Countries: A Systematic Review.* 3ie Systematic Review 24. London: International Initiative for Impact Evaluation.

Spence, Michael. 1973. "Job Market Signaling." *Quarterly Journal of Economics* 87 (3): 355–74.

SPHEIR (Strategic Partnerships for Higher Education Innovation and Reform). 2017. "Initial SPHEIR Partnerships Selected." Department for International Development, London. https://www.spheir.org.uk/latest-news/initial-spheir-partnerships-selected.

Springborg, Robert. 2011. "The Precarious Economics of Arab Springs." *Survival* 53 (6): 85–104. doi:10.1080/00396338.2011.636271.

Steenbergen-Hu, Saiying, Matthew C. Makel, and Paula Olszewski-Kubilius. 2016. "What One Hundred Years of Research Says about the Effects of Ability Grouping and Acceleration on K–12 Students' Academic Achievement. Findings of Two Second-Order Meta-Analyses." *Review of Educational Research* 86 (4): 849–99. doi: 10.3102/0034654316675417.

Teachers First. 2018. "Teachers First." http://teachersfirstegypt.com/about/what-is-tf/.

Temple, Judy A., and Arthur J. Reynolds. 2007. "Benefits and Costs of Investments in Preschool Education: Evidence from the Child–Parent

Centers and Related Programs." *Economics of Education Review* 26 (1): 126–44.
Thames, Mark Hoover, and Deborah Loewenberg Ball. 2010. "What Math Knowledge Does Teaching Require?" *Teaching Children Mathematics* 17 (4): 220–29.
Trade Arabia News Service. 2013. "MENA Tops Global Education Spend." Dubai, United Arab Emirates. http://www.tradearabia.com/news/EDU_229718.html.
Tzannatos, Zafiris, Ishac Diwan, and Joanna Abdel Ahad. 2016. "Rates of Return to Education in Twenty-Two Arab Countries; An Update and Comparison between MENA and the Rest of the World." ERF Working Paper 1007, Economic Research Forum, Giza, Egypt.
UIS (UNESCO Institute for Statistics) and UNICEF (United Nations Children's Fund). 2014. "Regional Report on Out-of-School Children." All in School: Middle East and North Africa Out-of-School Children Initiative (OOSCI), UIS, and UNICEF, Paris, October. http://www.oosci-mena.org/regional-overview.
Unangst, Lisa. 2017. "Germany's Innovative Strategies to Enroll Refugees." *Inside Higher Education,* January 18. https://www.insidehighered.com/blogs/world-view/germanys-innovative-strategies-enroll-refugees.
UNESCO (United Nations Educational, Scientific, and Cultural Organization). 1999. Declaration and Programme of Action on a Culture of Peace, Article A/4. UNESCO, Paris. http://www.un-documents.net/a53r243.htm.
———. 2011. *World Data on Education: Seventh Edition 2010–11.* Paris: UNESCO International Bureau of Education.
———. 2017a. *Global Education Monitoring Report—Accountability in Education: Meeting Our Commitments.* Paris: UNESCO.
———. 2017b. *The Why, What, and How of Competency-Based Curriculum Reforms: The Kenyan Experience.* Paris: International Bureau of Education, UNESCO.
UNHCR (United Nations High Commissioner for Refugees). 2018. "UNHCR Yemen Update, 15–31 May 2018." Geneva. https://reliefweb.int/sites/reliefweb.int/files/resources/Yemen%20Update%2015-31%20May%202018%20%28Final%29%20.pdf.
———. 2019a. "Syria Regional Refugee Response—Inter-agency Information Sharing Portal." Geneva. http://data.unhcr.org/syrianrefugees/regional.php.
———. 2019b. *UNHCR Mid-Year Trends 2018.* Geneva: UNHCR. https://www.unhcr.org/cgi-bin/texis/vtx/home/opendocAttachment.zip?COMID=5c77e8824.
UNICEF (United Nations Children's Fund). 2010. *Child Disciplinary Practices at Home: Evidence from a Range of Low- and Middle-Income Countries.* New York: UNICEF.
———. 2013. "Percentage of Children Aged 2–14 Who Experience Any Form of Violent Discipline (Physical Punishment and/or Psychological Agression)." UNICEF, Paris. http://www.childinfo.org/discipline_countrydata.php.
———. 2017. "Iraq Humanitarian Situation Report—June 2017." Paris. https://www.unicef.org/iraq/UNICEF_Iraq_Humanitarian_Situation_Report_-_June_2017.pdf.
———. 2018. "If Not in School—The Paths Children Cross in Yemen." Paris. https://www.unicef.org/infobycountry/files/IF_NOT_IN_SCHOOL_March2018_English.pdf.
———. No date. "Middle East and North Africa Out-of-School Initiative: Regional Overview." Paris. http://www.oosci-mena.org/regional-overview#report.
UN OCHA (United Nations Office for the Coordination of Humanitarian Affairs). 2018. *Humanitarian Bulletin Iraq,* May. https://reliefweb.int/sites/reliefweb.int/files/resources/FINAL%20OCHA%20Iraq%20Humanitarian%20Bulletin%20-%20May%202018.pdf.
UNRWA (United Nations Relief and Works Agency). 2019. "UNRWA in Figures 2018." UNRWA, Amman. https://www.unrwa.org/resources/about-unrwa/unrwa-figures-2018-2019.
UN Women (United Nations Entity for Gender Equality and Empowerment of Women) and Promundo. 2017. *Understanding Masculinities: Results from the International Men and Gender Equality Survey (IMAGES)—Middle East and North Africa.* Men and Women for Gender Equality Programme, UN Women Regional Office for Arab States. Paris: UN Women and Promundo.
USAID (U.S. Agency for International Development). 2018. Early Grade Reading Barometer. http://www.earlygradereadingbarometer.org/.
van Ginkel, Agatha. 2014. "Using an Additional Language as the Medium of Instruction: Transition in Mother Tongue-Based Multilingual Education." MTB-MLE Network Webinar. http://www.mlenetwork.org

/sites/default/files/van%20Ginkel%20-%20 Webinar%20Slides%20-%202014_0.pdf.
Vegas, Emiliana, and Lucrecia Santibáñez. 2010. *The Promise of Early Childhood Development in Latin America and the Caribbean.* Latin American Development Forum. Washington, DC: World Bank.
Witziers, Bob, Roel J. Bosker, and Meta L. Kruger. 2003. "Educational Leadership and Student Achievement: The Elusive Search for an Association." *Educational Administration Quarterly* 39 (3): 398–423.
Wong, Anny. 2017. "Insights from East Asia's High-Performing Education Systems: Leadership, Pragmatism, and Continuous Improvement." Background paper prepared for *Growing Smarter: Learning and Equitable Development in East Asia and Pacific,* World Bank, Washington, DC.
World Bank. 2004. *World Development Report 2004: Making Services Work for Poor People.* Washington, DC: World Bank.
———. 2005. *Expanding Opportunities and Building Competencies for Young People: A New Agenda for Secondary Education.* Washington, DC: World Bank.
———. 2008. *The Road Not Traveled: Education Reform in the Middle East and North Africa.* Washington, DC: World Bank. http://web.worldbank.org/archive/website01033/WEB/IMAGES/EDU_FLAG.PDF.
———. 2010. "SABER-Teachers Country Report: Egypt 2010." Systems Approach for Better Education Results (SABER) Country Report, World Bank, Washington, DC.
———. 2011. *The Road to Academic Excellence: The Making of World-Class Research Universities.* Washington, DC: World Bank.
———. 2012. *MENA Regional Synthesis on the Teacher Policies Surveys: Key Findings from Phase 1.* Washington, DC: World Bank.
———. 2013a. *Jobs for Shared Prosperity: Time for Action in the Middle East and North Africa.* Washington, DC: World Bank.
———. 2013b. "Rwanda: Education Resilience Case Report." Education Resilience Approaches (ERA) Program, Human Development Network, World Bank. Washington, DC.
———. 2013c. *Universities through the Looking Glass—Benchmarking University Governance to Enable Higher Education Modernization in MENA.* Washington, DC: World Bank.
———. 2013d. "What Matters Most for Teacher Policies: A Framework Paper." World Bank, Washington, DC.
———. 2015a. "Hashemite Kingdom of Jordan School Autonomy and Accountability: SABER Country Report 2015." Systems Approach for Better Education Results (SABER), World Bank, Washington, DC.
———. 2015b. "Inequality, Uprisings, and Conflict in the Arab World." *MENA Economic Monitor* 3 (October 15). World Bank, Washington, DC.
———. 2015c. *MENA Regional Synthesis on the Teacher Policies Survey: Key Findings from Phase 1.* Washington, DC: World Bank. https://openknowledge.worldbank.org/handle/10986/21490 License: CC BY 3.0 IGO.
———. 2015d. "Morocco School Autonomy and Accountability: SABER Country Report 2015." Systems Approach for Better Education Results (SABER), World Bank, Washington, DC.
———. 2015e. *World Development Report 2015: Mind, Society, and Behavior.* Washington, DC: World Bank.
———. 2016a. "Hashemite Kingdom of Jordan Education Sector Public Expenditure Review." Report ACS18935, World Bank, Washington, DC.
———. 2016b. *Making Politics Work for Development: Harnessing Transparency and Citizen Engagement.* Washington, DC: World Bank.
———. 2017a. "Building the Research Capacity of MENA Universities." Policy Note, World Bank, Washington, DC.
———. 2017b. "6th MENA Tertiary Education Conference—CMI Headquarters—June 2017." World Bank, Washington, DC.
———. 2018a. *Growing Smarter: Learning and Equitable Development in East Asia and Pacific.* East Asia and Pacific Regional Report. Washington, DC: World Bank.
———. 2018b. *Iraq Reconstruction and Investment.* Vol. 2: *Damage and Needs Assessment of Affected Governorates.* Washington, DC: World Bank.
———. 2018c. "Project Appraisal Document. Republic of Tunisia: Strengthening Foundations for Learning Project." World Bank, Washington, DC.
———. 2018d. "Project Appraisal Document. Supporting Egypt Education Reform Project." World Bank, Washington, DC.

———. 2018e. *World Development Report 2018: Learning to Realize Education's Promise.* Washington, DC: World Bank.

———. 2019. *World Development Report 2019: The Changing Nature of Work.* Washington, DC: World Bank.

———. Various years. Education Statistics (EdStats) database. Washington, DC. http://datatopics.worldbank.org/education/.

———. Various years. World Development Indicators database. Washington, DC. http://data.worldbank.org/data-catalog/world-development-indicators.

World Economic Forum. 2016. "Rich and Poor Teenagers Use the Web Differently—Here's What This Is Doing to Inequality." July 27. https://www.weforum.org/agenda/2016/07/rich-and-poor-teenagers-spend-a-similar-amount-of-time-online-so-why-aren-t-we-closing-the-digital-divide/.

Yoon, Kwang Suk, Teresa Duncan, Silvia Wen-Yu Lee, Beth Scarloss, and Kathy L. Shapley. 2007. "Reviewing the Evidence on How Teacher Professional Development Affects Student Achievement." Regional Education Laboratory, Institute of Education Sciences, U.S. Department of Education, Washington, DC.

Zhang, Junsen, Yaohui Zhao, Albert Park, and Xiaoqing Song. 2005. "Economic Returns to Schooling in Urban China, 1988 to 2001." *Journal of Comparative Economics* 33 (4): 730–52.

A New Lens on Education in MENA

Igor Kheyfets, Elisabeth Sedmik, Mohammed Audah, Laura Gregory, and Caroline Krafft*

Education has large untapped potential to contribute to human capital, well-being, and growth in the Middle East and North Africa (MENA) region. Realizing the potential of education can unleash its contributions to economic and social development. Investing in education as a form of human capital is important for countries' economic growth (Becker 1962; Mincer 1974; Sala-i-Martin, Doppelhofer, and Miller 2004). However, returns on investment in education are achieved only when education promotes learning and skills (Hanushek and Woessmann 2008). The *World Development Report 2018* finds a strong relationship between growth and learning outcomes (World Bank 2018). However, education's potential remains largely untapped in MENA.

Despite large investments in education over the last 50 years, impressive growth in enrollment rates, and gender parity at almost all levels of education, MENA has not been able to reap the full social and economic benefits of education. MENA has the lowest share of human capital in total wealth globally (Lange, Wodon, and Carey 2018), and the learning outcomes of MENA students are among the lowest in the world, as measured by international student assessments.[1]

Education systems in MENA have historically focused on conferring credentials rather than skills. As a result, young people in MENA lack foundational and other skills relevant for the workplace. In order to fulfill education's potential for economic and social development, MENA countries will need to commit to developing education systems that emphasize learning and skills. Only then can MENA countries achieve their full potential in developing human capital and meet the expectations and aspirations of its people.

MENA's economic and social challenges require a renewed focus on human capital development

Countries in the region face a broad array of social and economic challenges. While some countries are stable and high income, others are struggling economically or are beset by conflict. Iraq, Libya, the Syrian Arab Republic, and the Republic of Yemen are directly affected by conflict. Their neighbors—such as

---

* This chapter includes a summary section on higher education (p. 81), based on chapter 13, "Rethinking Tertiary Education: High-Level Skills and Research," by Jamil Salmi.

Jordan and Lebanon—are experiencing the spillover effects of these conflicts, which include hosting substantial numbers of refugees. Even countries in the MENA region that are stable and not hosting large refugee populations face major economic and social challenges. Some of these, like the Arab Republic of Egypt and Tunisia, are suffering from slow growth due to the economic downturns that followed the Arab Spring turmoil and a series of terrorist attacks (World Bank 2015). The high-income economies of the Gulf Cooperation Council (GCC) are experiencing moderate growth but also substantial fiscal challenges, primarily due to a decrease in oil prices from historically high levels.

Unemployment is highest among educated youth in MENA

Over the last decade, MENA economies did not create enough jobs to absorb all new labor market entrants. The result is a high rate of youth unemployment across the region—23 percent—more than double the unemployment rate of the general population within MENA countries (see figure 1.1). Unemployment is primarily a structural, rather than a business cycle–driven, problem. Demographics, including population growth and the large proportion of youth, contribute to high youth unemployment. By 2050, the MENA region will have to produce 300 million new jobs just to absorb the large youth population entering the labor market (Arezki et al. 2018). Additionally, unemployment is highest among youth with more education and those from better-off backgrounds who often defer accepting employment that is readily available in the expectation of attaining higher-quality jobs (Krafft and Assaad 2014).

Figure 1.2 presents youth unemployment rates by level of education for select countries. For male youths in Egypt, unemployment rates rise with education, from 7 percent for those with basic education to 15 percent for those with advanced (higher) education. For female youths in Egypt, the rates of unemployment range from 6 percent

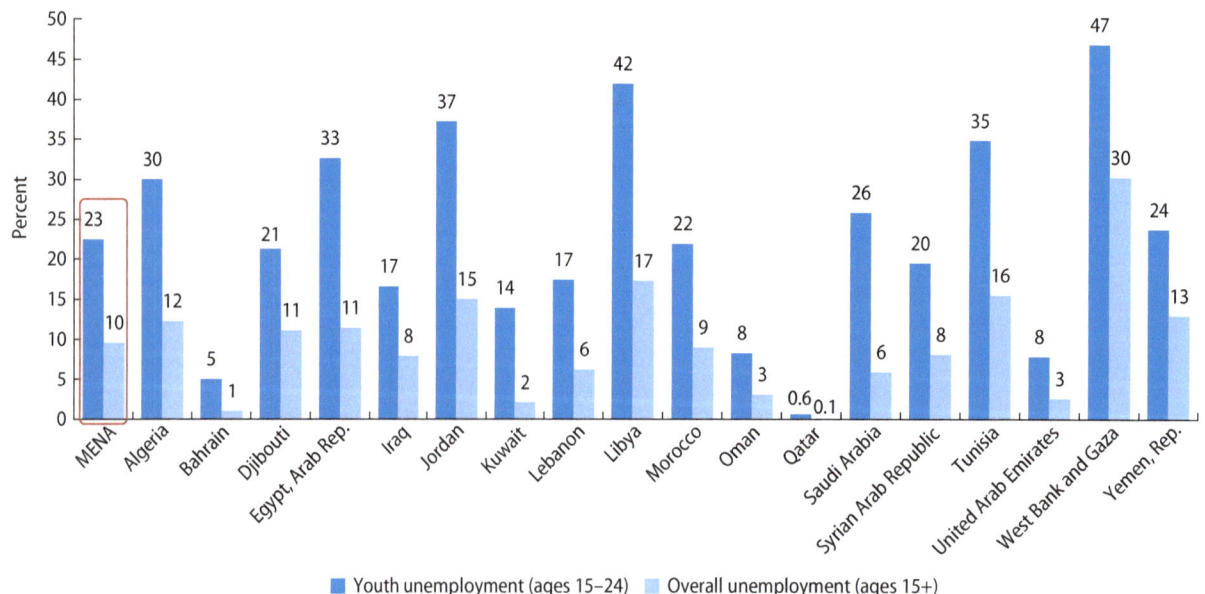

FIGURE 1.1 Youth unemployment rates are higher than overall unemployment rates across MENA

Overall (ages 15+) and youth (ages 15–24) unemployment rates, 2018

Source: International Labour Organization (ILO) ILOSTAT database, ILO modeled estimates for 2018.
Note: MENA average is the unweighted average of all economies presented in the figure.

FIGURE 1.2 Youth unemployment is highest among the most educated in many MENA economies

Youth (ages 15–24) unemployment rates, by gender and level of education, latest available year

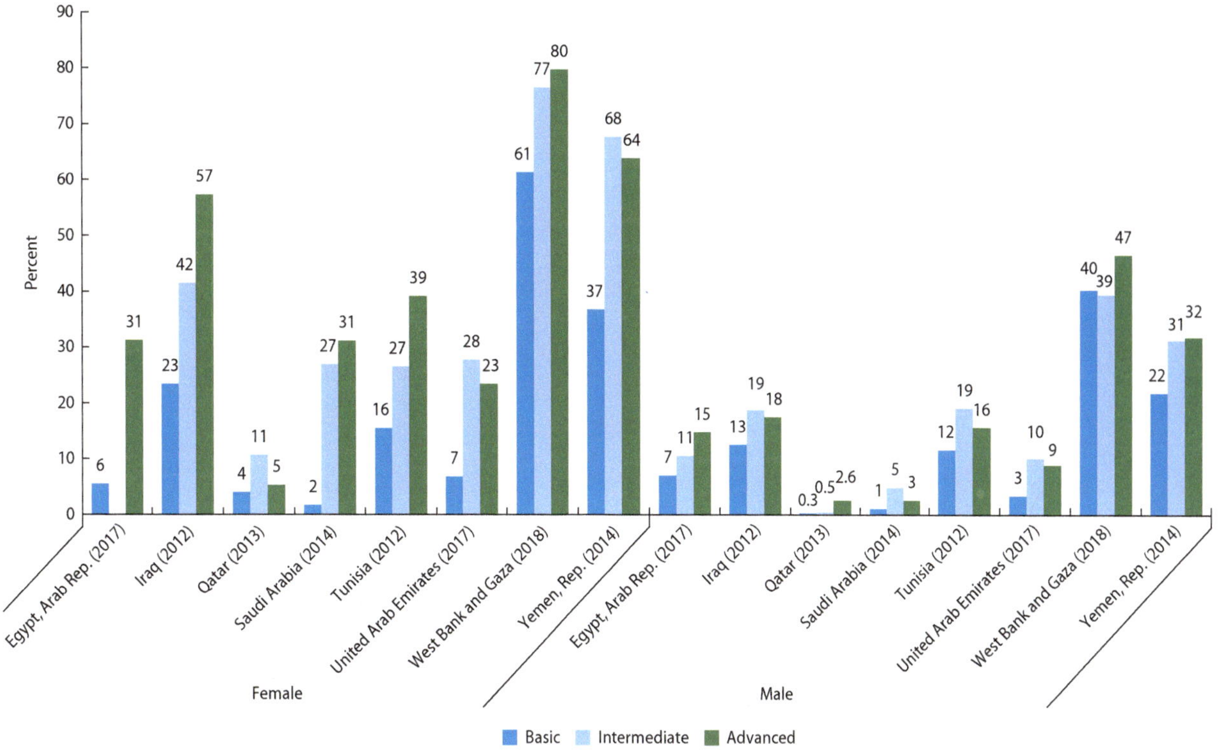

[Bar chart showing youth unemployment rates by country, gender, and education level]

Female:
- Egypt, Arab Rep. (2017): Basic 6, Advanced 31
- Iraq (2012): Basic 23, Intermediate 42, Advanced 57
- Qatar (2013): Basic 4, Intermediate 11, Advanced 5
- Saudi Arabia (2014): Basic 2, Intermediate 27, Advanced 31
- Tunisia (2012): Basic 16, Intermediate 27, Advanced 39
- United Arab Emirates (2017): Basic 7, Intermediate 28, Advanced 23
- West Bank and Gaza (2018): Basic 61, Intermediate 77, Advanced 80
- Yemen, Rep. (2014): Basic 37, Intermediate 68, Advanced 64

Male:
- Egypt, Arab Rep. (2017): Basic 7, Intermediate 11, Advanced 15
- Iraq (2012): Basic 13, Intermediate 19, Advanced 18
- Qatar (2013): Basic 0.3, Intermediate 0.5, Advanced 2.6
- Saudi Arabia (2014): Basic 1, Intermediate 5, Advanced 3
- Tunisia (2012): Basic 12, Intermediate 19, Advanced 16
- United Arab Emirates (2017): Basic 3, Intermediate 10, Advanced 9
- West Bank and Gaza (2018): Basic 40, Intermediate 39, Advanced 47
- Yemen, Rep. (2014): Basic 22, Intermediate 31, Advanced 32

Legend: Basic, Intermediate, Advanced

Source: International Labour Organization (ILO) ILOSTAT database.
Note: Basic education comprises primary education or lower-secondary education; intermediate education comprises upper-secondary or postsecondary nontertiary education; advanced education comprises short-cycle tertiary education, a bachelor's degree or equivalent education level, a master's degree or equivalent education level, or a doctoral degree or equivalent education level; all according to the 2011 International Standard Classification of Education (ISCED). No unemployment data were available for 15- to 24-year-old females with an intermediate level of education in the Arab Republic of Egypt for 2017 (the respective rate in 2014 was 32.9 percent).

for those with basic education to 31 percent for those with advanced (higher) education. In West Bank and Gaza, youth unemployment rates range from 39 to 47 percent for male youths and 61 to 80 percent for female youths.

Expectations of public sector jobs remain deeply entrenched in MENA societies

High rates of youth unemployment place substantial pressures on countries to generate jobs. Some national constitutions in the region guarantee the "right to work"; thus individuals expect the state to ensure that citizens will be employed. Some youths even view government employment as the only solution to unemployment (Barsoum 2015). Many people in the region believe that government, not the private sector, should provide employment opportunities, in part due to the higher quality of jobs in the public sector.[2] Protests around jobs were a critical element of the Jasmine Revolution in Tunisia during 2010–11, and such protests continue to the present day. These attitudes are a legacy of the government employment guarantees that were part of the social contract in the region during the 20th century (Assaad 1997, 2014).

The private sector's job-generating capacity remains underdeveloped in many MENA countries. The public sector is still a large and preferred employer (Barsoum 2015; Gatti et al. 2013). In Egypt, 30 percent of employment is in the public sector (Assaad and Krafft 2015). The situation is even more pronounced in most GCC countries. For example, in Saudi Arabia, 68 percent of employment is in the public sector, according to the ILOSTAT database (2014 data). The outsized role of government employment in some MENA countries, as well as the high wages in the public sector, crowd out private sector employment (Behar and Mok 2013; Nabli 2007). Government strategies to increase high-quality private sector employment have generally had little success thus far, resulting in limited or poor opportunities for new graduates (Dahi 2012; Salehi-Isfahani 2012; Springborg 2011).

Since at least the middle of the 20th century, the social contract in many MENA countries included a tacit agreement between the state and its citizens whereby the citizens accepted limited political freedom in return for free public services and subsidized goods, along with high levels of public employment (Assaad 2014). This model, although unsustainable in the long run and altered by subsequent structural reforms, left a lasting imprint on the region's education systems, economies, and labor markets. Namely, the emphasis on public employment led to an education system that is stuck in a "credentialist equilibrium," with credentials—such as degrees or diplomas—being valued above actual skills.

At the same time, companies in the private sector often report difficulty finding adequately skilled workers. This is especially the case for enterprises that are highly productive or in fast-changing industries. According to recent studies, one out of three firms surveyed in Iraq, Morocco, and Tunisia reported that the lack of an adequately educated workforce is a major or severe constraint for their business (see chapter 12). In addition, migration also affects the education and labor market decisions of youths in MENA (see box 1.1).

Returns to education are lower in MENA than in other regions of the world

Skills mismatches are a persistent problem in MENA, with workers' skills misaligned with what the labor market is demanding. There are symptoms of mismatch on both the supply and the demand sides of the labor market. The high unemployment rates of the educated show that the supply of highly educated workers exceeds the demand. This may indicate a low quality of learning in the skill areas demanded by the labor market, as employers note that university and vocational graduates lack the hard and soft skills required for their jobs (Gatti et al. 2013). This skills mismatch contributes to the low levels of private returns to education in the labor market.

An investment in one additional year of schooling can be expected, on average, to yield a stream of higher earnings in adulthood—leading to higher returns to completing additional education (Psacharopoulos and Patrinos 2018). The rate of return to education is typically calculated as the percentage increase in earnings for each additional year of schooling. Figure 1.3 shows the latest estimates for rates of return to an additional year of schooling by region (Psacharopoulos and Patrinos 2018). At 5.7 percent, the MENA region has the lowest average returns to education.

Both labor supply and demand may play a key role in these low returns. On the labor supply side, the human capital conferred by the education system tends to be of low quality, in terms of inadequate learning, which further contributes to low returns. The demand for workers with higher education credentials in the current education and economic system is also low. Rates of return to education vary across countries and levels of education, depending in part on the supply of and the demand for educated labor as well as the quality of education (Montenegro and Patrinos 2014). To generate higher returns to investment in education, it is important to build human capital through the development of key foundational and

Box 1.1 Migration affects education systems in MENA through three key channels

International migration flows—in the form of both forced displacement and labor migration—affect education systems in MENA in several important ways. While this topic is discussed at length in the previous MENA education flagship report (World Bank 2008), recent events have put migration at the center of many policy discussions throughout the region. Despite the importance of migration to MENA economies, the issue falls outside the scope of this report. However, migration affects MENA education systems through three key channels, which are highlighted here.

First, the migration of teachers from across MENA to countries of the GCC—and other parts of the world—has a potentially destabilizing impact on education systems in sending countries, many of which experience shortages of qualified teachers in certain subjects (such as mathematics and science). Second, migrant remittances are important for financing private education expenses in MENA. Total remittance transfers to MENA exceeded US$54 billion in 2017, accounting for at least 5 percent of gross domestic product (GDP) in seven MENA economies—Egypt, Jordan, Lebanon, Morocco, Tunisia, West Bank and Gaza, and the Republic of Yemen (World Bank n.d.). Household remittance receipts can increase the educational attainment of the children in those households (Ben Mim and Ben Ali 2012), while also contributing to the growth of educational inequality between households sending and those not sending migrants. Finally, the focus of large numbers of MENA students on entering the European labor market has the potential to distort their educational aspirations and influence their decisions about how much and what type of education to pursue (Ramos 2017).

Migration presents challenges, but can also lead to an economic "win-win" arrangement for both sending and receiving countries. Policies around migrant flows in both sets of countries matter a great deal in determining the net impact of migration on populations and education systems (World Bank 2008). Much more study of the topic is needed to identify the precise conditions under which effective migration, education, and labor policies can work in unison to maximize the benefits for individuals and societies from the movement of people.

Sources: Ben Mim and Ben Ali 2012; Ramos 2017; World Bank 2008, n.d.

21st-century skills that are likely to be in demand in the years and decades to come (see box 1.2) as well as to address the current constraints limiting the demand for educated labor.

Rates of return to education have been generally decreasing over time. The returns to another year of schooling tend to decline as the average number of years of schooling rises in an economy (Montenegro and Patrinos 2014). The MENA region has seen tremendous increases in educational attainment over the past decades. The decline in returns suggests that the growth in the labor supply of educated individuals has generally outpaced the growth in labor demand for educated individuals (Montenegro and Patrinos 2014).

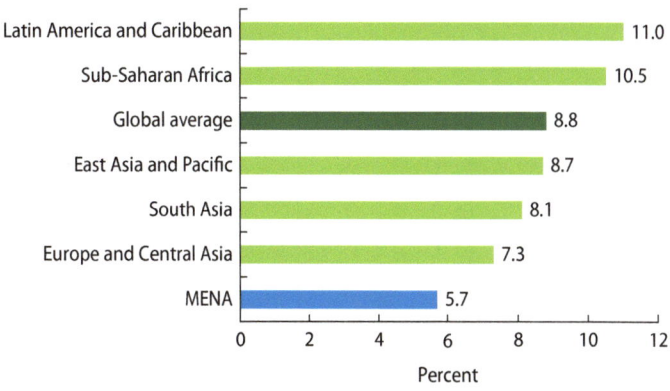

FIGURE 1.3 **Rates of return to education are lower in MENA than in other regions**

Rate of return to education, by region, latest estimate

Source: Psacharopoulos and Patrinos 2018.
Note: Each number represents the private rate of return, as a percentage increase in earnings, to an additional year of schooling.

Box 1.2 Technological change is driving the shift in labor market demand for skills

Technological change is among the main factors driving the shift in demand for skills in labor markets throughout the world. The *World Development Report 2019: The Changing Nature of Work* lists several ways in which technological change is affecting the demand for skills (World Bank 2019). Among them are (1) the decline in manufacturing employment; (2) the change in the relative wage premia of the skills that are rewarded in the labor market; (3) the disruption of production processes that is challenging the traditional boundaries of firms, expanding global value chains, and changing the geography of jobs; and (4) the change in how people work—for example, through the rise of the "gig economy," where organizations contract with independent workers for short-term engagements. Particularly important is the observation that relative wage premia are growing for skills that cannot be replaced by technology—namely, high-level cognitive skills, such as critical thinking, and socioemotional skills, such as managing and recognizing emotions that enhance teamwork.

In MENA, however, the picture of which skills are associated with higher rewards in the labor market is less clear. On average, MENA countries see lower returns to education than other parts of the world, in part because educational credentials correlate imperfectly with the skills they are supposed to confer. The adoption of digital technology in MENA can potentially help to boost the returns to education in the 21st century but also can increase income inequality between the tech-savvy workers employed in the booming sectors of the "new economy" and the less technologically inclined (older and poorer) ones in the traditional industries.

In the medium term, the demand for skills in MENA countries is likely to shift in the direction of those abilities that are commonly found in the "new economy." High-order cognitive skills (requiring at least a basic level of literacy and numeracy) and socioemotional skills (built on foundations that are developed in the early years) will be increasingly complemented by digital competencies and the ability to interact with modern technologies. By accelerating technological adoption and aligning education systems with the needs of the labor market, MENA countries would be better positioned to meet the demands of their citizens and economies for future prosperity.

Source: World Bank 2019.

For example, in Egypt, as the number of people with a vocational education has doubled, the return has halved (Krafft 2017); the supply of vocationally educated individuals is greater than the demand for their labor. Also, having more education than is needed for a job generates lower returns than having education that matches the job requirements (Hartog 2000).

Having credentials that do not confer labor market–relevant skills contributes to low returns to education across the MENA region. From the limited recent data that are available, it is evident that returns to education vary across the MENA region. While rates of return to education in Jordan and Tunisia are higher than those in Egypt, Kuwait, and West Bank and Gaza, all of these economies experience lower rates of return to education than the global average (see figure 1.4).

Although an in-depth analysis of labor market demand is beyond the scope of this report, the imperative of MENA education systems to improve the labor market outcomes of future workers lies at the core of the challenges facing the region. This report, therefore, focuses on the specific policy areas within education that will require special attention from policy makers and concerted efforts from all actors in society to ensure that the skills being imparted today serve the needs of future generations.

Human capital accounts for a smaller share of overall national wealth in MENA

Across the world, intangible wealth—embodied in people as human capital—constitutes the greatest share of total wealth, especially for high-income countries (Lange, Wodon, and Carey 2018). However, in MENA the share of human capital as a percentage of total wealth per capita is the lowest of all regions of the world (see table 1.1).

The degree to which human capital contributes to total wealth varies by country; however, all MENA countries have levels of human capital as a share of total wealth below the world average, with the exception of Lebanon (see table 1.2). On average, human capital as a share of total wealth in MENA (35 percent) is only about half the world average (64 percent). In Morocco, for example, total wealth per capita grew 45 percent from 2005 to 2014. Produced (physical) capital grew proportionately and natural capital more than doubled; however, human capital grew only 22 percent over the 10-year period (Lange, Wodon, and Carey 2018).

These estimates show that there is large, untapped potential for MENA countries to boost economic prosperity through improvements in their human capital endowments. To bring the region's share of human capital as a percentage of total wealth (currently 35 percent) toward the global average (64 percent), substantial efforts are needed to ensure that large expansions of schooling translate into learning and skills.

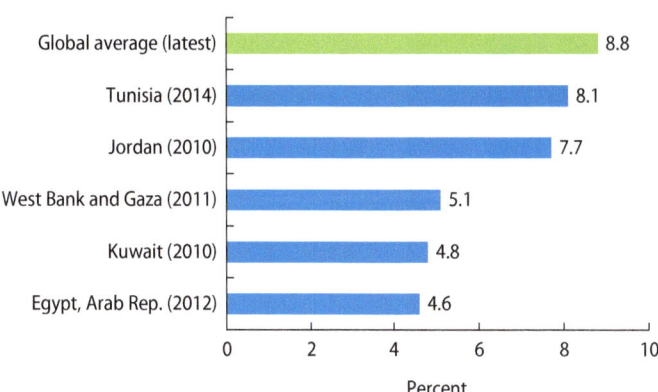

FIGURE 1.4 Rates of return to education in MENA are below the global average

Rate of return to education, by economy, latest estimate

Sources: Latest estimates of returns to education for an additional year of schooling are from Psacharopoulos and Patrinos 2018 for global average, Kuwait, and West Bank and Gaza, and from Krafft, Branson, and Flak 2019 for the Arab Republic of Egypt, Jordan, and Tunisia.
Note: Year of data used in the estimates is in parentheses. Most recent estimates since 2000 are reported.

Learning and skills are essential to build human capital

With substantial investments in quality education that emphasizes learning and skills development and complementary reforms in the economy, MENA countries will be able to use their human capital endowments to create faster economic growth and prosperity.

TABLE 1.1 Among regions, MENA has the lowest share of human capital as a percentage of total wealth

Human capital as a percentage of total wealth per capita, by region, 1995–2014

Region	1995	2000	2005	2010	2014	Annual growth
North America	80	80	78	76	77	1.1
Europe and Central Asia	63	64	63	62	62	1.4
East Asia and Pacific	72	69	63	61	60	2.3
Latin America and Caribbean	62	64	61	60	60	1.1
South Asia	48	53	55	51	51	4.0
Sub-Saharan Africa	36	40	38	45	50	1.6
MENA	**39**	**41**	**39**	**35**	**35**	**2.3**

Source: Summary of table 6.2 from Lange, Wodon, and Carey 2018, based on World Bank estimates.
Note: Figures are in constant 2014 U.S. dollars at market exchange rates.

TABLE 1.2 Most MENA economies have shares of human capital that are below the world average
Total wealth and human capital per capita and human capital as a share of total wealth, 2014

Economy	Total wealth per capita (US$)	Human capital per capita (US$)	Human capital as share of total wealth (%)
Lebanon	65,148	42,153	65
Egypt, Arab Rep.	38,470	22,591	59
Bahrain	270,311	157,679	58
Jordan	49,287	27,312	55
Tunisia	45,150	24,796	55
Djibouti	22,914	12,097	53
West Bank and Gaza	30,567	14,778	48
Oman	277,574	125,278	45
Morocco	40,488	16,490	41
Yemen, Rep.	22,909	9,002	39
United Arab Emirates	738,270	278,205	38
Qatar	1,597,125	562,650	35
Saudi Arabia	512,869	156,869	31
Kuwait	1,123,144	271,628	24
Iraq	101,705	15,473	15
MENA	158,892	54,871	35
World average	168,580	108,654	64

Source: Data on select countries in appendix B of Lange, Wodon, and Carey 2018, based on World Bank estimates.
Note: Figures are in constant 2014 U.S. dollars at market exchange rates.

Investments in education over the past five decades have achieved impressive expansion of access to school

Although MENA countries face a common challenge in needing to improve learning, they also share a common achievement in rapidly expanding access to education. Most countries have expanded access to education at a faster rate than the increase in their school-age population (see figure 1.5), which has led to large increases in enrollment rates. Between 1974 and 2016, the primary and secondary school-age population in MENA doubled, from 45 million to 90 million children. At the same time, school enrollment more than tripled, from 25 million to 83 million students. The MENA region experienced one of the fastest increases in school enrollment rates of any region in the world. Between 1974 and 2016, the average primary education gross enrollment rate (GER) in MENA increased from 77 percent to 105 percent.[3] The increase was even more pronounced for secondary education, where the GER more than doubled, from 31 percent to 79 percent over the same period.

Most MENA countries have achieved universal enrollment in primary education. They have also achieved gender parity at almost all education levels: full parity in primary and tertiary education and 9 females to every 10 males in secondary.[4] Despite substantial progress over the past decade, enrollment rates have stalled recently in some economies: in Jordan and Lebanon due to the influx of large numbers of Syrian refugees; and in Syria, West Bank and Gaza, and the Republic of Yemen due to ongoing conflict. In addition, secondary school enrollment levels are well below those of other middle-income countries around the world. While several countries—like Bahrain, Oman, and Saudi Arabia—have secondary GERs above 100 percent, others—like Djibouti, Syria, and the Republic of Yemen—are only around 50 percent. Even some middle-income countries—like Lebanon and Morocco—have secondary GERs below 70 percent.

FIGURE 1.5 Rapid population growth in MENA has been accompanied by large increases in school enrollment

Primary and secondary school-age population growth and enrollment growth, 1974–2016

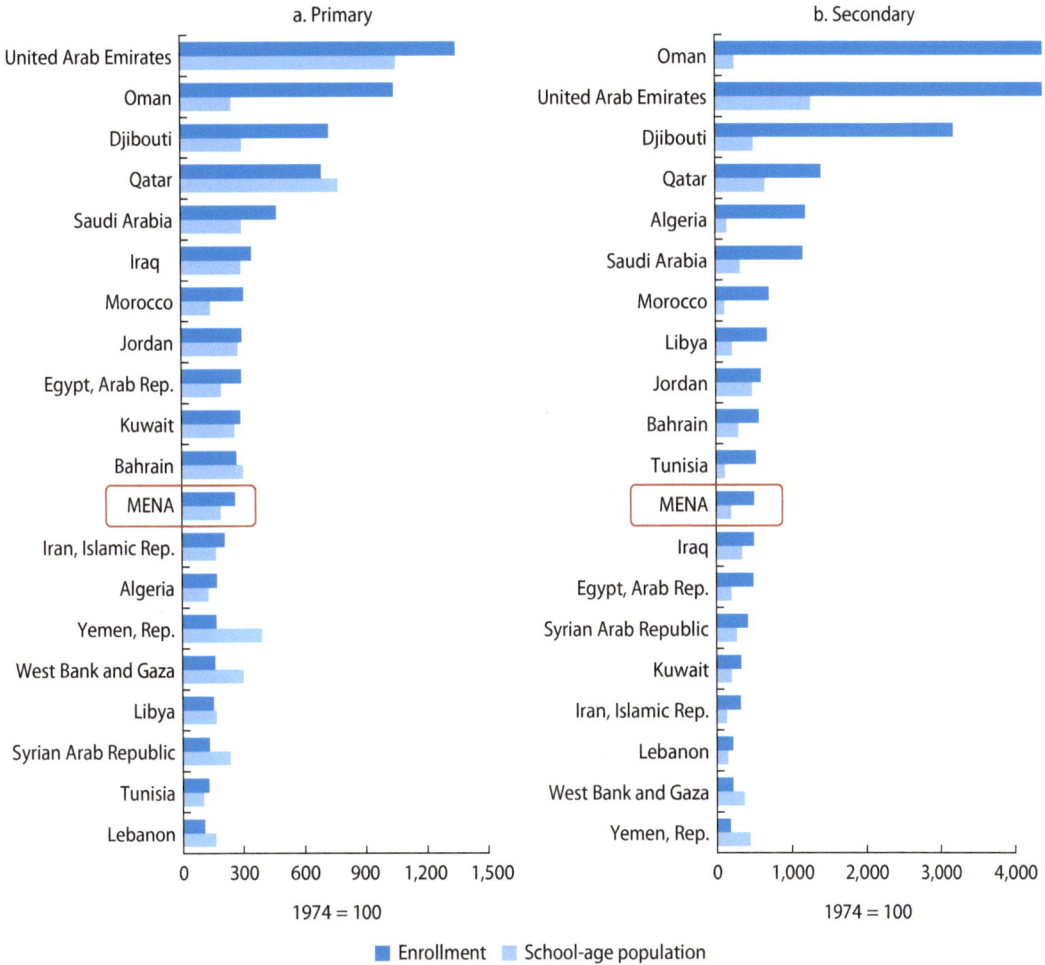

Source: World Bank EdStats database (http://datatopics.worldbank.org/education/).
Note: Base year for school enrollment is 1974 for all economies except Lebanon (1978 for primary enrollment and 1973 for secondary enrollment), Saudi Arabia (1979), West Bank and Gaza (1995), and the Republic of Yemen (1999). Latest year for school enrollment is 2016 for all economies except Algeria (2011 for secondary enrollment), the Islamic Republic of Iran (2015), Iraq (2007), Jordan (2014 for secondary enrollment), Kuwait (2015 for secondary enrollment), Libya (2006), Morocco (2012 for secondary enrollment), Saudi Arabia (2014 for secondary enrollment), the Syrian Arab Republic (2013), and the MENA regional average (2014). Last year of population data is 2016 for all economies except Iraq (2015), Jordan (2009 for primary school-age population), Libya (2015), and MENA (2014).

Access to postsecondary education has increased substantially over the past 50 years as well. In the early 1970s, only one country in the region had a tertiary GER above 10 percent—Lebanon, at 21 percent. Today, only one country is below 10 percent—Djibouti, at 5 percent—according to the latest available data. In 2014, the regional average tertiary GER was 38 percent, placing MENA on par with East Asia and the Pacific and above the world average.[5]

For countries to develop their human capital, learning must take place

Schooling is not the same as learning. MENA has not been able to benefit fully from its investments in education because the potential of education is achieved only when education confers the relevant skills that constitute human capital. Expanding education systems by increasing enrollment is not sufficient to deliver on that potential. The skills conferred by education are what determine education's contribution to economic growth, not just the years of schooling completed (Barro and Lee 2013; Hanushek and Woessmann 2008; World Bank 2018). As figure 1.6 shows, the relationship between learning outcomes, measured by test scores, and economic growth is much stronger than the relationship between years of schooling completed and economic growth.

In part due to education not living up to its potential, greater access to education has not translated into intergenerational economic mobility (see box 1.3). While the region's young people have attained higher education levels than their parents, they are often not able to translate their educational attainment into higher incomes (Narayan et al. 2018). While MENA has the highest absolute intergenerational *education mobility* compared with other regions in the world, it also has low intergenerational *income mobility*. In most other regions, educational mobility and income mobility are well correlated; this is not the case in MENA (Narayan et al. 2018) (see box 1.3).

In MENA, the substantial investments in schooling have not led to corresponding improvements in student learning and the acquisition of skills. When the actual years of schooling are adjusted for learning that takes place in schools, the result is a picture in which a school year is worth more in one country than in another. For example, while Jordan has actual years of schooling similar to those of Kazakhstan and New Zealand (around 11 years in each country), students in Jordan attain two to three fewer years of learning in these 11 years than students in the two other countries. The learning adjustment brings the number of years of schooling down to 10 for Kazakhstan, 9 for New Zealand, and 7 for Jordan. Put another way, students in Kazakhstan and New Zealand receive 30 to 40 percent more *effective* years of schooling than students in Jordan (see figure 1.7).[6]

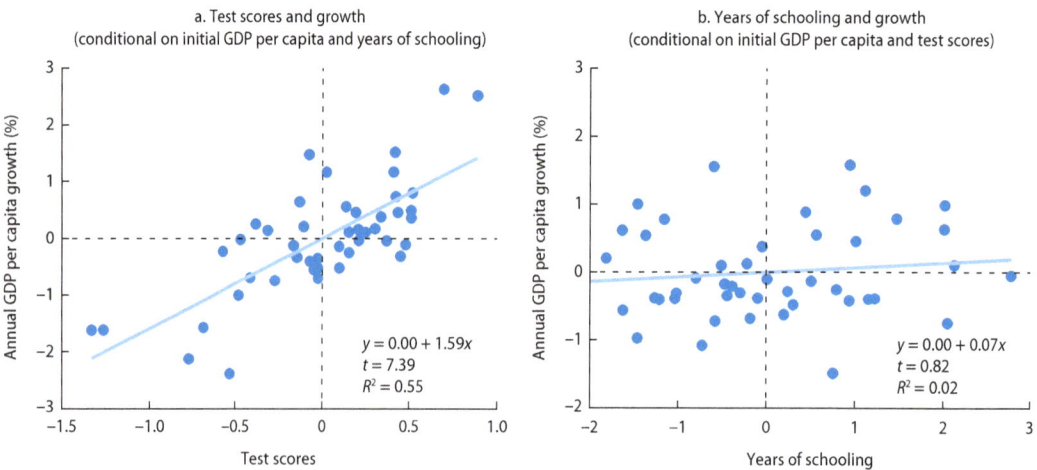

FIGURE 1.6 **What matters for growth is skills**

Annual average per capita growth in GDP, 1970–2015, conditional on test scores, years of schooling completed, and initial GDP per capita, selected countries

Source: World Bank 2018.

> **Box 1.3** **Income mobility lags behind educational mobility in MENA**
>
> Economic mobility across generations, also known as intergenerational mobility (IGM), is a key element of human and economic progress. Most parents would like to see their children earn a higher income, and with it a better life, than they have had themselves. At the same time, higher incomes and economic activity contribute to economic growth. Education is a key dimension of human progress and economic mobility. Narayan et al. (2018) measure the extent of IGM in education and how it has evolved across generations by comparing educational attainment of different generations and analyzing the improvements (mobility) in education from one to the next.
>
> MENA has the highest level of absolute mobility in education compared with any other region or with high-income countries. This means that the improvements in educational attainment ("absolute IGM in education") between two generation cohorts are larger in MENA than in other regions or high-income countries. In the average MENA country, roughly 60 percent of people born in the 1980s exhibit higher educational attainment than their parents, compared with only 35 percent of the same generation in the average economy of Africa.
>
> However, educational attainment of parents is still a strong predictor of children's education in MENA. The extent to which the educational attainment of an individual is independent of the education of his or her parents ("relative IGM in education") is relatively low in MENA compared with other developing regions.
>
> The achievements in absolute educational mobility in MENA do not translate into the labor market. Education and income mobility are highly correlated in most of East Asia, Eastern Europe and Central Asia, Latin America, and South Asia and in the high-income countries. However, income mobility in MENA lags behind educational mobility. Low income mobility may also be associated with low labor force participation rates, which are common in MENA (especially among women). Personal connections (*wasta*) and a focus on credentials over skills may also be associated with the disconnect between education and income mobility.
>
> *Source:* Narayan et al. 2018.

Data from the Trends in International Mathematics and Science Study (TIMSS) 2015 reveal that in MENA countries, on average, the effective years of schooling are 2.9 years less than the actual years of schooling—the low learning equates to approximately three lost years of education. This ranges from a difference of 2.2 years in Bahrain and Morocco to 3.9 years in Saudi Arabia and 4.2 years in Jordan.

International assessments help MENA countries to understand their learning gaps

How well students grasp the important aspects of countries' official curricula can be seen in international student assessments. Several MENA countries have participated in international student assessments such as TIMSS and the Progress in International Reading Literacy Study (PIRLS).[7] A common finding across these assessments is that students in MENA countries are not reaching the expected levels of subject knowledge. In fact, the average scores of MENA countries rank among the lowest of all countries participating in TIMSS and PIRLS (although mainly high- and middle-income countries have participated in these assessments). For example, figure 1.8 shows that the average TIMSS 2015 scores for grade 8 mathematics are lower in MENA countries than in most other participating countries.

Young people in MENA need to develop their foundational skills

International benchmarks of performance on TIMSS and PIRLS provide an indication of

FIGURE 1.7 When adjusted for learning, the number of years of effective schooling in MENA drops substantially

Actual years and learning-adjusted years of schooling among young people, ages 25–29

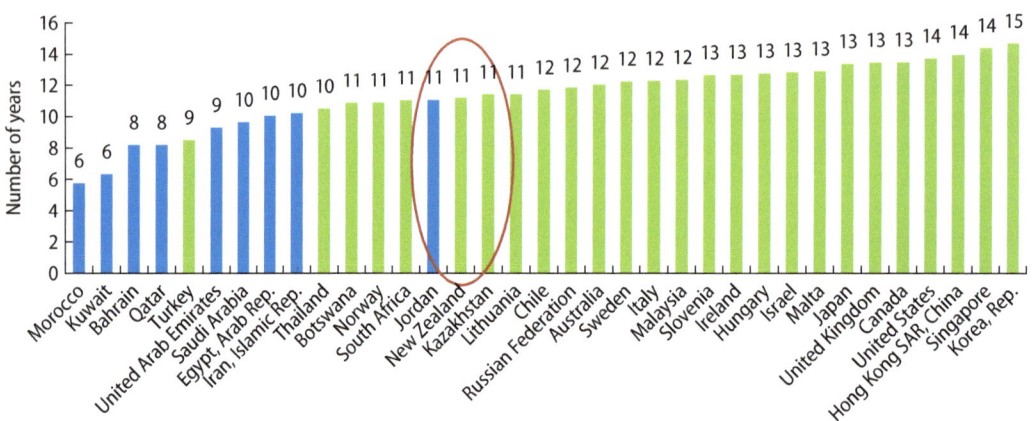

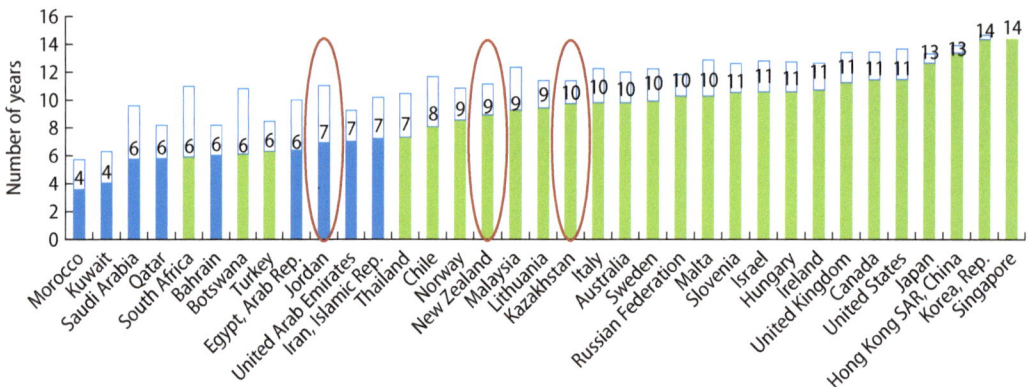

Sources: World Bank 2018, based on 2010 data from Barro and Lee 2013 and TIMSS 2015 (Mullis et al. 2016).
Note: For the purposes of this illustration, years of schooling are adjusted using the grade 8 mathematics results from the 2015 Trends in International Mathematics and Science Study (TIMSS). Results are compared with those of Singapore (highest-scoring economy). The figure highlights, for example, that while Jordan has actual years of schooling similar to those of Kazakhstan and New Zealand (around 11 years in each country), students in Jordan attain two to three fewer years of learning in these 11 years than students in the two other countries (10 years for Kazakhstan and 9 years for New Zealand).

what schoolchildren can do. The "low" international benchmark indicates a basic mastery of each subject at each grade level. For example, reaching the low international benchmark for grade 4 mathematics means that students have some basic mathematical knowledge—they can add and subtract whole numbers; show some understanding of one-digit multiplication, simple fractions, geometric shapes, and measurement; solve simple word problems; and read or complete simple graphs and tables (Mullis et al. 2016). In Kuwait, Morocco, and Saudi Arabia, less than 50 percent of grade 4 students in 2015 had this basic mathematical knowledge—only 33 percent, 41 percent, and 43 percent, respectively. By comparison, across all participating countries, 93 percent of grade 4

FIGURE 1.8 **MENA countries have some of the lowest results on international student assessments**
Average scale scores, by region, TIMSS 2015 grade 8 mathematics

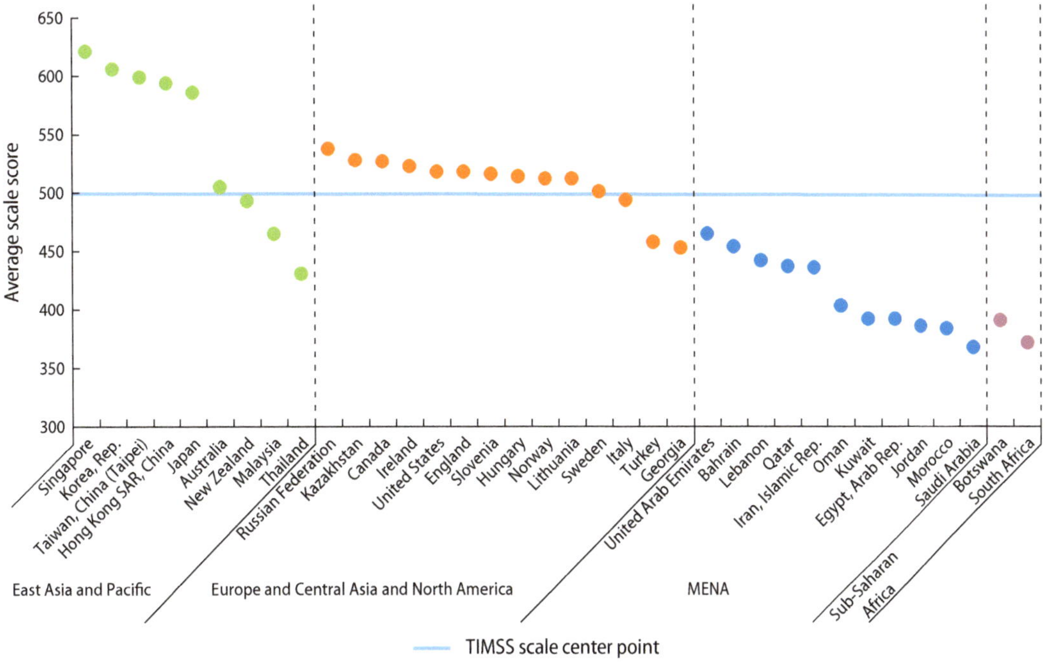

Source: Mullis et al. 2016.
Note: TIMSS = Trends in International Mathematics and Science Study.

students had mastered these basic mathematical skills.

MENA's learning crisis is apparent across primary and secondary grades as well as across different subject areas. No MENA country comes close to the international medians of percentage of students reaching the low international benchmarks, as shown in table 1.3. In Egypt, only 42 percent of grade 8 students have a basic understanding of science. In Morocco, just 36 percent of grade 4 students reach a minimum level of reading literacy.

The gaps between MENA countries and international averages tend to be greater at the primary than at the secondary school level. For countries that participated in TIMSS 2011 and 2015, it is possible to examine the same cohort of students who were in grade 4 in 2011 and grade 8 in 2015. In Bahrain, the Islamic Republic of Iran, Morocco, Oman, Qatar, and the United Arab Emirates, the gap between the average score for the country and the global average decreased between grades 4 and 8 (see figure 1.9).[8] This may indicate some catching up between grades 4 and 8. However, the potential for catch-up also highlights that a fundamental challenge for MENA countries is the deficit in early learning, which occurs before grade 4.

The Programme for International Student Assessment (PISA) measures what children at the age of 15 can do—that is, whether they can apply their knowledge and competencies in reading, mathematics, and science to real-world situations (Greaney and Kellaghan 2008).[9] Algeria, Jordan, Lebanon, Qatar, Tunisia, and the United Arab Emirates participated in the PISA 2015. Their 15-year-old students averaged two to four years of schooling behind those of Organisation for Economic Co-operation and Development (OECD) countries. Algeria and Lebanon, both joining PISA for the first time in 2015, found that more than two-thirds of their

TABLE 1.3 MENA countries have some of the lowest results on international student assessments
Percentage of students reaching low international benchmarks of performance on TIMSS 2011 and 2015 and PIRLS 2011 and 2016

Mathematics (TIMSS)					
Grade 4			Grade 8		
Country	2011	2015	Country	2011	2015
International median	90	93	International median	75	84
Bahrain[a]	67	72	Bahrain[a]	53	75
United Arab Emirates[a]	64	68	United Arab Emirates	73	73
Iran, Islamic Rep.	64	65	Lebanon	73	71
Qatar[a]	55	65	Iran, Islamic Rep.[a]	55	63
Oman[a]	46	60	Qatar[a]	54	63
Saudi Arabia[b]	55	43	Oman[a]	39	52
Morocco[a]	26	41	Egypt, Arab Rep.	n.a.	47
Kuwait[b]	30	23	Jordan[b]	55	45
			Morocco[a]	36	41
			Kuwait	n.a.	37
			Saudi Arabia[b]	47	34

Science (TIMSS)					
Grade 4			Grade 8		
Country	2011	2015	Country	2011	2015
International median	92	95	International median	79	84
Bahrain	70	72	United Arab Emirates	75	76
United Arab Emirates[a]	61	67	Bahrain[a]	70	73
Qatar[a]	50	64	Iran, Islamic Rep.[b]	79	73
Iran, Islamic Rep.[b]	72	61	Oman[a]	59	72
Oman[a]	45	61	Qatar[a]	58	70
Saudi Arabia[b]	63	48	Jordan[b]	72	63
Morocco[a]	16	35	Lebanon	54	50
Kuwait[b]	37	25	Kuwait	n.a.	49
			Saudi Arabia[b]	68	49
			Morocco[a]	39	47
			Egypt, Arab Rep.	n.a.	42

Reading (PIRLS)		
Grade 4		
Country	2011	2016
International median	95	96
United Arab Emirates[a]	64	68
Qatar[a]	60	66
Iran, Islamic Rep.[b]	76	65
Saudi Arabia	65	63
Oman[a]	47	59
Morocco[a]	21	36

Sources: Mullis et al. 2016, 2017.
Note: The international medians for 2011 and 2016 cannot be compared because the set of countries in each year is not the same. PIRLS = Progress in International Reading Literacy Study; TIMSS = Trends in International Mathematics and Science Study; n.a. = not applicable (the Arab Republic of Egypt and Kuwait did not participate in TIMSS for grade 8 in 2011).
a. Statistically significant increase between 2011 and 2015/2016.
b. Statistically significant decrease between 2011 and 2015/2016.

students did not meet a basic proficiency level in science, reading, and mathematics (see figure 1.10).

Results vary for those MENA countries that have participated in PISA over multiple years. In Tunisia and the United Arab Emirates, PISA scores have deteriorated over time.[10] In Tunisia, proficiency levels in all three subjects have declined over the last decade. PISA scores for Jordan remained stable over the four assessments from 2006 to 2015, and Qatar's results improved from 2012 to 2015 across all three subjects, although half of Qatar's students did not achieve basic proficiency.

MENA's postsecondary education is not contributing to scientific knowledge and innovation

The overall quality of postsecondary education in MENA, as measured by international university rankings, is low. Challenges in earlier schooling as well as challenges within postsecondary education contribute to low quality. Few MENA universities, for example, reached the top 500 of the Shanghai-based Academic Ranking of World Universities (see chapter 13). In most MENA countries, scientific productivity and technology transfer is low, although a few countries demonstrate strong capacity for innovation.[11] The Islamic Republic of Iran is an outlier in this respect, performing strongly across all measures, especially in its sizable production of domestic patents and its scientific and technical journal articles relative to national GDP.

The rate of technology transfer in some MENA countries deteriorated between 2012 and 2015: in the Republic of Yemen, from 46 patents to 7 patents, likely due to conflict, and in the Islamic Republic of Iran, from 5,227 patents to 2,880 patents. In Algeria, the number of patent grants fluctuated from 41 in 2012 to a high of 537 in 2014, declining to 74 in 2015. Overall, although progress is being made in places, MENA countries lag the world's leading economies in innovative capacity (Salmi 2017).

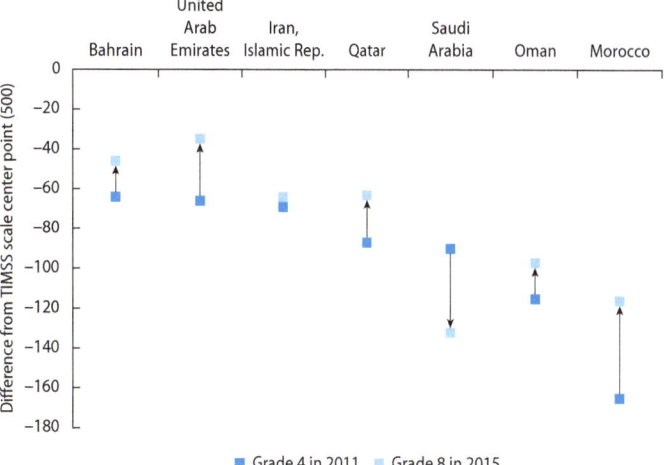

FIGURE 1.9 **Achievement gaps in MENA tend to be greater for primary school than for secondary school**

Test scores of 2011 grade 4 cohort as grade 8 students in 2015, difference from TIMSS scale center point

Source: Based on data from Mullis et al. 2016.
Note: TIMSS = Trends in International Mathematics and Science Study.

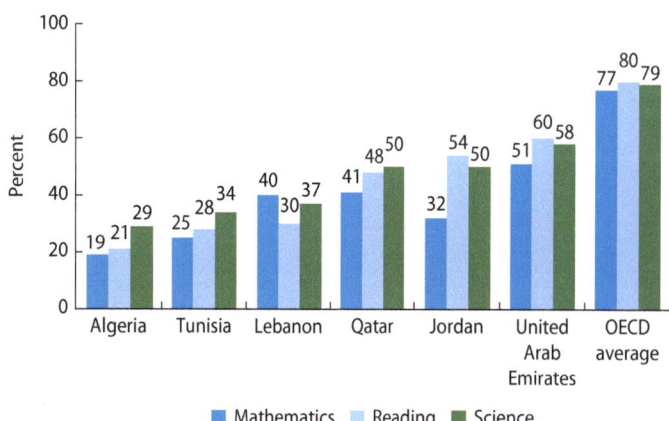

FIGURE 1.10 **Many children in MENA have not reached basic proficiency by age 15**

Percentage of 15-year-old students reaching basic proficiency, PISA 2015

Source: OECD 2016.
Note: OECD = Organisation for Economic Co-operation and Development; PISA = Programme for International Student Assessment.

Notes

1. World Bank EdStats database.
2. According to the 2019 Arab Youth Survey (ASDA'A BCW 2019), 78 percent of youths ages 18 to 24 surveyed across the Arab world believe that it should be the government's responsibility to provide jobs. This belief

varies from 71 percent in the Levant to 82 percent in the GCC.
3. The GER is the number of students enrolled in a specific level of education, regardless of age, as a percentage of the population in the official age group corresponding to that level of education. The GER can exceed 100 percent because it includes students who are younger or older than the official age range for a particular level of education.
4. World Bank EdStats database.
5. World Bank EdStats database.
6. These figures are calculated following the methodology presented in the *World Development Report 2018* (World Bank 2018), which adjusts the actual years of schooling, based on census data, with learning levels, based on the Trends in International Mathematics and Science Study (TIMSS) 2015 scores. A different but comparative method is employed as part of the Human Capital Index, introduced in the *World Development Report 2019* (World Bank 2019). The Human Capital Index uses current enrollment rates to gauge expected years of schooling that the current student generation will complete, which are then adjusted by the harmonized learning outcomes (HLO). The HLO combine onto a single scale an array of international standardized tests that vary by country. Both methodologies calculate a measure of learning-adjusted (actual or expected) years of schooling. Employing either methodology shows that, on average, the learning-adjusted years of schooling are one-third less than total years of schooling in MENA.
7. TIMSS and PIRLS measure students' mastery of official curricular elements common to participating countries in mathematics and science (grades 4 and 8) and reading (grade 4). See Mullis et al. (2016, 2017).
8. TIMSS scores are based on a range of 0 to 1,000 and were established in TIMSS 1995 based on the achievement distribution across all participating countries (treating each country equally). The scale center point is set at 500 to correspond to the mean overall achievement with a standard deviation of 100 points. Data from subsequent TIMSS assessments are linked to this scale to allow comparisons over time.
9. PISA is not based on shared elements of official curricula across participating countries.
10. In the United Arab Emirates, an increase in participation (from 83 percent of 15-year-olds in 2012 to 91 percent in 2015) may have contributed to the declining score.
11. Technology transfer refers to how research flows across national borders or from academia to the public and private sectors, using patent grants as a proxy.

References

Arezki, Rabah, Lili Mottaghi, Andrea Barone, Rachel Yuting Fan, Amani Abou Harb, Omer M. Karasapan, Hideki Matsunaga, Ha Nguyen, and Francois de Soyres. 2018. "Middle East and North Africa Economic Monitor, October 2018: A New Economy for Middle East and North Africa." World Bank, Washington, DC. https://openknowledge.worldbank.org/handle/10986/30436.

ASDA'A BCW. 2019. "A Call for Reform: 2019 Arab Youth Survey." ASDA'A, Dubai. http://arabyouthsurvey.com/.

Assaad, Ragui. 1997. "The Effects of Public Sector Hiring and Compensation Policies on the Egyptian Labor Market." *World Bank Economic Review* 11 (1): 85–118.

———. 2014. "Making Sense of Arab Labor Markets: The Enduring Legacy of Dualism." *IZA Journal of Labor and Development* 3 (1): 1–25.

Assaad, Ragui, and Caroline Krafft. 2015. "The Structure and Evolution of Employment in Egypt: 1998–2012." In *The Egyptian Labor Market in an Era of Revolution*, edited by Ragui Assaad and Caroline Krafft, 27–51. Oxford, U.K.: Oxford University Press.

Barro, Robert J., and Jong Wha Lee. 2013. "A New Data Set of Educational Attainment in the World, 1950–2010." *Journal of Development Economics* 104: 184–98.

Barsoum, Ghada. 2015. "Young People's Job Aspirations in Egypt and the Continued Preference for a Government Job." In *The Egyptian Labor Market in an Era of Revolution*, edited by Ragui Assaad and Caroline Krafft, 108–26. Oxford, U.K.: Oxford University Press.

Becker, Gary S. 1962. "Investment in Human Capital: A Theoretical Analysis." *Journal of Political Economy* 70 (5): 9–49.

Behar, Alberto, and Junghwan Mok. 2013. "Does Public-Sector Employment Fully Crowd Out Private-Sector Employment?" IMF Working Paper 13/146, International Monetary Fund, Washington, DC.

Ben Mim, Sami, and Mohamed Sami Ben Ali. 2012. "Through Which Channels Can Remittances Spur Economic Growth in MENA Countries?" *Economics: The Open-Access, Open-Assessment E-Journal* 6 (2012-33): 1–27. http://dx.doi.org/10.5018/economics-ejournal.ja.2012-33.

Dahi, Omar S. 2012. "The Political Economy of the Egyptian and Arab Revolt." *IDS Bulletin* 43 (1): 47–53. doi:10.1111/j.1759-5436.2012.00289.x.

Gatti, Roberta, Matteo Morgandi, Rebekka Grun, Stefanie Brodmann, Diego Angel-Urdinola, Juan Manuel Moreno, Daniela Marotta, Marc Schiffbauer, and Elizabeth Mata Lorenzo. 2013. *Jobs for Shared Prosperity: Time for Action in the Middle East and North Africa*. Washington, DC: World Bank.

Greaney, Vincent, and Thomas Kellaghan. 2008. *Assessing National Achievement Levels in Education*. Washington, DC: World Bank.

Hanushek, Eric A., and Ludger Woessmann. 2008. "The Role of Cognitive Skills in Economic Development." *Journal of Economic Literature* 46 (3): 607–68.

Hartog, Joop. 2000. "Over-Education and Earnings: Where Are We, Where Should We Go?" *Economics of Education Review* 19 (2): 131–47.

ILO (International Labour Organization). Various years. ILOSTAT database. Geneva: ILO. https://ilostat.ilo.org/.

Krafft, Caroline. 2017. "Is School the Best Route to Skills? Returns to Vocational School and Vocational Skills in Egypt." *Journal of Development Studies* 54 (7): 1–21.

Krafft, Caroline, and Ragui Assaad. 2014. "Why the Unemployment Rate Is a Misleading Indicator of Labor Market Health in Egypt." *Policy Perspective* 14, Economic Research Forum, Cairo.

Krafft, Caroline, Zea Branson, and Taylor Flak. 2019. "What's the Value of a Degree? Evidence from Egypt, Jordan, and Tunisia." *Compare: A Journal of Comparative and International Education*. doi:10.1080/03057925.2019.1590801.

Lange, Glenn-Marie, Quentin Wodon, and Kevin Carey. 2018. *The Changing Wealth of Nations 2018: Building a Sustainable Future*. Washington, DC: World Bank.

Mincer, Jacob. 1974. *Schooling, Experience, and Earnings*. Cambridge, MA: National Bureau of Economic Research.

Montenegro, Claudio E., and Harry Anthony Patrinos. 2014. "Comparable Estimates of Returns to Schooling around the World." Policy Research Working Paper 7020, World Bank, Washington, DC.

Mullis, Ina V. S., Michael O. Martin, Pierre Foy, and M. Hooper. 2016. *TIMSS 2015 International Results in Mathematics*. TIMSS and PIRLS International Study Center, Boston College, Boston, MA. http://timssandpirls.bc.edu/timss2015/international-results/.

———. 2017. *PIRLS 2016 International Results in Reading*. TIMSS and PIRLS International Study Center, Boston College, Boston, MA. http://timssandpirls.bc.edu/pirls2016/international-results/.

Nabli, M. 2007. *Breaking the Barriers to Higher Economic Growth: Better Governance and Deeper Reforms in the Middle East and North Africa*. Washington, DC: World Bank.

Narayan, Ambar, Roy Van der Weide, Alexandru Cojocaru, Christoph Lakner, Silvia Redaelli, Daniel Gerszon Mahler, Rakesh Gupta N. Ramasubbaiah, and Stefan Thewissen. 2018. *Fair Progress? Economic Mobility across Generations around the World*. Equity and Development. Washington, DC: World Bank. https://openknowledge.worldbank.org/handle/10986/28428.

OECD (Organisation for Economic Co-operation and Development). 2016. *PISA 2015 Results: Excellence and Equity in Education*. Vol. 1. Paris: OECD.

Psacharopoulos, George, and Harry Anthony Patrinos. 2018. "Returns to Investment in Education: A Decennial Review of the Global Literature." Policy Research Working Paper 8402, World Bank, Washington, DC. https://openknowledge.worldbank.org/handle/10986/29672.

Ramos, Raul. 2017. "Migration Aspirations among NEETs in Selected MENA Countries." IZA Discussion Paper 11146, Institute of Labor Economics, Bonn. http://ftp.iza.org/dp11146.pdf.

Sala-i-Martin, Xavier, Gernot Doppelhofer, and Ronald I. Miller. 2004. "Determinants of Long-Term Growth: A Bayesian Averaging of Classical Estimates (BACE) Approach." *American Economic Review* 94 (4): 813–35.

Salehi-Isfahani, Dhavad. 2012. "Education, Jobs, and Equity in the Middle East and North Africa." *Comparative Economic Studies* 54 (4): 843–61.

Salmi, Jamil. 2017. "Building the Research Capacity of MENA Universities." Background paper for this report, World Bank, Washington, DC.

Springborg, Robert. 2011. "The Precarious Economics of Arab Springs." *Survival* 53 (6): 85–104. doi:10.1080/00396338.2011.636271.

UIS (UNESCO Institute for Statistics). 2018. UIS. Stat database on education indicators. United Nations Educational, Scientific, and Cultural Organization (UNESCO), Paris. http://data.uis.unesco.org/.

UNESCO (United Nations Educational, Scientific, and Cultural Organization). 2011. International Standard Classification of Education (ISCED) database. Paris: UNESCO. http://uis.unesco.org/en/topic/international-standard-classification-education-isced.

World Bank. 2008. *The Road Not Traveled: Education Reform in the Middle East and North Africa*. Washington, DC: World Bank.

———. 2015. *Inequality, Uprisings, and Conflict in the Arab World*. MENA Economic Monitor. Washington, DC: World Bank.

———. 2018. *World Development Report 2018: Learning to Realize Education's Promise*. Washington, DC: World Bank.

———. 2019. *World Development Report 2019: The Changing Nature of Work*. Washington, DC: World Bank.

———. No data. "Remittances Data." Global Knowledge Partnership on Migration and Development (KNOMAD), World Bank, Washington, DC. https://www.knomad.org/data/remittances.

———. Various years. Education Statistics (EdStats) database. Washington, DC: World Bank. http://datatopics.worldbank.org/education/.

Behaviors, Norms, and the Political Economy of Education in MENA | 2

Safaa El Tayeb El-Kogali

Education does not occur in a vacuum; it is embedded in the complex interaction of factors at multiple levels. For decades, the countries in the Middle East and North Africa (MENA) have spent large proportions of their national income on education and have undertaken all kinds of reforms to fix the system and address the quantity and quality of education. Yet no MENA countries have managed to improve their learning outcomes to an international level of success. Why? Much of the research on education reform points to factors that are outside the MENA education system, including the political, economic, and social institutions that formally and informally interact with the education system and shape its outcomes.

This chapter examines the political economy of education within MENA and how these various forces interplay in a complex process. The chapter examines why reforms have not succeeded in bringing about positive outcomes, what key factors are holding back reforms, and what MENA countries can do to break out of this impasse.

Education is an inherently political and social process

Education is a political and social process as much as an individual journey. Governments have commonly used education to shape the identity of nations, to develop economies, and to define social structures and cultural norms. Education has been at the heart of the region's history and civilizations. In the past century, it has been central to the struggle for independence, to building the modern state and economy, and to defining its national identity. Governments as well as different interest groups use education to spread their vision and shape the minds of each generation. As such, education is a battlefield of different, often competing, visions and purposes (Purpel and Shapiro 1995).

The previous World Bank flagship report on education in MENA, *The Road Not Traveled*, demonstrated that, beyond the engineering of the education system, incentives and accountability mechanisms are weak in MENA countries, which helps to explain the low learning outcomes (World Bank 2008).

Poor accountability relationships in the political and administrative spheres weaken the incentives toward performance and policy implementation (World Bank 2015c). A rigorous review of the political economy of education systems in low- and middle-income countries further showed that, beyond capacity constraints, weak delivery systems, and poor administration and governance, vested interests, power relations, and lack of political will have influenced countries' education policies and outcomes (Kingdon et al. 2014).

Recent research on the development process and political economy adds a new dimension that focuses on behavior, social norms, and preferences, whereby beliefs about the nature of the problem and its solution shape the attitudes toward policies and reforms (Khemani 2017; World Bank 2015d). That is, "human sociality," whereby people associate and behave as members of a group and establish norms and patterns of cooperation, can influence education and impede reforms that they perceive would reduce their power or ability to extract benefits (Khemani 2017; Kingdon et al. 2014; World Bank 2015d). While it is not unusual for individuals or groups to resist a change that may jeopardize their interests or cause them to lose their position, they also may resist reforms because they believe that others are pursuing their own self-interest and that they therefore should be doing the same (Khemani 2017; World Bank 2015d).

The education process consists of a complex set of factors and actors at multiple levels. Factors outside the education system—political, economic, and social—formally and informally interact with the education system and shape its outcomes. Behavioral norms and ideological polarization among governments, interest groups, and citizens can hold countries back from delivering public goods (World Bank 2016).

Four tensions are holding back education in MENA

In MENA, education has been held back by these complex interactions, behavioral norms, and ideological polarization, which can be captured in four sets of tensions: credentials and skills, discipline and inquiry, control and autonomy, and tradition and modernity (see figure 2.1).

These tensions are deeply embedded in the region's history, culture, and political economy. They are reflected to varying degrees in all countries in the region, and, to a large extent, they define social and political relations. They have informed and shaped education policy in MENA countries since independence, and they are at the heart of current national discourses on education reforms. These tensions have held education systems back from evolving and delivering the skills that prepare students for their future. Schools and classrooms are the platforms where these tensions are exercised through curricula, pedagogy, and the norms that define interactions among principals, teachers, parents, and students. These tensions ultimately shape the education outcomes of young people in MENA and affect their lives as well as the economies and societies in which they live. In an increasingly connected world, the effects of these tensions can reach beyond the region's borders. Unless these tensions are addressed, MENA will not be able to reap the full benefits of education, no matter how much money is invested.

FIGURE 2.1 Four tensions are holding back education in MENA

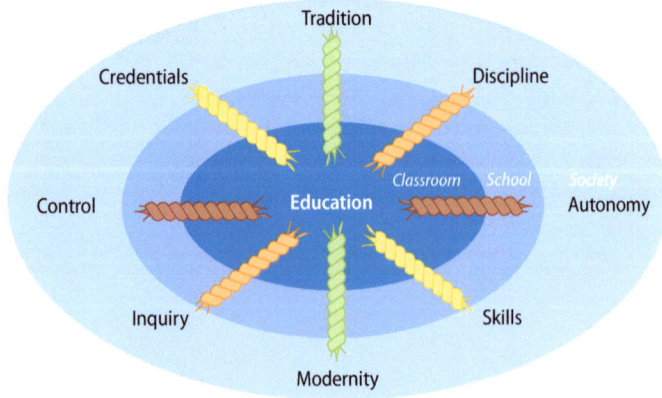

Source: World Bank.

Four features of these tensions are noteworthy. First, they are not mutually exclusive, and they coexist along a continuum. The challenge for countries is to determine where they want to be on the continuum and what balance would be optimal to deliver the desired outcomes. Second, the four tensions overlap in some areas and can reinforce each other. For example, notions of control and autonomy could also be associated with discipline and inquiry or tradition and modernity. Third, the tensions are neither unique to MENA nor time specific. Throughout history, countries across the world have struggled with these tensions in defining their goals and policies. Fourth, no one position applies to every country or region. Each country, based on its national development goals and vision, needs to decide where it wants to place its education system within these tensions.

Credentials and skills

The tension between credentials and skills has been a source of debate for almost 50 years. Since the 1970s, economists and sociologists have argued about the links between education, skills, and the labor market, using numerous theories and models, such as Becker's human capital theory (Becker 1962), Collins's credentialist theory (Collins 1979), and Spence's signaling model (Spence 1973). A credential in the form of a degree, diploma, or certificate is usually associated with the acquisition of a specific set of skills or knowledge. In the labor market, credentials signal productivity, based on the assumption that more years of education are associated with higher productivity (Page 2010). Credentials also bestow a certain status in society, where a higher degree is associated with higher status and figures in matters such as marriage.

The history of education as a tool to generate bureaucrats for the public sector shaped the current structure of the education system and labor market in MENA. Public sector employment was typically guaranteed for anyone who had a sufficient education credential—diploma or degree.

The requirement was more for the credential—the diploma or certificate—than for the skills. As a result, MENA countries have become societies in which there is little or no link between education credentials and skills (Assaad, Krafft, and Salehi-Isfahani 2018). In the meantime, little pressure has been placed on education institutions to ensure that credentials mean that the graduate possesses the relevant skills.

Although the size of the public sector as an employer has declined in many MENA countries, its legacy continues in the form of a "credentialist equilibrium" (Salehi-Isfahani 2012). In such an equilibrium, public sector employers communicate a strong demand for credentials, and the private sector's signals for skills are weak. Responding to market signals, students and families focus more on the credential (degree or diploma) and less on the skills and competencies that these credentials would ideally represent (see figure 2.2).

The credentialist equilibrium in MENA countries has been created in part by imbalances in the labor market, where the large public sector is the preferred employer (Barsoum 2015; World Bank 2013a). In addition to higher wages, the desire for public employment is motivated by greater prestige, more generous benefits, and a better work environment, particularly for women (Barsoum 2015). Expectations of the public sector are also high because employment opportunities are often treated as a right,

FIGURE 2.2 **MENA is stuck in a credentialist equilibrium**

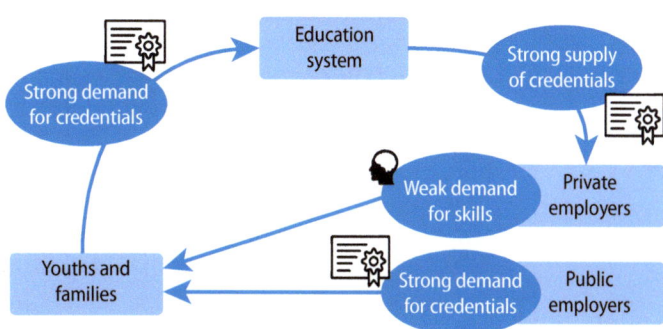

Source: Adapted from Assaad, Krafft, and Salehi-Isfahani 2018.

further disconnecting these opportunities from education. Several regional constitutions include the "right to work," engendering a common attitude that employment should be provided by the government and not by the private sector (Barsoum 2015). That attitude is a legacy of the government employment guarantees that were part of the region's social contract (Assaad 1997, 2014). The high wages and outsized role of government employment in MENA crowd out the private sector (Behar and Mok 2013; Nabli 2007), and government strategies to increase high-quality private sector employment have largely failed, resulting in poor or limited opportunities for new graduates (Dahi 2012; Salehi-Isfahani 2012; Springborg 2011) and reducing the demand for skills.

The notion of reducing public sector employment, a key aspect of a new Arab social contract, has gained little traction in the region (Devarajan and Ianchovichina 2018). Since the Arab Spring, calls for a new social contract have not yielded meaningful change in the role of the public sector. In fact, the Arab Republic of Egypt, Jordan, and Tunisia have all raised public salaries to stem further protests (Capital Economics 2017). While placating social discontent and temporarily supporting the economy, this approach also reinforces the notion that public sector employment is the only path to high salaries, career growth, and status within society—and so it will keep the region stuck in a credentialist equilibrium.

Discipline and inquiry

The terms *discipline* and *inquiry* have multiple meanings and uses. Here, *discipline* is defined as "the practice of training people to obey rules or a code of behavior" (*Oxford*) or "training that corrects, molds, or perfects the mental faculties or moral character" (*Merriam-Webster's*). *Inquiry* is defined as "an examination into facts or principles" (*Merriam-Webster's*). In societies with strong social norms, discipline is a key factor in ensuring adherence to norms. Although discipline is important, too much emphasis on discipline may constrict students' ability to learn, think, explore ideas, or question concepts. Inquiry, by contrast, allows students to understand their surroundings or contextualize concepts through questions and experimentation.

Some degree of discipline is important and necessary, but violent discipline negatively affects children's physical, psychological, and social development and hampers their learning and school performance, ultimately reducing human capital development (El-Kogali and Krafft 2015; UNICEF 2010). Violent child discipline is widespread in MENA. In a study of 50 countries or economies, UNICEF (2013) found that MENA has the highest percentage of children ages 2–14 years who are violently disciplined, ranging from 79 to 95 percent in Algeria, Egypt, Iraq, Morocco, the Syrian Arab Republic (preconflict), Tunisia, West Bank and Gaza, and the Republic of Yemen (El-Kogali and Krafft 2015).

Concepts of discipline and inquiry are closely linked to pedagogy and curricula, as well as to the day-to-day interactions of students with teachers; the emphasis on discipline leads to passive learning and memorization. Across MENA, curricula focus heavily on rote memorization, leaving little time for the development of critical thinking skills. According to teachers, the share of grade 8 students required to memorize mathematics and science rules, procedures, and facts for all or most lessons in many MENA countries is almost twice the international average (see figure 2.3). The share exceeds 50 percent in Egypt, the Islamic Republic of Iran, Jordan, Lebanon, Oman, and Saudi Arabia, which is far above that in many high-performing countries. For example, only 10 percent of grade 8 students in Canada and New Zealand are required to memorize during most mathematics lessons, 11 percent in Sweden and the United States, and 14 percent in Ireland and Singapore. Because of the emphasis on memorizing rules, procedures, facts, and principles, students are unable to show a basic understanding of everyday applications. In the 2015 Trends in

International Mathematics and Science Study (TIMSS), fewer than half of Morocco's grade 4 students could read a basic graph. And only about 55 percent of Egypt's and Saudi Arabia's grade 8 students could interpret a basic pictogram (Mullis et al. 2016).

The overemphasis on memorization of facts, principles, rules, and procedures does not negate the fact that some knowledge needs to be retained. Rather, it is a question of the degree of emphasis and the overall experience of the child in the classroom. Cognitive science provides information that allows a more nuanced understanding of the balance between rote memorization and higher-level processes such as discovery learning. The capacity to solve problems and to think critically about new material depends on background knowledge retained in one's memory (Kirschner, Sweller, and Clark 2006). Repeated reflective practice is fundamental to building flexible knowledge and skills. In addition, students need guidance from teachers to develop the knowledge and skills that can facilitate independent, complex cognitive work. Therefore, ideally there is a balance between rote memorization and high-level problem solving, and, depending on the task and level, it is a matter of striking the appropriate balance.

The tension between discipline and inquiry also reverberates in higher education, where it may hamper the push for solution-focused, multidisciplinary, high-impact research (World Bank 2017a). Effective postsecondary education programs emphasize practical training instead of theoretical knowledge. Mounting evidence provided by the cognitive and learning sciences indicates that interactive approaches facilitate an effective learning experience (Barkley, Cross, and Major 2005; Prince 2004). This combination allows future graduates to broaden their perspectives and equips them with the skills to enter the labor market. But postsecondary education programs in MENA are skewed toward theory over practice; they tend to have outdated curricula focused on theory and memorization, as opposed to practical knowledge and analytical reasoning (El Hassan 2013).

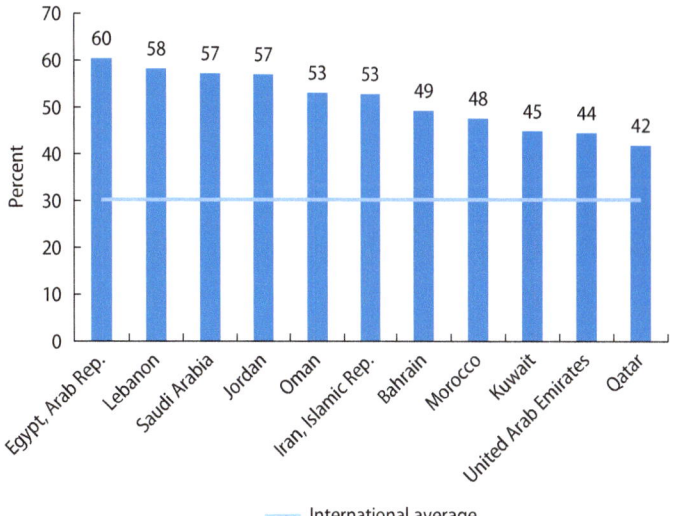

FIGURE 2.3 MENA students are more likely to be asked to memorize

Percentage of grade 8 students asked to memorize science facts and principles for every lesson or almost every lesson, 2015

Source: Martin et al. 2016.

The tension between discipline and inquiry also applies to relationships such as those between teachers and principals and between parents and their children. In many MENA countries, obedience is viewed as an especially important quality that children should be encouraged to learn at home. Inquiry-driven qualities, such as imagination and self-expression, are emphasized less often (see figure 2.4). Moreover, the tension between discipline and inquiry is also found in societies with strong social norms for class, gender, or hierarchy. For example, a recent comprehensive household survey of men and women ages 18–59 revealed that 90 percent of men and 58 percent of women in Egypt agree with the statement, "A man should have the final word about decisions in the home" (UN Women and Promundo 2017). Results were similar in West Bank and Gaza (80 percent of men and 48 percent of women) and Morocco (71 percent of men and 47 percent of women). These social norms may negatively affect the attitudes of girls and women toward inquiry and their right to ask questions both at home and in other settings such as school, university, or work.

FIGURE 2.4 Obedience plays a central role in children's education in MENA

Percentage of survey respondents who mentioned obedience, imagination, or self-expression as especially important qualities that children can be encouraged to learn at home

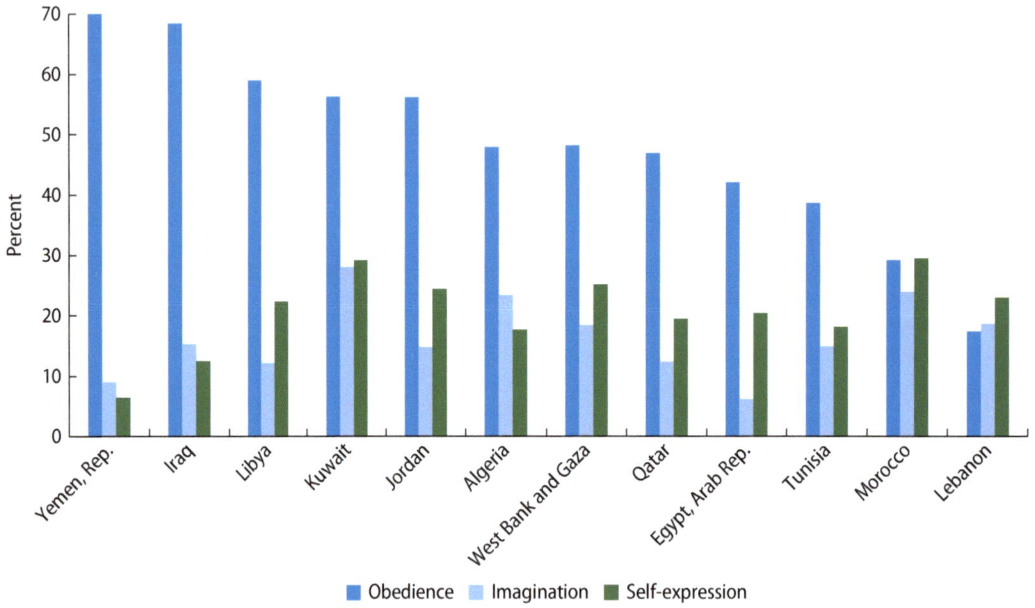

Source: World Values Survey, Wave 6 (2010–14), from Inglehart et al. 2014.
Note: These results are drawn from the following question: "Here is a list of qualities that children can be encouraged to learn at home. Which, if any, do you consider to be especially important? Please choose up to five." Potential answers included independence, hard work, feeling of responsibility, imagination, tolerance and respect for other people, thrift/saving money and things, determination/perseverance, religious faith, unselfishness, obedience, and self-expression.

Control and autonomy

The tension between control and autonomy is usually associated with the debate on decentralization of services and the balance of power between central ministries, regional offices, and schools. The goal of decentralization is typically to improve governance by fostering autonomy, accountability, and responsiveness to local conditions and needs. These attributes of decentralization in turn can improve student learning.

Over the past few decades, several MENA countries experimented with some aspects of decentralization, deconcentration, and devolution of authority from the central to the regional and school levels, but their education systems remain highly centralized. The success of attempted decentralization has varied. In some instances, the decision-making power was authorized but was not supported by the resources needed to implement decisions. For example, decentralization in Egypt in 2002–07 was not supported by sufficient financial resources (Ginsburg et al. 2010). Decentralization in Saudi Arabia in the 2000s appears to have been adequately funded, but the tasks and duties transferred to the local level were more administrative than geared toward the development of local schools (Almannie 2015). In other instances, a decentralized model was rolled out in a policy without putting in place the capacity to carry out the decentralized functions at the regional or school level. For example, Morocco's regional academies for education and training (académies régionales d'éducation et de formation) were only granted autonomy to manage some logistical and financial decisions based on guidelines provided by the central government (World Bank 2015b).

There is no magic formula for balancing centralized control and autonomy in education. It must be determined within the country context, with size, geography, and population distribution playing important roles in the decision. What is important is finding the balance in defining the roles and responsibilities of institutional actors (for example, the central government, local government, and communities) and defining the locus of control of the education processes and mechanisms used to steer the system (World Bank 2005). In other words, the balance between central control and autonomy should reflect the roles and responsibilities of central versus local governance and political versus professional power and accountability.

Limited autonomy at the school and classroom levels can constrain efforts by principals and teachers to be proactive in the learning process and prevent them from taking responsibility for student learning outcomes if they consider themselves as merely implementing a centralized approach (Akkary 2014). Teachers in MENA have far less decision-making responsibility than those in member countries of the Organisation for Economic Co-operation and Development (OECD). Studies in the Islamic Republic of Iran, Jordan, and Kuwait have found that central authorities maintain strict control of curricular content and teaching practices, leaving little autonomy for teachers (Afshar and Doosti 2016; Al-Yaseen and Al-Musaileem 2015; Namaghi 2009; World Bank 2015a).

Limited autonomy among teachers compromises job satisfaction and the development of student skills, in part because it impedes the ability of teachers to teach to the right level for their students, a critical element of effective teaching (Evans and Popova 2015). Limited autonomy at the regional, provincial, and school levels for the hiring and deployment of teachers also limits the ability to better match teacher characteristics with teaching needs.

Greater autonomy in higher education institutions tends to be associated with better performance (Aghion et al. 2009; World Bank 2011). However, most universities in MENA have very limited autonomy over academic, staffing, and financial matters. In 2012 the World Bank benchmarked the governance practices of 100 universities in Algeria, Egypt, Iraq, Lebanon, Morocco, Tunisia, and West Bank and Gaza (World Bank 2013b). Institutional autonomy was very low among public universities, with the local or central government making decisions about matters such as the academic program, hiring of teaching faculty, and fundraising. Private universities, by contrast, enjoyed much greater autonomy across all seven MENA economies surveyed (World Bank 2013b). In a follow-up survey in 2016, autonomy did not seem to have changed much for either public or private universities (World Bank 2017b). A comparison of self-assessment and actual scores revealed that public institutions perceive their autonomy to be higher than the autonomy score in the external evaluation, whereas private universities have a more accurate perception of their autonomy (World Bank 2017b).

Tradition and modernity

According to some scholars, the greatest challenge MENA countries face is aligning the development needs of a modern world and the moral imperatives of a religious society, resulting in tension between modernity and tradition (Cook 2000). The focus on tradition versus modernity, or the forces of change, can result in conflicts within education processes (Massialas and Jarrar 1987). This tension can be captured in the definition and purpose of education. In Arabic, *taaleem* (education) comes from the root word *ilm* (knowledge). The plural of *ilm* is *uloom* (science). *Taaleem* encompasses both learning and teaching—the acquisition and provision of knowledge or science. Education in Arabic is also *tarbiya*, which refers to education in the sense of growing or rearing. Its root word, *rabba,* means raising or bringing up. *Taaleem* and *tarbiya* have meanings similar to that of the Latin words *educere*—to lead forth and train—and *educare*—to rear and educate (Bass and Good 2004; Cook 1999).

At the center of the debate on tradition and modernity is the extent to which education should focus on the acquisition of knowledge or science (*taaleem*) versus the acquisition of values (*tarbiya*). This question is reflected in the evolution of the names given to ministries of education in MENA countries. Names have shifted between ministries of *tarbiya* and ministries of *taaleem*, with some countries settling on both names as ministries of *tarbiya* and *taaleem*.[1] When education ministries were established in the middle of the 20th century after independence in most MENA countries, they were called ministries of *maarif*—plural of *maarifa* (knowledge). Egypt, for example, began with the Ministry of *Maarif* and then shifted to the Ministry of *Taaleem*, and currently, it is the Ministry of *Tarbiya* and *Taaleem*. The change was a deliberate decision made during the tenure of President Jamal Abdel Nasser, who regarded education as the process required to form the complete person and to shape the Egyptian identity (Ahramonline 2015).

The values and principles reflected in education in the MENA region are shaped by a national discourse usually dominated by elites and powerful groups. Classrooms and curricula become the platforms on which the struggle between modernity and tradition are played out. The tension between tradition and modernity in defining the purpose of education is prevalent not only in MENA countries. Throughout history, countries worldwide have struggled to modernize while maintaining their cultural norms, values, and traditions, with education as the mechanism. In Japan, when the Meiji government (1868–1912) implemented reforms based on Western models of education, Japanese feared their identity and values would be lost. These fears led to the release of the Imperial Rescript of Education in 1890 emphasizing Japanese values and Confucian virtues. Since then, Japanese education policy has maintained a balance between retaining traditional Japanese values while adapting aspects of the world's best education systems (OECD 2010). Ernst Friedrich Schumacher, a British economist in the 1970s, argued that the purpose of education is to transmit the values "through which we look at, interpret, and experience the world" and that science "cannot produce ideas by which we could live . . . and is completely inapplicable to the conduct of our lives or the interpretation of the world" (Schumacher 1973). He believed that education was of no value if it did not transmit fundamental convictions. In other words, the purpose of education could be better understood not as *taaleem* but essentially as *tarbiya*.

The traditional values and fundamental convictions of MENA countries were established in Islam, which represents the foundation of national identity.[2] These values and convictions are at the heart of education. The proportion of instructional time devoted to religious education in most MENA countries is well above the average time that OECD countries spend on religious, ethics, and moral education (see chapter 7). Religious education also reflects traditional teaching practices that focus on memorization. The foundations of rote learning in MENA can be linked to the oral tradition among Arabs that predates Islam, which has also been used to preserve and spread Islamic teachings.

It is up to countries to determine the values they want to bestow on their citizens and how much time they want to dedicate to that. However, it is important that they recognize the trade-offs—in terms of limiting other learning—that are created by the time devoted to teaching religion. Countries can consider different approaches, such as introducing important values to students through activities such as art, sports, and debate, among others. It is also important to recognize the impact of traditional modes of teaching on learning. In many countries, attempts to reform the education system have been opposed as an attempt to change national character. In Jordan, for example, the introduction of curriculum reforms sparked public outrage, mainly by conservative religious groups who characterized the reforms as an attempt to undermine the kingdom's Islamic values and character (Kirdar 2017). Similarly, in Kuwait various groups have protested ongoing curriculum reforms as the imposition of imported concepts.

Modernizing does not mean importing a specific model. In many MENA countries, modernity is associated with foreign models and approaches and is used by both the proponents and opponents of change. Modernization is a process by which social norms evolve and are renewed; modernity can be in multiple forms. The issue is not replacing tradition with one form of modernity. Rather, it is allowing review of the traditional practices and norms that are holding back the potential of education and engaging in a process of renewal. Modernity is inevitable as the world changes. Countries need to prepare their students with the knowledge, skills, and values to engage with, adapt to, and succeed in a changing world.

Recognizing and addressing these constraints are critical for education in MENA

MENA countries are struggling with the four tensions—credentials and skills, discipline and inquiry, control and autonomy, and tradition and modernity—as diverging interests pull in different directions. Education reforms in MENA countries will be able to progress in a consistent and sustainable manner if they acknowledge and address the existence and impact of these tensions, as well as the competing interests that are constraining the learning and skills acquisition of future generations.

Notes

1. Seven economies use *tarbiya* in the official name of their ministry of education (Algeria, Iraq, Kuwait, Lebanon, Syria, Tunisia, and West Bank and Gaza); three use *taaleem* (Libya, Qatar, and Saudi Arabia); and seven use both *tarbiya* and *taaleem* (Bahrain, Egypt, Jordan, Morocco, Oman, the United Arab Emirates, and the Republic of Yemen).

2. Malta is the exception; it is classified as part of MENA in the World Bank's regional classifications.

References

Afshar, Hassan Soodmand, and Mehdi Doosti. 2016. "An Investigation into Factors Contributing to Iranian Secondary School English Teachers' Job Satisfaction and Dissatisfaction." *Research Papers in Education* 31 (3): 274–98.

Aghion, Philippe, Mathias Dewatripont, Caroline M. Hoxby, Andreu Mas-Colell, and André Sapir. 2009. "The Governance and Performance of Research Universities: Evidence from Europe and the U.S." NBER Working Paper 14851, National Bureau of Economic Research, Cambridge, MA.

Ahramonline. 2015. Ahramonline. http://www.ahram.org.eg/News/131704/4/448902/قضايا-واراء/فلسفة-مجانية-التعليم-فى-عدم-دبء-النصر.aspx.

Akkary, Rima K. 2014. "Facing the Challenges of Educational Reform in the Arab World." *Journal of Educational Change* 15 (2): 179–202.

Almannie, Mohamed A. 2015. "Leadership Role of School Superintendents in Saudi Arabia." *International Journal of Social Science Studies* 3 (3): 169–75.

Al-Yaseen, Wafaa Salem, and Mohammad Yousef Al-Musaileem. 2015. "Teacher Empowerment as an Important Component of Job Satisfaction: A Comparative Study of Teachers' Perspectives in Al-Farwaniya District, Kuwait." *Journal of Comparative and International Education* 45 (6): 863–85.

Assaad, Ragui. 1997. "The Effects of Public Sector Hiring and Compensation Policies on the Egyptian Labor Market." *World Bank Economic Review* 11 (1): 85–118.

———. 2014. "Making Sense of Arab Labor Markets: The Enduring Legacy of Dualism." *IZA Journal of Labor and Development* 3 (1): 1–25.

Assaad, Ragui, Caroline Krafft, and Djavad Salehi-Isfahani. 2018. "Does the Type of Higher Education Affect Labor Market Outcomes? Evidence from Egypt and Jordan." *Higher Education* 75 (6): 945–95.

Barkley, Elizabeth F., Patricia Cross, and Claire H. Major. 2005. *Collaborative Learning Techniques: A Handbook for College Faculty.* San Francisco: Jossey-Bass.

Barsoum, Ghada. 2015. "Young People's Job Aspirations in Egypt and the Continued

Preference for a Government Job." In *The Egyptian Labor Market in an Era of Revolution*, edited by Ragui Assaad and Caroline Krafft, 108–26. Oxford, U.K.: Oxford University Press.

Bass, Randall V., and J. W. Good. 2004. "Educare and Educere: Is a Balance Possible in the Educational System?" *Educational Forum* 68 (2): 161–68.

Becker, Gary S. 1962. "Investment in Human Capital: A Theoretical Analysis." *Journal of Political Economy* 70 (5): 9–49.

Behar, Alberto, and Junghwan Mok. 2013. "Does Public-Sector Employment Fully Crowd Out Private-Sector Employment?" IMF Working Paper WP/13/146, International Monetary Fund, Washington, DC.

Capital Economics. 2017. "Middle East Economics Focus." Singapore.

Collins, Randall. 1979. *The Credential Society: A Historical Sociology of Education and Stratification*. New York: Academic Press.

Cook, Bradley. 1999. "Islamic versus Western Conceptions of Education: Reflections on Egypt." *International Review of Education* 45 (3): 339–58.

———. 2000. "Egypt's National Education Debate." *Comparative Education* 36 (4): 477–90.

Dahi, Omar S. 2012. "The Political Economy of the Egyptian and Arab Revolt." *IDS Bulletin* 43 (1): 47–53. doi:10.1111/j.1759-5436.2012.00289.x.

Devarajan, Shantayanan, and Elena Ianchovichina. 2018. "A Broken Social Contract, Not High Inequality, Led to the Arab Spring." *Review of Income and Wealth* 64 (s1): s5–s25.

El Hassan, Karma. 2013. "Quality Assurance in Higher Education in Arab Region." *Higher Education and Management Policy* 24 (2): 73–84.

El-Kogali, Safaa, and Caroline Krafft. 2015. *Expanding Opportunities for the Next Generation: Early Childhood Development in the Middle East and North Africa*. Washington, DC: World Bank. https://openknowledge.worldbank.org/handle/10986/21287.

Evans, David, and Anna Popova. 2015. "What Really Works to Improve Learning in Developing Countries? An Analysis of Divergent Findings in Systematic Reviews." Policy Research Working Paper 7203, World Bank, Washington, DC.

Ginsburg, Mark, Nagwa Megahed, Mohammed Elmeski, and Nobuyuki Tanaka. 2010. "Reforming Educational Governance and Management in Egypt: National and International Actors and Dynamics." *Education Policy Analysis Archives* 18 (5): 1–54.

Inglehart, R., C. Haerpfer, A. Moreno, C. Welzel, K. Kizilova, J. Diez-Medrano, M. Lagos, P. Norris, E. Ponarin, and B. Puranen, eds. 2014. World Values Survey: Round Six—Country-Pooled Datafile Version. Madrid: JD Systems Institute. http://www.worldvaluessurvey.org/WVSDocumentationWV6.jsp.

Khemani, Stuti. 2017. "Political Economy of Reform." Policy Research Working Paper 8224, World Bank, Washington, DC.

Kingdon, Geeta Gandhi, Angela Little, Monazza Aslam, Shenila Rawal, Terry Moe, Harry Patrinos, Tara Beteille, Rukmini Banerji, Brent Parton, and Shailendra K. Sharma. 2014. *A Rigorous Review of the Political Economy of Education Systems in Developing Countries*. Education Rigorous Literature Review. London: Department for International Development.

Kirdar, Serra. 2017. *Education in the Arab World*. London: Bloomsbury Academic.

Kirschner, Paul A., John Sweller, and Richard E. Clark. 2006. "Why Minimal Guidance during Instruction Does Not Work: An Analysis of the Failure of Constructivist, Discovery, Problem-Based, Experiential, and Inquiry-Based Teaching." *Educational Psychologist* 41 (2): 75–86. https://doi.org/10.1207/s15326985ep4102_1.

Martin, Michael O., Ina V. S. Mullis, Pierre Foy, and M. Hooper. 2016. "TIMSS 2015 International Results in Science." TIMSS and PIRLS International Study Center, Boston College, Chestnut Hill, MA. http://timssandpirls.bc.edu/timss2015/international-results/.

Massialas, Byron G., and Samir A. Jarrar. 1987. "Conflicts in Education in the Arab World: The Present Challenge." *Arab Studies Quarterly* 9 (1): 35–52.

Mullis, Ina V. S., Michael O. Martin, Pierre Foy, and M. Hooper. 2016. "TIMSS 2015 International Results in Mathematics." TIMSS and PIRLS International Study Center, Boston College, Chestnut Hill, MA. http://timssandpirls.bc.edu/timss2015/international-results/.

Nabli, Mustapha. 2007. "Breaking the Barriers to Higher Economic Growth: Better Governance and Deeper Reforms in the Middle East and North Africa." World Bank, Washington, DC.

Namaghi, Seyyed Ali Ostovar. 2009. "A Data-Driven Conceptualization of Language Teacher Identity in the Context of Public High Schools in Iran." *Teacher Education Quarterly* 36 (2): 111–24.

OECD (Organisation for Economic Co-operation and Development). 2010. "Japan: A Story of Sustained Excellence." In *Strong Performers and Successful Reformers in Education: Lessons from PISA for the United States*, 137–76. Paris: OECD.

———. 2017. *Education at a Glance 2017: OECD Indicators*. Paris: OECD Publishing. https://doi.org/10.1787/eag-2017-en.

Page, M. E. 2010. "Signaling in the Labor Market." In *Economics of Education,* edited by Dominic J. Brewer and Patrick J. McEwan, 33–36. Oxford, U.K.: Elsevier.

Prince, Michael. 2004. "Does Active Learning Work? A Review of the Research." *Journal of Engineering Education* 93 (3): 223–31.

Purpel, David E., and Svi Shapiro. 1995. *Beyond Liberation and Excellence: Reconstructing the Public Discourse on Education*. Westport, CT: Bergin and Garvey.

Salehi-Isfahani, Djavad. 2012. "Education, Jobs, and Equity in the Middle East and North Africa." *Comparative Economic Studies* 54 (4): 843–61.

Schumacher, E. F. 1973. *Small Is Beautiful: A Study of Economics as If People Mattered*. London: Blond and Briggs.

Spence, Michael. 1973. "Job Market Signaling." *Quarterly Journal of Economics* 87 (3): 355–74.

Springborg, Robert. 2011. "The Precarious Economics of Arab Springs." *Survival* 53 (6): 85–104. doi:10.1080/00396338.2011.636271.

UNESCO (United Nations Educational, Scientific, and Cultural Organization). 2011. *World Data on Education: Seventh Edition 2010–11*. Paris: UNESCO International Bureau of Education.

UNICEF (United Nations Children's Fund). 2010. *Child Disciplinary Practices at Home: Evidence from a Range of Low- and Middle-Income Countries*. New York: UNICEF.

———. 2013. "Percentage of Children Aged 2–14 Who Experience Any Form of Violent Discipline (Physical Punishment and/or Psychological Aggression)." UNICEF, Paris. http://www.childinfo.org/discipline_countrydata.php.

UN Women (United Nations Entity for Gender Equality and Empowerment of Women) and Promundo. 2017. *Understanding Masculinities: Results from the International Men and Gender Equality Survey (IMAGES)—Middle East and North Africa*. Men and Women for Gender Equality Programme, UN Women Regional Office for Arab States. Paris: UN Women and Promundo.

World Bank. 2005. *Expanding Opportunities and Building Competencies for Young People: A New Agenda for Secondary Education*. Washington, DC: World Bank.

———. 2008. *The Road Not Traveled: Education Reform in the Middle East and North Africa*. Washington, DC: World Bank.

———. 2011. *The Road to Academic Excellence: The Making of World-Class Research Universities*. Washington, DC: World Bank.

———. 2013a. *Jobs for Shared Prosperity: Time for Action in the Middle East and North Africa*. Washington, DC: World Bank.

———. 2013b. *Universities through the Looking Glass: Benchmarking University Governance to Enable Higher Education Modernization in MENA*. Washington, DC: World Bank.

———. 2015a. "Hashemite Kingdom of Jordan School Autonomy and Accountability: SABER Country Report 2015." Systems Approach for Better Education Results (SABER), World Bank, Washington, DC.

———. 2015b. "Morocco School Autonomy and Accountability: SABER Country Report 2015." Systems Approach for Better Education Results (SABER), World Bank, Washington, DC.

———. 2015c. *Trust, Voice, and Incentives: Learning from Local Success Stories in Service Delivery in the Middle East and North Africa*. Washington, DC: World Bank.

———. 2015d. *World Development Report 2015: Mind, Society, and Behavior*. Washington, DC: World Bank.

———. 2016. *Making Politics Work for Development: Harnessing Transparency and Citizen Engagement*. Washington, DC: World Bank.

———. 2017a. "Building the Research Capacity of MENA Universities." Policy Note, World Bank, Washington, DC.

———. 2017b. "6th MENA Tertiary Education Conference—CMI Headquarters—June 2017." World Bank, Washington, DC.

Securing Learning for Children in Conflict and Crisis | 3

Noah Yarrow and Maja Capek

The Middle East and North Africa (MENA) region has experienced periods of violent conflict and protracted crises, forcing millions of people to leave their homes to seek safety, with major implications for education systems. Refugees and internally displaced persons (IDPs)[1] place substantial pressure on institutions and government services. Success or failure to provide education services for these groups will have large impacts on MENA's economies and societies for generations to come. Countries across MENA initially responded to the recent influx of refugees from neighboring countries with the assumption that the crises would be temporary. In practice, displacements and the conflicts that drive them have lasted many years. Both displaced children and host communities would benefit from longer-term policy approaches that support the resilience of individuals, schools, and education systems and contribute to the region's human capital.

To ensure that all children in host, refugee, and IDP communities can benefit from quality education to enhance their knowledge and skills, host countries in MENA can adopt policies to (1) increase access to education; (2) improve the learning experience for displaced children; and (3) strengthen resilience of their education systems.

One of the largest barriers to access that refugee and internally displaced children face is the cost of education. For older children, this cost goes beyond school fees and expenses for learning materials, as they face the opportunity cost of attending school instead of working to support their families. Other barriers to access include the lack of safe transportation to school. Safe transportation is particularly problematic for internally displaced children living close to active conflict zones and refugee children threatened by bullying and violence. Another important barrier is lack of adequate information about educational opportunities, keeping children from taking advantage of nearby formal and nonformal education services.

Even when children have access to education, trauma and challenges in adapting to a different curriculum or language of instruction often negatively affect learning. Host countries can improve children's learning through remedial education and enhance their well-being through psychosocial support services.

Long-term financial commitments of donors and integrated, sustainable policies across education, health, and social protection can strengthen the resilience of systems.

A coordinated push for quality education for the forcibly displaced and vulnerable children in MENA's host communities is needed to unlock opportunities for a better life in the future.

Remove barriers to education access

Refugees and IDPs make up a large share of the region's population, with MENA hosting more than a third of all refugees and about a quarter of all conflict-related IDPs worldwide (see figure 3.1; table 3.1). The Syrian conflict is the largest source of refugees and IDPs in MENA. Among them are around 2.6 million displaced children inside the Syrian Arab Republic and 2.1 million school-age Syrian refugees in other MENA countries who face great obstacles in accessing education services (Brussels Conference 2019; UN OCHA 2019). Only about 55 percent of school-age Syrian refugee children in the region are enrolled in formal education (Brussels Conference 2019; see figure 3.2).

Across the region, the enrollment rates of refugees and IDPs decrease as children get older, while refugee girls tend to be enrolled at slightly higher rates than boys across age groups (Brussels Conference 2019; UN OCHA 2018a; see figure 3.3). Older children are often expected to work in order to support the family or, particularly in the case of girls, get married and stop attending school (UNHCR, UNICEF, and WFP 2018). Reports from teachers in refugee contexts around the world also suggest that older children who may have spent a year or more in transition are reluctant to learn with younger children who are in the same or a lower grade as they were when their studies were interrupted (Save the Children 2018). The decline in enrollment for older children can also be linked to increased barriers to attendance (see box 3.1). For example, travel to secondary schools may be longer and more expensive, adding to the safety concerns of parents and children related to physical and verbal violence at or on their way to school

FIGURE 3.1 A large share of the world's IDPs and refugees live in MENA
Total number of IDPs and refugees, 2018

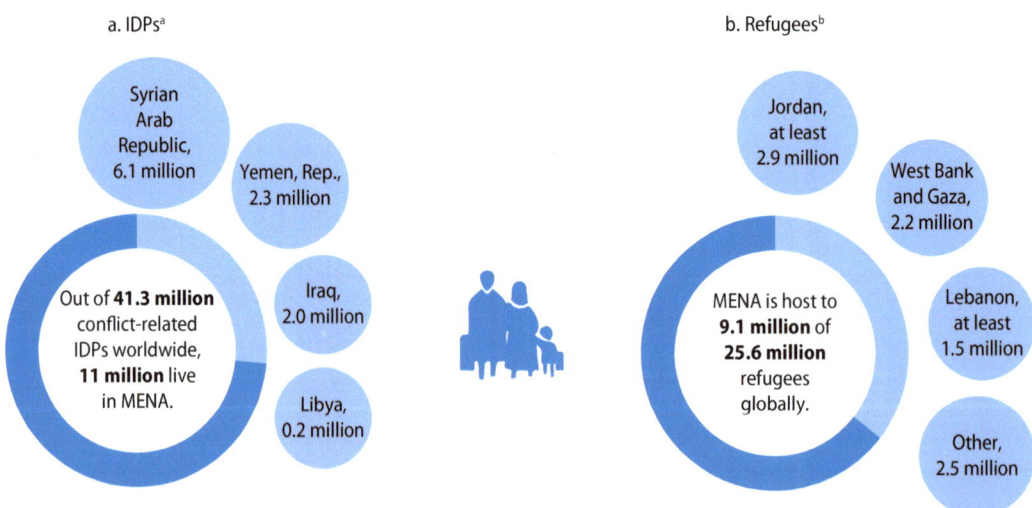

Sources: IDMC 2019; UNHCR 2019c; UNRWA 2019; World Bank.
Note: This figure highlights the MENA economies hosting the largest populations of internally displaced persons (IDPs) and refugees, respectively. Other MENA countries hosting large refugee populations include the Islamic Republic of Iran (1 million), the Syrian Arab Republic (0.6 million), Iraq (0.3 million), the Republic of Yemen (0.3 million), the Arab Republic of Egypt (0.2 million), Algeria (0.2 million), and Djibouti (0.02 million).
a. Total IDPs include conflict-related IDPs, but not displacements caused by natural disasters.
b. Total refugees globally are calculated as the sum of refugees registered with the United Nations High Commissioner for Refugees (UNHCR) and the United Nations Relief and Works Agency (UNRWA). Not all refugees are registered with UNHCR; thus the numbers presented are likely underestimates.

TABLE 3.1 **Total population, IDPs, and refugees in the world and in MENA**
Total population and number of IDPs and refugees (millions), 2018

Country	Population	Total IDPs[a]	Total refugees[b]	UNHCR-registered refugees	UNRWA-registered refugees
World	7,632.8	41.3	25.6	20.2	5.4
MENA	442.7	11.0	9.1	3.7	5.4
Iraq	39.3	2.0	0.3	0.3	—
Jordan	9.9	—	2.9	0.7[c]	2.2
Lebanon	6.1	<	1.5	1.0[c]	0.5
Syrian Arab Republic	18.3	6.1	0.6	<	0.6
Yemen, Rep.	28.9	2.3	0.3	0.3	—

Sources: IDMC 2019; UN 2017; UNHCR 2019c; UNRWA 2019.
Note: — = not available; < = number of people in the category is below 20,000.
a. Total IDPs (internally displaced persons) include conflict-related IDPs, but not displacements caused by natural disasters.
b. Total refugees are calculated as the sum of refugees registered with the United Nations High Commissioner for Refugees (UNHCR) and the United Nations Relief and Works Agency (UNRWA).
c. Not all refugees are registered with UNHCR in Jordan and Lebanon. The Government of Jordan estimates that more than 1.3 million Syrian refugees live in Jordan (Government of Jordan and UN 2018), while the Government of Lebanon estimates that Lebanon hosts 1.5 million Syrian refugees (Government of Lebanon and UN 2019).

(Save the Children 2018; UNHCR, UNICEF, and WFP 2018; UNICEF 2017a).

Evidence to guide policy makers on how to provide education services to refugees and IDPs is limited (see box 3.2). Education programs for these vulnerable populations often operate under extremely difficult conditions with limited resources. Although impact evaluations are costly and challenging to implement in these environments, for informed decision making at the policy level, it is crucial to generate more data on the effectiveness of different approaches to delivering education services. While many interventions focus on increasing the access of displaced children to education, attention to the quality dimension is essential to ensure that children are actually learning. So far, only a few isolated efforts have been made to assess the learning outcomes of children who are displaced and children who are from host communities (Assaad, Ginn, and Saleh 2018; Chemonics and DfID 2018; Comings 2018; IRC 2017; Tumen 2018). These efforts to evaluate the impacts of different arrangements for education service delivery on student learning are essential to find out how best to support these communities and advocate for better quality.

While evidence is scarce, host countries across the region face similar challenges, and promising practices have emerged to remove barriers to access and improve the quality of

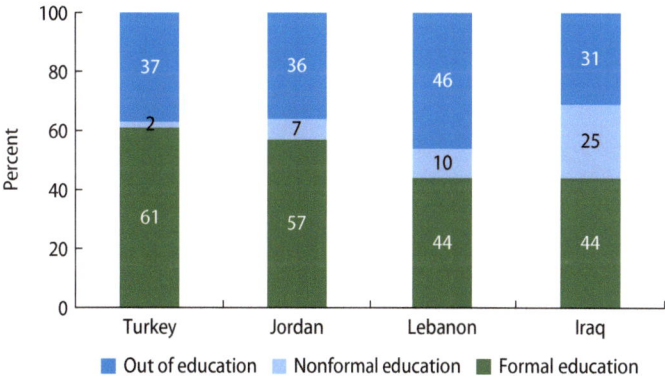

FIGURE 3.2 **Syrian refugees' enrollment in education differs across MENA**
Percentage of school-age Syrian refugees enrolled in formal or nonformal education, 2018–19

Source: Brussels Conference 2019.
Note: School age is defined as Syrian refugees between ages 5 and 17 years (except for Lebanon, where children and youths ages 3 to 18 are included, in line with the country's crisis response plan). Enrollment in nonformal education reflects only Syrian refugees who are not enrolled in formal education programs at the same time.

education (Save the Children, UNHCR, and Pearson 2017). The education policies discussed in the following sections cover these domains and consider mechanisms to strengthen resilience at the systems level.

Expand school infrastructure and the teaching workforce

At least 840,000 Syrian refugee children and youths under age 18 currently live in Jordan

FIGURE 3.3 **Refugees' enrollment drops with age**
Gross enrollment rate of refugees in Lebanese public schools, 2017–18

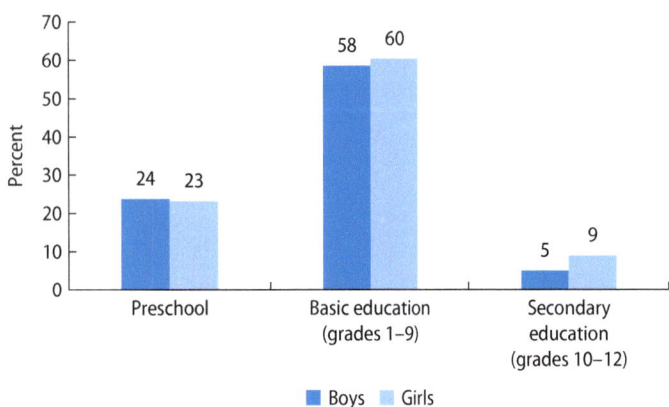

Sources: World Bank estimates based on MEHE Lebanon 2017, 2019a.

and Lebanon (UNHCR 2019b).[2] To accommodate this large influx of children, governments need to respond to a massive shortage of classrooms, learning materials, and qualified teachers. Jordan and Lebanon have made different choices about how to expand their education services, based on their current political context and recent history (Government of Jordan and UN 2018; Government of Lebanon and UN 2018).

To accommodate refugee children, Lebanon almost doubled the size of its national public education system in five years, something no country has ever done before. In the 2018–19 school year, non-Lebanese students made up an estimated 43 percent of

---

Box 3.1 Displaced within their countries' borders: IDPs' struggle to access education

At first glance, internally displaced and refugee children in MENA appear to face similar obstacles to accessing quality education: overcrowded classrooms, financial and administrative barriers, and a lack of capacity in the education system to meet students' needs for psychosocial support or provide catch-up classes for those who missed out on years of schooling. The negative coping mechanisms are similar across IDP and refugee contexts as well, with an increasing number of boys dropping out of school to work or girls dropping out to get married. However, a closer look reveals how violent conflict has severely eroded education systems in war-torn MENA countries.

School infrastructure has been heavily damaged. In Syria, more than a third of schools are damaged, destroyed, or being used for other purposes such as IDP shelters or military operations (UN OCHA 2019). The Yemeni education system has been hit even harder, with two-thirds of schools requiring major repairs (UNICEF 2018c). While violent conflict has subsided in Iraq, half of the schools in former conflict-affected areas still need to be rehabilitated (UN OCHA 2018a).

The reduced and often irregularly paid teacher workforce in conflict-affected countries is another key challenge to education quality. After eight years of crisis, more than a third of preconflict public school teachers have left Syria's formal education system (World Bank 2019). In the Republic of Yemen, half of the public school teachers in the 11 governorates most heavily affected by the conflict have not been paid their salaries since October 2016, forcing some to abandon their profession to secure their livelihoods (UN OCHA 2018b). In certain conflict-affected locations in Iraq, about a third of teachers are IDPs themselves, with very long commutes to school, which reduces the time they spend teaching because they arrive at school later and leave earlier than teachers living closer (UN OCHA 2018a).

At their peaks, the conflicts in Iraq and Syria extended into the classroom as part of the contest for legitimacy. Depending on the spheres of influence, education services were provided by the government, opposition groups, the Islamic State, or nongovernmental and international organizations. In Syrian areas controlled by the government,

box continues next page

Box 3.1 Displaced within their countries' borders: IDPs' struggle to access education *(continued)*

students would follow the prewar curriculum, while facilities overseen by opposition groups implemented revised versions of the Syrian curriculum (UNICEF 2015). With the Iraqi government having regained control over territories occupied by the Islamic State and the Syrian government in control of most Syrian provinces (Markusen 2018; Yee and Saad 2019), the patchwork of curricula and certification systems has been consolidated.

A vulnerable population that is sometimes overlooked in the current conflict is the approximately 445,000 refugees from West Bank and Gaza remaining in Syria. About 60 percent of them have been displaced inside Syria, sometimes cut off from essential support provided by the United Nations Relief and Works Agency (UNRWA), which still operates 104 schools in Syria and provides 48,000 children with education (UN OCHA 2019; UNRWA 2019).

As the dynamics and intensity of the conflicts in MENA change, so do migration flows. In Iraq and Libya, returnees[a] already far outnumber IDPs, with more than twice as many returnees as IDPs in each country (IOM 2019; UN OCHA 2018a). IDPs and refugees are likely to consider similar factors as they decide whether to move back to their home towns, including the level of peace, security, economic opportunities, access to basic services, and likelihood of asset restitution (World Bank 2019). This mobility calculus will continue to affect shifts in demand for and supply of education services in many locations across the region for years to come.

Sources: Brussels Conference 2019; IOM 2019; Markusen 2018; UNICEF 2015; UN OCHA 2018a, 2019; UNRWA 2019; World Bank 2019; Yee and Saad 2019.
a. Returnees are former refugees or IDPs who have returned to live in their country or locality of origin.

Box 3.2 Informing the global response to forced displacement: The need for better data

Little timely, high-quality data are available to inform evidence-based policy making in fragile contexts. Without good data on refugees and IDPs, it is difficult to design effective policies and programs, analyze the impact over time, and reach the most vulnerable with targeted interventions. Many fragile countries lack the financial resources and technical capacity to run functional statistics bureaus in a challenging environment (OECD 2018b). Active conflict zones make parts of the country inaccessible. Large and rapid population movements further complicate the collection of reliable data. To address these challenges, one-third of global funding for statistical development and capacity building between 2013 and 2015 was given to fragile countries (OECD 2018b).[a] In the absence of global standards, data on refugees and IDPs have been collected without harmonized terminology, methodology, and coordination (Suzuki and Sergeant 2018).

The *International Recommendations on Refugee Statistics* and the *Technical Report on Statistics of Internally Displaced Persons* constitute an important milestone to improve the availability and quality of data on forced displacement. Adopted by the United Nations (UN) Statistical Commission in March 2018, these reports take stock of existing data sources and collection practices, provide definitions of relevant terminology for statistical purposes, set guidelines for measurement, and include recommendations to strengthen national and international systems (EU and UN 2018a, 2018b).

Recognizing the need for better microdata on forced displacement, the World Bank and the

box continues next page

> **Box 3.2 Informing the global response to forced displacement: The need for better data** *(continued)*
>
> United Nations High Commissioner for Refugees (UNHCR) have joined forces to set up a joint data center that will collect, analyze, and disseminate population and socioeconomic data (UNHCR and World Bank 2018). To spur more independent research, ensuring open access to data on fragile states is a key objective of the joint data center. Operational data on program beneficiaries collected by multilateral and nongovernmental organizations (NGOs) could provide new insights into what works in fragile contexts. Rigorous anonymization protocols and safeguards could pave the way toward more open data. These ambitions, however, must carefully address data privacy and security concerns. Strong safeguards are necessary to ensure that data cannot be misused by any party to a conflict—for example, to identify and locate political adversaries (EU and UN 2018b).
>
> *Sources:* EU and UN 2018a, 2018b; Juran and Snow 2016; OECD 2018b; Suzuki and Sergeant 2018; UNHCR and World Bank 2018.
> a. In this context, "fragile countries" are countries listed in the fragility framework of the Organisation for Economic Co-operation and Development (OECD). While there is some overlap, the list differs from the World Bank's Harmonized List of Fragile Situations.

the total number of students enrolled in public education in Lebanon.[3] To accomplish this massive, rapid expansion, Lebanon operated second shifts in 346 public schools, with Lebanese-certified teachers as instructors (MEHE Lebanon 2019b). As part of this effort, the public system also provided free textbooks for all public school students and funds for schools to compensate for the abolition of enrollment fees (Government of Lebanon and UN 2018). This inclusive approach, where all benefits for refugee students were also made available to host-country students, was intended to reduce exclusion and the risk of social conflict. These results came at a financial cost, a portion of which has been supported by international donors. The results, which include 212,905 non-Lebanese children enrolled in public education in the 2018–19 school year (MEHE Lebanon 2019), are extraordinary, but still insufficient. More than half of the Syrian refugee children in Lebanon do not attend school (see figure 3.2).

Jordan expanded its formal education system by operating 209 double-shift public schools. While alleviating overcrowding and allowing more children to access education, double-shift schools reduce instructional time in both shifts and leave fewer opportunities for school-based extracurricular activities (Culbertson et al. 2016). Social cohesion is also a concern, as host community children and refugee children are often segregated by morning and afternoon shifts (Culbertson et al. 2016). The Government of Jordan also serves refugee children in camps[4] and provides nonformal education services run jointly by international organizations and the Ministry of Education (Government of Jordan and UN 2018). Nonformal education services do not lead to official certification; they are intended as a pathway to formal education and the reintegration of children who have missed out on years of schooling (UNICEF 2015). Children who lag three years or more behind their regular grade are not eligible to enroll in formal public schools, and nonformal education is their only lifeline to education (Salemi, Bowman, and Compton 2018).

Nonformal education includes catch-up courses, basic literacy programs, and learning support services such as the ones offered in the United Nations Children's Fund (UNICEF) Makani Centers (UNICEF 2017b). In the 2017–18 school year, these services alone reached more than 29,000 children, accounting for 13 percent of Jordan's school-age refugees (Brussels Conference 2018). Due to a shortfall in funding, this number dropped sharply to 17,600 children in 2018 (Brussels Conference 2019). While nonformal education is beneficial, children should ultimately be channeled to the formal education system, which provides diplomas recognized by potential employers and higher education institutions (see box 3.3).

Box 3.3 Great expectations, limited impact: EdTech for refugees

Internet penetration in the Middle East is above the world average (Internet World Stats 2019), and digital access extends to refugee populations throughout the region (UNHCR 2016a). Mobile phones are considered a basic survival tool and the main way in which the displaced can remain connected to their families and home communities (Wall, Campbell, and Jabek 2015). In the Za'atari Refugee Camp in Jordan, for example, a survey conducted in 2015 found that 86 percent of youths own mobile handsets and 83 percent own SIM cards (Maitland and Xu 2015). Most of the mobile handsets in Za'atari are smartphones. In other words, a relatively extensive digital infrastructure is in place that could be used to support education. With tablets also available at relatively low cost and already used in emergencies to support remote learning, governments and development partners have a variety of educational technology (EdTech) options at their disposal (GIZ 2016). However, this important opportunity has yet to demonstrate improvements in student learning outcomes.

MENA governments, NGOs, international donors, and the private sector are investing large sums in EdTech, some of it directed at refugee populations (Tauson and Stannard 2018). These investments consist of (1) developing digital learning content; (2) delivering the content; (3) training and mentoring teachers on the use of software and content; (4) maintaining and troubleshooting both the devices and the software; and (5) sharing learning results and data to improve the management of education information. Few organizations, institutions, or companies are able to provide all of these services, which is part of why the evidence base for EdTech continues to be weak. A comprehensive mapping of the EdTech literature found that the vast majority of publications are observational studies (Muyoya, Brugha, and Hollow 2016). Findings on technological innovations for refugee education suggest that blended learning designs that combine online and offline learning as well as mentoring and peer support are among the most promising approaches (UNESCO 2018b). Emerging evidence on the impact of smartphone learning games on literacy and well-being provides weak but modestly positive results (Comings 2018).

Digital content providers include Nafham, Tahrir Academy, and the UNICEF-UNRWA Joint Education Program, among others (Lewis and Thacker 2016). Some of the English-language content from Khan Academy and other platforms has been translated into Arabic. MENA-based content providers such as Nafham have followed the Khan format with original content, while others such as the Talal Abu-Ghazaleh International University, the Education Media Company in Morocco, and Bibliotheca Alexandrina in the Arab Republic of Egypt have created materials in Arabic, English, and French (Lewis and Thacker 2016). Most of the content on these platforms is for general use and was not developed specifically for educating refugees (Lewis and Thacker 2016). Even when developed specifically for refugees, free digital content "is often scattered and unaligned with education systems in which it is used" (UNESCO 2018b, 6). The current rush to leverage technology for refugee education has frequently led to the development of applications and platforms that do not address a clearly identified problem (Rutkin 2016). Further, distance-learning initiatives often fail to be adapted properly to the complex realities of refugees and IDPs (Tauson and Stannard 2018). These shortcomings suggest that the intended impact of EdTech is in many instances likely much greater than the actual impact on metrics that matter: student attendance, student persistence, and student learning.

Sources: Comings 2018; GIZ 2016; Lewis and Thacker 2016; Maitland and Xu 2015; Rutkin 2016; Tauson and Stannard 2018; UNESCO 2018b; UNHCR 2016a; Wall, Campbell, and Jabek 2015.

Provide financial relief and a safe learning environment

For many displaced families, the financial cost of educating their children is too high. In a representative survey of Syrian refugees in Lebanon, 40 percent of respondents named the cost of transportation or educational materials as the main reason why their children cannot attend school (UNHCR, UNICEF, and WFP 2018). Similarly, a survey conducted in the four governorates that host 80 percent of Syrian refugees in Jordan revealed that across six survey waves conducted between 2016 and 2018, the cost associated with schooling consistently featured among the top two reasons for dropping out of school (UNICEF 2018a). The data also suggest that financial pressures have different impacts on the school attendance of Syrian boys and girls. For boys, the need to work and contribute to family income is an important barrier for regular school attendance. For girls, the cost associated with safe transportation to school is a key barrier, particularly in the winter when it gets dark earlier (UNICEF 2017a).

Financial relief comes in many forms, including cash transfers, free transportation to school, and free school supplies. The evidence on the impact of cash transfers on the education of refugee children in MENA remains mixed. A review of UNHCR and UNICEF cash transfers in Jordan could not find substantial effects on school enrollment (ODI 2017).[5] However, families whose children were already enrolled in school spent more money on education when receiving cash assistance (ODI 2017). In Lebanon, a winter cash assistance program for Syrian refugees and vulnerable Lebanese households caused school enrollment to be 6 percentage points higher in the treatment group than in the control group (IRC 2014).[6] Since transportation is the main cost of schooling for many families, several programs have been launched to facilitate physical access to education. For example, the International Organization for Migration has been implementing a school bus system in parts of Jordan, Lebanon, and southeastern Turkey that operates throughout the summer, when Syrian refugee children attend catch-up and language classes (IOM 2018).

Attending school not only incurs direct costs, but also has high opportunity costs for youths. Teenage boys often do not enroll in school or eventually drop out to work and support their families. In 2017, almost one-fifth of Syrian refugee households in the four Jordanian governorates hosting the largest refugee populations reported that their child dropped out of school to provide for the family (UNICEF 2018a). In Lebanon, a quarter of Syrian refugee children ages 15 to 17 indicated that they were not attending school in order to work (UNHCR, UNICEF, and WFP 2018). Teenage girls are increasingly likely to drop out of school to get married (UNICEF 2017a). While about 13 percent of Syrian girls under age 18 got married in prewar Syria, today more than one-third of Syrian refugee girls in Lebanon marry before the age of 18 (Bartels et al. 2018). A study in Lebanon found that opinions about child marriage among Syrian refugees differ substantially by gender. Men are likely to report that child marriage is driven by financial hardship. Women, however, are more likely to think of child marriage as a measure to ensure that girls do not become victims of sexual and gender-based violence and harassment (Bartels et al. 2018). These different motivations have important implications for the design of programs aiming to prevent child marriage.

Along with financial barriers, safety and security concerns are the most important reasons preventing Syrian refugee children from attending school. Half of the respondents in a 2018 survey of refugees in Lebanon said they do not feel welcome in the country (GTS, OECD, and DfID 2018).[7] In a more recent survey of refugee families in Jordan, 17 percent named safety and security concerns, including bullying from children and teachers, as the main reason why their children do not attend school (UNICEF 2018a). Bullying of Syrian refugee children is also widespread in other host countries, including Lebanon and Turkey (Carlier 2018; Sirin and Rogers-Sirin 2015). Social and cultural differences can lead to tensions that negatively affect children's learning. Observational evidence suggests that curricula and pedagogy focused on the active participation of all students, including minorities and girls, can contribute to mitigating these tensions (Burde et al. 2015).

Inform parents and children about educational opportunities

Displaced families sometimes lack essential information about educational opportunities for their children, enrollment procedures, and the cost of schooling. In a 2018 survey of Syrian refugees in Lebanon, respondents explicitly mentioned educational opportunities as a topic about which they would like to receive more information (GTS, OECD, and DfID 2018). About 70 percent of respondents would like to receive face-to-face information, while 52 percent would like to receive text messages over the phone.[8] Informational barriers can be overcome with comprehensive campaigns. For example, in 2017, the Ministry of Education along with UN agencies and nongovernmental partners reached about 50,000 Syrian refugee households in Lebanon with a "Back-to-School" campaign, which involved community outreach and a social media campaign (UNICEF 2017c). In addition to information about enrollment procedures, the campaign provided school bags, stationery, and learning materials (UNICEF 2017c).

The current focus on increasing refugee enrollment in education is well placed. If not addressed early on, the enrollment rates of refugee children may remain low even decades after their arrival in the host country. For example, nearly 40 years after Afghan refugees arrived in Pakistan, their net enrollment in primary education stands at 29 percent, less than half the Pakistani national rate of 71 percent (UNESCO 2018a).

Parents may hesitate to send their children to school because they underestimate the returns to education. This concern is not unfounded: refugees in MENA are likely to earn less from investments in education than their host-country peers. For example, Jordan and Lebanon restrict refugee participation in the labor market, which has a negative impact on the expected returns to education for this population (Verme et al. 2016). In Jordan, work permits for refugees allow employment only in specific sectors, including agriculture, construction, and manufacturing (Krafft et al. 2018). Highly restrictive labor market policies suggest that returns to education will be lower for refugees than for host-country students, regardless of gender. Potential market saturation of low-skill labor also needs to be taken into account when estimating returns to investment in education. However, on the macroeconomic level, the long-term opportunity cost to the economy and society of not investing in human capital should be considered.

Reduce administrative requirements for admission to tertiary education

While ambitions in the tertiary education sector are high, the actual number of enrolled refugee students from MENA countries is very small, and there is no reliable data on IDPs' enrollment. In Lebanon, about 7,300 Syrian refugees were enrolled in universities in the academic year 2017–18, accounting for 5 percent of all university students (AUB Policy Institute 2019). This is in stark contrast to lower levels of education, where Syrian children make up around 50 percent of the student body (MEHE n.d.).[9] In Jordan, participation of refugees in higher education is similarly low. Rough estimates place gross enrollment at 8 percent, less than half of the 20 percent enrollment rate in pre-war Syria (Particip 2018). Financial barriers and lack of access to education credentials obtained in Syria are key obstacles that prevent refugees from enrolling in tertiary education (UNESCO 2018c; see box 3.4). To address these challenges, some local universities have started applying more flexible admission requirements (AUB Policy Institute 2019). MENA governments and international partners have also worked together to implement a variety of scholarship programs, but the needs are still far greater than the available funding (UNHCR 2019d).

Many civil society organizations have developed EdTech programs to help refugees overcome obstacles to enrolling in higher education. For example, Kiron Open Higher Education, a Berlin-based social startup, has partnered with established massive open online course (MOOC) providers such as edX and Coursera to offer online courses for refugees (Kiron 2018). DfID's Partnership for Digital Learning and Increased Access (PADILEIA) also aims to address the higher education needs of young people displaced by the Syrian crisis through blended academic programs, including MOOCs, targeted online learning, and classroom-based learning (SPHEIR 2019).

However, the proliferation of options and the lack of widely recognized certifications for completion limit the benefits for youth seeking to start or continue their studies.

While still at an early stage, the potential of blockchain technology is being discussed as a way to secure refugees' access to their credentials from previous educational achievements in the future (Grech and Camilleri 2017). The applicability of blockchain technology in a refugee context is already being tested by the World Food Programme, which runs its cash-for-food aid operation in Za'atari in Jordan through an identification system based on blockchain (Juskalian 2018).

Box 3.4 Learning from international experience: The European Qualifications Passport for Refugees

Piloted in Greece, Italy, Norway, and the United Kingdom in 2017, the European Qualifications Passport is an initiative that aims to provide refugees with a standardized document certifying their qualifications (Council of Europe 2017a). The Qualifications Passport includes information on educational achievements, language proficiency, work experience, and membership in professional organizations. The assessment of applicants takes about 1.5 months. Applicants have to submit a questionnaire before being invited to an in-person interview. Upon successful completion, applicants obtain the Qualifications Passport, which is valid for five years (Council of Europe 2017a). Their information is stored electronically in a common European database.

While the European Qualifications Passport is not "a substitute for identification or educational documentation" (Council of Europe 2017c, 2), it does provide refugees with a standardized document indicative of their credentials and skills. It explicitly does not guarantee admission to higher education institutions or recognition by potential employers. So far, refugees from Afghanistan, the Islamic Republic of Iran, Iraq, Syria, and West Bank and Gaza have participated in the assessment process (Council of Europe 2017b). Since the European Qualifications Passport is still in its trial phase and had only been issued to 249 individuals by the end of 2018 (Government of Norway 2019), it remains to be seen whether it can contribute effectively and cost-efficiently to facilitating access to higher education institutions and jobs.

Sources: Council of Europe 2017a, 2017b, 2017c; Government of Norway 2019.

Improve the learning experience of displaced children

Provide remedial education and address language of instruction challenges

Remedial and catch-up classes can be a lifeline for displaced children, many of whom have missed out on years of schooling. It is important that these classes be closely aligned with relevant curricula. If accelerated learning programs temporarily replace education in the formal system, it is imperative that there be a clear path toward reintegration.

A positive example from Lebanon is the Accelerated Learning Program, which condenses the national curriculum and delivers it in Arabic for refugee children who have been out of school so that they can enter the formal Lebanese system (Government of Lebanon and UN 2018). This approach was developed by the Center for Educational Research and Development with support from UNICEF.

Remedial education plays a particularly important role in contexts where children struggle with an unfamiliar language of instruction. An analysis of Programme for International Student Assessment (PISA) results revealed that the lower test scores of immigrant children as compared to host community students can be attributed largely to the fact that they speak a different language at home than in school (OECD 2018a). These students are also much less likely to feel "a sense of belonging" at school (OECD 2018a, 33).

For Syrian refugees in Lebanon, the language of instruction in school is often different from the language spoken at home. The curriculum prescribes English and French as languages of instruction for mathematics and science, while many refugee children are unfamiliar with these languages and lack support at home for acquiring them (UNICEF 2015).[10] The Ministry of Education and Higher Education of Lebanon does allow for some flexibility in the language of instruction for second-shift students, who are predominantly Syrian. However, as many teachers are trained and accustomed to teaching in English or French, and the math and science textbooks are in English or French, the ability of the system to implement this approach is limited. To realize the full potential of this approach, Arabic-language textbooks for subjects normally taught in a foreign language need to be developed, along with instructional support for teachers.

In Djibouti, the increase in refugee arrivals from the Republic of Yemen and the protracted nature of conflicts in Eritrea, Ethiopia, and Somalia have led to several policy changes. Djibouti has long been a place of emigration, immigration, and transit for the region. In 2018, Djibouti was host to more than 29,000 refugees and asylum seekers, of which almost 5,000 were Yemeni refugees (UNHCR 2019a). In past years, education services were provided primarily in English in camps, using a variety of curricula (UNHCR 2016b). Ministry of Education policy is that French is used exclusively in regular Djiboutian classrooms, while many refugees prefer to receive instruction in English because many intend to seek employment or envision future lives in Kenya, Somalia, or other places where English is likely to be more useful (IGAD 2018). In the Djibouti Declaration on Refugee Education,[11] the Government of Djibouti calls for progressive local integration of refugees (Intergovernmental Authority on Development 2017), mandating that the Djiboutian curriculum be used, but allowing instruction to take place in English.

Enhance children's well-being through psychosocial support

Displaced children and youths are at high risk of suffering from post-traumatic stress disorder, with different studies suggesting that between 50 and 90 percent of them may be affected (World Bank 2017b). Even after escaping conflict zones, internally displaced and refugee children continue to be exposed to severe adversity. Feeling accepted at school is strongly associated with better health, academic performance, and motivation (OECD 2018a). Focus group discussions indicate that bullying and violence experienced on their way to school have a severe impact on Syrian children's mental health in Jordan (International Medical Corps 2017). Some studies on conflict-affected populations suggest that "daily stressors in the host environment [are] actually more predictive of developing mental health problems than [is] past trauma" (World Bank 2017b, 11).

Exposure to violence and war, neglect, maltreatment, and bullying fundamentally affect children's ability to learn. Chronic stress is linked to cognitive effects, including trouble with attention, concentration, memory, and creativity (Bremner 2006). Mental health support has been shown to be more effective when embedded in community and education programs (World Bank 2017b). A resilience study in Lebanon found that refugee children who have concrete wishes concerning their future educational pathway display lower levels of post-traumatic stress and fewer emotional problems than those who do not (Giordano et al. 2014). Recreational and structured activities for psychosocial support are often a key component of nonformal education services such as the ones offered in UNICEF's Makani Centers in Jordan (UNICEF 2017b).

Neuroscience research and experience from trauma centers point to the healing effect of innovative treatments involving play, mindfulness techniques, theater, and movement (van der Kolk 2015). Several governments and NGOs around the world are applying this research in education programs with encouraging results. For example, arts, life skills, and team sports are an integral part of the Middle East Children's Institute, which supports out-of-school Syrian refugees and disadvantaged Jordanian youth. While the program has not been evaluated through an experimental study, an analysis of before-and-after test scores suggests that around 88 percent of regularly attending students show some degree of academic improvement and general well-being after three months of exposure to the program (MECI 2016). Further building on the power of arts and creativity, the Healing and Education through the Arts for Children (HEART) program by Save the Children has been implemented in Syria and refugee-hosting countries (Save the Children 2017). Through HEART, trained teachers and facilitators engage children in dancing, drawing, sculpting, singing, poetry, and other activities, building on local customs and traditions to promote children's self-expression and develop their socioemotional skills.

While these and other promising NGO-led programs are a step forward, there continues to be a massive shortage of teachers and school counselors who are trained to provide psychosocial support services within host countries' public education systems. Only a large-scale, coordinated effort to provide psychosocial support programs at the systems level can meet the enormous need and improve the well-being of traumatized children (Save the Children 2017).

Strengthen resilience at the systems level

The resilience discourse in education goes beyond individuals, schools, and communities to encompass the education system as a whole (World Bank 2013). Resilience can be defined as "the capacity of individuals, communities, and systems to survive, adapt, and grow in the face of stress and shocks" (Rockefeller Foundation 2017, n.p.). To build resilience, people, communities, and systems need to be "better prepared to withstand catastrophic events—both natural and manmade—and able to bounce back more quickly and emerge stronger from these shocks and stresses" (Rockefeller Foundation 2017, n.p.). In other words, a system's resilience can be assessed on the degree of its adaptive capacity in the face of shocks (Aschke and Zoch-Özel 2019).

MENA education systems have demonstrated resilience in many ways, even if resilience is often not an explicit part of the policy discourse. Examples of resilient adaptation in MENA include expanding existing services (for example, double shifts in schools), introducing coordinating and decision-making bodies between ministries and donor partners, and innovating new services (for example, psychosocial support training for teachers and other school professionals).

In the Republic of Yemen, local communities and teachers have demonstrated resilience in the education sector since the beginning of the conflict in 2015. Although most public school teachers have not received their salaries for two years or more, many teachers have continued working in the face of adversity (UNICEF 2018b). To alleviate their financial hardship and keep the education system from collapsing, UNICEF started paying incentives to almost 100,000 teachers and school-based staff in 2019, thus reaching approximately 50 percent of basic education teachers (UNICEF 2019). Local school committees added to the resilience of the education system. Parents' involvement in school management had already been established in select governorates in the Republic of Yemen prior to the conflict (World Bank 2015).

In Lebanon, the education system was able to absorb the large influx of Syrian refugees and almost doubled the number of children enrolled in its public school system in five years. What attributes of Lebanon's public education system contributed to this high degree of resilience and made it possible to increase enrollment rapidly? Prior to the Syrian crisis, Lebanon had excess capacity in schools, with low student-teacher ratios (World Bank 2017a). After the crisis began, many teachers were hired to expand access for refugees, but the number of teachers hired was lower than would otherwise be the case because of the preexisting inefficiency. In another instance of "serendipitous resilience" in Lebanon, long-standing legal constraints on the hiring of civil servants had led to the hiring of temporary, contractual teachers with lower levels of qualifications and benefits (World Bank 2017a). This mechanism was repurposed to hire additional teachers rapidly or expand the hours of existing teachers to instruct refugee students, particularly in the second shift. While low efficiency levels and existing policy mechanisms increased the resilience of the Lebanese public education system, these policy prescriptions are not likely to be helpful in other contexts given the uniqueness of the Lebanese experience.

The initial question of whether to integrate refugee students or to set up a parallel education system for them is an important one, with long-term impacts for both the host country and the refugee population. The selected approach depends on many variables, including the political concerns of the host country, the financing available domestically and internationally, the capacity and resilience of the education system, and particularly the expected length of refugee students' stay. As a short-term approach, a policy of establishing separate education service provision in camps may appear attractive to both host and refugee communities, especially if large amounts of external financing are available.

However, most refugee crises are protracted, with refugees staying in host countries for many years (Devictor and Do 2016). Ensuring sufficient funding for a parallel education system for refugees can be difficult, as the case of UNRWA has shown: UNRWA has suffered from chronic funding shortfalls for several years (UNRWA 2018). An intermediate approach—similar to that taken by both Jordan and Lebanon, which provide education services in the same schools with the same teachers (or similarly trained teachers) predominantly as part of a second shift—is a promising compromise as long as learning standards are maintained for both shifts and teachers are adequately supported.

Integrating refugee children into public schools can increase system coherence and sustainability. It can also trigger community pushback, as host community parents are concerned about potentially lowering the quality of the learning environment for their children. While it is difficult to estimate the impact of integrating refugee children in the public school system on education outcomes of the host population, evidence suggests that host populations are not adversely affected. For example, there is no evidence that Syrian refugees in Jordan have affected the education outcomes of Jordanian youth in terms of school entry, progression through basic and secondary schooling, or entry into tertiary education (Assaad, Ginn, and Saleh 2018). The absence of a significant impact may be attributed to the dual-shift system in schools, with Syrians mostly attending the second shift, while the vast majority of Jordanians attend the first shift. However, a study in the Netherlands found that even with a high concentration of recent immigrant children in the classroom, Dutch children's learning outcomes were not affected in math and only marginally and temporarily affected in language (Bossavie 2018). In Turkey, high school enrollment rates for Turkish youths increased in refugee-receiving regions, likely due to increased competition for low-skill jobs (Tumen 2018).

In the long run, integrating refugee children in the education system could facilitate their eventual integration in the labor market, and the country may benefit from an expanded workforce. The new Global Compact on Refugees suggests an emerging consensus that integration is the more effective approach (see box 3.5), although

---

Box 3.5 Sharing responsibility for the forcibly displaced: The Global Compact on Refugees

Following an extensive consultation process over almost two years, on December 17, 2018, the UN General Assembly adopted the Global Compact on Refugees (UN 2018b). This new framework aims to share responsibility for refugees more equitably, support host countries better, promote policies that strengthen refugees' self-reliance, and address root causes of conflict in the countries of origin (UN 2018a).

Jointly developed by UN member states, humanitarian and development organizations, and civil society, the Global Compact on Refugees relies on two main pillars: (1) the Comprehensive Refugee Response Framework (CRRF) and (2) a Program of Action. The CRRF puts refugees' inclusion in host communities' education systems and labor markets at the heart of the agenda (UNHCR 2018). It is currently being piloted in 15 countries mostly in Central America and Sub-Saharan Africa. The Program of Action lays out various high-level fora for pledging and coordinating financial and technical support. This includes a biannual Global Refugee Forum as well as ad hoc support platforms to be established for large-scale or complex refugee movements where the host needs major support. On education, the Global Compact's ambition is to ensure that refugee children can access education services within three months after their arrival in the host countries (UN 2018a).

While not legally binding, the Global Compact on Refugees sets the global stage and has the potential to promote change in international norms. It addresses gaps in the 1951 Geneva Convention and its 1967 Protocol, which acknowledged the international community's responsibility for refugees but failed to include explicit mechanisms for burden sharing (Türk and Dowden 2014). Having been adopted by an overwhelming majority of countries despite a challenging political environment, the widespread support for the Global Compact on Refugees gives reason for hope that it will prove an effective tool to galvanize international support for refugees and host countries.

Sources: Türk and Dowden 2014; UN 2018a, 2018b; UNHCR 2018.
Note: The Global Compact on Refugees was adopted by 181 countries. Hungary and the United States voted against the resolution; three countries abstained (the Dominican Republic, Eritrea, and Libya).

negative host community feelings are important to acknowledge and address and can have important political implications.

Rethink external funding mechanisms for education sectors in crisis

Unpredictable amounts of external funding make education sector planning in protracted crises exceedingly difficult. As ministries of education of countries in the region have limited capacity to pay for and deliver quality education services to their own populations, international partners often provide financial, technical, and implementation assistance in crises involving refugees and IDPs. Financing may flow from a donor into the national budget to pay for education services or may come from a donor to an agency such as UNICEF and be spent directly by UNICEF for education services. This makes financial flows and beneficiary counts for multinational crises such as the Syrian conflict difficult to track. Inconsistent and delayed reporting of funding by donors further complicates education sector planning (HRW 2017). For example, conflicting data on external education funding for Jordan suggest that the actual amount of financial resources received in 2016 may be anywhere between US$179 million and US$377 million (HRW 2017).

Education sector funding in emergencies should be adequate, timely, predictable, and not earmarked (Ayoub and Mahdi 2018). The absolute amount of money to finance education services is important, as are the time frame of availability and commitment as well as how the money can be spent. For example, it is much easier to hire and pay teachers and write contracts at the beginning of the academic year than to do so retroactively. Similarly, funds that can be used across nonformal education, formal education, technical and vocational education and training, and transportation to school are much more useful than funds that are earmarked for beneficiaries of specific genders or levels of education. Relatedly, long-term financing commitments of more than three years can allow ministries to plan, rather than simply obligating financing in one year and hoping that financing will be made available in future years. This is particularly important for education services, since there is much greater benefit to educating a student throughout the academic cycle, rather than just for one fiscal year, which is a common unit of time for donor financial commitments.

To increase the availability of multiyear funding for low-income, refugee-hosting countries, the World Bank Group set up a US$2 billion subwindow under the International Development Association (IDA) in 2017. Funding under the subwindow is provided on favorable terms and includes a grant element to support medium-term solutions that take a more developmental approach in protracted refugee crises. Fourteen countries were deemed eligible for financing under the subwindow, collectively hosting at least 6.4 million refugees (IDA 2019).[12] Similarly, the Global Concessional Financing Facility was piloted by the Islamic Development Bank, the UN, and the World Bank in 2016 to provide long-term financing to refugee-hosting middle-income countries, which so far has unlocked US$2.5 billion in concessional funds (GCFF 2018).

External funding can be an important catalyst for policy change. In many countries, refugees struggle to become self-reliant due to unfavorable policies regulating access to basic services and the labor market (Charles et al. 2018). The provision of external, multiyear funding opens opportunities to engage in intensive policy dialogue.

The different paths taken by countries in the region to provide education services for refugees and IDPs demonstrate how political, capacity, and financial variables interact as part of a dynamic system. The conflicts in Iraq, Libya, Syria, and the Republic of Yemen are expected to generate flows of refugees and IDPs for years to come. Although the

FIGURE 3.4 Policy approaches to deliver on displaced children's right to education

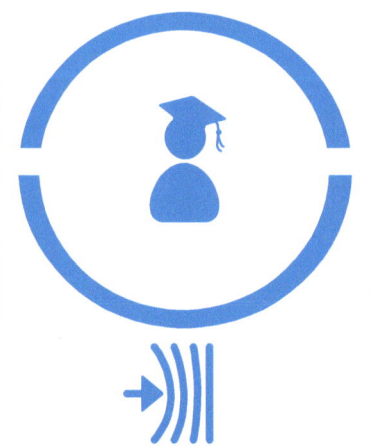

Remove barriers
- Reduce or abolish school fees
- Provide free and safe transportation to school
- Provide free textbooks
- Increase the supply of education services (build schools, hire teachers)
- Increase the demand for education services (community outreach, facilitate transfer from alternative learning to formal education)

Improve learning
- Match language of instruction to student's native language
- Train teachers to provide psychosocial support for vulnerable populations
- Provide remedial education, catch-up classes, and accelerated learning programs

Strengthen system resilience
- Obtain long-term donor and host financial commitments for coherent planning
- Integrate policies across systems (health, education, social protection)
- Expand the implementation capacity of line ministries
- Create information management systems with unique individual identification for education, health, and other services
- Create portable certification documents

Source: World Bank.

evidence base remains limited, the policies and approaches presented in figure 3.4, when adapted to existing implementation capacity, have shown promise for improving education services to vulnerable populations and host communities. Adaptive policy approaches that remove barriers, improve learning, and support resilience can help to ensure that all children within a country's borders have the opportunity to develop their full potential and contribute to society, economic growth, and innovation.

Notes

1. The international community defines "refugees" as people who are displaced beyond their nation's borders due to conflict or persecution founded on race, religion, nationality, political opinion, or membership in a particular social group (UNHCR 1951). Many MENA countries have not signed the 1951 Convention Relating to the Status of Refugees and its 1967 Protocol, including Jordan, Lebanon, and the Gulf Cooperation Council (GCC) countries (UN Treaty Collection 2017a, 2017b). No comparable legal framework applies specifically to IDPs, who are defined as people who flee their homes but remain within their nation's borders (UN 1998).
2. Data as of April 2019 based on the UNHCR Syria Regional Refugee Response Operational Portal (https://data2.unhcr.org/en/situations/syria). Since for various reasons not all refugees are registered, this number should be considered an underestimate.
3. This estimate is based on enrollment data for Lebanese public schools from the kindergarten level to secondary education for academic year 2018-19 (MEHE Lebanon 2018a, 2018b, 2019b).
4. About one-fifth of Syrian refugees in Jordan live in camps, while the rest live mostly in urban host communities (Government of Jordan and UN 2018).

5. The 2018 Post Distribution Monitoring Report of UNICEF's Hajati cash transfer program in Jordan suggests that school enrollment of children ages 6 to 8 and 12 to 16 increased, but it is not clear whether the relationship between the cash assistance and the increase in enrollment is causal (UNICEF 2018d).
6. The evaluation compared households living slightly more than 500 meters above sea level to those living slightly below. Due to the evaluation design, the results are representative only for Syrian refugees living around 500 meters above sea level. The impact on households living below that altitude could be larger because they spend less money on winter goods. For households living at higher altitude, the impact on school enrollment could be less pronounced because they spend more on heating fuel and other winter goods (Lehmann and Masterson 2014).
7. Interviews were conducted with 895 refugees (mostly Syrians, but also refugees from West Bank and Gaza) in all eight districts of Lebanon. Respondents had to have received aid within the last year. Means of each sample size were weighted according to the share of the population covered (GTS, OECD, and DfID 2018).
8. Percentages do not add up to 100 percent because respondents were allowed to choose multiple options.
9. This estimate includes Syrian refugees enrolled in both public and private formal education services. As mentioned previously in this chapter, in public education institutions from kindergarten to secondary level, Syrian refugees make up an estimated 43 percent of all children.
10. The Jordanian curriculum includes English as a foreign language, but, unlike Lebanon, English is not used as a language of instruction (UNICEF 2015).
11. The Djibouti Declaration was signed in December 2017 by all member states of the Intergovernmental Authority on Development, which includes Djibouti, Eritrea, Ethiopia, Kenya, Somalia, South Sudan, Sudan, and Uganda.
12. As of May 2019, 18 projects in nine countries have been approved across multiple sectors, totaling US$913 million.

References

Aschke, Victor, and Bettina Zoch-Özel. 2019. "Resilience in Development Cooperation: What Exactly Does That Mean?" Development in Brief 7, KfW Development Research, Frankfurt, May. https://www.kfw-entwicklungsbank.de/PDF/Download-Center/PDF-Dokumente-Development-Research/2019_05_16_EK_Resilienz_EN.pdf.

Assaad, Ragui, Thomas Ginn, and Mohamed Saleh. 2018. "Impact of Syrian Refugees in Jordan on Education Outcomes for Jordanian Youth." ERF Working Paper 1214, Economic Research Forum, Giza, September. https://erf.org.eg/publications/impact-of-syrian-refugees-in-jordan-on-education-outcomes-for-jordanian-youth/.

AUB Policy Institute. 2019. "Tertiary Education for Syrian Refugees in Lebanon." *Policy Brief #2/2019* (February). https://www.aub.edu.lb/ifi/Documents/publications/policy_briefs/2018-2019/20190402_tertiary_education_syrian_refugees_lebanon.pdf.

Ayoub, Bachir, and Dima Mahdi. 2018. "Making Aid Work in Lebanon." Joint Agency Briefing Paper, Lebanese Center for Policy Studies, Beirut; Oxfam, Oxford, U.K. https://www-cdn.oxfam.org/s3fs-public/file_attachments/bp-making-aid-work-lebanon-050418-en.pdf.

Bartels, Susan Andrea, Saja Michael, Sophie Roupetz, Stephanie Garbern, Lama Kilzar, Harveen Bergquist, Nour Bakhache, Colleen Davison, and Annie Buntig. 2018. "Making Sense of Child, Early, and Forced Marriage among Syrian Refugee Girls: A Mixed Methods Study in Lebanon." *BMJ Global Health* 3 (1): e000509.

Bossavie, Laurent. 2018. "The Effect of Immigrant Concentration at Schools on Natives' Achievement: Does Length of Stay in the Host Country Matter?" Policy Research Working Paper 8492, World Bank, Washington, DC. http://documents.worldbank.org/curated/en/702871529934288951/pdf/WPS8492-REVISED.pdf.

Bremner, J. Douglas. 2006. "Traumatic Stress: Effects on the Brain." *Dialogues in Clinical Neuroscience* 8 (4): 445–61. https://www.ncbi.nlm.nih.gov/pmc/articles/PMC3181836/pdf/DialoguesClinNeurosci-8-445.pdf.

Brussels Conference. 2018. "We Made a Promise—Ensuring Learning Pathways and Protection for Syrian Children and Youth." Presentation prepared for the Brussels II Conference, April 24–25. http://wos-education.org/uploads/brussels_report_2018/180412_Brussels_conference_report_Web_(hi-res).pdf.

———. 2019. "Investing in the Future: Protection and Learning for All Syrian Children and Youth." Report prepared for the Brussels III Conference, March 12–14. http://wos-education.org/uploads/reports/190227_Brussels_conference_report_2019_(hi-res).pdf.

Burde, Dana, Ozen Guven, Jo Kelcey, Heddy Lahmann, and Khaled Al-Abbadi. 2015. "What Works to Promote Children's Educational Access, Quality of Learning, and Wellbeing in Crisis-Affected Contexts." Education Rigorous Literature Review, Department for International Development, London. https://reliefweb.int/sites/reliefweb.int/files/resources/Education-in-Emergencies.pdf.

Carlier, Wannes. 2018. "The Widening Educational Gap for Syrian Refugee Children." Background report for the *KidsRights Report 2018*. KidsRights Foundation, Amsterdam. https://reliefweb.int/sites/reliefweb.int/files/resources/Background%20Report%202018%20-%20The%20Widening%20Educational%20Gap%20for%20Syrian%20Refugee%20Children_0.pdf.

Charles, Sarah, Cindy Huang, Lauren Post, and Kate Gough. 2018. "Five Ways to Improve the World Bank Funding for Refugees and Hosts in Low-Income Countries and Why These Dedicated Resources Matter More Than Ever." Center for Global Development, Washington, DC; International Rescue Committee, New York. https://www.cgdev.org/sites/default/files/five-ways-improve-world-bank-funding-refugees-and-hosts-low-income-countries-and-why.pdf.

Chemonics and DfID (Department for International Development). 2018. "Researching Education during Conflict: A Case Study from Syria." DfID, London. https://assets.publishing.service.gov.uk/media/5ac6006b40f0b62272a61518/DFID_researching_education_in_conflict_casestudy_syria.pdf.

Comings, John. 2018. "Assessing the Impact of Literacy Learning Games for Syrian Refugee Children: An Executive Overview of Antura and the Letters and Feed the Monster Impact Evaluations." World Vision and Foundation for Information Technology Education and Development, Washington, DC. https://allchildrenreading.org/wordpress/wp-content/uploads/2018/03/EduApp4Syria-IE-Summary-Web-Final-3.pdf.

Council of Europe. 2017a. "European Qualifications Passport for Refugees." Council of Europe, Strasbourg. https://www.coe.int/en/web/education/recognition-of-refugees-qualifications.

———. 2017b. "Second Evaluation for European Qualification Passport for Refugees Held in Greece." Council of Europe, Strasbourg. https://www.coe.int/en/web/education/-/second-evaluation-for-european-qualification-passport-for-refugees-held-in-greece.

———. 2017c. "What Is the European Qualifications Passport for Refugees?" Council of Europe, Strasbourg. https://rm.coe.int/168070016d.

Culbertson, Shelly, Tom Ling, Marie-Louise Henham, Jennie Corbett, Rita Karam, Paulina Pankowska, Catherine Saunders, Jacopo Bellasio, and Ben Baruch. 2016. *Evaluation of the Emergency Education Response for Syrian Refugee Children and Host Communities in Jordan*. Santa Monica, CA: RAND Corporation. https://www.rand.org/content/dam/rand/pubs/research_reports/RR1200/RR1203/RAND_RR1203.pdf.

Department of Statistics, Jordan. 2015. *National Population and Housing Census 2015*. Amman: Department of Statistics.

Devictor, Xavier, and Quy-Toan Do. 2016. "How Many Years Do Refugees Stay in Exile?" World Bank Development for Peace blog, September 15. http://blogs.worldbank.org/dev4peace/how-many-years-do-refugees-stay-exile.

EU (European Union) and UN (United Nations). 2018a. *Expert Group on Refugee and Internally Displaced Persons Statistics: International Recommendations on Refugee Statistics*. Luxembourg: Publications Office of the European Union. https://unstats.un.org/unsd/demographic-social/Standards-and-Methods/files/Principles_and_Recommendations/International-Migration/2018_1746_EN_08-E.pdf.

———. 2018b. *Technical Report on Statistics of Internally Displaced Persons: Current Practice and Recommendations for Improvement*. Luxembourg: Publications Office of the European Union. https://unstats.un.org/unsd/demographic-social/Standards-and-Methods/files/Technical-Report/national-reporting/Technical-report-on-statistics-of-IDPs-E.pdf.

GCFF (Global Concessional Financing Facility). 2018. *2017–18 Annual Report of the Global*

Concessional Financing Facility. Washington, DC: GCFF. https://globalcff.org/wp-content/uploads/2018/11/GCFF-Annual-Report-2018_181113.pdf.

Giordano, Francesca, Diego Boerchi, Veronica Hurtubia, Michel Maragel, Wissam Koteit, Lama Yazbek, and Cristina Castelli. 2014. "Risk and Protection in Mental Health among Syrian Children Displaced in Lebanon." Paper prepared for the "Second World Congress on Resilience: From Person to Society," Timisoara, Romania, May 8–10.

GIZ (Deutsche Gesellschaft für Internationale Zusammenarbeit). 2016. "Education in Conflict and Crisis: How Can Technology Make a Difference? A Landscape Review." GIZ, Bonn. https://allchildrenreading.org/wordpress/wp-content/uploads/2018/12/Landscape_Review_ICT4E_in_Conflict_and_Crisis.pdf.

Government of Jordan and UN (United Nations). 2018. "Jordan Response Plan for the Syria Crisis 2018–2020." Ministry of Planning and International Cooperation, Amman. https://www.dropbox.com/s/2y01rc0ctb3phwt/JRP%20Executive%20Summary%20Final%20Copy.pdf?dl=0.

Government of Lebanon and UN (United Nations). 2018. "Lebanon Crisis Response Plan 2017–2020, 2018 Update." Government of Lebanon, Beirut. https://reliefweb.int/sites/reliefweb.int/files/resources/LCRP2018_EN_Full_180122.pdf.

———. 2019. "Lebanon Crisis Response Plan 2017–2020, 2019 Update." Government of Lebanon, Beirut. https://reliefweb.int/sites/reliefweb.int/files/resources/67780.pdf.

Government of Norway. 2019. "Increased Support for the Qualifications Passport for Refugees." Press Release 86-19, Ministry of Education and Research, Oslo. https://www.regjeringen.no/en/aktuelt/increased-support-for-the-qualifications-passport-for-refugees/id2632111/.

Grech, Alexander, and Anthony F. Camilleri. 2017. *Blockchain in Education*. Joint Research Centre Science for Policy Report, edited by Andreia Inamorato dos Santos. Sevilla: European Commission. http://publications.jrc.ec.europa.eu/repository/bitstream/JRC108255/jrc108255_blockchain_in_education(1).pdf.

GTS (Ground Truth Solutions), OECD (Organisation for Economic Co-operation and Development), and DfID (Department for International Development). 2018. "Survey of Refugees and Humanitarian Staff in Lebanon." OECD, Paris, November 14. http://www.oecd.org/dac/conflict-fragility-resilience/docs/Survey%20_of_%20refugees_humanitarian_%20staff_Lebanon.pdf.

HRW (Human Rights Watch). 2017. "Following the Money: The Lack of Transparency in Donor Funding for Syrian Refugee Education." HRW, New York. https://www.hrw.org/sites/default/files/report_pdf/crdsyrianrefugees0917_web.pdf.

IDA (International Development Association). 2019. "IDA19 Special Theme: Fragility, Conflict and Violence." http://documents.worldbank.org/curated/en/515831563779134705/pdf/IDA19-Second-Replenishment-Meeting-Special-Theme-Fragility-Conflict-and-Violence.pdf.

IDMC (Internal Displacement Monitoring Centre). 2019. *Global Report on Internal Displacement 2019*. Nijmegen: IDMC. http://www.internal-displacement.org/sites/default/files/publications/documents/2019-IDMC-GRID.pdf.

IGAD (Intergovernmental Authority on Development). 2018. "2nd Meeting of IGAD Member States Education Experts Taskforce on Implementation of the Djibouti Declaration and Plan of Action on Refugee Education: Summary Report." Addis Ababa, Ethiopia, July 17–18. https://data2.unhcr.org/en/documents/download/65412.

Intergovernmental Authority on Development. 2017. "Djibouti Declaration on Regional Conference on Refugee Education in IGAD Member States—December 14, 2017." Intergovernmental Authority on Development, Djibouti. https://igad.int/attachments/article/1725/Djibouti%20Declaration%20on%20Refugee%20Education.pdf. Annex: https://www.globalcrrf.org/wp-content/uploads/2018/04/Djibouti-Plan-of-Action-on-Refugee-Education-in-IG.pdf.

International Medical Corps. 2017. "Understanding the Mental Health and Psychosocial Needs, and Service Utilization of Syrian Refugees and Jordanian Nationals: A Quantitative and Qualitative Analysis in the Kingdom of Jordan." United Nations High Commissioner for Refugees, Geneva. https://data2.unhcr.org/en/documents/download/62036.

Internet World Stats. 2019. "Internet Usage in the Middle East, Data for April 2019." Internet World Stats, Bogotá. http://www.internetworldstats.com/stats5.htm.

IOM (International Organization for Migration). 2018. "Bus Rides Boost Enrolment of Syrian Children in Turkish Schools." IOM Turkey. https://turkey.iom.int/stories/bus-rides-boost-enrolment-syrian-children-turkish-schools.

———. 2019. "IDP and Returnee Report, Round 24—Libya." Displacement Tracking Matrix, IOM, Geneva. https://www.globaldtm.info/libya/.

IRC (International Rescue Committee). 2014. "Emergency Economies: The Impact of Cash Assistance in Lebanon." IRC, New York. https://www.rescue.org/sites/default/files/document/631/emergencyeconomiesevaluationreport-lebanon2014.pdf.

———. 2017. "Impact of War on Syrian Children's Learning." IRC, New York. https://www.rescue.org/sites/default/files/document/1434/educationreportlearninglevelssyrianchildrenfinal.pdf.

Juran, Sabrina, and Rachel Snow. 2016. "The Potential of the 2010 Population and Housing Census Round for International Migration Analysis." Paper for Improving Data on International Migration: Towards Agenda 2030 and the Global Compact on Migration Conference, Berlin, December 2–3. https://gmdac.iom.int/sites/default/files/Data%20Availability%20on%20International%20Migration.pdf.

Juskalian, Russ. 2018. "Inside the Jordan Refugee Camp That Runs on Blockchain." *MIT Technology Review*, April 12. https://www.technologyreview.com/s/610806/inside-the-jordan-refugee-camp-that-runs-on-blockchain/.

Kiron. 2018. *Kiron Open Higher Education Annual Report 2017*. Berlin: Kiron Open Higher Education. https://kiron.ngo/wp-content/uploads/2018/04/Kiron_Annual_Report_2017.pdf.

Krafft, Caroline, Maia Sieverding, Colette Salemi, and Caitlyn Keo. 2018. "Syrian Refugees in Jordan: Demographics, Livelihoods, Education, and Health." ERF Working Paper 1184, Economic Research Forum, Giza. http://erf.org.eg/wp-content/uploads/2018/04/1184_Final.pdf.

Lehmann, Christian, and Daniel T. R. Masterson. 2014. "Impact Evaluation of a Cash-Transfer Programme for Syrian Refugees in Lebanon." *Field Exchange*. https://www.ennonline.net//fex/48/impactevaluation.

Lewis, Kent, and Simon Thacker. 2016. "ICT and the Education of Refugees: A Stocktaking of Innovative Approaches in the MENA Region." SABER-ICT Technical Paper 17, World Bank, Washington, DC. http://documents.worldbank.org/curated/en/236731492498454445/pdf/114274-WP-PUBLIC-MENA-ICT-Refugees-SABER-ICTno17.pdf.

Maitland, Carleen, and Ying Xu. 2015. "A Social Informatics Analysis of Refugee Mobile Phone Use: A Case Study of Za'atari Syrian Refugee Camp." Paper presented at the 43rd TPRC Research Conference on Communications, Information, and Internet Policy, Arlington, VA, September 24. https://papers.ssrn.com/sol3/papers.cfm?abstract_id=2588300.

Markusen, Maxwell B. 2018. "The Islamic State and the Persistent Threat of Extremism in Iraq." CSIS Brief, Center for Strategic and International Studies, Washington, DC. https://csis-prod.s3.amazonaws.com/s3fs-public/publication/181130_Markusen_ISIS_layout_v5_0.pdf?gMU9YfFRRiFMYHJoE30rcaDr0JCmxheo.

MECI (Middle East Children's Institute). 2016. *Annual Report 2016: Middle East Children's Institute, Jordan Office*. Amman: MECI. https://docs.wixstatic.com/ugd/697c3d_a35e1f9c49564dcbbcaa0c9f1058aafa.pdf.

MEHE (Ministry of Education and Higher Education), Lebanon. 2017. "RACE Lebanon, February 2017 Update Presentation." MEHE, Amman.

———. 2018a. "RACE II Fact Sheet, Issue: July 2018." MEHE, Amman. http://racepmulebanon.com/images/MEHE_REC_Fact_Sheet_July_2018.pdf.

———. 2018b. "RACE II Fact Sheet, Issue: November 2018." MEHE, Amman. http://racepmulebanon.com/images/fact-sheet-november-2018.pdf.

———. 2019a. "Enrollment Figures for Academic Year 2017–18." MEHE, Amman.

———. 2019b. "RACE II Fact Sheet, Issue: March 2019." MEHE, Amman. http://racepmulebanon.com/images/fact-sheet-march-2019.pdf.

———. No date. "RACE IIReaching All Children with Education – Lebanon." http://racepmulebanon.com/index.php/features-mainmenu-47/race2-article.

Muyoya, Chisenga, Meaghan Brugha, and David Hollow. 2016. "Education Technology Evidence Mapping Database." Jigsaw Consult, London. https://www.jigsawconsult.com/stories/3-dfid-mapping-education-technology.

ODI (Overseas Development Institute). 2017. "A Promise of Tomorrow: The Effects of UNHCR and UNICEF Cash Assistance on Syrian Refugees in Jordan." ODI, London. https://www.odi.org/sites/odi.org.uk/files/resource-documents/11877.pdf.

OECD (Organisation for Economic Co-operation and Development). 2018a. "The Resilience of Students with an Immigrant Background: Factors That Shape Well-Being." OECD, Paris. https://www.oecd-ilibrary.org/docserver/9789264292093-en.pdf?expires=1558964406&id=id&accname=guest&checksum=74D63656C67037D5441388C12A8E9932.

———. 2018b. *States of Fragility 2018*. Paris: OECD. http://www.oecd-ilibrary.org/deliver/9789264302075-en.pdf?itemId=/content/publication/9789264302075-en&mimeType=application/pdf.

Particip. 2018. "External Monitoring and Evaluation for the European Union Regional Trust Fund in Response to the Syrian Crisis, the 'Madad Fund'". https://ec.europa.eu/trustfund-syria-region/sites/tfsr/files/eutf_hedu_evaluation_report_0.pdf.

Rockefeller Foundation. 2017. "Resilience." https://www.rockefellerfoundation.org/our-work/topics/resilience/.

Rutkin, Aviva. 2016. "Phoning in Refugee Aid." *New Scientist* 230 (3069): 22–23.

Salemi, Colette, Jay A. Bowman, and Jennifer Compton. 2018. "Services for Syrian Refugee Children and Youth in Jordan: Forced Displacement, Foreign Aid, and Vulnerability." ERF Working Paper 1188, Economic Research Forum, Giza. http://erf.org.eg/wp-content/uploads/2018/05/WP-1188_Final.pdf.

Save the Children. 2017. "Invisible Wounds: The Impact of Six Years of War on the Mental Health of Syria's Children." Save the Children, Fairfield, CT. http://reliefweb.int/sites/reliefweb.int/files/resources/Invisible%20Wounds%20March%202017.pdf.

———. 2018. "Hear It from the Teachers: Getting Refugee Children Back to Learning." Save the Children, Fairfield, CT. https://www.savethechildren.org/content/dam/usa/reports/ed-cp/hear-it-from-the-teachers-refugee-education-report.pdf.

Save the Children, UNHCR (United Nations Office of the High Commissioner for Refugees), and Pearson. 2017. "Promising Practices in Refugee Education: Synthesis Report." Save the Children, Fairfield, CT. https://static1.squarespace.com/static/583af1fb414fb5b3977b6f89/t/59bd539d80bd5e7ca76704cd/1505579941493/Promising+Practices+in+Refugee+Education+Synthesis_Report_FINAL_WEB.pdf.

Sirin, Selcuk R., and Lauren Rogers-Sirin. 2015. "The Educational and Mental Health Needs of Syrian Refugee Children." Migration Policy Institute, Washington, DC. https://www.migrationpolicy.org/sites/default/files/publications/FCD-Sirin-Rogers-FINAL.pdf.

SPHEIR (Strategic Partnerships for Higher Education Innovation and Reform). 2019. "Partnership for Digital Learning and Increased Access (PADILEIA)." SPHEIR, Department for International Development, London. https://www.spheir.org.uk/partnership-profiles/partnership-digital-learning-and-increased-access.

Suzuki, Emi, and Caroline Mary Verney Sergeant. 2018. "World Bank Engagement through the Expert Group on Refugee and IDP Statistics (EGRIS)." World Bank Data blog, December 18. http://blogs.worldbank.org/opendata/world-bank-engagement-through-expert-group-refugee-and-idp-statistics-egris.

Tauson, Michaelle, and Luke Stannard. 2018. "EdTech for Learning in Emergencies and Displaced Settings: A Rigorous Review and Narrative Synthesis." Save the Children UK, London. https://resourcecentre.savethechildren.net/node/13238/pdf/edtech-learning.pdf.

Tumen, Semih. 2018. "The Impact of Low-Skill Refugees on Youth Education." IZA Discussion Paper 11869, Institute of Labor Economics, Bonn. http://ftp.iza.org/dp11869.pdf.

Türk, Volker, and Rebecca Dowden. 2014. "Protection Gaps." In *The Oxford Handbook of Refugee and Forced Migration Studies*, edited by Elena Fiddian-Qasmiyeh, Gil Loescher, Katy Long, and Nando Sigona. Oxford, U.K.: Oxford University Press. https://www.oxfordhandbooks.com/view/10.1093/oxfordhb/9780199652433.001.0001/oxfordhb-9780199652433-e-024?print=pdf.

UN (United Nations). 1998. "Guiding Principles on Internal Displacement." United Nations Economic and Social Council, Commission on Human Rights, New York. E/CN.4/1998/53/Add.2. https://documents-dds-ny.un.org/doc/UNDOC/GEN/G98/104/93/PDF/G9810493.pdf?OpenElement.

———. 2017. *World Population Prospects: The 2017 Revision*. New York: Department of Economic and Social Affairs, Population Division. https://population.un.org/wpp/DVD/Files/1_Indicators%20(Standard)/EXCEL_FILES/1_Population/WPP2017_POP_F01_1_TOTAL_POPULATION_BOTH_SEXES.xlsx.

———. 2018a. "Report of the United Nations High Commissioner for Refugees. Part II: Global Compact on Refugees." UN General Assembly, 73rd Session, Supplement 12, UN, New York. https://www.unhcr.org/gcr/GCR_English.pdf.

———. 2018b. "UN Affirms 'Historic' Global Compact to Support World's Refugees." *UN News*, December 17. https://news.un.org/en/story/2018/12/1028791.

UNESCO (United Nations Educational, Scientific, and Cultural Organization). 2018a. *Global Education Monitoring Report 2019: Migration, Displacement, and Education; Building Bridges, Not Walls*. Paris: UNESCO. https://unesdoc.unesco.org/ark:/48223/pf0000265866/PDF/265866eng.pdf.multi.

———. 2018b. *A Lifeline to Learning: Leveraging Technology to Support Education for Refugees*. Paris: UNESCO. https://unesdoc.unesco.org/ark:/48223/pf0000261278.

———. 2018c. "What a Waste: Ensure Migrants and Refugees' Qualifications and Prior Learning Are Recognized." Global Education Monitoring Report Policy Paper 37, UNESCO, Paris. https://unesdoc.unesco.org/ark:/48223/pf0000366312.

UNHCR (United Nations High Commissioner for Refugees). 1951. "1951 Convention Relating to the Status of Refugees." UNHCR, Geneva. http://www.unhcr.org/3b66c2aa10.pdf.

———. 2016a. "Connecting Refugees: How Internet and Mobile Connectivity Can Improve Refugee Well-Being and Transform Humanitarian Action." UNHCR, Geneva. https://www.unhcr.org/5770d43c4.pdf.

———. 2016b. "Education for Refugees: Priority Activities and Requirements Supporting Enrolment and Retention in 2016." UNHCR, Geneva. http://reporting.unhcr.org/sites/default/files/UNHCR%20Education%2020160810.pdf.

———. 2018. "Comprehensive Refugee Response Framework: Delivering More Comprehensive and Predictable Responses for Refugees." UNHCR, Geneva. https://www.unhcr.org/comprehensive-refugee-response-framework-crrf.html.

———. 2019a. "Djibouti Fact Sheet—January 2019." UNHCR, Geneva. http://reporting.unhcr.org/sites/default/files/UNHCR%20Djibouti%20Fact%20Sheet%20-%20January%202019.pdf.

———. 2019b. "Syria Regional Refugee Response." *Inter-Agency Information Sharing Portal*, June 3. https://data2.unhcr.org/en/situations/syria.

———. 2019c. *UNHCR Mid-Year Trends 2018*. Geneva: UNHCR. https://www.unhcr.org/cgi-bin/texis/vtx/home/opendocAttachment.zip?COMID=5c77e8824.

———. 2019d. "Education Activities for Refugees: Jordan, August 2019." https://reliefweb.int/sites/reliefweb.int/files/resources/70537.pdf.

UNHCR, UNICEF (United Nations Children's Fund), and WFP (World Food Programme). 2018. *VASyR 2018: Vulnerability Assessment of Syrian Refugees in Lebanon*. Geneva: UNHCR, December 25. https://data2.unhcr.org/en/documents/download/67380.

UNHCR, and World Bank. 2018. "UNHCR–World Bank Joint Data Center." Concept Note, World Bank, Washington, DC. http://pubdocs.worldbank.org/en/587131534367558386/FINAL-Joint-Data-Center-Concept-Note.pdf.

UNICEF (United Nations Children's Fund). 2015. *Curriculum, Accreditation, and Certification for Syrian Children in Syria, Turkey, Lebanon, Jordan, Iraq, and Egypt*. Amman: UNICEF MENA Regional Office. http://www.oosci-mena.org/uploads/1/wysiwyg/150527_CAC_for_Syrian_children_report_final.pdf.

———. 2017a. *Running on Empty II: A Longitudinal Welfare Study of Syrian Refugee Children Residing in Jordan's Host Communities*. New York: UNICEF. https://reliefweb.int/sites/reliefweb.int/files/resources/RUnningOnEmptyII_UNICEFJordanSep2017.pdf.

———. 2017b. *UNICEF Annual Report 2017: Jordan*. New York: UNICEF. https://www

.unicef.org/about/annualreport/files/Jordan_2017_COAR.pdf.

———. 2017c. *UNICEF Annual Report 2017: Lebanon.* New York: UNICEF. https://www.unicef.org/about/annualreport/files/Lebanon_2017_COAR.pdf.

———. 2018a. "Assessment of Syrian Refugee Children in Host Communities in Jordan." UNICEF Jordan Social Policy Section, Amman, February 26. https://www.unicef.org/jordan/Assessment_Syrians_in_Jordan_host_communities2018_online.pdf.

———. 2018b. "Despite Lack of Salaries, Female Yemeni Teachers Continue Their Efforts to Provide Children with a Better Future." UNICEF, Geneva. https://www.unicef.org/yemen/reallives_12746.html.

———. 2018c. "If Not in School—The Paths Children Cross in Yemen." UNICEF Yemen, Sanaa. https://reliefweb.int/sites/reliefweb.int/files/resources/IF%20NOT%20IN%20SCHOOL_March2018_English.pdf.

———. 2018d. *My Needs, Our Future: Hajati Cash Transfer Post Distribution Monitoring Report.* Geneva: UNICEF. https://www.unicef.org/jordan/media/146/file.

———. 2019. "To Keep Children in Education, UNICEF Starts Incentives for School-Based Staff in Yemen." Statement from Geert Cappelaere, UNICEF regional director for the Middle East and North Africa, UNICEF, New York. March. https://www.unicef.org/press-releases/keep-children-education-unicef-starts-incentives-school-based-staff-yemen.

UN OCHA (United Nations Office for the Coordination of Humanitarian Affairs). 2018a. "Humanitarian Needs Overview: Iraq." UN OCHA, Geneva, November. https://reliefweb.int/sites/reliefweb.int/files/resources/irq_2019_hno.pdf.

———. 2018b. "Humanitarian Needs Overview: Yemen." UN OCHA, Geneva, December 2018. https://reliefweb.int/sites/reliefweb.int/files/resources/2019_Yemen_HNO_FINAL.pdf.

———. 2018c. *Humanitarian Response Plan Monitoring Report, January–June 2018, Syrian Arab Republic.* Geneva: UN OCHA. https://www.humanitarianresponse.info/sites/www.humanitarianresponse.info/files/documents/files/2018_syria_mid_year_pmr_full.pdf.

———. 2019. *Humanitarian Needs Overview: Syrian Arab Republic.* Geneva: UN OCHA, March. https://www.humanitarianresponse.info/sites/www.humanitarianresponse.info/files/documents/files/2019_syr_hno_full.pdf.

UNRWA (United Nations Relief and Works Agency). 2018. "Statement of UNRWA Commissioner-General to the Advisory Commission." Press release, UNRWA, Amman. https://www.unrwa.org/newsroom/official-statements/statement-unrwa-commissioner-general-advisory-commission-Nov2018.

———. 2019. "UNRWA in Figures 2018." UNRWA, Amman. https://www.unrwa.org/resources/about-unrwa/unrwa-figures-2018-2019.

UN (United Nations) Treaty Collection. 2017a. *Status of Treaties: Convention Relating to the Status of Refugees—Geneva, 28 July 1951.* New York: UN. https://treaties.un.org/Pages/ViewDetailsII.aspx?src=TREATY&mtdsg_no=V-2&chapter=5&Temp=mtdsg2&clang=_en.

———. 2017b. *Status of Treaties: Protocol Relating to the Status of Refugees—New York, 31 January 1967.* New York: UN. https://treaties.un.org/Pages/ViewDetails.aspx?src=TREATY&mtdsg_no=V-5&chapter=5&clang=_en.

van der Kolk, Bessel. 2015. *The Body Keeps the Score: Mind, Brain, and Body in the Transformation of Trauma.* New York: Penguin.

Verme, Paolo, Chiara Gigliarano, Christina Wieder, Kerren Hedlung, Marc Petzoldt, and Marco Santacroce. 2016. *The Welfare of Syrian Refugees: Evidence from Jordan and Lebanon.* Washington, DC: World Bank. https://openknowledge.worldbank.org/bitstream/handle/10986/23228/9781464807701.pdf?sequence=21&isAllowed=y.

Wall, Melissa, Madeline Otis Campbell, and Dana Jabek. 2015. "Syrian Refugees and Information Precarity." *New Media and Society* 19 (2): 240–54.

World Bank. 2013. "What Matters Most for Education Resilience: A Framework Paper." SABER Working Paper 7, World Bank, Washington, DC, May. https://openknowledge.worldbank.org/bitstream/handle/10986/16550/788110NWP0Box30ucational0Resilience.pdf?sequence=1&isAllowed=y.

———. 2015. "Republic of Yemen: School Autonomy and Accountability." SABER Country Report 2015. World Bank,

Washington, DC. http://documents.worldbank.org/curated/en/947361505978236964/pdf/119783-BRI-PUBLIC-SABER-SAA-Yemen-Report-final-formatted.pdf.

———. 2017a. "Lebanon Education Public Expenditure Review 2017." World Bank, Washington, DC. http://documents.worldbank.org/curated/en/513651529680033141/pdf/127517-REVISED-Public-Expenditure-Review-Lebanon-2017-publish.pdf.

———. 2017b. "Mental Health among Displaced People and Refugees: Making the Case for Action at the World Bank Group." World Bank, Washington, DC. http://www.waspsocialpsychiatry.com/wp-content/uploads/2017/02/WBG_Web_MHDP_2017.pdf.

———. 2019. *The Mobility of Displaced Syrians: An Economic and Social Analysis*. Washington, DC: World Bank. https://openknowledge.worldbank.org/bitstream/handle/10986/31205/9781464814013.pdf?sequence=2&isAllowed=y.

Yee, Vivian, and Hwaida Saad. 2019. "Syrian Government Starts Campaign to Retake Last Opposition Stronghold of Idlib." *New York Times*, May 20. https://www.nytimes.com/2019/05/20/world/middleeast/syria-retaking-idlib.html.

Adopting a New Framework for Education in MENA

Safaa El Tayeb El-Kogali and Caroline Krafft

To realize the potential of education, countries in the Middle East and North Africa (MENA) need to establish an education system that prepares all students for a productive and successful future. Such a system would be responsive and flexible in order to nurture a culture of excellence and creativity in learning. It also would adopt new approaches—for instance, it would leverage disruptive technologies—so that it can offer young people the skills they need to define their trajectories in life and adapt to local, national, and global changes. Finally, it would be based on a shared national vision and would connect with the overall development goals of the country. All of society would be responsible for ensuring its success. To establish such a system, MENA countries need to adopt a new framework for education—one that includes a concerted *push* for learning, a wide-reaching *pull* for skills, and a new *pact* for education (see figure 4.1).[1]

Push for learning: Focus on learning, not just on schooling

The potential of education is achieved only when it confers the skills and knowledge that constitute human capital. In fact, the skills conferred through learning—not the years of schooling—are what determine education's contribution to economic growth (Barro and Lee 2013; Hanushek and Woessmann 2008; World Bank 2018)—see chapter 1.

MENA's learning crisis is apparent across primary and secondary grades and across different subject areas. No MENA country came close to the international medians for the percentage of students reaching the low international benchmarks of the recent Trends in International Mathematics and Science Study (TIMSS) and Progress in International Reading Literacy Study (PIRLS)—see chapter 1. Only 42 percent of grade 8 students in the Arab Republic of Egypt had a basic understanding of science (Martin et al. 2016). In Morocco, only 36 percent of grade 4 students reached minimum levels of reading literacy. According to the results of the 2015 Programme for International Student Assessment (PISA), students age 15 in Algeria, Jordan, Lebanon, Qatar, Tunisia, and the United Arab Emirates are on average two to four years of schooling behind 15-year-old students in the member countries of the Organisation for Economic Co-operation and Development (OECD) in applying their knowledge and competencies in reading, mathematics, and science to real-world situations. Algeria and Lebanon, both

FIGURE 4.1 "Push, pull, and pact" offers a new framework for education in MENA

Source: World Bank.

participating in PISA for the first time in 2015, found that more than two-thirds of their students did not meet a basic proficiency level in science, reading, and mathematics.

Low learning outcomes in MENA countries call for a push across several aspects of the educational process. To undertake a push for learning, countries need to focus on seven key areas:

1. Building the foundational skills—from early childhood development through the early grades of school—needed for future learning and success
2. Ensuring that teachers and school leaders, who are the most important inputs to the learning process, are qualified, well selected, effectively utilized, and incentivized to continue to develop professionally
3. Updating pedagogy and instructional practices to promote inquiry, creativity, and innovation
4. Addressing the language of instruction challenge, given the gap between spoken Arabic and modern standard Arabic
5. Applying learning assessments that regularly monitor student progress to ensure that students are learning
6. Giving all children, regardless of background or ability, an opportunity to learn—a requirement for raising learning outcomes at the national level
7. Leveraging technology to enhance the delivery of education and promote learning among students and educators, preparing students for an increasingly digital world.

The chapters and spotlights that follow address each of these areas.

Pull for skills: Complementary reforms are needed for education to achieve its potential

For education to reach its full potential, it must provide students with skills that satisfy the economic and social needs of each country. A push for learning would move education closer to fulfilling its potential, but it would be a second-best approach that would leave most of that potential untapped (Rodrik 2008).

A first-best approach involves multisystem reforms that align a push for learning with a pull for skills. It includes economic reforms to match the skills required in the labor market with those conferred by education and sought by parents and students. Multisystem reform would seek to address distortions in the education sector and beyond. For example, it would address signals and incentives from the labor market as well as implement reforms within the education sector. Without a realignment of the labor market that increases the demand for skills, the education sector's contribution to goals such as economic diversification will not be fully realized. Moreover, without civil service reforms that support hiring, motivating, and empowering the best teachers, the teaching profession would remain undervalued and learning would be compromised.

It is therefore important to understand how the education sector interacts with the economic, social, and political environments to achieve expected outcomes and to implement policies that address both the education system and labor market challenges.

Signaling for skills

Distortions in the labor market in MENA countries have led to an emphasis on credentials rather than skills (one of the tensions holding back education in MENA)—see chapter 2. To break out of the current credentialist equilibrium in MENA and move toward a skills equilibrium, employers need to send youths and families strong signals of the kinds of skills needed. For their part, these youths and families need to demand the relevant skills from the education system. The education system needs to respond by supplying the set of skills needed and signaling the skills acquired (see figure 4.2).

However, employers in MENA are not effectively communicating to (signaling) the education system or students and parents what skills they need. This weak signaling is exacerbated by the fact that, in most countries, private sector firms are disproportionately microenterprises, and these businesses lack the ability to send signals effectively to the region's education systems (Assaad, Krafft, and Salehi-Isfahani 2018). Moreover, these firms are not well positioned to receive signals from the education system. Currently, the signals are essentially for credentials (see box 4.1).

Rigid labor policies

MENA's rigid labor policies also constrain the pull for skills. For example, labor laws make it extremely difficult for employers to fire employees (World Bank 2013). This factor creates a disincentive for the private sector to take risks when hiring. Employers are therefore less likely to hire on a trial basis to learn about a candidate's skills, as is common practice in other parts of the world. That disincentive, coupled with the absence of information on the quality or productivity of graduates, means that firms tend to hire based on social networks.

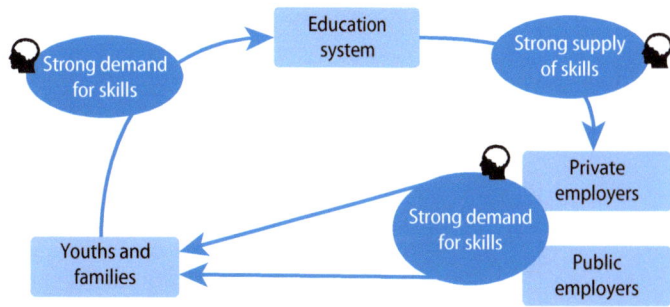

FIGURE 4.2 **MENA needs a skills equilibrium**

Source: Adapted from Assaad, Krafft, and Salehi-Isfahani 2018.

Personal connections, not skills, drive labor market outcomes in MENA, further dampening the demand for skills. A Gallup Poll conducted in 16 MENA economies found that, on average, 70 percent of respondents agreed that a personal connection is critical to securing a job (see figure 4.3). Families and students also lack incentives to focus on skills; in the labor market, measurable skills from education are rewarded much less, if at all, than social background or credentials (Assaad, Krafft, and Salehi-Isfahani 2018; Krafft and Assaad 2016; Krishnan et al. 2016).

Effective reforms, such as those in China, address both rigid labor policies and the education-specific challenges that contribute to low skills and poor signals. Previously in China, strict regulations, a lack of competition, and an inability to fire unproductive workers resulted in low productivity (Morrison 2011). Within the command economy, workers were guaranteed lifetime employment and assigned a job from which their employer was unable to terminate their appointment, with wages determined by seniority and education level (Meng, Shen, and Xue 2013). In the late 1970s, China successfully implemented multiple economic reforms, including giving more wage flexibility to firms

Box 4.1 Signaling in education is communicating about skills

Countries across MENA are not in a skills equilibrium. The Gulf Cooperation Council states are experiencing gaps between nationals and immigrant workers in terms of skills, labor prices, and labor mobility. There, policy makers are discussing the need for a fundamental reform of the skills system. For example, of the 23,000 annual new job seekers in Kuwait, some 10,000 would be unable to find suitable jobs. Placements for these job seekers would require the demand for labor to increase (employers wanting more of the kinds of workers currently produced by the education system) or education reforms to match skills more closely with the labor market (Hertog 2016).

Signaling is the process through which one party reveals some information about itself to another. For example, in the labor market employers do not immediately know the productive capabilities of their new hires. One prominent way in which applicants signal their abilities is through education (Arcidiacono, Bayer, and Hizmo 2010; Spence 1973). In the United States, the résumés of college graduates include information on grades, majors, and test scores. This information acts as a signal of ability and increases the likelihood that college graduates will be paid in line with their abilities. Most high school graduates have fewer ways in which to signal their abilities, although the financial returns to ability increase steeply with experience (Arcidiacono, Bayer, and Hizmo 2010).

In MENA, test scores do not currently appear to provide adequate information about ability (Assaad, Krafft, and Salehi-Isfahani 2018). In addition to making test scores more meaningful (by measuring skills more effectively), changes in labor policy could provide employers with the information and flexibility they need by, for example, encouraging trial periods of employment prior to long-term contracts. Together, these practices would send employers a more accurate signal of graduates' skills.

Signals from employers to students and education institutions are important as well. National employer surveys, with widely publicized reports and results, could be one route to signaling the skills that employers need. Career academies or other models of employer-school partnerships can give students information on the jobs available and the skills required. Partnerships that facilitate internships, mentoring, and other informational experiences may be effective (Lerman 2013).

and introducing a labor contracting system that moved away from lifetime tenure and gave state-owned enterprises the right to lay off workers. Following China's first national work conference in 1980, enterprises were granted more autonomy in hiring, and job seekers were given more autonomy to find jobs, including in the private sector (Brooks and Tao 2003). Wage flexibility, including instituting bonuses, has been gradually increased, and the share of bonuses in total wages for all enterprises increased from 2 percent of the wage bill in 1978 to 16 percent in 1997, effectively giving employees the incentive to perform well (Brooks and Tao 2003). Since 1997, earnings have almost doubled (Meng, Shen, and Xue 2013). Meanwhile, the reforms have led to higher returns to schooling (Zhang et al. 2005). Students have greater incentives to learn skills that will allow them to earn higher wages based on their skill set and productivity instead of their education credentials.

FIGURE 4.3 A personal connection (*wasta*) is critical to securing work in MENA

Percentage agreeing or disagreeing with the statement that a personal connection is critical to securing work

Country	Agree	Disagree
Lebanon	90	10
Jordan	85	12
Bahrain	79	18
Kuwait	79	19
Morocco	79	20
Yemen, Rep.	78	20
Tunisia	76	21
Egypt, Arab Rep.	75	23
Algeria	73	26
United Arab Emirates	72	19
West Bank and Gaza	67	29
Saudi Arabia	66	22
Iraq	64	30
Syrian Arab Republic	63	28
Libya	62	19
Qatar	58	24

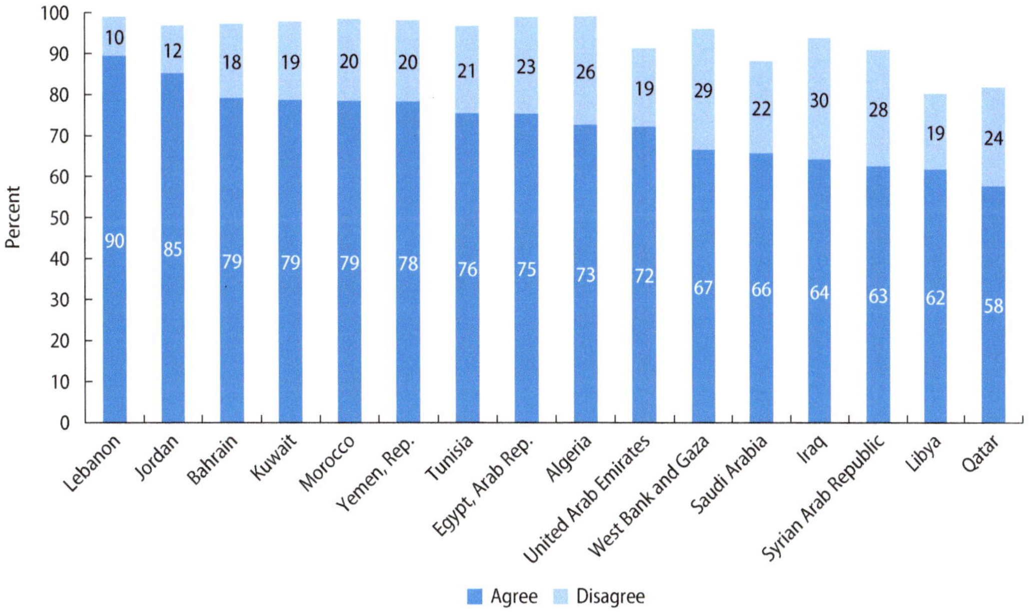

Source: Gallup Poll 2013.

A new education pact: Create a unified vision for education

In all countries, education is the subject of an ongoing national dialogue. In MENA, this national dialogue needs to be channeled toward a unified vision that takes into account the four tensions holding back education, the social norms that define them, and the local context. A shared vision also needs to take into account countries' development priorities, their economic opportunities, and their realities and resources so that the goals set are realistic and attainable.

To realize this unified vision, political will is critical. Moreover, the interests of a wide variety of stakeholders—including teachers, principals, inspectors, politicians, communities, employers, and students—need to be aligned through a powerful alliance. This effort would require strong leadership and shared accountability. It also would require bringing investments and resources in line with the vision's priorities. High-performing education systems—such as those of Japan, the Republic of Korea, and Singapore—are champions of strong education pacts that underscore the role of a unified vision for education across stakeholders. That vision includes *consistent* and *coherent* reforms to achieve human capital–driven economic growth (Wong 2017).

A critical role for national leaders

Political will and leadership are critical to rallying MENA around a new pact for education. Political leadership can initiate shifts in behavioral norms to push for education reform (Acemoglu and Jackson 2015). The national leaders of Japan, Korea, and Singapore, in championing education reforms, made education a national priority with a vision and clear goals and cultivated a consensus among stakeholders (World Bank 2018). Policies were built on the realization that the full potential of education can be achieved only through cross-sectoral policy alignment. The leaders succeeded in promoting a shared vision for education to which parents can aspire for their children's future (World Bank 2018) and a shared responsibility among all stakeholders for assuming their role in educational outcomes (Wong 2017).

MENA has produced many great leaders whose charisma and vision have led to remarkable progress. For example, Egyptian educator Taha Hussein, who became blind as a young child, went on to become one of the preeminent thinkers of his time, leaving his mark on an entire nation (Cachia 2014). Serving as minister of education in the early 1950s, he worked to massively expand public education and to abolish school fees. Considering education essential to human existence, Hussein famously said, "Education is like water and air" (Cook and El-Refaee 2017).

A unified vision for education

A new pact and shared vision require aligning political will and multiple interests in society. Experience has shown that reforms can succeed if there is strong political will to implement them. This means that politicians and interest groups have to refrain from using education as a tool to support their political views. An important step toward aligning political will and stakeholders' interests in education reform is to reduce the number of policy makers who have the power to veto policy reforms for political interests and to bring them in line with other stakeholders through a narrative of shared values (Acosta and Haddad 2014)—see box 4.2 for an example of a successful use of this approach in Peru.

To rally support for education reform in 2008, Australia's deputy prime minister developed clear outreach strategies that engaged the news media. She personally briefed the media on new proposals in advance, using stories about schools and students to humanize the narrative around reform. She also communicated with the business community through "boardroom lunches," highlighting the business case for reforms (Bruns and Schneider 2016). The minister of education of Ontario, Canada, regularly visited schools and school boards across the province when he was shadow minister, meeting with about 6,000 people in an effort to spend time with teachers, students, and parents to engage them in policy dialogue and establish trust (OECD 2011).

Recently, the president of Egypt has also been using the media and conferences to build support for education reforms. He has been advocating and supporting major reforms overhauling the education system, shifting from the traditional rote-learning, high-stakes examination system that focuses on credentials to a new system that focuses on learning and skills. He held several youth and education conferences to rally public support around the reforms, reassuring parents and students about the benefits of these reforms for them individually and for society and the economy as a whole. He announced that 2019 would be the year of education (Egyptian Gazette 2018).

Accountability to deliver results

Accountability is critical to improving learning. However, identifying who is accountable for learning outcomes is extremely difficult because different actors within and outside the education system interact to produce learning outcomes. Usually, educators, especially teachers, are the focus of accountability for student outcomes. Although teachers play a crucial role in student learning because they interact directly with students in the learning process, policy makers, school leaders, and parents, among others, also have an important role in shaping education outcomes. Therefore, accountability in education cannot be limited to any one individual or group (UNESCO 2017; World Bank 2004).

In a new education pact for MENA, accountability needs to go beyond the education system. There would be multiple accountability mechanisms, whereby

> **Box 4.2 Peru has found success in aligning interests**
>
> Through political will and alignment of stakeholders' interests, Peru succeeded in reducing the rate of stunted growth among children under age 5 in only six years. This was achieved by reducing the number of policy makers with veto power. These "veto players" were brought in line with other stakeholders through a shared set of values. Stakeholders were unified under a common policy platform and advocacy coalition, the Children's Malnutrition Initiative. This coalition was established to convene both government and nongovernment stakeholders around a single objective of making children's malnutrition central to the government's fight against poverty. During the 2006 presidential campaign, all candidates pledged to reduce malnutrition by 5 percentage points for children under 5 years of age within 5 years (5×5×5). Once elected, the president of Peru renewed his public commitment and set a target reduction of 9 percentage points and secured support from the prime minister, the minister for women and social development, and regional governors. Between 2005 and 2011, Peru reduced stunting by 10 percentage points.
>
> *Source:* Acosta and Haddad 2014.

citizens hold governments accountable, policy makers hold schools accountable, and principals hold teachers accountable. However, if the system as a whole is not aligned, conflicts and distortions will arise between the stakeholders at various levels (Burns, Köster, and Fuster 2016). System alignment toward greater accountability means that all stakeholders work collectively within a common vision for education and share responsibility for learning. These stakeholders (policy makers, school leaders, teachers, parents, employers, and students) must first hold themselves accountable to ensure learning while demanding accountability from others. For MENA countries to reap the full benefits of education, responsibility and accountability have to be shared collectively (see figure 4.4).

For accountability systems to be effective, the roles and responsibilities of the various stakeholders have to be clearly defined and understood. For example, a lack of understanding of the new roles for school administrators in Sweden resulted in varying approaches, which made it difficult to evaluate and compare learning across municipalities (Burns, Köster, and Fuster 2016). Moreover, when accountability lines are not clear, blame could be shifted among service providers, and citizens would not be able to determine who is responsible (UNESCO 2017). Without clearly defined roles and responsibilities, even well-designed accountability mechanisms can fail. For example, on the one hand, parental monitoring in school can be counterproductive if parents' involvement becomes too invasive and teachers are granted insufficient autonomy (World Bank 2008). On the other hand, if schools do not understand and recognize parents' role in the education system, they may not be responsive to legitimate parental initiatives and suggestions.

At the level of the education provider, teachers are responsible for monitoring and assessing their students' progress and for giving parents regular feedback. Teachers also should pursue ongoing professional development. School leaders are responsible for creating a school environment conducive to learning and for ensuring that teachers are delivering on learning by monitoring and empowering them.

FIGURE 4.4 Learning is a collective responsibility, and everyone is accountable

Policy makers
- Accountable for providing vision, leadership, and strategy for the education system to promote learning and skills
- Responsible for providing curricula, standards, and assessments development and effective and efficient management of resources (physical, financial, human, and information sharing)

School leaders
- Accountable for creating a school environment conducive to learning (safe, well-equipped, well connected)
- Responsible for monitoring, supporting, and empowering teachers to deliver learning and hold them accountable

Teachers
- Accountable for student learning progress in their classroom
- Responsible for monitoring student progress
- Responsible for undertaking continuous professional development and holding policy makers and school leaders accountable
- Responsible for sharing information on student progress with parents

Employers
- Responsible for sending the right signals to the education system and parents on skills required
- Accountable for rewarding skills not credentials

Parents
- Accountable for children going to and completing school
- Responsible for providing enabling learning environments at home, engaging in school activities, and seeking out feedback on student learning
- Responsible for holding policy makers, schools, and teachers accountable for learning by demanding qualified teachers, relevant curricula, and safe school environments

Civil society
- Responsible for demanding transparent communication of education inputs and outcomes

Media
- Accountable for reporting factual information and for correcting false claims
- Responsible for offering a platform for policy makers and other stakeholders to share information and promote greater transparency on education policies and other educational information
- Responsible for delivering news responsibly based on evidence and data

Students
- Responsible for being active and curious learners
- Responsible for demanding accountability and skills from schools, teachers, and policy makers
- Responsible for using technology and social media to exchange knowledge and learning and organize in a constructive manner

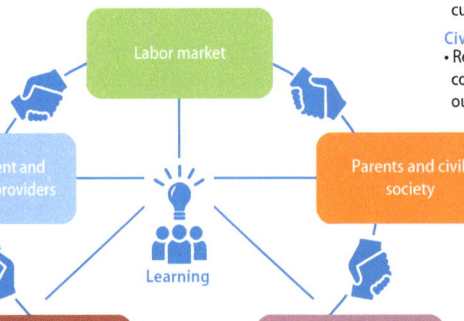

Source: World Bank.

Policy makers have the overall responsibility for providing vision and strategy and developing, leading, and supporting the implementation of education policies, developing curricula and standards, introducing national information systems that effectively monitor learning, and allocating resources at the national and regional levels (human, physical, and financial).

Parents are responsible for their children's education and for creating a supportive home environment. They are also responsible for engaging in school activities and monitoring their children's learning individually and collectively through parents' associations. Parents should also hold the education system (policy makers, schools, and teachers) accountable for their children's learning and demand qualified teachers, relevant curricula, and safe learning environments.

Employers also have a responsibility in the learning process. They need to signal to parents, students, and the education system what skills are needed in the labor market.

Finally, students are responsible for their learning; they must not be passive recipients. With their growing access to social media, students have access to massive amounts of learning resources. In many instances, they may have more access to information than their parents on global skills and knowledge and can demand these skills from the education system. Students can organize themselves to support their schools and hold service providers and educators to account.

The media play an important role in holding stakeholders accountable and in explaining complex issues. Social media are a growing major source of information in the world and in MENA countries, especially for youths, and they can serve as a platform for policy makers wishing to share information and promote greater transparency on education policy reforms. Social media also provide citizens with a mechanism to hold policy makers and educators accountable. And yet social media can also be exploited by interest groups to block important reforms and spread misinformation. In MENA countries such as Egypt, Jordan, and Kuwait, opponents of education reforms have launched strong social media campaigns against those reforms. Open channels for communication and debate are important to creating a pact around learning. Policy makers should engage with stakeholders through various channels to address concerns, correct information using evidence, and rally collective support for education reforms.

Beyond social media, technology can also be leveraged to establish accountability systems. Several countries are implementing education dashboards to facilitate open data and a move toward evidence-based policy making.

Note

1. The World Bank's *World Development Report 2018* highlights the global learning crisis (World Bank 2018). It sheds light on the dimensions of the crisis and proposes a way forward that is well aligned with the push, pull, and pact framework described here.

References

Acemoglu, Daron, and Matthew O. Jackson. 2015. "History, Expectations, and Leadership in the Evolution of Social Norms." *Review of Economic Studies* 82 (1): 1–34.

Acosta, Andrés Mejía, and Lawrence Haddad. 2014. "The Politics of Success in the Fight against Malnutrition in Peru." *Food Policy* 44: 26–35.

Arcidiacono, Peter, Patrick Bayer, and Aurel Hizmo. 2010. "Beyond Signaling and Human Capital: Education and the Revelation of Ability." *American Economic Journal: Applied Economics* 2 (4): 76–104.

Assaad, Ragui, Caroline Krafft, and Djavad Salehi-Isfahani. 2018. "Does the Type of Higher Education Affect Labor Market Outcomes? A Comparison of Egypt and Jordan." *Higher Education* 75 (6): 945–95.

Barro, Robert J., and Jong Wha Lee. 2013. "A New Data Set of Educational Attainment in the World, 1950–2010." *Journal of Development Economics* 104: 184–98.

Brooks, Ray, and Ran Tao. 2003. "China's Labor Market Performance and Challenges." IMF Working Paper WP/03/210, International Monetary Fund, Washington, DC. https://www.imf.org/external/pubs/ft/wp/2003/wp03210.pdf.

Bruns, Barbara, and Ben Ross Schneider. 2016. "Managing the Politics of Quality Reforms in Education: Policy Lessons from Global Experience." Paper commissioned for the International Commission on Financing Educational Opportunity, New York.

Burns, Tracey, Florian Köster, and Marc Fuster. 2016. *Education Governance in Action: Lessons from Case Studies*. Paris: OECD.

Cachia, Pierre. 2014. "Introduction." In *The Days: His Autobiography in Three Parts*, by Taha Hussein, 2–6. Cairo: American University in Cairo Press.

Cook, Bradley, and Engy El-Refaee. 2017. "Egypt: A Perpetual Reform Agenda." In *Education in the Arab World,* edited by Serra Kirdar, 285–305. London: Bloomsbury Academic.

Egyptian Gazette. 2018. "Sisi Declares 2019 Year of Education." http://www.egyptiangazette.net.eg/egypt-news/7407-sisi-declares-2019-year-of-education.html.

Gallup Poll. 2013. Gallup World Poll Survey 2013. Washington, DC.

Hanushek, Eric A., and Ludger Woessmann. 2008. "The Role of Cognitive Skills in Economic Development." *Journal of Economic Literature* 46 (3): 607–68.

Hertog, Steffen. 2016. "The Political Economy of Labour Markets and Migration in the Gulf: Workshop Proceedings," edited by Ribale Sleiman-Haidar. London School of Economics and Political Science, LSE Kuwait Programme, London.

Krafft, Caroline, and Ragui Assaad. 2016. "Inequality of Opportunity in the Labor Market for Higher Education Graduates in Egypt and Jordan." In *The Middle East Economies in Times of Transition,* edited by

Ishac Diwan and Ahmed Galal. New York: Palgrave Macmillan.

Krishnan, Nandini, Gabriel Lara Ibarra, Ambar Narayan, Sailesh Tiwari, and Tara Vishwanath. 2016. *Uneven Odds, Unequal Outcomes: Inequality of Opportunity in the Middle East and North Africa*. Directions in Development. Washington, DC: World Bank.

Lerman, Robert I. 2013. "Are Employability Skills Learned in U.S. Youth Education and Training Programs?" *IZA Journal of Labor Policy* 2 (1): 6.

Martin, M. O., I. V. S. Mullis, P. Foy, and M. Hooper. 2016. "TIMSS 2015 International Results in Science." TIMSS and PIRLS International Study Center, Boston College, Chestnut Hill, MA. http://timssandpirls.bc.edu/timss2015/international-results/.

Meng, Xin, Kailing Shen, and Sen Xue. 2013. "Economic Reform, Education Expansion, and Earnings Inequality for Urban Males in China, 1988–2009." *Journal of Comparative Economics* 41 (1): 227–44.

Morrison, Wayne M. 2011. "China's Economic Conditions." Congressional Research Service, Washington, DC.

OECD (Organisation for Economic Co-operation and Development). 2011. *Strong Performers and Successful Reformers in Education: Lessons from PISA for the United States*. Paris: OECD. http://www.oecd.org/pisa/46623978.pdf.

Rodrik, Dani. 2008. "Second-Best Institutions." *American Economic Review* 98 (2): 100–04.

Spence, Michael. 1973. "Job Market Signaling." *Quarterly Journal of Economics* 87 (3): 355–74.

UNESCO (United Nations Educational, Scientific, and Cultural Organization). 2017. *Global Education Monitoring Report—Accountability in Education: Meeting Our Commitments*. Paris: UNESCO.

Wong, Anny. 2017. "Insights from East Asia's High-Performing Education Systems: Leadership, Pragmatism, and Continuous Improvement." Background paper prepared for *Growing Smarter: Learning and Equitable Development in East Asia and Pacific*, World Bank, Washington, DC.

World Bank. 2004. *World Development Report 2004: Making Services Work for Poor People*. Washington, DC: World Bank.

———. 2008. *The Road Not Traveled: Education Reform in the Middle East and North Africa*. Washington, DC: World Bank. http://web.worldbank.org/archive/website01033/WEB/IMAGES/EDU_FLAG.PDF.

———. 2013. *Jobs for Shared Prosperity: Time for Action in the Middle East and North Africa*. Washington, DC: World Bank.

———. 2018. *World Development Report 2018: Learning to Realize Education's Promise*. Washington, DC: World Bank.

Zhang, Junsen, Yaohui Zhao, Albert Park, and Xiaoqing Song. 2005. "Economic Returns to Schooling in Urban China, 1988 to 2001." *Journal of Comparative Economics* 33 (4): 730–52.

# Establishing a Foundation for Lifelong Learning   5

Igor Kheyfets and
Samira Nikaein Towfighian

The early years of a child's life are the most crucial for learning. During this period, the brain undergoes its greatest development. Investments in learning during the early years and the early grades of school are, therefore, critical for laying the foundation of the cognitive and socioemotional skills that will be required to succeed in life and work. Investments made in the early years can yield higher returns than investments targeted at older populations (Heckman 2006). Yet access to early childhood education (ECE) remains low and unequal across the Middle East and North Africa (MENA). On average, only 31 percent of preschool-age children (ages 3 to 5 years) are enrolled in ECE.[1] Before starting primary school, many children are not developmentally on track in key foundational skills—such as literacy and numeracy—and they begin their formal education at a disadvantage. A push for investments in early learning through wide access to high-quality ECE is, therefore, a sound strategic direction for education systems throughout MENA. By ensuring that children come to school ready to learn and are off to a strong start in the early grades, education systems can maximize their contribution to their countries' social and economic development.

Intervene early for biggest impact

The period from in utero to age 6 is critical for children's development (Berlinski and Schady 2015; Heckman 2006; Leseman 2002). In these years, the brain undergoes its greatest development and the building blocks of the brain are formed (Center on the Developing Child 2009; Shonkoff and Garner 2012). Due to the rapid development of cognitive capacities during a child's early years, giving children a strong start is crucial to ensuring that they are ready to learn and succeed in life.

Investments in the early years have high returns

Investments in the early years can yield the highest returns in terms of future productivity by laying the foundation of cognitive and socioemotional skills (World Bank 2018). In contrast, if developmental growth in children is not supported from an early age—due to poor nutrition, a less nurturing home environment, or underinvestment in the development of cognitive skills—then children may arrive at school well behind their peers.

To take full advantage of the high potential returns to early learning, governments need to make adequate investments in expanding access to high-quality early childhood development (ECD) programs. Such programs include prenatal and neonatal parenting, nutrition, and health interventions as well as socioemotional and cognitive stimulation in the early years. However, by itself, expanded ECD coverage is not enough. Increasing access to low-quality programs does not produce the expected results in efficiency and equity (Britto, Boller, and Yoshikawa 2011). In contrast, high-quality ECD programs can boost children's intellectual and social development and help them to enter primary school ready to learn (Heckman 2006). Quality preschool education programs geared especially toward disadvantaged children can have a lifelong impact on beneficiaries' earnings and can even reduce crime (Elango et al. 2015; Schweinhart et al. 2005). These programs are also more cost-effective than other education interventions, such as reductions in class size, and help to close performance gaps by socioeconomic status, ethnicity, and geographic origin (Glewwe 2013; Heckman 2006).

Children must arrive at school ready to learn

When children start formal education, they need to be ready to learn. According to the Sustainable Development Goals (SDGs), specifically SDG 4.2, ensuring that all girls and boys have access to quality early childhood development, care, and preprimary education so that they are ready for primary education is critically important for ensuring inclusive and equitable lifelong learning opportunities for all (United Nations n.d.). Being ready for school requires that children develop a wide range of cognitive, social, emotional, and physical abilities early in life. Failing to do so can set children back—especially those from disadvantaged backgrounds—reducing their educational and economic opportunities later in life (El-Kogali and Krafft 2015).

However, in MENA there is evidence to suggest that, before children start school, they are not developmentally on track in terms of early literacy and numeracy. Except for Qatar, MENA countries that have undertaken the United Nations Children's Fund (UNICEF) Multiple Indicator Cluster Survey (MICS) have found low rates of 3- to 5-year-olds being developmentally on track in literacy and numeracy (see figure 5.1).[2] For example, only 18 percent of children in Iraq and West Bank and Gaza are deemed to be developmentally on track in early literacy and numeracy development. Only around 30 to 40 percent of children in Algeria, Oman, and Tunisia are found to be developmentally on track. While Qatar's proportion is higher, it is still below that of other high-income countries for which MICS data are available (Nikaein and Adams 2017).

Positive early experiences can push children onto a path for further learning in many ways, including having adequate nutrition in the early years (which contributes to physical health and cognitive development), early stimulation and positive interpersonal interactions (which contribute to children's social and emotional development), and access to play-based learning opportunities within and outside the home. Conversely, early negative experiences—such as the lack of formal early learning opportunities or lack of effective cognitive or socioemotional stimulation in the home—can hold children back from realizing their potential. Development outcomes can also interact; children who suffer from poor physical health will be at a disadvantage in their capacity for early learning and cognitive development. The various indicators and outcomes in early childhood interact and accumulate throughout early life, and the developmental experiences and outcomes that children accumulate in early childhood shape their subsequent learning, schooling, health, employment, social engagement, and, in general, life opportunities (El-Kogali and Krafft 2015).

Universalize preschool education

The importance of early childhood development is becoming increasingly recognized

FIGURE 5.1 Before they start school, many children are not developmentally on track

Percentage of 3- to 5-year-olds developmentally on track in literacy and numeracy

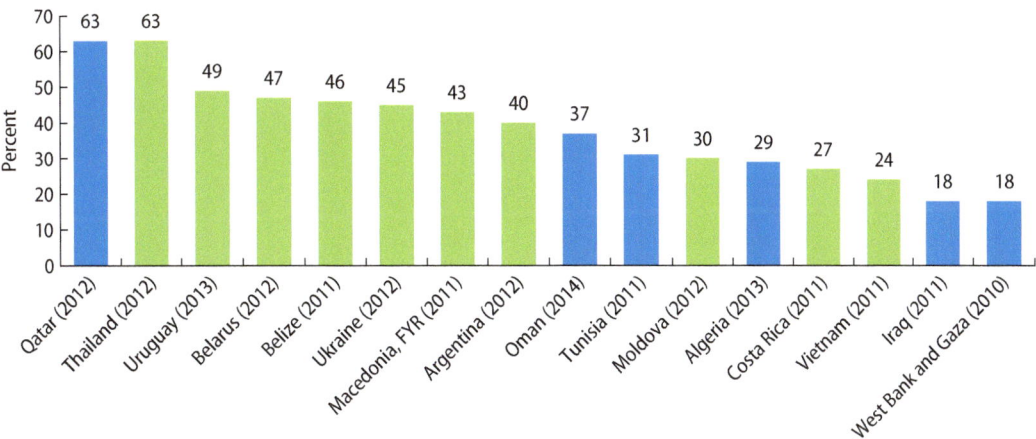

Source: UNICEF Multiple Indicator Cluster Survey (http://mics.unicef.org/).
Note: According to the survey, if a child can do at least two of the following, he or she is considered developmentally on track: identify or name at least 10 letters of the alphabet; read at least four simple, popular words; name and recognize the symbols of all numbers from 1 to 10.

across the region. As noted, SDG 4.2 has a target to ensure, by 2030, that all girls and boys have access to quality early childhood development, care, and preprimary education so that they are ready for primary education. Early childhood development is a key pillar of the regional Education for Competitiveness (E4C) initiative—launched by the Islamic Development Bank Group and the World Bank Group in 2014 and endorsed by MENA countries at the Meeting of Arab Ministers of Education in Amman in 2016 with the support of local, regional, and international partners.

Although access to preprimary education has increased in MENA, and several countries have recently made substantial investments in increasing access to education for 4- and 5-year-olds, coverage is still lagging and remains a challenge for many MENA countries. On average, MENA's gross enrollment ratio (GER) for preprimary-age children (3- to 5-year-olds) is just 31 percent—below every other region of the world except South Asia (see figure 5.2). However, coverage varies widely across the region. Some countries—such as Algeria, Lebanon, and the United Arab Emirates—are on their way to universal coverage, with GERs around 80 percent, while others have preprimary enrollment languishing in the single digits (see figure 5.3).

To improve early learning, countries with high ECE enrollment ratios can focus on improving the quality of education provided and raising children's key foundational skills. The expansion of compulsory preprimary education in Argentina in the 1990s, which successfully raised students' learning outcomes, can serve as an example. Among MENA countries, Algeria's introduction of a preprimary curriculum and the corresponding expansion of enrollment that followed is another important success story (see box 5.1).

Meanwhile countries with low ECE enrollment ratios can focus on the dual task of initiating high-quality ECE programs and scaling them up to reach all children. This effort can be particularly challenging in countries in which ECE-enabling policies are not well developed. The World Bank Systems Approach for Better Education Results (SABER) framework assessed ECD policies in Iraq (World Bank 2014), Tunisia (World Bank 2015), and the Republic of Yemen (World Bank 2013) and found that key ECD policy areas or programs were either latent or emerging. Examples of excellence in expanding the provision of quality ECE exist in MENA countries. The United Arab Emirates, for example, set the universalization of preschool education among the top

FIGURE 5.2 Preprimary enrollments are lower in MENA than in many other regions

Preprimary gross enrollment ratio, 1976, 1996, and 2016

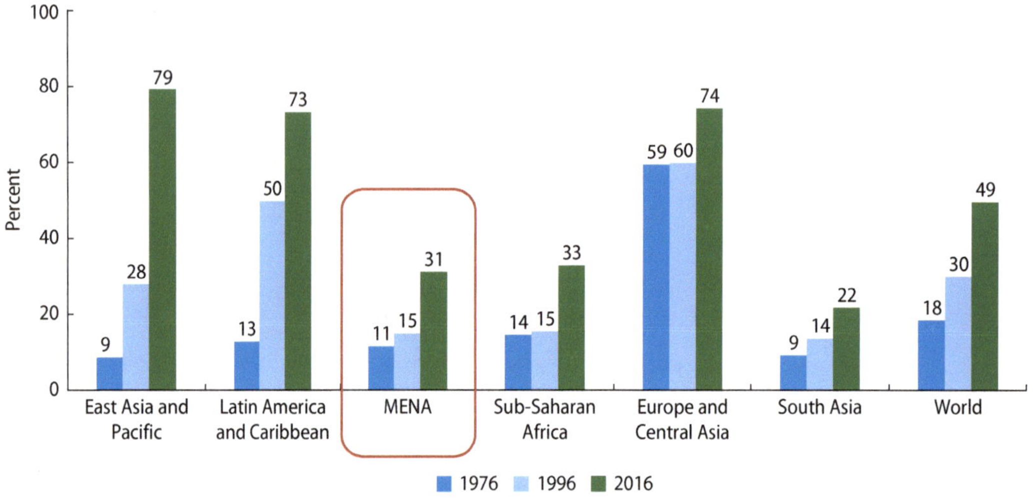

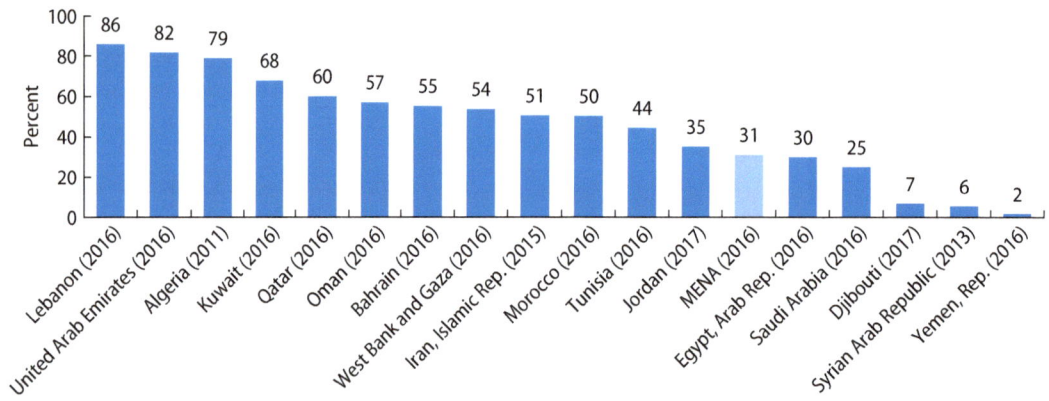

Source: World Bank EdStats database (http://datatopics.worldbank.org/education/), based on data from the UNESCO Institute for Statistics.

FIGURE 5.3 Large differences in preprimary enrollment ratios are found across MENA

Preprimary gross enrollment ratio

Sources: For all except Jordan, World Bank EdStats database (http://datatopics.worldbank.org/education/), based on data from the UNESCO Institute for Statistics. For Jordan, Queen Rania Center at the Jordan Ministry of Education, provided in August 2018.
Note: Data are for the latest available year between 2011 and 2017.

targets in its ambitious Vision 2021 national agenda (United Arab Emirates, Prime Minister's Office n.d.). The country is on pace to enroll 95 percent of its children in preschool by 2021, an increase of more than 30 percentage points since the 1990s (see box 5.2).

Target the most disadvantaged children

Inequalities of opportunity arise from the very beginning of life. Children born into difficult circumstances (starting in utero) are likely to fall behind in their health, nutrition, cognitive, social, and emotional development—all precursors to success in school. For example, at just 18 months of age, children's vocabulary differs by socioeconomic status of the parents (Center on the Developing Child 2009). By age 3, the vocabulary of a child whose parents have a college degree can be as much as three times larger than the vocabulary of a child whose parents have not completed high school

Box 5.1   **Universalizing access to preprimary education in Argentina and Algeria**

In 1993, a new Federal Education Law in Argentina expanded compulsory education to include the last year of preprimary school. A massive public school construction program began. Between 1993 and 1999, the government financed the construction of 3,531 new classrooms, creating approximately 176,550 new preschool places and building more classrooms in provinces with the lowest preprimary enrollment.

The expansion aimed to achieve two goals:

- Build on the developmental progress of children achieved at home and develop new age-appropriate competencies
- Provide early access to knowledge and skills to improve performance in the first years of primary education.

To achieve these goals, a specially designed curriculum was developed to build children's communication skills, personal autonomy and behavioral skills, social skills, logical and mathematical skills, and emotional skills. A subsequent impact evaluation found that one year of preprimary school increased average grade 3 test scores by 8 percent (equivalent to 0.23 standard deviations). The evaluation also concluded that preprimary school attendance positively affected students' self-control in grade 3 by improving attention, effort, class participation, and discipline.

At present, the public school system in Argentina comprises three years of preprimary education covering ages 3 to 5, although only the last two years are compulsory. The gross enrollment ratio in preprimary education was 73 percent in 2014, up from 48 percent in 1994.

Meanwhile, Algeria's expansion of preprimary enrollment is one of MENA's own success stories. In 1999, Algeria had a preprimary gross enrollment ratio of just 2 percent. By 2011, this had risen to 79 percent. How did Algeria expand early childhood education so quickly? In 2004, a preprimary curriculum was introduced along with a goal to increase gross enrollment to 80 percent by 2010. Algeria rapidly expanded government provision of preprimary services. As of 2014, it had the highest share of government provision in the region: 86 percent of preprimary education places were provided through the public sector. Expansion in private provision of preprimary education was also encouraged, with ongoing oversight of the curriculum in both public and private facilities.

Algeria's experience shows that it is possible for MENA countries to expand early childhood education rapidly.

Sources: Berlinski, Galiani, and Gertler 2009; El-Kogali and Krafft 2015; World Bank Edstats database.

Box 5.2   **Prioritizing early childhood education in the United Arab Emirates**

As part of its ambitious Vision 2021 national agenda, the United Arab Emirates has set a target of reaching 95 percent enrollment in preschool for the country's children by 2021. Embedded in its national goal of developing a first-rate education system, the expansion of access to preschool aims to provide all children with a solid foundation for learning from an early age. The United Arab Emirates is well on track to reach the 95 percent target.

As of 2016, the country's preprimary gross enrollment ratio was at 82 percent. The United Arab Emirates is, therefore, among the top performers of MENA in terms of preschool enrollment and has achieved a vast improvement from enrollment ratios of less than 30 percent in the 1970s and 60 percent in the 1990s.

The gradual expansion of ECE enrollment in the United Arab Emirates has been driven by the substantial growth in private provision of ECE services. More than four out of five preprimary students in the country are now enrolled in private institutions, up from half in the 1970s. The growth in private provision has been made possible by the country's conducive policy framework, which creates an enabling environment for private education providers. Dubai, one of the country's seven emirates, has led the way in expanding private education through a system of accountability and incentives at the preschool as well as the primary and secondary school levels. As of 2016–17, more than 94 percent of Dubai's preprimary students were enrolled in private institutions.

Sources: Thacker and Cuadra 2014; United Arab Emirates, Prime Minister's Office n.d.; World Bank Edstats database.

(Center on the Developing Child 2009). Inequality of opportunity exists where unequal outcomes are caused by factors beyond an individual's control.

Inequalities in early childhood development, care, and education have short- and long-term implications. When children reach the start of primary school, they are already set on different trajectories. Some children will have all they need for success in school and in adult life. Others will start their school life at a disadvantage, which will have knock-on effects throughout their schooling and beyond. Without intervention, the least advantaged children will gain less from primary school enrollment than the most advantaged children.

A recent study examines the extent of inequality of opportunity in early childhood in MENA and finds substantial differences appearing at the very start of life (El-Kogali and Krafft 2015). For example, there are variations between the prenatal and skilled delivery care provided to the most and least advantaged in the Arab Republic of Egypt, Iraq, and Morocco. Stunting is found to be much more common among the least (compared to the most) advantaged in Egypt, Iraq, Jordan, Morocco, the Syrian Arab Republic (preconflict), West Bank and Gaza, and the Republic of Yemen (preconflict). Inequalities in access to iodized salt, needed for healthy brain development, are high throughout MENA, with the exception of West Bank and Gaza. Moreover, the greatest inequalities are found in access to early childhood care and education.

Within overall low levels of ECE access in MENA, the most advantaged children are much more likely than the least advantaged to have access to early childhood care and education (El-Kogali and Krafft 2015). In many cases, the least advantaged have almost no access.[3] For example, in West Bank and Gaza, the 2014 MICS finds that children 3 to 5 years old from households in the wealthiest quintile are almost twice as likely to attend an organized ECE program as those from the poorest quintile; those whose mother is highly educated are almost twice as likely as those whose mother has only a basic education (see figure 5.4). Other countries in the region have even higher inequalities in access to early childhood education. For example, in Djibouti and Egypt, a most advantaged child is six times more likely to attend ECE than a least advantaged child (El-Kogali and Krafft 2015). In Iraq, Libya, and Tunisia, most advantaged children are 17 times more likely to attend ECE than least advantaged children.

Inequities may also exist in the quality of ECE. The Programme for International Student Assessment (PISA) 2015 results find that in MENA 15-year-olds who attended ECE perform better in science than those who did not attend. However, this analysis also finds that the difference in science scores is smaller for children from households with lower socioeconomic status (Dorn et al. 2017). This raises questions about equity in the quality of ECE provision. If the ECE available to those from poorer households is not as high quality as that available to those from the wealthiest households, then this result could be expected. Combined with the finding that starting ECE too early (at age 2 or before) is negatively correlated with PISA scores, the analysis concludes that the MENA region should focus on ensuring the provision of quality universal ECE for children ages 4 to 5.

FIGURE 5.4 **In West Bank and Gaza, opportunities for early childhood education are more likely for those from advantaged backgrounds**

Percentage of 3- to 5-year-olds attending an organized early childhood education program, by wealth quintile and by mother's education level, 2014

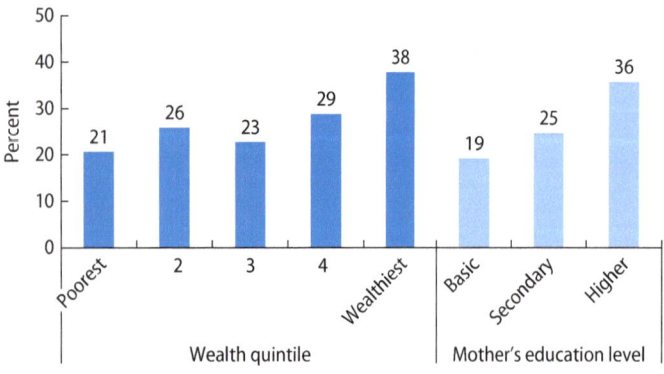

Source: UNICEF Multiple Indicator Cluster Survey (http://mics.unicef.org/).

Early childhood interventions can combat inequality

Providing access to quality ECE for all children and targeting interventions at the most disadvantaged and at-risk children from birth would give millions of children in the MENA region opportunities to develop the cognitive and socioemotional skills to thrive, thereby leveling the playing field. Box 5.3 provides an example of combatting inequality through early childhood education in the United States.

Accelerating the expansion of access to high-quality preprimary education to reach all children may require a change in policies throughout MENA. For example, countries may need to allocate more public funding for early childhood education either by increasing their public education budgets or reallocating resources from upper levels of education (such as higher education) toward the preprimary level. Constructing additional ECE facilities—or refurbishing existing primary schools to accommodate younger children—may be needed as well as providing training (or retraining) for sufficient numbers of early childhood educators. Finding innovative ways to partner with private education providers, while ensuring equitable access to children from all backgrounds, may be worthwhile in contexts where expanding

---

Box 5.3   Combatting inequality through ECE: An example from Boston

The Boston public prekindergarten (pre-K) program in the state of Massachusetts (United States) illustrates that children from a lower socioeconomic background benefit the most from high-quality center-based ECE. A quasi-experimental study analyzed the effect of one year of free full-day pre-K on 4-year-old children. While the results reveal significant positive impacts on the mathematics, literacy, and language skills of all children, children from lower-income families benefit relatively more, especially in the domains of numeracy and executive function (see figure B5.3.1).

To achieve a strong, positive impact on children's development, the quality of ECE service delivery is key. The success of the Boston public pre-K program is mostly credited to (1) a strong system of teacher recruitment and professional support and (2) the use of a research-based curriculum.

To promote pedagogical excellence, the Boston public pre-K program sets high educational requirements for its teaching workforce. Pre-K teachers need to be state-certified and obtain a master's degree, the same standards that K to 12 teachers must meet (Weiland 2016). Boston's public pre-K teachers are also paid on the same scale as K to 12 teachers. In addition, the pre-K staff benefit from on-the-job coaching with biweekly visits from ECD experts. Finally, classrooms are supported by paraprofessionals, resulting in a maximum adult-to-child ratio of 1:11.

Children's cognitive development is further supported through a research-based curriculum that enhances early literacy and numeracy skills. To ensure that the curriculum is implemented correctly, the state has developed concrete guidance for teachers and provided public pre-K facilities with all necessary learning materials.

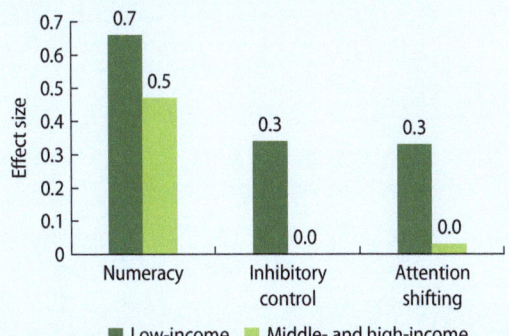

FIGURE B5.3.1 Low-income children benefit relatively more than do middle- and high-income children from early childhood education

Treatment effects of a Boston public prekindergarten program across selected domains, by children's socioeconomic status, 2008/09

Source: Weiland and Yoshikawa 2013.
Note: Effect sizes are expressed in standard deviations.

Sources: Center on the Developing Child 2009; Weiland 2016; Weiland and Yoshikawa 2013.

access through the public sector alone proves challenging. These policy changes require a concerted push by governments and other stakeholders to place early learning at the top of national strategic development agendas.

Build strong foundational skills in the early years

Many children in the MENA region begin their formal education by not being developmentally on track in terms of prereading skills (see, for example, figure 5.1). It is, therefore, vital that the early grades of school focus on building these important foundational skills, especially reading, in all children. Basic reading, writing, numeracy, and socioemotional skills set the foundation for learning throughout a child's life and into adulthood. Children need to have a good grasp of these foundational skills in the early grades of school—without which, they are at risk of falling behind, becoming disengaged, and not acquiring the increasingly more advanced skills demanded by today's fast-changing labor markets.

Ensure alignment between preprimary education and the early grades of school

Effective ECE programs can help children to arrive at school with the prerequisite skills to be able to learn. However, entering primary school classrooms, where a different educational philosophy is practiced, can be a difficult transition for young children. Going from play-based collaborative and child-centered learning to traditional teacher-centered instruction could undermine the positive impacts of even the most successful ECE programs. Instead, an alignment of instructional styles between preschool and primary grades is needed, with a focus on developmentally appropriate teaching and learning techniques for children in the early grades (OECD 2017).

Efforts are under way to align preprimary and primary grades in some MENA countries. For example, authorities in the United Arab Emirates are in the process of aligning grades 1 and 2 of primary school with preprimary education, which consists of two years of kindergarten, to create a holistic ECE cycle covering all children from ages 0 to 8. The objective of the reform is to ease the transition of children from kindergarten into primary education and to strengthen the development of key cognitive and socioemotional foundational skills. Similar efforts to align ECE with learning in the early grades have been undertaken across various Organisation for Economic Co-operation and Development (OECD) countries, such as New Zealand and Finland (see box 5.4).

After two or three years of schooling, many students still cannot read

The U.S. Agency for International Development (USAID) Early Grade Reading Assessments (EGRAs), several of which have been conducted in countries of the MENA region, provide information on the development of reading skills in the early grades of school.[4] These surveys show that reading is delayed for many children in the region. For example, more than one in three grade 2 children in Iraq, Morocco, and the Republic of Yemen cannot read a single word of connected text (see figure 5.5). By grade 3, this proportion drops, but still more than one in six children cannot read a single word of connected text after more than two full years of school. These results indicate that the initial grades of schooling are not as effective as they could be and that many students in the region start their early school life at a disadvantage, which is likely to affect their progress throughout subsequent years of schooling.

Early screening and intervention can boost foundational skills

Breaking down the skills and competencies, such as learning to read, into steps and being clear about the standards that should be achieved at each grade or level is important in helping teachers to assess their students and take the necessary actions. While new curricular reforms in the MENA region are beginning to focus on this level of detail,

> **Box 5.4** Unifying ECE curriculum in the national core curriculum of New Zealand and Finland

New Zealand's Te Whariki curriculum

New Zealand developed its ECE curriculum, Te Whariki, for children from birth to school entry. The curriculum is based on four principles (strands): (1) well-being, (2) belonging, (3) contributions of children, and (4) communications and exploration. To ensure that the contents of one curriculum framework are age-appropriate, the contents were developed for each age group within ECE: infants (0 to 18 months), toddlers (1.5 to 3 years), and young children (3 years to school entry age).

The ECE curriculum also is linked to the primary school curriculum. To smooth the transition from preschool to primary school, each strand of the ECE curriculum is linked to the learning areas and skills in the primary school curriculum. Conversely, the principles in the primary school curriculum are integrated in Te Whariki.

Finland's Act on Basic Education

Finland's Act on Basic Education aims to smooth children's path to school. With respect to ECE, the new core curricula for preprimary and basic (primary) education include specific goals for transition between the two levels.

The revised National Core Curriculum for Preprimary Education (2014) states:

> *It is important that early childhood education and care, of which preprimary education is a part, and basic education form an entity that proceeds consistently in terms of the child's growth and learning. ... The goal is that each child's learning path from early childhood education and care to preprimary education and further on to basic education is a flexible continuum founded on the needs of the child. ... The transitions from home or early childhood education and care attended by the child before his/her start in preprimary education, and from preprimary education to school, are important phases for children. A successful transition promotes a sense of security and well-being in children and supports their prerequisites for growth and learning.*

The revised core curriculum includes similar goals to ensure that ECE, preprimary school, and primary school staff have common objectives for the start of primary school and transitions between different settings.

In 2015, preprimary education for 6-year-olds became compulsory in Finland, and the curriculum for ECE underwent further changes. A revised version of the ECE curriculum was launched in October 2016.

Sources: OECD 2012, 2017.

---

a systematic review of research on teaching and learning finds no national standards for reading (in Arabic) in Egypt, Iraq, Jordan, Morocco, or the Republic of Yemen (Boyle, Al Ajjawi, and Xiang 2014). A close examination of the curricula in Egypt and Jordan notes that they do not guide students on the vocabulary differences between colloquial Arabic and literary Arabic (Gove, Brombacher, and Ward-Brent 2017). Across the countries studied, whole-word recognition (*tariqa hijaiyah*) is employed, whereas phonics (*tariqa sawtiya*) is frequently neglected. In addition, textbooks have few exercises in which students can manipulate letters and sounds to create words. Instead, the curriculum jumps directly to reading and reproducing full texts (Boyle, Al Ajjawi, and Xiang 2014).

The good news is that early grade reading interventions can make a substantial difference. A review of the evidence from 18 early grade reading programs finds that almost all are effective and several are highly cost-effective (Graham and Kelly 2018). Several countries in the region have made concerted efforts to address literacy in the early grades. The most successful parts of Egypt's early grade reading program include the following elements: model lessons focused on student-centered learning, classroom management, library use and management, and effective supervision and coaching. These elements are in addition to the core components of the program, which include a review of phonics and the introduction of new phonetic aspects, vocabulary development, and reading comprehension (Gove, Brombacher, and Ward-Brent 2017). In Jordan, the most successful schools implementing a reading intervention have supervisors who visit frequently and teachers who consistently check their students' understanding (both through oral questioning and checking of written work) (USAID 2014a). In Morocco, however, a lack of specialized teacher training in reading instruction and assessment of students' reading skills, combined with a lack of supplementary reading materials, leaves teachers ill-equipped to support children's reading development in the early grades (USAID 2014b).

A recent study shows that early literacy interventions can positively affect cognitive and socioemotional development, even in fragile, violent, and conflict-affected parts of the region. Two digital early literacy apps, (1) Antura and the Letters and (2) Feed the Monster, recently entered in the EduApp4Syria competition, providing encouraging evidence that smartphone learning games may build basic Arabic literacy skills and improve the psychosocial well-being of Syrian refugee children (Comings 2018).

A focused effort to build foundational skills for learning in England (see box 5.5) highlights the importance of assessing and monitoring students' early skills acquisition to identify weaknesses and progression so that teachers can determine the best strategies for their students, particularly those requiring additional support.

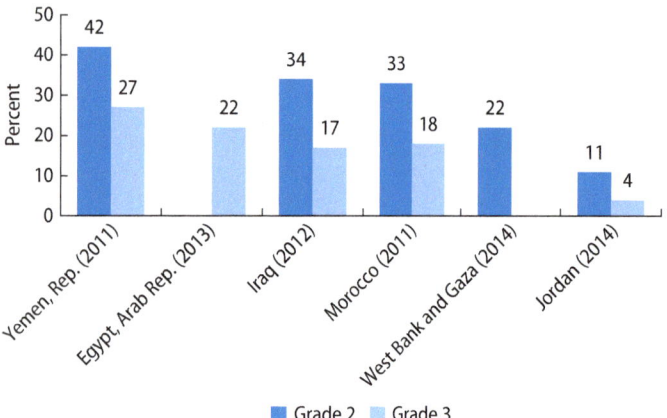

FIGURE 5.5 **Many children in MENA cannot read a single word after two or three years of schooling**
Percentage of grade 2 and grade 3 students who cannot read a single word of connected text

Source: USAID Early Grade Reading Barometer (http://www.earlygradereadingbarometer.org/).
Note: Data for the Arab Republic of Egypt and for West Bank and Gaza are available for one grade only.

Box 5.5   Screening for literacy and numeracy development in England

In 2012, England introduced a regular phonics screening check of all 6-year-olds. This simple screening tool, designed to ascertain if children are on track to become fluent readers, is credited with helping to improve reading instruction and outcomes for children learning to read. The Department for Education estimates that the number of 6-year-olds on track to become fluent readers increased by 154,000 between 2012 and 2018. England's increasing scores in grade 4 reading literacy between the 2011 and 2016 Progress in International Reading Literacy Study (PIRLS) assessments may reflect this close individual monitoring of early grade reading development over that time period.

Attention is now turning to numeracy and, in particular, multiplication tables. In February 2018, the Department for Education announced that some schools started piloting a multiplication table check of their 8- to 9-year-old students. The test, which is on-screen and takes 5 minutes, helps teachers to monitor the progress of their students in remembering multiplication tables up to 12 × 12. Although results will be published at the school level, the test is designed to give minimal stress to students and teachers. The initiative aims to reduce the burden of testing on children and teachers and provide a more accurate measure of student progress. The initiative was planned to roll out in June 2019 and be mandatory in June 2020.

Source: Department for Education and the Rt Hon Nick Gibb MP 2018.

To improve readiness to learn in the early years, education policies in MENA should focus on aligning preprimary schooling with primary grades to achieve a smoother transition for young children. Piloting early childhood and early grade interventions to identify which ones successfully boost children's foundational skills is an effective strategy to maximize the use of scarce resources. Measuring ECD outcomes through early grade literacy and numeracy assessments can shed further light on the key drivers of early learning and monitor whether children are able to build the key foundational skills from a young age. Improving learning in the early years can provide a critical push to propel subsequent learning.

Notes

1. World Bank EdStats database.
2. According to the MICS, a child is considered developmentally on track if he or she can do at least two of the following: identify or name at least 10 letters of the alphabet; read at least four simple, popular words; name and recognize the symbols of all numbers from 1 to 10.
3. Following El-Kogali and Krafft (2015), this analysis defines a "most advantaged" child as "a child who has parents with secondary or higher education and is from the richest 20 percent of households," while a "least advantaged" child is "a child who lives in the poorest 20 percent of households and with uneducated parents."
4. USAID Early Grade Reading Barometer.

References

Berlinski, Samuel, Sebastian Galiani, and Paul Gertler. 2009. "The Effect of Pre-Primary Education on Primary School Performance." *Journal of Public Economics* 93 (1–2): 219–34.

Berlinski, Samuel, and Norbert Schady, eds. 2015. *The Early Years: Child Well-Being and the Role of Public Policy*. Washington, DC: Inter-American Development Bank.

Boyle, Helen N., Samah Al Ajjawi, and Yuanyuan Xiang. 2014. "Topical Analysis of Early Grade Reading Instruction." EdData II: Task Order 15: Data for Education Programming in Asia and Middle East, U.S. Agency for International Development, Washington, DC.

Britto, Pia Rebello, Kimberly Boller, and Hirokazu Yoshikawa. 2011. "Quality of Early Childhood Development Programs in Global Contexts: Rationale for Investment, Conceptual Framework, and Implications for Equity." *Social Policy Report* 25 (2): 1–31. https://eric.ed.gov/?id=ED519240.

Center on the Developing Child. 2009. "Five Numbers to Remember about Early Childhood Development." Center on the Developing Child, Harvard University, Cambridge, MA. https://developingchild.harvard.edu/resources/five-numbers-to-remember-about-early-childhood-development/.

Comings, John P. 2018. "Assessing the Impact of Literacy Learning Games for Syrian Refugee Children: An Executive Overview of Antura and the Letters and Feed the Monster Impact Evaluations." World Vision, Washington, DC; Foundation for Information Technology Education and Development, Quezon City, Philippines.

Department for Education and the Rt Hon Nick Gibb MP. 2018. "Multiplication Tables Check Trials to Begin in Schools." Department for Education, London, February 14. https://www.gov.uk/government/news/multiplication-tables-check-trials-to-begin-in-schools.

Dorn, Emma, Marc Krawitz, Chadi Moujaes, Mona Mourshed, Stephen Hall, and Dirk Schmautzer. 2017. "Drivers of Student Performance: Insights from the Middle East and North Africa." McKinsey and Company, New York. https://www.mckinsey.com/industries/social-sector/our-insights/drivers-of-student-performance-insights-from-the-middle-east-and-north-africa.

Elango, Sneha, Jorge Luis Garcia, James Heckman, and Andrés Hojman. 2015. "Early Childhood Education." NBER Working Paper 21766, National Bureau of Economic Research, Cambridge, MA. http://www.nber.org/papers/w21766.

El-Kogali, Safaa, and Caroline Krafft. 2015. *Expanding Opportunities for the Next Generation*. Washington, DC: World Bank.

Glewwe, Paul. 2013. *Education Policy in Developing Countries*. Chicago: University of Chicago Press.

Gove, Amber, Aarnout Brombacher, and Michelle Ward-Brent. 2017. "Sparking a Reading Revolution: Results of Early Literacy

Interventions in Egypt and Jordan." *New Directions for Child Adolescent Development* 155 (Spring): 97–115.

Graham, Jimmy, and Sean Kelly. 2018. "How Effective Are Early Grade Reading Interventions? A Review of the Evidence." Policy Research Working Paper 8292, World Bank, Washington, DC. http://documents.worldbank.org/curated/en/289341514995676575/How-effective-are-early-grade-reading-interventions-a-review-of-the-evidence.

Heckman, James J. 2006. "Skill Formation and the Economics of Investing in Disadvantaged Children." *Science* 312: 1900–02.

Leseman, Paul. 2002. "Early Childhood Education and Care for Children from Low-Income or Minority Backgrounds." A paper for discussion at the OECD Oslo Workshop, June 6–7.

Nikaein, Samira, and Lindsay Sarah Adams. 2017. "Early Childhood Development in Qatar: Status and Opportunities for the Future." Working paper, World Bank, Washington, DC.

OECD (Organisation for Economic Co-operation and Development). 2012. *Starting Strong III: A Quality Toolbox for Early Childhood Education and Care*. Paris: OECD. http://dx.doi.org/10.1787/9789264123564-en.

———. 2017. *Starting Strong V: Transitions from Early Childhood Education and Care to Primary Education*. Paris: OECD. http://dx.doi.org/10.1787/9789264276253-en.

Schweinhart, Lawrence J., Jeanne Montie, Zongping Xiang, W. Steven Bernett, Clive R. Belfield, and Milagros Nores. 2005. *Lifetime Effects: The High/Scope Perry Preschool Study through Age 40*. Ypsilanti, MI: High/Scope Press.

Shonkoff, Jack P., and Andrew S. Garner. 2012. "The Lifelong Effects of Early Childhood Adversity and Toxic Stress." *Pediatrics* 129 (1): 232–46.

Thacker, Simon, and Ernesto Cuadra. 2014. *The Road Traveled: Dubai's Journey towards Improving Private Education—A World Bank Review*. MENA Development Report. Washington, DC: World Bank. https://openknowledge.worldbank.org/handle/10986/23963.

UNICEF (United Nations Children's Fund). Various years. Multiple Indicator Cluster Surveys (MICS). New York: UNICEF. http://mics.unicef.org/.

United Arab Emirates, Prime Minister's Office. No date. *Vision 2021*. Abu Dhabi: Prime Minister's Office. https://www.vision2021.ae/en/national-agenda-2021/list/card/enrollment-rate-in-preschools-(public-and-private).

United Nations. No date. "Sustainable Development Goal 4." Sustainable Development Goals Knowledge Platform. https://sustainabledevelopment.un.org/sdg4.

USAID (U.S. Agency for International Development). 2014a. "Education Data for Decision Making (EdData II): National Early Grade Literacy and Numeracy Survey—Jordan." Intervention Impact Analysis Report, USAID, Washington, DC. http://pdf.usaid.gov/pdf_docs/PA00KH3M.pdf.

———. 2014b. "Research on Reading in Morocco: Analysis of Initial Teacher Training." Final Report: Component 2, USAID, Washington, DC.

———. Various years. Early Grade Reading Barometer. Washington, DC: USAID. http://www.earlygradereadingbarometer.org/.

Weiland, Christina. 2016. "Launching Preschool 2.0: A Road Map to High-Quality Public Programs at Scale." *Behavioral Science and Policy* 2 (1): 37–46.

Weiland, Christina, and Hirokazu Yoshikawa. 2013. "Impacts of a Prekindergarten Program on Children's Mathematics, Language, Executive Function, and Emotional Skills." *Child Development* 84 (6): 2112–30.

World Bank. 2013. "Yemen Early Childhood Development: SABER Country Report 2013." Systems Approach for Better Education Results (SABER) Country Report, World Bank, Washington, DC. https://openknowledge.worldbank.org/handle/10986/20151.

———. 2014. "Iraq Early Childhood Development: SABER Country Report 2014." Systems Approach for Better Education Results (SABER) Country Report, World Bank, Washington, DC. https://openknowledge.worldbank.org/handle/10986/29522.

———. 2015. "Tunisia Early Childhood Development: SABER Country Report 2015." Systems Approach for Better Education Results (SABER) Country Report, World Bank, Washington, DC. http://documents.worldbank.org/curated/en/986461492508159495/Rapport-du-pays-de-d%C3%A9veloppement-de-la-petite-enfance-SABER-Tunisie-2015.

———. 2018. *World Development Report 2018: Learning to Realize Education's Promise*. Washington, DC: World Bank.

———. Various years. World Bank Education Statistics (EdStats) database. Washington, DC: World Bank. http://datatopics.worldbank.org/education/.

Ensuring Inclusive and Equitable Learning

6

Laura Gregory and
May Bend

Unequal opportunities to learn and progress in school have effects at both the individual and national levels.[1] At the individual level, access to education is a basic human right recognized in the Universal Declaration of Human Rights (1948) and the United Nations Convention on the Rights of the Child (1989). With education, individuals can improve their length of life, earnings, health, and prospects. At the national level, inequalities in learning lower the average level of human capital, thereby affecting economic growth (Klasen 2002). A quality education for all is a sound and strategic government investment decision because it contributes to economic prosperity, poverty reduction, and social inclusion. Without the skills that education develops, governments bear greater social and economic costs in relation to health, welfare, and social security (OECD 2018).

Ensuring universal access to high-quality early childhood education is a clear way to level the playing field, as shown in chapter 5. Removing barriers that prevent children from completing a full course of primary and secondary schooling is also paramount, because well-being and earnings rise with educational attainment. Recognizing disparities where they exist and addressing them through targeted resources and interventions, particularly for the most vulnerable populations, can help to reduce the inequalities found in the region. Raising the learning outcomes of all children will require systematic monitoring of the gap between top and bottom performers and innovative solutions to improve learning experiences for all children.

Remove barriers to access

While impressive efforts have been made across the Middle East and North Africa (MENA) to provide educational opportunities, millions of children are still out of school—around 14 million in 2017. This number includes around 2.9 million children of primary-school age, 3.1 million of lower-secondary-school age, and 7.6 million of upper-secondary-school age.[2] In the MENA region, barriers to access can include unequal distribution of education resources and high out-of-pocket costs. In addition, where children are living in violent contexts ridden with conflict, these fragile conditions pose a barrier to education, negatively affecting learning, along with the development of cognitive and socioemotional skills (see chapter 3).

Focus more resources on children from the poorest households because they are the most likely to be excluded

Large enrollment gaps exist in MENA, particularly between the richest and the poorest children (see figure 6.1). For example, in Morocco, more than half of all children of primary-school age in the poorest quintile of households are out of school compared with 6 percent of children in the richest quintile. Gaps in the rates of out-of-school children also occur by gender and location (urban vs. rural).

Poverty is an important factor in equality of access because it affects exclusion in both direct and indirect ways (UIS and UNICEF 2014). Direct effects of poverty limit children's access to education through financial constraints facing their families, which leave them unable to afford school fees or other education-related expenses. But poverty's indirect effects are equally important. Children from poor families tend to live in rural or remote areas, where school infrastructure is often scarce; they are more likely than their more advantaged peers to be affected by child labor or child marriage (both important causes of dropout in their own right); and they are also less likely to have well-educated parents or to benefit from preprimary education (both important positive predictors of school enrollment).

Although child marriage has declined over time, it continues to be one of the most prominent barriers to schooling (Nguyen and Wodon 2015). The earlier a girl marries, the more likely she is to drop out of school, resulting in lower levels of educational attainment. For example, in the Arab Republic of Egypt, 28 percent of dropouts from secondary and vocational education and training are reportedly due to child marriage (Wodon, Nguyen, et al. 2017). Legal protections against child marriage tend to be weaker in MENA, where 73 percent of girls who are married between the ages of 10 and 17 are not legally safeguarded (Wodon, Tavares, et al. 2017). Potential policies to protect girls from child marriage include (1) establish a legal marriage age, (2) require parental consent, and (3) require judicial consent. However, the enforcement of these regulations continues to be a challenge in rural and isolated areas, where the practice is most widely spread, depriving these girls of an education and the opportunity to reach their full potential.

FIGURE 6.1 In MENA, household wealth disparities translate into large enrollment gaps

Percentage of children of primary school age who are not in school

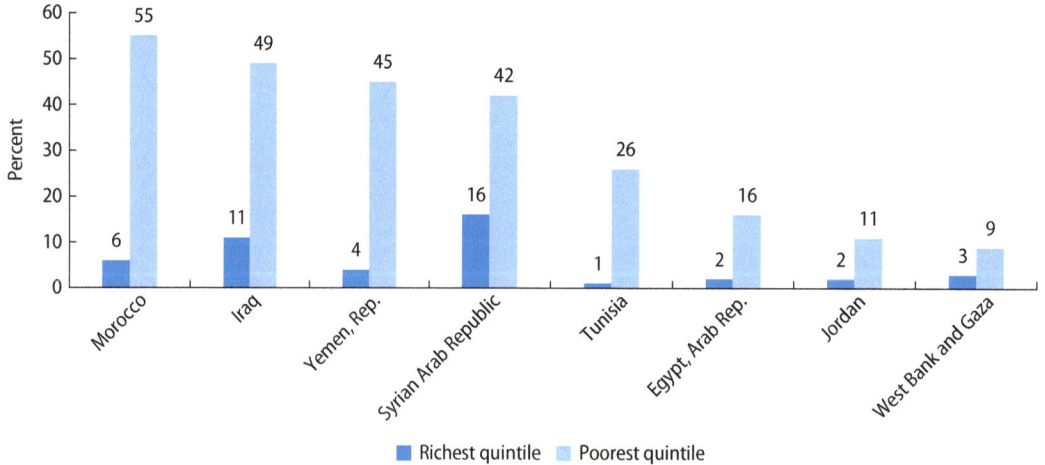

Source: WID.World World Inequality Database on Education (https://wid.world/).
Note: Data are for the following years: Arab Republic of Egypt (2014); Iraq (2011); Jordan (2012); Morocco (2003); Syrian Arab Republic (2006); Tunisia (2011); West Bank and Gaza (2014); Republic of Yemen (2006).

Reduce or offset out-of-pocket education expenses because they reinforce inequality of opportunity

Private spending on education is substantial in the MENA region and tends to be regressive. Poorer households typically spend a larger share of their income on education-related expenses than wealthier households. Based on available data covering six MENA countries from 2002 to 2015, World Bank estimates suggest that private spending on education in MENA is substantially above the average for Organisation for Economic Co-operation and Development (OECD) countries (discussed in more detail in chapter 11).[3] Not surprisingly, household spending on education is large in countries where government expenditure on education as a share of gross domestic product (GDP) is below international benchmarks. In addition, public spending that is geared toward richer households can exacerbate inequality of opportunity.

Moreover, public spending on education can be regressive in some countries where children from wealthier households are more likely to enroll in (public) school than children from poorer households. For example, in Djibouti, public expenditure per child enrolled in primary education is 1.5 times higher for the richest income quartile than for the poorest. At the secondary level, the disparity factor increases to 11 (World Bank 2006). In education systems where fewer children from poorer households are able to access public education, public spending tends to benefit wealthier households disproportionately. The poor-rich disparity in benefiting from government expenditure on education is usually greatest at the tertiary education level, which few students from disadvantaged backgrounds reach in many countries. This situation can further exacerbate inequality of opportunity (Krafft and Alawode 2018; UIS et al. 2018).

High levels of private spending in low- and middle-income countries raise serious concerns about the regressive nature of private payments. In West Bank and Gaza, inequalities in educational access with regard to income appear to be relatively small, but household expenditure on education varies enormously (the richest households spend more than 80 times more on education than the poorest households—approximately US$800 versus US$10 per year, respectively) (World Bank 2007). In Djibouti, parents spend up to 12 percent of their monthly income on school fees and other education-related costs (World Bank 2006).

In countries for which participation in basic education requires out-of-pocket expenditures (whether direct or indirect), children from households that can afford to make the necessary payments often enjoy a greater degree of access and opportunity. In contrast, children whose families cannot afford to pay for school—either through formal school fees or through informal payments for expenses such as materials, uniforms, and transportation—can be shut out from enjoying the full benefits of schooling. This is of particular concern in countries in which public schools either do not reach all of the population or provide an inferior education to what students receive in schools with paid attendance.

MENA governments can remove barriers to education access by focusing more resources on children from the poorest households, who are the most likely to be excluded. One effective means of removing barriers is through conditional cash transfer (CCT) programs. CCTs target resources to disadvantaged groups and have proven to be an effective means of preventing dropout in countries around the world. Bolsa Família in Brazil and Oportunidades in Mexico are two of the longest-running and most widely researched CCT programs in the world. Both show positive impacts on the education trajectories of participants.

While well-designed and carefully implemented CCTs often prove to be an effective policy response to offset the economic barriers to education, they are relatively uncommon in the MENA region. Morocco's Tayssir program is one of the few examples from the region, and it has been proven to raise school attendance (Benhassine et al. 2015). This program, which began in 2009, conditions financial support for the most vulnerable households on school enrollment of primary-school-age children. The Government of Morocco has expanded the program, and it now reaches almost 700,000 students (see World Bank n.d.).

Recognize and address learning gaps by supporting the lowest-performing students and schools

Inequality exists not only in access to education but also in its quality, leading to substantial learning gaps between students of different socioeconomic levels and exacerbating intergenerational inequities. As is often seen in countries across the world, academic performance is positively correlated with the economic, social, and cultural status (ESCS) of the student's household. This can result in substantial disparities in performance for students from high-ESCS households compared with those from low-ESCS households. Figure 6.2 shows Programme for International Student Assessment (PISA) scores for students from the top quarter of ESCS households in each country compared with those in the bottom quarter. Based on these data, Lebanon has the greatest gap in socioeconomic performance, equal to a difference of more than two full years of schooling.

Focus more resources on the bottom performers to reduce achievement gaps

While average levels of student performance on international assessments in key subjects have been low, student performance varies widely within each country. In fact, MENA countries have some of the widest disparities in student performance on international assessments. In many high-income countries, such as Canada, Estonia, Finland, and Japan, high levels of academic performance exist alongside low levels of academic inequality; in these countries, the link between test

FIGURE 6.2 **In MENA, socioeconomic differences translate into persistent learning gaps**

Average score of 15-year-old students on the PISA science literacy scale, by national quarters of the PISA index of economic, social, and cultural status (ESCS), 2015

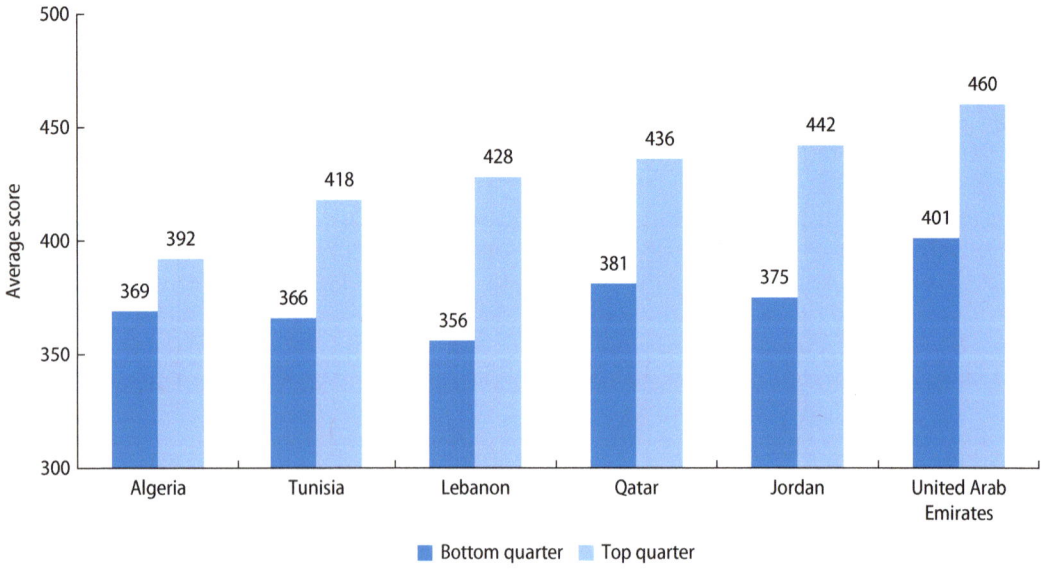

Source: OECD 2016.
Note: PISA = Programme for International Student Assessment.

scores and socioeconomic status is generally weak. In contrast, MENA countries exhibit some of the widest disparities in student performance on international assessments (see figure 6.3). All nine of the MENA countries that participated in the 2015 grade 4 Trends in International Mathematics and Science Study (TIMSS) mathematics assessment were among the 13 countries with the widest gaps between the top and bottom quarters of performance. Improving performance among those at the bottom would provide the most rapid improvement in overall levels of learning.

Gaps in performance are narrowing in some countries and increasing in others

The inequality map is changing within MENA: some countries are closing the achievement gap between their best and poorest performers, while the gap in others appears to be widening. Table 6.1 shows the MENA countries that participated in the grade 8 TIMSS 2015 assessment ordered by the amount of increase in their average scores from 2011 to 2015 in mathematics and science. In Bahrain, the Islamic Republic of Iran, Morocco, Oman, and Qatar,

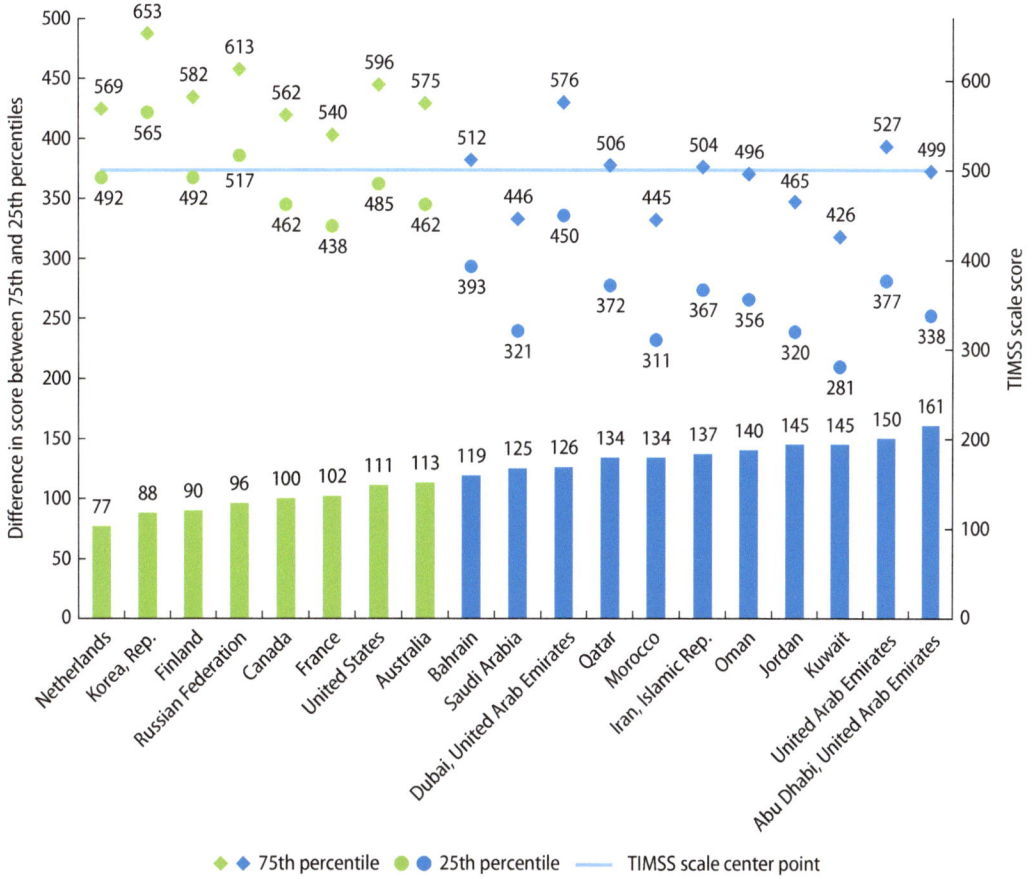

FIGURE 6.3 MENA has the biggest gaps in student achievement between top and bottom performers
Difference in scale score between the 75th and 25th percentiles of grade 4 mathematics achievement, TIMSS 2015

Source: Mullis et al. 2016.
Note: Includes all participating MENA countries (blue) and a selection of other countries. The diamonds represent the 75th percentile scores, and the circles represent the 25th percentile scores in the selected comparison countries. The blue horizontal line represents the TIMSS scale center point, which is the mean of the overall achievement distribution in 1995 (kept constant over the years). TIMSS = Trends in International Mathematics and Science Study.

TABLE 6.1 **MENA's student achievement gaps have both narrowed and widened**
Change in grade 8 TIMSS average achievement, 10th and 90th percentiles, 2011 and 2015

	Average score		Change in		
Country	2011	2015	Average score	10th percentile	90th percentile
Mathematics					
Bahrain	409	454	45	72	19
Oman	366	403	37	54	22
Qatar	410	437	27	40	20
Iran, Islamic Rep.	415	436	21	20	23
Morocco	371	384	13	20	8
United Arab Emirates	456	465	9	−4	23
Lebanon	449	442	−7	−7	−7
Jordan	406	386	−20	−8	−22
Saudi Arabia	394	368	−26	−13	−35
Science					
Qatar	419	457	38	52	19
Oman	420	455	35	54	19
Morocco	376	393	17	18	16
Bahrain	452	466	14	12	18
United Arab Emirates	465	477	12	−3	22
Lebanon	406	398	−8	−13	−2
Iran, Islamic Rep.	474	456	−18	−16	−19
Jordan	449	426	−23	−15	−21
Saudi Arabia	436	396	−40	−59	−20

Source: Mullis et al. 2016, 72.
Note: TIMSS = Trends in International Mathematics and Science Study.

mathematics scores increased at both ends of the distribution—the low performers at the 10th percentile and the top performers at the 90th percentile. For mathematics, Bahrain, Oman, and Qatar made substantial advances among the lowest-scoring students; for science, this improvement occurred in Oman and Qatar. The United Arab Emirates is a notable case in this regard, with gains at the top of the spectrum and declines at the bottom, meaning that the top students are performing better, but the lowest performers are faring worse.

Target resources to in-need geographic regions

Geography plays a role in learning opportunities across MENA. While some countries provide better education services in urban areas, this is not always the case and depends on the local context. Inequalities in education provision lead to varying learning outcomes that occur across geographic locations and are often linked to socioeconomic circumstances. Students from urban areas tend to be significantly more advantaged in countries such as Morocco and Saudi Arabia.[4] There is less of a difference in countries such as Lebanon and Oman. Differences in urban and rural learning outcomes are common in MENA, but whether it is urban or rural students who tend to have higher achievement differs by country. Accordingly, for MENA countries to tackle inequalities in educational achievement, each country needs to have a geographic lens for targeting resources to the specific urban or rural areas that are falling behind.

Improve the quality of boys' education and address MENA's gender paradox

With regard to gender equality, MENA has a unique paradox. Gender parity in access to education has been achieved in most countries. However, in some countries, access to secondary school for girls still needs to improve. However, MENA's gender paradox lies in the advantage of females in learning outcomes and their disadvantage in labor market participation. MENA has some of the largest learning gaps in favor of girls, yet the lowest female labor force participation rates in the world. That is, while the push to learn exists, there is no corresponding pull from the labor market. This amounts to a loss of talent or missed opportunity across the region—for men, due to their underperformance in learning, and for women, due to their inability to reap economic benefits from the human capital investments they have accrued.

Gender gaps in learning appear early and persist throughout the educational levels

Gender gaps in learning manifest early. By grade 2, girls outperform boys in MENA countries in reading (see figure 6.4). The Early Grade Reading Assessments (EGRA) in West Bank, for example, show that the difference between girls and boys in the percentage who cannot read a single word of connected text is 10 percentage points—27 percent of boys cannot read a single word compared with 17 percent of girls. Across all countries taking the EGRA (in 2010–15), the gap is the most pronounced for MENA countries.

MENA has the largest gender disparities in student achievement, with boys consistently scoring lower than girls

Not only are learning outcomes in MENA strikingly low, they are also among the most gender unequal in the world. Figure 6.5 shows the countries in the 2015 TIMSS grade 4 science assessment with the highest point differences in favor of girls. The MENA region has 8 out of the 10 countries with the largest gaps, with Saudi Arabian girls outperforming boys by almost a standard deviation in test scores. Given that learning outcomes

FIGURE 6.4 **Gender gaps in MENA start early**
Difference (girls – boys) in oral reading fluency (percentage unable to read a single word of connected text), EGRA grade 2

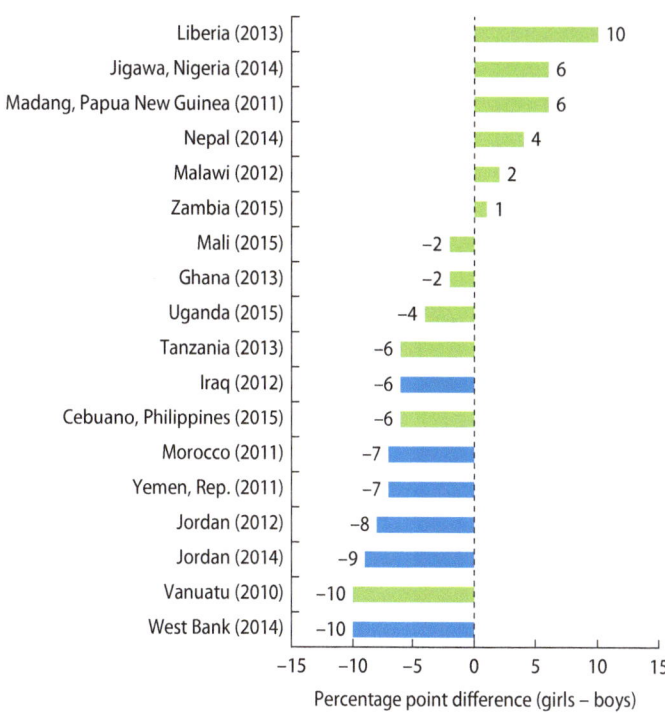

Source: USAID Early Grade Reading Barometer (https://earlygradereadingbarometer.org/).
Note: EGRA = Early Grade Reading Assessment.

FIGURE 6.5 **MENA has the largest gender gaps in test scores**
Score point difference in science (girls – boys), countries with the highest score point difference, TIMSS grade 4, 2015

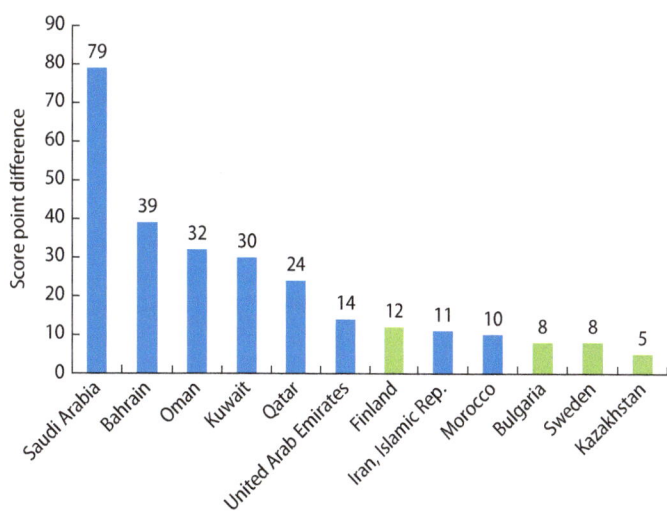

Source: Martin et al. 2016.
Note: The difference between girls and boys in the Islamic Republic of Iran is not statistically significant. TIMSS = Trends in International Mathematics and Science Study.

for all MENA students are low, the pervasive gender gap amounts to a learning crisis for boys in the region. In short, the underperformance of MENA's boys, a phenomenon on a scale not seen elsewhere in the world, requires a push for education systems to address the quality of boys' education.

Education systems in the MENA region need to meet the learning needs of boys

The early manifestation of gender gaps in foundational skills such as literacy and numeracy points to the need to address the specific learning needs of boys in the early grades. Indeed, interventions that are not targeted to boys and to students in need of additional support may exacerbate the gender gap (see box 6.1).

The gender gap in learning lingers on through primary and into secondary school. At grade 4 and grade 8, most countries participating in the TIMSS 2015 with gender gaps in favor of girls were from the MENA region (Martin et al. 2016; Mullis et al. 2016). Likewise, at age 15, large gender differences in favor of girls were found in all MENA countries that participated in the PISA 2015 reading assessment and in most MENA countries in science and mathematics (OECD 2016). Jordan, Qatar, and the United Arab Emirates had some of the biggest gender gaps, equivalent to girls having approximately one additional year of schooling in science and two additional years in reading.

The message from these assessments of student achievement could not be clearer. Education systems in the MENA region are not meeting the learning needs of boys. The inefficiencies and costs associated with this loss of learning are substantial, spanning from economic to social. The results of student assessments clearly indicate that systems are currently not working for boys. Further examining the reasons for poor learning among boys and identifying policies to address them could be a helpful first step (see, for example, Ridge 2014).

Box 6.1 **Early grade literacy and numeracy interventions in Jordan have had different impacts on girls and boys**

Early grade literacy and numeracy interventions need to be gender targeted, specifically in single-sex school environments. The 2014 U.S. Agency for International Development (USAID) report on the Jordan National Early Grade Literacy and Numeracy Survey found that boys did not benefit from an early grade reading intervention to the extent that girls benefited (USAID 2014).

Jordan's 2012 Early Grade Reading Assessment (EGRA) and Early Grade Mathematics Assessment (EGMA) found that children in the early grades were not reading with comprehension or understanding mathematics as expected. A one-year pilot intervention was conducted, in which teachers spent the first 15 minutes of each reading and mathematics class revisiting and reinforcing foundational skills.

The intervention was successful for girls—girls made significant gains on all EGRA and EGMA subtasks. However, boys did not benefit from the intervention; in fact, there were no significant gains on any of the EGRA or EGMA subtasks.

Students in all-girl schools performed better than students in mixed schools, who in turn performed better than students in all-boy schools (all differences were statistically significant). In MENA countries, where single-sex schools are common and where gender gaps in favor of girls are pronounced, it will be important to increase learning levels by paying attention to gender-specific elements of teaching and learning.

Source: USAID 2014.

MENA's gender paradox undermines human capital development

The large gender gap in learning has important implications for females, particularly in the labor market, where women are underrepresented. Female labor force participation in the MENA region is the lowest in the world (World Bank 2017). On average across all MENA countries, only 20 percent of women ages 15 or older participate in the labor force (see figure 6.6). The percentage point difference in labor force participation for men and women ages 15 or older is most pronounced in Algeria, Iraq, Jordan, Saudi Arabia, and West Bank and Gaza. In short, there is not a sufficient pull for women to enter MENA's workforce.

This paradox—whereby girls outperform boys in learning from the early years all the way to adulthood but women are not equally represented in the labor market—reflects substantial underutilization of human capital.

An important means of combating MENA's gender paradox is to use targeted interventions to increase access to learning opportunities. For example, the innovative Ishraq program in Egypt, targeted at girls who have dropped out of school, has improved girls' literacy skills and self-confidence and led to greater mobility and participation of girls in the local community. Launched in 2001, Ishraq is a multidimensional program for girls ages 12 to 15 that combines literacy, life skills, and nutrition with sports and financial education. Classes are held at youth centers and focus on mobilizing communities around issues important for girls through partnerships. The program has directly reached 3,321 girls and 1,775 boys in 54 villages, as well as more than 5,000 parents and community leaders across five of the most disadvantaged governorates in Upper Egypt (Selim et al. 2013).

Increase resources for special needs to reduce inequality

Across the world, more attention is being paid to the education of children with physical disabilities, learning difficulties, and other special educational needs. While policies vary by the

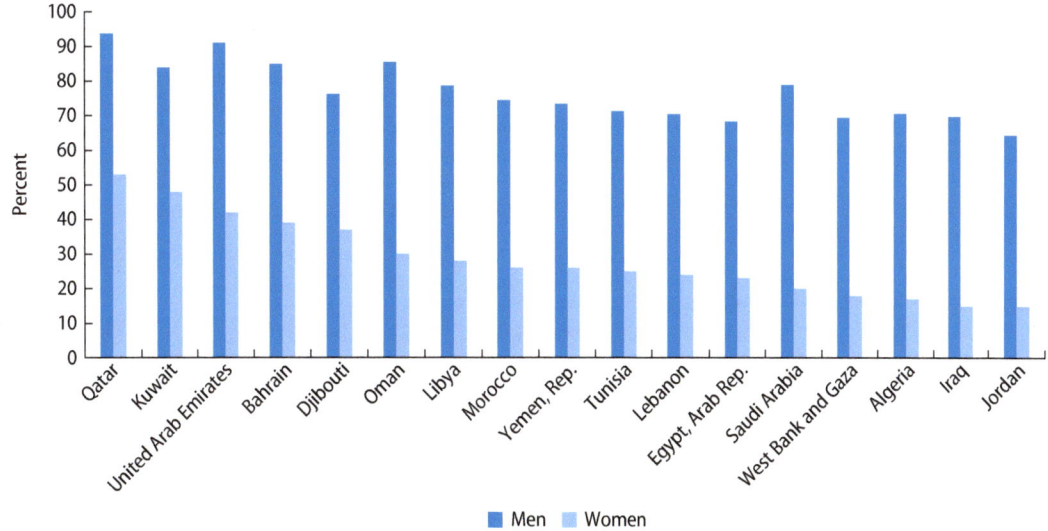

FIGURE 6.6 **Female labor force participation is low in MENA**
Labor force participation rates for men and women ages 15 and older, 2016 (ILO modeled estimates)

Source: World Bank 2017.
Note: ILO = International Labour Organization.

education setting—including special schools, special classes in integrated schools, or inclusive classrooms—there is broad agreement that inclusive classrooms, where children learn alongside their peers, are desirable (UNESCO 2001). In addition, there is a better understanding across the world of how children learn and the appropriate developmental milestones. Learning difficulties are being picked up at earlier stages. Promising efforts are taking place internationally to recognize the needs of these students and to personalize their schooling experiences so that their needs are met (Deng and Harris 2008).

Some MENA countries have established policies to protect the rights of children and youths with disabilities, including the right to receive appropriate education. For example, Tunisia adopted measures to integrate children with minor disabilities into regular schools, and both Jordan and Tunisia declared their commitment to providing educational services for children with special needs, among others (Save the Children 2008). However, negative attitudes toward disability and special education exist in MENA, and awareness needs to be increased (see box 6.2).

Although estimates suggest that nearly 53 million persons with disabilities live in MENA, most countries of the region still have a limited supply of special education services. Reasons may include (1) inadequate facilities, (2) unqualified teacher workforce and inappropriate curricula, (3) lack of funding, and (4) negative attitudes toward disability and special education (Alkhateeb and Hadidi 2015).

Although several MENA countries (for example, Jordan, Kuwait, Qatar, Saudi Arabia, and the United Arab Emirates) have developed regulations and policies to create barrier-free accessible environments for students with disabilities, physical inaccessibility and inadequate school facilities remain a challenge. There is also a serious shortage of support personnel such as school psychologists, sign-language interpreters, speech and language pathologists, and physical and occupational therapists (Alkhateeb and Hadidi 2015). Similarly, training programs for special education teachers lack adequate standards and practical activities in the classroom. Curricula for special education programs are almost nonexistent in most MENA countries (Alkhateeb and Hadidi 2015). These factors pose a challenge to the implementation of inclusive models in countries of the MENA region and ultimately to the integration of students with special needs in the mainstream education system.

Major sources of special education funding in MENA countries include governments, international development agencies, parents, and NGOs (Alkhateeb and Hadidi 2015). Existing public special education institutions and programs face financial constraints that prevent them from investing in

---

Box 6.2   Negative attitudes toward disability and special education exist in MENA

Abuse and mistreatment of disabled people, particularly girls and women, still occur in some countries of the region. In fact, women and girls with disabilities are more likely to suffer gender violence and abuse at home. Furthermore, studies conducted in MENA countries have shown a lack of awareness of disability issues and the rights of students with special needs among schoolteachers, senior-level administrators, the public, and health care providers.

Negative attitudes toward persons with disabilities and special education hamper efforts by governments, the private sector, and nongovernmental organizations (NGOs) to expand inclusive education services so that special needs children and youths can enjoy fulfilling lives and develop successfully in society.

Source: Al Thani 2007.

facility improvement, capacity strengthening of special education teachers, and tailored curriculum development. Similarly, most private special education schools and centers in MENA countries also deal with fund-raising difficulties. In both rich and poor MENA countries, lack of funding for public and private institutions and initiatives reflects the lack of awareness in the region about the importance of inclusive education and high-quality education services for students with special needs.

Increasing retention through targeted programs can help students with learning challenges to stay in school. Morocco's Urgency program, implemented between 2009 and 2012, expanded support units in schools to identify children and youths who are at risk of dropping out and provided pedagogical support to enhance their chances of remaining in school. These units included the head teacher, teachers, local associations, and parents. These support units exist in more than 1,000 schools and provide support for 38,000 students and remedial lessons for 450,000 students. Targeted programs can also help students at risk of dropping out to stay in school. Tunisia has established national programs to prevent early school leaving in primary and lower secondary, including the Social Action Program (UIS and UNICEF 2014). This initiative tasked social units in schools with identifying students' difficulties and social-adjustment problems. Social units were composed of social workers, psychologists, doctors, and school directors to provide targeted support to struggling children. The program reached nearly 2,300 students between 2006 and 2007 and covered nearly 40 percent of schools.

Across MENA, a push is needed to create a more inclusive and equitable learning system. By expanding access to high-quality early childhood development programs, removing barriers to access, and identifying and addressing disparities where they exist, MENA governments can design, target, and scale up innovative efforts to address inequalities in education access and learning. Indeed, in several countries vulnerable groups are receiving targeted interventions aimed at ensuring that students stay in school and develop skills they will need for the rest of their lives.

Notes

1. Inequality of opportunity exists where unequal outcomes are caused by factors beyond an individual's control.
2. United Nations Educational, Scientific, and Cultural Organization (UNESCO) Institute for Statistics (UIS) data retrieved from the World Bank EdStats database.
3. Limited data are available on household spending for education in MENA countries, and what little are available tend to be out of date. This information should not be considered comprehensive.
4. UIS World Inequality Database on Education.

References

Alkhateeb, Jamal, and Muna Hadidi. 2015. "Special Education in Arab Countries: Current Challenges." *International Journal of Disability Development and Education* 62 (5): 518–30.

Al Thani, Hissa. 2007. "Disability in the Arab Region: Current Situation and Prospects." *Journal of Adult Education and Development* 68: n.p.

Benhassine, Najy, Florencia Devoto, Esther Duflo, Pascaline Dupas, and Victor Pouliquen. 2015. "Turning a Shove into a Nudge? A 'Labeled Cash Transfer' for Education." *American Economic Journal: Economic Policy* 7 (3): 86–125. https://www.povertyactionlab.org/evaluation/cash-transfers-education-morocco.

Deng, Meng, and Kymberly Harris. 2008. "Meeting the Needs of Students with Disabilities in General Education Classrooms in China." *Teacher Education and Special Education* 31 (3): 195–207.

Klasen, Stephan. 2002. "Low Schooling for Girls, Slower Growth for All?" *World Bank Economic Review* 16 (3): 343–73.

Krafft, Caroline and Halimat Alawode. 2018 "Inequality of Opportunity in Higher Education in the Middle East and North Africa." *International Journal of Educational Development* 62: 234–44.

Martin, Michael O., Ina V. S. Mullis, Pierre Foy, and M. Hooper. 2016. "TIMSS 2015 International Results in Science." TIMSS and PIRLS International Study Center, Boston College, Chestnut Hill, MA. http://timssandpirls.bc.edu/timss2015/international-results/.

Mullis, Ina V. S., Michael O. Martin, Pierre Foy, and M. Hooper. 2016. "TIMSS 2015 International Results in Mathematics." TIMSS and PIRLS International Study Center, Boston College, Chestnut Hill, MA. http://timssandpirls.bc.edu/timss2015/international-results/.

Nguyen, Minh Cong, and Quentin Wodon. 2015. "Global and Regional Trends in Child Marriage." *Review of Faith and International Affairs* 13 (3): 23–31.

OECD (Organisation for Economic Co-operation and Development). 2016. *PISA 2015 Results: Excellence and Equity in Education*. Vol. 1. Paris: OECD.

———. 2018. "Ten Steps to Equity in Education." Policy Brief, OECD, Paris. http://oecd.org/education/school/39989494.pdf.

Ridge, Natasha. 2014. *Education and the Reverse Gender Divide in the Gulf States*. New York: Teachers College Press.

Save the Children. 2008. *Child Rights Situation Analysis for Middle East and North Africa Region*. Stockholm: Save the Children.

Selim, Mona, Nahla Abdel-Tawab, Khaled Elsayed, Asmaa El Badawy, and Heba El Kalaawy. 2013. "The Ishraq Program for Out-of-School Girls: From Pilot to Scale-Up." Population Council, Cairo.

UIS (UNESCO Institute for Statistics). Various years. World Inequality Database on Education. Paris: UIS. https://www.education-inequalities.org/.

UIS, FHI 360, Oxford Policy Management, and REAL (Research for Equitable Access and Learning) Centre, University of Cambridge. 2018. *Handbook on Measuring Equity in Education*. Montreal: UIS. http://uis.unesco.org/en/news/new-report-how-measure-equity-education.

UIS and UNICEF (United Nations Children's Fund). 2014. *Regional Report on Out-of-School Children*. All in School: Middle East and North Africa Out-of-School Children Initiative (OOSCI). Paris: UIS and UNICEF, October. http://www.oosci-mena.org/regional-overview.

UNESCO (United Nations Educational, Scientific, and Cultural Organization). 2001. *Understanding and Responding to Children's Needs in Inclusive Classrooms*. Paris: UNESCO.

USAID (U.S. Agency for International Development). 2014. "Education Data for Decision Making (EdData II): National Early Grade Literacy and Numeracy Survey—Jordan." Intervention Impact Analysis Report, USAID, Washington, DC. http://pdf.usaid.gov/pdf_docs/PA00KH3M.pdf.

———. Various years. Early Grade Reading Barometer. Washington, DC: USAID. http://www.earlygradereadingbarometer.org/.

Wodon, Quenton, Minh Cibg Nguyen, Ali Yedan, and J. Edmeades. 2017. *Economic Impacts of Child Marriage: Educational Attainment*. Washington, DC: World Bank. http://www.right-to-education.org/resource/economic-impacts-child-marriage-educational-attainment.

Wodon, Quenton, Paula Tavares, Oliver Fiala, Alexis Le Nestour, and Lisa Wise. 2017. *Ending Child Marriage: Child Marriage Laws and Their Limitations*. Washington, DC: World Bank.

World Bank. 2006. "Republic of Djibouti Public Expenditure Review: Making Public Finances Work for Growth and Poverty Reduction." World Bank, Washington, DC. http://documents.worldbank.org/curated/en/458211468245383445/Djibouti-Public-Expenditure-Review-PER-making-public-finances-work-for-growth-and-poverty-reduction.

———. 2007. "West Bank and Gaza Public Expenditure Review: From Crisis to Greater Fiscal Independence." Vol. 2, World Bank, Washington, DC. https://openknowledge.worldbank.org/handle/10986/7807.

———. 2017. *World Development Indicators 2017*. Washington, DC: World Bank. https://openknowledge.worldbank.org/handle/10986/26447.

———. No date. "Morocco: Can Cash Transfers Help a Country Reach Universal Primary School Education?" World Bank, Washington, DC. https://www.worldbank.org/en/programs/sief-trust-fund/brief/morocco-can-cash-transfers-make-a-difference-in-childrens-schooling.

———. Various years. Education Statistics (EdStats) database. Washington, DC: World Bank. http://datatopics.worldbank.org/education/.

SPOTLIGHT 1

CHOOSING A LANGUAGE OF INSTRUCTION

May Bend and
Laura Gregory

The complex linguistic situation common to countries in the Middle East and North Africa (MENA) adds educational difficulties for students. The choice of a language of instruction (LOI) is especially complicated—shaped by culture, history, and current economic and political trends—when opportunities for social and economic advancement are higher in a language that is not a student's mother tongue. For decades, tensions between modernity and tradition have affected the LOI in MENA countries, and changing the LOI has been one of the key education reforms in several MENA countries.

First, MENA faces the challenge of using modern standard Arabic (MSA)—also known as classical Arabic—in the classroom, which amounts to a new language that children must learn when they start school. Second, some MENA countries have populations with multiple first languages, leading to difficult political decisions regarding the choice of LOI. Third, as globalization increases, the need for MENA's students to learn a second, or even a third, language is growing. The use of a foreign language for instruction has been a topic of debate in MENA countries, with major implications for learning.

Changes in the LOI have sometimes led to unintended consequences. For example, the 1980s movement of Algerian and Tunisian public education away from instruction in French and toward MSA increased educational inequality, as elites put their children into French-speaking schools, instead of leading to the intended increase in classical Arabic skills. Furthermore, students who did not learn French were at a disadvantage for future economic opportunities, as higher-income positions continued to require French fluency (Benrabah 2007; Lefevre 2015).

Learning in a new language is a complex task. Finding a balance between adequate learning time in children's mother tongue, the tradition of MSA, and the economic and social importance of learning foreign languages poses an important challenge for MENA countries.

Modern standard Arabic

A unique challenge for Arabic-instruction education systems is the required mastery of MSA (Abadzi 2014). From a purely pedagogical viewpoint, the use of classical Arabic as the LOI is challenging for large segments of the population because of the linguistic distance between the living form of Arabic spoken at home and the traditional, erudite language used as the official language in most MENA nations.

Classical Arabic originated from pre-Islamic central Arabian tribes and acquired a privileged, sacred status as the language of the Quran. While it was codified after centuries of written tradition and has remained more or less unaltered for the last thousand years, the versions of the Arabic language spoken in the various countries of the region evolved over the centuries. The spoken Arabic languages—their phonetics, vocabulary, morphology, grammar, and structure—have changed considerably (Al-Huri 2015).

As an LOI, MSA is difficult to learn. For example, the absence of vowels makes it necessary to understand what the words mean before being able to read them, which is not always straightforward. Consequently, students may struggle to acquire basic literacy skills and may feel substantial linguistic insecurity due to their lack of identification and familiarity with MSA (Maamouri 1998). Indeed, research has shown that all students in the MENA region may be at a linguistic disadvantage because students learn MSA as if it were a second language (Abadzi 2014; Bouhlila 2011; Ibrahim and Aharon-Peretz 2005; Salmi 1987). Features of the language mean that it is more difficult to identify letters in Arabic than in Roman script (taking experienced readers about three times longer), and the deletion of vowels at grades 3–4 creates visual crowding, slowing down reading and requiring a reliance on context and memorization (Abadzi 2014). If students fail to achieve both oral and written comprehension of MSA in early primary school, their future studies are limited to memorizing and regurgitating information without synthesizing the information. Where teachers are themselves not comfortable operating in MSA, the problem is exacerbated (Salmi 1987).

Some MENA countries have addressed the MSA/dual-language challenge by designing curricular materials and providing additional support in the early grades. For example, interventions funded by the U.S. Agency for International Development (USAID) and implemented in conjunction with the ministries of education in the Arab Republic of Egypt and Jordan have shown promise and are being scaled up. In Jordan the intervention included implementing daily time for low-performing students to practice foundational skills in reading and mathematics. Beyond enhanced curricular emphasis on foundational skills, the intervention provided teachers with 10 days of training and additional in-school coaching on how to target remedial support to students who need it. As a result, not only did the number of low-performing students decrease, but the number of high-performing students increased. In Egypt the program included eight days of teacher training in addition to curriculum inputs. Grade 2 students who received six months of intervention improved their performance by an entire grade level (Gove, Brombacher, and Ward-Brent 2017). A phonics-based program in Egypt, the USAID's Girls' Improved Learning Outcomes project, has also yielded promising outcomes (Abadzi 2012).

Multiple local languages

MENA countries often have communities speaking languages other than Arabic, for example, Amazigh and Tamazight in the three Northern African MENA countries or Kurdish in Iraq and the Syrian Arab Republic. These linguistic groups represent a substantial share of the total population (35 percent in Morocco, 15–30 percent in Algeria, 18 percent in Iraq, 12 percent in Syria, and 4 percent in Libya), but they have not historically been schooled in their mother tongue (Absi 2008; Suleiman 1999). The consensus among educational experts is that learning takes place more effectively when young children are taught to write and read in their own language (Benson 2005; Carter 2003; Salmi 1987). As several nations consider moving to instruction in local languages to improve learning, policies must be put in place to ensure its successful implementation.

Instruction in a foreign language

Mastery of students' mother tongue does not guarantee economic opportunity, and families recognize this fact. For example, in Algeria, parents who speak Tamazight at home have reported being reluctant to educate their children in Tamazight schools for fear of limiting their future career opportunities (Hayat Chaif 2015). University graduates in Egypt who studied in English earn more after graduation than those studying in Arabic (Assaad, Krafft, and Salehi-Isfahani 2018). As they move through the education system, MENA students need to receive training in languages that provide access to economic advancement in increasingly globalized labor markets.

Before students can learn *in* an LOI, they need to have learned enough *of* the LOI.

This is because every language has a vocabulary threshold required to understand simple text. For example, in order to understand English texts, students must understand at least 5,000 words in English. Typically, children come to school knowing 4,000 to 6,000 words in their mother tongue. On average, children can learn four vocabulary words per hour of second language instruction. Thus it takes 1,000 or more schooling hours to build sufficient vocabulary to begin learning in a second language (van Ginkel 2014).

If teaching in a second language is needed, when should it become the primary LOI? The critical period hypothesis claims that children are born with an innate language faculty that diminishes with age, and therefore it is important to tap into these innate mechanisms before the critical age when they disappear (Johnson and Newport 1989; Krashen 1975). Assuming that this is true, is younger really better when learning a foreign language in the classroom? It depends on what is meant by "better." If "better" means faster vocabulary acquisition, the research shows that older children outperform younger children because their greater cognitive maturity helps them to make the best of second language instruction (Muñoz 2006; Myles 2017). Indeed, studies indicate that efficiency in formal language learning increases with age, so older students (those over the age of 12) appear to have an advantage over younger learners (Singleton and Lengyel 1995; Thompson and Gaddes 2005).

A recent study in England compared how children ages 5, 7, and 11 learn French in the classroom. All children were complete beginners at the start of the project and received two hours a week of similar instruction from the same teacher over 19 weeks. This study found that the older children learn faster, as they are better able to use a range of cognitive strategies to aid their learning and that they are able to use their more advanced literacy skills to support foreign language learning (Myles 2017).

Perhaps the most ambitious piece of research investigating the role of age in early foreign language learning in the classroom is the Barcelona Age Factor project (Muñoz 2006). Muñoz and her team capitalized on the fact that the government changed, in rapid succession, the age at which English was introduced in the classroom, creating a natural experiment whereby they were able to compare second language learners who started at 8, 11, 14, and more than 18 years of age. The team of researchers was able to follow a large number of these learners over a long period of time (learners were tested after 200, 416, and 726 hours of instruction). They then compared the students' learning on a wide range of measures by testing speaking, listening, writing, and reading skills. They found that, with the same amount of instruction, late starters were consistently faster and more efficient learners on all measures. Nevertheless, several other studies have shown that younger children are more enthusiastic second language learners than older children (Cable et al. 2010; Myles 2017). In short, evidence is mixed on whether second languages are best learned earlier, when cognitive plasticity is greater, or later, when maturity and study habits ideally are better developed.

Begin in the child's mother tongue

Among education experts, consensus exists that learning during the early grades takes place most effectively when young children are taught to write and read in their mother tongue (Salmi 1987). Accordingly, students should be given adequate instructional time in their mother tongue to ensure fluency before being exposed to a foreign LOI.

Language capital—the ability to communicate in the mother tongue—is generally acquired at home and strengthened at school. However, when early schooling, or a substantial portion of early schooling, takes place in a second language, development of language fluency is interrupted. Poor language skills can result in time spent memorizing terminology in the LOI rather than understanding concepts. Essentially, students' ability to develop higher conceptual functioning is limited by their lack of first language vocabulary for information digested in a foreign language (Salmi 1987; Yip, Tsang, and Cheung 2003), which, in turn, has a detrimental impact on their ability to learn classroom material and to perform on examinations in the LOI (Marsh, Hau, and Kong 2002; Yip, Tsang, and Cheung 2003). Poor language skills result in lower numeracy skills, which show up in international tests based on word problems (Toll and Van Luit 2014; Yore, Pimm, and Tuan 2007).

For these reasons, research suggests that children should be taught primarily in their mother tongue during the early years, with limited hours of instruction in a second language (to capitalize on the enthusiasm of young language learners). The use of second or third languages for instruction should take place in later years of schooling, after students have had sufficient time to build fluency in their mother tongue and to acquire the necessary base of vocabulary to engage with subject material upon introduction of a foreign LOI. The quality of language acquisition during the earlier grades has important implications for learning later in life.

Increase research into Arabic-language learning

The challenges of MSA are well known, but there are few proven interventions to help overcome them. Cognitive science holds potential to improve understanding of the complexities and point to ways to improve the learning of Arabic (Abadzi 2014). Where research suggests potential solutions, a variety of interventions should be designed, implemented, and evaluated in schools so that the benefits, if any, can be measured.

Improve foreign language instruction at all levels

Across MENA, lack of mastery of foreign languages by many secondary school graduates adds a degree of difficulty for those who pursue university education in English or French. In Dubai, public school studies take place in both Arabic and English, beginning in grade 1. Science and mathematics in all grades are taught in English, while Arabic language, social studies, and geography are taught in Arabic (Ofori-Attah 2008). Thus students have to master a second language to succeed in mathematics.

While the goal of training students for global business is admirable, this structure places students without sufficient language support at a disadvantage, often privileging those in urban or higher-wealth families. In Algeria, Morocco, and Tunisia, science and mathematics are taught in French at the secondary level. However, only 30 percent of Tunisians, most of whom live near the capital, are fluent in written and spoken French. In Algeria, urban populations are fluent in French, but only 55 percent of rural populations are. A similar dynamic occurs in Morocco. Students in areas without French fluency suffer in education access and achievement (Lefevre 2015). On the Trends in International Mathematics and Science Study (TIMSS) tests in 2007 and 2015, students being tested in their mother tongue performed better than those being tested in a language they did not speak at home (Mullis et al. 2016). If mathematics (or any other subject) is to be taught in a second language, then adequate support for learning this language must be incorporated.

LOI has also been contentious and problematic at the tertiary education level, pointing to a need for improved foreign language instruction at all levels. Most Arab countries use either English or French as the LOI for mathematics, engineering, medical sciences, and other sciences. Qatar's rapid expansion of higher education institutions using English as the LOI generated resistance (MacLeod and Abou-El-Kheir 2016). Tunisia's system remains in two languages, with Arabic used for all social sciences and French used for science, technology, engineering, and mathematics studies (Battenburg 1997; Stevens 1983). Recently, the Ministry of Higher Education in the Kurdistan Region of Iraq commissioned a study of its 13 state universities to examine the impact of English-medium instruction. Just over 63 percent of instructors were satisfied with their own level of English and, despite English being the official LOI, only 30 percent spoke English all the time or almost all the time in lectures. English was used for written materials and homework, but instructors widely stated that their students' language level was insufficient for English-medium studies, despite the 12 years of English-language studies in prior levels of education (Borg 2015).

At any education level, employing an LOI that is not the students' mother tongue requires training teachers, providing adequate curriculum and classroom resources, and offering more support for students.

References

Abadzi, Helen. 2012. "Developing Cross-Language Metrics for Reading Fluency Measurement: Some Issues and Options (English)." Global Partnership for Education (GPE) Working Paper 6, World Bank, Washington, DC.

———. 2014. "Efficient Reading for Arab Students: Implications from Neurocognitive Research." Paper presented at the World Summit of Innovation in Education (WISE), Doha, Qatar.

Absi, Samir Abu. 2008. "Language-in-Education in the Arab Middle East." *Annual Review of Applied Linguistics* 2: 129–43. https://www.cambridge.org/core/journals/annual-review-of-applied-linguistics/article/languageineducation-in-the-arab-middle-east/894745FAD9CDEE839907166F938DDFB7.

Al-Huri, Ibrahim. 2015. "Arabic Language: Historic and Sociolinguistic Characteristics." *English Literature and Language Review* 1 (4): 28–56. https://www.researchgate.net/publication/307167761_Arabic_Language_Historic_and_Sociolinguistic_Characteristics.

Assaad, Ragui, Caroline Krafft, and Djavad Salehi-Isfahani. 2018. "Does the Type of Higher Education Affect Labor Market Outcomes? Evidence from Egypt and Jordan." *Higher Education* 75 (6): 945–95. doi:10.1007/s10734-017-0179-0.

Battenburg, John D. 1997. "English Versus French: Language Rivalry in Tunisia." *World Englishes* 16 (2): 281–90. doi:10.1111/1467-971X.00062.

Benrabah, Mohamed. 2007. "The Language Planning Situation in Algeria." *Current Issues in Language Planning* 6 (4): 379–502.

Benson, Carol. 2005. "The Importance of Mother Tongue–Based Schooling for Educational Quality." Study commissioned for the *2005 EFA Global Monitoring Report*, UNESCO, Paris. https://mlephil.wordpress.com/2009/09/26/the-importance-of-mother-tongue-based-schooling-for-educational-quality/.

Borg, Simon. 2015. "Researching Language Teacher Education." In *The Continuum Companion to Research Methods in Applied Linguistics*, edited by Brian Paltridge and Aek Phakiti, 541–60. London: Bloomsbury.

Bouhlila, Donia S. 2011. "The Quality of Secondary Education in the Middle East and North Africa: What Can We Learn from TIMSS' Results?" *Compare: A Journal of Comparative and International Education* 41 (3): 327–52.

Cable, Carrie, Patricia Driscoll, Rosamond Mitchell, Sue Sing, Teresa Cremin, Justine Earl, Ian Eyres, Bernardette Holmes, and Cynthia Martin, with Barbara Heins. 2010. "Language Learning at Key Stage 2: A Longitudinal Study; Final Report." Research Report DCSF-RR198, Department of Schools, Children, and Families, London.

Carter, Ronald. 2003. "Language Awareness." *ELT Journal* 57 (1): 64–65. https://eric.ed.gov/?id=EJ661136.

Gove, Amber, Aarnout Brombacher, and Michelle Ward-Brent. 2017. "Sparking a Reading Revolution: Results of Early Literacy Interventions in Egypt and Jordan." *New Directions for Child and Adolescent Development* 155 (special issue): 97–115.

Hayat Chaif, Rim. 2015. "In Algeria, the Berber Language Can't Get an Educational Foothold." *Al-Fanar Media,* July 27. https://www.al-fanarmedia.org/2015/07/in-algeria-the-berber-language-cant-get-an-educational-foothold/.

Ibrahim, Raphiq, and Judith Aharon-Peretz. 2005. "Is Literary Arabic a Second Language for Native Arab Speakers? Evidence from Semantic Priming Study." *Journal of Psycholinguistic Research* 34 (1): 51–70.

Johnson, Jacqueline, and Elissa Newport. 1989. "Critical Period Effects in Second Language Learning: The Influence of Maturational State on the Acquisition of English as a Second Language." *Cognitive Psychology* 21 (1): 60–99.

Krashen, Stephen D. 1975. "The Critical Period for Language Acquisition and Its Possible Bases." *Annals of the New York Academy of Sciences* 263 (1): 211–24. doi:10.1111/j.1749-6632.1975.tb41585.x.

Lefevre, Raphael. 2015. "The Coming of North Africa's 'Language Wars.'" *Journal of North African Studies* 20 (4): 499–502. doi:10.1080/13629387.2015.1072917.

Maamouri, Mohamed. 1998. "Language Education and Human Development: Arabic Diglossia and Its Impact on the Quality of Education in the Arab Region." Mediterranean Development Forum, World Bank, Washington, DC.

MacLeod, Paul, and Amir Abou-El-Kheir. 2016. "Qatar's English Education Policy in K-12 and Higher Education: Rapid Development, Radical Reform and Transition to a New Way Forward." In *English Language Education Policy in the Middle East and North Africa*, edited by Robert Kirkpatrick, 171–97. New York: Springer.

Marsh, Herbert W., Kit-Tai Hau, and Chit-Kwon Kong. 2002. "Multilevel Causal Ordering of Academic Self-Concept and Achievement: Influence of Language of Instruction (English Compared with Chinese) for Hong Kong Students." *American Educational Research Journal* 39 (3): 727–63.

Mullis, Ina V. S., Michael O. Martin, Pierre Foy, and M. Hooper. 2016. "TIMSS 2015 International Results in Mathematics." TIMSS and PIRLS International Study Center, Boston College, Chestnut Hill, MA. http://timssandpirls.bc.edu/timss2015/international-results/.

Muñoz, Carmen. 2006. *Age and the Rate of Foreign Language Learning*. Trowbridge, U.K.: Cromwell Press.

Myles, Florence. 2017. "Learning Foreign Languages in Primary Schools: Is Younger Better?" Policy Paper, Multilingualism: Empowering Individuals, Transforming Societies (MEITS), Cambridge, U.K.

Ofori-Attah, Kwabena. 2008. *Going to School in the Middle East and North Africa (Global School Room)*. Santa Barbara, CA: Greenwood.

Salmi, Jamil. 1987. "Language and Schooling in Morocco." *International Journal of Educational Development* 7 (1): 21–31.

Singleton, David, and Zsolt Lengyel. 1995. *The Age Factor in Second Language Acquisition*. Bristol, U.K.: Multilingual Matters.

Stevens, Paul B. 1983. "Ambivalence, Modernisation, and Language Attitudes: French and Arabic in Tunisia." *Journal of Multilingual and Multicultural Development* 4 (2–3): 101–14. doi:10.1080/01434632.1983.9994105.

Suleiman, Yasir. 1999. *Language and Society in the Middle East and North Africa*. London: Routledge. https://doi.org/10.4324/9781315829272.

Thompson, Tim, and Matt Gaddes. 2005. "The Importance of Teaching Pronunciation to Adult Learners." *Asian EFL Journal* 39 (2): 3–22.

Toll, Sylke W. M., and J. E. H. Van Luit. 2014. "The Developmental Relationship between Language and Low Early Numeracy Skills throughout Kindergarten." *Exceptional Children* 81 (1): 64–78. https://doi.org/10.1177/0014402914532233.

van Ginkel, Agatha. 2014. "Using an Additional Language as the Medium of Instruction: Transition in Mother Tongue–Based Multilingual Education." MTB-MLE Network Webinar. http://www.mlenetwork.org/sites/default/files/van%20Ginkel%20-%20Webinar%20Slides%20-%202014_0.pdf.

Yip, Din Yan, Wing Kwong Tsang, and Sin Pui Cheung. 2003. "Evaluation of the Effects of Medium of Instruction on the Science Learning of Hong Kong Secondary Students: Performance on the Science Achievement Test." *Bilingual Research Journal* 27 (2): 295–331. doi.org/10.1080/15235882.2003.10162808.

Yore, Larry D., David Pimm, and Hsiao-Lin Tuan. 2007. "The Literacy Component of Mathematical and Scientific Literacy." *International Journal of Science and Math Education* 5 (4): 559–89. https://doi.org/10.1007/s10763-007-9089-4.

Modernizing Curricula, Instruction, and Assessment to Improve Learning

7

Laura Gregory and
May Bend

Teaching and learning are multifaceted and complex processes. Children arrive at school with diverse backgrounds, life experiences, and individual characteristics. Teachers interact with children in a multitude of ways, themselves having a variety of backgrounds, experiences, and teaching styles. Curricula, instructional practices, and school and classroom environments shape the student experience. It is not surprising, then, that there is no easy fix to improve learning. Nevertheless, the low learning outcomes in the Middle East and North Africa (MENA) region call for a push across many aspects of the educational process—from curricula (what is being taught), to instruction (how it is being taught), to assessment (how learning is determined).

Modernizing curricula means moving from an expectation that students will memorize facts, rules, and procedures to an expectation that they will develop a broader range of higher-order skills to solve problems and think creatively. These types of skills align better with students' lifelong needs and to the communities and economies in which they live. Modern instructional practices not only promote these higher-order skills but also can maximize each student's potential through having teachers move from instructional practices that involve students as passive listeners and watchers to those that engage students in lessons and that adapt lessons to students' needs, readiness, and background. Good-quality resources, both human and physical, and a nurturing school environment—for girls and boys—are essential. Finally, by modernizing assessment systems, countries can help to move from a focus on rote memorization and credentials (as commonly seen in the high-stakes exit examinations in the region) to the use of assessments for deeper forms of learning and regular classroom assessments for timely feedback to students and teachers.

Modernize curricula to meet students' needs

Learning is a complex process that combines multiple interacting factors. Official curricula determine the content that education systems intend their students to learn. The official curriculum, instructional practices, school and classroom environment (including infrastructure, learning materials, and leadership), and student assessment combine to produce the learning that happens in schools (see figure 7.1). This process is embedded within

FIGURE 7.1 **Learning is a complex process that involves multiple actors and factors**

A framework for learning: How learning opportunities are shaped

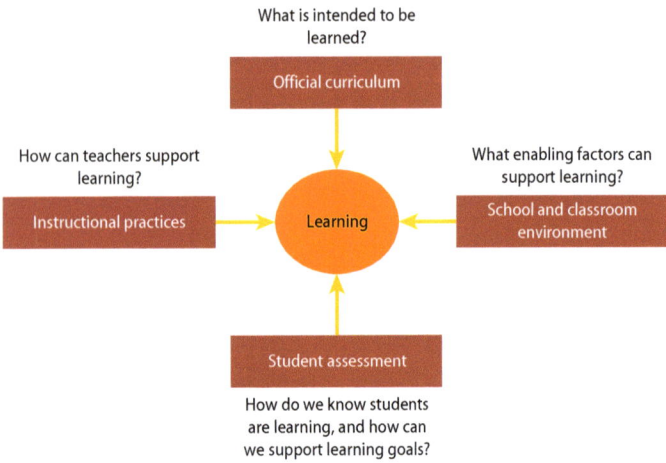

Source: World Bank.

the political, economic, social, and cultural contexts in which the child and the school are situated.

Across the world, many curriculum reforms are moving toward expressing outcomes in terms of competencies and skills and away from defining curriculum content only in terms of the subject material taught (UNESCO 2017). This shift represents a greater push for learning, as the focus moves from the acquisition of facts to what students are able to do *with* their learning—that is, the skills and competencies students have acquired as a result of the education process (see box 7.1). In this respect, competency-based learning is student centered.

However, across MENA, curricula by and large continue to focus heavily on factual recall

---

Box 7.1 Competency-based learning

Competency-based learning refers to systems of instruction and assessment based on students demonstrating that they have acquired the knowledge and skills (competencies) they are expected to learn as they progress through education. The goal of a competency-based curriculum is therefore to provide schools and teachers with learning standards that support student acquisition of the knowledge and skills that society deems to be essential for success in school, work, and adult life. According to the United Nations Educational, Scientific, and Cultural Organization (UNESCO), a competency-based curriculum is one that emphasizes what learners are expected to do rather than what they are expected to know (UNESCO 2017).

Internationally, countries take a variety of approaches to creating and implementing a competency-based curriculum. Within U.S. public schools, competency-based systems use state learning standards to determine academic expectations and define "proficiency" in a given course, subject area, or grade level (although other sets of standards may also be used, including standards developed by districts and schools or by subject-area organizations). Several high-scoring East Asian education systems (Hong Kong SAR, China; Japan; the Republic of Korea; and Singapore) have begun to legislate and implement competency-based curricula to help students to develop 21st-century skills. These education systems have reduced the relative weight of subject-centered education and introduced competency-based learning through the application of new theories of intelligence, with the aim of developing student capabilities along with well-being. Among these countries, some (like Korea) prescribe the curriculum, and others (like Japan) set general guidelines, leaving the specifics up to schools and teachers (Cheng 2017; Moon 2007).

A few MENA countries have recently begun to explore competency-based learning. Through its Integrated Education Reform Program, Kuwait is in the midst of transforming its curricula, instruction, and assessment methods. The government's program is aiming to embed a modern, personalized approach to teaching and learning. This approach focuses on the student, emphasizes applied knowledge, and caters to different learning abilities. Local education professionals have developed a national curriculum framework, along with curricula standards for all subjects and grades. Competency-based textbooks are being developed in line with the new standards as well as a national assessment to gauge progress at the national, school, and student levels.

FIGURE 7.2 **MENA students are more likely to be asked to memorize**

Percentage of grade 8 students asked to memorize science facts and principles for every lesson or almost every lesson, 2015

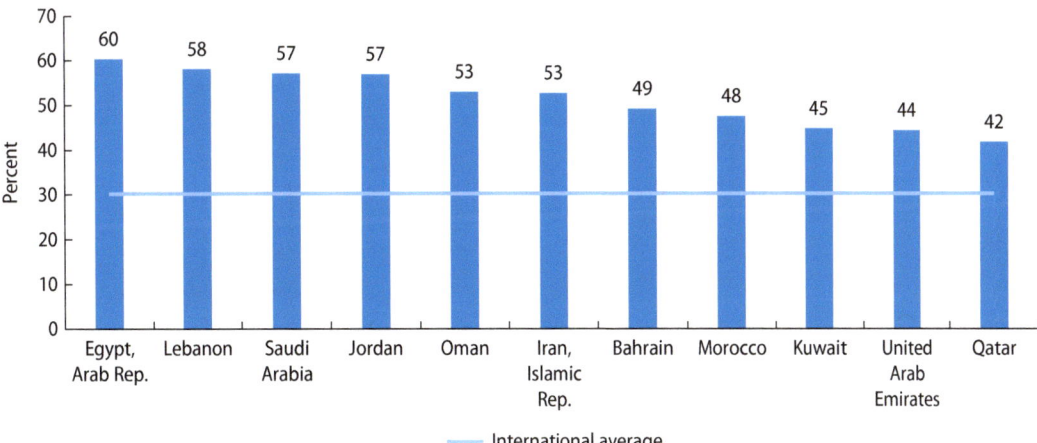

Source: Based on data from Martin et al. 2016.

and rote memorization, leaving little time for development of critical thinking skills. For example, the share of grade 8 students required to memorize mathematics and science rules, procedures, facts, and principles for all or most lessons is almost twice the international average in many MENA countries. More than half of grade 8 students in the Arab Republic of Egypt, the Islamic Republic of Iran, Jordan, Lebanon, Oman, and Saudi Arabia are asked to memorize science facts and principles every lesson or almost every lesson (see figure 7.2). This share is far above that of many high-performing countries. For example, only 2–3 percent of grade 8 students in New Zealand and Norway and less than 10 percent in Australia, Sweden, the United Kingdom, and the United States are required to memorize during most science lessons.

Students in some MENA countries are given very few opportunities to challenge their thinking and engage in high-level thought processes. For example, in Morocco and Saudi Arabia, around 20 percent of grade 8 students are never asked by their teacher to complete challenging science exercises that would require them to go beyond the instruction (see figure 7.3). This share is far higher than the international average of 5 percent of students never being asked to complete challenging exercises. Curricula that focus on low-level skills (such as factual recall) instead of critical thinking skills are not meeting the needs of students in the 21st century.

The overemphasis on memorization and lack of emphasis on critical thinking can stem from the curricula, from teaching practices, or from a combination of both. For example, a recent curriculum review for West Bank and Gaza revealed an overconcentration on memorization to the detriment of problem-solving skills (GIZ 2013a). However, in examining civics education practices in Lebanese schools, Akar (2016) noted that teachers do not feel that their students can learn what they need to know through the dialogic practices (learning through dialogue) prescribed in the curriculum. Instead, teachers use didactic methods, with the teacher as the expert and students as the receiver of knowledge, usually in lecture style. In this way, the experience of students in MENA's classrooms is markedly different from that of students in other parts of the world and may explain the region's low results in international student assessments.

Religious education, which forms a substantial part of curricula in the MENA region, uses predominantly memorization strategies. In fact, the foundations of rote

FIGURE 7.3 Several MENA countries do not consistently challenge students beyond the instruction
Percentage of grade 8 students who are never asked to complete challenging science exercises that require them to go beyond the instruction, 2015

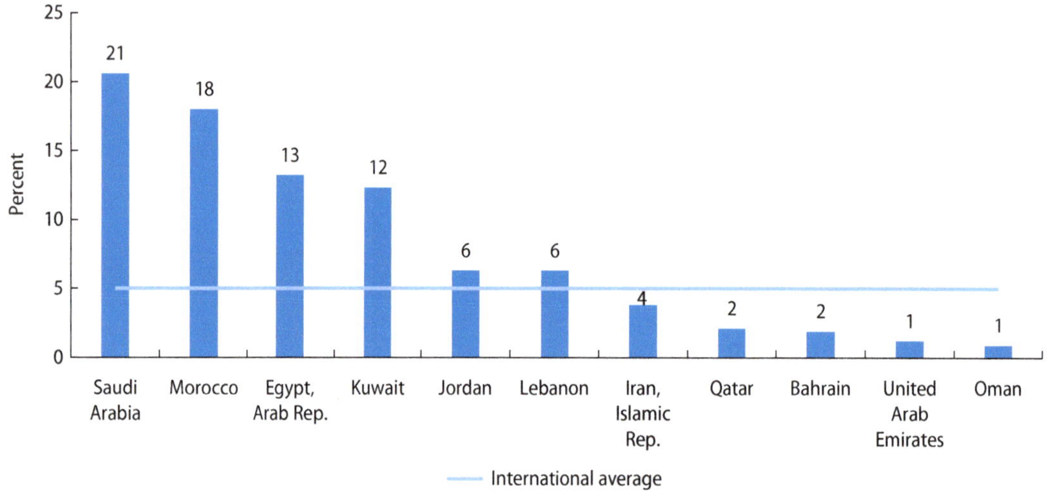

Country	Percent
Saudi Arabia	21
Morocco	18
Egypt, Arab Rep.	13
Kuwait	12
Jordan	6
Lebanon	6
Iran, Islamic Rep.	4
Qatar	2
Bahrain	2
United Arab Emirates	1
Oman	1

— International average

Source: Based on data from Martin et al. 2016.

learning in the MENA region can be linked to an oral tradition predating Islam that encourages memorization to preserve and spread Islamic teachings. The proportion of instructional time devoted to religious education in most MENA countries is well above the average time that Organisation for Economic Co-operation and Development (OECD) countries spend on religious, ethics, or moral education (see figure 7.4). For example, based on the most recent comparable information available, grade 1 students in Bahrain, Iraq, Kuwait, Morocco, Oman, Saudi Arabia, the United Arab Emirates, and the Republic of Yemen spend more than double the OECD average of 5 percent. The emphasis on memorization in religious education further contributes to memorization as a large part of MENA children's school day.

As a result of memorizing texts, rules, procedures, facts, and principles, students are often unable to show basic understanding in everyday applications. For example, in the 2015 Trends in International Mathematics and Science Study (TIMSS) assessment, less than half of Morocco's grade 4 students could read a basic graph. Likewise, only about 55 percent of grade 8 students in Egypt and Saudi Arabia could interpret a basic pictogram (Mullis et al. 2016). Curricula that encourage application and critical thinking instead of memorization are likely to meet the future needs of students.

The overemphasis on memorization of facts, principles, rules, and procedures does not negate the fact that some knowledge needs to be retained; instead, it is a question of the degree of emphasis and overall experience of the child in the classroom. Cognitive science provides information that allows a more nuanced understanding of the balance between rote memorization and higher-level processes such as discovery learning (see box 7.2). The capacity to solve problems and think critically about new material depends on the background knowledge retained in one's memory (Kirschner, Sweller, and Clark 2006). Repeated reflective practice is fundamental to building flexible knowledge and skills. In addition, students need guidance from teachers in order to develop the knowledge and skills that can facilitate independent, complex cognitive work. Therefore, a balance needs to be struck between rote memorization and high-level problem solving, and the appropriate emphasis depends on the task and skill level.

FIGURE 7.4 Substantial time is devoted to religious education in MENA

Percentage of instructional time allocated to religious education in grade 1 of primary school

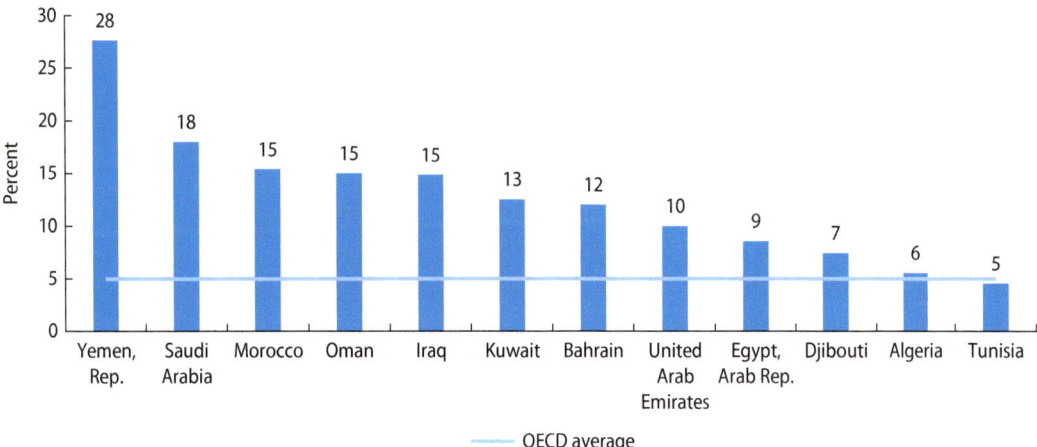

Sources: OECD 2017a for OECD average (refers to all grades of primary school); UNESCO 2011 for Algeria (2004), Bahrain (2004), Djibouti (2008), Iraq (2011), Kuwait (2004), Oman (2004), Tunisia (2008), and the Republic of Yemen (2004); World Bank calculations using various online sources for the Arab Republic of Egypt (2014), Morocco (2016), Saudi Arabia (2017), and the United Arab Emirates (2016).
Note: OECD = Organisation for Economic Co-operation and Development.

Box 7.2 Balancing repetition and high-level problem solving

To develop high-level knowledge and skills, students need opportunities to grapple with cognitive challenges in the classroom (Stigler and Hiebert 2009). Such practice must happen repeatedly before real mastery can be attained (Dunlosky et al. 2013; Ericsson, Krampe, and Tesch-Römer 1993; Willingham 2010). As novice learners, students initially attain inflexible, shallow knowledge; they can develop the deeper knowledge of structures, relationships, and principles that facilitate expert problem solving through repeated engagement (Willingham 2010). Empirical evidence suggests that the human brain cannot develop high-level problem-solving skills that can be applied effectively across all topics or domains. However, when students internalize extensive knowledge of a domain and learn to recognize connections within that body of knowledge, they can then use this deep knowledge to think critically about new domains (Pellegrino and Hilton 2012; Schneider and Stern 2010; Stigler and Hiebert 2009).

Research on classroom learning suggests that problem-solving and meta-cognitive strategies should be taught explicitly, but within the context of a particular subject area (Abrami et al. 2008; Pellegrino and Hilton 2012). While novice learners must engage actively with new material, they also require expert guidance in order to structure both the topical content and the learning process. Without adequate guidance, learners can become frustrated and lose motivation, or they can draw factually erroneous conclusions (Kirschner, Sweller, and Clark 2006). To provide such guidance effectively, teachers need training in how students learn, including an understanding of how the brain works as well as familiarity with how knowledge is structured in specific subject areas (Kirschner, Sweller, and Clark 2006; Willingham 2010).

An alternative to "discipline-based" or "subject-based" curricula, in which subject content is taught separately with distinct curricula and methods, is an interdisciplinary curriculum approach. This type of curriculum approach has become more common around the world (Jacobs 1989), particularly at the primary school level. An interdisciplinary curriculum allows for multiple skills and competencies to be gained in a subject area that may previously have been taught in isolation. The issue of curriculum reform and the predominance of memorization is a complex and contentious one in the region, and approaches will be nation specific. However, education systems can consider several practical options to broaden the skill sets and raise the learning levels of students, including through integrating subjects with an interdisciplinary approach (Thobani 2007). For example, several East Asian countries are reducing their primary and secondary curricula with a focus on the integrated development of 21st-century skills. Hong Kong SAR, China, has recently reduced its curriculum to four key learning areas. Japan has eliminated 30 percent of its formal curriculum, and Singapore has cut one-third of the formal curriculum (Cheng 2017).

Align curricula with children's lifelong skills needs

Curricula in education systems across MENA reflect the belief that education should provide academic content, workforce preparation, and social and civic development. Reforms over the last few decades have added, for example, life skills, foreign languages, problem-solving approaches, and more science, mathematics, and information technology to the curriculum (Alayan, Rohde, and Dhouib 2012). The legislative rhetoric concerning what schools and teachers should teach in MENA countries emphasizes mastery of Arabic and foreign languages, awareness of human rights, desire for international cooperation, awareness of environmental and conservation issues, critical thinking, and research skills. For example, Saudi Arabia's education legislation states that students should have the skills and knowledge to contribute to society economically and culturally and to build up their communities. The curriculum document of the United Arab Emirates states that the education system trains students for physical, intellectual, and emotional development and prepares them for their future. Morocco's goals focus on acquiring language, developing the appropriate social skills and civic understanding, and preparing students for future careers (UNESCO 2011).

However, the material studied and pedagogical approaches used in many MENA classrooms are not linked to students' everyday lives. Material covered in the curricula is decontextualized from students' day-to-day life, is presented as a set of facts and processes to be memorized, and is presented in a manner that does not encourage independent learning and investigation (Bouhlila 2011). This decontextualization is likely to contribute to poor absorption of the material. Connections between theory and practice are left unexplored, as are links between past and present (Alrebh and Al-Mabuk 2016). Not only does decontextualization lead to poor learning, but lack of relevance to real life makes students less interested in the topic. For example, secondary school students show low levels of interest in mathematics, which could be remedied by making the content applicable to real-life situations and tying it to other subjects under study (GIZ 2013b). Relevance is particularly important in programs that are intended to align closely with the workplace (see box 7.3).

The cognitive and learning sciences provide mounting evidence that interactive approaches facilitate an effective learning experience (Barkley, Cross, and Major 2005; Prince 2004). This combination allows future graduates to broaden their perspectives and equips them with the skills expected in the labor market. However, the curriculum of postsecondary education programs in MENA tends to be outdated, to focus on theory and memorization as

> **Box 7.3** **Relevance in vocational education**
>
> In some MENA countries, vocational tracks that include religious, technical, industrial, agricultural, and commercial education are growing. Algeria has partnered with public and private companies to increase enrollment in vocational tracks by creating suitable programs in construction, public works, electricity, agriculture, and tourism (Oxford Business Group 2015). Bahrain introduced apprenticeships in 2007/08 (Al-Mudhahki 2017). Since the 2011 revolution, the Tunisian Ministry of Education has been developing a reform plan, which includes restructuring its vocational education tracks (Oxford Business Group 2017), and other countries across the region are interested in making vocational education work better for students and for the labor market.
>
> Issues of relevance in vocational education are very important, as vocational education works best when schools collaborate with employers. In Egypt, vocational schools suffer from a lack of appropriate facilities and hands-on learning opportunities (Krafft 2017). The tracks have failed to adapt appropriately to available jobs and may be too rigid in their structure, failing to provide students with a broad enough foundation for employment.
>
> *Sources:* Krafft 2017; Oxford Business Group 2015, 2017.

opposed to practical knowledge and analytical reasoning (El Hassan 2013), and to be skewed toward theory over practice. Additionally, higher education institutions provide limited opportunities for leadership development through extracurricular activities and curricular enrichment. Tunisia has attempted to address this issue through information technologies and soft skills certification. However, systemwide change is needed. For instance, students graduating with a business degree lack entrepreneurial skills (Oxford Business Group 2017). Meeting students' needs for employability and life skills will be difficult without a curriculum more relevant to the world of work and without a shift from textbook-based education to interactive learning.

In some cases, countries have adopted curricula from outside the region without taking sufficient measures to ensure a good fit with core goals and local needs. For instance, imported curricula in the Gulf Cooperation Council (GCC) states often have not been adapted to reflect local cultural knowledge or, indeed, the Arabic language, even though these are key education goals (Bashshur 2010). A review of a curriculum used in Bahrain and Saudi Arabia found that an Arabic-language translation had inadvertently resulted in the omission of higher-order thinking lessons and activities (GIZ 2013a).

Allow time for effective learning

The amount of time a student is expected to be in school varies across countries in the region. Some countries, such as Oman and Saudi Arabia, have recently moved to increase instructional time, albeit from a low base. The TIMSS 2015 provides information from school principals on the total instructional hours per year in their school. In grade 4, the median number of hours per year ranged from 630 hours in the Islamic Republic of Iran—well below the median of 857 hours across all participating countries—to 1,050 hours in Qatar.[1] In grade 8, the median instructional time reported by school principals ranged from 900 hours in the Islamic Republic of Iran to 1,404 hours in Morocco, compared with a median of 992 hours across all participating countries (Mullis et al. 2016). However, the practice of suspending classes during examination times in some MENA countries, combined with high rates of student and teacher absenteeism, means that the implemented number of instructional hours is likely to be substantially less.

Often, the intended curriculum in MENA countries is not implemented or is implemented only partially. The learning that is intended by the official curricula cannot be met if insufficient time is allocated for mastery. Additional factors, including inadequate resources, lack of appropriate training or ineffective training of teachers, insufficient time on task, misaligned incentives, or the way curricula were developed, may also contribute. In West Bank and Gaza, the curriculum includes more material than teachers can realistically teach during a school year (GIZ 2013a), and this is likely to be the case in other MENA countries as well. A review of five MENA countries found that 36 to 43 percent of the time allocated was not used, revealing a possible area for improvement through better-engaged classroom hours (Millot and Lane 2002).

Encourage instructional practices that maximize children's potential

Beyond curriculum content and time allocation, the experience of students in the classroom rests on decisions made by teachers as to how they will deliver the curriculum. Whether lessons are well planned (with variety and in innovative ways to capture the attention of students) or whether they are given little thought and preparation (with methods that do not engage students) makes a difference to how well children's potential can be maximized in the classroom. When children are engaged and motivated, their attention will be captivated and learning will be more likely to occur.

Align instructional practices with learning goals

While curricula in the MENA region are based heavily on lower-order skills and memorization, pedagogical practices are mainly teacher centered, placing students in the role of passive learners. For example, passive listening is widespread in almost every mathematics and science lesson in the region. Around 80 percent or more of grade 4 students are asked to listen to their teacher explain mathematics content in almost every lesson in Bahrain, the Islamic Republic of Iran, Morocco, Oman, Qatar, and Saudi Arabia (see figure 7.5). This share compares to just 27 percent in New Zealand, 35 percent in Norway and Singapore, and around 45 percent in Australia, Canada, Germany, and Sweden.

When not listening to content, students are passive watchers. MENA's grade 4 students are much more likely to be asked to watch their teacher conduct an experiment every day—66 percent in Morocco, 64 percent in Oman, 59 percent in the Islamic Republic of Iran, 56 percent in Saudi Arabia, 52 percent in Kuwait, and 47 percent in Bahrain (Mullis et al. 2016). This share compares with the international average of 22 percent and less than 5 percent in Denmark, France, Germany, the Netherlands, New Zealand, and Northern Ireland. As illustrated in figure 7.5, of all countries participating in TIMSS, pedagogy in most MENA countries has the highest levels of both rote memorization and teacher-centered practices.

Active learning is generally defined as any instructional method that engages children and young people directly in the learning process. In short, active learning requires children and young people to engage in meaningful learning activities and to think about what they are doing. While this definition could include traditional activities such as homework, in practice active learning refers to activities that are introduced into the classroom. For example, active learning includes discussion, practice, review, application, problem solving, and group exploration of new concepts. The core element of active learning is the child's planned involvement and engagement in the learning process. In contrast to traditional teacher-directed learning, where children and young people are viewed as passive recipients of knowledge provided by the teacher, active learning puts children and young people firmly at the center of the learning process (Estyn 2017).

FIGURE 7.5 Rote memorization and teacher-centered practices prevail in most MENA countries

Percentage of students who listen to the teacher explain new mathematics content and are asked to memorize mathematics facts and procedures every day or almost every day, grade 4, 2015

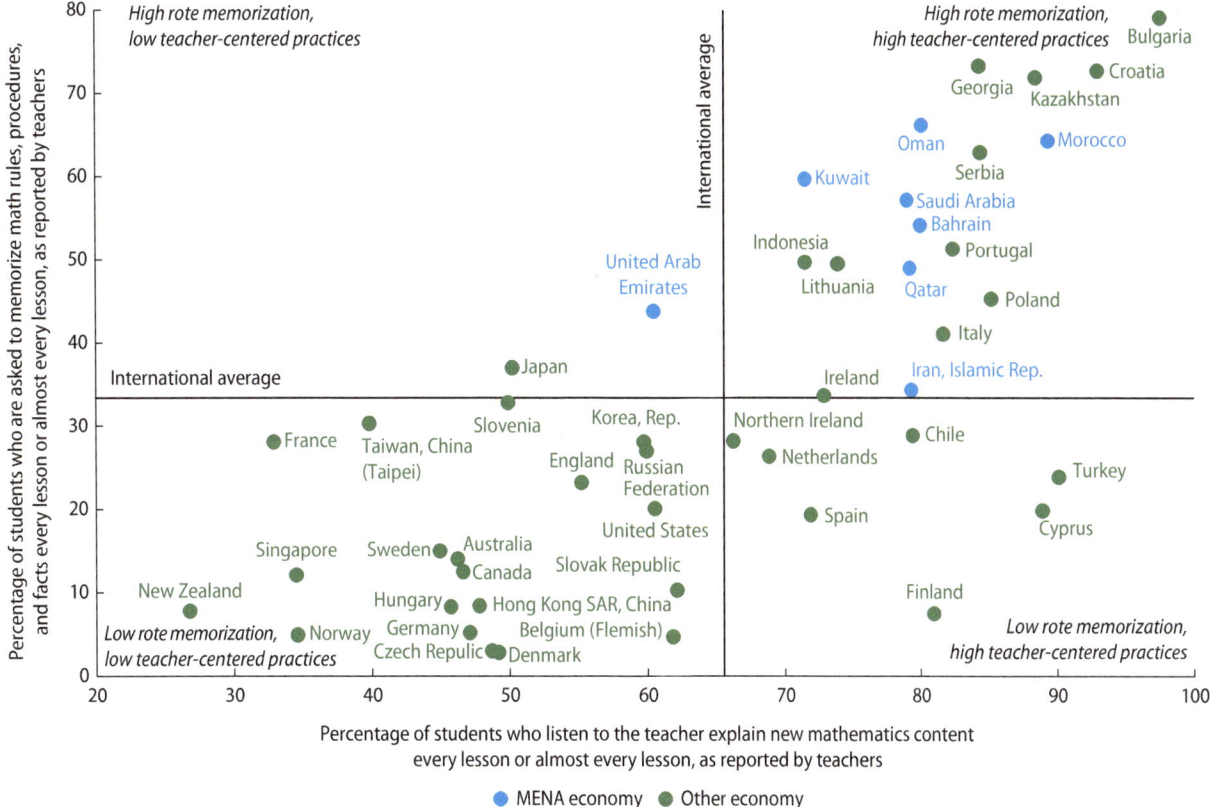

Source: Mullis et al. 2016.
Note: Teacher-centered practices are considered high if they require a passive student role, such as listening to teacher explanations.

As an example, over the last five years, Wales has undertaken substantial education system reform focused on the curriculum and associated pedagogy. The reform places active learning approaches at the center of the curriculum because "adult-directed" learning leaves teachers with too little flexibility to react to students' interests and imagination and hinders students' decision making on how and what they learn. This approach can lead to students being less confident in applying their skills and learning independently (Estyn 2017).

Pay attention to individual learning

When students do not have the prerequisite knowledge or skills to engage effectively with a lesson, they are likely to struggle with the new material. A lack of the prerequisite knowledge or skills in mathematics was found to be a severe limitation for a third of grade 8 mathematics students across all participating TIMSS 2015 countries, as perceived by their teachers. In MENA, this share rises to 51 percent in Jordan, 58 percent in the Islamic Republic of Iran, and a striking 62 percent in Morocco (Mullis et al. 2016).

Adhering rigidly to curricula that are beyond students' comprehension is counterproductive. Instead, MENA classrooms could implement pedagogical practices that match teaching to students' learning—also known as teaching at the right level, or adaptive instruction. These practices have been consistently found to improve student learning around the world (Evans and Popova 2015) and can be teacher led or supplemented with computer-based applications.

Between 2013 and 2015, at least six systematic meta-analyses examined the interventions that improve learning outcomes in low- and middle-income countries (Conn 2014; Glewwe et al. 2014; Kremer, Brannen, and Glennerster 2013; Krishnaratne, White, and Carpenter 2013; McEwan 2015; Murnane and Ganimian 2014). Across the reviews, pedagogical interventions (including computer-assisted learning) that tailor teaching to student skill levels ranked among the top three most effective means of improving student learning in low- and middle-income countries. The other two were repeated teacher training interventions, often linked to another pedagogical intervention, and improved accountability through contracts or performance incentives (Evans and Popova 2015).

One of these meta-reviews (McEwan 2015) examined 77 randomized control trials to determine which learning interventions are most effective (have the largest effect size) in improving the learning of primary-level students in low- and middle-income countries. It found that the largest average effect sizes are for treatments that incorporate instructional materials (0.08); computers or instructional technology (0.15); teacher training (0.12); smaller classes, smaller learning groups within classes, or ability grouping (0.12); contract or volunteer teachers (0.10); and student and teacher performance incentives (0.09). These categories are not exclusive.

Teacher-led adaptive instruction is based on diagnostic assessments to gauge students' learning levels. One method is to group students according to learning levels for part of their schooling and to use teaching materials matched to their level. While this approach may sound intuitive, it diverges considerably from the approach used in many education systems, including in MENA, where teaching is based on age-expected levels of learning prescribed by the national curriculum. This method can be successful in some situations; however, there are judgments to be made about when this method is appropriate, since grouping by ability can have adverse effects, and teachers can use other methods to individualize lessons while keeping mixed-ability groups (Mavroudi et al. 2015).

Teacher-led adaptive instruction has been successful in specific situations. For example, in India grouping students into different ability groups (for part of their school day) has been found to improve student learning significantly. Successful models include (1) interventions that take place on normal school days, whether taught by regular teachers during a designated segment of school hours (in separate groups) or taught by volunteers as after-school classes, and (2) intensive volunteer-taught "learning camps" for several hours a day over 10 or 20 consecutive days. Both configurations include learning materials and teacher-volunteer training (Banerjee et al. 2016).

In Singapore, students take screening tests at the beginning of grade 1, and those who are behind in reading receive additional daily support (OECD 2011). In India, Pratham Foundation trained local volunteers for a week in reading pedagogy and encouraged them to run after-school reading programs. An experimental study of the program found that literacy increased among students in grades 3 to 4 by 8 percent. Children who could read a letter at the beginning of the program were 26 percentage points more likely to read and understand a story by the end of the program than the control group (Banerjee 2012).

Another effective configuration, known as differentiated instruction, groups students within existing classrooms into small groups based on their prior achievement in the subject being taught. This configuration can take place in normal lessons, but it requires skilled teachers and considerable preparation to differentiate instruction effectively (Gates Foundation n.d.; Tomlinson 2014).

An alternative model of adaptive instruction consists of remedial lessons only for students who are falling behind their peers. In a low-cost experiment in India, young women from the local community were hired to teach basic literacy and numeracy to groups of 15 to 20 underperforming students. This model led to significant gains in test scores, especially among the lowest-performing children (Banerjee et al. 2007). In Canada and Finland, for example, extensive personalized support is available to any student who is struggling with expected levels of learning, especially during the formative years of primary school (World Bank 2018).

Evidence suggests that such targeted interventions and remedial lessons are more effective than other models of level-appropriate instruction, such as grade repetition and between-class ability grouping. Grade repetition, which is practiced in some MENA countries, requires students who do not pass year-end examinations to repeat the prior school year rather than progressing with their peers (OECD 2016). Between-class ability grouping entails grouping students in the same grade into classes based on their prior achievement, so that classes are homogeneous in learning levels. Although a randomized control trial in Kenyan primary schools found that between-class ability grouping improved student achievement (Duflo, Dupas, and Kremer 2011), this result may have been due in part to a research design that helped teachers to adapt teaching to student levels. A meta-analysis of 100 years of research on ability grouping found that such between-class grouping did not, in fact, benefit students (Steenbergen-Hu, Makel, and Olszewski-Kubilius 2016).

Provide useful teaching resources

For children to learn, teachers need to have the right resources and support materials. Traditionally, the textbook has been central to schooling in MENA countries and in some cases is considered akin to the curriculum. While textbooks are useful resources for both students and teachers, their overuse can mean that students do not experience other types of learning such as discovery, hands-on experiences, collaborative tasks, and so on. In addition, where textbooks are not well developed or adapted to meet the needs of their audience, their effectiveness may be further eroded.

The development, selection, and use of textbooks is an important consideration. Often, textbooks are chosen without the use of selection criteria related to how well their content and approach promote learning (Jobrack 2012). Instead, more superficial factors such as design are often the basis of selection. In addition, it is important for persons with experience of what works well in the classroom to be involved in textbook development. Without this element of instructional experience, textbooks are likely to be less engaging to the intended audience.

In several MENA countries, crammed curricula often lead to "teaching to the textbook" according to a predefined time schedule. Such a schedule limits the ability of teachers to use more dynamic teaching methods, such as introducing an idea and adapting lessons based on how well students have absorbed the material. In this more dynamic scenario, the textbook is a resource for the lesson rather than the "curriculum" itself. In more dynamic teaching styles, teachers can use a range of sample lesson plans and supplemental materials to meet the needs of individual students.

An overreliance on factual recall and rote memorization often means an overreliance on textbook use as well. While activities that promote discovery learning, problem solving, and critical thinking can emanate from textbooks, teachers' guides and lesson plan examples are what can help teachers to present the material in a more engaging way. In several MENA countries, including Egypt, the Islamic Republic of Iran, Lebanon, and Saudi Arabia, 50 percent or more of grade 8 students are asked to read their science textbooks every lesson (see figure 7.6). Not only does this leave little time for other learning activities, but if the textbooks are not based on sound pedagogical principles or designed by experienced practitioners, the experience for students may be less than engaging and result in limited depth of knowledge and understanding.

FIGURE 7.6   Some MENA countries rely heavily on textbooks
Percentage of grade 8 students asked to read their science textbook or other material every lesson or almost every lesson, 2015

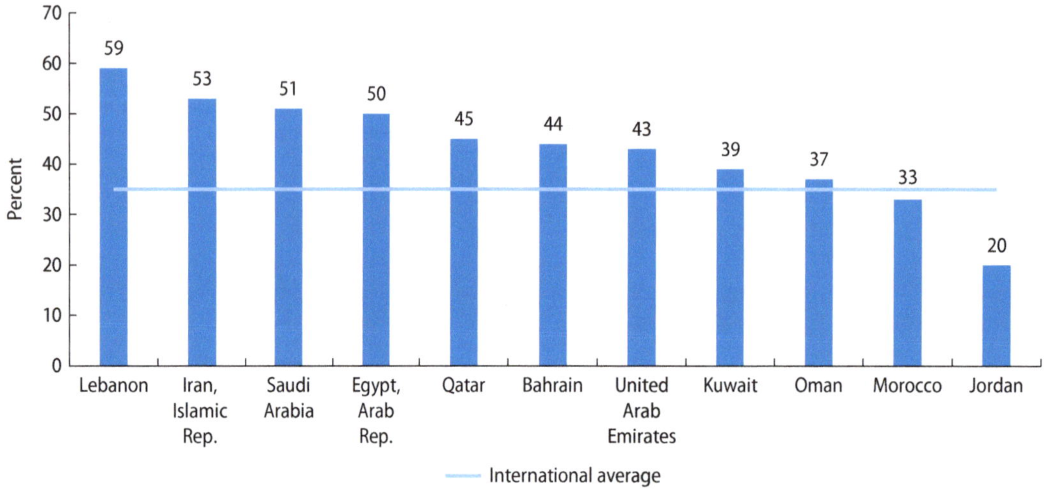

Country	Percent
Lebanon	59
Iran, Islamic Rep.	53
Saudi Arabia	51
Egypt, Arab Rep.	50
Qatar	45
Bahrain	44
United Arab Emirates	43
Kuwait	39
Oman	37
Morocco	33
Jordan	20

— International average

Sources: Jobrack 2012; Mullis et al. 2016.

Box 7.4   Moving from poor to fair: The role of scripted lessons in structured pedagogy

Structured pedagogy can be modeled in many ways, including curriculum supported by worksheets, step-by-step lesson plans, or even scripted lessons. The purpose of scripted lessons—also referred to as prescriptive pedagogy—is to provide scaffolding and motivation for low-skill teachers and principals (Westbrook et al. 2013). With supportive evidence from five different education systems, Westbrook et al. (2013) recommend that this method of intervention be used only for systems trying to move from "poor" performance to "fair" performance.[a] Fair performance means that students have achieved basic literacy and numeracy. To meet basic educational needs, scripted lessons stabilize systems with standardized instructional practice and reduce variation among classrooms and schools.

Successful structured pedagogy programs require several interacting elements (Snilstveit et al. 2015). Teaching and learning materials need to be structured and sequenced to fit both the intended content and the classroom contexts in question. These materials must be provided to teachers and students in adequate quantities and at appropriate times. Moreover, teachers require high-quality and sustained training in delivering the structured content and should be able to provide feedback to the entities creating the resources.

Sources: Snilstveit et al. 2015; Westbrook et al. 2013.
a. Chile (2001–05), Madhya Pradesh, India (2006+), Minas Gerais, Brazil (2003+), Western Cape, South Africa (2003+), and Ghana (2003+).

Countries around the world, particularly those with low-skill teachers, have found success with the use of structured pedagogy programs (see box 7.4 for a description of these programs). Such programs typically include training courses for teachers and learning resources for both teachers and students. In addition to improving instructional quality for the topic concerned, structured pedagogy programs can change existing classroom practice because they incorporate learning activities and pedagogical training. In a review of 420 scholarly analyses of educational interventions in low- and middle-income countries, structured pedagogy interventions had the largest and most consistently positive effects on student learning outcomes. Although none of the structured pedagogy interventions reviewed had taken place in MENA, some of the interventions were in countries performing at similar levels on TIMSS and the Programme for International Student Assessment (PISA), such as Chile, Costa Rica, and South Africa (Snilstveit et al. 2015). A variety of scripted lessons and teacher coaching can help to overcome deficits in teacher skills in low-performing education systems (Mourshed, Chijioke, and Barber 2010). This approach can be an important short- to medium-term intervention until teachers' professional skills are developed further.

Using instructional practices that maximize children's potential could start with policies that encourage student-centered instructional methods linked to clear learning standards in a competency-based curriculum. Faculties of education, where new entrants to teaching gain the latest knowledge and skills of effective pedagogical methods, are the starting point for embedding good techniques. For practicing teachers, high-profile systemwide in-service teacher training programs can indicate that the top is focusing on the need to move toward student-centered instructional methods. Lessons should be targeted to the students' skill level. The sharing of lesson plans—and scripted lessons where teacher capacity is low—can encourage and support teachers in trying something new.

Provide classroom environments conducive to learning

In addition to modernizing curricula and instructional practices to maximize children's potential, the school and classroom environment must be conducive to, and even promote, learning. This environment includes the appropriate physical environment as well as the ethos and atmosphere created by school leaders and teachers, all of which influence the experience of the child while in formal learning settings.

School buildings, multiple shifts, and overcrowding are problems

Many students in MENA are in schools where the principal perceives that instruction is severely impeded by shortages or inadequacies in the school buildings and grounds. Across all countries participating in TIMSS 2015, 18 percent of students are in schools in which shortages or inadequacies in the school buildings and grounds severely affect instruction (Mullis et al. 2016).[2] In stark contrast, all participating MENA countries reported even higher proportions (with the exception of Lebanon).

Across MENA, in conflict- and nonconflict-affected countries and in wealthy and poor countries, issues of poor school infrastructure and overcrowding are apparent. In Libya, 25 percent of public schools are unable to provide access to drinking water, and just 37 percent of public schools have a waste collection-disposal system (UNICEF 2012). Saudi Arabia struggles with overcrowded classrooms, despite having additional schools in rented buildings and multiple-shift school days where needed. Although Saudi Arabia's education regulations stipulate a maximum of 30 students in classes in government school buildings and 20 students in rented buildings, according to teachers it is now common to find more than 40 students in classrooms. Overcrowding makes it difficult for teachers to teach and students to learn, because there is not enough time for in-depth discussion of schoolwork in overly full classes (Al-Sughair 2014). Egypt also stands out, with more than 40 percent of students in schools in which the principal feels that infrastructure (school buildings and grounds) severely hinders teaching (Mullis et al. 2016).

In some areas, severe overcrowding leads to the need for double- or even triple-shift schools. In a multiple-shift system, schools cater to two or more entirely separate groups of students during each school day. The first group typically attends from early morning until midday, and the second attends from midday through late afternoon. Each group uses the same buildings and equipment.

In some school systems, the two groups are taught by the same teachers, and in other systems they are taught by different teachers. Multiple-shift schooling may create problems. The school day, especially in triple-session systems, is often shortened, which implies that quality is being sacrificed for quantity—students are losing time for classroom learning and extracurricular activities. In addition, if teachers work in more than one session, they are likely to be tired, causing further deterioration in quality (Batra 1998).

Furthermore, multiple-shift systems are sometimes accused of causing social problems because children are in school for shorter periods of time and so have more idle time to roam the streets and cause trouble (Batra 1998). Even when schools successfully circumvent these issues, the public often views multiple-shift schools as being of inferior quality; they are less attractive to teachers and parents (see, for example, Batra 1998). This perception exacerbates inequality, with multiple-shift schools relying on lower-quality teachers and enrolling predominantly poorer students (Herrán and Rodríguez 2000; Nhundu 2000).

Embracing multiple-shift schools is a feasible option in the face of medium-term resource constraints, but longer-term solutions must be prioritized. In recent years, MENA has expanded education, and this expansion has contributed to overcrowding and, in some cases, the need for multiple-shift schools (Heyne and Gebel 2012). While seeing multiple-shift schools as a solution for the medium term may make it seem worth investing time and energy to improve their effectiveness, little evidence exists that this improvement is likely or even possible given the shorter school hours and the social stigma attached to multiple-shift schools (Herrán and Rodríguez 2000). Time is of the essence, as this dilemma will come into sharper focus as MENA countries face increasing pressure from larger numbers of primary education graduates (Linden 2001). Ultimately, the wisest choice for MENA is to invest the resources necessary in providing adequate school infrastructure for single-shift schools with uncrowded classrooms as soon as possible.

The school experience differs for boys and girls

Many schools in MENA are segregated by gender, particularly at the secondary level. In most cases, girls are taught by women, and boys are taught by men. The exceptions are Lebanon and Morocco, where girls and boys are generally educated together at all levels. In Saudi Arabia, where the gender difference in student achievement is the greatest, girls and boys are educated separately beginning in grade 1. In Jordan and Oman, public schools are coeducational until around grade 4 and then gender segregated. In other GCC countries, the predominance of coeducational private schools means that at least a quarter to half of all students are educated in a coeducational environment (Ripley 2017).

The school and classroom environments differ substantially between all-girls and all-boys schools, and so the learning experiences of girls and boys in single-sex schools can be vastly different. For example, as shown in the following section, MENA classrooms manage student behavior using outdated and harmful techniques, which can be particularly harsh in all-boys schools (Ridge 2014).

Given the substantial differences in learning outcomes between girls and boys across MENA, it is important to examine how the learning environment differs between all-girls and all-boys schools. In Oman, an interdisciplinary project undertaken between 2011 and 2014 studied the gender gap in student performance and its implications—this was called "The Male Dilemma." The project found that, among the many factors contributing to lower academic performance among boys, all-girls schools had more learning materials, student participation, and attentiveness in class (Osman et al. 2014). In addition, female teachers provided more assistance and feedback to students and allowed more creativity and expression of ideas than male teachers in all-boys schools.

Addressing the differences in learning experiences between all-girls and all-boys schools will require taking a closer look at aspects of the teaching profession as perceived by male and female teachers and the gendered ways in which they may experience teacher training. Research reveals that men have a poor perception of the teaching profession, which may lead to inferior performance among male teachers in the classroom and low learning outcomes for boys (Ridge 2014). Suggestions for policy actions include public campaigns highlighting the importance of using male role models in lessons and identifying and encouraging top-performing male teachers to raise their voices and allow others to learn from them.

Given the pervasive underperformance of boys in the MENA region and the stark differences in the schooling experiences of boys and girls, it is time to elevate the discussion of boys' education and the appropriate and constructive management of student behavior in classrooms to create positive learning environments for all. One particularly important reason to pay attention to the quality of boys' education is that boys may be more affected by school quality than girls, be more harmed by bad schools, and gain more from strong schools (Autor et al. 2016).

Schools and classrooms should be positive places of learning

Classrooms should be positive places of learning. Across the region, high rates of student and teacher absenteeism are signs of poor school and classroom climates (Ezzine 2009); a positive environment in which students feel a sense of belonging is more conducive to learning.

The learning environment in MENA schools is safer and more encouraging in all-girls schools than in all-boys schools. Analysis of the TIMSS 2015 data for this report found that, across the region, girls feel a greater sense of belonging to schools, experience less bullying, and feel more encouraged to succeed academically than boys. At age 15, students—both boys and girls—in Qatar, Tunisia, and the United Arab Emirates have some of the highest levels of exposure to bullying among participating PISA 2015 countries, while Tunisia has one of the worst disciplinary climates. In an unpublished U.S. Agency for International Development study (quoted in Ripley 2017), classroom observations in Jordan revealed a climate in which male teachers in all-boys schools are more likely than female teachers in all-girls schools to react to a student's incorrect answer with belittling or punishment. In the same study, boys are much more likely than girls to complain about teachers shouting at and beating students. In addition to concerns about the welfare of children, the time spent on misguided methods of managing student behavior is time lost from learning.

Developing a positive learning environment will require taking another look at student behavior management techniques. Now is the time to elevate the discussion of managing student behavior in classrooms, particularly for all-boys schools, and to equip teachers with methods that will encourage learning and create positive learning environments. Changing the way teachers manage their students would benefit from intensive in-service training and incentives. All-boys schools have particular challenges, and their teachers need to know and understand how to use teaching techniques that work best for these situations. This understanding could be taught explicitly in preservice and in-service teacher training—teacher standards should be clear, and teachers should be monitored. An example comes from Western Australia, where teachers complained to their union about poor student behavior in classrooms. This complaint led to a collaboration between the teachers' union and the state authority for education, resulting in the rollout of a highly regarded in-service training program for teachers across the state, follow-up mentoring support from trainers, and teachers feeling better equipped to cope with challenging student behavior (Virgona 2012).

Adequate teaching and learning materials are needed to promote learning

Shortages and inadequacies of learning and teaching materials are impeding teaching in MENA. This problem is more pronounced in MENA countries than in other countries participating in TIMSS 2015. Learning and teaching materials include books and writing materials, as well as concrete objects or materials to help students to understand concepts, quantities, and procedures.[3] A lack of basic inputs, such as learning and teaching materials, can hinder the implementation of curriculum and therefore student learning. On average, more than 20 percent of MENA students participating in TIMSS 2015 were in schools with inadequate mathematics materials,[4] compared with only 12 percent across all participating countries. The shortfall is even more pronounced in science, where 32 percent of MENA students are in schools with inadequate science materials, compared with 21 percent, on average, across all participating countries (see figure 7.7).

Use assessment methods to adapt instruction and promote higher-order skills

While large-scale national and international assessments can catalyze education reform at the policy level, public examinations and formative classroom assessments have the potential to generate powerful incentives for efforts to improve learning for students, teachers, and schools. However, if used inappropriately, public examinations can reinforce shallow forms of learning, and classroom assessment can consume valuable lesson time without enhancing student learning.

Frequent, high-quality classroom assessment can be a powerful tool for learning

There is compelling evidence that formative classroom assessments—the types of assessment procedures that teachers use during the learning process so that they can modify their activities and approaches in response—can raise learning outcomes by providing feedback to students on how to improve their performance and understanding (Black and Wiliam 2010; Hattie and Timperley 2007;

FIGURE 7.7 Inadequacy of mathematics or science materials affects instruction for many students across MENA

Percentage of grade 8 students whose school's capacity to provide instruction is affected by a shortage or inadequacy of mathematics or science teaching and learning materials, as reported by school principals, 2015

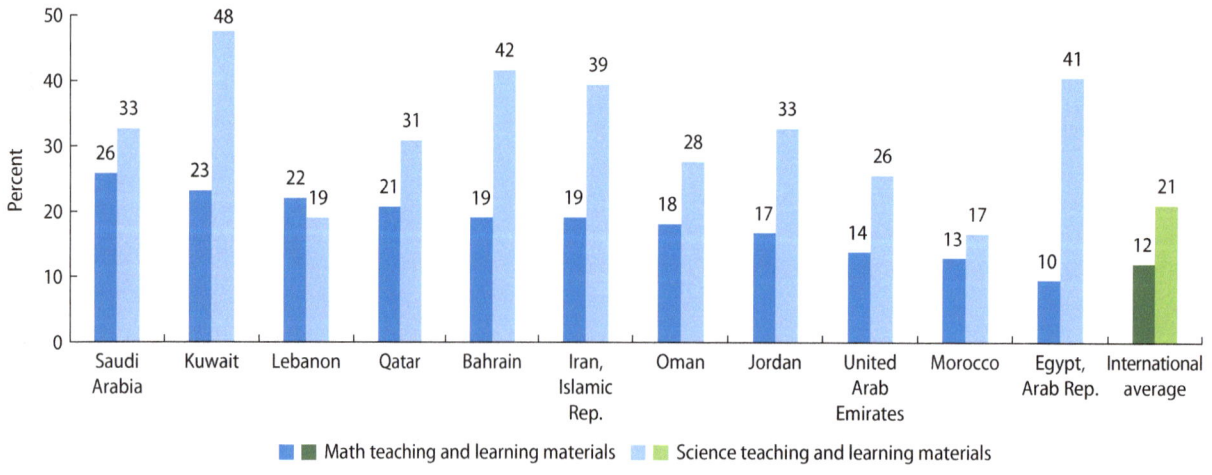

Source: Mullis et al. 2016.

Roediger, Putnam, and Smith 2011). Classroom assessment techniques can include verbal questioning and feedback; written quizzes; students holding up response cards or miniature whiteboards to give the teacher a real-time snapshot of classwide understanding; or activities requiring students to retrieve and apply newly acquired knowledge. With today's technology, mobile devices and applications can be used for similar purposes (see box 7.5 for one successful model of classroom assessment).

While teachers in the MENA region regularly assess students, classroom assessments are often ineffective. More than 70 percent of students in MENA countries participating in TIMSS 2015 have had teachers who reported placing a major emphasis on monitoring students' progress in mathematics through students' ongoing work or classroom tests (Mullis et al. 2016). Yet, across MENA countries, classroom assessments are rarely used to adapt instruction or provide meaningful feedback to students. For instance, only one in four teachers in Jordan reported using classroom assessments to inform lesson planning (Rabie et al. 2017). Failure to do so limits the potential of classroom assessments to improve student learning.

High-stakes examinations often overemphasize rote recall

As shown in spotlight 2 on measuring learning, public examinations can strongly influence teaching and learning. High-stakes public examinations in some MENA countries exacerbate the pull for low-level instead of high-level skills, through their emphasis on factual recall over critical thinking.

Assessments focused on complex tasks may generate stronger incentives for higher-order skills development. Given the global demand for higher-order cognitive skills, growing attention is being paid to assessment formats—such as task-based assessments—that replace narrow, superficial question-and-answer approaches with complex tasks testing deeper forms of learning (Wagner 2011). Reforms of high-stakes examinations

---

Box 7.5 Using peer instruction to assess, challenge, and engage in science, technology, engineering, and mathematics lessons

Peer instruction is a model for science and mathematics instruction that incorporates dialogue, problem solving, and formative classroom assessment. It follows a sequence:

1. The teacher explains a concept.
2. The teacher poses a problem focused on the concept, which requires deep understanding rather than straightforward formulaic application.
3. Students think about the problem and arrive at an answer individually.
4. Students discuss the problem with a partner.
5. Students show the teacher their postdiscussion answer.
6. The teacher explains the correct answer.

Although developed for Harvard undergraduates studying physics, peer instruction has improved student learning in many settings, including in India's low-cost Avanti Learning Centers, where students have a 40 percent success rate in a challenging tertiary entrance examination, compared with a 1 percent success rate among students with similar background characteristics who are not in Avanti Learning Centers.

Peer instruction can be adapted to national education systems by developing a bank of challenging problems testing students' understanding of key concepts in the curriculum. When implemented correctly, peer instruction has the potential to augment classroom assessments, giving teachers valuable information to inform their pedagogical practice.

Sources: Mazur 1997; Wagner and Dintersmith 2015.

in MENA hold promise for transforming the teaching and learning process and creating a pull for skills.

Noncognitive and socioemotional skills are critically important for student achievement

Noncognitive skills encompass a range of abilities; for example, conscientiousness, perseverance, and teamwork. These skills are critically important for student achievement, both in and beyond the classroom (Heckman 2006; Schanzenbach et al. 2016; World Economic Forum 2016). Noncognitive skills form a critical piece of workers' skill sets, which are composed of cognitive, noncognitive, and job-specific skills. Research at the international, national, and school levels is increasingly looking at how education systems affect the development of these skills. Demand for these skills will continue to change as economies and labor market needs evolve, with trends such as automation causing fundamental shifts. For many countries, a big question for the future will be how their education systems can move to support, develop, and assess in-demand noncognitive skills more effectively.

Among education policy makers, there is growing interest in personal qualities other than cognitive ability that determine success, including self-control, grit, growth mind-set, and many others (Duckworth 2016; Dweck 2007; Mischel 2014). However, attempts to measure such qualities for the purposes of educational policy and practice are more recent (see spotlight 2). The measures in use today have both advantages and limitations. In determining which tool to use for measuring noncognitive skills, policy makers would do well to consider the purpose for which they are assessing these skills. Furthermore, it may make sense to combine or use a variety of measurements or to adapt questions (if a questionnaire is used) or tasks to the specific pedagogical situation and skill being targeted.

Despite the inherent challenges, measuring the existence of noncognitive skills against other key variables such as educational attainment and employment may be illuminating for MENA countries. While some measurement efforts have emerged in this area—such as the Big 5 Personality Test, the Grit Scale, and others—the MENA region has generally lagged in developing contextually appropriate tools for measuring socioemotional skills. However, some developments are under way in the region. The Measuring Early Learning Quality and Outcomes (MELQO) is an initiative of the World Bank, UNESCO, United Nations Children's Fund (UNICEF), and the Brookings Institution, which aims to improve the quality, feasibility, and accessibility of population-based measures of early childhood environments and learning outcomes associated with readiness for primary education around the world. Initiated in 2014, MELQO was designed to generate efficiently locally relevant data on children's learning and development at the start of school and preprimary learning environments, with specific relevance for informing national early childhood development policy and global monitoring (UNESCO et al. 2017). Through a consultative process designed to draw on the best experiences in measuring early childhood development to date, MELQO has developed modules for country adaptation, measuring socioemotional and cognitive skills among children between four and six years (MODEL) and the quality of children's learning environments (MELE).

Notes

1. As reported by school principals in TIMSS 2015.
2. As reported by the school principals.
3. Examples are mathematics tools such as blocks, counters, and geo-shapes that contribute to improving mathematical skills and conceptual development (Swan and Marshall 2010) or science kits that contain equipment for student-led experiments (UNESCO 2015).
4. As reported by school principals.

References

Abrami, Philip C., Robert M. Bernard, Evgueni Borokhovski, Anne Wade, Michael A. Surkes, Rana Tamim, and Dai Zhang. 2008. "Instructional Interventions Affecting Critical Thinking Skills and Dispositions: A Stage 1 Meta-Analysis." *Review of Educational Research* 78 (4): 1102–34.

Akar, Bassel. 2016. "Dialogic Pedagogies in Educational Settings for Active Citizenship, Social Cohesion, and Peacebuilding in Lebanon." *Education, Citizenship, and Social Justice* 11 (1): 44–62. doi:10.1177/1746197915626081.

Alayan, Samira, Achim Rohde, and Sarhan Dhouib, eds. 2012. *The Politics of Education Reform in the Middle East: Self and Other in Textbooks and Curricula*. New York: Berghahn Books.

Al-Mudhahki, Jawaher S. 2017. "Bahrain: Moving towards a Knowledge-Based Economy." In *Education in the Arab World*, edited by Serra Kirdar, 217–42. London: Bloomsbury Academic.

Alrebh, Abdulla F., and Radhi Al-Mabuk. 2016. "Teaching for Democracy in Post-Arab Spring." In *Education and the Arab Spring*, edited by Eid Mohamed, Hannah R. Gerber, and Slimane Aboulkacem, 3–23. Rotterdam: Sense Publishers.

Al-Sughair, Jubail. 2014. "Overcrowded Saudi Classrooms 'Hampering Learning Process.'" *Arab News*, October 15.

Autor, David, David Figlio, Krzysztof Karbownik, Jeffrey Roth, and Melanie Wasserman. 2016. "School Quality and the Gender Gap in Educational Achievement." *American Economic Review* 106 (5): 289–95.

Banerjee, Abhijit. 2012. "Teaching at the Right Level." Presentation, Delhi, India, July 26. https://www.povertyactionlab.org/sites/default/files/documents/Session%201%20-%20Teaching%20to%20the%20Level.pdf.

Banerjee, Abhijit, Rukmini Banerji, James Berry, Esther Duflo, Harini Kannan, Shobhini Mukherji, Marc Shotland, and Michael Walton. 2016. Mainstreaming an Effective Intervention: Evidence from Randomized Evaluations of 'Teaching at the Right Level' in India." NBER Working Paper 22746, National Bureau of Economic Research, Cambridge, MA.

Banerjee, Abhijit V., Shawin Cole, Esther Linden, and Leigh Duflo. 2007. "Remedying Education: Evidence from Two Randomized Experiments in India." *Quarterly Journal of Economics* 122 (3): 1235–64.

Barkley, Elizabeth F., Patricia Cross, and Claire H. Major. 2005. *Collaborative Learning Techniques: A Handbook for College Faculty*. San Francisco: Jossey-Bass.

Bashshur, Munir. 2010. "Observations from the Edge of the Deluge: Are We Going Too Far, Too Fast in Our Educational Transformation in the Arab Gulf?" In *Trajectories of Education in the Arab World: Legacies and Challenges*, edited by Osama Abi-Mershed, 247–72. New York: Routledge.

Batra, Sunil. 1998. *Problems and Prospects of Double Shift Schools: A Study of Assam and Madhya Pradesh*. Delhi: Centre for Education, Action, and Research.

Black, Paul, and Dylan Wiliam. 2010. "Inside the Black Box: Raising Standards through Classroom Assessment." *Phi Delta Kappan* 92 (1): 81–90. https://doi.org/10.1177/003172171009200119.

Bouhlila, Donia S. 2011. "The Quality of Secondary Education in the Middle East and North Africa: What Can We Learn from TIMSS' Results?" *Compare* 41 (3): 327–52.

Cheng, Kai-ming. 2017. *Advancing 21st Century Competencies in East Asian Education Systems*. New York: Center for Global Education, Asia Society.

Conn, Katherine M. 2014. "Identifying Effective Education Interventions in Sub-Saharan Africa: A Meta-Analysis of Rigorous Impact Evaluations." PhD diss., Columbia University, New York.

Duckworth, Angela. 2016. *Grit: The Power of Passion and Perseverance*. New York: Scribner.

Duflo, Esther, Pascaline Dupas, and Michael Kremer. 2011. "Peer Effects, Teacher Incentives, and the Impact of Tracking: Evidence from a Randomized Evaluation in Kenya." *American Economic Review* 101 (5): 1739–74.

Dunlosky, John, Katherine A. Rawson, Elizabeth J. Marsh, Mitchell J. Nathan, and Daniel T. Willingham. 2013. "Improving Students' Learning with Effective Learning Techniques: Promising Directions from Cognitive and Educational Psychology." *Psychological Science in the Public Interest* 14 (1): 4–58. https://doi.org/10.1177/1529100612453266.

Dweck, Carol S. 2007. *Mindset: The New Psychology of Success*. New York: Ballantine Books.

El Hassan, K. 2013. "Quality Assurance in Higher Education in 20 MENA Economies." *Higher Education Management and Policy* 24 (2): 73–84. http://dx.doi.org/10.1787/hemp-24-5k3w5pdwjg9t.

Ericsson, K. Anders, Ralf T. Krampe, and Clemens Tesch-Römer. 1993. "The Role of Deliberate Practice in the Acquisition of Expert Performance." *Psychological Review* 100 (3): 363–406. https://doi.org/10.1037/0033-295X.100.3.363.

Estyn. 2017. "Active and Experiential Learning: Effective Foundation Phase Practice in Delivering Literacy and Numeracy in Year 1 and Year 2." Estyn, Cardiff. https://www.estyn.gov.wales/sites/www.estyn.gov.wales/files/documents/Estyn%20Active%20and%20experiential%20learning_E_Accessible_1.pdf.

Evans, David, and Anna Popova. 2015. "What Really Works to Improve Learning in Developing Countries? An Analysis of Divergent Findings in Systematic Reviews." Policy Research Working Paper 7203, World Bank, Washington, DC.

Ezzine, Mourad. 2009. "Education in the Arab World: Shift to Quality in Math, Science, and Technology Faltering." MENA Knowledge and Learning Quick Note 2 (February), World Bank, Washington, DC. http://web.worldbank.org/archive/website01418/WEB/IMAGES/QUICK-31.PDF.

Gates Foundation. No date. "Teaching All Students to High Standards in Mixed-Ability Classrooms." Gates Foundation, Seattle, WA.

GIZ (Deutsche Gesellschaft für Internationale Zusammenarbeit). 2013a. "All Children Learning, Middle East and North Africa 2013, Summary Report." Paper prepared for the All Children Learning Workshop, GIZ, Rabat, December 3.

———. 2013b. *Early Primary Mathematics Education in Arab Countries of the Middle East and North Africa*. Eschborn: GIZ.

Glewwe, Paul W., Eric A. Hanushek, Sarah D. Humpage, and Renato Ravina. 2014. "School Resources and Educational Outcomes in Developing Countries: A Review of the Literature from 1990 to 2010." In *Education Policy in Developing Countries*, edited by Paul Glewwe, 13–64. Chicago: University of Chicago Press.

Hattie, John, and Helen Timperley. 2007. "The Power of Feedback." *Review of Educational Research* 77 (1): 81–112.

Heckman, James J. 2006. "Skill Formation and the Economics of Investing in Disadvantaged Children." *Science* 312 (5782): 1900–02. http://science.sciencemag.org/content/312/5782/1900.full.

Herrán, Carlos Alberto, and Alberto Rodríguez. 2000. *Secondary Education in Brazil: Time to Move Forward*. Washington, DC: World Bank.

Heyne, Stephanie, and Michael Gebel. 2012. "Education and Labor Market Entry in Middle East and Northern African Countries: Chances and Constraints in Times of Increasing Uncertainty." Proposal for a presentation at the 7th conference on employment and development, Institute of Labor Economics (IZA) and World Bank, New Delhi, November 5–6. http://conference.iza.org/conference_files/worldb2012/heyne_s8181.pdf.

Jacobs, H. H. 1989. *Interdisciplinary Curriculum: Design and Implementation*. Alexandria, VA: Association for Supervision and Curriculum Development.

Jobrack, Beverlee. 2012. *Tyranny of the Textbook: An Insider Exposes How Educational Materials Undermine Reforms*. Plymouth: Rowman and Littlefield.

Kirschner, Paul A., John Sweller, and Richard E. Clark. 2006. "Why Minimal Guidance during Instruction Does Not Work: An Analysis of the Failure of Constructivist, Discovery, Problem-Based, Experiential, and Inquiry-Based Teaching." *Educational Psychologist* 41 (2): 75–86. https://doi.org/10.1207/s15326985ep4102_1.

Krafft, Caroline. 2017. "Is School the Best Route to Skills? Returns to Vocational School and Vocational Skills in Egypt." *Journal of Development Studies* 54 (7): 1–21.

Kremer, Michael, Conner Brannen, and Rachel Glennerster. 2013. "The Challenge of Education and Learning in the Developing World." *Science* 340 (6130): 297–300.

Krishnaratne, Shari, Howard White, and Ella Carpenter. 2013. "Quality Education for All Children? What Works in Education in Developing Countries." 3ie Working Paper 20, International Initiative for Impact Evaluation, International Food Policy Research Institute, Washington, DC.

Linden, Toby. 2001. "Double-Shift Secondary Schools: Possibilities and Issues." Human Development Network, Secondary Education Series, working paper, World Bank, Washington, DC.

Martin, Michael O., Ina V. S. Mullis, Pierre Foy, and M. Hooper. 2016. "TIMSS 2015 International Results in Science." TIMSS and PIRLS International Study Center, Boston College, Chestnut Hill, MA. http://timssandpirls.bc.edu/timss2015/international-results/.

Mavroudi, Anna, Thanasis Hadzilacos, Dimistris Kalles, and Andreas Gregoriades. 2015. "Teacher-Led Design of an Adaptive Learning Environment." *Interactive Learning Environments* 24 (8): 1996–2010.

Mazur, Eric. 1997. *Peer Instruction: A User's Manual*. Upper Saddle River, NJ: Prentice Hall.

McEwan, Patrick J. 2015. "Improving Learning in Primary Schools of Developing Countries: A Meta-Analysis of Randomized Experiments." *Review of Educational Research* 85 (3): 353–94.

Millot, Benoît, and Julia Lane. 2002. "The Efficient Use of Time in Education." *Education Economics* 10 (2): 209–28. doi:10.1080/09645290210126922.

Mischel, Walter. 2014. *The Marshmallow Test: Why Self Control Is the Engine of Success*. Boston, MA: Little, Brown and Company.

Moon, Yong-lin. 2007. "Education Reform and Competency-Based Education." *Asia Pacific Education Review* 8 (2): 337–41.

Mourshed, Mona, Chinezi Chijioke, and Michael Barber. 2010. *How the World's Most Improved School Systems Keep Getting Better*. London: McKinsey and Company.

Mullis, Ina V. S., Michael O. Martin, Pierre Foy, and M. Hooper. 2016. "TIMSS 2015 International Results in Mathematics." TIMSS and PIRLS International Study Center, Boston College, Chestnut Hill, MA.

Murnane, Richard J., and Alejandro J. Ganimian. 2014. "Improving Educational Outcomes in Developing Countries: Lessons from Rigorous Evaluations." NBER Working Paper 20284, National Bureau of Economic Research, Cambridge, MA. http://www.nber.org/papers/w20284.

Nhundu, Tichatonga J. 2000. "Headteacher and Teacher Perspectives of Multiple-Shift School Practices: A Zimbabwean Experience." *International Studies in Education Administration* 28 (1): 42–56.

OECD (Organisation for Economic Co-operation and Development). 2011. *Strong Performers and Successful Reformers in Education: Lessons from PISA for the United States*. Paris: OECD Publishing.

———. 2016. *PISA 2015 Results*. Vol. 2: *Policies and Practices for Successful Schools*. Paris: OECD Publishing. http://dx.doi.org/10.1787/9789264267510-en.

———. 2017. *Education at a Glance 2017: OECD Indicators*. Paris: OECD Publishing. https://doi.org/10.1787/eag-2017-en.

Osman, Mohamed E., Thuwayba A. Al Barwani, Abdo M. Al Mekhlafi, and Mustafa B. Ab Sheiba. 2014. "Gender Gap in Students Performance: Implications on the Labor Market and the Fabric of Society." Sultan Qaboos University and the Research Council of Oman.

Oxford Business Group. 2015. *The Report: Algeria 2015*. London: Oxford Business Group. https://oxfordbusinessgroup.com/algeria-2015.

———. 2017. *The Report: Tunisia 2017*. London: Oxford Business Group. https://oxfordbusinessgroup.com/overview/track-series-reforms-are-set-overhaul-sector.

Pellegrino, James W., and Margaret L. Hilton, eds. 2012. *Education for Life and Work: Developing Transferable Knowledge and Skills in the 21st Century*. Washington, DC: National Academies Press. http://nap.edu/13398.

Prince, Michael. 2004. "Does Active Learning Work? A Review of the Research." *Journal of Engineering Education* 93 (3): 223–31.

Rabie, Tamer Samah, Samira Nikaein Towfighian, Cari Clark, and Melani Cammett. 2017. *The Last Mile to Quality Service Delivery in Jordan*. Directions in Development—Human Development. Washington, DC: World Bank. https://openknowledge.worldbank.org/handle/10986/26577.

Ridge, Natasha. 2014. *Education and the Reverse Gender Divide in the Gulf States*. New York: Teachers College Press.

Ripley, Amanda. 2017. "Boys Are Not Defective." *The Atlantic*, September 21. https://www.theatlantic.com/education/archive/2017/09/boys-are-not-defective/540204/.

Roediger, H. L. III, Adam L. Putnam, and Megan A. Smith. 2011. "Ten Benefits of Testing and Their Applications to Educational Practice." In *The Psychology of Learning and Motivation*, Vol. 55: *The Psychology of Learning and Motivation: Cognition in Education*, edited by

Jose P. Mestre and Brian H. Ross, 1–36. San Diego: Elsevier Academic Press.

Schanzenbach, Diane Whitmore, Ryan Nunn, Lauren Bauer, Megan Mumford, and Audrey Breitwieser. 2016. "Seven Facts on Noncognitive Skills from Education to the Labor Market." The Hamilton Project, Brookings Institution, Washington, DC, October 4.

Schneider, Michael, and Elsbeth Stern. 2010. "The Cognitive Perspective on Learning: Ten Cornerstone Findings." In *The Nature of Learning: Using Research to Inspire Practice*, edited by Hannah Dumont, David Istance, and Francisco Benavides, 69–90. Paris: OECD Publishing.

Snilstveit, Birte, Jennifer Stevenson, Daniel Phillips, Martina Vojtkova, Emma Gallagher, Tanja Schmidt, Hannah Jobse, Maisie Geelen, Maria Grazia Pastorello, and John Eyers. 2015. *Interventions for Improving Learning Outcomes and Access to Education in Low- and Middle-Income Countries: A Systematic Review*. 3ie Systematic Review 24. London: International Initiative for Impact Evaluation.

Steenbergen-Hu, Saiying, Matthew C. Makel, and Paula Olszewski-Kubilius. 2016. "What One Hundred Years of Research Says about the Effects of Ability Grouping and Acceleration on K–12 Students' Academic Achievement; Findings of Two Second-Order Meta-Analyses." *Review of Educational Research* 86 (4): 849–99. doi:10.3102/0034654316675417.

Stigler, James W., and James Hiebert. 2009. "Closing the Teaching Gap." *Phi Delta Kappan* 91 (3): 32–37. https://doi.org/10.1177/003172170909100307.

Swan, Paul, and Linda Marshall. 2010. "Revisiting Mathematics Manipulative Materials." *Australian Primary Mathematics Classroom* 15 (2): 13–19.

Thobani, Shiraz. 2007. The Dilemma of Islam as School Knowledge in Muslim Education." *Asia Pacific Journal of Education* 27 (1): 11–25.

Tomlinson, Carol Ann. 2014. *The Differentiated Classroom: Responding to the Needs of All Learners*, 2d ed. Alexandria, VA: Association for Supervision and Curriculum Development.

UNESCO (United Nations Educational, Scientific, and Cultural Organization). 2011. World Data on Education: Seventh Edition 2010–11 database. Geneva: International Bureau of Education. http://www.ibe.unesco.org/en/document/world-data-education-seventh-edition-2010-11.

———. 2015. "Curriculum and Materials." IIEP Learning Portal. https://learningportal.iiep.unesco.org/en/improve-learning/curriculum-materials/supplementary-learning-materials.

———. 2017. "The Why, What, and How of Competency-Based Curriculum Reforms: The Kenyan Experience." In-Progress Reflection 11, International Bureau of Education, UNESCO, Geneva.

UNESCO (United Nations Educational, Scientific, and Cultural Organization), UNICEF (United Nations Children's Fund), World Bank, and Brookings Institution Center for Universal Education. 2017. *Overview: MELQO: Measuring Early Learning Quality and Outcomes*. Paris: UNESCO. https://unesdoc.unesco.org/ark:/48223/pf0000248053.

UNICEF (United Nations Children's Fund). 2012. *Nationwide School Assessment: Libya*. Paris: UNICEF. http://washinschoolsmapping.com/wengine/wp-content/uploads/2015/10/Libya_Nationwide-assessment-report-english.pdf.

Virgona, Lynette. 2012. "Teachers Are the Key: Strategies for Instructional Improvement." In *2009–2017 ACER Research Conferences*. Camberwell: Australian Council for Educational Research. https://research.acer.edu.au/research_conference/RC2012/28august/5.

Wagner, Daniel A. 2011. "Smaller, Quicker, Cheaper: Improving Learning Assessments for Developing Countries." International Institute of Educational Planning, UNESCO, Paris. http://www.literacy.org/sites/literacy.org/files/publications/213663e.pdf.

Wagner, Tony, and Ted Dintersmith. 2015. *Most Likely to Succeed: Preparing Our Kids for the Innovation Era*. New York: Simon and Schuster.

Westbrook, Jo, Naureen Durrani, Rhona Brown, David Orr, John Pryor, Janet Boddy, and Francesca Salvi. 2013. *Pedagogy, Curriculum, Teaching Practices and Teacher Education in Developing Countries: Final Report*. Centre for International Development, University of Sussex.

Willingham, Daniel T. 2010. *Why Don't Students Like School? A Cognitive Scientist Answers Questions about How the Mind Works and What It Means for the Classroom*. San Francisco: Jossey Bass.

World Bank. 2018. *World Development Report 2018: Learning to Realize Education's Promise*. Washington, DC: World Bank.

World Economic Forum. 2016. "The Future of Jobs: Employment, Skills, and Workforce Strategy for the Fourth Industrial Revolution." World Economic Forum, Cologny, Switzerland, January.

SPOTLIGHT 2

MEASURING LEARNING

Laura Gregory and
Elisabeth Sedmik

Learning is a key goal of education systems, but without accurate information on learning, policy makers cannot make informed decisions. Assessment, therefore, is both an important learning tool (for students) and a key source of data (for teachers and education decision makers). There are several ways to monitor and assess student learning, each serving different purposes (Clarke 2012; World Bank 2018).

- A teacher may use *formative classroom assessment* during a lesson to measure how well students understand the material. This is an example of a "low-stakes" assessment, in that the results do not have long-term implications for student placement, but instead inform the teacher and student about the instructional process.
- In contrast, *public examinations* evaluate how well students have mastered a certain domain of knowledge and skills, usually at the end of a phase of education. These examinations are often "high-stakes" assessments, in that their results influence students' progression through the education system.
- Finally, *national and international large-scale assessments* of student learning provide educators and policy makers with comparative information that enables them to take stock of what is working and what needs to improve.

Although both public examinations and national and international assessments can yield countrywide data on student learning, it is important to distinguish between their different purposes. Public examinations evaluate or certify individual students. In contrast, national or international large-scale assessments monitor educational progress at the collective level and have low stakes for individual students, thus allowing for more rigorous comparison of educational progress over time (Clarke 2012; Greaney and Kellaghan 2008). The distinction between public examinations and national and international assessments is not always straightforward.

Such examinations can create perverse incentives that have a negative impact on student learning environments. This is the case, for example, when national assessments have low stakes for students but affect school funding or teacher promotions. If school funding depends on test scores, inequity could increase as schools located in areas with ample physical and human capital resources receive more funding than those located in areas with fewer resources. Likewise, when teacher promotions depend solely on student test scores, teachers are motivated to teach to the test, and this focus on examination scores can lead to overuse of rote memorization, factual recall, and even cheating, as documented in Jordan and Morocco (Buckner and Hodges 2015), as well as Lebanon (Bacha, Bahous, and Nabhani 2012). Therefore, clarity about the purpose of an assessment program can enhance its utility.

National and international large-scale student assessments monitor education system progress

National and international large-scale student assessments are often used to measure and monitor student learning at a collective level. These assessments are generally limited to certain grades, subject areas, and schooling years. They often involve a representative sample of students; in some countries, all students in a given grade are tested each year.[1] These assessments are useful for (1) tracking within-country trends in student learning, (2) measuring against learning targets, and (3) providing points of comparison with other countries. Some countries implement national assessments of learning, which can focus on national curricula and measure within-country education goals tied to national education policy. Developing and implementing regular national assessments require financial resources and technical capacity.

Large-scale assessments can inform policy and drive improvements

High-profile international and national assessments often receive media and public attention, leading to demand for reform (Greaney and Kellaghan 2008). Unfortunately, in several countries in the Middle East and North Africa (MENA), the public is often unaware of poor assessment results because they are not openly discussed, or, in the case of national assessments, the results are not made publicly available.

Major international student assessments include the Trends in International Mathematics and Science Study (TIMSS), which is conducted every four years, and the Progress in International Reading Literacy Study (PIRLS), which is conducted every five years. In addition, the Programme for International Student Assessment (PISA) studies the performance of 15-year-olds in mathematics, science, and reading every three years.

Some international assessments have also been designed for low- and middle-income countries with limited financial resources and technical capacity. These assessments are sometimes used to stand in for national assessments, often adapted to reflect student progress in the education systems of the countries in which they are given. The Early Grade Reading Assessment (EGRA) and Early Grade Mathematics Assessment (EGMA) measure within-country trends in student learning during the early years. Each assessment takes an average of 15 to 20 minutes per student, and scoring does not require knowledge of statistical techniques (Gove et al. 2013). Similarly, the PAL Network coordinates volunteer-led, household-based assessments of basic literacy and numeracy in 14 countries (PAL Network n.d.). The Organisation for Economic Co-operation and Development (OECD) recently launched PISA for Development, an initiative to adapt PISA assessment instruments to the needs of low- and middle-income countries (OECD 2016). In addition, the International Association for the Evaluation of Educational Achievement is developing the Literacy and Numeracy Assessment (LaNA).[2] Although these assessments are not tied to national education policy goals, they do provide a means of basic assessment and comparative benchmarking of student progress that would not otherwise take place.

More MENA countries are undertaking large-scale assessments

The number of national and international assessments of student achievement has increased in the region since the mid-1990s. This expansion provides important pieces of information on what students have learned and what they can do. Table S2.1 shows the various national and international assessments of student achievement undertaken in MENA countries since 1995, illustrating the surge in participation that began in 2007. In 1995, just two countries (the Islamic Republic of Iran and Kuwait) participated in TIMSS, while 11 MENA countries participated in 2019.

But few countries are using the results to inform decisions

While MENA countries are increasingly participating in large-scale international assessments and many are, or have begun, applying national assessments on a regular basis,

TABLE S2.1 Participation in national and international student assessments has surged in MENA since 2007
MENA economies undertaking national and international student assessments, 1995–2019

Economy	1995	1996	1997	1998	1999	2000	2001	2002	2003	2004	2005	2006	2007	2008	2009	2010	2011	2012	2013	2014	2015	2016	2017	2018	2019
Algeria													○								◇				
Bahrain									•				•		◇	◇	○◇	◇		◇	•○	◂			○
Djibouti																			×					+	
Egypt, Arab Rep.									•			◇	◇	◇	×◇	◇	×	×	×	×	•	◂			◇
Iran, Islamic Rep.	○				•		◂		○			◂	○•	•			○• ◂				○	◂			○
Iraq																		×+						◇	
Jordan					•							□	•	◇	□		•	□× +		×+	○• □			□	○
Kuwait	○				•		◂				◇	◂	○•				○				○	◂			○
Lebanon									•				•	◆			•				• □	×	◇	×□	•
Libya																									
Morocco					•		◂		○			◂	○•	◇			○•◂ +				○	◇ ◂		□	○
Oman											◇						○• ◂				○	◂			○
Qatar												□◂	○•		□		○•◂	□			○• □	◂		□	○
Saudi Arabia									•				•	◆			○•◂				○ ◇	◂		◇	○•×◇
Syrian Arab Republic					•								•				•								
Tunisia									○□			□	○•	◇	□		○•	□			□			□	○
United Arab Emirates															□[a]		○•◂			×	○• □	◂		□	•
West Bank and Gaza									•		◇		•				•			×				×	
Yemen, Rep.					◇				○		◇		○				○×								

+ EGMA × EGRA ◇ National or other assessment ▲ PIRLS grade 4 □ PISA ○ TIMSS grade 4 • TIMSS grade 8 ◆ TIMSS Advanced[b]

Source: Compiled by the World Bank, based on information from country task teams and international assessment organizations.
Note: Includes participating countries for which results were not reported because of sampling or other issues. EGMA = Early Grade Mathematics Assessment; EGRA = Early Grade Reading Assessment; PIRLS = Progress in International Reading Literacy Study; PISA = Programme for International Student Assessment; TIMSS = Trends in International Mathematics and Science Study.
a. The 2009 PISA scores pertain to the PISA 2009+ reported score for the United Arab Emirates (Dubai participated in 2009, and the remaining emirates participated in 2010).
b. TIMSS Advanced assesses the advanced mathematics and physics knowledge and skills of students in their final year of secondary school who have taken courses in advanced mathematics and physics. TIMSS Advanced was administered in 1995, 2008, and 2015.

few are using the results to inform education policy and pedagogical practices. Jordan is an exception, as it has been sharing the results of its national assessment with the public, allowing education stakeholders the opportunity to respond to the status quo and participate in efforts to make improvements (Obeidat and Dawani 2014). Examples from countries in other regions illustrate how the best use can be made of these rich sources of information; for example, Chile's Sistema de Medición de la Calidad de la Educación (Education Quality Measurement System) has carried out census-based assessments since 1988 and publishes the results at both the national and school levels. The Chile example demonstrates that publishing results can nurture a culture of evaluation that makes all actors accountable (Meckes and Carrasco 2010).

At the local level, several MENA countries have used student assessment results to evaluate and inform education initiatives. For example, EGRA results have been used successfully to determine effect sizes of small-scale reading interventions, such as in the Arab Republic of Egypt and Jordan, which have informed scaling up of these programs to a national level (USAID 2012, 2014). In addition, a few years ago, Lebanon finished gathering EGRA baseline data in a set of schools for grades 2 and 3 (2015, 2016) and is currently gathering endline data for both grades to assess improvements in reading outcomes following implementation of a teacher training intervention.

While EGRAs and EGMAs are not nationally representative, they have the potential to affect national policy positively by serving as evaluation tools for local education initiatives, thus providing data on which programs (or aspects of programs) might be scaled successfully to a national level. In cases where EGRA and EGMA assessments have been undertaken at a nationally representative level, their results can serve to gauge how policies are working and can provide information on the following:

- How learning outcomes vary across geographic areas and demographic groups, thus informing improved targeting (to regions, resources, or districts, for example) of reforms
- How new curricula, teacher training, or teaching methods should be developed and implemented
- How benchmarks can be set to enable tracking of progress and increase accountability.

Public examinations can catalyze reform but also can create perverse incentives

While large-sale national and international assessments can catalyze education reform at the policy level, public examinations can generate powerful incentives for change at the school, teacher, and student levels (Kellaghan and Greaney 2001; Madaus, Russell, and Higgins 2009). However, if used inappropriately, public examinations can reinforce shallow forms of learning, and preparation can consume valuable lesson time without enhancing student learning. In many MENA countries, students receive one of the only measures of their learning through high-stakes year-end examinations. These high-stakes examinations are typically used to determine grade progression. More regular feedback on students' learning progress could be very helpful to students. In addition, high-stakes assessments often lead to perverse incentives that negatively affect behavior among teachers, students, and parents and limit learning outcomes.

Public examinations are high stakes and overemphasize rote recall

Public examinations can strongly influence teaching and learning, but this influence has mixed effects. While one analysis of cross-country PISA data found that exit examinations have a large positive effect on student achievement (Woessmann et al. 2009), another PISA analysis did not find a significant correlation between standardized testing and achievement (OECD 2016). Some smaller-scale studies have found that teachers respond to high-stakes tests with increased diligence and focus (Hamilton 2003; Koretz 2008). However, teachers have also responded by narrowing lesson content to match test coverage, allocating excessive classroom time to test preparation, focusing on students whose performance hovers around grade boundaries, or assigning low-performing students to special-needs categories that exempt them from testing (Hamilton 2003; Kellaghan and Greaney 1992; Koretz 2008). In some cases, the introduction of high-stakes examinations has resulted in a rise in student test scores on the high-stakes test without corresponding improvements in low-stakes tests, suggesting that the improvements in high-stakes scores did not translate into broader learning gains (Hamilton 2003; Koretz 2008).

In MENA, high-stakes examinations reinforce a focus on credentials rather than skills acquisition (Salehi-Isfahani 2012). In addition to the lack of widespread and systematic formative assessments, high-stakes examinations in MENA are misaligned with goals for the acquisition of relevant knowledge and skills. High-stakes examinations in MENA countries at the end of secondary school are used to ration progression into further—tertiary—education. As the sole determinant of progression to higher education in many cases, learning, especially in the last years of secondary education, emphasizes this high-stakes examination rather than the acquisition of broader skills and learning to learn.

Furthermore, the high-stakes examinations at the end of secondary education in the MENA region tend to emphasize straightforward recall and procedural applications, leading to cramming, private tutoring, and rote memorization (Akar 2016; Shuayb 2012). The *Tawjihi* in Jordan and West Bank and Gaza or the *Thanaweya Amma* in Egypt are used to determine whether a student can enroll in a specific university or faculty, which in turn determines his or her future occupational opportunities and social standing. High-stakes examinations focused on recall lead to teaching methods that focus on memorization of facts and procedures, and, ultimately, to students who have not developed lifelong skills such as critical thinking and learning to learn, both of which are increasingly important in today's world (World Bank 2019). In Egypt, 53 percent of students utilize private tutoring, and a further 10 percent utilize paid study groups (Assaad and Krafft 2015).

Regarding equity, students from higher socioeconomic backgrounds are more likely to receive tutoring and therefore to achieve higher test scores, exacerbating inequality of learning outcomes among students from different socioeconomic backgrounds. In addition, widespread private tutoring by schoolteachers creates an economic disincentive to cover material adequately during class, further exacerbating inequalities in education outcomes (Assaad and Krafft 2015).

Even at lower grades, year-end school examinations affect opportunities for children to progress through grades, which can negatively influence teaching practices. Lebanon's students are tested monthly in class, take two examinations every year, and sit national examinations at the end of grades 9 and 12. In the Islamic Republic of Iran and Jordan, students may pass on to the next level provided they do not fail more than three subjects in their year-end examinations. These examinations or summative assessments are intended to measure whether students have mastered the necessary content. They also serve to channel students into education tracks. However, their high-stakes nature often results in teachers emphasizing memorization for examinations over problem-solving skills (Akar 2016; Shuayb 2012). Morocco has implemented a system of examinations at each level (Mullis and Martin 2013). These examinations are intended to channel students into educational and vocational tracks; as such, they run the risk that teachers will use didactic rather than dialogic teaching methods (Akar 2016; Shuayb 2012).

Recognizing the inherent risks, several MENA countries have reduced the focus on high-stakes examinations, especially during the early grades. Jordan, Kuwait, and

Lebanon have abolished high-stakes examinations that ration progression between grades 1 and 3. Their example might guide further reforms in other MENA countries aimed at ensuring that high-stakes examinations are rationed, do not create perverse incentives for teachers and students, and test higher-order thinking skills.

Recently, East Asian countries with historically high scores on PISA and TIMSS have made efforts to reduce high-stakes testing in upper-secondary school, introducing more process-oriented and student-centered assessment measures. For example, in an effort to eliminate "teaching to the test" and to support 21st-century skills and curricular reforms focused on learning to learn, in 2014 Japan proposed the Prospective University Entrant Scholastic Abilities Evaluation Test, an alternative examination to be implemented from 2019 forward. The examination will deemphasize rote memorization, while prioritizing students' thinking ability, expression, and reasoning skills (Kimura and Tatsuno 2017). In a similar effort to promote student learning, the Republic of Korea has implemented an "exam-free semester." In order for lower-secondary students to discover their dreams and talents free from the pressure of midterm and final exams, Korea allows teachers to make flexible use of the curriculum for a period of one semester, which encourages student participation through discussion and practice and enables various activities such as career exploration. The exam-free semester was introduced in 2013, pilot-tested for two years, and then implemented nationwide in 2016 (Cheng 2017).

Task-based assessments can measure higher-order skills

In some education systems, examinations have been replaced with a series of complex tasks that students complete over an extended period of time in order to demonstrate their learning (Darling-Hammond 2017). Task-based assessments can be incorporated into curricular subjects or conducted as a stand-alone subject. For example, students attending schools within the New York Performance Standards Consortium are certified for graduation based on portfolios of complex tasks in which they apply their knowledge and skills across different subjects, such as an argumentative literary analysis or an original scientific experiment (Guha et al. 2018). In Singapore, preuniversity students take a stand-alone subject called Project Work as part of the A-level examination. In Project Work, groups of four or five students investigate a problem in their local context, research possible solutions, and deliver an oral presentation of their findings. Students receive a final grade reflecting both individual and group performance (Examinations and Assessment Board Singapore 2017).

Besides task-based assessments linked to specific topics or subject areas, another form of task-based assessment focuses on testing generic higher-order cognitive skills. While these assessments are standardized sit-down tests, they differ substantially from traditional content-oriented exams. One such test, the Collegiate Learning Assessment (CLA+), is a computer-based test of students' critical thinking and written communication capabilities. In addition to multiple-choice questions testing different types of reasoning and argumentation, the CLA+ includes a performance task, in which students craft practical written responses to a real-world scenario based on several authentic sources in different formats, such as newspaper articles, statistical reports, and interview transcripts (Council for Aid to Education 2017). Some U.S. universities use the CLA+ to measure gains in students' skills over the course of their tertiary education, providing a common metric of educational value added across different academic disciplines (Benjamin 2014; Hardison and Vilamovska 2009). Similar assessments of complex generic skills at the secondary level include the College and Work Readiness Assessment, developed by the institution behind the CLA+ (Wagner 2010; Zahner 2013), and the PISA 2015 Collaborative Problem Solving test (OECD 2017).

To promote skills development, MENA countries may benefit from exploring task-based assessments. Task-based assessments are a relatively recent development, and various forms are being adopted by a growing number of schools and education systems around the world to promote deeper learning and complex skills development (Darling-Hammond 2017; Guha et al. 2018; Wagner 2010). In MENA, Lebanon has conducted some small-scale studies on the feasibility of using a task-based assessment rather than an intelligence quotient test to identify students for gifted education programs (Sarouphim 2009, 2015). In Oman, examination grades incorporate scores from written tests as well as classroom-based assessment tasks (World Bank 2013). However, affecting a systemwide shift to task-based assessment can be difficult, as in Malaysia's experience (see box S2.1).

Box S2.1 Malaysia faced various challenges in introducing task-based assessment

In 2011, Malaysia's Ministry of Education launched a new task-based assessment system for primary and lower-secondary education. This assessment system was part of a push to develop students' critical thinking, creativity, and socioemotional skills and was introduced under the banner of the Malaysia Education Blueprint 2013–2025. However, there have been considerable challenges to implementing this policy program.

Overambitious implementation timelines did not adequately prepare teachers and systems to facilitate skills development. Between 1999 and 2011, Malaysia charted the largest declines in mathematics and science performance among all countries participating in TIMSS. Consequently, the government was under pressure to raise student outcomes rapidly. Major initiatives to develop 21st-century skills were implemented too hastily for adequate preparation. A revised lower-secondary examination, which replaced multiple-choice items with open-ended questions, was announced just months before students were tested, leaving both students and teachers unprepared and anxious. Similarly, a new assessment system based on in-class tasks—a radical departure from the long-established centralized examinations—was instituted nationwide before teachers had been briefed on assessment standards.

Education monitoring systems, which traditionally prioritized procedural compliance, were not adequately adapted for assessing complex skills. When the in-class task-based assessment system was first introduced, it mandated extensive reporting in complicated physical files and a sluggish online database. The reporting requirements were later streamlined, but only after triggering widespread disillusionment with the assessment system—and after consuming countless hours of teacher effort that would have been better channeled toward developing high-quality assessments. The mismatch between routine modes of monitoring and nonroutine skills development was also evident in assessment, where teachers accustomed to rigid marking schemes were unsure of how to award credit for open-ended questions and did not receive adequate training to do so.

After a fractious start, the revised examination formats are gradually gaining public acceptance. The shift to assessing the depth rather than the breadth of students' knowledge requires not only new approaches to teaching and learning, but also a different conception of educational success. It is too early to tell whether meaningful changes have occurred in classroom practice or students' cognitive and socioemotional skills, but there appears to be growing public acceptance of the new assessments. While the first few cycles of the new assessments met with considerable hostility from students, teachers, and parents who were caught off-guard by the rapid changes, the 2017 reformatting of the primary school exit assessment—which emphasized performance in classroom tasks, co-curricular activities, and physical fitness alongside standardized test scores—received a warmer response (Menon and Rajaendram 2017; Mior and Atikah 2017).

Sources: Hwa 2016; Ministry of Education Malaysia 2013, 2017.

Noncognitive and socioemotional skills should be assessed alongside cognitive skills

One important means of supporting the development of noncognitive skills within education systems is for noncognitive skills assessment to be conducted alongside cognitive skills assessment. However, there are substantial challenges in determining the extent to which students are developing these key skills. Confusion over terminology, including the descriptor *noncognitive*, complicates defining the bounds of this broad category of personal qualities, obscuring agreement on the specific attributes worth measuring. In addition, noncognitive skills tend to be process oriented, while traditional cognitive assessments focus on outcome measures ("the right answer" rather than the personal qualities that supported the student in arriving at the answer).

Despite these difficulties, several promising measures of noncognitive skills have been developed, and there is a growing body of literature on improving what is available (OECD 2016). In particular, self-report questionnaires, teacher-report questionnaires, and performance tasks reveal that each approach is imperfect in its own way and can affect its suitability for program evaluation, accountability, individual diagnosis, and practice improvement. Self-report and teacher-report questionnaires are the most common approaches to assessing students' personal qualities and are widely used by education researchers and practitioners alike (Duckworth and Yeagar 2015). Questionnaires are cheap, quick, reliable, and, in many cases, remarkably predictive of objectively measured outcomes. Arguably, self-report questionnaires are better suited than any other measure for assessing internal psychological states, like feelings of belonging (Duckworth and Yeagar 2015).

Notes

1. For example, Chile's Sistema de Medición de la Calidad de la Educación tests all students in grades 2, 4, 6, and 8 (basic education) and in grades 10 and 11 (second and third years of secondary education) every year.
2. See https://www.iea.nl/lana.

References

Akar, Bassel. 2016. "Dialogic Pedagogies in Educational Settings for Active Citizenship, Social Cohesion, and Peacebuilding in Lebanon." *Education, Citizenship, and Social Justice* 11 (1): 44–62. doi:10.1177/1746197915626081.

Assaad, Ragui, and Caroline Krafft. 2015. "The Evolution of Labor Supply and Unemployment in the Egyptian Economy: 1988–2012." In *The Egyptian Labor Market in an Era of Revolution,* edited by Ragui Assaad and Caroline Krafft, 1–26. Oxford, U.K.: Oxford University Press.

Bacha, Nahla Nola, Rima Bahous, and Mona Nabhani. 2012. "High Schoolers' Views on Academic Integrity." *Research Papers in Education* 27 (3): 365–81. https://www.tandfonline.com/doi/ref/10.1080/02671522.2010.550010?scroll=top.

Benjamin, Roger. 2014. "Two Questions about Critical-Thinking Tests in Higher Education." *Change: The Magazine of Higher Learning* 46 (2): 24–31.

Buckner, Elizabeth, and Rebecca Hodges. 2015. "Cheating or Cheated? Surviving Secondary Exit Exams in a Neoliberal Era." *Compare: A Journal of Comparative and International Education* 46 (4): 603–23. https://doi.org/10.1080/03057925.2015.1088379.

Cheng, Kai-ming. 2017. "Advancing 21st Century Competencies in East Asian Education Systems." Center for Global Education, Asia Society, New York.

Clarke, Marguerite. 2012. "What Matters Most for Student Assessment Systems: A Framework Paper." SABER Student Assessment Working Paper 1, World Bank, Washington, DC. https://openknowledge.worldbank.org/handle/10986/17471.

Council for Aid to Education. 2017. *CLA+ Student Guide.* New York: Council for Aid to Education. http://cae.org/images/uploads/pdf/CLA_Student_Guide_Institution.pdf.

Darling-Hammond, Linda. 2017. "Teacher Education around the World: What Can We Learn from International Practice?" *European Journal of Teacher Education* 40 (3): 291–309. doi:10.1080/02619768.2017.13315399.

Duckworth, Angela, and Scott Yeagar. 2015. "Measurement Matters: Assessing Personal Qualities Other Than Cognitive Ability for Educational Purposes." *Educational Researcher* 44 (4): 237–51. http://journals.sagepub.com/doi/abs/10.3102/0013189X15584327.

Examinations and Assessment Board Singapore. 2017. "Project Work: Singapore-Cambridge General Certificate of Education Advanced Level Higher 1 (2018): (Syllabus 8808)." https://www.seab.gov.sg/docs/default-source/national-examinations/gce-a-level/8808_2018.pdf.

Gove, Amber, Samir Habib, Benjamin Piper, and Wendi Ralaingita. 2013. "Classroom-Up Policy Change: Early Reading and Math Assessments at Work." *Research in Comparative and International Education* 8 (3): 373–86.

Greaney, Vincent, and Thomas Kellaghan. 2008. *Assessing National Achievement Levels in Education: National Assessments of Educational Achievement*. Washington, DC: World Bank. https://openknowledge.worldbank.org/handle/10986/6904.

Guha, Roneeta, Tony Wagner, Linda Darling-Hammond, Terri Taylor, and Diane Curtis. 2018. *The Promise of Performance Assessments: Innovations in High School Learning and College Admission*. Palo Alto, CA: Learning Policy Institute.

Hamilton, Laura. 2003. "Assessment as a Policy Tool." *Review of Research in Education* 27 (1): 25–68. doi:https://doi.org/10.3102/0091732X027001025.

Hardison, Chaitra M., and Anna-Marie Vilamovska. 2009. *The Collegiate Learning Assessment: Setting Standards for Performance at a College or University*. Technical Report TR-663-CAE. Santa Monica, CA: RAND Corporation.

Hwa, Yue-Yi. 2016. "From Drills to Skills? Cultivating Critical Thinking, Creativity, Communication, and Collaboration through Malaysian Schools." Working paper, Penang Institute, Kuala Lumpur, August. https://penanginstitute.org/wp-content/uploads/jml/files/research_papers/HwaYY_Four_Cs_working_paper_28October2016.pdf.

Kellaghan, Thomas, and Vincent Greaney. 1992. "Using Examinations to Improve Education: A Study in Fourteen African Countries." Technical Paper WTP165, Africa Technical Department Series, World Bank, Washington, DC.

———. 2001. *Using Assessment to Improve the Quality of Education*. Paris: UNESCO: International Institute for Educational Planning.

Kimura, Daisuke, and Madoka Tatsuno. 2017. "Advancing 21st Century Competencies in Japan." Center for Global Education, Asia Society, New York. https://asiasociety.org/files/21st-century-competencies-japan.pdf.

Koretz, Daniel. 2008. "Test-Based Educational Accountability: Research Evidence and Implications." *Zeitschrift für Pädagogik* 54 (6): 777–90.

Madaus, George F., Michael Russell, and Jennifer Higgins. 2009. *The Paradoxes of High Stakes Testing*. Charlotte, NC: Information Age Publishing.

Meckes, Lorena, and Rafael Carrasco. 2010. "Two Decades of SIMCE: An Overview of the National Assessment System in Chile." *Assessment in Education: Principles, Policy, and Practice* 17 (2): 233–48. doi:10.1080/09695941003696214.

Menon, Sandhya, and Rebecca Rajaendram. 2017. "Parents and Pupils Welcome PPSR." *Star Online,* November 24. https://www.thestar.com.my/news/nation/2017/11/24/parents-and-pupils-welcome-ppsr-it-is-a-good-system-that-encourages-youngsters-to-do-more-all-at-onc/.

Ministry of Education Malaysia. 2013. *Malaysia Education Blueprint 2013–2015 (Preschool to Post-Secondary Education)*. Putrajaya: Ministry of Education Malaysia. https://planipolis.iiep.unesco.org/sites/planipolis/files/ressources/malaysia_blueprint.pdf.

———. 2017. "Pelaporan Pentaksiran Sekolah Rendah (PPSR)." *Negaraku*, November 25. https://www.negaraku.co/pelaporan-pentaksiran-sekolah-rendah/.

Mior, Alia, and Qistina Atikah. 2017. "Bouquets and Brickbats: New Primary School Assessment Report Sparks Heated Debate on Social Media." *New Straits Times,* November 23. https://www.nst.com.my/news/nation/2017/11/306561/bouquets-and-brickbats-new-primary-school-assessment-report-sparks-heated.

Mullis, Ina V. S., and Michael O. Martin, eds. 2013. "TIMSS 2015 Assessment Frameworks." TIMSS and PIRLS International Study Center, Boston College, Chestnut Hill, MA. http://timssandpirls.bc.edu/timss2015/frameworks.html.

Obeidat, Osamha, and Zaina Dawani. 2014. "Disseminating and Using Student Assessment Information in Jordan." SABER Student Assessment Working Paper 12, World Bank, Washington, DC.

OECD (Organisation for Economic Co-operation and Development). 2016. *PISA 2015 Results*.

Vol. 2: *Policies and Practices for Successful Schools*. Paris: OECD Publishing. doi: http://dx.doi.org/10.1787/9789264267510-en.

———. 2017. *PISA 2015 Results (Volume V): Collaborative Problem Solving*. Paris: OECD Publishing. http://dx.doi.org/10.1787/9789264285521-en.

PAL Network. No date. "People's Action for Learning: What We Do." http://palnetwork.org/what-we-do/.

Salehi-Isfahani, D. 2012. "Education, Jobs, and Equity in the Middle East and North Africa." *Comparative Economic Studies* 54 (4): 843–61.

Sarouphim, Ketty M. 2009. "The Use of a Performance Assessment for Identifying Gifted Lebanese Students: Is DISCOVER Effective?" *Journal for the Education of the Gifted* 33 (2): 275–95.

———. 2015. "Slowly but Surely: Small Steps toward Establishing Gifted Education Programs in Lebanon." *Journal for the Education of the Gifted* 38 (2): 196–211.

Shuayb, Maha. 2012. "Social Cohesion in Secondary Schools in Lebanon." In *Rethinking Education for Social Cohesion: International Case Studies,* edited by Maha Shuay, 137–53. London: Palgrave Macmillan.

USAID (U.S. Agency for International Development). 2012. "EdData II: Student Performance in Reading and Mathematics, Pedagogic Practice, and School Management in Jordan." Report prepared by RTI International for USAID, Washington, DC. https://Earlygradereadingbarometer.org/files/EGRA%20in%20Jordan.pdf.

———. 2014. "Education Data for Decision Making (EdData II): National Early Grade Literacy and Numeracy Survey—Jordan." Intervention Impact Analysis Report, USAID, Washington, DC. http://pdf.usaid.gov/pdf_docs/PA00KH3M.pdf.

Wagner, Tony. 2010. *The Global Achievement Gap: Why Even Our Best Schools Don't Teach the New Survival Skills Our Children Need—and What We Can Do About It*. New York: Basic Books.

Woessmann, Ludger, Elke Luedemann, Gabriela Schuetz, and Martin R. West. 2009. *School Accountability, Autonomy, and Choice around the World*. Cheltenham: Edward Elgar Publishing.

World Bank. 2013. *Education in Oman: The Drive for Quality*. Vol. 2: *Main Report*. Washington, DC: World Bank. http://documents.worldbank.org/curated/en/280091468098656732/Main-report.

———. 2018. *World Development Report 2018: Learning to Realize Education's Promise*. Washington, DC: World Bank.

———. 2019. *World Development Report 2019: The Changing Nature of Work*. Washington, DC: World Bank.

Zahner, Doris. 2013. *CWRA+ Standard Setting Study Final Report*. New York: Council for Aid to Education. http://cae.org/images/uploads/pdf/cwra_ss.pdf.

Leveraging Education Technology

8

Mariam Nusrat Adil, Venkatesh Sundararaman, and May Bend

Over the last decade, new technologies have emerged and spread globally, disrupting the lives of billions and changing the nature of work. Consequently, the kinds of skills needed to succeed in the labor market are changing as well (World Bank 2019). The role of technology as a shaper of demand in the future of work is certain, but its role as a catalyst for the delivery of education holds great untapped potential in the region. Indeed, technology is changing how today's students are being prepared to enter the future workforce—that is, it is influencing not only the ends of education but also the means. Technology presents a unique opportunity to deliver high-quality education in a more efficient and effective manner.

The Middle East and North Africa (MENA) region has the capacity and resources to leverage technology to create education systems that will build its human capital. However, the power of education to build human capital and to create change depends on its quality, its access to complementary economic and social environments, and its ability to leverage technology smartly.

A 2015 study by the Organisation for Economic Co-operation and Development (OECD) using Programme for International Student Assessment (PISA) data notes, "The *reality* in our schools lags considerably behind the *promise* of technology" (OECD 2015). The available evidence is mixed at best regarding the effectiveness of the use of technology for improving student performance, specifically, learning outcomes in language, mathematics, and science. In fact, the OECD study points to a rather perverse set of outcomes, one in which the frequency of classroom computer use is associated with significantly worse learning outcomes, even after controlling for a variety of household and social characteristics. The report concludes that investing heavily in information and communication technology (ICT) services and infrastructure is less likely to prepare students for life in a digital world than ensuring that all children meet basic proficiency levels in reading and mathematics (OECD 2015).

Based on a review of more than 100 experimental (randomized control trials and regression discontinuity design) studies on the impacts of education technology (EdTech) across the world, Escueta et al. (2017) provide a comprehensive analysis of the evidence regarding EdTech's ability to improve student learning and summarize

> **Box 8.1** **Introducing disruptive technology in the classroom: From the blackboard to ICTs**
>
> The blackboard was invented in the early 19th century when colleges and universities were starting to experiment with the lecture approach (Horn 2017, referring to a speech by David Dockterman). The blackboard spread quickly, and efforts to migrate this new technology to school classrooms soon began. This process proved to be complicated, given that the typical classroom at the time had multiple grades, with children of different ages and abilities under the tutelage of one teacher. The blackboard was not useful in such a setting. Many years would pass before classrooms were reorganized as they are today, and blackboards finally proved their worth in single-grade environments.
>
> Over the past couple of decades, the introduction of ICTs into the classroom has followed a similar path. ICTs have not fundamentally altered our approach to classroom teaching, thus limiting their ability to affect student learning positively. The fundamental structure of the classroom is still oriented to a time when students needed to focus forward to a blackboard and the teacher used the blackboard to share information that students could not access on their own.
>
> With today's online devices, students can access information, methods, formulas, and problem-solving techniques, learn to play the piano, watch and perform laboratory experiments, or learn how best to shoot a basketball or hit a tennis ball—all from the relative safety of their desk.
>
> Classrooms as we currently know them could potentially disappear. How children learn can be fundamentally altered and dramatically improved. For the next EdTech technology revolution to take place, a fundamental shift in teaching and classroom organization is necessary, just as it was for successful introduction of the blackboard.
>
> *Sources:* Horn 2017, citing Mackey 2010, referring to a speech by David Dockterman. Also see Buzbee 2014; Muttappallymyalil et al. 2016.

their findings across four broad themes: (1) access to technology, (2) computer-assisted learning, (3) behavioral interventions, and (4) online courses. They find that the most promising interventions include computer-assisted learning and behavioral interventions, while interventions that merely provide access to technologies and online courses are less impactful (see box 8.1).

Digital technology is altering all facets of life in MENA

Although we cannot be certain that the use of EdTech will improve learning outcomes across MENA, we can predict with confidence that the following will occur in the not-so-distant future:

- MENA's youths will inherit a world dominated by technology, where digital skills will likely need to be part of their foundational skill set.
- The ability of youths to understand, use, navigate, modify, and adapt digital technology for a wide variety of applications will be critical to their future success.

Remarkable technological advances have occurred in the past 10 years. A bewildering number of new disruptive technologies appear on the market every day and are having dramatic effects on how we communicate, search for information, read, coordinate, socialize, conduct business, and so on. The pace of this change has been exponential.[1] At the time of the last World Bank MENA education flagship report in 2008, the iPhone was one year old, Twitter was just taking off, and Facebook users numbered around 145 million globally (Guardian 2014; World Bank 2008). By 2016, there were 107 mobile subscriptions per 100 persons in MENA countries (World Bank World Development Indicators database), and by 2017 there were almost 100 million active social media users (Radcliffe and Lam 2018). Of the 2.1 billion current Facebook users, more than 100 million are in MENA. The social network WhatsApp, which was launched in 2009, has 1.5 billion users globally. Today, more than two-thirds of young Arabs use Facebook and WhatsApp. Furthermore, YouTube, which was three years old in 2008, currently has 1.5 billion users globally, and Saudi Arabia is its biggest market in per capita consumption. Young Saudi Arabians ages 15 to 24 spend on average 72 minutes a day watching online videos (Radcliffe and Lam 2018).

In MENA, digital technologies have begun to alter all facets of life. Countries in the region are seeking ways to integrate digital technologies further into their national and regional development plans. Initiatives such as Dubai Plan 2021 and Vision 2030 of Saudi Arabia are expected to result in far-reaching changes in government social contracts with citizens and noncitizens. Smart cities are expected to mushroom all over the region, with cities like Abu Dhabi, Doha, and Dubai leading the way. These cities are gearing up for a future where highly connected, participatory societies engage with one another and where big data, artificial intelligence, machine learning, and deep learning drive service delivery (McKinsey 2016).

Although MENA's businesses and public sector are looking for ways to expand the use of digital technologies, citizens have been the ones driving the adoption of technology across the region thus far. Bahrain, Qatar, and the United Arab Emirates have more than 100 percent smartphone adoption rates, which are higher than in the United States (McKinsey 2016). Mobile broadband connections are expected to grow from half of all connections to nearly 70 percent by decade's end, with the number of smartphones increasing almost 60 percent (or 167 million new smartphones) for a total of nearly 463 million smartphones. By 2020, it is foreseen that approximately half of all MENA residents will have access to mobile Internet services and become consumers of social media, e-commerce, financial and social services, and a range of entertainment services (GSM Association 2017).[2]

Rapid penetration of technology and the myriad opportunities it presents entice citizens and policy makers to invest in digital technologies and attempt to leapfrog constraints in current service delivery mechanisms. Across the region, three underlying factors will keep access to general technology on the front burner: (1) governments' desire to diversify their economies, (2) efforts by businesses to remain globally competitive by extending the reach of digital technologies in their respective areas, and (3) the opportunity offered by digital technology to support learning for all and perhaps contribute to leveling the playing field for women in the region. A technology-driven future will require children to be technologically savvy and education systems to support them in becoming so.

Innovations in EdTech are disrupting the education sector

The world and the region have seen a sharp increase in EdTech, ICT applications aimed at improving education. Investments in EdTech reached a record US$9.5 billion in 2017 (Shulman 2018). Khan Academy, which opened its doors in 2008, uses YouTube to provide lessons to millions. In 2017, revenue from the global EdTech market was estimated at US$17.7 billion (Business Wire 2018).[3]

Several factors have fueled this growth: recognition of the importance of education for economic growth; a flattening or even decline of public financing for education, thereby creating space for private sector participation; and—perhaps most important—efforts to disrupt this sector through technology in hopes of increasing student learning and leapfrogging ahead in international education rankings.

Leverage technology for a stronger push for learning

Although many other sectors have already borne the brunt of technological disruption, the education sector has not changed substantially in its principal mode of delivery over the last 150 years—globally and in MENA. Technology offers a unique opportunity to deliver high-quality education in a more efficient and effective manner. If leveraged smartly, technology can help MENA countries to advance their education systems and support learning.

Several conditions in MENA today support greater adoption of EdTech, including a young, dynamic, and tech-savvy population, an education market valued at about US$100 billion (Al Masah Capital 2012), and countries that, on average, allocate about a fifth of their budget to education (Trade Arabia News Service 2013; World Bank 2008). All of this points to an environment conducive to the use and growth of EdTech. Many online platforms in MENA provide Arabic learning content. Some of the English-language content from Khan Academy and others has been translated into Arabic. MENA-based content providers such as Nafham have followed the Khan Academy format, producing original content that uses curricula from several countries in the region, along with crowdsourcing to upload lessons. Others—such as Talal Abu-Ghazaleh International University in Lebanon, the Education Media Company in Morocco, and Bibliotheca Alexandrina in the Arab Republic of Egypt—have created digital content in different languages. Some initiatives allow qualified refugees to access online courses (see chapter 3).

While MENA's education sector has witnessed several innovative EdTech solutions, the core systems continue to face ongoing challenges—poorly prepared teachers, teaching-learning processes that emphasize rote memorization over critical thinking, relatively low rates of participation in early childhood education, poor learning outcomes during the early years that persist throughout schooling, teaching and assessment systems that do not challenge children and fail to inculcate a growth mind-set, and a curriculum that does not fully emphasize 21st-century skills.

Expand ICT infrastructure for wider reach of EdTech solutions

Accessing EdTech solutions and platforms requires ICT infrastructure. In MENA, even countries with modest budgets have made substantial investments in school ICT infrastructure (Lightfoot 2011). ICTs are available in most MENA schools, averaging about 2.7 computers for every 10 grade 8 students. This is below the international average of 4.0 (Mullis et al. 2016). Cross-country variability is quite wide, with 10.5 computers for every 10 students in Qatar and only 1.0 computer for every 50 students in the Islamic Republic of Iran (see figure 8.1).

Across MENA, the staffing needed to support ICT-based learning is not yet in place. Traditional approaches to the teaching-learning process are carried over into the classroom. For example, classroom observations in Bahrain, Jordan, and the United Arab Emirates revealed limited autonomy and lack of clear teacher instructions in the majority of classrooms where ICT is being used (Lightfoot 2011). Studies also note that investments in ICT infrastructure are underutilized. For example, approximately a quarter of all students in Bahrain, Egypt, the Islamic Republic of Iran, and Jordan use computers only once or twice a month or do not use them at all (see figure 8.2).

Leverage the strong public support for education technology in MENA

Families, students, and the broader community in the region strongly support further integration of digital technology in classrooms to change the nature of education and

FIGURE 8.1 Computers are available in MENA schools, although coverage varies considerably

Number of computers (including tablets) available for student use in school for every 10 grade 8 students, 2015

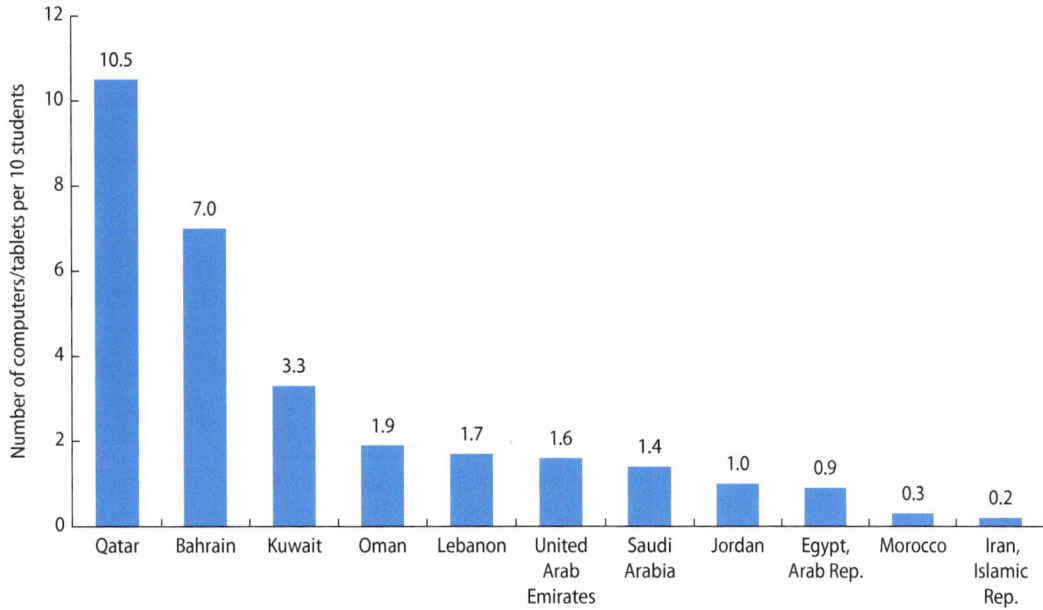

Source: Mullis et al. 2016.

FIGURE 8.2 Students in MENA rarely use computers in math or science classes

Percentage of grade 8 students who never or almost never use school computers to practice mathematics or science skills and procedures, as reported by teachers, 2015

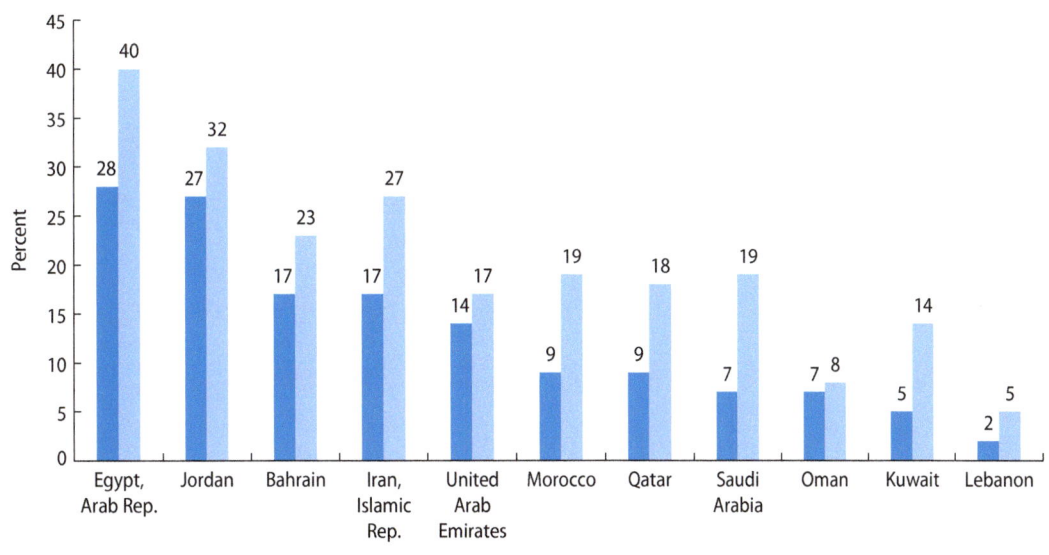

Source: Mullis et al. 2016.

FIGURE 8.3 Public support for EdTech reform is strong in MENA

Percentage of respondents who agreed with the following statements on Internet access, social media, and education reform, 2013

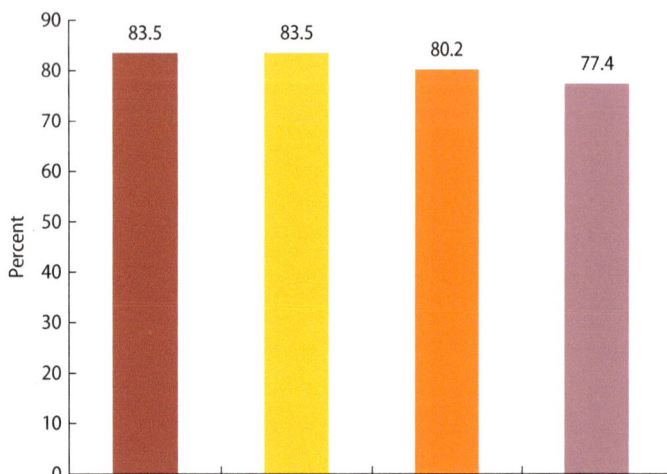

- **Internet access:** The government and the private sector should partner to universally provide schools and academic institutions with Internet access in my country.
- **Computers for students:** The government and the private sector should partner to universally provide students in schools with Internet access devices in my country (such as tablets, personal computers, laptops, and desktops).
- **Educational institutions:** Educational institutions in my country should promote the use of interactive technologies (such as social media) among teachers and students in classes.
- **Curriculum reforms:** On a national level, the ministry of education and higher education institutions and organizations should promote using social media in different curricula.

Source: ASMR 2013.

training systems in their countries. In a survey on social media and education reform across 13 of MENA's countries, a majority of respondents supported ICTs in the classroom (ASMR 2013). Of those surveyed, 84 percent felt that universal Internet access should be a norm and that children in schools should be able to access the Internet on individualized personal devices. More than 75 percent felt that social media should be part of the school curriculum (see figure 8.3).

Nevertheless, those surveyed also recognized that some aspects of access to technology could have detrimental effects on student learning. Responding to whether school students should be allowed to engage in a range of computer-related activities, almost 80 percent noted that they would be happy to have their kids use "collaborative web tools" in classwork, but less than 40 percent felt that students should be allowed to use social networking media in class (see figure 8.4).

Providing access to technology is not enough

The mere act of ensuring that students have access to technology yields varying results (Escueta et al. 2017). A recent analysis of PISA results for MENA countries found that

FIGURE 8.4 Most people in MENA approve of ICT use in the classroom

Percentage of respondents who agreed that children should be allowed to engage in specific ICT-related activities in school, 2013

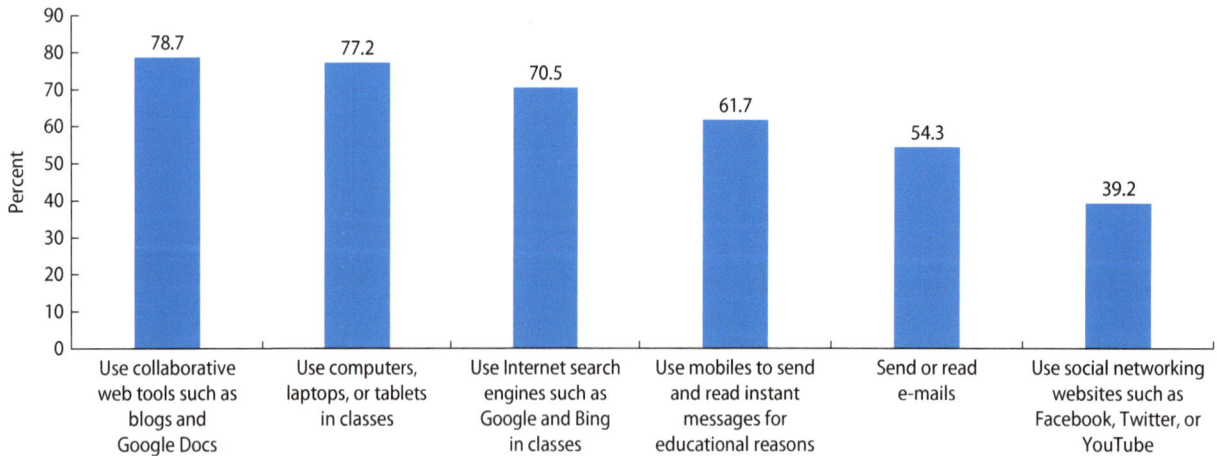

Source: ASMR 2013.
Note: ICT = information and communication technology.

access to technology alone does not help to solve problems related to student outcomes (McKinsey 2017). The study found that the association with adding an additional computer to classrooms is small, ranging from 0.2 to 1.1 PISA points per device added. The same study also found that supplying computers to teachers has a larger positive association; adding a teacher computer per classroom is associated with six times higher student PISA scores, than adding a student computer.[4]

Although increasing access to computers and the Internet may not, on its own, measurably improve academic achievement, it has been successful in increasing the ease of using technology and the time spent learning to use digital devices. In this sense, online connectivity in the classroom is a necessary, but not sufficient, condition for improving student learning outcomes aided by EdTech solutions.

Blended learning approaches have yielded promising results

Programs that pair face-to-face classroom learning with online components of the curriculum work well when delivered to students through structured online and in-class settings, where teachers are trained to facilitate this interaction. In essence, blended learning takes place any time a student learns through a combination of supervised school experiences away from home and online content delivery with some element of student control over time, place, path, and pace (Horn and Staker 2011). With blended learning, classroom and online experiences are tailored to reinforce one another (Horn and Staker 2012).

When paired with adequate teacher training in the use of technology and management of blended curricula, blended learning might improve the quality of teaching and learning in MENA schools and help the region to move away from antiquated teaching methods (Forbes Middle East 2013). With skillfully employed blended learning opportunities, MENA countries could leapfrog into the 21st century by teaching students how to engage in lifelong learning aided by technology. However, even in more advanced economies, such changes are proving to be difficult, given their costs and the need to train teachers in the use of EdTech.

Interest in blended learning programs is beginning to take root in MENA countries (Forbes Middle East 2013). For example, blended learning models are being used in the tertiary sector of the United Arab Emirates (Tamim 2017). A review of these models emphasized that a student-centered approach is the most important factor for success. Algeria, Bahrain, Egypt, the Islamic Republic of Iran, Israel, Jordan, Kuwait, Morocco, Oman, Qatar, Saudi Arabia, and the United Arab Emirates also have blended learning programs. While most examples are in the tertiary space, Kuwait, Qatar, Saudi Arabia, and the United Arab Emirates have rapidly growing programs at the basic education level (Weber and Hamlaoui 2018).

Computer-assisted blended learning interventions, particularly in mathematics, have shown positive learning outcomes on par with more traditional interventions, such as smaller class sizes, longer school days, and private provision of in-person tutoring (Escueta et al. 2017). Blended learning courses (or computer-assisted learning) produce similar outcomes to (and in some cases better outcomes than) in-person courses. An up-front investment in blended learning, paired with the necessary teacher training in their use, could improve schooling in MENA. Blended learning, when appropriately adapted to context and introduced by teachers trained to facilitate digital learning, offers a promising avenue for MENA education policy makers to explore.

Online courses have grown rapidly in popularity

Distance learning, or correspondence courses, have a long history in higher education in the United States, of which conventional online courses (COCs) became a natural online extension over the last decades. These courses are typically offered as part of a degree program that consists entirely of online courses or that includes blended learning courses. Experimental research on COCs has compared online and face-to-face courses to evaluate whether COCs are a viable substitute for fully in-person education. Of the nine courses evaluated by Escueta et al. (2017), all were consistent with the hypothesis that, without some degree of face-to-face teaching, learning outcomes are likely to suffer. In contrast, blended learning approaches have not yet been found to underperform purely face-to-face courses significantly. The Aldarayn Academy, the Arab E-Learning Academy, and the Tahrir Academy are three online program academies that existed before massive open online courses (MOOCs) were introduced to MENA in 2012.[5]

MOOCs have taken online courses to the next level. They make it possible for learners to take classes from reputable universities around the world on a wide range of topics and increasingly provide recognized credits for courses completed. MOOCs are growing rapidly in popularity, even though some efficiency issues remain to be addressed.

Several MOOC platforms are working in MENA, including homegrown efforts to produce MOOCs that cater to Arabic-language speakers. MOOC platforms popular in MENA include Rwaq, Nafham, and Edraak. The Rwaq platform offers a wide variety of courses in Arabic for Arab students by Arab professors. In 2015, Rwaq catered to more than 330,000 individuals, of which about 70 percent were male and between the ages of 17 and 34 years (Sallam 2017). Nafham is a free online K–12 educational Arabic video platform that crowdsources short videos for students and teachers. After first starting to create education video content for the Egyptian market, Nafham is now regional, and its content is used in Algeria, Kuwait, and Saudi Arabia and is a key tool for children displaced by the Syrian conflict.[6] Edraak offers free online courses for Arabic-speaking learners. The platform is decidedly regional in nature and is a product of the Queen Rania Foundation's work for education and development. Course content consists of both originally created courses and edX (free online) courses that are translated into Arabic (Pirkle 2014). Both platforms have reached millions of users from around the region (Jordan Times 2017).

The need to go from teaching and training millions to helping billions learn will require access to ubiquitous learning platforms that keep learners interested, are adaptive enough to deliver *personalized courses* matching student ability and effort, and are affordable enough to maintain, and ideally improve, educational equity (particularly in higher education). New methods to certify learning and exploit competency-based curricula and modularized programs by linking them to MicroMasters programs and nano credentials will likely have important impacts in the coming years (Escueta et al. 2017). Over the past decade, MENA has seen rapid growth in software-driven EdTech initiatives resulting in the widespread use of locally developed web-based and mobile-based learning platforms that cut across regional borders. Currently, there are more than 270 EdTech start-ups in MENA (D'Cunha 2018), bringing their vast experience from around the world and establishing a strong foothold in the region.[7]

Experimental research on the learning impacts of online courses is in the early stages. Because fully in-person classes outperform completely online courses, online courses are best employed only in areas where the alternative is nothing at all. Nevertheless, COCs do offer a range of other benefits, such as their relatively low cost and ability to cater to people who are otherwise fully employed, enabling them to take and complete courses at their preferred pace of study. Furthermore, Internet access and online courses offer girls and women opportunities to learn, extend their social influence, and grow their own businesses.

Technology-based "nudges" can promote behavioral change in education

Drawing on insights from behavioral economics, behavioral interventions are relatively new on the education landscape where they are proving useful in a wide variety of settings. Behavioral interventions are part of an increasingly fashionable area of research referred to as "nudges," an approach that presents choices to beneficiaries without changing the costs of these choices in any real way.[8] Typically, nudges reach users in the form of text messages reminding parents to register children for early childhood development programs or to review their children's secondary report card or alerting university students that it is time to submit student loan materials (Escueta et al. 2017; Pugatch and Wilson 2018).

Many governments in MENA are actively thinking about using nudge tactics to improve outcomes in education, including governments in Kuwait, Lebanon, Qatar, Saudi Arabia, and the United Arab Emirates. Given that behavioral change would have to underpin many of the changes envisioned in documents, such as Abu Dhabi's Economic Vision 2030, the United Arab Emirates' Vision 2021, and Saudi Arabia's Vision 2030, nudge units in these countries are identifying ways by which governments can employ behavioral economics techniques to help people to make the right choice, resulting in outcomes that have both individual and societal benefits.[9]

The existing experimental evidence consistently shows that technology-enabled behavioral interventions can have meaningful, if modest, impacts on a variety of education-related outcomes, at extremely low costs. Notably, they do so effectively at all ages—by connecting with parents during the early years and by motivating tertiary students, all through highly automated and inexpensive text messaging systems. MENA needs low-cost interventions, particularly during the early years where it is working to expand access to quality early childhood development and early learning programs. Behavioral EdTech initiatives have proven effective at increasing parental involvement, one of the key factors in early learning. Research on large-scale behavioral interventions remains in its infancy. Nevertheless, given the substantial results found thus far at the tertiary level, learning more about which approaches to mind-set changes are most effective and in which contexts could be important for MENA countries as they work to improve learning at all ages (Weissmüller 2019).

Online textbooks can facilitate access to information

Until about 30 years ago, the role of the teacher was not only to teach course content, but also to direct the student to potential resources outside the school premises. The teacher was the conduit for the flow of information to students. The World Wide Web and search engines like Google have altered their tasks forever. Today teachers need to guide students on how to search for information, and they need to support the growth of critical thinkers who can discern and discriminate between all of the information available to them, organizing, prioritizing, and synthesizing vast amounts of data.

One generation ago, at the start of the school year, students would carefully cover their textbooks in brown paper or even newspapers so as not to damage the book through the year. Students in many parts of the world today carry their entire set of textbooks across several grades on a single electronic device. The textbooks are now interactive in some cases and allow for a much more interesting interaction with the student. These developments are not new to MENA. On one end of the spectrum are mobile apps that provide online interactive libraries like Rawy Kids from Egypt or Kitabi Book Reader from Lebanon and those that use entertainment and games to encourage learning, such as Sho'lah, which is the first Arabic personal brain trainer, with more than 3 million downloads, and Loujee, which is a "smart" Arabic toy aimed at learning-through-play (Arab News 2016). Recently, two smartphone app-based games had encouraging early reading results in the conflict-ridden Syrian Arab Republic: Antura and the Letters and Feed the Monster, both of which showed positive learning results on initial impact evaluations and won awards at the 2017 EduApp4Syria competition (Comings 2018).

Combining these kinds of textbooks and learning materials with state-of-the art virtual reality and augmented reality platforms offers students a means to learn about various topics in ways hitherto not experienced in any classroom. Virtual reality technology is likely to allow students to practice laboratory experiments or engage in the practical side of training without having to bear the substantial recurrent costs of laboratory and practical training consumables. Both virtual and augmented reality resources are growing in MENA schools, allowing teachers to engage with their students on a wide range of topics and giving children experiences that they might not have had otherwise, while at the same time further incentivizing student participation in schooling activities.

Continued exploration and use of digital textbooks in MENA could improve the delivery of education services by providing a resource that can be updated easily across a wide variety of income levels and geographies. The movement toward digital textbooks comes with a set of challenges that can only be identified as they are being rolled out or experienced. A necessary condition is online connectivity and successful dissemination of devices loaded with up-to-date digital textbooks, along with continued maintenance of devices. Once this infrastructure is in place, it could provide substantial gains in education efficiency and course content delivery.

Smart classrooms are the classrooms of the future

Countries in MENA, and particularly in the Gulf Cooperation Council, are beginning to make substantial investments in 21st-century classrooms—referred to as smart classrooms. The early versions of smart classrooms simply put some device—a laptop or a tablet or a desktop—in front of the child, without fundamentally changing how the classroom was organized. Today's smart classrooms are very different and include multidimensional learning spaces that can support a blended learning style of online and face-to-face education. These classrooms have efficient infrastructure, which provides a learning-management system that allows students and teachers to use, design, and develop online digital content, supports behavioral interventions, and creates safe and exciting learning spaces for children with teachers who are trained to function in such environments.

Initiatives to bring smart classrooms to MENA are on the rise. Major private sector tech companies have set up shop in the region in an effort to support transformation of classrooms into 21st-century learning centers. Recognizing that teaching critical 21st-century skills in schools will require a cadre of teachers well versed in facilitating student learning in such environments, the Smart Learning Center in the United Arab Emirates aims to develop and build teacher capacity to use technology to deliver strong education content across MENA countries (Deloitte 2017). Such a regional resource is critical to ensure that teachers are well trained to teach in classrooms where student-centered approaches are adopted and self-paced and where student-directed learning shapes the teaching-learning process, not one where teachers dominate students through lectures. Such changes in the role of the teacher in the classroom tug at the very foundations of the education sector and will necessarily uproot a century of schooling, requiring more support for teachers both before (teacher training) and during (ongoing professional development, both onsite and offsite) service.

Evidence in the United States and elsewhere on the success of nascent smart classrooms is mixed at best, showing unreliable impacts on student learning to date (Robinson 2017). This is a very newly emerging and high-cost area of EdTech that MENA policy makers could continue to research while putting in place the basic infrastructure for EdTech solutions: online connectivity, access to computers and tablets for teachers and students, and teacher training on the use of blended learning approaches.

Navigating the technological landscape can be tricky

The bewildering volume of new technological resources entering the education market on an almost daily basis challenges education administrators and policy makers to identify, evaluate, and procure the best of these resources for their schools. Navigating the ever-changing terrain of new EdTech options is challenging, and governments are wise to do so being equipped with the best available research. To this end, the U.S. Department of Education recently launched a free online tool—the EdTech Rapid Cycle Evaluation Coach—that guides school administrators through this minefield and is a test bed that schools and school districts can use to compare different technologies and software.[10] Newman, Jaciw, and Lazarev (2018) have released a set of guidelines on how to conduct and report research related to EdTech impacts in K–12 schools in the United States.

Evaluation platforms could be a useful tool for MENA's education administrators and policy makers. Given the rapid pace with which new EdTech products are entering the market and the growth of cloud computing, which permits greater access to big data, their promise to support evaluation of EdTech is worth examining in order to drive evidence-based solutions.

Notes

1. To put this in perspective, consider the following: the Apple iPhone (2007), Amazon Kindle (2007), Facebook (initiated in late 2006), Android operating system (2007), the apps revolution (2007), Twitter (2007), Airbnb (2008), and Uber (2009) are products and services that have become household names even in remote corners of the world, and every one of them is only about a decade old.
2. Mobile connections vary widely across countries. Kuwait and Qatar lead the way in the proportion of mobile broadband connections (more than 85 percent), while West Bank and Gaza has yet to get 3G coverage off the ground.
3. However, these figures vary quite considerably depending on the source of this information.
4. They also found that computers have a greater association with scores in countries where ICT penetration is low. Adding a teacher computer in the North African countries that took PISA (Algeria and Tunisia), for example, was associated with higher PISA scores by 24.5 points. Doing the same in the two Gulf Cooperation Council countries (Qatar and the United Arab Emirates), where classroom technology is more common, was associated with an increase of just 1.1 PISA points.
5. For more information on these academies, see Sallam (2017).
6. See https://www.nafham.com/.
7. Although the number of EdTech companies (and the amount being spent) may seem very high, it is still a small fraction compared with the number in more advanced economies and larger countries like China and India.
8. Nudges could include information to increase access to or participation in colleges or to improve outcomes for students already enrolled and guide them to appropriate resources within such settings, such as tutorial classes or guidance counselors.
9. For example, getting people to eat healthfully and exercise has enormous implications in the medium to long term, both for health outcomes and for public health budgets.
10. See Office of Educational Technology, U.S. Department of Education (https://tech.ed.gov/rce/).

References

Al Masah Capital. 2012. "MENA Education Report." Dubai. http://www.almasahcapital.com/images/reports/report_89.pdf.

Arab News. 2016. "8 Educational Apps from MENA That Are Changing Classrooms and Education." *Arab News*, April 25. http://www.arabnews.com/science-technology/news/915356.

ASMR (Arab Social Media Report). 2013. "Transforming Education in the Arab World: Breaking Barriers in the Age of Social Learning." Dubai School of Government. June. http://www.arabsocialmediareport.com/UserManagement/PDF/ASMR_5_Report_Final.pdf.

Business Wire. 2018. "Growth Opportunities in the Education Technology Market—Forecast to 2022." *Business Wire*, January 11. https://www.businesswire.com/news/home/20180111006109/en/Growth-Opportunities-Global-Education-Technology-Market-2017.

Buzbee, Lewis. 2014. "The Simple Genius of the Blackboard: Why the Board-Centered Classroom Is Still the Best Place to Teach and Learn." *Slate*, October 15. http://www.slate.com/articles/life/education/2014/10/a_history_of_the_blackboard_how_the_blackboard_became_an_effective_and_ubiquitous.html.

Comings, John. 2018. "Assessing the Impact of Literacy Learning Games for Syrian Refugee Children: An Executive Overview of Antura and the Letters and Feed the Monster Impact Evaluations." World Vision, Washington, DC; Foundation for Information Technology Education and Development, Quezon, Philippines.

D'Cunha, Suparna Dutt. 2018. "Why the Middle East's Booming Student Population Makes It a Perfect Site for Education Tech Startups." *Forbes*, March 19. https://www.forbes.com/sites/suparnadutt/2018/03/19/edtech-startups-are-plugging-an-innovation-gap-in-education-in-the-middle-east/#7b584894fa47.

Deloitte. 2017. "National Transformation in the Middle East: A Digital Journey." Deloitte and Touche (Middle East), Beirut. https://www2.deloitte.com/content/dam/Deloitte/xe/Documents/technology-media-telecommunications/dtme_tmt_national-transformation-in-the-middleeast/National%20Transformation%20in%20the%20Middle%20East%20-%20A%20Digital%20Journey.pdf.

Escueta, Maya, Vincent Quan, Andre Joshua Nickow, and Philip Oreopoulos. 2017. "Education Technology: An Evidence-Based Review." NBER Working Paper 23744, National Bureau of Economic Research, Cambridge, MA.

Forbes Middle East. 2013. "Creating the Right Mix for Blended Learning." Dubai.

GSM Association. 2017. "The Mobile Economy, Middle East and North Africa 2017." London.

Guardian. 2014. "Facebook: 10 Years of Social Networking, in Numbers." *Guardian*, February 4. https://www.theguardian.com/news/datablog/2014/feb/04/facebook-in-numbers-statistics.

Horn, Michael B. 2017. "New Research Answers Whether Technology Is Good or Bad for Learning." *Forbes*, November 14. https://www.forbes.com/sites/michaelhorn/2017/11/14/new-research-answers-whether-technology-is-good-or-bad-for-learning/.

Horn, Michael B., and Heather Staker. 2011. "The Rise of K–12 Blended Learning." Innosight Institute, Lexington, MA.

———. 2012. "Classifying K–12 Blended Learning." Innosight Institute, Lexington, MA.

Jordan Times. 2017. "EdTech Outreach Spreads Regionally as Online Course Subscriptions Reach 1m Mark." *Jordan Times*, February 26. http://www.jordantimes.com/news/local/edraak-outreach-spreads-regionally-online-course-subscriptions-reach-1m-mark.

Lightfoot, Michael. 2011. "Promoting the Knowledge Economy in the Arab World." Sage Open, 1–8. http://journals.sagepub.com/doi/abs/10.1177/2158244011417457.

Mackey, Katherine. 2010. "Cramming." Christensen Institute (blog), October 19. https://www.christenseninstitute.org/blog/cramming/.

McKinsey. 2016. "Digital Middle East: Transforming the Region into a Leading Digital Economy." McKinsey and Company, Washington, DC, October. https://www.mckinsey.com/~/media/mckinsey/featured%20insights/middle%20east%20and%20africa/digital%20middle%20east%20transforming%20the%20region%20into%20a%20leading%20digital%20economy/digital-middle-east-final-updated.ashx.

———. 2017. "Drivers of Student Performance: Insights from the Middle East and North Africa." McKinsey and Company, Washington, DC. https://www.mckinsey.com/industries/social-sector/our-insights/drivers-of-student

-performance-insights-from-the-middle-east-and-north-africa.

Mullis, Ina V. S., Michael O. Martin, Pierre Foy, and M. Hooper. 2016. "TIMSS 2015 International Results in Mathematics." TIMSS and PIRLS International Study Center, Boston College, Chestnut Hill, MA.

Muttappallymyalil, Jayakumary, Susuruth Mendis, Lisha Jenny John, Nisha Shanthakumari, Jayadevan Sreedharan, and Rizwana B. Shaikh. 2016. "Evolution of Technology in Teaching: Blackboard and Beyond in Medical Education [Review Article]." *Nepal Journal of Epidemiology* 6 (3): 588–94.

Newman, Denis, Andrew P. Jaciw, and Valeriy Lazarev. 2018. "Guidelines for Conducting and Reporting EdTech Impact Research in U.S. K–12 Schools." Empirical Education, Palo Alto, CA. https://www.empiricaleducation.com/pdfs/guidelines.pdf.

OECD (Organisation for Economic Co-operation and Development). 2015. "Students, Computers, and Learning: Making the Connection." PISA Series, OECD Publishing, Paris. http://dx.doi.org/10.1787/9789264239555-en.

Pirkle, Hayden. 2014. "Arabic MOOC Platform Edraak Launches to Bring Quality Education to the Region." Wamda, Dubai. https://www.wamda.com/2014/06/first-arabic-mooc-platform-launches-quality-education.

Pugatch, Todd, and Nicholas Wilson. 2018. "Nudging Study Habits: A Field Experiment on Peer Tutoring in Higher Education." *Economics of Education Review* 62: 151–61. https://doi.org/10.1016/j.econedurev.2017.11.003.

Radcliffe, Damian, and Amanda Lam. 2018. "Social Media in the Middle East: The Story of 2017." University of Oregon, Eugene. https://ssrn.com/abstract=3124077 or http://dx.doi.org/10.2139/ssrn.3124077.

Robinson, Melia. 2017. "Tech Billionaires Spent $170 Million on a New Kind of School—Now Classrooms Are Shrinking and Some Parents Say Their Kids Are 'Guinea Pigs.'" *Business Insider*, November 21. http://www.businessinsider.com/altschool-why-parents-leaving-2017-11.

Sallam, Marwan H. 2017. "A Review of MOOCs in the Arab World." *Creative Education* 8 (4): 564–73. https://doi.org/10.4236/ce.2017.84044.

Shulman, Robyn D. 2018. "EdTech Investments Rise to a Historical $9.5 Billion: What Your Startup Needs to Know." *Forbes*, January 26. https://www.forbes.com/sites/robynshulman/2018/01/26/EdTech-investments-rise-to-a-historical-9-5-billion-what-your-startup-needs-to-know/.

Tamim, Rana M. 2017. "Blended Learning for Learner Empowerment: Voices from the Middle East." *Journal of Research on Technology in Education* 50 (1): 70–83.

Trade Arabia News Service. 2013. "MENA Tops Global Education Spend." Dubai. http://www.tradearabia.com/news/EDU_229718.html.

Weber, Alan S., and Sihem Hamlaoui, eds. 2018. *E-Learning in the Middle East and North Africa (MENA) Region*. New York: Springer International Publishing.

Weissmüller, Kristina S. 2019. "Return of the Behavioural Paradigm? The Discourse on Nudging in Higher Education Research." KPM Center for Public Management, University of Bern. https://ksweissmueller.github.io/files/Weissmueller_Manuscript_Nudging_(unblinded).pdf.

World Bank. 2008. *The Road Not Traveled: Education Reform in the Middle East and North Africa*. MENA Development Report. Washington, DC: World Bank.

———. 2019. *World Development Report 2019: The Changing Nature of Work*. Washington, DC: World Bank.

———. Various years. World Development Indicators database. Washington, DC: World Bank.

Empowering Teachers to Lead the Way to Better Student Learning

9

Lianqin Wang, Bob Prouty, Manal Bakur N Quota, and Angela Demas

Effective teachers have a profound impact on students' learning and their educational and career aspirations. Teacher effectiveness is the most important school-related factor influencing student achievement (Darling-Hammond 2000; Hanushek 2005; Mourshed, Chijioke, and Barber 2010). It is paramount that education systems recruit, train, and support students with the greatest potential to become effective teachers. Effective teachers are knowledgeable in both pedagogy and their subject areas, adapt and innovate their teaching practices to facilitate students' critical thinking, and support learning for students with different learning styles (Hightower et al. 2011; Metzler and Woessmann 2012; OECD 2012).

This chapter analyzes challenges in developing effective teachers in Middle East and North Africa (MENA) countries and recommends a series of reforms that include (1) changing recruitment processes to attract the best potential teachers and better respond to local needs and priorities; (2) equipping teachers (through preservice and in-service training) with up-to-date skills to strengthen teaching practice; (3) establishing a more rigorous teacher assessment mechanism that links performance to career advancement; and (4) targeting greater support to the teachers who need it most, such as teachers in rural areas and those who are new to the profession.

Recruit the best and prepare them to be effective teachers

Since teachers are the single most important school-related factor influencing student achievement, it is important for education systems to recruit those with the greatest potential, prepare them to enter the profession with confidence and the necessary skills, and nurture their careers to ensure sustained improvements in performance across schools.

Attract and select high-caliber candidates into teacher education programs

Attracting and selecting highly qualified candidates for initial teacher education programs is the first step in the long-term process of building an effective teaching force. International experience shows that selectivity standards should be raised to ensure that the best candidates are selected into initial teacher education programs and that these candidates have a reasonable opportunity to be hired after graduation. In raising these standards, a broad view of good teaching that goes beyond academic skills should be applied (Barber and Mourshed 2007; Bruns and Luque 2015). In most MENA countries, the screening process for initial teacher education is dependent on test scores from secondary school graduation examinations (World Bank 2015a). As can be seen from the Finnish example in box 9.1, this is a necessary but insufficient basis for selection. Other criteria, such as teacher creativity, engagement with education issues, and ability to work well with others, should also be considered.

Although acceptance into initial teacher education programs is relatively competitive in countries such as the Arab Republic of Egypt, Jordan, Lebanon, and Tunisia, the education sector remains less competitive than many other sectors (World Bank 2015a). In Egypt, for instance, the required secondary school passing grade on the national examination is 96–98 percent for admission to medical school, but only 80–88 percent for science and mathematics and 75–85 percent for education and literature (World Bank 2010b). While policies are changing in MENA countries to mandate a bachelor's degree for entering the teaching profession, several countries still have large proportions of teachers in the system with less than this level of education (World Bank SABER database). For example, only 42 percent of Morocco's grade 4 teachers have a bachelor's degree or higher, compared with 96 percent of Qatar's teachers and 93 percent of the United Arab Emirates' teachers (Mullis et al. 2017).

In addition to raising selectivity standards, high-performing education systems also design and implement policies to make the teaching profession attractive for the best high school graduates (World Bank 2013). Incentives to attract and retain talented candidates into the teaching profession may

---

Box 9.1 Selection of initial teacher education candidates in Finland

Finland's process for selecting teachers for initial education programs is considered key to its education system's success. This selection process stems from a reform implemented in the 1970s that strengthened teacher education programs and made entering teacher education programs highly selective. At present, universities with teacher education programs admit only about 10 percent of applicants.

Applicants to teacher education programs must have passed the Finnish matriculation examination at the end of secondary education or completed a three-year vocational education program. After meeting these minimum requirements, they must undergo a selection process that involves two stages:

- *Phase I.* An examination is used to assess applicants' academic learning skills. It is based entirely on a written test drawn from six wide-ranging academic and professional articles that students review in advance. This test seeks to identify candidates who engage deeply and intellectually with key concepts in education. Students who perform well in this first phase are invited to the second phase.
- *Phase II.* An examination is used to test candidates' personality, knowledge, and overall suitability to become a teacher. It includes a combination of written questions and aptitude tests to assess applicants' skills, motivation, and commitment, varying slightly depending on the university. Most universities require candidates to demonstrate that they can create ideas, plan, and work well with others and ultimately invite applicants to individual interviews. For the final selection, universities usually consider applicants' results from the first phase of the process (the test), their grades on the Finnish matriculation examination, or their performance in vocational education programs as well as their merits in arts, sports, and any other activities that the selecting university deems relevant to the teaching profession.

Sources: Barber and Mourshed 2007; Crouch 2015; OECD 2015.

include scholarships and tuition support, opportunities to progress and grow in the teaching career, competitive salaries, and other benefits such as housing assistance. In addition, evidence shows that pay compression can play a key role in the decline in the average aptitude of individuals who decide to enter the teaching profession (Hoxby and Leigh 2004). In some MENA countries, teachers are offered competitive starting packages, but the evolution of their salaries over time is relatively moderate. After 15 years, teachers can expect to earn between 1.2 and 1.5 times more than their initial salary (World Bank 2015a). Such compressed salary scales within the teaching career may affect how appealing the teaching profession is for talented candidates in MENA.

Taken together, these factors highlight the need for MENA to develop policies to attract and select high-caliber teacher candidates. Without talented and committed teacher candidates, MENA's education systems have a weak foundation on which to align the teaching force with the demands of 21st-century schools. Some initiatives are under way. Jordan, for example, has embarked on a reform to decompress teacher salary scales to attract motivated candidates and provide ongoing opportunities for growth over the course of a teaching career (World Bank 2016a).

Strengthen pedagogical skills and include classroom practice in preservice programs

In MENA, the quality of preservice teacher training varies widely. Teacher preservice training programs often do not give adequate time for hands-on classroom teaching experience. In addition, since graduates from preservice programs often require further pedagogical training, increasing the emphasis on pedagogical theory in preservice training is also likely to be warranted (Male and Al-Bazzaz 2015). Furthermore, pedagogical theory in preservice training should be clearly linked with hands-on practice. In Morocco, for example, few links exist between classroom theory and hands-on practice programs—officials in charge of these two types of training rarely communicate or work with one another (USAID 2014).

The importance of practical experience for trainee teachers can be expressed by an analogy with the medical profession—if it is not acceptable for doctors to practice without a substantial period of guided training, it should not be acceptable for teachers to work independently immediately after graduation (McBeath 2006). Most high-performing education systems require teacher entrants to have considerable classroom experience before becoming independent teachers (Darling-Hammond, Wei, and Andree 2010; Ingersoll 2007). Initial teacher education programs in New York City that focus on practical experience were found to be particularly effective for first-year teachers (Boyd et al. 2009). By introducing practical experience early, students will develop their pedagogical skills and gain a realistic understanding of the roles and responsibilities of a teacher. To strengthen and modernize pedagogical practices in MENA, greater emphasis should be placed on the development of generic and subject-oriented pedagogical knowledge and skills.

Several countries in the MENA region have initiated efforts to improve the preparation of future teachers. For instance, Kuwait has strengthened hands-on practical aspects of preservice training programs. Kuwait's College of Basic Education now provides students with in-school placements during the last year of their program, with the aim of preparing them for their tasks in the classroom (Male and Al-Bazzaz 2015). A follow-up study found that this practice provided many prospective teachers with their first real opportunity to evaluate their own aptitude for teaching; as a result, some chose not to enter the profession. The study recommended that practical training be introduced earlier in the program and that a more careful assessment of teaching aptitude be made upon program entry. Some MENA universities have also begun to place more emphasis on developing practical teaching skills for future teachers. Oman, for instance, has identified this as an area of urgent priority (Ministry of Education, Oman, and World Bank 2012).

Revamp teacher hiring policy and practice

Different practices exist worldwide for granting teaching positions to education graduates. Many advanced education systems have rigorous processes for selecting the best-performing graduates of initial teacher education programs for teaching positions, often requiring them to hold certificates or licenses. The oldest and most established licensing systems are in the United States, where state teaching licenses ensure a consistent set of standards—namely, that teachers have graduated with a certain level of teaching proficiency recognized by all schools (see box 9.2). In the absence of such standards, graduates' proficiency varies widely depending on their particular teacher training program.

Most MENA countries require new teacher candidates to have a university degree, but they generally do not apply hiring criteria and processes that look beyond the academic degree to assess the candidates' subject knowledge and pedagogical and other skills. Of the 10 MENA countries that participated in the Trends in International Mathematics and Science Study (TIMSS) 2015, only 4 required teacher candidates to pass qualifying examinations for selection to

---

Box 9.2 Teacher licensing in the United States

A teacher licensing system establishes a minimum set of standards required for teachers to teach, allowing education systems to certify a teacher's competence. Licensing standards can be tailored to include specific standards for different grade levels, regions, or school types.

The United States mandates that teachers hold teacher licenses to be able to teach. Licensure requirements vary by state, subject, and grade level. Requirements can include a minimum education level (bachelor's degree) with a minimum passing grade, student teaching experience, completion of a teacher preparation program, a master's degree, or an approved state licensure examination, depending on individual state mandates. This licensure examination frequently assesses teachers' competencies in the content areas and grade levels they wish to teach. Teachers must also renew their licenses regularly to remain in the teaching profession. Requirements for renewal may be similar to those for first-time licenses.

Some states may even require different types of licenses for teachers to move up in the profession's career ladder and link them with compensation and benefits. For example, Massachusetts has three types of licenses, with different requirements:

- *Preliminary license.* Requirements include a bachelor's degree and passing scores on the appropriate Massachusetts Tests for Educator Licensure.
- *Initial license.* Requirements include a preliminary license, plus the completion of an approved teacher preparation program.
- *Professional license.* Requirements include an initial license plus the completion of an approved master's degree program, the completion of an approved alternative program, achievement of National Board Certification, or three years of teaching combined with completion of a one-year induction program. Once an educator receives a professional license, he or she must attend workshops or take courses to earn the professional development points necessary for the certificate to be renewed.

In addition, in many states, teacher licensure programs also allow alternative pathways to enter the profession for individuals who hold a bachelor's degree in an area different from teaching. For example, a chemist can become a chemistry teacher if he or she complies with certain requirements, which vary from state to state. These requirements usually include participating in teacher preparation programs and passing a state licensure examination, among others.

Sources: Cavalluzzo 2004; Darling-Hammond 2017; Teacher Certification Center 2018.

teaching posts: Lebanon, Morocco, Qatar, and Saudi Arabia (Mullis et al. 2016). In most high-performing education systems, teachers are hired at the school level (Barber and Mourshed 2007; Bruns and Luque 2015), which allows the school to identify a better match between teacher characteristics and teaching needs. Such experience could be useful for MENA countries if teacher hiring and assignment still take place at the central level.

Support new teachers with a carefully designed induction program

The first year of teaching is the most challenging for most teachers. Research shows this year to be of vital importance in establishing the methods and testing the ideas that will be the cornerstone of a teaching career (Rivkin, Hanushek, and Kain 2005). An induction phase incorporating this first year provides a useful bridge between preservice teacher education and long-term continuing professional development (Glazerman et al. 2010). Effective induction programs invest a substantial amount of teachers' time in collaborative professional development activities, with a strong focus on mentoring and coaching from more experienced teachers (Darling-Hammond et al. 2017; Liang, Kidwai, and Zhang 2016).

Recognizing the importance of induction for providing support and guidance to novice teachers, several MENA countries offer nonmandatory induction programs (World Bank 2015a). However, the quality of induction matters. In 2009, the Omani induction program shifted from familiarizing new teachers with information on rules and procedures to a more comprehensive program where teachers learn about classroom activities, evaluation, curriculum, new teaching methods, relations between teachers, students, and administrators, student behaviors, examples of good lessons, and school and teacher roles and responsibilities. The program involves two-week courses delivered in three blocks in September, October, and February each year and focuses on teaching practices and policies as well as the curriculum (Ministry of Education, Oman, and World Bank 2012).

Induction programs in MENA should provide an opportunity for new teachers to gain real classroom teaching skills plus offer opportunities for collaborative professional development, including mentoring and coaching by more experienced teachers. Given the shortage of practical experience currently provided in initial teacher education programs, MENA countries could place greater emphasis on using the induction period to strengthen new teachers' capacity to deliver content knowledge effectively through improved pedagogical, classroom management, and other related skills.

Strengthen continuous professional support to teachers

Given the pace of change in technology, research, and labor market needs, teachers need to be empowered with opportunities to update their knowledge and skills continuously through professional development. While advanced education systems use various forms of professional development—such as mentoring, tutoring, online or in-person classes, and research opportunities—there is no one-size-fits-all solution. The key is for professional development programs to be structured with as much care as the curriculum itself, including opportunities that enable teachers to grow and improve continually on the job so that they can lead the way for better student learning (Darling-Hammond et al. 2017). Some characteristics shared by high-performing education systems provide useful examples for MENA, as described in this chapter.

Expand professional development opportunities, particularly for teachers who work in rural and remote areas

While teachers need to strengthen and update their content knowledge and pedagogical skills to improve learning, some MENA countries do not provide sufficient opportunities for professional development. Compared with many countries in the world, countries in MENA allocate fewer days for professional development. In some countries, fewer than three days annually are devoted to this purpose. By way of comparison, teachers in the Republic of Korea, the Netherlands, and Sweden spend more than 14 days in professional development per year (World Bank 2012, 2013). Some MENA economies—for example, Lebanon, West Bank and Gaza, and the Republic of Yemen—do not require teachers to complete a minimum amount of professional development (World Bank 2012). Participation in inservice professional development varies greatly among MENA countries (see figure 9.1). Countries need to analyze teachers' professional development needs and develop a strategy to help them to benefit from professional growth. Requiring a minimum amount of participation in quality, targeted professional development can establish an expectation for teachers' continued learning. Due to geographic constraints, teachers in rural and remote areas often have fewer opportunities to engage in professional development activities and will need additional support (World Bank 2015a).

Focus professional development on teachers' skills in delivery of content

Teachers' subject-matter knowledge strongly predicts student learning (Glewwe et al. 2013; Metzler and Woessmann 2012). A teaching credential should signify (1) strong knowledge of subject-matter content, (2) the teaching skills to deliver this content effectively, and (3) the ability to address specific learning challenges (Loughran, Berry, and Mulhall 2012; Shulman and Shulman 2004; Thames and Ball 2010). In many MENA countries, an insufficient number of teachers have appropriate subject knowledge, indicated by low levels of education and shortage of teachers with specialization in critical areas (see figure 9.2). In 2016 Morocco conducted the Service Delivery Indicators Survey in Education, which found that the majority of grade 4 teachers do not have the minimum skills and knowledge to teach Arabic and French languages. Although results in mathematics are considerably better, still about one-third of teachers cannot pass the evaluation test with a score of

FIGURE 9.1 Some MENA countries provide insufficient professional development opportunities for teachers

Percentage of teachers participating in professional development in the past three months, by region

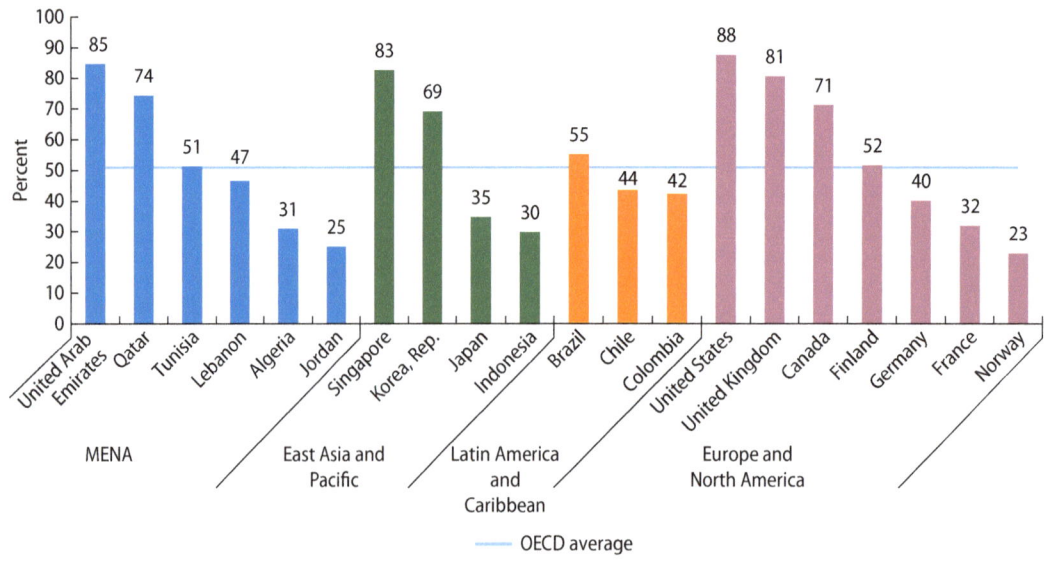

Source: OECD 2016.
Note: OECD = Organisation for Economic Co-operation and Development.

FIGURE 9.2 In MENA, the number of teachers with appropriate subject knowledge may be insufficient

Percentage of grade 8 students attending schools where instruction is affected by a shortage of teachers with specialization in mathematics

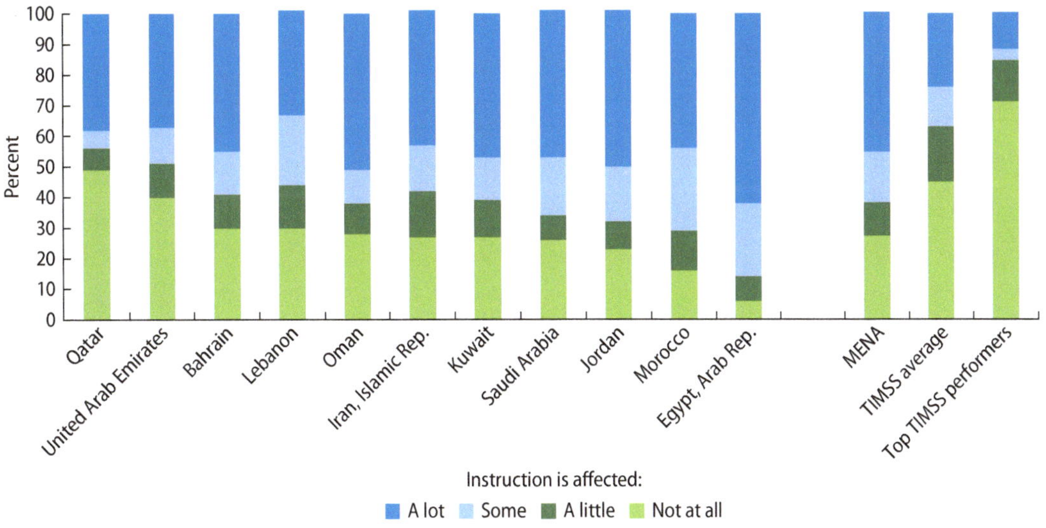

[Stacked bar chart showing percentages for Qatar, United Arab Emirates, Bahrain, Lebanon, Oman, Iran Islamic Rep., Kuwait, Saudi Arabia, Jordan, Morocco, Egypt Arab Rep., MENA, TIMSS average, and Top TIMSS performers. Legend — Instruction is affected: A lot, Some, A little, Not at all.]

Source: Mullis et al. 2016.
Note: TIMSS = Trends in International Mathematics and Science Study.

80 percent or more (ONDH 2017). In terms of pedagogy, MENA teachers often employ traditional teaching methods that discourage student participation, independent initiative, and critical thinking (Kirdar and Brock 2017). This result is also indicated in the TIMSS data (see figure 9.3).

Intensive, content-focused professional development programs can improve teachers' subject-matter knowledge and their ability to use this knowledge in their teaching (Jensen et al. 2016). Professional development programs also need to improve teaching skills, such as mastering pedagogical processes to deliver content knowledge effectively to all types of students and to support students' creative and higher-order learning processes (Loughran, Berry, and Mulhall 2012; Shulman and Shulman 2004; Thames and Ball 2010). Research shows that training programs that teach pedagogy specific to subject areas, such as how to teach a mathematics class effectively, with follow-up visits in which trainers observe and support teachers in the classroom, are highly effective (Darling-Hammond et al. 2009).

Such practices have not yet been widely introduced in MENA countries.

Improve the effectiveness of professional development through collaborative and reflective approaches

Professional development is most effective in changing classroom practice when teachers work collaboratively. It should be organized around team-oriented, school-based classroom instructional improvement and pedagogy-specific subject areas. Teachers should be provided with continuous support and follow-up (Brown, Smith, and Stein 1995; Darling-Hammond et al. 2017; Evans and Popova 2015; Yoon et al. 2007). A growing body of evidence shows that such approaches can improve teacher performance (Barber and Mourshed 2007; Rockoff 2008). Collaboration allows teachers to benefit from each other's knowledge and skills and creates opportunities for sharing and mentoring (Angrist and Lavy 2001; Borko 2004; Darling-Hammond et al. 2017). The Organisation for Economic Co-operation

FIGURE 9.3 Teachers in MENA often employ traditional teaching methods
Percentage of grade 8 students whose teachers report reliance on memorizing in mathematics

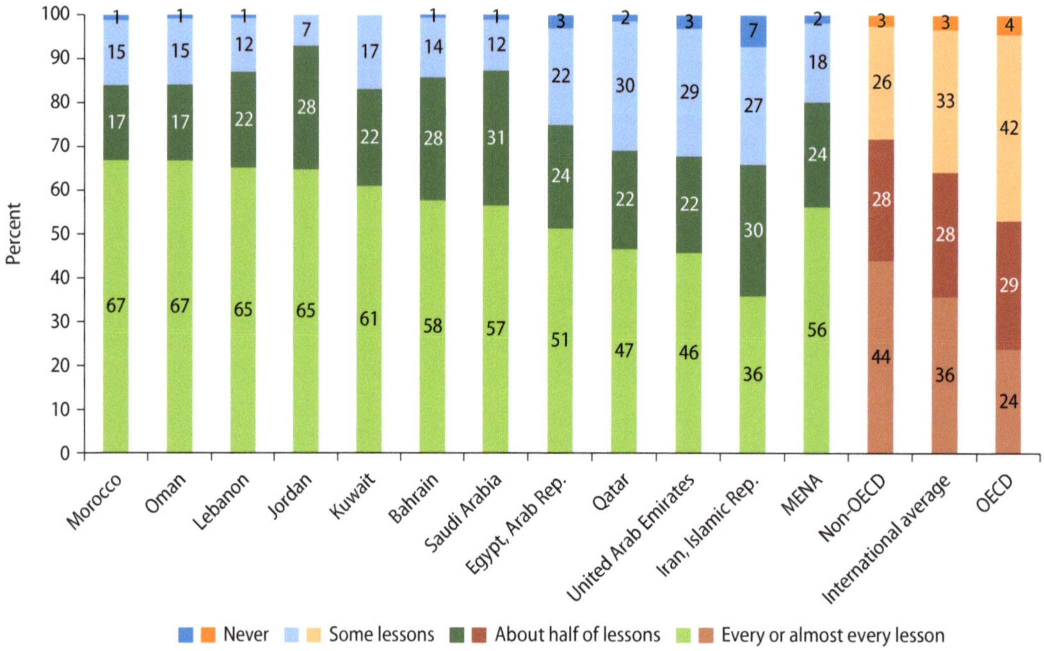

Country	Never	Some lessons	About half of lessons	Every or almost every lesson
Morocco	1	15	17	67
Oman	1	15	17	67
Lebanon	1	12	22	65
Jordan	7	—	28	65
Kuwait	1	17	22	61
Bahrain	1	14	28	58
Saudi Arabia	1	12	31	57
Egypt, Arab Rep.	3	22	24	51
Qatar	2	30	22	47
United Arab Emirates	3	29	22	46
Iran, Islamic Rep.	7	27	30	36
MENA	2	18	24	56
Non-OECD	3	26	28	44
International average	3	33	28	36
OECD	4	42	29	24

Source: Mullis et al. 2016.
Note: OECD = Organisation for Economic Co-operation and Development.

and Development (OECD) Teaching and Learning International Survey (TALIS) 2013, conducted in 34 countries, shows that participating in peer networks is a key element of teacher professionalism and is associated with teacher satisfaction and self-efficacy (OECD 2014). High-performing countries in East Asia and elsewhere have practiced collaborative approaches in professional development for decades, with positive results (Evans and Popova 2015; World Bank 2018c; Yoon et al. 2007).

Changing teachers' methods and behaviors requires challenging their existing theories of learning. Reflecting on preconceptions, being challenged by new ideas, and receiving support to try different approaches are all part of the process of change. To make professional development effective, it is important to introduce teachers to the "why," not just the "what" and "how," of professional development. This can help teachers to understand the demands for change and to move past the feelings of dislocation and loss that come with a push for education reform (CPRE 2017).

The collaborative and reflective approaches in high-performing countries such as Australia, Canada, China, Finland, and Singapore include lesson study groups, teaching-research groups, and communities of practice to perform key professional development functions, such as the following (Darling-Hammond et al. 2017):

• *Curriculum planning and assessment.* Teachers collaborate to develop curriculum units and lessons at the school level, and they frequently develop, use, and review school-based performance assessments to evaluate student learning outcomes. This process helps teachers to understand the standards and curriculum goals thoroughly and to share their knowledge of content and teaching practices. In conjunction with mentoring programs, the approach is particularly valuable in helping

new teachers and low-performing teachers to learn from their mentors in the context of their day-to-day work environment (Darling-Hammond et al. 2017).
- *Research.* Teachers gain a solid grounding of research methods in their preparation programs and are expected to be able to conduct their own practical research. In this way, teachers develop their knowledge about student learning and can use that knowledge to improve their teaching practice (Darling-Hammond et al. 2017).
- *Teacher-led professional learning.* Teachers take the lead in developing professional learning offerings that provide more structured learning by teachers, for teachers. Teachers lead professional learning not only in school-based contexts, but also in more formal settings outside the school. Platforms for teachers to lead professional learning include professional networks, professional focus groups, and professional learning communities. Teachers' unions also play an important role (Darling-Hammond et al. 2017).

Shanghai, for example, has practiced a collaborative professional development approach for decades. Its teaching-research groups offer some insights on how they nurture teachers' professional growth and support those teachers who need it most, such as new or low-performing teachers (see box 9.3).

Collaborative approaches of this nature yield a positive impact. The Opportunity Culture program in the United States, for instance, relies on multiclassroom leaders (MCLs), who are excellent teachers, to lead a teaching team and provide guidance and frequent on-the-job coaching while continuing to teach (Public Impact 2018). Evidence shows that most students who receive treatment under an MCL model achieve higher math scores (Backes and Hansen 2018).

Some MENA countries have started implementing collaborative approaches for their in-service education programs. Table 9.1 shows countries that have already implemented some of these initiatives; box 9.4 presents examples in Egypt and Jordan. MENA could benefit from international experiences and its own regional experience to mainstream such approaches gradually and to tailor them to individual contexts. It would be important for MENA countries to collect their own data to evaluate how these approaches affect student learning. Emphasis can be placed on how new or low-performing teachers benefit from these professional development opportunities. To accomplish this, the school day needs to be structured so that teachers have time to participate in these activities.

Link professional learning to teacher career advancement

It is important to create incentives to motivate teachers to participate in professional development and to apply the new skills in their teaching practice. In most well-functioning systems, teachers' career advancement is tied to professional learning (Darling-Hammond et al. 2017). Knowledgeable and experienced teachers lead professional learning for newer and less-knowledgeable teachers; they become part of the school leadership team and help to manage instructional leadership in the school and, in some cases, beyond the school. Such incentives will take different forms in different countries. In Australia, continuing professional development is a prerequisite for maintaining certification and registration. China offers incentives for teacher learning by sponsoring teaching competitions in which teachers conduct lessons in front of a panel of judges and many observers (who are mainly teachers too). Incentives for professional learning in Canada's Ontario Province include a salary structure that rewards teachers for obtaining additional qualifications that upgrade their knowledge and enhance their practice (Darling-Hammond et al. 2017).

MENA countries could also consider locally targeted incentive mechanisms, such as linking professional development activities to career advancement or licensing to motivate teachers both to participate in

Box 9.3 **Teaching-research groups in Shanghai**

Shanghai provides an example of teachers working together in teaching-research groups to improve continually. These groups are at the school, district, provincial or municipal, and national levels. The groups normally meet for two to three hours every week. In every group, major activities include the following:

- *Professional development.* Teachers are organized in subject groups to focus on lesson planning and to bring the curriculum to the appropriate grade level of the student. Teachers also plan together and observe and assess each other's lessons. They conduct peer observations in their own school and in other schools. This openness creates a stronger collective set of ideals from which to gauge strong teaching versus weak teaching. The practice allows teachers to hold images of "good teaching" in their minds and to maintain the drive toward individual improvement by being immersed in an overall culture that allows teachers to see colleagues perform on a regular basis.
- *Coaching and guidance.* Senior teachers provide guidance and coaching to junior teachers in a wide range of teaching activities, with regular discussions about examination design and teaching experience. The groups are especially useful for new teachers, who participate in group activities, receive guidance from experienced teachers, and gain expertise on a wide range of teaching topics. The leader of the group often coaches new teachers. This mentoring includes lesson observations and critiques.
- *Research.* The group spends much of its time developing hypotheses, collecting evidence, analyzing the evidence, and developing conclusions. The goal of the research is to improve educational practices for individual teachers as well as the school. To accomplish this goal, the group's members meet weekly. Each research group is led by a teacher who is recognized in the school as high-performing. The leader can be higher on the teaching ladder or a promising young teacher. The school principal works closely with the heads of the research groups, who serve as an informal council or cabinet offering advice.
- *Performance evaluations.* The group is also an important mechanism for evaluating teacher performance. Teachers in the same group often evaluate each other during group activities. The group leader has a responsibility to provide feedback in annual teacher performance evaluations.

The group's collaborative nature helps the entire teaching community to grow. Such groups create a constructive work environment and allow teachers to create close bonds. The tiered network of groups at the school, district, and municipal levels allows for quick and far-reaching dissemination of curricula, best practices, and other ideas on teaching and learning.

Sources: Liang, Kidwai, and Zhang 2016; NCEE 2016b; World Bank 2018a.

TABLE 9.1 **MENA countries are implementing a variety of collaborative approaches in teacher professional development**

Types of collaborative approaches implemented, by country

Country	Observation visits	Teacher networks	School networks	Teacher research	Mentoring or coaching
Egypt, Arab Rep.				✓	✓
Jordan	✓	✓	✓	✓	✓
Lebanon	✓	✓	✓		✓
Qatar	✓				✓
Tunisia	✓	✓	✓	✓	✓

Sources: Based on World Bank Systems Approach for Better Education Results (SABER)-Teachers Country Reports: For the Arab Republic of Egypt, World Bank 2010b; for Jordan, World Bank 2010c; for Lebanon, World Bank 2010d; for Qatar, World Bank 2018b; and for Tunisia, World Bank 2011.

> **Box 9.4 Professional development experiences in MENA**
>
> **Egypt's Teachers First**
>
> Teachers First is a professional development program that aims to change teachers' behaviors so that they can successfully instill 21st-century skills in their students and enable them to thrive in a technology-driven, highly competitive, and globally connected world (Teachers First n.d). To this end, it combines formal workshops with ongoing mentoring and an online platform.
>
> The Teachers First behavior framework was developed for Egypt by the Open University and is based on the United Nations Educational, Scientific, and Cultural Organization (UNESCO) Competency Framework for Teachers. Participating teachers have access to the three components of the program: (1) an application for smartphones and tablets, which approves, assesses, and evaluates the continuity of behavioral improvement inside classes and facilitates communication among teachers; (2) continuous support through mentorship and coaching activities; and (3) communities of practice, which facilitate best-practice sharing.
>
> The pilot program began in 2015 with 500 participating teachers, and the objective was to reach 10,000 teachers, 1,000 schools, and 1,000,000 students within 18 months. By 2019, it had reached almost 500,000 teachers and millions of students in more than 14,000 schools (Imagine Education 2019).
>
> **Jordan's professional development approach**
>
> Jordan has made important progress in improving its professional development policies. All Jordanian teachers are obliged to complete at least 20 hours of professional development on a yearly basis provided by several types of institutions, such as the Ministry of Education, local educational authorities, and schools. In addition, some universities provide professional development opportunities for teachers.
>
> Professional development includes traditional training, such as courses, workshops, conferences, and seminars, plus collaborative activities—qualification programs, observation visits to other schools, participation in teacher networks, and mentoring, among others. The content of these activities covers both administrative support and aspects related to teaching, such as subject-matter knowledge, curriculum teaching, alignment of curriculum with standards, classroom management, instructional practices, and guidance to teach students with special needs.
>
> The Queen Rania Teacher Academy draws on the expertise of its partners, Columbia University Teachers College and Columbia University Middle East Research Center, to develop both long-term and short-term programs to raise the quality of teaching in Jordan. Since its establishment in 2009, the academy has supported teacher training and strengthened school communities through a variety of approaches.
>
> *Sources:* Imagine Education 2019; QRTA 2019; World Bank 2016b.

continuous learning and to apply the lessons learned to their teaching practice. It is only when the gains from wide-scale professional development programs are used and maintained that desired changes in education systems will occur. For example, Saudi Arabia's Khebrat program, in which teachers and other educators experience a one-year intensive theoretical and practical training in high-performing countries, is producing a cadre of teachers with required skills.[1] How well these skills are harnessed will determine the effectiveness of this initiative in bringing about change and modernizing teaching practices across the system.

Use teacher assessment to strengthen support and accountability

International experiences show that it is crucial to use multiple sources of information to assess teacher performance, as they complement each other. Assessment instruments may include, but are not necessarily limited to, (1) students' performance in learning assessments; (2) teacher subject-knowledge assessments; (3) pedagogical practices assessments; (4) classroom observations; (5) teaching portfolios; and (6) feedback from students and parents. International experience suggests that none of these approaches separately can produce a balanced and objective evaluation of teacher performance. As a result, a combination of different instruments and approaches is most appropriate (World Bank 2013).

In MENA, most countries have monitoring and evaluation systems in place to oversee teachers (see table 9.2). These systems vary from supervising bodies, such as those in Morocco, to regular teacher evaluations, like those in Egypt, where teachers are obliged to participate in both internal and external evaluations. Both internal and external evaluations are informed by the principal's individual assessment and classroom observation and consider these criteria: knowledge of subject matter, curriculum compliance, teaching processes (including methods used to assess students as well as their classroom participation), lesson planning, use of homework and technological tools in the classroom, and students' academic achievement (World Bank 2015a). In other countries, like Tunisia, external evaluations are generally carried out in the early years of a teacher's career, and internal evaluations are led exclusively by the principal and informed by a self-assessment (World Bank 2011). Although criteria are extensive (for example, compliance with the curriculum, teaching methods, assessment methods, teacher-student interactions, student achievement, and teacher attendance), they are based mainly on the principal's point of view. MENA countries could benefit from integrating the views of peer teachers, parents, and students into teacher assessments.

In high-performing education systems such as Singapore, Ontario (Canada), and Massachusetts (United States), promotions are linked to evaluation results, and underperforming teachers can be dismissed. These systems use the results of teacher assessments to identify opportunities for improvement and to draft improvement plans that tailor collaborative professional development opportunities to teachers' needs (World Bank 2015b). While MENA countries are developing their teacher evaluation systems, more emphasis could be placed on using evaluation results to improve classroom practice and to strengthen teacher support and accountability mechanisms.

Provide meaningful incentives to motivate and reward teachers

No education system will be successful unless it provides incentives for teacher effort, although a system's overall incentives structure will vary by context (World Bank 2018c). Incentives, whether financial or professional, need to be meaningful to make a difference.

Pay-for-performance based on student test scores has shown mixed results internationally

International research provides little reason to believe that financial incentives should be

TABLE 9.2 Many MENA economies have systems in place to monitor teacher performance
Teacher evaluation systems, by economy

Economy	Students' achievement	Teaching processes	Parents' feedback[a]	Students' feedback	Colleagues' feedback[a]
Djibouti		✓			
Egypt, Arab Rep.	✓	✓			
Jordan	✓	✓			
Lebanon		✓			
Tunisia	✓	✓			
West Bank and Gaza		✓			
Yemen, Rep.	✓	✓		✓	

Sources: Based on World Bank Systems Approach for Better Education Results (SABER)-Teachers Country Reports: for Djibouti, World Bank 2010a; for the Arab Republic of Egypt, World Bank 2010b; for Jordan, World Bank 2010c; for Lebanon, World Bank 2010d; for Tunisia, World Bank 2011; for West Bank and Gaza, World Bank 2010f; and for the Republic of Yemen, World Bank 2010e.
a. Parents' and colleagues' feedback do not form part of teacher evaluation systems in any of the MENA economies listed in the table.

the primary way to motivate teachers to improve student learning. In New York City, financial incentives were found to hurt learning outcomes (Fryer 2013). A review of performance-pay programs found the same results, which were ascribed to the unintended consequence of narrowing teaching to the elements tested (Neal 2011). Similar results were found in a study on the issue of "free riding" associated with performance pay, by which many teachers received bonuses for results that would have occurred even without the program (Goodman and Turner 2012).

Despite these findings from the United States, financial incentives should not be dismissed entirely. The small impact of financial incentives found in the New York City study could be attributed to the complexity of the program design and teachers' feeling that they had little control over student learning (Fryer 2013). A study in India, in which teachers' financial incentives were set at 3 percent of annual pay, found that students in incentive schools outperformed those in control schools by 0.28 and 0.16 standard deviation in mathematics and language tests, respectively. Students scored significantly higher on "conceptual" as well as "mechanical" components of the tests, suggesting that the gains in test scores represented an actual increase in learning outcomes. Incentive schools also performed better on subjects for which there were no incentives, suggesting positive spillovers (Muralidharan and Sundararaman 2011). Another study found modest positive effects in Kenya, where teacher bonuses were linked to examination results (Glewwe, Ilias, and Kremer 2010). A recent World Bank study also found potential longer-term benefits, noting that restructuring teacher pay both to remunerate competitively and to provide returns for good performance may improve the quality of candidates entering the teaching profession or the performance of teachers (World Bank 2018c). In addition, a recent review of impact evaluations of educational initiatives in 56 countries found that incentives can increase teacher effort and student achievement from very low levels when they are adequately designed and based on behaviors that teachers can fully control, such as attendance (Ganimian and Murnane 2016).

Professional incentives for teachers have the potential to improve student learning

While merit pay systems may be warranted in some contexts, international evidence is clear that well-chosen professional incentives have even greater potential. Changes to career ladders and other forms of recognition for teachers have been shown to have more substantial motivational effects in several high-performing countries (Darling-Hammond et al. 2017; Liang, Kidwai, and Zhang 2016). These countries create structures within school systems that promote professional learning and enable teachers to take on new responsibilities based on their interests and skills. These systems also use appraisal processes to identify talent and accomplishment. Shanghai provides a good model in which teachers are evaluated systematically and fairly, with career advancement mechanisms. Teachers have opportunities to advance professionally throughout their teaching career through a four-level ranking system (Liang, Kidwai, and Zhang 2016; World Bank 2018a). Australia, Canada, and Singapore have similar career ladders or career pathways that reward teachers' knowledge, skills, and contributions (NCEE 2016a).

Teachers' career advancement in most MENA countries depends mainly on years of service, which does not reward performance (World Bank 2012). Indeed, in many MENA countries, low-performing teachers are rarely sanctioned. The lack of sanctions for poor performance encourages behaviors such as teacher absenteeism in the region (IEA 2015). The potential of professional incentives may also be limited by school leaders' relative lack of authority over teacher performance, as the power to hire and fire lies with central government authorities. Increased efforts need to be made to reform the incentive systems to promote good teaching and learning and to provide rewarding career pathways. These types of initiatives may require the reform of civil service rules and regulations that would support incentive and accountability systems.

MENA countries also lack incentive systems for placing teachers where they are most needed. In eight MENA countries examined in depth through the World Bank Systems Approach for Better Education Results (SABER)-Teachers studies,[2] five received the lowest ratings possible (latent and emerging) for the policy goal of "matching teachers' skills with students' needs." Only Egypt, Jordan, and Tunisia were found to provide some type of incentives for teachers who teach in hard-to-staff schools, including those serving vulnerable children in rural and isolated areas. Teachers have few incentives to work in the weakest schools, where the need for their skills is highest. Iraq is a counterexample within the region, registering as one of the best performers in this area, with monetary incentives and improved opportunities for promotion for teachers working in hard-to-staff areas in the country. Egypt, Jordan, and Tunisia also provide some types of incentives. However, these incentives are not enough to attract and retain sufficient numbers of qualified teachers in remote and unattractive areas (World Bank 2010b, 2010c, 2011).

The lack of incentive systems for placing teachers where they are needed most is an impediment to reform, since the most effective way to improve student learning is to bridge the gap between high- and low-performing schools and between high- and low-performing teachers (Merilainen and Pietarinen 2002). MENA countries should look to develop policies that incentivize teachers to work where they are needed most (see, for example, Ministry of Education, Oman, and World Bank 2012).

The degree of autonomy accorded to teachers is an important professional incentive

In the MENA countries that participated in the Programme for International Student Assessment (PISA) 2015, teachers were found to have far less decision-making responsibility than those in OECD countries (see figure 9.4). Studies in the Islamic Republic of Iran, Jordan, and Kuwait found that central authorities maintain strict control over curricular content and teaching practices, leaving little autonomy for teachers (Afshar and Doosti 2016; Al-Yaseen and Al-Musaileem 2015; Namaghi 2009).

Such disempowerment among teachers compromises job satisfaction and the development of students' skills, in part because it impedes the ability of teachers to teach to the right level of students, a critical element of effective teaching (Evans and Popova 2015). Ultimately, MENA school systems need to find the balance between autonomy and accountability that will best support learning and provide schools with the resources and flexibility they need to establish and achieve ambitious goals for student learning.

Notes

1. For news from the Khebrat host countries, see Master (2018); University of Leicester (2018); University of Queensland (2018).

FIGURE 9.4 **Teachers in MENA have less autonomy than teachers in OECD countries**
Percentage of 15-year-old students attending schools in which teachers have considerable responsibility for instructional decisions, PISA 2015

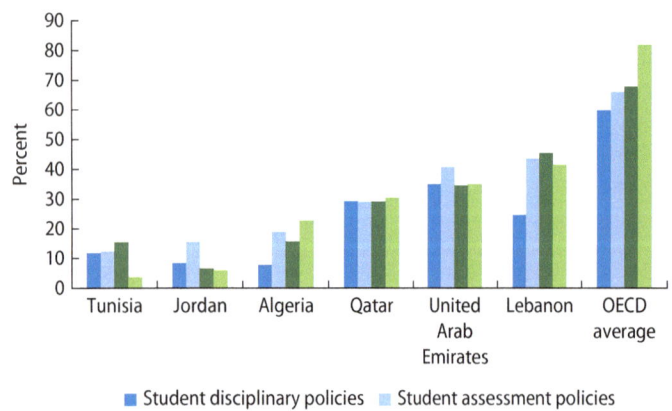

Source: OECD 2016.
Note: OECD = Organisation for Economic Co-operation and Development; PISA = Programme for International Student Assessment.

2. SABER provides education systems analyses, assessments, diagnosis, and opportunities for dialogue and measures policy dialogue on a four-point scale from latent to advanced.

References

Afshar, Hassan Soodmand, and Mehdi Doosti. 2016. "An Investigation into Factors Contributing to Iranian Secondary School English Teachers' Job Satisfaction and Dissatisfaction." *Research Papers in Education* 31 (3): 274–98.

Al-Yaseen, Wafaa Salem, and Mohammad Yousef Al-Musaileem. 2015. "Teacher Empowerment as an Important Component of Job Satisfaction: A Comparative Study of Teachers' Perspectives in Al-Farwaniya District, Kuwait." *Journal of Comparative and International Education* 45 (6): 863–85.

Angrist, Joshua, and Victor Lavy. 2001. "Does Teacher Training Affect Pupil Learning? Evidence from Matched Comparisons in Jerusalem Public Schools." *Journal of Labor Economics* 19 (2): 343–69.

Backes, Ben, and Michael Hansen. 2018. "Reaching Further and Learning More? Evaluating Public Impact's Opportunity Culture Initiative." Calder Working Paper 181, National Center for Analysis of Longitudinal Data in Education Research, Washington, DC, January. https://caldercenter.org/sites/default/files/WP%20181_0.pdf.

Barber, Michael, and Mona Mourshed. 2007. "How the World's Best-Performing School Systems Come Out on Top." McKinsey and Company, Washington, DC.

Borko, Hilda. 2004. "Professional Development and Teacher Learning: Mapping the Terrain." *Educational Researcher* 33 (8): 3–15.

Boyd, Donald, Pamela Grossman, Hamilton Lankford, Susanna Loeb, and James Wyckoff. 2009. "Teacher Preparation and Student Achievement." *Journal for Educational Evaluation and Policy Analysis* 31 (4): 416–40.

Brown, C. A., M. S. Smith, and M. K. Stein. 1995. "Linking Teacher Support to Enhanced Classroom Instruction." Paper presented at the annual meeting of the American Educational Research Association, New York.

Bruns, Barbara, and Javier Luque. 2015. *Great Teachers: How to Raise Student Learning in Latin America and the Caribbean.* Washington, DC: World Bank.

Cavalluzzo, Linda C. 2004. "Is National Board Certification an Effective Signal of Teacher Quality?" CNA Corporation, Alexandria, VA.

CPRE (Consortium for Policy Research in Education). 2017. "Robert Evans: Introducing Teachers to the 'Why,' Not Just the 'What' and 'How' of Professional Development." Video, CPRE Knowledge Hub, University of Pennsylvania Graduate School of Education, December 1. http://www.cprehub.org/content/emerging-insights-effective-professional-development?video_id=347.

Crouch, David. 2015. "Highly Trained, Respected, and Free: Why Finland's Teachers Are Different." *Guardian*, June 17. https://www.theguardian.com/education/2015/jun/17/highly-trained-respected-and-free-why-finlands-teachers-are-different.

Darling-Hammond, Linda. 2000. "Teacher Quality and Student Achievement: A Review of State Policy Evidence." *Education Policy Analysis Archives* 8 (1): 1–44.

———. 2017. "Teacher Education around the World: What Can We Learn from International Practice?" *European Journal of Teacher Education* 40 (3): 291–309.

Darling-Hammond, Linda, Dion Burns, Carol Campbell, A. Lin Goodwin, and Karen Hammerness. 2017. *Empowered Educators: How High-Performing Systems Shape Teaching Quality around the World.* Hoboken, NJ: Jossey-Bass.

Darling-Hammond, Linda, Ruth Chung Wei, and Alethea Andree. 2010. "How High-Achieving Countries Develop Great Teachers." Research Brief, Stanford Center for Opportunity Policy in Education, Stanford University, Stanford, CA.

Darling-Hammond, Linda, Ruth Chung Wei, Alethea Andree, Nikole Richardson, and Stelios Orphanos. 2009. *Professional Learning in the Learning Profession: A Status Report on Teacher Development in the United States and Abroad.* Dallas, TX: National Staff Development Council.

Evans, David, and Anna Popova. 2015. "What Really Works to Improve Learning in Developing Countries? An Analysis of Divergent Findings in Systematic Reviews." Policy Research Working Paper 7203, World Bank, Washington, DC.

Fryer, Roland G. 2013. "Teacher Incentives and Student Achievement: Evidence from New York City Public Schools." *Journal of Labor Economics* 31 (2): 373–427.

Ganimian, Alejandro, and Richard Murnane. 2016. "Improving Educational Outcomes in Developing Countries: Lessons from Rigorous Impact Evaluations." NBER Working Paper 20284, National Bureau of Economic Research, Cambridge, MA.

Glazerman, Steven, Eric Isenberg, Sarah Dolfin, Martha Bleeker, Amy Johnson, and Matthew Grider. 2010. *Impacts of Comprehensive Teacher Induction: Final Results from a Randomized Controlled Study*. Washington, DC: Institute of Education Sciences. https://ies.ed.gov/ncee/pubs/20104027/pdf/20104027.pdf.

Glewwe, Paul, Eric A. Hanushek, Sarah D. Humpage, and Renato Ravina. 2013. "School Resources and Educational Outcomes in Developing Countries: A Review of the Literature from 1990 to 2010." In *Education Policy in Developing Countries*, edited by Paul Glewwe, 13–64. Chicago: University of Chicago Press.

Glewwe, Paul, Nauman Ilias, and Michael Kremer. 2010. "Teacher Incentives." *American Economic Journal: Applied Economics* 2 (3): 205–27.

Goodman, Sarena F., and Lesley J. Turner. 2012. "The Design of Teacher Incentive Pay and Educational Outcomes: Evidence from the New York City Bonus Program." *Journal of Labor Economics* 31 (2): 409–20.

Hanushek, Eric A. 2005. "Why Quality Matters in Education." *Finance and Development* 42 (2): 15–19.

Hightower, Amy M., Rachael C. Delgado, Sterling C. Lloyd, Rebecca Wittenstein, Kacy Sellers, and Christopher B. Swanson. 2011. *Improving Student Learning by Supporting Quality Teaching: Key Issues, Effective Strategies*. Bethesda, MD: Editorial Projects in Education.

Hoxby, C. M., and A. Leigh. 2004. "Pulled Away or Pushed Out? Explaining the Decline of Teacher Aptitude in the United States." *American Economic Review* 94 (2): 236–40.

IEA (International Association for the Evaluation of Educational Achievement). 2015. Trends in International Mathematics and Science Study–TIMSS 2015 database. Chestnut Hill, MA: IEA. https://timssandpirls.bc.edu/timss2015/international-database/.

Imagine Education. 2019. "Teachers First Goes from Impact to Sustainability across Egypt." Imagine Education, Chantilly, VA. https://www.imagine.education/1264-2/.

Ingersoll, Richard. 2007. "Misdiagnosing the Teacher Quality Problem." CPRE Policy Brief, University of Pennsylvania, Philadelphia.

Jensen, Ben, Julie Sonnemann, Katie Roberts-Hull, and Amélie Hunter. 2016. "Beyond PD: Teacher Professional Learning in High-Performing Systems." National Center on Education and the Economy, Washington, DC.

Kirdar, Serra, and Colin Brock. 2017. *Education in the Arab World*. Oxford, U.K. Bloomsbury Publishing.

Liang, Xiaoyan, Huma Kidwai, and Minxuan Zhang. 2016. *How Shanghai Does It—Insights and Lessons from the Highest-Ranking Education System in the World*. Washington, DC: World Bank.

Loughran, John, Amanda Berry, and Pamela Mulhall. 2012. *Understanding and Developing Science Teachers' Pedagogical Content Knowledge*, 2d ed. Rotterdam: Sense Publishers.

Male, Trevor, and Abdulghani Al-Bazzaz. 2015. "Enhancing Initial Teacher Education in Kuwait: 'Cooking on a Low Heat.'" Unpublished paper, April 15. https://www.researchgate.net/publication/283720072_Enhancing_Initial_Teacher_Education_in_Kuwait_%27Cooking_on_a_Low_Heat%27.

Master, Farida. 2018. "Educators from Saudi Arabia Keen to Learn from Local College." Times online, June 21. https://www.times.co.nz/news/educators-from-saudi-arabia-keen-to-learn-from-local-college/.

McBeath, Angus. 2006. "Getting Districtwide Results." Cross City Campaign for Urban Schools Reform, Chicago.

Merilainen, Matti, and Janne Pietarinen. 2002. "Primary Teachers' Professional Development in the Context of Small Rural Schools." Paper presented at the European Conference on Educational Research, University of Lisbon, September 11–14.

Metzler, Johannes, and Ludger Woessmann. 2012. "The Impact of Teacher Subject Knowledge on Student Achievement: Evidence from Within-Teacher Within-Student Variation." *Journal of Development Economics* 99 (2): 486–96.

Ministry of Education, Oman, and World Bank. 2012. *Education in Oman: The Drive for Quality*. Washington, DC: World Bank.

Mourshed, Mona, Chinezi Chijioke, and Michael Barber. 2010. *How the World's Most Improved School Systems Keep Getting Better*. London: McKinsey and Company.

Mullis, Ina V. S., Michael O. Martin, Pierre Foy, and M. Hooper. 2016. "TIMSS 2015 International Results in Mathematics." TIMSS and PIRLS International Study Center, Boston College, Chestnut Hill, MA. http://timssandpirls.bc.edu/timss2015/international-results/.

———. 2017. "PIRLS 2016 International Results in Reading." TIMSS and PIRLS International Study Center, Boston College, Chestnut Hill, MA. http://timssandpirls.bc.edu/pirls2016/international-results/.

Muralidharan, Karthik, and Venkatesh Sundararaman. 2011. "Teacher Performance Pay: Experimental Evidence from India." *Journal of Political Economy* 119 (1): 39–77.

Namaghi, Seyyed Ali Ostovar. 2009. "A Data-Driven Conceptualization of Language Teacher Identity in the Context of Public High Schools in Iran." *Teacher Education Quarterly* 36 (2): 111–24.

NCEE (National Center on Education and the Economy). 2016a. "Developing High-Quality Teaching." Empowered Educators: How High-Performing Systems Shape Teaching Quality around the World Policy Brief, NCEE, Washington, DC. http://ncee.org/wp-content/uploads/2017/02/ProfLearningPolicyBrief.pdf.

———. 2016b. "Shanghai: Culture, Policy, and Practice." Empowered Educators: How High-Performing Systems Shape Teaching Quality around the World Country Brief, NCEE, Washington, DC. https://edpolicy.stanford.edu/sites/default/files/ShanghaiCountryBrief.pdf.

Neal, Derrick. 2011. "The Design of Performance Pay in Education." In *Handbook of Economics of Education*, Vol. 4, edited by Eric A. Hanushek and Stephen J. Machin, 495–550. New York: North-Holland.

OECD (Organisation for Economic Co-operation and Development). 2012. *Preparing Teachers and Developing School Leaders for the 21st Century: Lessons from around the World.* Paris: OECD.

———. 2014. *TALIS 2013 Results: An International Perspective on Teaching and Learning.* Paris: OECD. http://www.oecd.org/edu/school/Alberta%20(Canada)%20National%20TALIS%202013%20report.pdf.

———. 2015. *Education Policy Outlook 2015: Making Reforms Happen.* Paris: OECD. http://dx.doi.org/10.1787/9789264225442-en.

———. 2016. *PISA 2015 Results.* Vol. 2: *Policies and Practices for Successful Schools.* Paris: OECD. http://dx.doi.org/10.1787/9789264267510-en.

ONDH (Observatoire National du Développement Humain). 2017. "Enquête sur les Indicateurs de Prestation de Services en Éducation (IPSE) au Maroc." Rapport technique, ONDH, Rabat. http://www.ondh.ma/sites/default/files/documents/rapport_ipse_vf.pdf.

Public Impact. 2018. "Opportunity Culture." Public Impact, Chapel Hill, NC. http://opportunityculture.org/.

QRTA (Queen Rania Teacher Academy). 2019. "The Queen Rania Teacher Academy." https://www.queenrania.jo/en/initiatives/queen-rania-teacher-academy.

Rivkin, S. G., E. A. Hanushek, and J. F. Kain. 2005. "Teachers, Schools, and Academic Achievement." *Econometrica* 73 (2): 417–58.

Rockoff, J. E. 2008. "Does Mentoring Reduce Turnover and Improve Skills of New Employees? Evidence from Teachers in New York City." NBER Working Paper 13868, National Bureau of Economic Research, Cambridge, MA.

Shulman, Lee S., and Judith H. Shulman. 2004. "How and What Teachers Learn: A Shifting Perspective." *Journal of Curriculum Studies* 36 (2): 257–71.

Teacher Certification Center. 2018. "The Massachusetts Teaching and Certification Resource." Teacher Certification Center, Malden, MA. https://www.teachercertificationdegrees.com/certification/massachusetts/.

Teachers First. No date. "Teachers First Egypt." http://teachersfirstegypt.com/.

Thames, Mark Hoover, and Deborah Loewenberg Ball. 2010. "What Math Knowledge Does Teaching Require?" *Teaching Children Mathematics* 17 (4): 220–29.

University of Leicester. 2018. "Leicester Plays Part in Modernisation of Saudi Education System." University of Leicester News, May 23. https://www2.le.ac.uk/news/blog/2018-archive/may/leicester-plays-part-in-modernisation-of-saudi-education-system.

University of Queensland. 2018. "Building Leadership for Change through School Immersion." Institute of Continuing and TESOL Education, University of Queensland, St. Lucia, May 24. https://icte.uq.edu.au/blog/2018/05/building-leadership-change-through-school-immersion-%D8%AE%D8%A8%D8%B1%D8%A7%D8%AA.

USAID (U.S. Agency for International Development). 2014. *Research on Reading in Morocco: Analysis of Initial Teacher Training Final Report; Component 2.* Prepared by Research Triangle Institute and Varly Project. Washington, DC: USAID.

World Bank. 2010a. "SABER-Teachers Country Report: Djibouti 2010." SABER Country Report, World Bank, Washington, DC.

———. 2010b. "SABER-Teachers Country Report: Egypt 2010." SABER Country Report, World Bank, Washington, DC.

———. 2010c. "SABER-Teachers Country Report: Jordan 2010." SABER Country Report, World Bank, Washington, DC.

———. 2010d. "SABER-Teachers Country Report: Lebanon 2010." SABER Country Report, World Bank, Washington, DC.

———. 2010e. "SABER-Teachers Country Report: Republic of Yemen 2010." SABER Country Report, World Bank, Washington, DC.

———. 2010f. "SABER-Teachers Country Report: West Bank and Gaza 2010." SABER Country Report, World Bank, Washington, DC.

———. 2011. "SABER-Teachers Country Report: Tunisia 2011." SABER Country Report, World Bank, Washington, DC.

———. 2012. "MENA Regional Synthesis on the Teacher Policies Surveys: Key Findings from Phase 1." World Bank, Washington, DC.

———. 2013. "What Matters Most for Teacher Policies: A Framework Paper." World Bank, Washington, DC.

———. 2015a. "MENA Regional Synthesis on the Teacher Policies Survey: Key Findings from Phase 1." World Bank, Washington, DC.

———. 2015b. "SABER-Teachers Country Report: Singapore 2015." SABER Country Report, World Bank, Washington, DC.

———. 2016a. "Hashemite Kingdom of Jordan Education Sector Public Expenditure Review." Report ACS18935, World Bank, Washington, DC.

———. 2016b. "Hashemite Kingdom of Jordan School Autonomy and Accountability Country Report 2015." SABER Country Report, World Bank, Washington, DC.

———. 2018a. *Growing Smart: Learning and Growth in East Asia and Pacific.* Washington, DC: World Bank.

———. 2018b. "SABER-Teachers Country Report: Qatar 2018." SABER Country Report, World Bank, Washington, DC.

———. 2018c. *World Development Report 2018: Learning to Realize Education's Promise.* Washington, DC: World Bank.

———. Various years. Systems Approach for Better Education Results (SABER) database. Washington, DC: World Bank. http://saber.worldbank.org/index.cfm?indx=4.

Yoon, Kwang Suk, Teresa Duncan, Silvia Wen-Yu Lee, Beth Scarloss, and Kathy L. Shapley. 2007. "Reviewing the Evidence on How Teacher Professional Development Affects Student Achievement." Regional Education Laboratory, Institute of Education Sciences, U.S. Department of Education, Washington, DC.

Developing Effective School Leadership | 10

Lianqin Wang, Angela Demas, Manal Bakur N Quota, and Bob Prouty

Effective schools are characterized by strong school leadership support for teaching and learning (Barber and Mourshed 2007; World Bank 2018b). Among school factors, research consistently identifies leadership as second only to classroom teaching in its impact on student learning (Jensen, Downing, and Clark 2017b; Leithwood, Harris, and Hopkins 2008). School leaders have an indirect but powerful effect on student achievement through their interactions with teachers and their ability to shape school culture (Pont, Nusche, and Moorman 2008; Witziers, Bosker, and Kruger 2003).

Recognizing the importance of school leaders and the challenges that many countries in the Middle East and North Africa (MENA) region face in developing effective leadership, this chapter highlights transformational reforms that have helped school principals to move away from their traditional role as administrators and toward becoming instructional leaders. Developing effective school leadership starts with the selection and preparation of skilled, well-equipped principals. In MENA countries, reshaping the policy and practice of the recruitment and professional development of principals is warranted, along with granting schools more autonomy so that school leaders can better address the local needs of their students and communities. Successful change depends on principals who are appropriately selected, supported, and given the needed blend of autonomy and accountability to perform.

Transform the role of the school principal from administrator to instructional leader

Improving teaching and learning requires school principals to be instructional leaders who can lead, guide, and monitor instructional practices related to pedagogy and curriculum (Jensen, Downing, and Clark 2017b; OECD 2016c). Such leadership is a strong predictor of whether and how teachers collaborate and engage in a reflective dialogue about their teaching practices (OECD 2016b). The practice of collaborating and pooling expertise allows instructional staff to meet students' needs better and improves the content and pedagogical knowledge of individual teachers. Instructional leadership fosters a school environment that focuses more on academic success, which in turn enhances student learning. For example, higher average mathematics achievement is associated with principals' reports of greater school emphasis on academic success (see figure 10.1).

FIGURE 10.1 **Schools in MENA that emphasize academic success have better student learning**
TIMSS grade 8 mathematics average scale score, by principal's emphasis on academic success, 2015

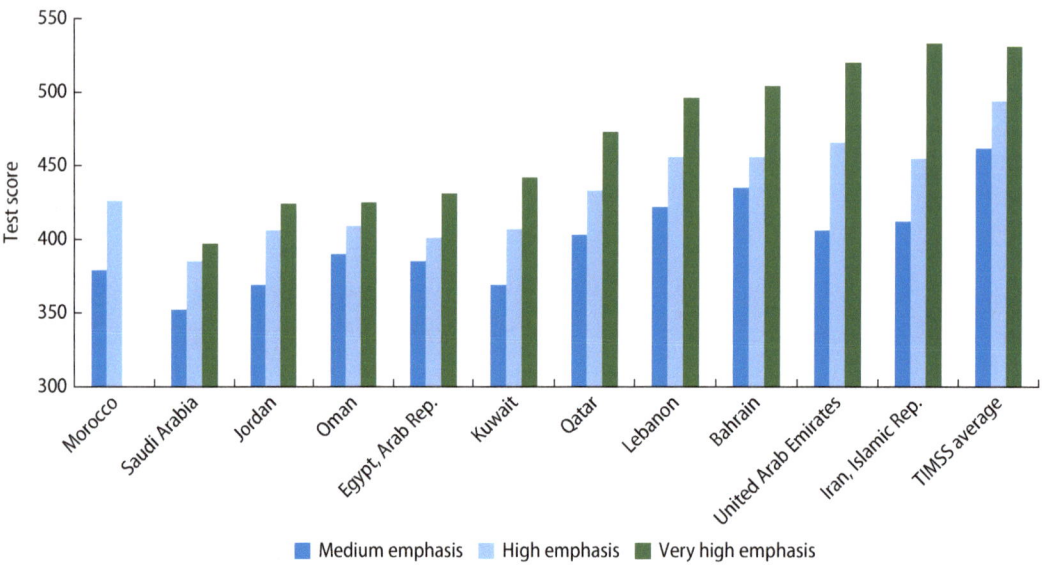

Source: Mullis, Martin, Foy, et al. 2016.
Note: TIMSS = Trends in International Mathematics and Science Study.

Instructional leadership can improve learning through positive changes in the context in which learning occurs. For example, in Boston, Massachusetts, principals and school coaches play a key role in leading sessions using assessment data to facilitate joint planning and analysis of teaching practices. Some schools using this approach are built on an open environment that encourages collaboration among teachers and invites parents and members of the community to participate (Barber and Mourshed 2007). However, this focus on instructional leadership is rare in MENA countries. In Lebanon and Morocco, for instance, principals are not required to provide guidance on teaching or to evaluate teacher performance (World Bank SABER-Teachers database). Primary school directors in Tunisia can make few decisions to improve teaching and learning and have weak incentives to improve student achievement (World Bank 2018a).

Instructional leadership is most effective when principals share decision-making processes with other stakeholders (Jensen, Downing, and Clark 2017b; Leithwood and Mascall 2008). Known as distributed leadership, this approach creates an instructional leadership team with a shared sense of purpose within the school (Jensen, Downing, and Clark 2017b; OECD 2016b). For example, in the province of Ontario in Canada; Hong Kong SAR, China; Shanghai; and Singapore a new principal will already have had the opportunity to provide instructional leadership as a teacher through shared responsibility for curriculum improvement or through participation in professional learning communities and in-school lessons and research groups. These opportunities for leadership at the teacher level eventually influence the roles and responsibilities of principals and leadership teams (Jensen, Downing, and Clark 2017a, 2017b, 2017c).

A study of 85 principals from an education district in Kuwait found that an inclusive management style for building a shared vision in which all voices are heard is important for teacher motivation and that successful school principals are aware of the limits of an individual leadership approach and the importance of collaborative work (Alsaeedi and Male 2013). Distributed leadership occurs when decision-making authority is shared with others, and it is correlated with improvements in student learning (Hallinger and Heck 2011). The transformational approach adopted by principals in Singapore provides insights into the process of fostering distributed leadership (see box 10.1).

Professional development can help to shift the role of school principals toward instructional leadership. The 2013 Organisation for Economic Co-operation and Development (OECD) Teaching and Learning International Survey (TALIS) found that principals who attend instructional leadership programs are more frequently engaged in instructional leadership activities in their schools and more likely to create opportunities for collaborative learning in school (OECD 2016c). This indicates the positive impact of training in transforming school principals into instructional leaders. New Zealand is one of the countries investing heavily in such training programs (see box 10.2).

Many challenges are inherent in the reskilling process for existing school principals. Principals who have difficulty making the transition will need additional support. Shanghai, for instance, uses an approach that centers on flexible and temporary transfer or rotation of high-performing school leaders to low-performing schools and provides incentives for career advancement. At the same time, some of the less effective principals are assigned to shadow high-performing principals for a few months so that they can learn quickly and effectively (Liang, Kidwai, and Zhang 2016).

In some MENA countries, instructional leadership tends to be considered the responsibility of district-level supervisors, but evidence suggests that supervisors do not play this role effectively in all countries. In Tunisia, for example, primary education inspectors conduct regular classroom visits and give feedback to individual teachers, but the approach is seldom effective in promoting and supporting school-level professional interaction among teachers. The observation methods used by inspectors are outdated, and observations happen at most twice a year; for improvement to occur, teachers need to receive feedback much more often. Inspectors are also responsible for delivering professional development, but the style of this delivery is a traditional lecture-based approach,

---

Box 10.1 Distributed and collaborative school leadership in Singapore

Singapore has one of the world's leading education systems, which was established quickly—within a few decades—partly due to strong leadership.

To reduce workload and create a sense of collaboration, principals adopt a distributed and transformational leadership approach, in which they train and use their middle managers to support instructional leadership. In doing so, principals leverage the subject-matter expertise of middle managers to provide subject-specific instructional feedback. Principals evaluate teachers and provide mentoring and feedback to them during the process. When they identify areas for improvement in teacher instruction, principals strategically gain teachers' trust, making them more receptive to suggested changes.

The transformational leadership approach allows school principals to monitor, assess, and provide feedback to teachers efficiently and thoroughly. The approach fosters a sense of community and collaboration, allowing principals to delegate monitoring tasks and provide effective instructional leadership.

Sources: Ng et al. 2015; Nguyen, Ng, and Yap 2017.

> **Box 10.2 Training school principals to become effective instructional leaders in New Zealand**
>
> New Zealand's Ministry of Education (MOE) provides new principals with extensive support and training. Principals receive training in three domains: instructional leadership, critical thinking and interpersonal skills, and management abilities. Training is provided through small groups as well as personalized mentorship on demand. Principals also have access to a regional management support group composed of trainers, principals, and regional MOE officials. Additionally, interactive informational resources for new principals are posted on the MOE website. The MOE continues to provide instructional leadership support for principals as they become more experienced, including online tools for assessment, best practices in teaching, and learning toolkits. Beginning in 2017, the system was improved to (1) build greater equity and excellence in a small number of national priority areas, including mathematics, science, reading and writing, and digital fluency; (2) enhance schools' capacity for evaluation; (3) tailor training better to the needs and contexts of individual schools; and (4) support leadership and professional education networks as a potential source of professional learning and development.
>
> *Sources:* "Communities of Learning" and "Information for Aspiring Principals" (Ministry of Education New Zealand n.d.).

which does not lead to changes in teacher practices (World Bank 2018b). In addition to upgrading teachers' skills, inspectors or supervisors will need to provide support for schools and liaison between schools and MOEs, while giving principals the mandate to provide instructional leadership and the training necessary to support them in their new role (OECD 2016b, 2016c). In MENA countries where principals provide instructional leadership, such as Jordan, there is a lack of programs to support the continuous development of these leadership skills (World Bank 2010).

Given the degree and importance of transference between principal and teacher, transforming all principals into instructional leaders is one of the most effective investments a country can make to improve student learning. MENA countries could benefit from investments to help school principals to improve teaching practices and student learning. Successful change depends on how principals are selected, supported, and given the necessary blend of autonomy and accountability to perform.

Modernize criteria and processes to select new school leaders

The selection and preparation of talented new principals are important steps in developing effective school leadership. Most MENA countries employ multiple criteria for screening and selecting school principals but place the heaviest weight on academic qualifications and teaching experience (Mullis, Martin, Goh, et al. 2016). In Oman, for example, school principals are chosen according to seniority and experience in teaching and classroom management. Some school principals have a degree in educational leadership in addition to teaching qualifications. Potential school principals in Bahrain are required to have teaching experience, to have been promoted from teacher to senior teacher and then to assistant principal, or to have experience as an adviser or education specialist. Some principals in Saudi Arabia have a degree in educational leadership in addition to teaching qualifications. In Lebanon, leadership training programs are the main route for preparing to become a principal, and principals must pass an interview and a year-long training program in leadership and supervision. The Arab

Republic of Egypt has rigorous professional requirements: all school principals must have a minimum of 15 years of teaching experience and a minimum of 5 years of administrative experience. Candidates for the position of principal must hold a tertiary education degree and are required to complete specific training. They also must pass a written test, successfully complete a supervised internship, and participate in an induction and mentoring program (Mullis, Martin, Goh, et al. 2016).

On average, school principals in MENA have less formal education than principals in other regions (see figure 10.2). In some MENA countries, good candidates have few incentives to apply for leadership positions, as principals are not paid more than teachers with equivalent years of service (World Bank SABER database).

Internationally, the process for selecting, preparing, and recruiting school principals varies. For example, Singapore selects potential school leaders through a talent management process that identifies and develops talent. Singapore's MOE uses data from its educator evaluation system to cultivate a pool of strong candidates and shape its selection decisions. These data also inform leadership development programs, which can be highly responsive to individual participants' needs (Jensen, Downing, and Clark 2017b). Most systems in the world do not have Singapore's talent management system. Instead, teacher leaders apply for and finance their own qualification training program and then wait for a position to open. This is known as the "aspiration" approach. In Hong Kong SAR, China, for instance, aspiring principals self-nominate to undertake the Certification for Principalship (Jensen, Downing, and Clark 2017a).

The Jiading District in Shanghai takes a similar but somewhat more stringent approach. Candidates are required to have a school principal eligibility certificate prior to becoming a candidate for a principalship. The requirements for the certificate include a written test, appropriate academic credentials, and a minimum number of years of service in teaching and school management. Prior to becoming a principal, candidates receive regular training in the necessary leadership and management skills. If there is an opening for a school principal position, the district office will select from the pool of candidates who have met these requirements (Liang, Kidwai, and Zhang 2016).

MENA countries could consider putting in place transparent, merit-based mechanisms to identify potential candidates for school principals and provide the right professional and financial incentives so that the best potential candidates will apply. Academic qualifications and good teaching abilities are important, but not sufficient; leadership qualities are also essential (Bush, Kiggundu, and Moorosi 2011; Van der Westhuizen, Mosoge, and Van Vuuren 2004).

Empower school leaders with professional development and rewarding career pathways

Once new principals are hired, it is critical to empower them with continuous professional

FIGURE 10.2 On average, school principals in MENA have lower education levels than principals elsewhere

Percentage of grade 4 students, by principal's formal level of education

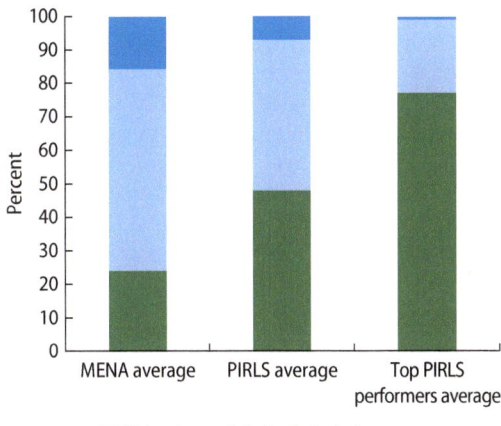

Source: Mullis et al. 2017.
Note: PIRLS = Progress in International Reading Literacy Study.

development opportunities. In-service training is equally important for principals who have been in the position for a long time. Training is important because a principal's role changes over time along with school demands (Jensen, Downing, and Clark 2017b; OECD 2013). As technology, research, and labor market needs are changing rapidly, school leaders must be able to update their knowledge and skills regularly. While professional development for principals needs to be tailored to the local context and needs, many high-performing systems share some core elements that are worth highlighting (Jensen, Downing, and Clark 2017b; World Bank 2018b):

- Leadership development is structured to reflect the principal's vision for the school, including the way a system expects its teachers to act, the kind of schools the system wants, and the system's vision for how schools improve.
- School leaders are trained to manage professional learning organizations through instructional and collaborative leadership. This means that the principal is not the sole instructional and curriculum leader, but instead appoints leaders and shares oversight.
- Leadership development is tied to practical problems that are actionable, uses problem-solving approaches in a real school environment, and is supported by mentors.
- School leadership programs build skills for a dynamic work environment by developing leaders' resilience, critical thinking skills, and the ability to adapt practices for new situations.
- Leadership development programs continue throughout a leader's career, through a systematic and comprehensive approach that is career-long and systemwide.

While most education systems in MENA have established requirements for school principals, more than half of those participating in the Trends in International Mathematics and Science Study (TIMSS) 2015 had not updated these requirements for at least 10 years (Mullis, Martin, Goh, et al. 2016). A review of school leadership using the Systems Approach for Better Education Results (SABER)-Teachers assessment tool in nine MENA countries found that most countries did not have well-established policies in place to support strong school leadership (World Bank SABER-Teachers database). These countries either do not invest sufficiently in school leadership development (except Egypt) or do not have a clear policy that principals are mandated to implement to improve instructional practice (except Egypt, Jordan, and Tunisia). The ongoing reform efforts in many MENA countries have recognized the importance of school leadership and have started to prioritize school leadership development. Kuwait, for example, has launched school leadership programs as part of a comprehensive reform.

Many countries have developed ways to make the profession of school principal more rewarding and flexible. In Flemish Belgium, former principals can become directors of a community of schools that collaborate on issues such as career guidance for students, course provision, and special needs education. England has created a Leadership Development Framework that provides a pathway of programs and standards that extend across a school leader's career, including opportunities for experienced school leaders to provide support for other head teachers (Pont, Nusche, and Moorman 2008). In Shanghai, the career ladder of school principals has four levels, which are aligned with job performance (see box 10.3).

These international experiences show that career ladders offer school leaders a structured path for professional growth and provide incentive structures that reward performance and results. In turn, school leaders are more willing to develop their expertise, to collaborate with other colleagues, and to coach and mentor their less experienced peers. Career ladders also encourage expert teachers and school leaders to move into positions in which they are most needed and can make greater contributions, leading to more equitable systems.

> **Box 10.3** **School principals' career ladders in Shanghai**
>
> Since the early 1990s, China has focused on making sure that the most capable instructional experts are leading schools. All school principals come from the teaching ranks, and many of them maintain teaching duties after moving into principal positions.
>
> In order to encourage continued professional growth and motivate principals for high performance, Shanghai introduced a career ladder for principals in 1993. To encourage innovation and competition among principals and improve student learning, the ladder has a four-level structure tied to the pay scale. The ladder articulates educational requirements, expected professional skills, continuing professional development requirements, and performance appraisal processes for school principals.
>
> Requirements are specified for principals at each level. For instance, master principals, the top level on the ladder, not only must have senior qualifications, but also should have an outstanding record of education theory and teaching research and be recognized provincially and even nationally as influential leaders in education. To be promoted one rank up, principals must achieve a rating of "excellent" in one annual assessment or a rating of "qualified" in two consecutive assessments.
>
> Principals and teachers participate in an innovative approach for bringing up low-performing schools by matching them with high-performing schools. The high-performing school is contracted to support and develop the low-performing school. Principals are also encouraged to work in less developed areas. Their promotion on the career ladder takes such contributions into consideration.
>
> Shanghai has rapidly strengthened its school leadership effectiveness since the ladder's inception. Combined with the teacher career ladder, Shanghai has built an entire career path for teachers and principals. Beginning-level principals are selected from excellent teachers on the high level of the teacher career ladder.
>
> *Sources:* Jensen, Downing, and Clark 2017c; Liang, Kidwai, and Zhang 2016; NCEE 2016.

Provide school leaders with more authority to support teaching and learning

The role that school principals play in school governance processes is critical to school quality (Bruns, Filmer, and Patrinos 2011; Demas and Arcia 2015). Providing school leaders with decision-making power and resources can give them more direct influence on the performance of teachers and other school personnel. Such authority may encourage teachers to be more responsive to students' learning needs. This approach can be more effective than central decision making, which is far removed from the point of delivery and has little ability to incentivize teachers to improve learning (World Bank 2018b).

In MENA, a school principal's authority to determine resource needs, budgeting, and personnel management is relatively low (OECD 2016b; World Bank 2015). Most principals in MENA's public schools do not have the authority to select teachers for their school or to fire underperforming or chronically absent teachers. In contrast, many OECD countries (Denmark, Ireland, the Netherlands, New Zealand, Slovenia, Switzerland, the United Kingdom, and the United States) grant the school principal a substantial role in hiring and firing teachers (see figure 10.3). Of the six MENA countries participating in the Programme for International Student Assessment (PISA) 2015, the three with the highest mathematics scores (Lebanon, Qatar, and the United Arab Emirates) give principals a similar level of responsibility for school governance as OECD countries, although more studies are needed to demonstrate whether the correlation between school governance and student performance is causal.

In Tunisia, primary school directors do not have access to financial resources. Although by policy they are explicitly required to

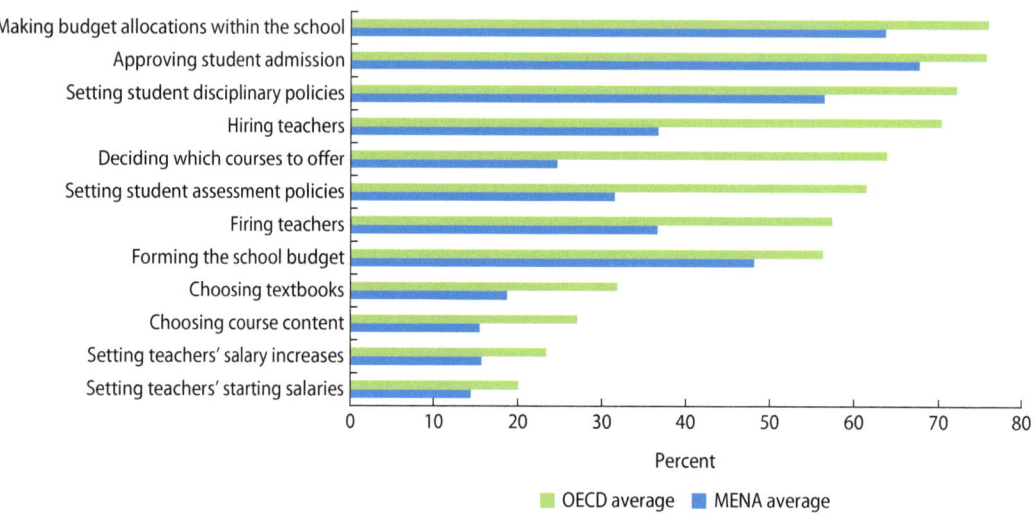

FIGURE 10.3 **School principals in MENA have less authority than those in OECD countries**
Percentage of students in schools in which the principal has considerable responsibility for ...

Source: OECD 2016a.
Note: OECD = Organisation for Economic Co-operation and Development.

provide guidance to teachers on curriculum and teaching-related tasks, in practice this role is often left to pedagogical counselors and inspectors who make periodic visits. Tunisia's school directors do not have authority to determine the selection or removal of teachers in their schools. School directors do not have decision-making authority to reward strong performance. Recognizing these governance issues in primary education, Tunisia has designed a project to empower school leaders and strengthen school management, which will be implemented in the coming years (World Bank 2018a).

Greater autonomy for principals alone is unlikely to be successful unless there is a solid foundation for good accountability (Bruns, Filmer, and Patrinos 2011; Demas and Arcia 2015). Qatar's independent school model was a groundbreaking reform in the region. It created mechanisms for school autonomy and accountability and demonstrated the potential of a results-based approach. However, the model was ultimately discontinued after 2013 and came under intense criticism for failing to achieve the anticipated results. Among many lessons learned from Qatar's experience is the importance of developing the capacity and accountability for school-level leaders to exercise their authority skillfully and responsibly. The reform effort also illustrates the need for active engagement of local actors, including teachers and parents, in developing policy and making decisions regarding implementation (Paschyn 2013).

MENA countries will need to grant school principals greater autonomy so that they can make instructional and administrative decisions based on local needs. At the same time, school leaders will have to show improvement in their schools' student learning outcomes to demonstrate accountability. A transformational change such as this requires new policies and implementation support from all stakeholders.

References

Alsaeedi, Farraj, and Trevor Male. 2013. "Transformational Leadership and Globalization: Attitudes of School Principals in Kuwait." *Educational Management Administration and Leadership* 41 (5): 640–57. http://journals.sagepub.com/doi/abs/10.1177/1741143213488588?journalCode=emad.

Barber, Michael, and Mona Mourshed. 2007. "How the World's Best-Performing School Systems Come Out on Top." McKinsey and Company, Washington, DC.

Bruns, Barbara, Deon Filmer, and Harry Anthony Patrinos. 2011. *Making Schools Work: New Evidence on Accountability Reforms.* Washington, DC: World Bank.

Bush, Tony, Edith Kiggundu, and Pontso Moorosi. 2011. "Preparing New Principals in South Africa: The ACE School Leadership Programme." *South African Journal of Education* 31 (1): 31–43.

Demas, Angela, and Gustavo J. Arcia. 2015. "What Matters Most for Autonomy and Accountability: A Framework Paper." SABER Working Paper 9, World Bank, Washington, DC.

Hallinger, Philip, and Ronald H. Heck. 2011. "Exploring the Journey of School Improvement: Classifying and Analyzing Patterns of Change in School Improvement Processes and Learning Outcomes." *School Effectiveness and School Improvement: An International Journal of Research, Policy, and Practice* 22 (1): 1–27. http://dx.doi.org/10.1080/09243453.2010.536322.

Jensen, Ben, Phoebe Downing, and Anna Clark. 2017a. "Preparing to Lead: Hong Kong Preparation for Principalship Program; Case Studies for School Leadership Development Programs in High-Performing Education Systems." National Center on Education and the Economy, Washington, DC. http://ncee.org/wp-content/uploads/2017/09/PreparingtoLeadHongKong092617.pdf.

———. 2017b. "Preparing to Lead: Lessons in Principal Development from High-Performing Education Systems." National Center on Education and the Economy, Washington, DC. http://ncee.org/wp-content/uploads/2017/10/PreparingtoLeadFINAL101817.pdf.

———. 2017c. "Preparing to Lead: Shanghai Continuing Professional Development; Case Studies for School Leadership Development Programs in High-Performing Education Systems." National Center on Education and the Economy, Washington, DC.

Leithwood, Kenneth, Alma Harris, and David Hopkins. 2008. "Seven Strong Claims about Successful School Leadership." *School Leadership and Management* 28 (1): 27–42. https://doi.org/10.1080/13632430701800060.

Leithwood, Kenneth, and Blair Mascall. 2008. "Collective Leadership Effects on Student Achievement." *Educational Administration Quarterly* 44 (4): 529–61.

Liang, Xiaoyan, Huma Kidwai, and Minxuan Zhang. 2016. *How Shanghai Does It—Insights and Lessons from the Highest-Ranking Education System in the World.* Washington, DC: World Bank.

Ministry of Education New Zealand. No date. "Communities of Learning." https://www.education.govt.nz/communities-of-learning/.

———. No date. "Information for Aspiring Principals." http://www.educationalleaders.govt.nz/Aspiring-principals/.

Mullis, Ina V. S., Michael O. Martin, Pierre Foy, and M. Hooper. 2016. "TIMSS 2015 International Results in Mathematics." TIMSS and PIRLS International Study Center, Boston College, Chestnut Hill, MA. http://timssandpirls.bc.edu/timss2015/international-results/.

———. 2017. "PIRLS 2016 International Results in Reading." TIMSS and PIRLS International Study Center, Boston College, Chestnut Hill, MA. http://timssandpirls.bc.edu/pirls2016/international-results/.

Mullis, Ina V. S., Michael O. Martin, Shirley Goh, and Kerry Cotter, eds. 2016. *TIMSS 2015 Encyclopedia: Education Policy and Curriculum in Mathematics and Science.* Chestnut Hill, MA: Boston College, TIMSS and PIRLS International Study Center. http://timssandpirls.bc.edu/timss2015/encyclopedia/.

NCEE (National Center on Education and the Economy). 2016. "Shanghai: Culture, Policy, and Practice." Empower Educators: How High-Performing Systems Shape Teaching Quality around the World Country Brief, NCEE, Washington, DC.

Ng, Foo Seong David, Thanh Dong Nguyen, Koon Siak Benjamin Wong, and Kim Weng William Choy. 2015. "Instructional Leadership Practices in Singapore." *School Leadership and Management* 35 (4): 388–407.

Nguyen, Dong Thanh, David Ng, and Pui San Yap. 2017. "Instructional Leadership Structure in Singapore: A Co-Existence of Hierarchy and Heterarchy." *Journal of Educational Administration* 55 (2): 147–67.

OECD (Organisation for Economic Co-operation and Development). 2013. *PISA 2012 Results: Excellence through Equity: Giving Every Student the Chance to Succeed.* Paris: OECD Publishing.

———. 2016a. *PISA 2015 Results.* Vol. 2: *Policies and Practices for Successful Schools.* Paris: OECD Publishing. http://www.keepeek.com/Digital-Asset-Management/oecd/education/pisa-2015-results-volume-ii_9789264267510-en#page1n.

———. 2016b. *School Leadership for Developing Professional Learning Communities.* Teaching in Focus 15. Paris: OECD.

———. 2016c. *School Leadership for Learning: Insights from TALIS 2013.* Paris: OECD. http://dx.doi.org/10.1787/9789264258341-en.

Paschyn, Christina Maria. 2013. "Zig-Zagging Education Policies Leave Qatari Students Behind." Al-Fanar Media, October 25. https://www.al-fanarmedia.org/2013/10/zig-zagging-education-policies-leave-qatari-students-behind/.

Pont, Beatriz, Deborah Nusche, and Hunter Moorman. 2008. *Improving School Leadership.* Vol. 1. Paris: OECD. http://www.oecd.org/education/school/44374889.pdf.

Van der Westhuizen, Philip C., M. J. Mosoge, and H. J. Van Vuuren. 2004. "Capacity-Building for Educational Managers in South Africa: A Case Study of the Mpumalanga Province." *International Journal of Educational Development* 24 (6): 705–19.

Witziers, Bob, Roel Bosker, and Meta Kruger. 2003. "Educational Leadership and Student Achievement: The Elusive Search for an Association." *Educational Administration Quarterly* 39 (3): 398–423.

World Bank. 2010. "Jordan SABER-Teacher Country Report: Jordan 2010." SABER Country Report, World Bank, Washington, DC.

———. 2015. *MENA Regional Synthesis on the Teacher Policies Survey: Key Findings from Phase 1.* Washington, DC: World Bank. https://openknowledge.worldbank.org/handle/10986/21490.

———. 2018a. "Republic of Tunisia: Strengthening Foundations for Learning Project." Project Appraisal Document, World Bank, Washington, DC.

———. 2018b. *World Development Report 2018: Learning to Realize Education's Promise.* Washington, DC: World Bank.

———. Various years. Systems Approach for Better Education Results (SABER)-Teachers database. Washington, DC: World Bank. http://saber.worldbank.org/index.cfm?indx=8&pd=1&sub=0.

Prioritizing Investments to Promote Learning and Skills

11

Igor Kheyfets and
Mohammed Audah

In the Middle East and North Africa (MENA), governments have allocated substantial resources to meet the education demands of growing populations. Most countries have been able to expand access to education at a faster rate than the increase in their school-age populations (see chapter 1), which has led to impressive gains in school enrollment. Today, in some countries—like Tunisia—education accounts for one-fifth of all government spending (World Bank EdStats database). For the region as a whole, public investment in education has declined slightly since 2000. However, while adequate public funding is necessary, it is not sufficient to ensure learning. As has often been noted, "It's *how*, not simply *how much*, that counts" (Vegas and Coffin 2012; World Bank 2018).

Within education budgets, the allocation of spending is often misaligned with national strategic goals, such as improving learning outcomes. MENA countries spend large shares of their education budgets on staff salaries, which may crowd out investment in other important inputs that enable learning. Sufficient investments in early childhood education (ECE) and in the early grades of schooling are also needed to ensure that students build basic foundational skills that enable them to learn effectively in later stages of education. Countries in which public education spending is skewed toward the tertiary level may need to realign their investment priorities to be more conducive to achieving early learning goals.

Invest sufficient public resources in education

To reach their education goals, countries must make adequate investments in their education systems. Large public investments may be needed at times of system expansion or reform, and consistent investments are needed to sustain quality learning over time. Governments that place the improvement of learning outcomes at the center of their policy agendas need to ensure that adequate domestic resources are allocated to strengthening their education systems. These resources should be allocated equitably, used efficiently, and managed with clear links between public budgets and education results (see spotlight 3).

MENA governments have allocated substantial resources to education

Nearly 50 million more children were enrolled in school in the MENA region at the turn of the new millennium than in 1970.

More than half of the increase was due to greater numbers of girls enrolling in school (World Bank EdStats database). Substantial financial efforts have made this possible. Between the 1970s and the 1990s, many countries in the region made concerted efforts to increase their public expenditures on education.[1] Some countries—like the Arab Republic of Egypt and Morocco—aimed to achieve universal enrollment in primary education. Others—like most countries of the Gulf Cooperation Council (GCC)—moved toward universal coverage in secondary education. Saudi Arabia was among the countries that managed to do both (see box 11.1).

Across MENA, tremendous progress has been made in expanding access to schooling through larger public investments in education. In the early 1970s, the median national education budget in MENA accounted for around 3 percent of gross domestic product (GDP). By 2000, that number had doubled to 6 percent, and more than 20 percent of national public budgets was spent on education (see figure 11.1). In some countries—like Djibouti and the Republic of Yemen—education's share of the national budget reached 30 percent around the turn of the century, a level not seen in MENA either before or since.

After 2000, the region witnessed a steady decline in public spending on education as a

Box 11.1 Public spending and expansion of access to education in Saudi Arabia

In 1979, Saudi Arabia's modest gross enrollment ratio (GER) of 57 percent in primary education was among the lowest in the region. Similarly, the 27 percent GER in secondary education placed the country among the bottom third of all MENA countries. Fewer than 800,000 children were enrolled in primary school, and fewer than 300,000 were enrolled in secondary school. In both levels, only 36 to 37 percent were girls. Over the following decades, Saudi Arabian authorities invested substantial resources in expanding access to education, successfully increasing GERs to 93 percent for primary and 86 percent for secondary education by 2005 (when the major expansion of access to schooling had been completed). Among girls, GERs rose more than 50 percentage points during this time, reaching gender parity. These gains came at a substantial cost to the Saudi Arabian public budget. Between 1981 and 1998, the share of GDP spent on education more than doubled—from 4 to 8 percent. This impressive investment yielded equally impressive results: 4.6 million more students were enrolled in the country's primary and secondary schools by 2005 (see figure B11.1.1).

FIGURE B11.1.1 **Saudi Arabia rapidly expanded school enrollments**
Enrollment trends, by level of education, 1979 and 2005

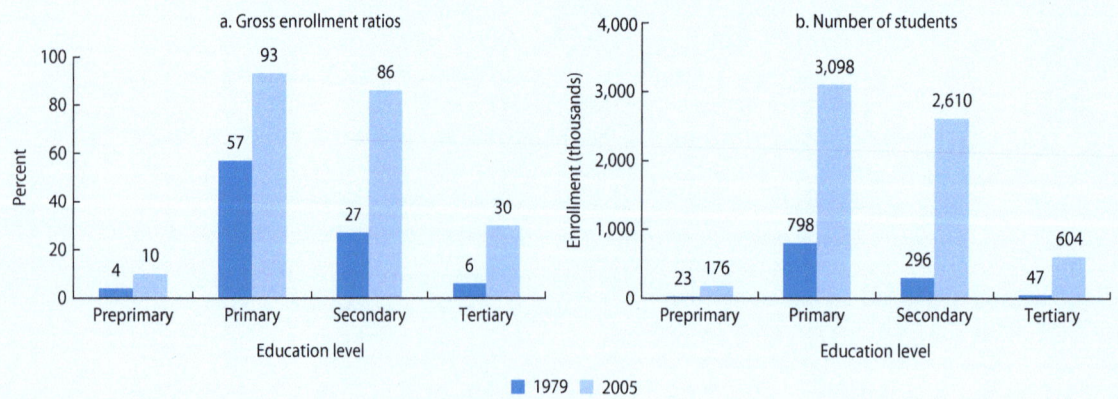

Source: World Bank EdStats database (http://datatopics.worldbank.org/education/).

FIGURE 11.1 **Public spending on education in MENA grew steadily to 2000, then declined**

Government expenditure on education as a percentage of GDP and of total government expenditure

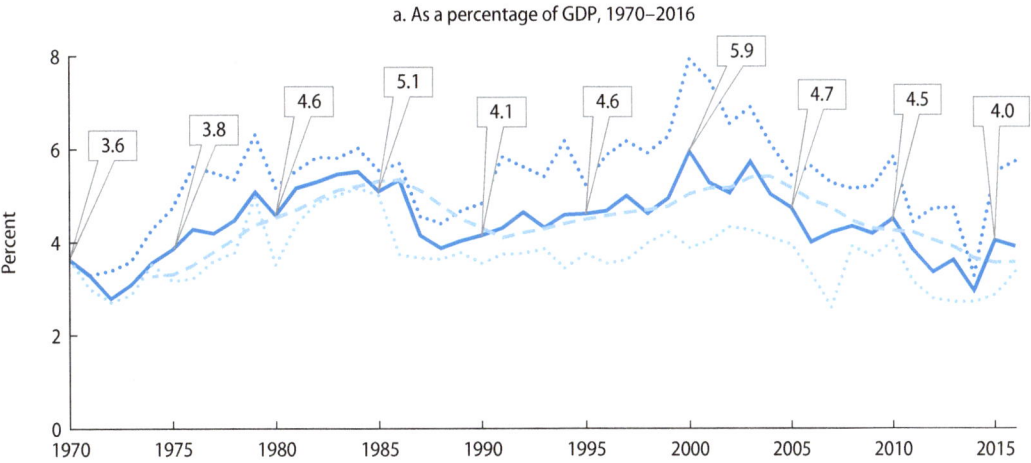

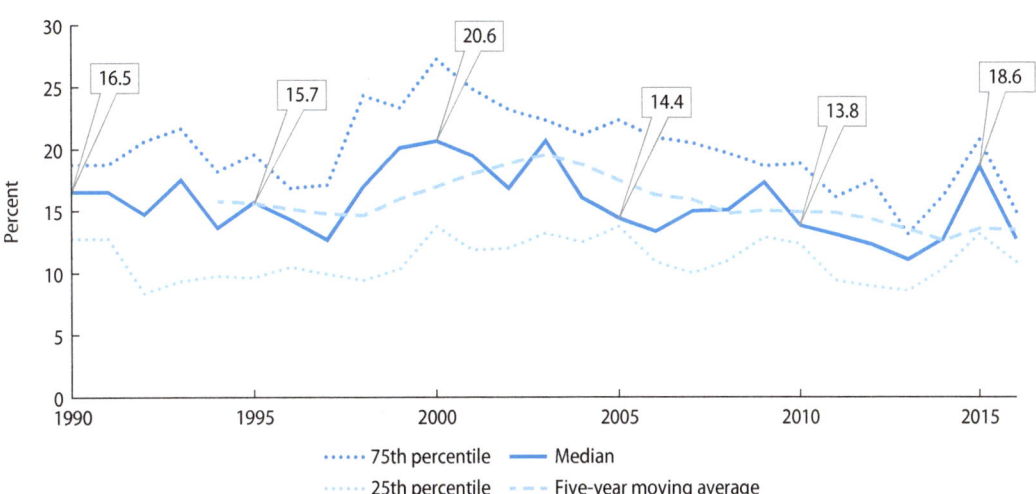

Source: World Bank EdStats database (http://datatopics.worldbank.org/education/).
Note: MENA regional medians (and corresponding interquartile ranges) are computed as the median of all national data points available in a given year. Due to sporadic reporting across countries, the medians are sensitive to the selection of countries included in the calculation for any given year. However, the results displayed are not substantially affected by the changing composition of countries used to calculate the median. The five-year moving average is included as a robustness check.

share of GDP and total government expenditure. By 2016, the median education budget had shrunk to approximately 4 percent of GDP, and only 13 percent of national budgets was spent on education. A few countries—like Oman and Tunisia—still invest more than 6 percent of GDP in education (see figure 11.2). However, most have cut back their public spending to below 4 percent of GDP. Bahrain and Lebanon are behind the rest of the region, with less than 3 percent of GDP and less than 10 percent of their budgets going to education. Not surprisingly, private funding from households makes up much of the funding gap in these countries.

FIGURE 11.2 Large variations exist in public spending on education across MENA

Government expenditures on education as a percentage of GDP and of total government expenditure, 2016 or latest available year

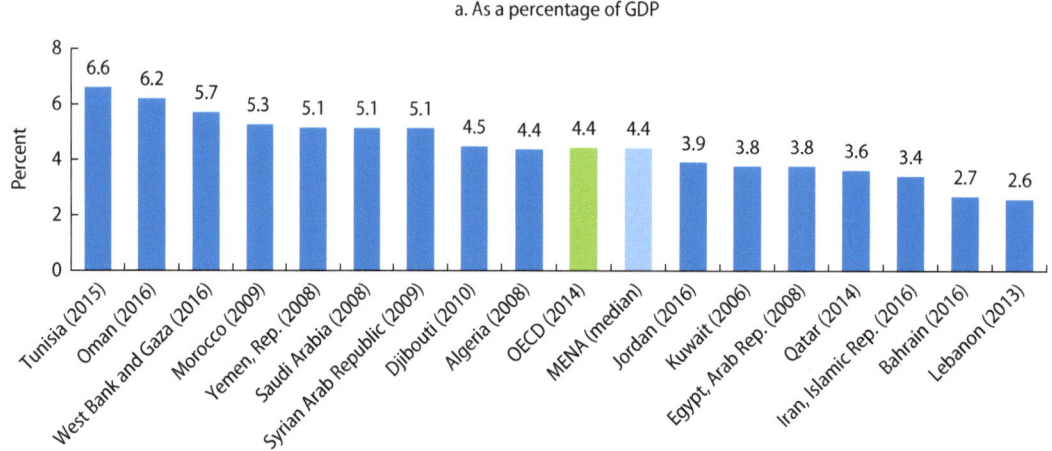

a. As a percentage of GDP

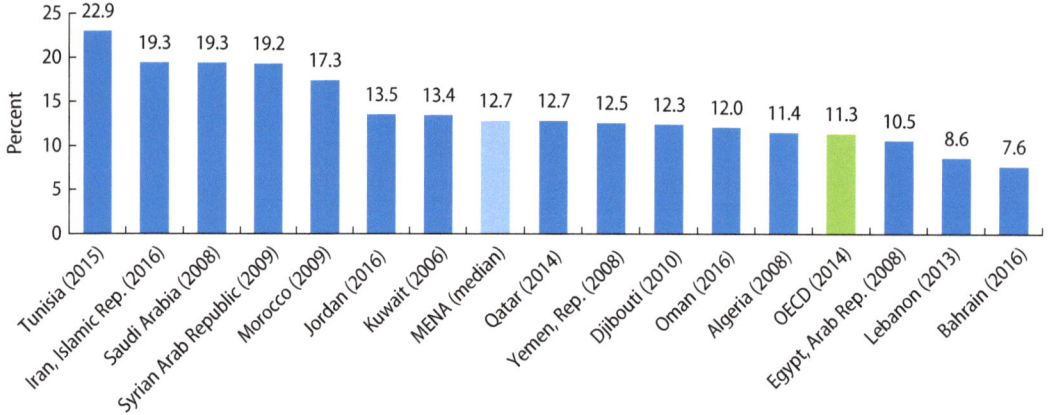

b. As a percentage of total government expenditure

Sources: OECD 2017a; World Bank EdStats database (http://datatopics.worldbank.org/education/).
Note: Data are for the latest available year between 2006 and 2016. MENA regional medians are computed as the median of the latest available year's figures for each country. The OECD average is as reported in OECD (2017a, tables B2.3 and B4.1). OECD = Organisation for Economic Co-operation and Development.

In countries with insufficient public investment, private payments often make up the difference

While comprehensive and reliable information on private expenditures on education is difficult to obtain, some countries in MENA where data are available tend to have relatively high levels of private spending.[2] Based on available data covering six MENA countries from 2002 to 2015, World Bank estimates suggest that private spending on education in MENA is substantially above the Organisation for Economic Co-operation and Development (OECD) average (see figure 11.3). Strikingly, in West Bank and Gaza, where estimated private expenditure amounts to approximately 5 percent of GDP, and in Lebanon, where estimated private expenditure amounts to at least 3 percent of GDP, households collectively spend as much on education as does the state (see figure 11.2). In Bahrain, Kuwait, and Morocco, households finance 20 to 33 percent of all education spending. By comparison, in an average OECD country, private expenditure accounts for about 15 percent of all education expenditure.[3]

Allocate resources toward learning

Even when the overall level of investment in education is high enough, the allocation of spending within the sector has an important influence on the level of learning. Underinvestment in ECE or the early years of schooling, for example, may lead to children failing to develop early in life the foundational skills necessary for learning at the later stages of education. Similarly, committing large shares of the education budget to salary spending may crowd out investment in other quality-enhancing inputs.

Underinvestment in early learning contrasts with large outlays for higher education

Government spending on education is skewed more heavily toward the tertiary level in some MENA countries (see figure 11.4). At the same time, public investment in early learning opportunities may be lower than would be optimal. Algeria, the Islamic Republic of Iran, Kuwait, and Lebanon all exceed the OECD average of 24 percent of public education budgets spent on tertiary education. At the same time, the tertiary GERs in MENA, with the exception of the Islamic Republic of Iran, are far below the 70 percent observed in the OECD, which should require lower relative spending levels rather than higher ones.

Expanding access to preprimary education has been a challenge for many MENA countries. On average, MENA enrolls only 31 percent of children of preschool age, compared with 49 percent worldwide. While the leading countries—Algeria, Lebanon, and

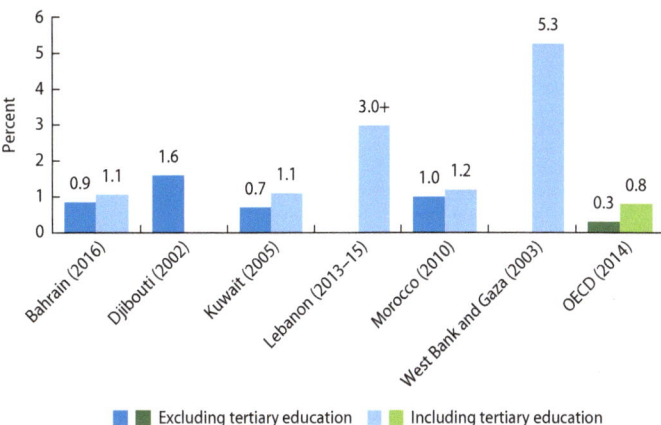

FIGURE 11.3 **High private spending on education is common in MENA**
Estimated private expenditure on education as a percentage of GDP, latest available year

■ Excluding tertiary education   ■ Including tertiary education

Sources: OECD 2017a; UNESCO Institute for Statistics UIS.Stat database (http://data.uis.unesco.org/); World Bank 2006, 2007b, 2017.
Note: Data are not available for "excluding tertiary education" for Lebanon or West Bank and Gaza or for "including tertiary education" for Djibouti. Year(s) of data on which the estimates are based are listed in parentheses beside the economy name. For Bahrain, Kuwait, and Morocco, "Initial household funding of education" from the UNESCO Institute for Statistics database is used (UIS n.d.). For Lebanon, "3.0+" indicates an estimate of at least 3.0 percent. OECD = Organisation for Economic Co-operation and Development.

FIGURE 11.4 **Public investments in education in MENA disproportionately focus on tertiary education**
Tertiary gross enrollment ratio (GER) and percentage of government education expenditure spent on tertiary education, 2016 or latest available year

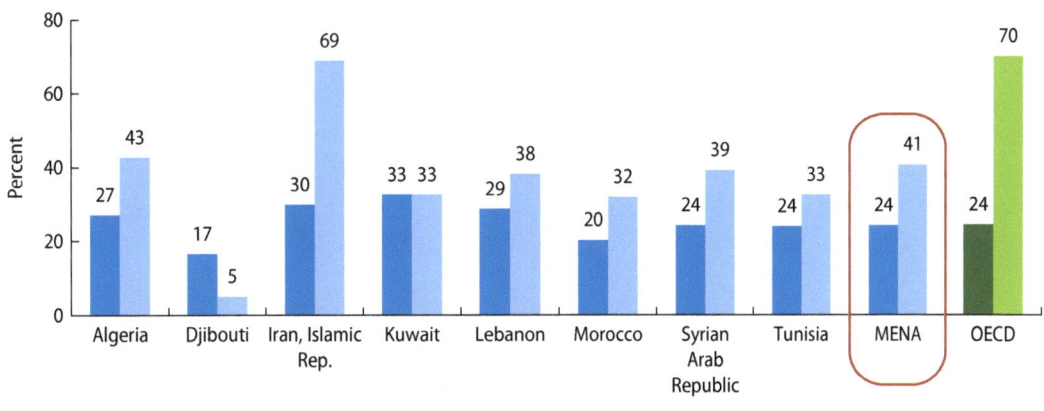

■ Expenditure on tertiary education as a percentage of government expenditure on education   ■ Tertiary GER

Sources: OECD 2017a; World Bank EdStats database (http://datatopics.worldbank.org/education/).
Note: Data are for the latest available year between 2006 and 2016. MENA average expenditure is computed as the median of the latest available figures for each country between 2006 and 2016. OECD = Organisation for Economic Co-operation and Development.

the United Arab Emirates—have at least 75 percent of their young children enrolled in ECE, several others are far behind. Djibouti, the Syrian Arab Republic, and the Republic of Yemen have fewer than 10 percent of children enrolled in ECE (see figure 11.5).

Governments in MENA generally underinvest in the provision of ECE. Based on the little international data available, no MENA country spends more than 0.4 percent of GDP on ECE from the public budget. Most spend far less (well below 0.2 percent). In comparison, the average OECD country invests about 0.7 to 0.8 percent of GDP on ECE, and some countries—like Sweden—invest as much as 1.3 percent of GDP in ECE (see box 11.2). With young and growing populations that consistently show low levels of foundational skills, public investment in high-quality early learning programs for all children is a key policy priority for the MENA region.

Substantial capital investments respond to the needs of growing student populations

MENA's vibrant demographic growth has required a long-running expansion of the region's education infrastructure. As a result, education budgets of many MENA countries place a heavy emphasis on capital investment. Capital investment includes the construction of new schools and the rehabilitation and expansion of existing facilities as well as the procurement of school equipment and other physical assets. With high fertility rates in many parts of the region, countries will continue to face pressures to expand their education infrastructure until at least 2030, when demographic growth may begin to slow.[4]

Today, some countries, such as Kuwait and Qatar, spend more than 20 percent of their education budgets on capital investment (see figure 11.6).[5] Lebanon and Morocco follow, devoting more than 13 percent of spending to capital investment. Such levels of capital investment are often needed to meet the demand for education infrastructure in countries with growing school-age populations.

To ensure that large capital expenditures are used efficiently, effective budget planning is required in the sphere of public capital investment. MENA education systems are often characterized by ad hoc budget requests for capital projects that are not well rooted in sector strategic priorities (Beschel and Ahern 2012). As a result, approval processes can be long and unpredictable, and capital investment decisions may not be linked to clear sector needs. Several countries around the world

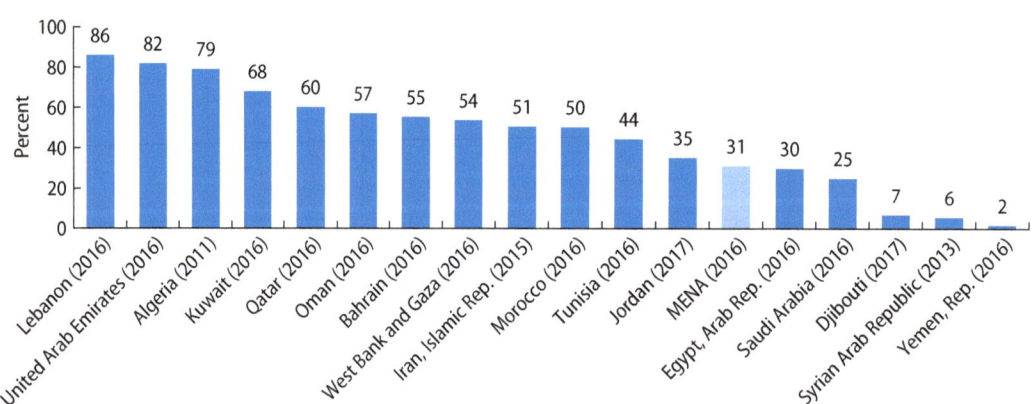

FIGURE 11.5 Large differences in preprimary enrollment ratios are found across MENA
Preprimary gross enrollment ratio

Sources: For all except Jordan, World Bank EdStats database (http://datatopics.worldbank.org/education/), based on data from the UNESCO Institute for Statistics UIS.Stat database (http://data.uis.unesco.org/). For Jordan, data from the Queen Rania Center at the Jordan Ministry of Education, provided in August 2018.
Note: Data are for the latest available year between 2011 and 2017.

Box 11.2 Growing public investment in early learning: The cases of Finland and Sweden

Between 1999 and 2014, Finland and Sweden—two high-performing Scandinavian countries—made large investments in expanding the coverage of their preschool systems. Finland's preprimary GER grew from 47 to 80 percent, while Sweden's increased from 76 to 96 percent during this time. The cost of this expansion was substantial. Both countries' public education budgets increased as a share of GDP: from below 6 to 7 percent in Finland and from approximately 7 to 8 percent in Sweden. The share of their education budgets dedicated to preprimary education more than doubled (from 5 to 11 percent in Finland and from 7 to 17 percent in Sweden) to pay for this expansion.

At the same time, higher levels of education—especially the university sector—received smaller shares of the education budget in both countries. Finland's tertiary education sector shrank as a share of all education spending, from 34 to 28 percent, while Sweden's tertiary education sector decreased slightly, from 27 to 25 percent. In absolute terms, both countries' funding for tertiary education remained at a relatively constant 2 percent of GDP during this time (and tertiary enrollment ratios remained flat). The clear priority being given to expanding early learning in the early 2000s earned both Finland and Sweden praise as the top OECD countries for public investment in ECE (OECD 2017a).

Sources: OECD 2017a; World Bank EdStats database (http://datatopics.worldbank.org/education/).

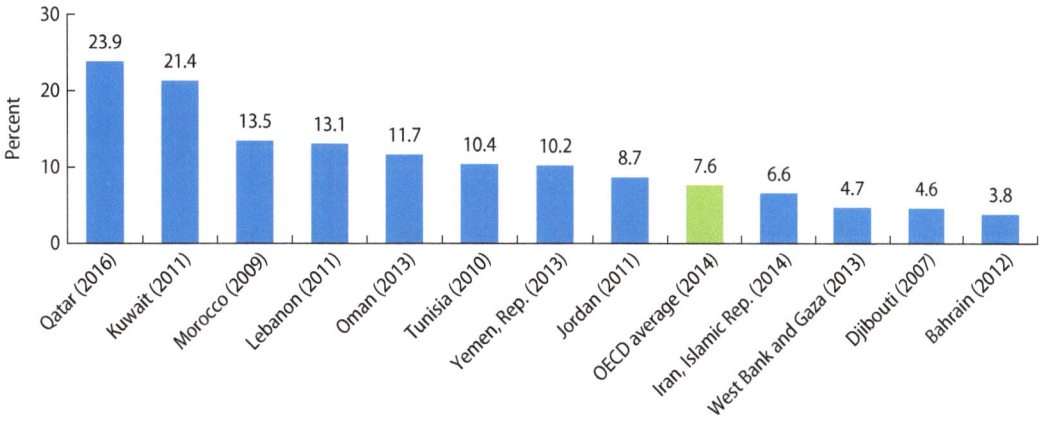

FIGURE 11.6 **Large capital budgets reflect the demographic needs of many MENA economies**
Capital expenditure as a percentage of all public education spending, 2016 or latest available year

Sources: World Bank staff estimates based on data from OECD 2017a and World Bank EdStats database (http://datatopics.worldbank.org/education/).
Note: Data are for the latest available year between 2007 and 2016. Estimates for the following include primary and secondary education only: Jordan, Kuwait, Morocco, the Republic of Yemen, and the OECD average (including postsecondary, nontertiary). OECD = Organisation for Economic Co-operation and Development.

have addressed this issue by adopting national infrastructure plans (NIPs) that cover the education sector. NIPs allow for long-term planning of school infrastructure investment supported by robust analyses of actual and projected needs. Box 11.3 describes several examples that may be relevant to MENA countries.[6]

Salaries make up the largest share of recurrent education spending, leaving little room for other important inputs

Many countries in MENA spend more than 80 percent of their recurrent public education budgets—that is, all budget spending except capital investment—on personnel

Box 11.3 Capital budgeting in education: The use of national infrastructure plans

Capital budgeting can be integrated into sectoral policy making through the use of national infrastructure plans. In education, these are often called national school infrastructure plans or national education infrastructure strategies. These approaches combine evidence-based policy making (where decisions are made on the basis of relevant sector data) with medium- and long-term strategic planning. With a NIP in place, the decision about whether or not to build a school in a particular location can be made by thoroughly analyzing relative needs across different localities and by applying transparent selection criteria to timely and accurate data. This approach to infrastructure planning is preferable to an ad hoc approach, as each investment can be viewed through the lens of the strategic needs of the sector and country.

In Peru, the Ministry of Education partnered with local academics to devise a strategy for reducing seismic vulnerability of education facilities. This information then fed into the creation of the National School Infrastructure Plan 2025. In Romania, the government designed a holistic and evidence-based model to inform decisions about investments in education infrastructure by strengthening their existing Education Management Information System and monitoring and evaluation mechanisms, identifying education infrastructure needs at the subnational level, and developing of a set of criteria to prioritize investments.

Sources: Beschel and Ahern 2012; Teixeira, Amoroso, and Gresham 2017; Universidad de los Andes and World Bank 2017.

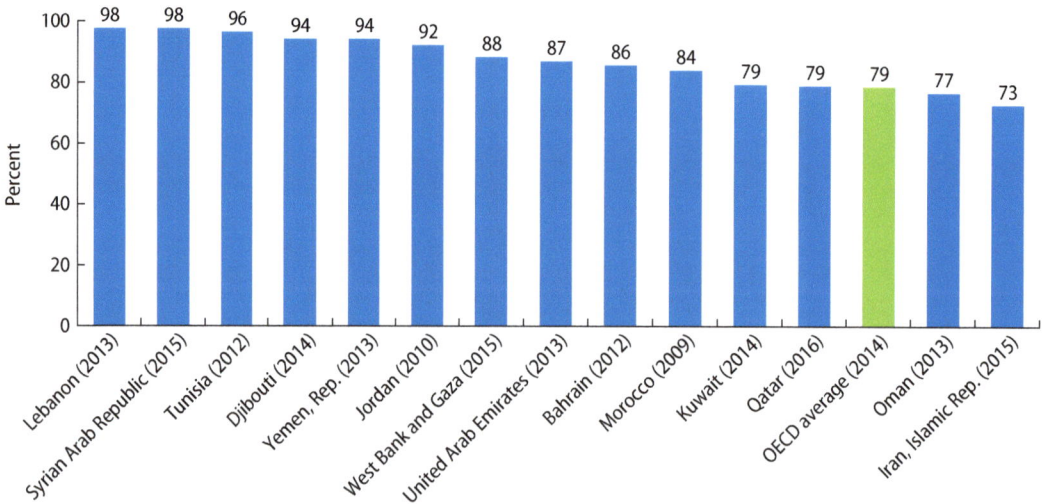

FIGURE 11.7 **A wage bill's high share can crowd out other important education spending in MENA**
Staff salaries as a percentage of recurrent public education spending, 2016 or latest available year

Sources: World Bank staff estimates based on data from OECD (OECD 2017a) and World Bank EdStats database (http://datatopics.worldbank.org/education/).
Note: Data are for the latest available year between 2009 and 2016. Estimates for the following include primary and secondary education only: Djibouti, Jordan, Kuwait, Morocco, the Syrian Arab Republic, Tunisia, the United Arab Emirates, the Republic of Yemen, and the OECD average (including postsecondary, nontertiary). OECD = Organisation for Economic Co-operation and Development.

costs (see figure 11.7). Lebanon leads the way with 98 percent, while many others—Djibouti, Jordan, Syria, Tunisia, and the Republic of Yemen—spend more than 90 percent of recurrent expenditure on salaries. While teachers are clearly the most important contributors to learning in the classroom, inputs such as teaching and learning materials are also critical. When less than 10 percent of the recurrent education budget is allocated to nonsalary spending, there is little room for financing the day-to-day operation of schools, and other important investments that contribute to learning are crowded out, such as teaching and learning materials, professional development, and school rehabilitation and maintenance.[7] Adequate funding of nonsalary categories in education budgets is crucial for ensuring that large public investments translate into education results. Unbalanced allocations between wage bill expenses and investments in nonsalary recurrent spending, as well as capital investment, can lead to inefficiencies in the use of existing financial resources.

Manage the teacher workforce efficiently

Despite MENA countries' large investments in teachers, such investments can make a positive contribution to student learning only if human resources are managed and used efficiently and deployed in areas where they are needed. If teachers are not present in the classroom or are lacking in certain key subjects, then the substantial investments that countries make in their education systems—whose largest share is devoted to financing teacher salaries—may not lead to learning.

Learning can only happen with an adequate number of qualified teachers

Having an adequate number of qualified teachers in the classroom is the basic prerequisite for learning. However, students in some MENA countries are taught in classes so large that effective instruction can be difficult. A handful of countries in the region report having among the largest class sizes of all countries participating in the Trends in International Mathematics and Science Study (TIMSS) 2015. Average class size for grade 8 mathematics varies from a high of 43 students in Egypt to a low of 25 in Lebanon (see figure 11.8). Egypt, Jordan, and Morocco have some of the largest classes among TIMSS participants, while GCC countries have class sizes generally in line with the international average of TIMSS participants and those found in East Asia (though still higher than in countries like Australia and Sweden).

Meanwhile, student-teacher ratios (STRs) in some MENA countries are substantially below their average class sizes. For example, Egypt's STR is 23 in primary education, but only 15 in secondary education (15 students per teacher compared with average grade 8 class size of 43). Wide disparities between STRs and average class sizes may indicate

FIGURE 11.8 Class size varies across MENA, with the Arab Republic of Egypt and Morocco having among the largest classes

Students per class for grade 8 mathematics, as reported by the teacher, TIMSS 2015

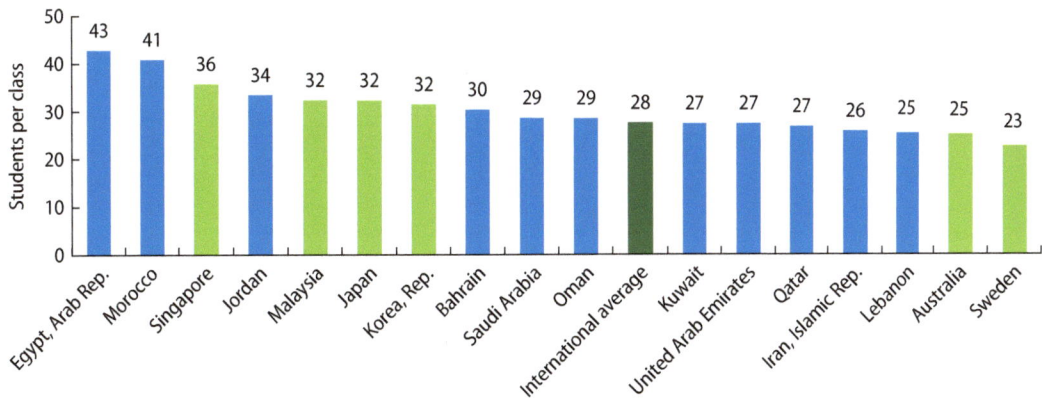

Source: IEA 2015.
Note: TIMSS = Trends in International Mathematics and Science Study.

inefficient use of teaching staff (due to relatively low teaching hours, for example). The differences in the two ratios depend on several factors: the number of classes or students for which a teacher is responsible, the amount of instruction time compared with the length of teachers' working days, the proportion of time teachers spend teaching, how students are grouped within classes, and use of team teaching (Shewbridge et al. 2016).

STRs vary widely across MENA countries in both primary and secondary education. In primary school, STRs range from a high of 30 students per teacher in Djibouti to a low of 9 in Kuwait (see figure 11.9). At the lower end, Bahrain, Lebanon, Qatar, and Saudi Arabia join Kuwait, with STRs around 12. A similar pattern holds at the secondary level, where Kuwait and Lebanon average 8 students per teacher. Only Djibouti and West Bank and Gaza have relatively high secondary STRs, at 23 and 20, respectively.

Decisions to invest in smaller classes and lower STRs can be costly. Countries all over the world face trade-offs when deciding whether to spend scarce resources on hiring additional teachers or financing other educational inputs (see box 11.4). Investing in professional development, working conditions, and higher salaries for current and future teachers can often prove to be more effective at increasing student learning than employing more teachers to reduce class sizes. The same is true for greater investment in technology or the use of teaching assistants in the classroom (OECD 2017b). Investments in the hiring of additional teachers to reduce class sizes should be targeted to areas where class sizes are particularly large and act as a constraint on learning. However, STRs should be reduced in tandem with other education system reforms, such as changing pedagogy in order to capture the potential benefits of smaller classes, where greater numbers of teachers can be used most effectively (OECD 2017b).

Although countries in MENA employ large numbers of teachers, many countries also experience teacher shortages, especially in mathematics and science. On average across MENA, 45 percent of students in grade 8 are estimated to attend schools whose capacity to provide instruction is affected "a lot" by the shortage of qualified mathematics teachers, and 46 percent are in schools constrained by the shortage of qualified science teachers (IEA 2015). For example, in Egypt, 69 percent of grade 8 students attend schools that face substantial shortages of specialized science teachers, according to TIMSS 2015, and 62 percent are in schools that have

FIGURE 11.9 **Student-teacher ratios vary widely across MENA**

Student-teacher ratios in primary and secondary education, 2016 or latest available year

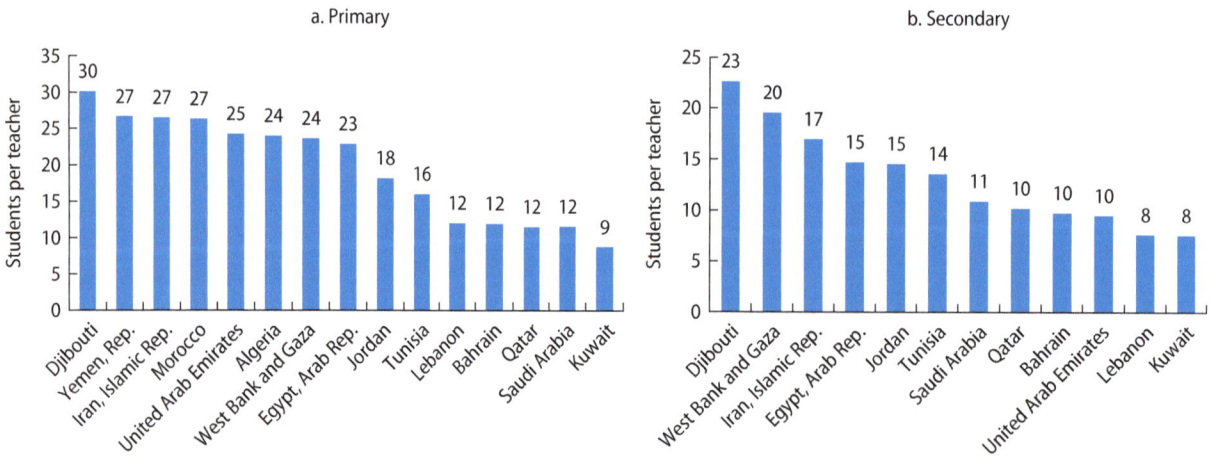

Source: World Bank EdStats database (http://datatopics.worldbank.org/education/).
Note: Data are for the latest available year between 2011 and 2016.

> **Box 11.4 Class size policies across the OECD**
>
> The average class size among OECD member countries is approximately 21 students in primary and 23 students in lower-secondary education. However, some high-performing systems such as Shanghai (China) and Singapore choose to have larger classes to free up teacher time for professional learning and self-improvement in their everyday practice.
>
> The trade-offs between investing in smaller class sizes versus investing in alternative educational inputs are inherent in all education systems. On the one hand, some evidence suggests that smaller classes may have a positive impact on educational attainment and student behavior. Research from England indicates that students in smaller classes are the focus of a teacher's attention for more time, and there is more active interaction between students and teachers and more student engagement (Department for Education, United Kingdom 2011). A study from Denmark estimated that reducing class sizes by 5 percent during all compulsory schooling—from about 18 to 17 students per class—would extend expected enrollment in postcompulsory schooling by about 1 percent (approximately 0.04 year or 8 days of additional schooling), which translates into a 0.2 percent increase in expected lifetime earnings (Bingley, Jensen, and Walker 2005).
>
> On the other hand, the potential benefits of small classes need to be weighed against other investments, such as the improvement of teacher education, professional development, and employment conditions or the more widespread use of assistant teachers and other professionals who can support qualified teachers. Trade-offs often exist between investing in *more* human resources by maintaining small classes and investing in *better* human resources and new approaches to teaching (including through greater use of technology). A synthesis of more than 800 studies relating to student achievement concluded that value for money in raising performance is better achieved through interventions other than class size reduction (Hattie 2009). This result is supported by research finding that increasing teacher effectiveness has greater value for money than reducing class sizes and suggests assigning the most effective teachers to the largest classes to maximize the potential benefits (Hanushek 2011; Rivkin, Hanushek, and Kain 2005).
>
> With the exception of situations in which initial class sizes are very large—above approximately 30 students per class—most estimates suggest that expected benefits in terms of education outcomes from a reduction in class size are typically modest. Given the high cost of such interventions, other alternatives are frequently found to be more cost-effective at improving students' learning outcomes.
>
> *Sources:* OECD 2017b; Santiago et al. 2016; Shewbridge et al. 2016.

shortages of specialized mathematics teachers (see figure 11.10). Even in the relatively well-off countries of the GCC, shortages of mathematics and science teachers are well in excess of the OECD levels of 11 and 12 percent, respectively.

Efficient teacher utilization requires sufficient working hours and low absenteeism

Even in countries where teachers are deployed in adequate numbers, they are often not used efficiently. In MENA, low numbers of working hours for teachers and high rates of teacher absenteeism are common. Only half of the MENA countries surveyed in 2010 required working hours for teachers that were comparable to those of the top-performing countries (World Bank 2015). Only Egypt (1,760 hours) and Tunisia (1,680 hours) were within the range of top-performing countries such as Japan, the Republic of Korea, and New Zealand (1,554 to 1,960 hours per year). Meanwhile, Djibouti, Jordan, Lebanon, West Bank and Gaza, and the Republic of Yemen were all well below this range (see figure 11.11). For instance, the working hours required in Lebanon of primary (864 hours) and secondary (640 hours) education teachers were less than half of those observed in top-performing countries.

FIGURE 11.10 Students across MENA face shortages of qualified mathematics and science teachers

Percentage of grade 8 students attending schools whose capacity to provide instruction is affected "a lot" by a shortage of teachers with specialization in mathematics or science, TIMSS 2015

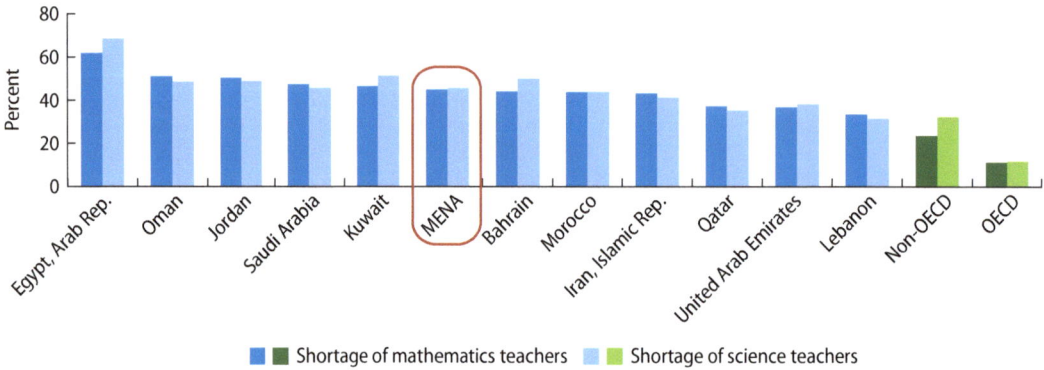

Source: IEA 2015.
Note: OECD = Organisation for Economic Co-operation and Development; TIMSS = Trends in International Mathematics and Science Study.

FIGURE 11.11 The required working hours for teachers in MENA are well below those in top-performing countries

Statutory teaching and total working time required for teachers in primary education in selected MENA (2010) and OECD (2007) economies

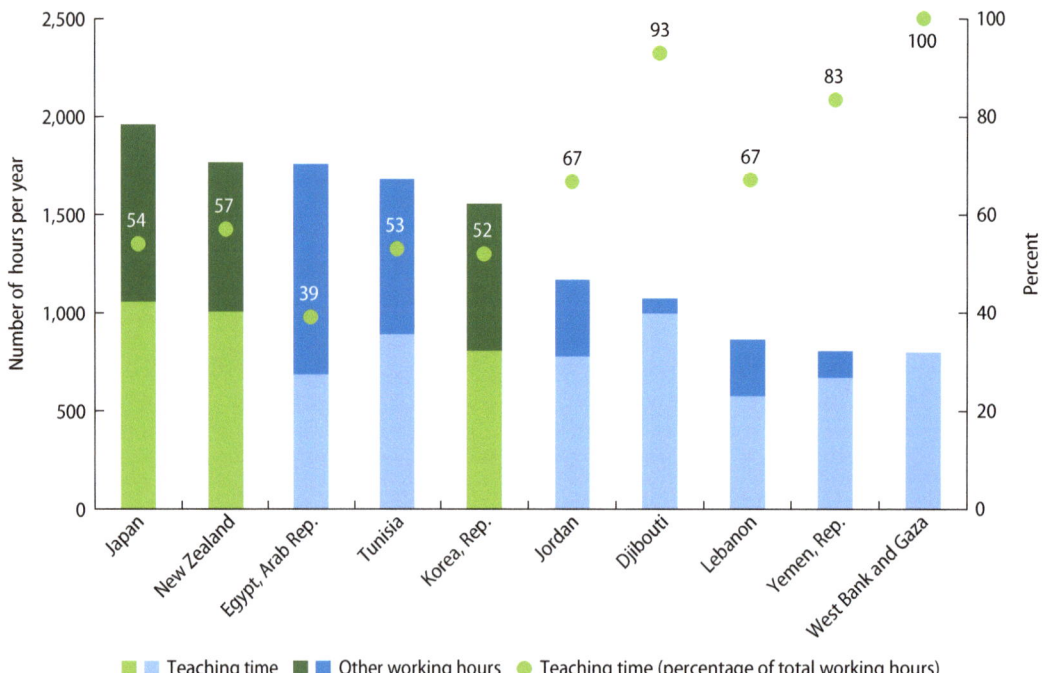

Source: World Bank 2015.
Note: OECD = Organisation for Economic Co-operation and Development.

At the same time, teachers in MENA are expected to spend a higher proportion of their working time teaching than their counterparts in OECD countries. The same survey indicates that, while the top-performing countries typically require less than 60 percent of a teacher's working hours to be spent teaching, MENA countries are usually above this threshold.[8] In some MENA economies—such as the Republic of Yemen (83 percent), Djibouti (93 percent), and West Bank and Gaza (100 percent)—nearly all of a teacher's working time is supposed to be spent teaching, leaving little room for professional development, collaboration, and other nonteaching tasks.[9]

Teacher absenteeism is another chronic problem plaguing MENA school systems. Among the MENA countries participating in TIMSS 2015, an average of 16 percent of students in grade 8 were enrolled in schools whose principals reported teacher absenteeism to be a "serious problem" (see figure 11.12). The problem is most acute in Morocco (affecting 28 percent of students), followed by Saudi Arabia, Oman, and Egypt. By comparison, only 4 percent of grade 8 students across the OECD were enrolled in schools with serious problems with teacher absenteeism. Similarly, low levels of absenteeism were observed in the Islamic Republic of Iran (2 percent) and the United Arab Emirates (7 percent).

A closer study of the Moroccan school system provides a more detailed look at the detrimental effect of teacher absenteeism. In the schools visited by the research team in 2016, 4 percent of teachers were absent from school, and an additional 6 percent were in school but absent from class (see table 11.1). This absence

FIGURE 11.12 **Teacher absenteeism is prevalent throughout MENA**

Percentage of grade 8 students attending schools whose principal reports that teacher absenteeism is a "serious problem," TIMSS 2015

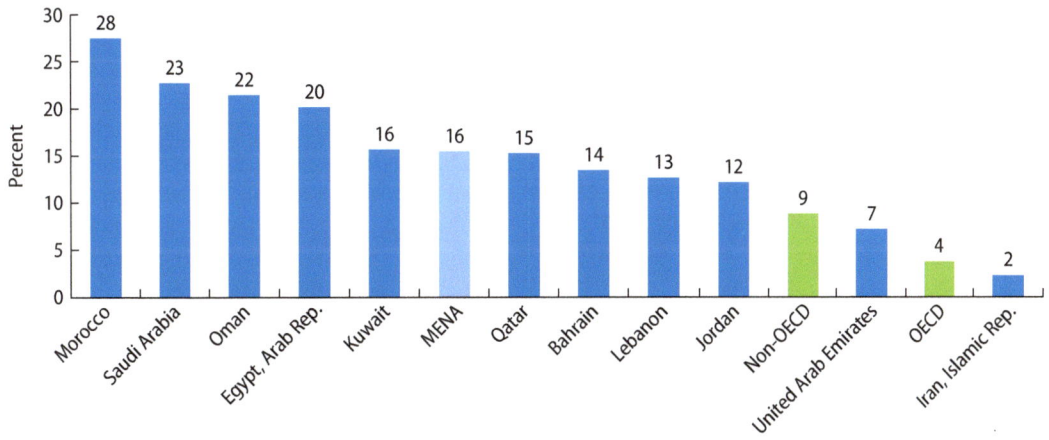

Source: IEA 2015.
Note: OECD = Organisation for Economic Co-operation and Development; TIMSS = Trends in International Mathematics and Science Study.

TABLE 11.1 **Teacher absenteeism affects teaching time in Morocco**

Teacher effort service delivery indicators, by school type, 2016

Indicator	Public			Private	Total
	Urban	Rural	Total		
Absence from school (percent)	3.2	5.2	4.8	1.7	4.4
Absence from class (percent)	3.6	6.4	5.9	2.7	5.5
Teaching time (planned)	4 hrs., 34 mins.	4 hrs., 23 mins.	4 hrs., 26 mins.	5 hrs., 51 mins.	4 hrs., 37 mins.
Teaching time (actual)	4 hrs., 15 mins.	3 hrs., 51 mins.	3 hrs., 56 mins.	5 hrs., 25 mins.	4 hrs., 9 mins.
Teaching time lost (actual − planned)	−19 mins. (−7%)	−32 mins. (−12%)	−30 mins. (−11%)	−26 mins. (−7%)	−28 mins. (−10%)

Source: ONDH 2017.

TABLE 11.2 A lack of key educational inputs affects many students in Morocco
Percentage of grade 4 students who lack selected inputs, by school type, 2016

	Public				
Indicator	Urban	Rural	Total	Private	Total
Students without a textbook	6.3	16.0	13.8	2.3	12.3
Mathematics textbook	1.6	25.9	22.5	0.7	20.0
French textbook	1.5	12.7	10.3	0.3	8.9
Arabic textbook	10.5	11.9	11.4	4.4	10.4
Students without a pencil	5.0	11.2	9.8	0.7	8.6
Students without a notebook	8.5	16.1	14.4	5.7	13.3
Classrooms without minimum teaching resources	30.6	37.3	35.7	11.6	32.5

Source: ONDH 2017.
Note: Classrooms without minimum teaching resources are those in which 90 percent of students do not have pencils and notebooks.

reduced average teaching time by 28 minutes (or 10 percent) for grade 4 students. The effect was larger in rural public schools than in urban public schools or in private schools. On average, rural public school teachers were three times more likely to be absent from school than private school teachers, resulting in students from rural public schools receiving almost 30 percent less instruction time than those from private schools (ONDH 2017).

Availability of instructional materials allows teachers to teach effectively

Even when teachers are in the classroom for an adequate number of hours, they may not be able to help students to learn effectively when they lack necessary instructional materials. Textbooks and other learning materials are often not available until late in the school year, especially in schools located in remote or hard-to-reach areas. In Morocco, for example, a shortage of textbooks in rural public schools (where 16 percent of grade 4 students did not have a textbook) left those students at a disadvantage compared with their peers in urban public schools (where 6 percent lacked a textbook) and those in private schools (where 2 percent lacked a textbook) (see table 11.2). Students in rural public schools were also twice as likely as their urban peers to be without a pencil or a notebook. Overall, one in three Moroccan classrooms surveyed did not have the minimum teaching resources for at least 90 percent of grade 4 students (ONDH 2017).

In Oman, 73 percent of principals indicated that a shortage of instructional materials hindered their school's capacity to provide instruction (IEA 2015). This is well above the international average of 48 percent. In Algeria, although almost all lower-secondary schools have basic furniture and usable office equipment, a substantial proportion lack essential pedagogical material, and 33 percent of schools do not have basic scientific equipment and lab materials (Suchaut 2006; World Bank 2007a).

MENA countries have made tremendous progress in expanding access to education over the last four decades, at a substantial cost to the public purse. The next challenge is to ensure that these investments translate into improved learning outcomes for the region's students. This effort will require maintaining the momentum for adequate public investment, ensuring that financial and human resources are allocated equitably and used efficiently, and forging stronger links between resource allocations and education sector results. Only then can the promise of education for all translate into better learning outcomes and life prospects for the next generation of MENA's citizens.

Notes

1. More than US$2 trillion in public funds have been spent on education in MENA since the 1970s (based on World Bank estimates from EdStats data), which is approximately equal to the annual GDP of India.

2. National education accounts (NEAs) offer a new and promising avenue for systematically collecting comprehensive data on education expenditures from national sources. This approach should be used widely to enhance the availability of comparable information on public and private funding of education around the world. For comprehensive guidelines on the preparation of NEAs, see http://uis.unesco.org/en/news/national-education-accounts.
3. This is comparable to the 15 percent of education spending attributable to households in Djibouti. However, Djibouti's estimate excludes spending on tertiary education; if it were included, the share of private spending would likely rise. By comparison, the OECD average for the private share of education spending *excluding* tertiary is around 8 percent.
4. Based on United Nations population projections, countries such as Algeria, Djibouti, the Islamic Republic of Iran, Lebanon, Libya, Morocco, Oman, Saudi Arabia, and Tunisia are likely to see their preschool- and school-age populations (ages 0 to 19 years) peak by around 2030. Other countries, such as Bahrain, Egypt, Jordan, Syria, and the Republic of Yemen, will experience this peak between 2040 and 2055. Only Iraq, Kuwait, Qatar, the United Arab Emirates, and West Bank and Gaza are projected to see continuing growth in their youth populations into the second half of the century (United Nations Population Division 2017).
5. Some GCC countries started expanding their education infrastructure networks later than other MENA countries and thus appear as outliers. The large education infrastructure projects in the 1960s to 1990s accounted for a substantial share of education spending in many MENA countries—such as Egypt, Jordan, and Lebanon—in previous decades. Many countries outside the GCC also depend on donor financing to pay for their investments in education capital; these investments are not captured completely in the internationally comparable data, thus leading to potential underestimates of capital investment in some countries.
6. For a more detailed discussion of effective approaches to education budgeting, see spotlight 3.
7. By comparison, OECD member countries spend on average 21 percent of their recurrent education budgets on items other than staff compensation. Some high-performing countries—such as Finland (36 percent), the Republic of Korea (30 percent), and the United Kingdom (28 percent)—spend well above that amount on nonsalary inputs (OECD 2017a).
8. Egypt is a notable exception, where only 39 percent of a teacher's statutory working time is expected to be spent teaching. At the time of the analysis, Egyptian teachers had enough time to fulfill their duties, but legislation at the time (2010) was unclear on how working time should be distributed across various tasks. As a result, teachers spent most of their time on lesson planning and preparation and administrative tasks (World Bank 2015).
9. However, the survey, which collects data on *statutory* working hours, cannot capture the *actual* working hours of teachers.

References

Beschel, Robert P., Jr., and Mark Ahern. 2012. *Public Financial Management Reform in the Middle East and North Africa: An Overview of Regional Experience*. Washington, DC: World Bank. https://openknowledge.worldbank.org/handle/10986/9368.

Bingley, Paul, Vibeke Myrup Jensen, and Ian Walker. 2005. "The Effects of School Class Size on Length of Post-Compulsory Education: Some Cost-Benefit Analysis." IZA Discussion Paper 1605, Institute for the Study of Labor, Bonn. http://ssrn.com/abstract=731683.

Department for Education, United Kingdom. 2011. "Class Size and Education in England: Evidence Report." Research Report DFE-RR169, Economics, Evaluation, and Appraisal Team, Education Standards Analysis and Research Division, London. www.gov.uk/government/uploads/system/uploads/attachment_data/file/183364/DFE-RR169.pdf.

Hanushek, Eric A. 2011. "The Economic Value of Higher Teacher Quality." *Economics of Education Review* 30 (3): 466–79. http://hanushek.stanford.edu/publications/economic-value-higher-teacher-quality.

Hattie, John. 2009. *Visible Learning: A Synthesis of Over 800 Meta-Analyses Relating to Achievement*. London: Routledge.

IEA (International Association for the Evaluation of Educational Achievement). 2015. Trends in International Mathematics and Science

Study—TIMSS 2015 Database. Chestnut Hill, MA: Boston College, IEA. https://timssandpirls.bc.edu/timss2015/international-database/.

OECD (Organisation for Economic Co-operation and Development). 2017a. *Education at a Glance 2017: OECD Indicators*. Paris: OECD. http://dx.doi.org/10.1787/eag-2017-en.

———. 2017b. *The Funding of School Education: Connecting Resources and Learning*. Paris: OECD. http://dx.doi.org/10.1787/9789264276147-en.

ONDH (National Observatory for Human Development). 2017. "Enquête sur les Indicateurs de Prestation de Services en Éducation (IPSE) au Maroc." ONDH, Rabat. http://www.ondh.ma/fr/presentation-resultats-letude-indicateurs-prestation-services-rendus-etablissements-scolaires-au.

Rivkin, Steven G., Eric A. Hanushek, and John F. Kain. 2005. "Teachers, Schools, and Academic Achievement." *Econometrica* 73 (2): 417–58. http://hanushek.stanford.edu/sites/default/files/publications/Rivkin%2BHanushek%2BKain%202005%20Ecta%2073%282%29.pdf.

Santiago, Paulo, Gábor Halász, Rosalind Levacic, and Claire Shewbridge. 2016. *OECD Reviews of School Resources: Slovak Republic 2015*. Paris: OECD. http://dx.doi.org/10.1787/9789264247567-en.

Shewbridge, Claire, Jan Herczyński, Thomas Radinger, and Julie Sonnemann. 2016. *OECD Reviews of School Resources: Czech Republic 2016*. Paris: OECD. http://dx.doi.org/10.1787/9789264262379-en.

Suchaut, Bruno. 2006. "Analyse des acquisitions des élèves de l'enseignement secondaire en Algérie." Unpublished report, Université de Bourgogne et Irédu, CNRS (French National Center for Scientific Research).

Teixeira, Janssen, Jeremie Amoroso, and James Gresham. 2017. "Why Education Infrastructure Matters for Learning." *Education for Global Development* (blog), October 3. http://blogs.worldbank.org/education/why-education-infrastructure-matters-learning.

UIS (UNESCO Institute for Statistics). No date. "Initial Household Funding of Education as % of GDP." UIS Indicators, UIS, Montreal. http://uis.unesco.org/indicator/edu-fin-fund_gdp-hh.

———. Various years. UIS.Stat database. Montreal: UIS. http://data.uis.unesco.org.

United Nations Population Division. 2017. *World Population Prospects 2017*. New York: United Nations Population Division. https://population.un.org/wpp/.

Universidad de los Andes and World Bank. 2017. "Seismic Risk Reduction Strategy for Public School Buildings in Peru." Technical Note, World Bank, Washington, DC. https://openknowledge.worldbank.org/handle/10986/29051.

Vegas, Emiliana, and Chelsea Coffin. 2012. "Education Finance: It's How, Not Simply How Much, That Counts." Education Notes. World Bank, Washington, DC. https://openknowledge.worldbank.org/handle/10986/10056.

World Bank. 2006. "Republic of Djibouti Public Expenditure Review: Making Public Finances Work for Growth and Poverty Reduction." World Bank, Washington, DC. http://documents.worldbank.org/curated/en/458211468245383445/Djibouti-Public-Expenditure-Review-PER-making-public-finances-work-for-growth-and-poverty-reduction.

———. 2007a. "People's Democratic Republic of Algeria Public Expenditure Review: Assuring High-Quality Public Investment." Vol. 1: "Main Report," World Bank, Washington, DC. https://openknowledge.worldbank.org/handle/10986/7880.

———. 2007b. "West Bank and Gaza Public Expenditure Review: From Crisis to Greater Fiscal Independence." Vol. 2, World Bank, Washington, DC. https://openknowledge.worldbank.org/handle/10986/7807.

———. 2015. "MENA Regional Synthesis on the Teacher Policies Survey: Key Findings from Phase 1." World Bank, Washington, DC. https://openknowledge.worldbank.org/handle/10986/21490.

———. 2017. "Lebanon: Education Public Expenditure Review 2017." World Bank, Washington, DC. https://openknowledge.worldbank.org/handle/10986/30065.

———. 2018. *World Development Report 2018: Learning to Realize Education's Promise*. Washington, DC: World Bank. http://www.worldbank.org/en/publication/wdr2018.

———. No date. Education Statistics (EdStats) database. Washington, DC: World Bank. http://datatopics.worldbank.org/education/.

SPOTLIGHT 3

LINKING BUDGET MANAGEMENT TO LEARNING

Igor Kheyfets

Spending must target learning. Across the Middle East and North Africa (MENA) region, many governments have moved toward modernizing their budget management practices to improve the transparency, efficiency, and accountability of public service provision in all spheres, including education (Beschel and Ahern 2012). By making learning the central (and measurable) objective of education systems and aligning public budgets to meet this goal, governments can spend the funds devoted to education more efficiently. This effort requires high-level strategic planning, clear links between spending and results, and timely budget execution.

Link budgets to strategic national and education priorities

Nearly every country in the world has a national strategic framework to guide its long-term policy planning. Many of these frameworks are set out in formal national development plans (NDPs) or similar high-level strategic documents. In MENA, at least 10 such plans are currently under implementation (IIEP n.d.). Many countries also have education sector plans (ESPs), subsector plans, or national education strategies that provide overall strategic guidance to education policy making.[1]

Higher-level strategic documents can inform education budget preparation in several ways. One way is to lay out specific education objectives with clear indicators to be achieved within the (usually long-term) time frame of the NDP. A second way is to set out in the NDP the general strategic directions to be prioritized in each sector, which then cascade down into sectoral plans such as ESPs or action plans of the respective line ministries. A third way is to prepare stand-alone sector strategic documents like ESPs that are not linked explicitly to a national vision document but can be guided implicitly through strategic policy pronouncements from the head of state, for example.

The United Arab Emirates' Vision 2021 employs a combination of the first and second approaches. The high-level national strategic document lays out eight concrete key performance indicators (KPIs) to be achieved in the education sector by 2021 (see table S3.1). These KPIs then cascade into the strategic plan of the Ministry of Education, whose 2017–21 implementation period is aligned with the time frame of the national Vision 2021. In that sense, both the country's and the education ministry's objectives are aligned and are tied to specific, measurable, achievable, relevant, and time-bound (SMART) indicators (IEG 2012).

Budget for education with an explicit focus on learning

Targeting spending to learning requires concentrating on outputs and outcomes, not just inputs. Performance-based budgeting (PBB)—also known as "results-based budgeting" or "output-based budgeting"—seeks to introduce explicit measures of performance directly into the budgeting process.

TABLE S3.1 United Arab Emirates Vision 2021 lays out national key performance indicators for the education sector
National agenda priority: First-rate education system

Indicator	Latest result	2021 target
1. Average PISA score	Mathematics: rank 38 Science: rank 36 Reading: rank 36 (PISA 2015)	Among the top 20 countries
2. Average TIMSS score	Mathematics, grade 4: rank 35 Science, grade 4: rank 35 Mathematics, grade 8: rank 19 Science, grade 8: rank 22 (TIMSS 2015)	Among the top 15 countries
3. Upper-secondary graduation rate (percent)	97.9 (2017)	98
4. Enrollment rate in preschools (public and private) (percent)	92.6 (2017)	95
5. Percentage of students with high skills in Arabic, according to national tests	67.8 (2017)	90
6. Percentage of schools with high-quality teachers	32.0 (2017)	100
7. Percentage of schools with highly effective school leadership	28.0 (2017)	100
8. Enrollment rate in university foundation year (percent)[a]	44.8 (2017)	0

Sources: Ministry of Education, United Arab Emirates n.d.; Prime Minister's Office, United Arab Emirates n.d.
Notes: PISA = Programme for International Student Assessment; TIMSS = Trends in International Mathematics and Science Study.
a. The foundation year is a program to strengthen Arabic, English, mathematics, and information technology skills of incoming university students. Under Vision 2021, the foundation year is planned to be phased out.

Performance-based budgets are often organized around programs with specific performance indicators that can be used to measure the effectiveness of budget implementation. Ministries of education that receive budgets under a PBB system would receive allocations to achieve certain sectoral outputs (for example, increasing preprimary enrollment) rather than to finance certain amounts of inputs (such as salaries or capital costs).

In Jordan, Morocco, and Tunisia, ministries of education have been early adopters of those countries' PBB systems (Beschel and Ahern 2012; OECD 2010). In Western Europe and other countries of the Organisation for Economic Co-operation and Development (OECD), PBB approaches have been employed for some time. The Netherlands, for example, introduced proto-PBB approaches as far back as the 1970s and moved its entire public sector to program and performance budgeting in 1999. Such reforms make it easier for ministries of finance to hold line ministries accountable for results linked to specific budget allocations, while also helping line ministries to align their activities with the achievement of their strategic sectoral policy agendas (Beschel and Ahern 2012; OECD 2010).

Improve budget execution rates to smooth service delivery

Even in countries with robust strategic planning and budget formulation systems in place, public expenditures may fail to produce the desired results. A problem seen in many education systems is lagging budget execution, which can be observed in the differences between the amounts budgeted and those actually spent. Underexecution of budgets can occur for many reasons—from revenue shortages brought about by weak revenue collection systems to late disbursements or lengthy procurement procedures and internal controls. For example, in countries such as Jordan, Lebanon, and Morocco, having different agencies involved in signing off on certain budget expenditures causes substantial delays in public procurement. In some MENA countries (notably Iraq), the delays caused by lengthy and burdensome budget control procedures explain delays in capital projects (Beschel and Ahern 2012). In Tunisia, the development budget in education (which finances capital investment) is frequently underexecuted by as much as 8 percent per year.[2] In Algeria, the investment budget for education was underexecuted by 15 to 26 percent between 2002 and 2004 (World Bank 2007).

Improving budget execution rates can start with a review of the relevant administrative procedures to identify key bottlenecks. Depending on the underlying causes, budget execution can be improved by simplifying and streamlining existing procedures; strengthening the management, planning, and procurement capacities of key agencies and departments; introducing internal management systems and practices that improve coordination across units and clarify their responsibilities; improving education management information systems and data flows between data systems for education and those for finance, procurement, and human resource management; and streamlining the planning and execution of capital projects, as was done in Iraq (Beschel and Ahern 2012).

Notes

1. The International Institute for Educational Planning of the United Nations Educational, Scientific, and Cultural Organization maintains a database of national education plans, high-level strategic documents, and policy frameworks on its Planipolis website (IIEP n.d.).
2. See the Tunisia BOOST database (http://boost.worldbank.org/country/tunisia).

References

Beschel, Robert P., Jr., and Mark Ahern. 2012. *Public Financial Management Reform in the Middle East and North Africa: An Overview of Regional Experience.* Washington, DC: World Bank. https://openknowledge.worldbank.org/handle/10986/9368.

IEG (Independent Evaluation Group). 2012. "Designing a Results Framework for Achieving Results: A How-To Guide." World Bank, Washington, DC. http://siteresources.worldbank.org/EXTEVACAPDEV/Resources/designing_results_framework.pdf.

IIEP (International Institute for Educational Planning). No date. "Planipolis: A Portal of National Education Plans and Policies." United Nations Educational, Scientific, and Cultural Organization (UNESCO), Paris. http://planipolis.iiep.unesco.org/.

Ministry of Education, United Arab Emirates. No date. "Ministry of Education Strategic Plan 2017–2021." Ministry of Education, Dubai. https://www.moe.gov.ae/En/AboutTheMinistry/Pages/MinistryStrategy.aspx.

OECD (Organisation for Economic Co-operation and Development). 2010. *Progress in Public Management in the Middle East and North Africa: Case Studies on Policy Reform.* Paris: OECD. http://dx.doi.org/10.1787/9789264082076-en.

Prime Minister's Office, United Arab Emirates. No date. "Vision 2021." Prime Minister's Office, Dubai. https://www.vision2021.ae/en/national-agenda-2021/list/first-rate-circle.

World Bank. 2007. "People's Democratic Republic of Algeria Public Expenditure Review: Assuring High Quality Public Investment." Vol. 1: "Main Report." World Bank, Washington, DC. https://openknowledge.worldbank.org/handle/10986/7880.

———. Various years. BOOST database. Washington, DC: World Bank. http://boost.worldbank.org/country/.

Strengthening Skills by Linking Education to the Labor Market | 12

Almedina Music and Caroline Krafft

To reap the benefits of education, the Middle East and North Africa (MENA) will have to align its *push for learning* with a *pull for skills*. After leaving school, many young people in MENA are not able to find work or they secure jobs with limited prospects.[1] Youths are often stuck in low-wage, unstable, informal jobs with limited social protection, or jobs that offer few opportunities to strengthen their skills or increase their employability for better jobs. In the Arab Republic of Egypt, for example, informality is two times more common among workers 15 to 24 years old than among workers 35 to 54 years old (Gatti et al. 2012). Unless the labor market is realigned to increase the demand for skills, the potential contribution of the education sector to the economy will not be fully realized. To align the skills that young people acquire more closely with those that the labor market requires, employers have a role to play in providing on-the-job training. Improving the flow of labor market information for the decision making of employers and students may also facilitate school-to-work transitions.

Workplace training can provide students with job-relevant skills

Skills training programs are more successful when the private sector is involved in developing curricula and training methods or in providing on-the-job training (World Bank 2019). Workplace training comes in different forms: short-term programs, apprenticeship schemes at the upper-secondary school level, internship programs for university students, informal training, and many others. Training programs are designed to improve labor market outcomes, raise productivity, and reduce employee turnover (World Bank 2018b).[2]

The evidence on the effects of youth training programs is mixed. Most of the literature on programs in high- or middle-income countries finds limited effects on employment outcomes (Card, Kluve, and Weber 2010; Datta et al. 2018; Kluve et al. 2019; McKenzie 2017). However, some programs have shown positive effects on employment and earnings. In Nepal, a large youth training intervention generated an increase in nonfarm employment of 10 percentage points and sizable gains in monthly earnings (Chakravarty et al. 2019). In India, a subsidized vocational education program for women residing in low-income households led to higher probability of employment and higher earnings. Results were sustained over the medium term (Maitra and Mani 2017). In Kenya, the Ninaweza Youth Empowerment program, which integrates information and communication technology, life skills, internship training, and job placement support for youths, shows positive impacts on labor market outcomes (World Bank 2018b). Colombia's Jóvenes en Acción (Youth in Action) program combines classroom instruction with on-the-job training at private companies. The probability of formal employment and earnings rose in the short term and has been sustained in the long run (Attanasio, Kugler, and Meghir 2011; Attanasio et al. 2015).

Many active labor market policies (ALMPs) in MENA have not been successful in addressing youth unemployment. In Tunisia, employers who hired subsidized graduates were usually hiring anyway, and graduates receiving the subsidy were the most employable (Broecke 2013). A job-matching program that matched more than 1,000 individuals in Jordan led to only 15 jobs (Groh et al. 2015). Some ALMPs, however, may have positive effects other than employment. A program in Tunisia used the process of writing an undergraduate thesis to teach students basic entrepreneurial skills (Brodmann, Grun, and Premand 2011). Students were mentored by professors and private sector coaches to develop business plans. The initial results showed that the program motivated students and gave them confidence to take risks.[3]

Effective engagement with the private sector is crucial for successful workplace training.[4] However, nearly 80 percent of Egyptian employers report, for example, no active cooperation with vocational and training institutions (Álvarez-Galván 2015). In addition, the level of employer engagement varies greatly across different economic sectors and occupational fields. In Egypt, the highest reported level of engagement is in the industrial sector, with 33 percent of employers reporting cooperation with vocational education and training, but engagement falls to only 5 percent in the commercial sector. Social services and tourism and hotels have similar levels of cooperation with employers (20 percent), while the medical sector also experiences a moderate level of cooperation as evidenced by the number of employers participating (13 percent) (SPU, MOHE 2012).

Vocational schools suffer from a lack of appropriate facilities and hands-on learning opportunities (Krafft 2017). In Egypt, 41 percent of workers are in jobs requiring a technical skill; the share is 34 percent in Tunisia. Only around a quarter (25–27 percent) of workers in jobs requiring a technical skill acquired it through regular schooling (see figure 12.1). In Egypt, a further 12 percent acquired the skill through technical education. Other routes, including on-the-job training, learning from a craftsperson, vocational training, or from a contractor, were common. Vocational training and contractors were a particularly common route in Tunisia, while craftspeople were a major source of skills in Egypt.

Those entering vocational education and training in MENA often lack basic skills (Krafft 2017). Mostly there is no coordinated action plan to deal with this challenge, and disadvantaged students do not receive coherent and systematic support in most cases. Vocational training programs are often related directly to specific occupations. If this type of program is to become more attractive to prospective students, switching between academic and vocational tracks needs to be easier, and the quality of options at the upper-secondary level needs to improve more generally. In Singapore since the early 1990s, publicity campaigns showed that vocational education and technical jobs are not second-best options in a technology-driven world; enormous state investment has gone into upgrading technical and vocational education and training (TVET) programs at all levels. Today, nearly two-thirds of all postsecondary enrollments are in TVET programs with state-of-the-art facilities and equipment

FIGURE 12.1 **Only a quarter of workers in Egypt and Tunisia acquired their technical skills through regular schooling**
Percentage of workers with technical skills reporting source of skills

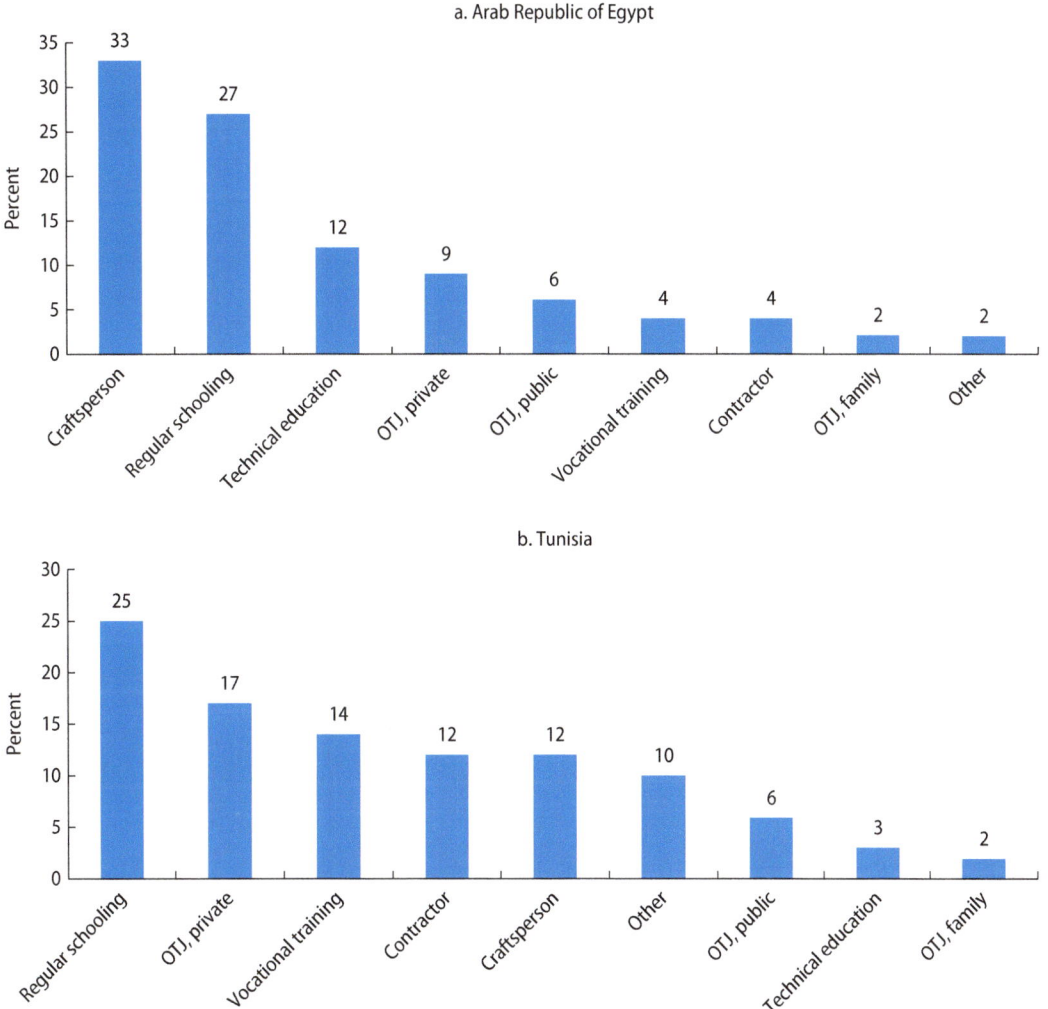

Sources: Calculations based on the Economic Research Forum Egypt Labor Market Panel Survey 2012 (http://www.erfdataportal.com/index.php/catalog/45) and Tunisia Labor Market Panel Survey 2014 (http://erfdataportal.com/index.php/catalog/105).
Note: The panels show the source of technical skills for those in jobs requiring a technical skill among wage workers ages 15–64. OTJ = on-the-job (training).

and top-quality instructors with industry experience (World Bank 2018a).

MENA countries recognize these issues and increasingly foster public-private partnerships to provide more students with the opportunity to work as part of their studies. In Algeria, enrollment in vocational tracks has increased. The Algerian government has partnered with public and private companies to create suitable programs in construction, public works, electricity, agriculture, and tourism (Oxford Business Group 2015). Since the 2011 revolution, the Tunisian Ministry of Education has been developing a reform plan, which includes restructuring its vocational education tracks (Oxford Business Group 2017). Other countries across the region are interested in making vocational education work better for students and for the labor market.

In Saudi Arabia, several large private companies have developed industry-specific apprenticeship programs. One of the oldest examples is Saudi Aramco's apprenticeship program, which was designed to support national strategic objectives but also reduces the burden of finding nonuniversity graduates who require substantial retraining.[5]

The World Bank Education to Work Transition Project for West Bank and Gaza aims to develop and implement employment-oriented education programs in partnership with the private sector (World Bank 2012). Higher education institutions can compete for funds by proposing new and innovative study programs that respond to the needs of the labor market. The unemployment rate of graduates from participating institutions has been reduced by 9.7 percent[6] alongside other achievements.

Companies in MENA report difficulties in finding an adequately skilled workforce

In Iraq, Morocco, Tunisia, and the Republic of Yemen, the share of companies reporting challenges in finding an adequately skilled workforce is above the average level seen in both lower-middle-income and upper-middle-income economies (see figure 12.2). In these four countries, every third firm surveyed reported that the scarcity of an adequately educated workforce is a major or a severe constraint for their business. Yet in Djibouti and West Bank and Gaza the share of companies reporting challenges is below the average in lower-middle-income economies, and Jordan and Lebanon have rates below those of upper-middle-income countries. Employer surveys indicate greater demand for socioemotional skills and higher-order cognitive skills than for basic cognitive or technical skills (Cunningham and Villaseñor 2016). High-paying jobs increasingly require social skills, with technological change providing one possible explanation (Deming 2017).

Across MENA economies the intensity of training provided by firms is low. In other words, firm-provided training in the region is lagging far behind firm-provided training in other countries (see figure 12.3). Firms in Djibouti, Lebanon, Morocco, and Tunisia

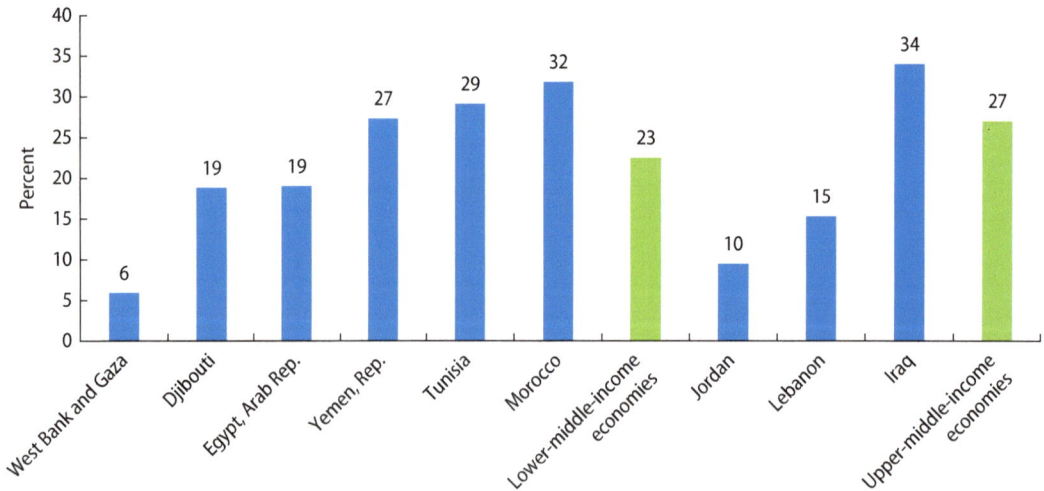

FIGURE 12.2 **Firms in MENA vary in whether they face an inadequately educated workforce**
Percentage of firms reporting an inadequately educated workforce as a major or very severe constraint

Sources: World Bank Enterprise Surveys, most recent available year (http://www.enterprisesurveys.org/).

FIGURE 12.3   **Firms in MENA have below-average rates of formal training**
Percentage of firms offering formal training

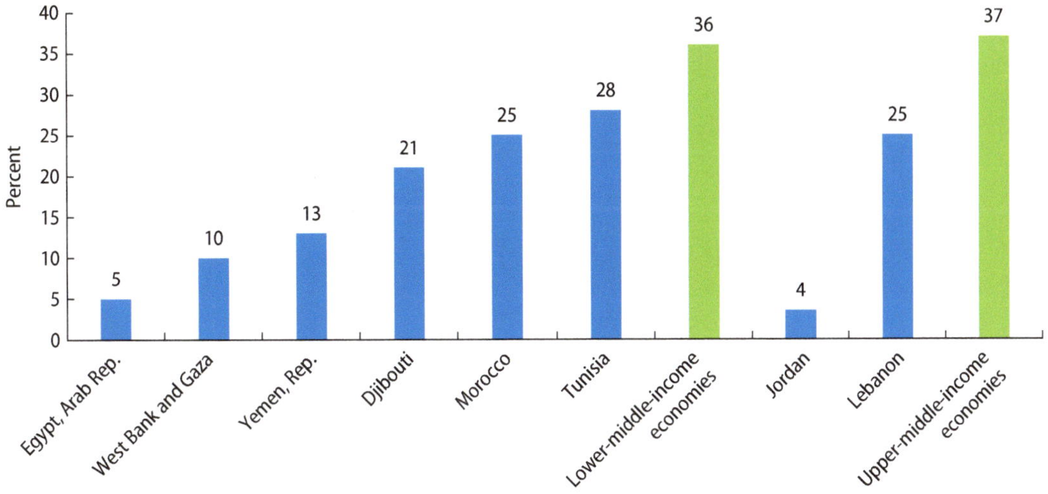

Country/Group	Percent
Egypt, Arab Rep.	5
West Bank and Gaza	10
Yemen, Rep.	13
Djibouti	21
Morocco	25
Tunisia	28
Lower-middle-income economies	36
Jordan	4
Lebanon	25
Upper-middle-income economies	37

Sources: World Bank Enterprise Surveys, most recent available year (http://www.enterprisesurveys.org/).

provide relatively more training, but less than the average in economically similar countries. In MENA countries, firms with a larger share of young workers are more likely to provide training to their workers. In fact, the higher the share of university-educated employees, the higher the probability of providing training (EBRD, EIB, and World Bank 2016).

The intensity and quality of the training received in the workplace is crucial. This is even more true in a fast-changing world, where updating skills is the key to workers' relevance and longevity. An estimated 41 percent of all work activities in Kuwait are susceptible to automation, as are 46 percent in Bahrain and Saudi Arabia, 47 percent in the United Arab Emirates, 49 percent in Egypt, 50 percent in Morocco, and 52 percent in Qatar (World Economic Forum 2017). In addition, whether jobs are declining, stable, or growing, their skills profile is changing substantially. The World Economic Forum's Future of Jobs analysis found that, by 2020, 21 percent of core skills in the countries of the Gulf Cooperation Council will be different from the skills that were needed in 2015 (World Economic Forum 2017).

Improving labor market information flows can help both students and employers

Better communication between the education system and employers to identify what skills are in high demand and increase those skills within the education system can improve student outcomes. Improved communication will be a necessary part of moving away from a credentialist equilibrium to a skills equilibrium. If employers shift from focusing on credentials to demanding skills and communicating the skills that are in demand, parents and students will then demand skills from the education system. National employer surveys, with widely publicized reports and results, could be one route to signal the skills that employers demand. In most MENA countries, private sector firms are disproportionately microenterprises. These businesses lack the ability to send signals effectively to education systems (Assaad, Krafft, and Salehi-Isfahani 2018), so surveys and other intentional links are required.

Career guidance is one way to communicate to future employees what type of studies and skills are most sought after in the labor market. Career information programs often provide direction on coursework selection and career planning, usually on an individual basis in schools and universities (OECD 2010; OECD and EC 2004). Career information can be especially useful for students who lack family or social networks that can provide meaningful direction. Many countries have experimented with mechanisms to integrate career guidance with national lifelong learning strategies. Still, evidence is limited on how career information initiatives affect students' choices, training trajectories, and outcomes (Hooley 2014; Hooley and Dodd 2015; Kluve et al. 2019).

Across countries, the breadth and depth of programs vary substantially, highlighting the need for a well-articulated vision, cohesive strategy, and robust quality assurance mechanisms linked to funding. Successful career guidance programs have clear objectives and measure outcomes to track program performance. They also offer different pathways for participants from diverse backgrounds, so skilled career guidance staff can tailor skills development trajectories to students' needs (OECD and EC 2004).

In MENA, career guidance for students is inadequate. Most students at the higher-education level aim to work in the public sector, where few jobs are available (Assaad, Krafft, and Salehi-Isfahani 2018). However, if students do not have enough information to guide their educational choices, the gap between labor market demands and the corresponding supply of graduates might increase in certain specializations. Chile established online platforms where students can access information on employability and future earnings by degree as well as the required courses for specific occupations (World Bank 2019). The Mexican Ministry for Education has developed an innovative method to equip students with labor market information: "Career guidance in my memory" (*Orientación vocacional en mi memoria*), a USB stick distributed to students. It includes a set of questions that help students to understand their strengths and professional interests and provides information on education institutions and some data on labor market outcomes such as employment opportunities after graduation (SEMS 2010). Generally, digital solutions can improve access to information, and online job platforms have been taking advantage of this information to improve job-matching capacity (Aguerrevere, Langan, and Mnif 2018).

Notes

1. Youth unemployment rates in the MENA region are the highest in the world, reaching 30 percent in 2017. See World Bank World Development Indicators database.
2. A trained workforce contributes to higher firm productivity (see, for example, Almeida and de Faria 2014; Gonzales-Velosa, Rosas, and Flores 2016; Rosholm, Nielsen, and Dabalen 2007; Tan and López-Acevedo 2003).
3. A male participant from Tunis explained, "I have become more independent. My behavior has changed. I use my new skills. I am more disciplined." Students also explained that the program expanded their professional networks by giving them opportunities to interact with mentors. "I now have a social network. I know whom to consult," said a female participant.
4. What does successful workplace training look like? Countries with well-developed systems, such as Austria, Denmark, Germany, Norway, and Switzerland, have formalized an engagement with employers and other stakeholders, with clear pathways for youths to enter into training (OECD and ILO 2017). Successful programs have invested in a close and trusted relationship between the private and the public sectors. Comprehensive and labor market–oriented pathways are built around demanded occupations.
5. See the Aramco website (https://www.saudiaramco.com/en/careers/saudi-applicants/non-employee-programs/high-school-and-diploma-graduates/apne) and the Chevron website (http://careers.chevron.com/find-a-job/saudi-arabia).
6. World Bank Education to Work Transition Project 2018 data.

References

Aguerrevere, Gabriela, Patricia Langan, and Ali Mnif. 2018. "Using Technology to Promote Youth Employment: How to Develop Digital Solutions." *Jobs and Development* (World Bank blog), January 22. https://blogs.worldbank.org/jobs/using-technology-promote-youth-employment-how-develop-digital-solutions.

Almeida, Rita Kullberg, and Marta Lince de Faria. 2014. "The Wage Returns to On-the-Job Training: Evidence from Matched Employer-Employee Data." *IZA Journal of Labor and Development* 3 (1): 1–33.

Álvarez-Galván, José Luis. 2015. *A Skills beyond School Review of Egypt*. OECD Reviews of Vocational Education and Training. Paris: OECD.

Assaad, Ragui, Caroline Krafft, and Djavad Salehi-Isfahani. 2018. "Does the Type of Higher Education Affect Labor Market Outcomes? Evidence from Egypt and Jordan." *Higher Education* 75 (6): 945–95.

Attanasio, Orazio, Arlen Guarin, Carlos Medina, and Costas Meghir. 2015. "Long-Term Impacts of Vouchers for Vocational Training: Experimental Evidence from Colombia." NBER Working Paper 21390, National Bureau of Economic Research, Cambridge, MA.

Attanasio, Orazio, Adriana Kugler, and Costas Meghir. 2011. "Subsidizing Vocational Training for Disadvantaged Youth in Colombia: Evidence from a Randomized Trial." *American Economic Journal: Applied Economics* 3 (3): 188–220.

Brodmann, Stefanie, Rebekka Grun, and Patrick Premand. 2011. "Can Unemployed Youth Create Their Own Jobs? The Tunisia Business Plan Thesis Competition." Fast Brief 83 (March), MNA Knowledge and Learning, World Bank, Washington, DC.

Broecke, Stijn. 2013. "Tackling Graduate Unemployment in North Africa through Employment Subsidies: A Look at the SIVP Programme in Tunisia." *IZA Journal of Labor Policy* 2 (1): 1–19.

Card, David, Jochen Kluve, and Andrea Weber. 2010. "Active Labour Market Policy Evaluations: A Meta-Analysis." *Economic Journal* 120 (548): F451–77.

Chakravarty, Shubha, Mattias Lundberg, Plamen Nikolov, and Juliane Zenker. 2019. "Vocational Training Programs and Youth Labor Market Outcomes: Evidence from Nepal." *Journal of Development Economics* 136: 71–110.

Cunningham, Wendy, and Paula Villaseñor. 2016. "Employer Voices, Employer Demands, and Implications for Public Skills Development Policy Connecting the Labor and Education Sectors." *World Bank Research Observer* 31 (1): 102–34.

Datta, Namita, Angela Elzir Assy, Johanne Buba, Sara Johansson de Silva, and Samantha Watson. 2018. "Integrated Youth Employment Programs: A Stocktake of Evidence on What Works in Youth Employment Programs." Jobs Working Paper 24, World Bank, Washington, DC.

Deming, David J. 2017. "The Growing Importance of Social Skills in the Labor Market." *Quarterly Journal of Economics* 132 (4): 1593–640.

EBRD (European Bank for Reconstruction and Development), EIB (European Investment Bank), and World Bank. 2016. *What's Holding Back the Private Sector in MENA? Lessons from the Enterprise Survey*. Washington, DC: World Bank.

Economic Research Forum. 2012. Egypt Labor Market Panel Surveys (ELMPS) 2012 database. Giza: Economic Research Forum. http://www.erfdataportal.com/index.php/catalog/45.

———. 2014. Tunisia—Labor Market Panel Survey (TLMPS), 2014 database. Giza: Economic Research Forum. http://www.erfdataportal.com/index.php/catalog/105.

Gatti, Roberta, Diego Angel-Urdinola, Joana Silva, and Andreas Bodor. 2012. *Striving for Better Jobs: The Challenge of Informality in the Middle East and North Africa*. Washington, DC: World Bank.

Gonzales-Velosa, Carolina, David Rosas, and Roberto Flores. 2016. "On-the Job Training in Latin America and the Caribbean: Recent Evidence." In *Firm Innovation and Productivity in Latin America and the Caribbean*, edited by Matteo Grazzi and Carlo Pietrobelli. New York: Palgrave Macmillan.

Groh, Matthew, David McKenzie, Nour Shammout, and Tara Vishwanath. 2015. "Testing the Importance of Search Frictions and Matching through a Randomized Experiment in Jordan." *IZA Journal of Labor Economics* 4 (7).

Hooley, Tristram. 2014. "The Evidence Base on Lifelong Guidance: A Guide to Key Findings for Effective Policy and Practice." ELGPN Tools 3, European Lifelong Guidance Policy Network, Finnish Institute for Educational Research, University of Jyväskylä.

Hooley, Tristram, and Vanessa Dodd. 2015. "The Economic Benefits of Career Guidance." Research paper, Careers England, Chorley, U.K.

Kluve, Jochen, Susana Puerto, David A. Robalino, José Manuel Romero, Friederike Rother, Jonathan Stöterau, Felix Weidenkaff, and Marc Witte. 2019. "Do Youth Employment Programs Improve Labor Market Outcomes? A Quantitative Review." *World Development* 114: 237–53.

Krafft, Caroline. 2017. "Is School the Best Route to Skills? Returns to Vocational School and Vocational Skills in Egypt." *Journal of Development Studies* 54 (7): 1–21.

Maitra, Pushkar, and Subha Mani. 2017. "Learning and Earning: Evidence from a Randomized Evaluation in India." *Labour Economics* 45: 116–30.

McKenzie, David. 2017. "How Effective Are Active Labor Market Policies in Developing Countries? A Critical Review of Recent Evidence." *World Bank Research Observer* 32 (2): 127–54.

OECD (Organisation for Economic Co-operation and Development). 2010. *Learning for Jobs: Synthesis Report.* OECD Reviews of Vocational Education and Training Series. Paris: OECD.

OECD (Organisation for Economic Co-operation and Development) and EC (European Commission). 2004. *Career Guidance: A Handbook for Policy Makers.* Paris: OECD.

OECD (Organisation for Economic Co-operation and Development) and ILO (International Labour Organization). 2017. *Engaging Employers in Apprenticeship Opportunities.* Paris: OECD. http://dx.doi.org/10.1787/9789264266681-en.

Oxford Business Group. 2015. *The Report: Algeria 2015.* London. https://oxfordbusinessgroup.com/algeria-2015.

———. 2017. *The Report: Tunisia 2017.* London. https://oxfordbusinessgroup.com/overview/track-series-reforms-are-set-overhaul-sector.

Rosholm, Michael, Helena Skyt Nielsen, and Andrew Dabalen. 2007. "Evaluation of Training in African Enterprises." *Journal of Development Economics* 84 (1): 310–29.

SEMS (Subsecretaria de Educación Media Superior). 2010. "Orientación vocacional en mi memoria: SEMS, Mexico D.F. http://sems.gob.mx/en/sems/orientacion_vocacional_en_mi_memoria.

SPU (Strategic Planning Unit), MOHE (Ministry of Higher Education of Egypt). 2012. "Post-Secondary Vocational Education and Training in Egypt." Country Background Report, OECD, Paris.

Tan, Hong, and Gladys López-Acevedo. 2003. "Mexico: In-Firm Training for the Knowledge Economy." Policy Research Working Paper 2957, World Bank, Washington, DC.

World Bank. 2012. "West Bank and Gaza—Education to Work Transition Project." World Bank, Washington, DC. http://documents.worldbank.org/curated/en/375471468321832951/West-Bank-and-Gaza-Education-to-Work-Transition-Project.

———. 2018a. *Growing Smarter: Learning and Equitable Development in East Asia and Pacific.* East Asia and Pacific Regional Report. Washington, DC: World Bank.

———. 2018b. *World Development Report 2018: Learning to Realize Education's Promise.* Washington, DC: World Bank.

———. 2019. *World Development Report 2019: The Changing Nature of Work.* Washington, DC: World Bank.

———. Various years. World Bank Enterprise Surveys database. Washington, DC: World Bank. http://www.enterprisesurveys.org/.

———. Various years. World Development Indicators database. Washington, DC: World Bank. https://databank.worldbank.org/data/source/world-development-indicators.

World Economic Forum. 2017. "The Future of Jobs and Skills in the Middle East and North Africa: Preparing the Region for the Fourth Industrial Revolution." Executive Briefing, World Economic Forum, Geneva.

Rethinking Tertiary Education: High-Level Skills and Research | 13

Jamil Salmi

A growing body of research indicates that tertiary education contributes to the long-term prosperity of any nation (Salmi 2017a). Tertiary education offers high-level skills for an adaptable labor force, including scientists, professionals, technicians, and teachers in basic and secondary education as well as future government, civil service, and business leaders. It also generates new knowledge through basic and applied research and provides a platform for accessing the existing store of global knowledge and adapting it to local use. An innovative tertiary education system facilitates sustainable transformation and growth throughout the economy (Salmi 2017a).

Tertiary institutions also contribute substantially to positive social outcomes, such as improved health and welfare, better civic participation, good governance, and protection of human and environmental rights (McMahon and Oketch 2013; OECD 2012; Oketch, McCowan, and Schendel 2014). In order to realize these economic and social outcomes, tertiary systems and institutions need to have the capacity to provide a high-quality education that equips students with the skills necessary to thrive in current economic and social circumstances and to adapt to future changes and innovations.

Tertiary education needs to confer skills relevant to the labor market and to focus on high-quality research

The performance of tertiary education institutions in the Middle East and North Africa (MENA) can be measured at two levels: first, the quality and relevance of their graduates and, second, their research output. In the first instance, the current educational experience in MENA universities can generally be described as traditional, based on rigid and often outdated curricula that emphasize memorization of content over development of critical reasoning and analytical skills. The tendency to focus on the theoretical rather than on practical ways of learning gives precedence to the ability to recite theoretical concepts (knowing what to say) rather than the ability to solve problems (knowing how to perform). A combination of narrow content and disconnected context makes it difficult to broaden students' perspectives and equip them with the labor market skills and attitudes they will need to adapt to labor market developments. The high levels of graduate unemployment found in many MENA countries confirm the mismatch between what students learn and the skills that graduates need to achieve successful labor market outcomes (Salmi 2017b).

Global rankings can be a useful proxy with which to assess the research strength of universities in MENA countries from an international viewpoint. In spite of the methodological limitations of ranking systems, international rankings help to identify top universities that generate knowledge through their cutting-edge research, offer high-quality teaching with innovative curricula and teaching methods, and produce graduates with the necessary high-level skills to excel in global labor markets (Salmi 2017b). For example, the Shanghai Ranking is the leading publication of international rankings; it does not rely on subjective reputational surveys but uses only objective indicators. In 2017, the Shanghai Ranking listed only three MENA countries—the Arab Republic of Egypt, the Islamic Republic of Iran, and Saudi Arabia—with universities in the top 500 (Shanghai Ranking n.d).

The Leiden Ranking[1] also confirms the weak performance of MENA universities. One of the most highly cited publications of rankings, the Leiden Ranking objectively measures the number of publications of universities and their impact. The 2017 edition ranks 900 universities worldwide according to their output of publications in the Web of Science database in the following five fields: (1) biomedical and health sciences, (2) life and earth sciences, (3) mathematics and computer science, (4) natural sciences and engineering, and (5) social sciences and humanities. Only five MENA countries—Egypt, the Islamic Republic of Iran, Lebanon, Saudi Arabia, and Tunisia—have universities with enough scientific publications to appear in the 2017 edition of the ranking (Leiden University 2017).[2] The top-ranked MENA university, the University of Tehran, is ranked 195, followed by King Saud University, which is ranked 229. In general, MENA universities fall far below Southeast Asian universities.[3] Because MENA universities have low research capacity and production, they cannot serve as engines of innovation for local and national economies. Overall, as evidenced by its international rankings, MENA needs to improve the quality of its tertiary education system.

Attracting the best, investing adequate resources, and operating under enabling governance systems are key determinants of university performance

Well-performing universities depend on highly sought graduates, leading-edge research, and dynamic knowledge and technology transfer. As such, the outstanding performance of these universities can be attributed to three complementary sets of factors: (1) a high concentration of talent (academics and students), (2) enough resources to offer a rich learning environment and support advanced research, and (3) enabling governance features that encourage strategic vision, innovation, and flexibility (Salmi 2009). These features enable institutions to make decisions in an autonomous manner and to manage resources without being encumbered by bureaucracy. The configuration of results in research, learning, and technology transfer depends on the nature and specific mission of each tertiary education institution (research intensive, teaching, applied science). However, these three sets of factors have to be aligned for any type of tertiary education institution to succeed (Salmi 2009).

Adequate academic preparation among incoming students is one of the major challenges facing MENA universities (Salmi 2017a). In many countries in the region, incoming students are inadequately prepared for tertiary education due to the poor quality of secondary education, as discussed in this report. Those who have been strongly prepared for tertiary-level academic work tend to leave the country to study elsewhere. In other words, the brain drain is a serious issue in several countries. A growing proportion of doctoral graduates from MENA countries are staying in Europe and North America after completing their studies.

A factor that has accelerated brain drain in some MENA countries is the fact that the richest universities in the Gulf Cooperation Council countries have attracted large numbers of top academics from MENA. These universities have sufficient resources to pay competitive salaries and purchase advanced scientific equipment (Salmi 2017a).

Among the numerous factors influencing the performance of tertiary education systems and institutions around the world, recent research has identified governance as the most important determinant (Aghion et al. 2009; Salmi 2009, 2011). A good governance structure and favorable regulatory conditions can promote innovative behavior among autonomous tertiary education institutions, enable the development of strong quality assurance systems, and facilitate the design of innovative financing mechanisms that encourage improved performance. Therefore, in their efforts to support tertiary education institutions interested in transforming their approach to education, national authorities in MENA countries might encourage more autonomous governance, better quality assurance mechanisms, and performance-based budget allocation mechanisms. Presently, universities in the region have few incentives to improve the quality of their graduates and research production.

Rethinking tertiary education: The way forward

To improve the quality and relevance of their tertiary system, MENA countries could produce a comprehensive vision and strategic plan for tertiary education reform. Based on international experience, the appropriate sequence of a reform process at the tertiary level follows the four steps shown in figure 13.1 and discussed further below (Salmi 2017b).

A vision that aligns tertiary education with skills for the future

A first step for thinking about possible reforms in MENA countries consists of

FIGURE 13.1 Four steps can be taken toward successful tertiary education reform in MENA
Proposed sequence for reform design and implementation

Source: Elaborated by Jamil Salmi.

formulating a vision for the future of tertiary education. The vision would define the mission and role of tertiary education as well as the guiding principles that would orient growth of the system; outline policies to improve equity, quality, and relevance; and channel efforts to strengthen the research capacity of the country.

Once formulated, the vision would be translated into a comprehensive strategic plan that articulates quantitative targets for expanding coverage and reducing disparities. The plan also would set out overall goals for improving quality and enhancing program relevance. Additionally, and as needed, the plan would revisit the institutional configuration of the entire tertiary education system. The plan would also outline those reforms necessary to establish appropriate conditions for the effective operation of tertiary education institutions, including supportive quality assurance mechanisms, favorable governance, and sustainable financing.

Strategic reforms to translate the vision into reality

The most effective reforms are designed as a set of coherent, mutually reinforcing interventions aimed at improving the operation of the entire tertiary education system (Salmi 2017b). Denmark, for example, initiated a series of reforms in 2002–03 that included changing the governance arrangements at the national and institutional levels (Holm-Nielsen 2017). These changes brought the university sector under the authority of the Ministry of Industry and Innovation and strengthened the role of the board by moving from an elected university president to an international, competitive selection process. This change resulted in more funding for university research and several university mergers, enabling universities to achieve a critical mass in research and boost their scientific production while improving the global competitiveness of Danish universities.

MENA countries keen on reforming and transforming their tertiary education system could identify and design a set of interventions most appropriate to reach their long-term goals. By doing so, they could ensure better results in the following key areas of performance.

Increasing equity in tertiary education access

To ensure that tertiary education is accessible, MENA governments need to eliminate all financial and nonmonetary barriers that may affect the ability of students from disadvantaged groups (low income, girls, rural, language or ethnic groups, persons with disability) to pursue a tertiary education. Well-targeted scholarship and student loan programs should be in place for that purpose rather than universally free higher education. International experience shows that the most effective interventions for removing the nonfinancial barriers facing underrepresented groups include academic and career counseling, outreach and bridge programs linking universities and high schools, affirmative action programs, and measures to increase retention and reduce dropouts (Salmi and Malee Bassett 2014).

Improving quality and relevance of tertiary education institutions, programs, and courses

To improve the quality of tertiary education programs, MENA universities could introduce innovative curricular and pedagogical practices that stimulate independent learning and foster intellectual curiosity. International experience suggests a few lessons regarding how best to accomplish this (Salmi 2017b). Some countries—for example, the United Kingdom—have found it convenient to require all doctoral candidates to get a teaching certificate before completing their doctorate. This is a first step in acknowledging the importance of good teaching for future university professors. Second, it is important to offer appropriate incentives that reward teaching excellence on par with outstanding research. Professors can be given the necessary time to work on improving their teaching performance, similar to the emphasis given to allotting adequate time for research. Finally, early integration of teaching and research is a powerful way of making the educational experience more stimulating and effective and encouraging students to think creatively to find innovative solutions to the big challenges facing the economy and society.

Strengthening links with industry is an effective way of increasing the relevance of tertiary education programs in MENA countries. Universities can use a large variety of mechanisms, including internships for undergraduate students, in-company placements of research students and academics, and use of industry practitioners as visiting lecturers. Incorporating training for entrepreneurship into regular university programs can also help to bring them closer to the productive sectors. Finally, universities may consider establishing cooperative learning programs that alternate on-campus learning periods with regular in-firm internships, following the model developed by the University of Waterloo in Canada (University of Waterloo n.d.).

At the national level, almost all MENA countries already have a quality assurance agency (Salmi 2015). Their main task, moving forward, is to make sure that each tertiary education institution puts in place a well-functioning quality assurance unit and develops a strong self-evaluation culture. Quality assurance agencies could also focus on learning outcomes rather than inputs and processes. This process would encourage tertiary education institutions to be innovative, instead of traditional, in their educational outlook.

Strengthening quantity, relevance, and impact of the research output of universities

It is important to strengthen the research capacity of universities, clearly recognizing the role that they can play as part of the national innovation system within the countries' science and technology strategy. For MENA countries to achieve this goal, governments will need to facilitate more flexible governance arrangements for research-intensive universities. Each country could generate a clear science and technology development strategy at the national level, encouraging strong links between academia and industry (Salmi 2017b). In addition, sufficient funding will be needed for innovative research.

Academic mobility is very low in MENA universities. To reduce inbreeding at the institutional level, universities could define rules to limit the number of doctoral graduates recruited directly after they finish their research degree by establishing promotion criteria that take into consideration experience in foreign academic settings—including at least a short stay at a good-quality foreign university and joint doctoral programs with partner universities (Salmi 2017b).

By setting up their own incubators or closely linking up with industrial parks, the strongest MENA universities could contribute directly to innovative ways of producing goods and services (Yusuf and Nabeshima 2007). Systematic efforts are needed to undertake industry-oriented research and seek opportunities to commercialize technology.

Each research-focused university could define areas of excellence that are different from those of other universities and that are directly relevant to the regional environment. Research universities that have rapidly achieved a high level of performance have done so by concentrating their efforts to reach excellence on niche programs and research areas (Salmi 2011). For example, through this niche-seeking strategy, Moscow Higher School of Economics and Hong Kong University of Science and Technology have successfully built a critical mass of excellence in teaching and research much faster than comprehensive universities in their respective countries (Altbach and Salmi 2011).

MENA research-intensive universities could encourage, through appropriate financial and academic incentives, the design of research programs based on solution-focused research questions (Yusuf and Nabeshima 2007). This effort could link the main development challenges of their economies directly to the geographic regions where the universities are located, allowing a more systematic meshing of disciplines across faculties and institutes and resulting in higher-impact research.

Launch the reform, taking political risks into consideration

As MENA countries prepare to launch tertiary reform initiatives, it is important to consider incentives and stakeholder buy-in. The extent to which governments rely on positive incentives to encourage change, rather than mandatory edicts to impose reforms, has a positive influence on outcomes (Salmi 2017b). Tertiary education institutions and actors tend to respond more readily to constructive stimuli. Ultimately, tertiary education reform is most feasible within a supportive policy environment in which all participants fundamentally agree on the scope, pace, and direction of reform (Salmi 2017b). Engaging with the views of all stakeholders ensures greater likelihood of positive outcomes when implementing reforms.

Focus on structural measures to ensure the sustainability of reforms

Successfully launching tertiary education reform is necessary, but not sufficient; equally important to the reform's success is putting in place conditions that can guarantee its sustained positive impact over the long run. Doing so involves two dimensions: one linked to the reform process and one related to the content of reforms. In the first instance, the reform packages should be presented and adopted as national programs, not as partisan initiatives of a single political party or the governing majority. Such an approach is the only way to ensure that the consensus achieved when launching a reform has a durable effect. The set of reforms could include enabling measures to facilitate the long-term durability of the proposed changes. Appropriate governance and sustainable financing are the most important enabling conditions (Salmi 2017b).

Modernizing governance for greater accountability

International experience shows that autonomous institutions are more responsive to incentives for improved performance and efficient use of available resources. A series of recent case studies on emerging research universities indicates that fully autonomous institutions are not constrained by externally imposed regulations and can, as a result, manage their resources—human and financial—with more flexibility in order to strengthen performance (Altbach and Salmi 2011).

It is important that MENA authorities allow public universities to be free to determine their own employment conditions, such as the ability to hire and fire staff, if and when needed, and to set the remuneration conditions to encourage academic staff to engage in research. Flexible procurement rules are also needed to accelerate and simplify the purchase of goods and services. In addition, MENA universities need to have independent fiscal control, including the ability to reallocate resources internally according to self-determined criteria. Independent fiscal control is necessary so that institutions can strengthen weak academic units, cross-subsidize programs, and fund new initiatives quickly and flexibly in response to evolving needs (Altbach and Salmi 2011).

Autonomous universities would be in a better position to introduce performance elements to reward those academics and researchers who perform best (Eastermann, Nokkala, and Steinel 2011). MENA governments could consider two options to help their public universities to introduce performance elements into the personnel status of academics. The first would be to maintain the civil service status of academic staff and establish benefits and rewards to recognize the performance and contributions of individual staff. The second would be to eliminate the civil service status of academic staff and make each university the employer of its academic and administrative staff, as has happened in Finland. Research-intensive universities in MENA countries would develop and post their own criteria for recruitment and establish their own salary scale and package of benefits (Salmi 2013).

Public universities in several Western European countries have brought in additional benefits to reward outstanding academic performance (Salmi 2016). In France and Germany, for example, universities benefiting from excellence initiatives commenced special incentives to support postdoctoral researchers, create tenure tracks for talented young researchers, and offer salary supplements for senior professors. The University of Montpellier set up attractive postdoctoral programs, tenure tracks, and high-profile positions combining higher incomes and dedicated research support. Heidelberg University developed a new human resources policy whereby promotion is not linked directly to seniority anymore but is associated with a performance-based system of bonuses that recognizes good research and teaching as well as successful participation in administrative tasks (Salmi 2017a).

The MENA University Governance Screening Card (UGSC) could be a useful tool for reflecting on the governance of tertiary education institutions (see box 13.1). It highlights areas that require development and change.

Ensuring sustainable financing to meet long-term prosperity

Whether tertiary education can be financially sustainable in MENA depends on how the education system in each country addresses

> **Box 13.1** **The MENA University Governance Screening Card (UGSC)**
>
> The UGSC was developed by the World Bank and the Marseille Center for Mediterranean Integration in 2010 as a benchmarking tool to assess the extent to which MENA's tertiary education institutions are following governance practices aligned with their institutional goals, national policies, and international trends. The tool was first applied in 2011–12 and was revised in 2016. Since 2015, it has been implemented in more than 100 universities from eight MENA countries.
>
> The UGSC captures the multidimensional nature of governance, including (1) overall context, mission, and goals; (2) management; (3) autonomy; (4) accountability; and (5) participation in decision making. The UGSC uses an institution-based approach that focuses on universities and higher education institutions as opposed to national systems or country ratings. The UGSC has the capacity to:
>
> - Identify strengths and weaknesses at individual institutions
> - Identify trends at the national level
> - Identify trends and practices by type of institution
> - Generate interest for reforms at the institutional, national, and regional levels. The tool can be accessed through the following link: http://cmimarseille.org/.
>
> *Sources:* Karim 2016; World Bank and MCI 2013, 2017.

the following questions about financial needs, funding sources, and allocated resources.

- *Strategic decisions that influence the medium- and long-term financing needs.* What institutional configuration would allow for a balanced and affordable tertiary education system? The size and shape of the tertiary education system affect the amount of public funding needed. It makes a huge difference, for the public purse, whether the system expands through expensive public universities or less expensive short-duration institutions such as community colleges or technical institutes. The development of online education and private institutions also helps to alleviate government budgets.
- *Resource mobilization options.* How can public and private funding sources be mobilized in the most effective manner? What are efficient and equitable student aid mechanisms to maintain equality of opportunities?
- *Resource allocation approaches.* What are appropriate performance-based mechanisms to distribute public resources in a manner that encourages innovation and rewards performance?

Notes

1. The CWTS Leiden Ranking is based on the database produced by Thomson Reuters, called "Web of Science bibliographic." See http://www.leidenranking.com/.
2. See https://www.leidenranking.com/ranking/2017/list.
3. For example, China, the Republic of Korea, and Singapore each have at least one university in the top 100.

References

Aghion, Philippe, Mathias Dewatripont, Caroline Hoxby, Andreu Mas-Colell, and André Sapir. 2009. "The Governance and Performance of Research Universities: Evidence from Europe and the U.S." NBER Working Paper 14851, National Bureau of Economic Research, Cambridge, MA.

Altbach, Philip G., and Jamil Salmi, eds. 2011. *The Road to Academic Excellence: Emerging Research Universities in Developing and Transition Countries.* Directions in Development. Washington, DC: World Bank.

Eastermann, Thomas, Terhi Nokkala, and Monika Steinel. 2011. *University Autonomy in Europe II: The Scorecard.* Brussels: European University Association. http://www.eua.be/Libraries/Publications

/University_Autonomy_in_Europe_II_-_The_Scorecard.sflb.ashx.

Holm-Nielsen, Lauritz. 2017. "Opportunities for Change—University Reforms in Denmark." CYD Foundation Study 1-2017, Aarhus University, Aarhus, Denmark.

Karim, J. Nasr. 2016. "University Governance Changing the Higher Education Paradigm in MENA." Marseille Center for Mediterranean Integration (blog), May 27. http://cmimarseille.org/blog/university-governance-changing-higher-education-paradigm-mena.

Leiden University. 2017. *CWTS Leiden Ranking of 2017*. Leiden: Leiden University. http://www.leidenranking.com/ranking/2017/list.

McMahon, Walter W., and Moses Oketch. 2013. "Education's Effects on Individual Life Chances and on Development: An Overview." *British Journal of Educational Studies* 61 (1): 79–107.

OECD (Organisation for Economic Co-operation and Development). 2012. *Higher Education in Regional and City Development: Southern Arizona, United States, 2011*. Paris: OECD.

Oketch, Moses, Tristan McCowan, and Rebecca Schendel. 2014. "The Impact of Tertiary Education on Development: A Rigourous Literature Review." EPPI-Centre Report 2205, U.K. Department for International Development, London. http://r4d.dfid.gov.uk/.

Salmi, Jamil. 2009. *The Challenge of Establishing World-Class Universities*. Directions in Development. Washington, DC: World Bank.

———. 2011. "The Challenge of Establishing World-Class Research Universities in Developing Countries." In *Leadership for World-Class Universities: Challenges for Developing Countries*, edited by Philip G. Altbach. New York and London: Routledge.

———. 2013. "Formas exitosas de gobierno universitario en el mundo." CYD Foundation Study 03/2013, CYD Foundation, Barcelona.

———. 2015. *Is Big Brother Watching You? The Evolving Role of the State in Regulating and Conducting Quality Assurance*. Washington, DC: Council of Higher Education Accreditation.

———. 2016. "Excellence Strategies and the Creation of World-Class Universities." In *Global Rankings and the Geopolitics of Higher Education: Understanding the Influence and Impact of Rankings on Higher Education, Policy, and Society*, edited by Ellen Hazelkorn. London: Routledge.

———. 2017a. *The Tertiary Education Imperative: Knowledge, Skills, and Values for Development*. Boston, MA: Sense Publishers.

———. 2017b. "Building the Research Capacity of MENA Universities." Background paper, World Bank, Washington, DC.

Salmi, Jamil, and Roberta Malee Bassett. 2014. "The Equity Imperative in Tertiary Education: Promoting Fairness and Efficiency." *International Review of Education* 60 (3): 361–77.

Shanghai Ranking. No date. *Academic Ranking of World Universities*. Shanghai Ranking Consultancy, Shanghai. http://www.shanghairanking.com/ARWU2018.html.

University of Waterloo. No date. "Co-op at Waterloo." https://uwaterloo.ca/future-students/co-op.

World Bank and MCI (Marseille Center for Mediterranean Integration). 2013. *Benchmarking Governance as a Tool for Promoting Change*. Washington, DC: World Bank.

———. 2017. "6th MENA Tertiary Education Conference: Towards Competitiveness and Equity in Tertiary Education in the MENA Region; Collaboration for Good Governance, Sustainable Financing, and Internationalization," Marseille, France, June 15–16. MCI, Marseille; World Bank, Washington, DC. http://cmimarseille.org/sites/default/files/newsite/library/files/en/One-pagers.pdf.

Yusuf, Shahid, and Kaoru Nabeshima. 2007. *How Universities Promote Economic Growth*. Washington, DC: World Bank.

Strengthening Accountability for Better Learning Outcomes | 14

Lianqin Wang, Manal Bakur N Quota, Angela Demas, and Bob Prouty

Accountability is critical to improving learning. Accountability in education implies a systemwide obligation to monitor student learning, identify problems, and work out how to solve them (UNESCO 2017). It requires efforts by persons within the education system, such as teachers and school leaders, along with support and pressure for change by actors outside the system, such as parents and communities (UNESCO 2017; World Bank 2004).

Countries in the Middle East and North Africa (MENA) have established learning goals for students—an important step toward greater accountability—but few countries use these goals effectively to monitor and improve learning outcomes. The inspection systems in the region often emphasize compliance with rules and standards, rather than provision of instructional or professional support. Furthermore, the highly centralized education systems in MENA do not grant school principals the authority to exercise key accountability mechanisms. The focus on credentials rather than skills has reduced the pressure to hold education systems accountable for enhancing learning. Compared with parents in other regions, MENA parents are less involved in school decision making. MENA countries should shift to results-based monitoring and evaluation (M&E) systems, transform the inspection systems to support teaching and learning, and increase school autonomy for better accountability. School-level accountability can be enhanced further by making information widely available to communities and parents so that they have the means to hold schools accountable and can engage effectively as part of the overall accountability system. Media and technology also play an important role in strengthening accountability systems.

Establish accountability mechanisms within education systems

For accountability systems to be effective, the roles and responsibilities of stakeholders must be clearly defined and understood. Teachers are responsible for monitoring and assessing students' progress and for giving parents regular feedback. School leaders are responsible for creating a school environment conducive to learning and for monitoring and empowering teachers to ensure that they are delivering on learning. Policy makers have overall responsibility for providing vision and strategy. They develop, lead, and support the implementation of education policies, develop curricula and standards, introduce national information systems that monitor learning, and allocate resources at the national and regional levels (human, physical, and financial). Some of these topics are discussed in other chapters. This chapter highlights key issues that shape accountability in the education system.

Develop results-based monitoring and evaluation

Defining clear student learning goals and standards for what students should know and be able to do after completing each school year is a key element in strengthening accountability. Standards should be adequately reflected in the curricula, and M&E mechanisms should be in place (Fuhrman and Elmore 1994). By measuring the extent to which student learning standards are met, education systems can identify underperforming schools and students in a timely fashion, allowing for concrete actions to support these schools and students.

Ministries of education (MOEs) in most MENA countries have succeeded in defining learning objectives. These objectives are articulated in national curricula outlining program content and intended levels of subject-matter mastery for teachers and students. Of the 10 MENA countries that participated in the Systems Approach for Better Education Results (SABER) Teacher Survey, 8 are rated as "established" or above for their ability to communicate to teachers what students should learn (see box 14.1 for more information on SABER).[1] Likewise, the 2015 Programme for International Student Assessment (PISA) survey results indicate that the majority of 15-year-old students attend schools that have written performance standards and

---

Box 14.1   Systems Approach for Better Education Results (SABER)

SABER is a diagnostic tool developed by the World Bank and launched in 2012 that collects and analyzes comparative data and knowledge on education systems around the world. SABER evaluates the quality of countries' education policies against evidence-based global standards, with the aim of helping countries to strengthen their education systems systematically. This evaluation is based on measures and topics that can be compared easily across education systems around the world.

As of April 2019, the SABER program covers the following domains of education:

- Early childhood development
- Education management information systems
- Education resilience approaches
- Engaging the private sector
- Equity and inclusion
- Information and communication technologies
- School autonomy and accountability
- School finance
- School health and school feeding
- Student assessment
- Teachers
- Tertiary education
- Workforce development.

As part of its methods, SABER identifies and assesses the education policies that matter most in helping countries to achieve education results. By analyzing policy intent, SABER informs critical dialogue at the policy level, which then affects learning at the school level. SABER aggregates policy levers to a set of policy goals per topic. Countries can be assessed, depending on the level of development of their education systems with respect to each goal. SABER is part of the feedback loop that ensures that all education systems, especially those serving the poorest and most marginalized students, are achieving the results needed to boost learning worldwide.

Source: World Bank n.d.

self-evaluations, along with systematically recorded student outcomes (see figure 14.1).

However, many of the region's MOEs have not used learning objectives effectively to monitor learning outcomes or to introduce inquiry-based approaches to teaching and learning. Although MENA countries conduct learning assessments, few use assessment results to address weaknesses in student performance (World Bank 2018c). Inputs and compliance with related policies are often monitored, but the objectives and standards are rarely used to assess learning outcomes (Devlin 2010). This missing link may partially explain the low results for MENA countries participating in international assessments.

High-performing education systems such as those in Australia, France, Japan, Massachusetts (United States), the Netherlands, and Ontario (Canada) have established student learning goals and standards that serve as a guide for designing and implementing school improvement plans, conducting teacher preservice and in-service training, applying teacher assessments, designing M&E mechanisms, as well as assigning resources and funding. These systems use assessment results to provide feedback on teaching practices and to identify underperforming schools and students so that targeted interventions can be developed (Clarke 2012; Jaimovich 2014; Resnick, Nolan, and Resnick 1995). Schools in Australia place strong emphasis on using assessment data to inform instruction. In some schools, teachers administer an array of assessments in literacy and numeracy and work as teams to analyze the data to create a well-rounded picture of student learning (NCEE 2016).

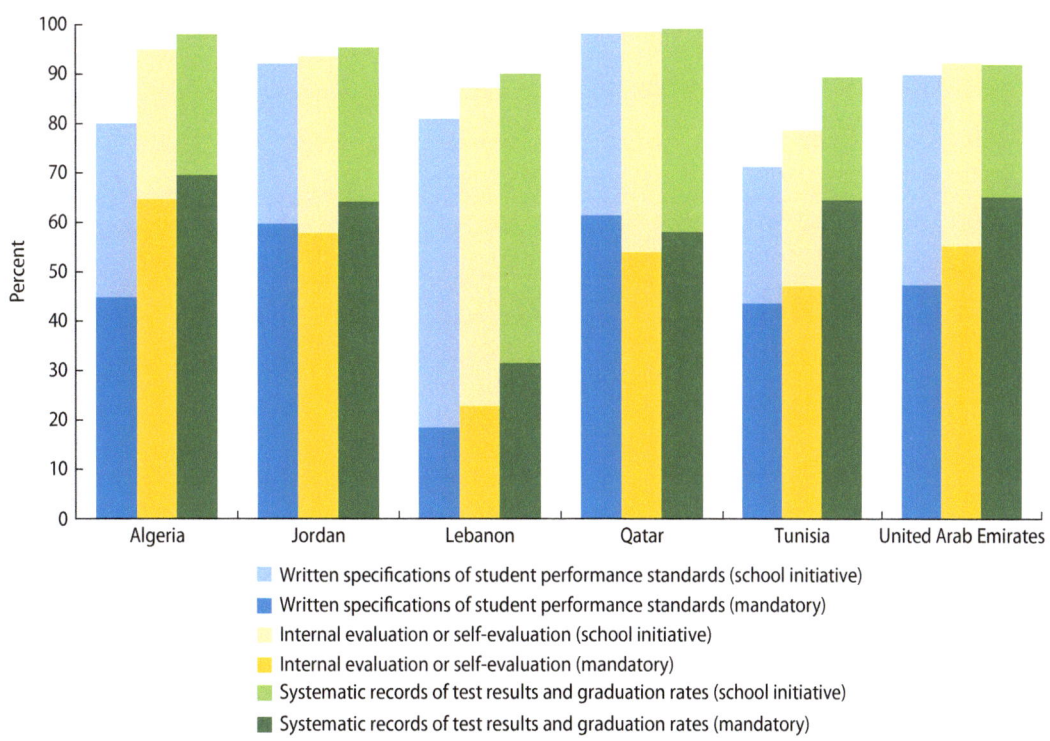

FIGURE 14.1 Many MENA countries have developed school monitoring mechanisms

Percentage of 15-year-old students attending schools in which quality assurance arrangements exist, PISA 2015

Source: OECD 2016.
Note: PISA = Programme for International Student Assessment.

Although opportunities for teachers to learn about the national assessment results in MENA are still limited, some countries are making notable progress.[2] Bahrain, for example, uses international results in a variety of ways to inform decision making, including tracking the impact of reforms on student achievement levels and informing resource allocation (World Bank 2018c). Jordan's education reform of the 1990s also provides an example of policy makers improving stakeholder access to information on student learning, which has had a positive impact on student performance (see box 14.2). The Jordanian experience demonstrates that, with effective use of data, it is possible to improve accountability for better learning outcomes.

To achieve the goals of education, MENA countries will need to establish more rigorous M&E mechanisms that are based on evidence and focused on results. Such an approach requires moving away from traditional input and process-driven methods. Shifting to a focus on results requires more accurate data and information for taking action. Assessing learning and acting on evidence are important elements of accountability systems (World Bank 2018b).

Strengthen supervision and other support to schools

School inspectors provide the most visible form of performance monitoring in many MENA school systems; they are a very important component of accountability systems.

Box 14.2 Jordan's education reform: Evidence-supported accountability

Jordan became the first Arab country to participate in the International Assessment of Educational Progress (IAEP), which assesses 13-year-old students in mathematics and science. Among the 19 countries that participated in the 1991 IAEP, Jordan ranked near the bottom. These results offered tangible evidence of Jordan's poor student learning outcomes and came as a shock to the country.

In response, Jordan accelerated education reform efforts. The curriculum was reviewed, and new learning materials were developed. Jordan evaluated teacher qualifications and introduced a university bridge program to upgrade teacher skills substantially. The bridge program essentially eliminated the two-year teacher education programs by requiring all two-year programs to be consolidated with four-year institutes, thereby extending teacher training.

This reform entailed several key actions. Focusing on evidence, the government (1) established expert committees to investigate the causes of poor performance, (2) examined the IAEP test item by item and compared results to the curricula, (3) established benchmarks for 13-year-olds' achievement, (4) identified strengths and weaknesses in the teaching of each subject, (5) compared the performance of students to inform teacher training, and (6) analyzed characteristics related to achievement.

Jordan's National Center for Human Resources Development (NCHRD), established in 1990, was designed as a longitudinal system to monitor student learning achievements and assess instructional quality at the basic education level. A key focus of NCHRD has been to produce and disseminate reports to develop a feedback loop between the parties researching the education system and those implementing changes. Through these efforts, Jordan has made remarkable gains in educational quality. Between 1997 and 2007, Jordan made more progress on the Trends in International Mathematics and Science Study (TIMSS) science test than any other participating country, although the more recent 2015 results showed a drop.

Throughout this phase, Jordan laid a foundation for reform efforts with sound research and evidence-based policy choices. The focus was on three objectives: (1) seeking and gaining access to data, (2) analyzing learning determinants and benchmarking against other countries, and (3) using evidence in policy making.

Source: Abdul-Hamid, Abu-Lebdeh, and Patrinos 2011.

Among the six MENA countries that participated in PISA 2015, the proportion of students attending schools receiving school inspections ranged from 61 percent in Tunisia to 96 percent in Qatar (OECD 2016). Throughout the region, school inspectors visit schools a few times a year and prepare administrative reports. The inspection reports are based on standardized lesson plans and schedules that are centrally developed for all teachers (World Bank 2008), focusing on teachers' progress through the curriculum, not on student learning results. These inspection reports may influence the career paths of teachers and school administrators. In addition, inspectors have traditionally been trained to emphasize compliance with rules and standards, rather than to provide instructional or professional support. Changing the focus from inspection and supervision to instructional support will require new models to monitor, evaluate, and support schools.

Evidence shows that more decentralized collaborative approaches to supervision can be very effective in helping schools to improve instructional practices and increase student performance when they are aligned with other efforts to give schools more autonomy and accountability (OECD 2011). In 2015, for example, the Scottish government produced the fourth version of "How Good Is Our School?"—a framework that can be adapted and used with school leaders, teachers, students, parents, and partners across the school community to support collaborative enquiry for self-evaluation. This self-evaluation allows schools to identify their own features of effective practice and to develop a shared understanding of what to do next, which can inform their school and district improvement plans. This framework also addresses the need to close the gap in attainment and achievement experienced by the most disadvantaged children (Education Scotland 2015).

Support systems targeting underperforming municipalities and schools are another important accountability measure. For example, the Commonwealth of Massachusetts and Boston Public Schools created support systems in which administrative, pedagogical, and strategic planning experts are available to provide assistance to underperforming schools (see box 14.3). Similarly, in Helsinki, Finland, schools are organized into networks of about 25 schools. These networks are under the responsibility of district leaders and offer instructional improvement assistance (Jaimovich 2014). Other smaller support structures, such as those in the Netherlands and New Zealand, act as brokers and are responsible for hiring technical assistance providers who work directly with schools to help them to improve student achievement (Jaimovich 2014).

MENA countries have great potential to use the supervision and other support systems already in place for improving learning, if they develop incentive systems to transform traditional compliance inspection into support for teaching and learning and promote collaborative efforts at the school level. In Dubai the use of school self-evaluations in private schools encourages school personnel to collaborate with external supervisors for school improvement (Alkutich 2016). Cuadra and Thacker (2014) note the importance of both explicit (opportunity to attract additional resources, for instance) and implicit (professional satisfaction from positive feedback, for example) incentives for improving supervision systems in MENA. Moreover, central governments need to reconsider their functions and budget priorities to bring them closer to the learner by providing greater support to schools. This support could be in the form of more human and financial resources targeted to disadvantaged geographic areas, social groups, and weak schools. Substantial improvements in countries' overall student learning could also be made by a commitment to bringing up bottom-performing districts and schools. This approach is a proven path toward overall education excellence and inclusion; it has led Finland to become one of the top international performer for many years (Sahlberg 2014).

Shift to greater local and school-level autonomy for enhanced accountability

Countries around the world, including most Organisation for Economic Co-operation and Development (OECD) countries, have moved

> **Box 14.3** **Boston Public Schools' support systems**
>
> In the U.S. decentralized education system, the federal government incentivizes reforms and sets quality standards, but states have the autonomy to design policies and monitor the provision of education services. Service delivery is the responsibility of local governments and school districts, which are directly accountable to their constituents.
>
> Boston Public Schools is the largest school district in Massachusetts, serving nearly 125 schools and 57,000 students, of whom 78 percent have low socioeconomic status. To provide support for underperforming schools, Boston Public Schools has established a system in which each network provides pedagogical and administrative support services to 15 or 16 schools. The network's team includes a language specialist, a mathematics specialist, and support for teacher effectiveness, special education, human resources, data management, education technology, infrastructure, and finance.
>
> Underperforming schools receive support from the network and from the state government, including district and school assistance centers (DSACs). DSACs help schools with self-assessment, improvement plans and monitoring, access to professional networks, opportunities for sharing best practices, and strategies for improving finances and strengthening capacity. These schools can also receive funding from the state government to pay for private licensed providers who can help them to hone their pedagogical and teaching practices and increase their management and administrative capacity. In Massachusetts, chronically underperforming schools are required to close.
>
> *Sources:* Jaimovich 2014; Massachusetts Department of Education 2018; OECD 2015.

toward more decentralized approaches in education (Busemeyer 2012). The core idea involves shifting decision making on some key functions, including human and financial resources management, away from centralized government structures and toward lower administrative units such as governorates, school districts, or individual schools. Regional and district authorities can be instrumental in mobilizing resources. They can respond with greater agility to urgent needs by removing institutional barriers and building capacity at the school level (Brixi, Lust, and Woolcock 2015; Lewis 2016). The goal of decentralization is typically to improve governance by fostering autonomy, accountability, and responsiveness to local conditions and needs. These attributes, in turn, can improve student learning (King and Özler 2004).

Most education systems in MENA have highly centralized management structures. These structures have limited ability to identify and respond to the individual needs of schools and their students. For instance, as discussed in the preceding chapters, in most MENA countries, the current central decision-making process for teacher recruitment is removed from local needs and often results in human resource wastage or inefficiencies and a mismatch between school needs and service delivery. Also, school principals often do not have the authority to exercise key accountability mechanisms such as removing nonperforming teachers from the classroom. The levels of decision-making authority across countries within the region are documented in table 14.1.

Decentralizing the education system requires consistent and strong leadership across administrative units. Whereas principals can create conditions that encourage excellence in teaching, district leaders can create conditions that encourage excellence in leadership (Levin, Datnow, and Carrier 2012) by providing resources, tools, and information for quality assurance and performance monitoring. Districts are also well positioned to provide comparative and individual school analysis, helping schools to understand their own level of performance in relation to that of neighboring schools and the wider system—for instance, as has been done through the Data Must Speak program (UNICEF n.d.).

TABLE 14.1 **Most decisions on education policy and inputs are made at the central level in MENA**
Level of education decision-making authority, by economy, 2015

Policy	Algeria	Bahrain	Djibouti	Egypt, Arab Rep.	Iran, Islamic Rep.	Iraq	Jordan	Kuwait	Lebanon	Libya	Morocco	Oman	Qatar	Saudi Arabia	Syrian Arab Republic	Tunisia	United Arab Emirates	West Bank and Gaza	Yemen, Rep.
National strategy	♦	♦	♦	♦	♦	♦	♦	♦	♦	♦	♦	♦	♦	♦	♦	♦	♦	♦	♦
Planning				♦			♦			♦			♦	♦					
Establishment of input and infrastructure norms			♦	♦□			□	♦	♦	♦			♦	♦		♦□	♦	♦	♦□
Finance				♦									♦	♦					
Resource allocation	○		♦	♦□			○	♦	●	♦	□		○				○	○	
Human resource management			♦	♦				□	♦		♦			♦	♦				
Principal selection			♦	♦			□	♦			♦	□		♦	♦				
Teacher selection			♦	♦			♦	♦		♦	♦			♦	♦				
Teacher deployment			♦	♦			□	♦			♦	□		♦					
Teacher training			♦	♦□				♦□	♦	♦□				♦	♦				
Establishment of teacher responsibility			♦	♦				♦	♦					♦	♦				
Supervision of teachers			♦□	□			□	♦□	♦□	♦□				♦	□	♦□		♦	□
Firing of teachers	□		♦	♦				♦	♦	○	♦			○			♦	○	
Pedagogy			♦	♦				♦	♦		♦			♦					
Curriculum design	♦		♦	♦			♦	♦	♦○	♦				♦	♦		♦	♦○	
Standards setting			♦	♦	♦			♦	♦	♦	♦			♦	♦		♦		♦
Examination management			♦	♦□	♦□		♦	♦□	♦	♦				♦		♦		♦□	♦□

Source: Compiled from World Bank SABER database (http://saber.worldbank.org/index.cfm).
Note: ♦ = central ministry; □ = provincial and regional administration; ○ = schools.

It is unrealistic to expect that greater accountability at the school level will improve results unless schools also have greater decision-making authority over their operations. By transferring core managerial responsibilities to schools, school autonomy with proper support can (1) foster local ownership and accountability; (2) reflect local priorities, values, and needs through increased participation of parents and the community; and (3) give teachers the opportunity to build a strong instructional program on a foundation of personal commitment to students and their parents. Increased school autonomy and improved accountability can lead to improved learning by aligning teacher and parent incentives. Studies have shown a causal link between school autonomy and efficiency in resource use (Demas and Arcia 2015; UNICEF 2015), with small to moderate positive effects on efficiency and learning (Carr-Hill, Rolleston, and Schendel 2016). Effects are stronger in middle-income and more advantaged communities than in low-income and disadvantaged communities. While the impact of such decentralization depends on its design and the country context, the managerial capacity of the school leadership is an important factor for obtaining positive outcomes (Bloom et al. 2015; Hanushek, Link, and Woessmann 2013).

Experience with more school autonomy and accountability in MENA shows potential, although so far the scope of implementation has been limited. In the Arab Republic of Egypt, the Education Reform Program piloted this approach in seven governorates, allocating resources to schools by formula funding. Schools received assistance to prepare school improvement plans (World Bank 2018a). Staff at the governorate and school levels received support to improve their ability to carry out their roles. Teachers were trained to assist students in improving their analytical problem-solving skills. Jordan, Lebanon, and Morocco have experimented with school-based programs for many years, but they still fall short in producing and using good-quality data at the school level (Brixi, Lust, and Woolcock 2015). However, Jordan's experiences suggest pockets of success with improved education services, stronger community engagement, and a heightened sense of school accountability (Brixi, Lust, and Woolcock 2015). These achievements could be strengthened by taking a more holistic approach to change in which the central MOEs provide far greater support to school leadership. Since greater school autonomy and accountability demand higher school-level capacity, the central government and district level must be accountable for ensuring that school leaders have the incentives to change and that schools have what they need to succeed.

In light of MENA's overly centralized education systems, countries are encouraged to consider increasing local and school autonomy by granting more authority to schools to manage human and financial resources as well as instruction (including the hiring and firing of teachers). Schools can be more accountable if they are empowered with more authority and supported by capacity development for school leaders and teachers.

Some MENA countries have already started a process for school improvement and accountability. The school improvement program in Jordan, for instance, was implemented in 35 field directorates and 2,778 schools between 2011 and 2016. The program improved the capacity of schools to develop and implement plans and improved the accountability of MOE staff at the central and field directorates. Parents got involved in developing school improvement plans, countersigning school expenditures, and meeting regularly with school staff to discuss students' results. An accountability unit, the Education Quality Accountability Unit, was set up in the MOE and is fully staffed and operational (World Bank 2018d).

Involve communities and parents in accountability systems

The engagement of communities and parents in monitoring school performance has been shown to contribute to student learning, particularly when parents are involved in deciding how and what to monitor (Zeitlin et al. 2011). Buy-in from parents is a key step toward a new pact for education in which the interests of a wide variety of stakeholders—including teachers, principals, inspectors, politicians, communities, employers, and students—are aligned.

Raise parents' expectation for learning

In all education systems, it is a natural reflex of parents, students, and teachers to focus on the credentials that signify completion of a course of study. When tightly linked to achievement of learning and skills, the credential helps parents to know whether their child has obtained all of the skills necessary for obtaining employment or for continuing an education program. But when the credential is increasingly decoupled from achievement of learning and skills, as is currently the case in many MENA countries, the focus on credentials enables weak systems to persist without making the necessary course corrections. Getting credentials drives what and how teachers teach and students learn. As a result, less attention is given to developing students' skills than to scoring well on high-stakes examinations. In some cases, focusing on examination scores without developing the underlying skills has led to high levels of cheating in assessments, as documented in Jordan and Morocco (Buckner and Hodges 2015) as well as in Lebanon (Bacha, Bahous, and Nabhani 2012).

Parental involvement in school programs can be an important lever for MOEs to bring additional pressure for bottom-up change within the system. These ministries could lead a national dialogue to engage government, educators, parents, civil society, and all stakeholders in understanding what roles they can play. This effort could lead to a greater push to improve student learning outcomes, including a focus on skills rather than on credentials.

Innovative approaches to communication can be developed to involve communities in raising expectations of learning. An approach that has proven effective in the health sector and that could be adapted to the education sector in MENA is known as social and behavior change communications (SBCC) (Storey and Figueroa 2012) (see box 14.4). Mobile phones and other information and communication technology can be useful tools to support communication, but it is important to understand how mutual signaling occurs between the education sector and stakeholders such as parents and employers and on developing a communications strategy based on this information.

Empower parents with information to support school-level accountability

For parents to play a strong role and insist on accountability, school data must be accessible to the community. Government officials and the public have differing interests when it comes to data—government officials need information to set policies and to reallocate resources, while parents and communities need information to make sure that their own children are succeeding. These purposes are complementary, and both are needed. Parents can also use such information to put pressure on schools to raise standards and improve results (Brixi, Lust, and Woolcock 2015; World Bank 2018b). Many education systems in high-income countries welcome such pressure and channel it toward continuous improvement. Low- and middle-income countries are also exploring this approach, such as Kenya, where enabling parents to hold teachers and schools accountable has had positive impacts on student learning (Duflo, Dupas, and Kremer 2011). In MENA, where teacher absenteeism is prevalent, this approach could be particularly useful.

In addition to school data on student and teacher absenteeism, the availability of comparative results of national examinations and learning assessments can help parents to monitor the performance of their children's school and hold it accountable. Such information can give parents a voice in the educational process and empower them to promote their children's learning and academic

---

Box 14.4 Social and behavior change communications (SBCC)

SBCC focuses on the community as the unit of change. SBCC is an evidence-based process of using communication, usually as part of a broader intervention, to promote behaviors that lead to improvements in outcomes. Explicit emphasis is placed on changes in behavior as an outcome, seeking to understand why people do what they do and how to support positive change. Given the growing understanding that behaviors take place in a particular context and that change must be supported from multiple levels of influence, SBCC is designed to influence social norms in support of long-term, sustainable change in behaviors; to strengthen community engagement; to influence decision makers, family, and peer networks; to influence policy development; and to increase demand (USAID 2017). To improve the focus on learning outcomes and skills, SBCC would need to deepen awareness among all stakeholders (including parents, students, educators, and employers) of the importance of focusing on skills rather than on credentials so that graduates are well prepared for the job market.

Source: Storey and Figueroa 2012.

growth (Weiss, Lopez, and Rosenberg 2010). Another way to strengthen accountability and the flow of communications is to share school-level data through school report cards (IIEP 2018) (see box 14.5). However, these approaches may not be effective if there is limited capacity within the system to respond effectively to positive pressure; there is also the potential for adverse effects such as further burdening the most vulnerable (Read and Atinc 2016). A forum for dialogue with parents should be in place, and schools need the authority and quick-response capacity to shift resources and improve the flow of communications to maintain both trust and accountability.

Strengthening school-level information sharing in the MENA region will require new approaches to empowering parents and other stakeholders. Jordan is one of the most advanced education systems in the region in data collection and analysis. Yet even Jordan does not have a policy requiring that analysis of public examination results be distributed to parents. The National Center for Human Resources Development in Jordan routinely conducts comparative analyses of the national examination results and submits a report to the education directorates, but not to parents (World Bank 2016a). This means that parents are not routinely equipped with the information needed to make informed decisions on where and when—as well as how—to engage in dialogue with schools to improve performance and to bring positive pressure to bear.

Establish institutional arrangements for parents to participate in school management

Many education systems create institutional arrangements that involve the community in decision-making processes. For instance, Finland, Massachusetts (United States), and Ontario (Canada) have local education management units, such as school boards and districts, that oversee administrative and academic management and report to the state level. In New Zealand, schools are managed by democratically elected school boards,

---

Box 14.5 **Using school report cards to promote transparency and accountability**

School report cards are a good example of using school data to strengthen education systems. School report cards can cover a wide range of aspects regarding the effectiveness of an individual school, including student achievement, teacher qualifications, school facility conditions, teaching resources, and other important indicators of school quality and achievement. The information presented in the school report card provides the school community, including students and parents, the opportunity to ensure that a school has received an appropriate amount of resources and is meeting student needs. Many countries have adopted school report cards as a means of sharing school-level data.

To ensure that school report cards are used to their full potential as a means of promoting transparency and accountability, the following key factors need to be considered:

- Creating legal provisions for the disclosure of school data
- Selecting data that are critical to monitoring financial, management, or pedagogical accountability
- Designing mechanisms enabling "fair comparisons" between schools
- Training school management committees, teachers, parents, and community groups on how data can be used to demand accountability
- Introducing a legal grievance redress mechanism for parents and communities.

By taking advantage of open school data and using school report cards effectively, governments can involve the school community at-large in shaping the education system and ensuring education transparency and accountability at the local and national levels.

Source: IIEP 2018.

which have a direct relationship with the central level (Jaimovich 2014). In El Salvador, the Community Managed Schools Program (EDUCO), established in 1992, gave parents power and responsibility for schools, including the hiring and firing of teachers. The EDUCO quickly increased enrollment in rural areas and positively affected student learning outcomes (Jimenez and Sawada 1998). EDUCO was intended to decentralize education by strengthening the direct involvement and participation of parents. However, the program was ended in 2010 due to cost inefficiency and a newly elected Salvadoran government, which was dissatisfied with the program's labor relationship between teachers and communities (Florez et al. 2015). This case offers some important lessons for the design and implementation of programs to improve the involvement of communities and parents in education.

Many MENA countries have school management committees (SMCs), but few of these committees have a substantive voice in school affairs (Brixi, Lust, and Woolcock 2015). In Morocco, for example, SMCs have been widely established, yet their functionality and effectiveness are weak. The SMCs are not authorized to handle funds, and their composition is unbalanced, with little representation from individuals outside of school personnel. SMC members do not have clear roles and can lose motivation because they lack influence on school affairs. Parent-teacher meetings often represent the only other substantial opportunity for interaction between parents and the school, but these meetings are typically infrequent and of short duration, providing limited opportunity for meaningful engagement (World Bank 2016b).

There is little systematic research on the extent of parental and community involvement with schools in MENA, but several promising initiatives are emerging. For example, parents in the United Arab Emirates are regularly invited to participate in school activities, including workshops for students (Al-Taneiji 2012). Egypt's New Schools Program has been implemented in more than 90 communities and engages community actors in school management, including actions to address learning and other school issues (CARE 2016).

Provide a home environment that supports learning

To learn, children need to feel safe and supported in their learning environments. The home environment provides the foundation for children's learning and should be considered as an element of the accountability system (UNESCO 2017). Education success is positively affected by home learning opportunities such as when parents read to their children and when learning resources are available at home. The benefit of in-home exposure to literary Arabic was evidenced in a recent study, showing that children from literate middle-income families with spoken Arabic could retell short stories told in literary Arabic and that recent additions of modern standard Arabic children's literature, home reading, and cartoon programming fostered fluency among preprimary children (Leikin, Ibrahim, and Eghbaria 2013).

Before entering school, children in MENA countries are less prepared for literacy learning than children in other regions. On average, across all countries that participated in the Progress in International Reading Literacy Study (PIRLS) 2016, 39 percent of grade 4 students had a parent who reported often having engaged in literacy activities with their child during the preprimary years. However, MENA countries that participated in PIRLS 2016 all reported lower percentages (see figure 14.2).

The assessment also found an alarming lack of resources for in-home learning. For example, 74 percent of homes of grade 4 students in Egypt and 70 percent of those in Morocco had 10 or fewer children's books. In Oman, 38 percent of grade 4 students had 10 or fewer children's books in the home, down from 55 percent in 2011 (IEA 2013; Mullis et al. 2017).

MENA parents are behind their international peers in providing their children with a supportive home environment for learning.

Awareness campaigns and capacity building could be a means of improving this situation, since many parents may not understand the relationship between home environment and school achievement or may not have sufficient skills and tools with which to support their children's learning development. Such efforts could improve children's learning and strengthen the education pact through which the home and community become important links in the chain of education system accountability.

FIGURE 14.2 **Few children in MENA benefit from sufficient literacy activities at home**
Percentage of grade 4 students whose parents reported often doing early literacy activities with their child before primary school

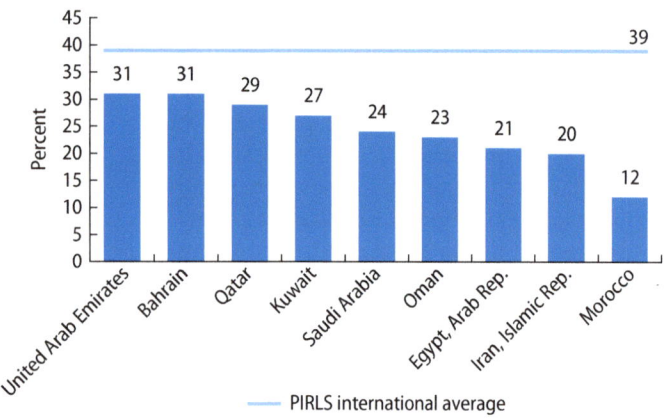

Source: Mullis et al. 2017.
Note: PIRLS = Progress in International Reading Literacy Study.

Use media and technology to support accountability systems

Social media are a major source of information in the world and in MENA countries, especially for youths, and they can serve as a platform for policy makers wishing to share information and promote greater transparency on education policy reforms. Social media also provide citizens with a mechanism to hold policy makers and educators accountable. And yet social media can also be exploited by interest groups to block important reforms and spread misinformation. Open channels for communication and debate are important to creating a pact around learning. Policy makers should engage with stakeholders through various channels to address concerns, correct information using evidence, and rally collective support for education reforms. Civil society is responsible for demanding transparent communication of education inputs and outcomes.

Technology can also be leveraged to establish accountability systems. Several countries are implementing education dashboards to facilitate open data and a move toward evidence-based policy making. The government of Egypt has effectively leveraged modern technology to promote accountability (see box 14.6).

Box 14.6 **Using technology in Egypt's education sector to ensure accountability**

Egypt has embarked on ambitious accountability reforms in the education sector using modern technology. These reforms are enhancing accountability through the following channels:

- Increasing the amount of data and information available to policy makers and the public, thereby improving accountability for resource allocation and service delivery
- Enhancing transparency around student assessments and citizens' trust of assessment results
- Strengthening accountability across key stakeholders, giving the community and parents a greater voice in policy making
- Creating a better compact between the Ministry of Education and Technical Education and schools by improving district-level management.

Source: World Bank 2018a.

Notes

1. A rating of "established" indicates that the standards for what students must know and be able to do at both the subnational and national levels are set. Djibouti and West Bank and Gaza were rated as "emerging," meaning that the policy in place reflects some good practices but is still being developed.
2. The following SABER-Student Assessment Country Reports were reviewed: Bahrain (2013), the Arab Republic of Egypt (2013), Iraq (2013), Jordan (2014), Lebanon (2013), Libya (2015), Morocco (2015), Oman (2013), the Syrian Arab Republic (2013), Tunisia (2013), the United Arab Emirates (2013), West Bank and Gaza (2013), and the Republic of Yemen (2013). (See World Bank 2013a–2013j; 2014; 2015a and 2015b.)

References

Abdul-Hamid, Husein, Khattab M. Abu-Lebdeh, and Harry Anthony Patrinos. 2011. "Assessment Testing Can Be Used to Inform Policy Decisions: The Case of Jordan." Policy Research Working Paper 5890, World Bank, Washington, DC. https://openknowledge.worldbank.org/handle/10986/3658.

Alkutich, Muhamad. 2016. "Examining the Impact of School Inspection on Teaching and Learning: Dubai Private Schools as a Case Study." Master's thesis, British University, Dubai. https://www.grin.com/document/358814.

Al-Taneiji, Shaikah. 2012. "The Role of Leadership in Engaging Parents in United Arab Emirate Schools." *International Education Studies* 6 (1): 153–65. https://files.eric.ed.gov/fulltext/EJ1067113.pdf.

Bacha, Nahla Nola, Rima Bahous, and Mona Nabhani. 2012. "High Schoolers' Views on Academic Integrity." *Research Papers in Education* 27 (3): 365–81. https://www.tandfonline.com/doi/ref/10.1080/02671522.2010.550010?scroll=top.

Bloom, Nicholas, Renata Lemos, Raffaella Sadun, and John Van Reenen. 2015. "Does Management Matter in Schools?" *Economic Journal* 125 (584): 647–74.

Brixi, Hana, Ellen Marie Lust, and Michael Woolcock. 2015. *Trust, Voice, and Incentives: Learning from Local Success Stories in Service Delivery in the Middle East and North Africa.* Washington, DC: World Bank. https://openknowledge.worldbank.org/handle/10986/21607.

Buckner, Elizabeth, and Rebecca Hodges. 2015. "Cheating or Cheated? Surviving Secondary Exit Exams in a Neoliberal Era." *Compare: A Journal of Comparative and International Education* 46 (4): 603–23. https://doi.org/10.1080/03057925.2015.1088379.

Busemeyer, Marius R. 2012. "Two Decades of Decentralization in Education Governance: Lessons Learned and Future Outlook for Local Stakeholders." Paper presented at Conference on Effective Local Governance in Education, Organisation for Economic Co-operation and Development, Warsaw, April 16.

CARE. 2016. "CARE Egypt's Legacy 2005–2015." CARE, Cairo. https://www.care.org/sites/default/files/documents/egypt_legacy-report-final.pdf.

Carr-Hill, Roy, Caine Rolleston, and Rebecca Schendel. 2016. "The Effects of School-Based Decision Making on Educational Outcomes in Low- and Middle-Income Contexts: A Systematic Review." Campbell Systematic Reviews 2016:9, Campbell Collaboration, Oslo.

Clarke, M. 2012. "What Matters Most for Student Assessment Systems: A Framework Paper." SABER Working Paper 1, World Bank, Washington, DC.

Cuadra, Ernesto, and Simon Thacker. 2014. *The Road Traveled: Dubai's Journey towards Improving Private Education.* MENA Development Report. Washington, DC: World Bank.

Demas, Angela, and Gustavo J. Arcia. 2015. "What Matters Most for Autonomy and Accountability: A Framework Paper." SABER Working Paper 9, World Bank, Washington, DC.

Devlin, Julia C. 2010. *Challenges of Economic Development in the Middle East and North Africa Region.* Singapore: World Scientific Publishing.

Duflo, Esther, Pascaline Dupas, and Michael Kremer. 2011. "Peer Effects, Teacher Incentives, and the Impact of Tracking: Evidence from a Randomized Evaluation in Kenya." NBER Working Paper 14475, National Bureau of Economic Research, Cambridge, MA.

Education Scotland. 2015. *How Good Is Our School?* 4th ed. Livingston: Education Scotland. https://files.eric.ed.gov/fulltext/ED574051.pdf.

Florez, Ana, Audrey Moore, Samuel Field, and Jochen Kluve. 2015. *Evaluating the Impact of Closing a Community-Managed Schools Programme in El Salvador*. New Delhi: International Initiative for Impact Evaluation.

Fuhrman, Susan, and Richard F. Elmore. 1994. *The Governance of Curriculum: 1994 Yearbook of the ASCD*. Alexandria, VA: Association for Supervision and Curriculum Development.

Hanushek, Erik, Susanne Link, and Ludger Woessmann. 2013. "Does School Autonomy Make Sense Everywhere? Panel Estimates from PISA." *Journal of Development Economics* 104: 212–32.

IEA (International Association for the Evaluation of Educational Achievement). 2013. PIRLS 2011 International Database. Boston, MA: Boston College, TIMSS and PIRLS International Study Center. https://timssandpirls.bc.edu/pirls2011/international-database.html.

IIEP (International Institute for Education Planning). 2018. "10 Ways to Promote Transparency and Accountability in Education." IIEP, United Nations Educational, Scientific, and Cultural Organization, Paris. http://www.iiep.unesco.org/en/10-ways-promote-transparency-and-accountability-education-4307.

Jaimovich, Analía. 2014. *Institutional Architecture for School Improvement*. Washington, DC: Inter-American Development Bank.

Jimenez, Emmanuel, and Yasuyuki S. Sawada. 1998. "Do Community-Managed Schools Work? An Evaluation of El Salvador's EDUCO Program." Impact Evaluation of Education Reforms Working Paper, World Bank, Washington, DC.

King, Elizabeth M., and Berk Özler. 2004. *What's Decentralization Got to Do with Learning? School Autonomy and Student Performance*. Washington, DC: World Bank.

Leikin, Mark, Raphiq Ibrahim, and Hazar Eghbaria. 2013. "The Influence of Diglossia in Arabic on Narrative Ability: Evidence from Analysis of the Linguistic and Narrative Structure of Discourse among Pre-School Children." *Reading and Writing* 27 (4): 733–47. http://link.springer.com/article/10.1007/s11145-013-9462-3.

Levin, Ben, Amanda Datnow, and Nathalie Carrier. 2012. "Changing School District Practices." Student at the Center Series, Jobs for the Future, Boston, MA. http://www.jff.org/sites/default/files/publications/materials/Changing%20School%20District%20Practices.pdf.

Lewis, Laura. 2016. "Leadership Development Guidance Note." Background paper for *The Learning Generation: Investing in Education for a Changing World*, Education Commission, Washington, DC.

Massachusetts Department of Education. 2018. "Mass. Teachers Are Making a Difference in Classrooms across the State." Department of Elementary and Secondary Education (blog). http://www.doe.mass.edu/.

Mullis, Ina V. S., Michael O. Martin, Pierre Foy, and M. Hooper. 2017. "PIRLS 2016 International Results in Reading." TIMSS and PIRLS International Study Center, Boston College, Chestnut Hill, MA. http://timssandpirls.bc.edu/pirls2016/international-results/.

NCEE (National Center on Education and the Economy). 2016. "Developing High-Quality Teaching." Empower Educators: How High-Performing Systems Shape Teaching Quality around the World Policy Brief, World Bank, Washington, DC.

OECD (Organisation for Economic Co-operation and Development). 2011. "School Autonomy and Accountability: Are They Related to Student Performance?" PISA in Focus 9, OECD Publishing, Paris.

———. 2015. "PISA (Programme for International Student Assessment) 2015: Massachusetts Country Note." OECD, Paris.

———. 2016. *PISA 2015 Results*. Vol. 2: *Policies and Practices for Successful Schools*. Paris: OECD. http://dx.doi.org/10.1787/9789264267510-en.

Read, Lindsay, and Tamar Atinc. 2016. "From Data to Learning: The Role of Social Accountability in Education Systems." Education Plus Development (blog), December 21. https://www.brookings.edu/blog/education-plus-development/2016/12/21/from-data-to-learning-the-role-of-social-accountability-in-education-systems/.

Resnick, Lauren B., Katherine J. Nolan, and Daniel P. Resnick. 1995. "Benchmarking Education Standards." *Educational Evaluation and Policy Analysis* 17 (4): 438–61.

Sahlberg, Pasi. 2014. *Finnish Lessons 2.0: What Can the World Learn from Educational Change in Finland?* 2d ed. New York: Teachers College Press.

Storey, Douglas, and Maria Elena Figueroa. 2012. "Toward a Global Theory of Health Behavior and Social Change." In *Handbook of Global*

Health Communication, edited by Rafael Obregón and Silvio Waisbord, 70–94. San Francisco: John Wiley and Sons.

UNESCO (United Nations Educational, Scientific, and Cultural Organization). 2017. "Global Education Monitoring Report Summary 2017/8: Accountability in Education; Meeting Our Commitments." UNESCO, Paris.

UNICEF (United Nations Children's Fund). 2015. UNICEF MENARO database. New York: Paris. https://open.unicef.org/post-document/menaro-oa5-2015/.

———. No date. "Data Must Speak." UNICEF, New York. https://www.unicef.org/education/data-must-speak.

USAID (U.S. Agency for International Development). 2017. "Designing a Social and Behavior Change Communication Strategy." Health Communication Capacity Collaborative, Washington, DC. https://sbccimplementationkits.org/courses/designing-a-social-and-behavior-change-communication-strategy/.

Weiss, Heather B., M. Elena Lopez, and Heidi Rosenberg. 2010. "Beyond Random Acts: Family, School, and Community Engagement as an Integral Part of Education Reform." Harvard Family Research Project (December), Southwest Educational Development Laboratory, U.S. Department of Education, Washington, DC. https://www.sedl.org/connections/engagement_forum/beyond_random_acts.pdf.

World Bank. 2004. *World Development Report 2004: Making Services Work for Poor People.* Washington, DC: World Bank.

———. 2008. *The Road Not Traveled: Education Reform in the Middle East and North Africa.* Washington, DC: World Bank.

———. 2013a. "SABER Student Assessment Country Report: Bahrain 2013." Systems Approach for Better Education Results (SABER) Country Report: Student Assessment, World Bank, Washington, DC. https://hubs.worldbank.org/docs/imagebank/Pages/docProfile.aspx?nodeid=26374677.

———. 2013b. "SABER Student Assessment Country Report: Arab Republic of Egypt 2013." Systems Approach for Better Education Results (SABER) Country Report: Student Assessment, World Bank, Washington, DC. https://hubs.worldbank.org/docs/imagebank/pages/docprofile.aspx?nodeid=26374673.

———. 2013c. "SABER Student Assessment Country Report: Iraq 2013." Systems Approach for Better Education Results (SABER) Country Report: Student Assessment, World Bank, Washington, DC. https://hubs.worldbank.org/docs/imagebank/pages/docprofile.aspx?nodeid=26374671.

———. 2013d. "SABER Student Assessment Country Report: Lebanon 2013." Systems Approach for Better Education Results (SABER) Country Report: Student Assessment, World Bank, Washington, DC. https://hubs.worldbank.org/docs/imagebank/pages/docprofile.aspx?nodeid=20137625.

———. 2013e. "SABER Student Assessment Country Report: Oman 2013." Systems Approach for Better Education Results (SABER) Country Report: Student Assessment, World Bank, Washington, DC. https://hubs.worldbank.org/docs/imagebank/pages/docprofile.aspx?nodeid=26374674.

———. 2013f. "SABER Student Assessment Country Report: Republic of Yemen 2013." Systems Approach for Better Education Results (SABER) Country Report: Student Assessment, World Bank, Washington, DC. https://hubs.worldbank.org/docs/imagebank/pages/docprofile.aspx?nodeid=26374664.

———. 2013g. "SABER Student Assessment Country Report: Syria 2013." Systems Approach for Better Education Results (SABER) Country Report: Student Assessment, World Bank, Washington, DC. https://hubs.worldbank.org/docs/imagebank/pages/docprofile.aspx?nodeid=27368417.

———. 2013h. "SABER Student Assessment Country Report: Tunisia 2013." Systems Approach for Better Education Results (SABER) Country Report: Student Assessment, World Bank, Washington, DC. https://hubs.worldbank.org/docs/imagebank/pages/docprofile.aspx?nodeid=26374663.

———. 2013i. "SABER Student Assessment Country Report: United Arab Emirates 2013." Systems Approach for Better Education Results (SABER) Country Report: Student Assessment, World Bank, Washington, DC. https://hubs.worldbank.org/docs/imagebank/pages/docprofile.aspx?nodeid=26374666.

———. 2013j. "SABER Student Assessment Country Report: West Bank and Gaza 2013." Systems Approach for Better Education Results (SABER) Country Report: Student Assessment, World Bank, Washington, DC. https://hubs.worldbank.org/docs/imagebank/pages/docprofile.aspx?nodeid=26374667.

World Bank. 2014. "SABER Student Assessment Country Report: Jordan." Systems Approach for Better Education Results (SABER) Country Report: Student Assessment, World Bank, Washington, DC. https://hubs.worldbank.org/docs/imagebank/pages/docprofile.aspx?nodeid=27368835.

———. 2015a. "SABER Student Assessment Country Report: Libya 2015." Systems Approach for Better Education Results (SABER) Country Report Student Assessment, World Bank, Washington, DC. https://hubs.worldbank.org/docs/imagebank/Pages/docProfile.aspx?nodeid=27369103.

———. 2015b. "SABER Student Assessment Country Report: Morocco 2015." Systems Approach for Better Education Results (SABER) Country Report: Student Assessment, World Bank, Washington, DC. https://hubs.worldbank.org/docs/imagebank/pages/docprofile.aspx?nodeid=27368416.

———. 2016a. "SABER School Autonomy and Accountability: Jordan Country Report 2015." SABER Country Report, World Bank, Washington, DC.

———. 2016b. "SABER School Autonomy and Accountability: Morocco Country Report 2015." SABER Country Report, World Bank, Washington, DC.

———. 2018a. "Project Appraisal Document: Supporting Egypt Education Reform Project." World Bank, Washington, DC.

———. 2018b. *World Development Report 2018: Learning to Realize Education's Promise.* Washington, DC: World Bank.

———. 2018c. "SABER Student Assessments Ratings and Data." World Bank, Washington, DC. http://saber.worldbank.org/index.cfm?indx=8&pd=5&sub=1.

———. 2018d. "World Bank Education." Information compiled by Jordan Country Team, World Bank, Washington, DC.

———. No date. SABER—Systems Approach for Better Education Results database. World Bank, Washington, DC. http://saber.worldbank.org/index.cfm.

Zeitlin, Andrew, Lawrence Bategeka, Madina Guloba, Ibrahim Kasirye, and Frederick Mugisha. 2011. "Management and Motivation in Ugandan Primary Schools: Impact Evaluation Final Report." Improving Institutions for Pro-Poor Growth, University of Oxford, Oxford, U.K. http://www.iig.ox.ac.uk/.

Conclusion | 15

Safaa El Tayeb El-Kogali and Caroline Krafft

How can countries in the Middle East and North Africa (MENA) region achieve the full potential of education? The chapters in this book examine the status of education in the MENA region, recognizing the variations between and within countries. They present a political economy characterization of the tensions that are holding back the potential of education in MENA. They also propose a new push-pull-pact framework to address the challenges. Within this framework, the chapters highlight the common issues, challenges, and constraints that exist inside and outside the region's education systems and describe the challenges that are keeping MENA countries from reaping the potential benefits of education for their citizens.

Understanding countries' education investments, learning process, measurement of learning, and roles played by stakeholders is a critical first step to achieving the potential of education. The process of education is not only technical but also political, cultural, and social. Recognizing the multidimensional nature of education helps to identify the stakeholders and tensions that constrain learning at the society, school, and classroom levels. Each chapter offers specific policy options and solutions, sharing successful examples that can help to tap into this potential.

This conclusion offers some key lessons for policy reforms that countries can adopt and adapt to their specific conditions in order to achieve the potential of education.

Offering lessons for effective education reform

No solution fits all: Implementing a reform will not achieve the same results across all contexts

There are multiple models for transforming education. Finland and the Republic of Korea were both top scorers in the 2015 Programme for International Student Assessment (PISA), a signal of strong learning. Yet the two education systems leading to this learning are quite different (see box 15.1). A variety of models for education can help countries to achieve their goals. There is not one, singular, or uniform "best practice" for reforming or running an education system. The most effective education model for a country will depend on its current capabilities as well as its political, economic, and social context. This context determines what is feasible and what will work. Emphasizing different goals

> **Box 15.1** **Finland and the Republic of Korea rely on different successful education models**
>
> Both Finland and Korea have successful, high-performing education systems, and yet these systems differ greatly. Korea is known for its rigorous, test-driven system, while Finland has a more accommodating, flexible system with no mandated standardized tests, except for college entrance exams (Darling-Hammond, Wei, and Andree 2010). A high school student in Korea spends, on average, 10 hours a day at school and is under immense pressure from his or her family to do well (Ellinger and Beckham 1997). By contrast, Finland allows students to take courses at their own pace in their final years of schooling, enabling them to learn the material better without stresses and on their own time (Morgan 2014). There is no clearly "right" education system—they both promote learning.
>
> Despite their differing environments, there are a few distinct similarities. Both countries are committed to providing equal learning opportunities to students. In Korea, teachers are rotated to different schools every five to seven years, creating more chances for exceptional teachers to interact with disadvantaged students (Morgan 2016). PISA revealed that the opportunities to learn in Finland are essentially the same throughout the country (Morgan 2016). Finnish schools offer welfare services and free early academic support for students who need help in reading, writing, or math (Morgan 2014, 2016), all of which help to diminish preexisting inequalities among students, enabling them to learn.
>
> In addition, both countries invest in, and develop, accomplished teachers. In Finland, teaching is a highly respected profession that is often perceived to be more important than medicine or law. Finland admits only the top 10 percent of students to the teacher education program. Teachers come out of the five-year intensive program well prepared, allowing them to have more autonomy to teach the way they feel is most effective (Morgan 2014). The program involves a wide variety of training, including observing teachers in the classroom, practicing teaching lessons to students, as well as preparing students to become researchers and practitioners. In Korea, teachers are required to take 90 hours of professional development courses every three years to enhance their teaching. One Korean professional development program, in particular, offers an advanced certificate, which often leads to an increase in salary and sometimes a promotion (Darling-Hammond, Wei, and Andree 2010).

of education, such as social mobility or job training, also can lead to different education models.

For education reforms to be successful, they must be coherent with other system elements

An enormous body of research has been produced on what works in education in the decade since the last MENA education flagship report was published (World Bank 2008). A rich proliferation of high-quality experiments in education has occurred in an attempt to disentangle cause and effect. Yet, notably, reviews of what works in education still do not find consistent results (Evans and Popova 2015; Glewwe et al. 2013; Kremer, Brannen, and Glennerster 2013; McEwan 2015). Researchers are beginning to recognize that the question of "what works" is insufficient. The often-contradictory results of studies of "what works" become more informative when we ask, "When does it work?" "Why does it work?" or "What else has to happen for it to work?" Solitary education reforms, on their own, are likely to be ineffective or less effective than combinations of interventions. A few examples illustrate the importance of ensuring that reforms are coherent and coordinated and that they complement existing systems:

- Early childhood development programs have enormous potential to improve learning outcomes, but they are ineffective when program quality is low (Bouguen et al. 2013; Jung and Hasan 2014; Temple and Reynolds 2007) or when they are not available to the most at-risk populations (Karoly 2017).

- An early literacy program, when implemented by a nongovernmental organization with complementary teaching materials, had enormous effects on early literacy. When teaching materials were omitted during scale-up by the government, the intervention had insignificant effects on literacy (Kerwin and Thornton 2015).
- Simply providing technology (computers) to children—a solitary reform—has no effect on learning (Cristia et al. 2012). However, computer-assisted learning for mathematics, delivered as an after-school complement to in-school learning, improved mathematics scores (Lai, Khaddage, and Knezek 2013).
- Skills and entrepreneurship training programs, on their own, tend to be ineffective at improving labor market outcomes. However, skills and financial capital together can be an effective intervention for generating income and employment (Bausch et al. 2017; Blattman and Ralston 2015; Cho and Honorati 2014).

These studies illustrate how reforms—and education systems—need to be coherent and coordinated, so that all of the pieces work together and complement each other. A "pick-and-choose" approach, or piecemeal reform, will not work.

Reforms should vary across countries, depending on what is feasible in education, economic, or social reform

Successful reforms depend on understanding existing constraints (Rodrik 2008). For example, countries like Jordan and Lebanon face a large influx of refugees due to the conflict in the Syrian Arab Republic, so any reforms to their education systems must consider the need to accommodate refugee children in the system and the specific constraints associated with them. Another example is when coordination between the education sector and labor market is not feasible and the information necessary to provide specific, in-demand job skills is not available, the education system should focus on foundational skills. When coordination between the education sector and the labor market is feasible, more specific job skills can be a focus of education, because educators would know the skills employers need. Conditions that enable or hinder program success are a crucial aspect of successful reforms. The effectiveness of different policy options often depends on whether complementary conditions are in place. For example, school-based decision making may be less effective in disadvantaged contexts where parents are less able to participate effectively (Carr-Hill, Rolleston, and Schendel 2016).

The success of reforms also depends on how the reforms are designed, introduced, approved, and implemented

For example, Mexico's president Carlos Salinas started introducing reforms and negotiating with the teachers' union after his first three years in power. He also used tactful negotiations instead of confrontation, which led to successful reforms (Grindle 2004; Kingdon et al. 2014). In contrast, Tunisia's Minister of Education Néji Jalloul took on the Tunisian General Labor Union soon after taking office and approached reforms in a confrontational manner, leading to the reforms being blocked and costing him his position.

MENA has already undertaken many policy reforms within the education sector, but often with insufficient attention to how the education sector interacts with broader societal trends and incentives. The tendency of reform efforts in the region to ignore complementarities or constraints is one reason for the lack of progress in student learning. Other reasons relate to the misalignment of education investments with learning priorities, issues of pedagogy, curricula, lack of assessments and accountabilities, misaligned interests, and political and social tensions. Technology is changing how today's students are prepared to enter the future workforce—that is, it is influencing not only the ends of education but also the means. Technology can provide a unique opportunity to help education systems to be more efficient and effective. If leveraged smartly, technology can offer an opportunity for MENA countries to advance their education systems and support learning.

Education cannot do it alone, and education is everyone's responsibility

The skills acquisition process is affected by a wide variety of actors and factors, such as the private sector, civil society, the macroeconomic environment, or broader trends in technology like the Internet and social media. This is why education reform is a dynamic and complex process. Comprehensive reform beyond the education system, particularly in the labor market, will be required to address persistent shortfalls in learning outcomes. Such approaches may, for instance, address signals and incentives from the labor market in addition to implementing reform within the education sector. For these reasons, it is important to discuss and agree on reform processes and priorities both within and beyond the education sector. Ultimately, education is everyone's responsibility and requires commitment and action within and beyond the education system.

Unleashing the potential of education

MENA countries can enjoy the full benefits of education only when a push for learning is coupled with a pull for skills and a social pact for education. Specifically, MENA will realize the potential of education when (1) priority is given to learning; (2) focus is placed on the early years of schooling and learning opportunities are distributed equally, including for those affected by conflict; (3) curricula are updated and educators are empowered; (4) employers communicate their demands for skills; (5) all stakeholders agree on a common vision for education and jointly take responsibility for its outcomes and are held accountable for clearly defined roles; and (6) resources are aligned with priorities. These changes will require a joint effort to address the four tensions holding education back in the MENA countries.

Improving education is not the responsibility of educators alone; it involves all members of society—politicians, businesspeople, and community and religious leaders as well as parents, teachers, school principals, and students themselves. By far the most difficult task is dealing with varying and often opposing views, strongly held convictions, and divergent interests. But it is not impossible. Countries with high-performing education systems have succeeded in rallying support around a common vision and shared responsibility.

MENA has the history, culture, and resources to leap into a future founded on a learned society and a knowledge economy. The region has great expectations and aspirations. Unleashing the potential of education is attainable, but it will take a new pact to elevate education not only as a national priority but also as a national emergency. The question is: Are its leaders ready, and do they have the will and grit, to see through the implementation of policy reforms?

References

Bausch, Jonas, Paul Dyer, Drew Gardiner, Jochen Kluve, and Sonja Kovacevic. 2017. "The Impact of Skills Training on the Financial Behaviour, Employability, and Educational Choices of Rural Young People: Findings from a Randomized Controlled Trial in Morocco." Impact Report 6, International Labour Organization, Geneva.

Blattman, Christopher, and Laura Ralston. 2015. "Generating Employment in Poor and Fragile States: Evidence for Labor Market and Entrepreneurship Programs." Working Paper, SSRN Electronic Journal. http://dx.doi.org/10.2139/ssrn.2622220.

Bouguen, Adrien, Deon Filmer, Karen Macours, and Sophie Naudeau. 2013. "Impact Evaluation of Three Types of Early Childhood Development Interventions in Cambodia." Policy Research Working Paper 6540, World Bank, Washington, DC.

Carr-Hill, Roy, Caine Rolleston, and Rebecca Schendel. 2016. *The Effects of School-Based Decision Making on Educational Outcomes in Low- and Middle-Income Contexts: A Systematic Review.* Campbell Systematic Review 2016: 9. Oslo: Campbell Collaboration.

Cho, Yoonyoung, and Maddalena Honorati. 2014. "Entrepreneurship Programs in Developing Countries: A Meta Regression Analysis." *Labour Economics* 28: 110–30.

Cristia, Julian, Pablo Ibarraran, Santiago Cueto, Ana Santiago, and Eugenio Severin. 2012. "Technology and Child Development: Evidence from the One Laptop per Child Program." IZA Discussion Paper 6401, Institute for the Study of Labor, Bonn.

Darling-Hammond, Linda, Ruth Chung Wei, and Alethea Andree. 2010. "How High-Achieving Countries Develop Great Teachers." Research Brief, Stanford University, Stanford, CA.

Ellinger, Thomas R., and Garry M. Beckham. 1997. "South Korea: Placing Education on Top of the Family Agenda." *Phi Delta Kappan* 78 (8): 624–25.

Evans, David, and Anna Popova. 2015. "What Really Works to Improve Learning in Developing Countries? An Analysis of Divergent Findings in Systematic Reviews." Policy Research Working Paper 7203, World Bank, Washington, DC.

Glewwe, Paul, Eric A. Hanushek, Sarah Humpage, and Renato Ravina. 2013. "School Resources and Educational Outcomes in Developing Countries: A Review of the Literature from 1990 to 2010." In *Education Policy in Developing Countries*, edited by Paul Glewwe, 13–64. Chicago: University of Chicago Press.

Grindle, Merilee S. 2004. "Good Enough Governance: Poverty Reduction and Reform in Developing Countries." *Governance: An International Journal of Policy, Administration, and Institutions* 17 (4): 525–48.

Jung, Haeil, and Amer Hasan. 2014. "The Impact of Early Childhood Education on Early Achievement Gaps: Evidence from the Indonesia Early Childhood Education and Development (ECED) Project." Policy Research Working Paper 6794, World Bank, Washington, DC.

Karoly, Lynn A. 2017. *Investing in the Early Years: The Costs and Benefits of Investing in Early Childhood in New Hampshire.* RR-1890-E. Santa Monica, CA: RAND Corporation. https://www.rand.org/pubs/research_reports/RR1890.html.

Kerwin, Jason T., and Rebecca Thornton. 2015. "Making the Grade: Understanding What Works for Teaching Literacy in Rural Uganda." PSC Research Report 15-842. Population Studies Center, Institute for Social Research, University of Michigan.

Kingdon, Geeta Gandhi, Angela Little, Monazza Aslam, Shenila Rawal, Terry Moe, Harry Patrinos, Tara Beteille, Rukmini Banerji, Brent Parton, and Shailendra K. Sharma. 2014. *A Rigorous Review of the Political Economy of Education Systems in Developing Countries.* Education Rigorous Literature Review. London: Department for International Development.

Kremer, Michael, Conner Brannen, and Rachel Glennerster. 2013. "The Challenge of Education and Learning in the Developing World." *Science* 340 (6130): 297–300.

Lai, Kwok-Wing, Ferial Khaddage, and Gerald Knezek. 2013. "Blending Student Technology Experiences in Formal and Informal Learning." *Journal of Computer Assisted Learning* 29 (5): 414–25.

McEwan, Patrick J. 2015. "Improving Learning in Primary Schools of Developing Countries: A Meta-Analysis of Randomized Experiments." *Review of Educational Research* 85 (3): 353–94.

Morgan, Hani. 2014. "The Education System in Finland: A Success Story Other Countries Can Emulate." *Childhood Education* 90 (6): 453–57.

———. 2016. "Lessons from the World's Most Successful Nations in International Testing." *Multicultural Education* 24 (1): 56–60.

Rodrik, Dani. 2008. "Second-Best Institutions." *American Economic Review* 98 (2): 100–04.

Temple, Judy A., and Arthur J. Reynolds. 2007. "Benefits and Costs of Investments in Preschool Education: Evidence from the Child-Parent Centers and Related Programs." *Economics of Education Review* 26 (1): 126–44.

World Bank. 2008. *The Road Not Traveled: Education Reform in the Middle East and North Africa.* MENA Development Report. Washington, DC: World Bank.

Appendix: Overview of MENA Policy Recommendations

TABLE A.1 Overview of MENA policy recommendations

Challenges	Policy directions	Examples	Responsible actors
Chapter 3: Securing learning for children in conflict and crisis			
Remove barriers to education			
Children in or near conflict zones face safety issues preventing them from accessing education services. Refugee children have reported bullying and security incidents on their way to school. Additional concerns stem from children having to travel long distances to reach the nearest school.	Provide safe, free transportation to school through security escorts or shuttle buses. Where feasible and appropriate, pilot innovative education technology (EdTech) solutions and mobile learning kits for remote learning in areas where formal education services are not accessible.	The governments of Iraq, Jordan, and Turkey have cooperated with the International Organization for Migration, which operates school buses transporting Syrian refugee children to school and catch-up classes.	Ministry of education, in cooperation with local nongovernmental organizations (NGOs) and international organizations, undertakes needs assessments and targets vulnerable communities, where parents are inclined to keep children at home due to safety concerns.
A substantial share of children who are refugees or internally displaced persons (IDPs) do not attend school because of the cost associated with school attendance.	Eliminate school fees and provide textbooks and learning materials free of charge.	Lebanon abolished enrollment fees and provides free textbooks for *all* children attending public schools. The German Academic Exchange Service and other institutions provide scholarships to Syrian refugees living in the Middle East and North Africa (MENA) region.	Ministry of education and ministry of finance, with support from the international donor community, develop a multiyear budget that includes schooling for refugees and vulnerable host communities.
Destroyed school infrastructure and the arrival of large numbers of IDPs and refugees have led to overcrowded schools in conflict countries and host communities.	Operate double-shift schools, supplement public education with nonformal education services, and repair or rebuild school infrastructure in areas where conflict has subsided.	Lebanon operates 346 double-shift schools, with most refugee children attending the second shift. About 17,600 school-age refugees in Jordan are enrolled in nonformal education services offered by international organizations and local NGOs.	Ministry of education assesses and maps demand for education services, expands the teacher workforce, and enhances the capacity of the public education system.

table continues next page

TABLE A.1 Overview of MENA policy recommendations *(continued)*

Challenges	Policy directions	Examples	Responsible actors
Chapter 3: Securing learning for children in conflict and crisis *(continued)*			
Remove barriers to education *(continued)*			
The lack of credentials from previous education slows the enrollment process for refugees and IDPs and often makes it impossible for them to pursue a tertiary education.	Relax administrative enrollment requirements for refugees and IDPs who do not have documentation of their educational achievements. Establish tests to determine the appropriate education level and procedures to determine equivalency of previously obtained degrees with local certification requirements.	The European Qualifications Passport for Refugees provides refugees with an official document listing their degrees, language competencies, and other credentials relevant for pursuing further education or employment.	Ministry of education reduces administrative enrollment requirements for refugees and coordinates with private tertiary education providers to facilitate access.
Improve the learning experience of displaced children			
Refugee children are confronted with unfamiliar languages of instruction and curricula (for example, instruction in English or French in Lebanon and Turkish in Turkey); internally displaced children can be affected by a change in dialect or language as well (for example, Arabic- and Kurdish-speaking children in Iraq).	Offer language classes to familiarize displaced children with a new language of instruction. Teach displaced children in their native language, where appropriate and politically feasible. Use host community curriculum in protracted conflicts so that children have a better chance of eventually being integrated into the local labor market.	Many governments, international organizations, and local NGOs provide specialized language support for refugee children such as extra hours of instruction in the afternoon (for example, in Germany and Turkey). Djibouti mandates the use of Djiboutian curriculum but allows instruction for refugees to take place in English.	Ministry of education ensures that language of instruction does not create a prohibitive barrier for refugees' learning process and adapts curricula to be conflict sensitive where appropriate.
Refugee and internally displaced children who have fled war and destruction have experienced trauma that can inhibit their learning.	Provide psychosocial support such as arts and music therapy in public schools and create safe learning and play spaces in camps and at NGO sites.	NGOs like Save the Children implement programs such as Healing and Education through Arts (Jordan). Lebanon is training teachers and school counselors in psychosocial support and conflict-sensitive classroom management.	Ministry of education trains teachers or deploys counselors to provide psychosocial support. NGOs integrate psychosocial support in nonformal education.
Children who have missed out on years of schooling need remedial education and accelerated learning programs (ALPs) to catch up and keep up with the material covered in school.	Offer remedial education and support services for children who have trouble following the regular class content. Provide ALPs for children who have missed out on years of schooling to bridge the gap and provide a pathway to the formal education system.	United Nations Children's Fund (UNICEF) and others provide remedial education in nonformal education centers throughout MENA. Lebanon offers an ALP that condenses the national curriculum and delivers it in Arabic for refugee children.	Ministry of education, international organizations, and local NGOs coordinate remedial education services and establish a clear pathway to formal education.
Strengthen resilience at the systems level			
Unpredictability in the amount of external funding makes education sector planning exceedingly difficult in protracted crises and can destabilize the entire education system.	In emergencies provide education sector funding that is adequate, timely, predictable, and not earmarked. Make funding available in the first half of the calendar year for planning and implementation during the following academic year.	Multiyear funding commitments and transparent reporting of donors are expected at the annual Brussels Conference, where donors gather to debate the status of access to and quality of education for Syrian refugees and support for host communities.	Donor community coordinates with host countries and establishes mechanisms for transparent and regular reporting, timely transfer of pledged funds, and multiyear commitments.

table continues next page

TABLE A.1 Overview of MENA policy recommendations (continued)

Challenges	Policy directions	Examples	Responsible actors
Chapter 5: Establishing a foundation for lifelong learning			
Intervene early for biggest impact			
Early learning interventions have some of the highest returns on investment for individuals and societies. However, many countries fail to prioritize universal access to preschool and cognitive development during the early years. As a result, children do not arrive in school ready to learn.	Place early learning and development of key foundational skills at the top of the national productivity and growth agenda. Expand access to high-quality preschool programs. Target resources toward the most vulnerable children to ensure that no one is left behind during this critical period for the development of key foundational skills.	The United Arab Emirates has placed great emphasis on increasing preschool coverage as part of its Vision 2021 national agenda. The country is on track to achieve the target of 95 percent early childhood education (ECE) coverage in public and private preschools by 2021.	Ministry of education explicitly sets universal early learning as a priority and ensures that it is reflected in the budget. Ministry of finance adequately funds early learning programs, especially those targeting poor children.
Universalize preschool education			
Most MENA children do not have access to quality ECE programs. The preprimary gross enrollment ratio for 3- to 5-year-olds in MENA was just 31 percent in 2016 compared with a global average of 49 percent. MENA ranked below every other region except South Asia. Preprimary enrollment ratios are particularly low in Djibouti, the Arab Republic of Egypt, Saudi Arabia, the Syrian Arab Republic, and the Republic of Yemen.	Accelerate expansion of access to high-quality preprimary education, which will require (1) reallocating financial resources to the early years, (2) training early childhood educators, (3) refurbishing existing spaces, and (4) constructing new spaces.	Starting in 1993, Argentina began implementing a wide-reaching national program to expand compulsory preprimary education, which was shown to have significant positive impacts on students' learning outcomes lasting into grade 3. Algeria and the United Arab Emirates are good examples of effective ECE expansions in the MENA region.	Ministry of education organizes increased provision of high-quality preschool education, designs incentives for private providers to expand access for the most vulnerable, and informs parents about the benefits of ECE. Ministry of finance prioritizes funding from the public budget for increasing the public provision of high-quality preschool education and financial incentives for private providers.
Build strong foundational skills in the early years			
After two or three years of schooling, many MENA students cannot read. More than one in three children in grade 2 in Iraq, Morocco, and the Republic of Yemen could not read a single word of connected text on the 2011/2012 Early Grade Reading Assessment (EGRA), indicating that the early grades are not as effective as they might be in teaching children to read.	Improve readiness to learn before school and ensure that, once in school, children are gaining age-appropriate literacy and numeracy skills. Pilot early grade learning interventions to boost the foundational skills of literacy and numeracy in the early grades and scale up successful ones.	In Jordan, daily time is allocated for low-performing students to practice foundational skills in reading and mathematics. England's literacy screening checks highlight the importance of assessing and monitoring students' early acquisition of skills to identify weaknesses and target additional support to students in need.	Ministry of education, university faculties of education, school leaders, teachers, and parents develop and implement effective foundational learning programs during the early grades.

table continues next page

TABLE A.1 **Overview of MENA policy recommendations** *(continued)*

Challenges	Policy directions	Examples	Responsible actors
Chapter 6: Ensuring inclusive and equitable learning			
Remove barriers to access			
Primary completion is universal, but completion of upper-secondary education and transition to university (and good jobs in the labor market) are limited to children and youths from more advantaged households (for example, in Egypt, Jordan, and Tunisia).	Equalize access to education—at all levels—across the MENA region. Focus more resources on children and youths from the poorest households, as they are the most likely to be excluded. Offset private spending on education, because it reinforces inequality of opportunity.	Countries such as Canada, Estonia, Finland, and Japan have high levels of academic performance alongside low levels of inequality in access and learning. In these countries, the link between test scores and socioeconomic status is generally weak.	Ministry of education sets universal secondary education enrollment ratios and learning as top priorities, ensuring that resources are allocated toward achieving these goals.
Recognize and address learning gaps by supporting the lowest-performing students and schools			
Among MENA's 15-year-olds, the economic, social, and cultural status of their families is strongly correlated with their learning achievement, as demonstrated by the Programme for International Student Assessment (PISA) 2015 results. Based on these data, Lebanon shows the greatest gap in learning achievement by socioeconomic status—one that equates to a difference of more than two full years of schooling.	Monitor the proportion of children not reaching expected levels of learning and provide support to those students and schools achieving below expectations.	Between the Trends in International Mathematics and Science Study (TIMSS) 2011 and 2015, Bahrain, Oman, and Qatar made substantial advances among the lowest-scoring mathematics students; Oman and Qatar also made substantial advances in science.	Ministry of education uses large-scale, system-level student assessments to monitor learning gaps and provides additional support to identified areas of need. Ministry of finance prioritizes these efforts.
Target resources to in-need geographic regions			
Significant inequalities exist in education by socioeconomic and geographic circumstances across MENA. Students from urban areas in Morocco and Saudi Arabia receive higher-quality education than students from rural areas; in Lebanon, PISA 2015 scores show a two-year gap in science literacy between national quarters of the PISA index of economic, social, and cultural status.	Monitor gaps in student achievement by socioeconomic and geographic circumstances. Identify areas of need and devote additional resources to the lowest-performing students and schools.	High-performing countries monitor school outcomes and intervene when necessary by providing required resources.	Ministry of education organizes and ministry of finance prioritizes initiatives such as designing and implementing suitable data systems and monitoring processes and supervising ongoing implementation and evaluation.

table continues next page

TABLE A.1 Overview of MENA policy recommendations *(continued)*

Challenges	Policy directions	Examples	Responsible actors
Chapter 6: Ensuring inclusive and equitable learning *(continued)*			
Improve the quality of boys' education and address MENA's gender paradox			
Substantial inequalities exist in the quality of education between all-boys and all-girls schools in many MENA countries. Student assessments indicate that systems are not working for boys in many MENA countries. For example, in TIMSS 2015, the seven countries with the largest gender gaps in grade 8 science—Bahrain, Jordan, Kuwait, Oman, Qatar, Saudi Arabia, and the United Arab Emirates— were all in MENA, and achievement favored girls.	Improve the training of teachers and principals—particularly those in underperforming schools, which are often all-boys schools in the region—to equip them with a range of effective student-centered teaching and classroom management techniques, including setting high expectations for all students. Identify top-performing teachers and leaders from all-boys schools and raise their voices to allow others to learn from them.	Between 2011 and 2014, Oman undertook a study, "The Male Dilemma," to understand the factors contributing to differences in academic performance between boys and girls.	Ministry of education strengthens teacher recruitment and training for all-boys schools. School leaders organize teacher training.
Increase resources for special needs to reduce inequality			
Suitable interventions for students with specific learning difficulties and special educational needs are lacking in MENA.	Embed systems of early detection of learning difficulties and special education needs in schools. Pilot and scale up interventions to improve the quality of education service provision for students with special needs.	Jordan and Tunisia have declared their commitment to provide education services for children with special needs, and Tunisia has also adopted measures to integrate children with minor disabilities into regular schools. Finnish teachers are trained to identify students who are slipping behind, and a teacher is dedicated to those students.	Ministry of education declares commitment to services for children with special needs and puts in place policies to identify and support students in need of additional support. School leaders and teacher trainers ensure that teachers are aware of the need for early detection of learning difficulties and understand the new policies on how to address these needs.
Chapter 7: Modernizing curricula, instruction, and assessment to improve learning			
Modernize curricula to meet students' needs			
Across MENA, curricula are focused on learning facts to gain knowledge, leaving little room for students to think creatively, engage in cooperative experiences, or apply understanding to real-life situations. Competencies such as flexibility, teamwork, and problem solving are essential for success in future labor markets.	Update and modernize curricula to promote the development of 21st-century skills; in particular, (1) move from memorization to higher-order skills and a broader range of competencies, (2) align curricula with children's need to develop lifelong skills, and (3) allow sufficient time for effective learning.	In Oman, recent curricular reforms aim to (1) introduce new subjects, (2) limit the amount of theoretical content, (3) make learning more meaningful by relating content to students' practical world, and (4) reduce the emphasis on memorization.	Ministry of education and curricula developers review curricula. University faculties of education ensure strong links between the curricula and teacher education.

table continues next page

TABLE A.1 Overview of MENA policy recommendations *(continued)*

Challenges	Policy directions	Examples	Responsible actors
Chapter 7: Modernizing curricula, instruction, and assessment to improve learning *(continued)*			
Encourage instructional practices that maximize children's potential			
Across the region, pedagogical methods (how the curriculum is delivered) emphasize rote memorization and low-level skills over critical thinking skills, resulting in low learning outcomes.	Align instructional practices with learning goals by improving teacher training so that teachers use instructional practices that maximize children's potential, starting with policies that encourage student-centered instructional methods, paying attention to individual learning, and employing structured pedagogy, such as lesson plans and scripted lessons, particularly where teacher capacity is low. Provide teachers with useful and high-quality resources. Attract and retain the best teachers and amplify their influence as mentors.	Finland improved education by implementing long-term policies on excellence in teaching, including attracting and retaining a high-quality teaching workforce and training teachers to examine their own practices systematically. Kuwait is embarking on systemwide reforms concentrating on student-focused classroom practices.	Ministry of education sets standards for initial teacher education and monitors quality. University faculties of education review curricula and teaching methods to ensure new teachers have these skills. Teacher training providers review their curricula to ensure that teachers are continuing to develop these skills. Ministry of education purchases or develops high-quality materials to support teachers in providing instructional practices that maximize children's potential.
Provide classroom environments conducive to learning			
The intended curriculum is often not implemented in MENA countries due to inadequate resources, including insufficient teachers, teaching and learning materials, and school infrastructure.	Allow enough time (in the year) for effective learning and avoid multishift school days, wherever possible. Provide sufficient teachers and teaching and learning materials to all schools and students.	Oman and Saudi Arabia have recently moved to increase instructional time, although instructional time is still low by international comparison.	Ministry of finance prioritizes adequate budgets for conducive classroom environments. Ministry of education monitors classroom environments and targets resources where needed. School leaders are trained and incentivized to improve their schools' environments.
Use assessment methods to adapt instruction and promote higher-order skills			
Although MENA's teachers regularly assess students, classroom assessments are not always used to identify misunderstandings or adapt instruction to students' learning needs. For example, only one in four teachers in Jordan reported using classroom assessments to inform lesson planning.	Build the capacity of teachers to develop and use formative and task-based assessments so that they can (1) determine students' prior learning achievement, (2) assess acquisition of cognitive and noncognitive (including socioemotional) skills, and (3) adapt pedagogical strategies to students' needs.	Lebanon has conducted some small-scale studies to explore using task-based assessments (rather than intelligence quotient tests) to identify students for gifted education programs. In Oman, examination grades incorporate scores from classroom-based assessment tasks.	Ministry of education, teacher training institutes, university faculties of education, and others responsible for initial and practicing teachers improve teachers' skills in using assessments for learning.

table continues next page

TABLE A.1 Overview of MENA policy recommendations *(continued)*

Challenges	Policy directions	Examples	Responsible actors
Chapter 7: Modernizing curricula, instruction, and assessment to improve learning *(continued)*			
Use assessment methods to adapt instruction and promote higher-order skills *(continued)*			
High-stakes examinations, such as the *Tawjihi* in Jordan and West Bank and Gaza or the *Thanaweya Amma* in Egypt, overemphasize rote recall and reinforce the acquisition of credentials over skills.	Replace high-stakes examination systems that contribute to cramming and private tutoring with other forms of assessment. Focus on classroom assessments that are aligned with intended student learning outcomes and test skills beyond low-level factual recall.	Jordan, Kuwait, and Lebanon have abolished high-stakes examinations that ration progress between grades 1 and 3. The Republic of Korea has an "exam-free semester" for lower-secondary students. In 2019, Japan will implement a university entrance examination that deemphasizes rote memorization, while prioritizing students' thinking, expression, and reasoning skills.	Ministry of education reforms examination systems.
MENA countries are increasingly participating in large-scale, system-level student assessments, but few are using the results to inform education decision making. For example, in 2015 Saudi Arabia developed a national assessment program that has been applied every year, although results are yet to be released to the public.	Use large-scale, system-level student assessments to inform education policy decisions by making results available to the public and making data sets available to researchers.	Jordan shares the results of its national assessment with the public, allowing education stakeholders the opportunity to respond to the status quo and participate in efforts to make improvements.	Ministry of education and related agencies publish the results of large-scale, system-level student assessments and make databases available to researchers.
Chapter 8: Leveraging education technology			
Ensure that investments in technology respond to the changing nature of work and leverage technology as a delivery catalyst			
Several countries have made large investments in information and communication technology (ICT), with little impact to date. Technology investments in the education sector are often in the shape of one-off, boutique interventions. Skills that technology can replace are fading in demand, but skills that complement technology are becoming highly valued.	Take a holistic approach to investing in technology that recognizes the demand-shaping role of technology and leverages it as a catalyst for service delivery. Make investments that shape demand by building skills that are critical for the future of work and begin focusing on equipping youths with the skills that are relevant for the digital economy rather than with credentials. Make investments that catalyze the delivery of education more efficiently. Couple technology interventions with a renewed focus on empowering teachers and school leaders and innovating pedagogical and assessment practices. Harness the power of technologies to support and steer teachers in their classroom practices; for example, through online training, connections to other teachers, and rapid provision of support materials and lesson plans.	AWS Educate builds cloud computing skills for the future workforce. Similarly, Microsoft launched the One Million Arab Coders initiative that offers an intensive curriculum to prepare Arab coders to develop solutions on the cloud, while Code.org mainstreams computer science education in schools by providing curriculum for K–12 computer science. Egypt has undertaken ambitious reforms to leverage technology for delivering student assessments and assisting classroom learning practices. The Egypt Knowledge Bank hosts digital learning assets for a wide range of curriculum competencies, while the grade 10 exams are in the process of being moved from paper to computer. Digital platforms and libraries can expand access to state-of-the-art knowledge and online learning. Platforms like Edraak and Nafham have immense potential when delivered to students through structured online and in-class settings in which teachers are trained to facilitate this interaction.	Ministry of education supports the notion that ICTs are accepted tools of the future for teaching and learning, helps to build the core capacities of teachers to use ICT tools in their classrooms, supports the development of ICT infrastructure (both hardware and software), establishes academic, curricular, and use standards for ICT in schools, and works closely with the private sector in developing and implementing appropriate course content.

table continues next page

TABLE A.1 **Overview of MENA policy recommendations** *(continued)*

Challenges	Policy directions	Examples	Responsible actors
Chapter 9: Empowering teachers to lead the way to better student learning			
Recruit the best and prepare them to be effective teachers			
In some cases, the policy and process for selecting new teachers are inadequate. Where teacher selection processes exist, their requirements are sometimes not sufficiently stringent to ensure that new teachers have the necessary competencies to enter the profession (for example, in Lebanon and Saudi Arabia). In countries with stringent requirements for the teacher selection process, implementation can be challenging (for example, in Kuwait and Morocco).	Establish a policy and regulations to attract the best candidates to teacher education programs in higher education and establish rigorous teacher selection processes for assigning teaching positions. Include requirements such as high levels of educational attainment (at least a bachelor's degree), a minimum amount of previous practical experience, and passing grades in subject-knowledge and pedagogical assessments, conduct interviews to assess skills and motivations, and update requirements according to emerging needs, among others. Strengthen the capacity of the ministry of education to coordinate and manage selection processes and teacher licensure programs.	In Finland, only 10 percent of applicants will gain acceptance to teacher education programs. Initial selection is based entirely on a written test drawn from six wide-ranging academic and professional articles that students study in advance. In Morocco, teacher candidates must have a three-year bachelor's program, pass a written test, and interview to enter the Teacher Certification Center, where they study pedagogy for one additional year. In the United States, licensure requirements may include having a minimum education level, passing a state licensure exam, and having teaching experience. Teachers must renew their license every few years.	Ministry of education and higher education, ministry of civil services, universities, and other legislative branches establish an enabling framework for transparent and functional teacher selection and assignment processes. Human resources unit within ministry of education organizes a national selection process with support from regional and local governments and schools, when possible. Ministry of finance allocates resources for selection process.
Strengthen continuous professional support to teachers			
The first year of teaching is the most challenging, but first-year teachers receive little support. The number of teachers with appropriate subject-matter knowledge is insufficient. Where in-service training programs exist but the methodology is traditional, a one-off workshop may be needed, rather than continuous professional development and support programs embedded in schools (for example, in Morocco and many Gulf Cooperation Council [GCC] countries). Many countries do not link professional development with career advancement, reducing the incentives for meaningful teacher engagement and limiting the opportunities to identify and promote teachers with the greatest ability.	Develop teacher induction programs focusing on classroom practices and teaching skills. Introduce a minimum amount of professional development, with a focus on improved pedagogical practices and subject knowledge, and link professional development with career improvement opportunities. Introduce collaborative professional development models such as teacher research groups and teacher networks in schools and across schools, with emphasis on mentoring and coaching by more experienced teachers and sharing of good practices. Continue to experiment with collaborative and other innovative models and to monitor, evaluate, and scale up lessons from pilots.	Oman's induction program involves three two-week courses focused on teaching practices and policies as well as the curriculum. Egypt, Lebanon, Qatar, and Tunisia have professional development policies in place that focus on improved pedagogical practices. Egypt's Teachers First program provides continued mentorship and coaching and fosters participation in communities of practice. In Shanghai, research groups at all school levels meet two to three hours every week to discuss curriculum and best practices.	Ministry of education develops the model and creates an enabling environment. Ministry of finance provides seed funding, and school leaders build time into teachers' workday for capacity building and piloting. School leaders and teachers are in charge of their own professional development and actively link with other schools.

table continues next page

TABLE A.1 Overview of MENA policy recommendations *(continued)*

Challenges	Policy directions	Examples	Responsible actors
Chapter 9: Empowering teachers to lead the way to better student learning *(continued)*			
Use teacher assessment to strengthen support and accountability			
Teaching standards and mechanisms to monitor and assess teachers are lacking (for example, in the Republic of Yemen). Existing teaching standards and oversight mechanisms focus on compliance with administrative tasks instead of practices to improve learning (for example, in Djibouti, Lebanon, and West Bank and Gaza). Where teacher assessments exist, results are not used effectively to improve classroom practice and participate in professional development opportunities. Consequences of evaluations are also unclear (for example in Egypt, Jordan, and Tunisia).	Establish and update teaching standards to be adequately aligned with the curriculum; introduce supervisory mechanisms to monitor teachers' attendance and compliance with teaching standards; develop a supervisory body within the ministry of education capable of visiting schools periodically. Introduce teacher assessments, including several methods, such as evaluations of both subject knowledge and pedagogical practice, as well as classroom observations, the principal's assessment, and parents' and students' assessments. Incorporate several instruments in teacher assessments, including classroom observations, evaluations of subject knowledge and pedagogical practices, lesson planning capacity, student learning results, assessments by principals and peers, and inputs by parents and students, and link results of teacher assessments with classroom practice and professional development.	Morocco has established an inspection force that visits schools every three years. Egyptian schools evaluate teachers at least twice a year. Both internal and external examinations are informed by the principal's individual assessment and classroom observation. Principals in Ontario, Canada, conduct a teacher appraisal program twice a year based on competency statements. Classroom observations are used to assess teachers.	Ministry of education develops a supervisory body, designs and applies teacher evaluations based on international evidence, and, with the support of state and local governments, helps schools to oversee teacher performance and to conduct regular evaluations. Empowered school leaders communicate with the ministry of education regarding teachers. Regional and local governments along with school leaders collaborate on teacher assessments and foster transparency.
Provide meaningful incentives to motivate and reward teachers			
Lack of incentives for qualified teachers serving vulnerable populations makes it difficult to place teachers where they are needed most. The failure to sanction low-performing teachers can lead to a loss of learning opportunities for students.	Introduce incentives for teachers who teach in rural and isolated areas or who teach critical subjects with a shortage of teachers. Provide well-chosen professional incentives, rather than financial incentives, to support improved teaching. Improve the design and implementation of incentives that reward behaviors that teachers can change. Link career advancement to the results of teacher assessments and performance in the classroom.	Qatar is considering career pathways to motivate teachers to perform. Australia, Canada, and Singapore have career ladders that reward teachers' knowledge and skills. Chronically underperforming teachers are not allowed to continue teaching.	Ministry of education defines the teachers' career ladder and assesses and revises incentives already in place. It identifies teachers who serve in vulnerable areas and teach critical subjects and designs incentives accordingly. Ministry of finance budgets incentives in line with teacher workforce and projects salary expenditures. Local governments, school leaders, education NGOs, and the private sector offer nonmonetary incentives (for example, teaching awards and enhanced professional development opportunities).

table continues next page

TABLE A.1 **Overview of MENA policy recommendations** *(continued)*

Challenges	Policy directions	Examples	Responsible actors
Chapter 10: Developing effective school leadership			
Transform the role of the school principal from administrator to instructional leader			
School principals in most MENA countries hold purely administrative roles, with few instructional responsibilities. Where principals are expected to provide instructional leadership, they often lack guidance or an adequate support system (for example, in Jordan).	Support the shift to instructional leadership, formally give principals an instructional leadership mandate, provide them with appropriate training and mentoring, and train supervisors to address learning issues. Support distributed leadership models and deconceptualize the supervisor's role to provide support for principals in instructional leadership.	Kuwait's School Leadership Program supported pilot schools with greater autonomy and participatory and team-based approaches for planning. New Zealand supports collaborative instructional leadership for principals. Singapore supports collaborative school leadership that enables subject-specific instructional feedback.	Ministry of education creates training support, establishes technical support for school restructuring, and provides reskilling opportunities for supervisors to support principals. Higher education and training institutions create professional development curriculum to support instructional leadership. Ministry of finance supports pilot experiences with devolved budget responsibilities.
Modernize criteria and processes to select new school leaders			
In some cases, selection processes for principals are not transparent, and principals have low education levels (for example, in the Islamic Republic of Iran). Where clear teacher selection processes exist, criteria are often limited to academic qualifications and teaching experience (for example, in Bahrain, Jordan, and Oman). Where selection processes are transparent, they often require a postgraduate education degree, but are often highly centralized processes (for example, in Egypt and Qatar).	Establish criteria for merit-based hiring of principals, increase minimum experience requirements, and develop specialized leadership training programs. Establish multiple criteria for principals, including management experience and expertise. Develop a pool of candidates through talent management. Create a certification process as part of preparing and selecting principals. Build the capacity of district education offices to take the lead in selecting principals. Establish supervised internship and induction programs as an extension to the selection process.	Egypt has created rigorous professional requirements for school principals. Kuwait, Qatar, and Saudi Arabia have created professional development programs for principals. Qatar and the United Arab Emirates require an educational leadership license for principals. Shanghai requires candidates to have a school principal eligibility certificate and provides prior training in leadership and management skills. Shanghai also supports the district education office in selecting principals based on fit with the needs of individual schools. The process includes training in leadership and management.	Ministry of education develops merit-based recruitment, selection, and certification requirements and provides internship and induction programs and capacity building for district offices. Higher education and training institutions create leadership training and management skills programs.
Empower school leaders with professional development and rewarding career pathways			
In some cases, there is little or no professional development for school principals (for example, in Djibouti and Morocco). Often, limited career pathways prevent the emergence of school leadership as a professional option attracting high-caliber personnel (for example, in Lebanon and Tunisia). Where strong school leadership programs are implemented, evaluation of pilots for system scaling up and support is limited (for example, in Egypt and some GCC countries).	Establish prior leadership training for principals and provide continuous in-service professional development, with regular evaluation of training effectiveness. Initiate the process of developing career pathways for school leaders and link career pathways to systemwide goals and priorities. Provide technical support for collaborative school leadership, pilot greater autonomy for teacher selection and management, and establish multifaceted training programs for school leaders.	Egypt has created rigorous professional requirements for school principals. New Zealand has a centrally funded leadership support training program targeted to the needs of individual schools. Kuwait, Qatar, and Saudi Arabia are developing career pathways for school leaders. Shanghai rotates high-performing school leaders to low-performing schools with incentives for career advancement.	Higher education and training institutions create professional development curricula that also support career pathways. Ministry of education creates enabling environment. Ministry of finance develops procedures for increased budget autonomy at the school level.

table continues next page

TABLE A.1 Overview of MENA policy recommendations *(continued)*

Challenges	Policy directions	Examples	Responsible actors
Chapter 10: Developing effective school leadership *(continued)*			
Provide school leaders with more authority to support teaching and learning			
In almost all MENA countries, school principals have limited autonomy to manage human and financial resources and have insufficient authority in making instructional and other decisions. Often, school principals have limited capacity to implement more school-based management.	Grant school principals more autonomy to make instructional and administrative decisions suitable for improving teaching and learning in their schools. Build capacity for school leaders to exercise more autonomy and accountability to improve learning.	Qatar's independent school model created mechanisms for school autonomy and accountability and demonstrated the potential of a results-based approach (but failed to account sufficiently for pushback linked to the change process). Lebanon, Qatar, and the United Arab Emirates give principals a similar level of responsibility for school governance as Organisation for Economic Co-operation and Development (OECD) countries do and have had good results on mathematics performance.	Ministry of education works with other relevant authorities to develop policies. It designs implementation and creates training and other capacity development support.
Chapter 11: Prioritizing investments to promote learning and skills			
Invest sufficient public resources in education			
In some countries, public education investment is insufficient to meet the basic learning needs of large numbers of children (for example, in Lebanon). Where public education investment is sufficient to get most children enrolled in school, gaps in coverage and learning opportunities remain among vulnerable groups (for example, in Jordan). In other countries, public education investment is adequate, but inefficiencies remain (for example, in many GCC countries).	Allocate a sufficient share of the national public budget to education to ensure minimum basic learning conditions for all children. Target additional resources to address the needs of underperforming students and vulnerable populations. In addition to ensuring adequate public spending, crowd in private investment for education (where possible), while addressing equity concerns that can arise from regressive private spending.	Saudi Arabia's massive scale-up of public spending on education between the 1970s and 1990s led 4.6 million more children to be enrolled in school by 2005 compared to 1979. Tunisia's Social Action Program and Morocco's Urgency Program are two examples of targeted interventions that identify students at risk of dropping out and provide additional pedagogical and psychosocial support to help them to remain in school. In MENA, private spending on education is common but is often regressive; education authorities in Dubai, United Arab Emirates, aim to minimize this negative impact by capping private school fees and linking the fee levels that private schools can charge with performance.	Ministry of finance allocates adequate funding to ensure basic learning conditions for all children. Ministry of education and local authorities use scarce resources efficiently to enroll all children and work with other relevant actors to develop and implement regulations governing private financing and private provision of education. Ministry of education, ministry of finance, and ministry of social policy work together to ensure that social programs are well designed, are adequately funded, and reach vulnerable populations.

table continues next page

TABLE A.1 **Overview of MENA policy recommendations** *(continued)*

Challenges	Policy directions	Examples	Responsible actors
Chapter 11: Prioritizing investments to promote learning and skills *(continued)*			
Allocate resources toward learning			
Public spending is skewed toward upper levels of education—especially higher education—that few children from poor households are able to reach (for example, in the Islamic Republic of Iran, Kuwait, and Lebanon). Employee compensation accounts for more than 90 percent of all recurrent education spending in some countries, crowding out investment in other important inputs (for example, in Jordan).	Prioritize public investment in early learning, building foundational skills in preschool and basic education. Ensure that nonsalary expenses are adequately budgeted and financed, allowing for timely provision of key educational inputs that contribute to learning (such as teaching and learning materials, professional development, and school rehabilitation and maintenance).	In the early 2000s, Finland and Sweden shifted substantial public expenditure toward expanding preprimary education. By 2014, they were spending 11 and 17 percent, respectively, of their public education budgets on preprimary education (more than double the share in 1999). As a result, enrollment rates rose by 33 and 20 points, respectively, to 80 percent in Finland and 96 percent in Sweden.	Ministry of education explicitly sets universal early learning as a priority and ensures that this focus is reflected in the budget. It budgets adequate amounts for nonsalary education expenses. Ministry of finance adequately funds early learning programs, especially those targeting poor children. It ensures that nonsalary education expenses are financed accordingly.
Manage the teacher workforce efficiently			
Some countries lack sufficient numbers of teachers overall or in certain subjects (such as mathematics and science in Egypt), while others face widespread teacher absenteeism (for example, in Morocco). Teachers' working hours are low by international standards (for example, in Djibouti, Jordan, Lebanon, West Bank and Gaza, and the Republic of Yemen), or insufficient time is allocated to nonteaching activities (such as professional development and collaborative activities). Class sizes and student-teacher ratios are too low in some GCC countries, while in other countries excessive numbers of teachers and nonteaching staff crowd out investment in nonsalary quality-enhancing inputs.	Ensure that teacher salaries are competitive, especially in hard-to-staff subjects like mathematics and science. Monitor teacher effort, punish absenteeism, and encourage accountability. Mandate numbers of working and teaching hours that are high enough in comparison to top-performing systems, while allowing sufficient nonteaching time for professional development, collaboration, and lesson preparation. Gradually reduce the number of excessive teaching and nonteaching staff, where feasible (for example, in densely populated areas with small class sizes) and reallocate resources to nonsalary inputs.	In North Carolina, United States, a policy of "charging" teachers US$50 per day for missing work after using a certain number of sick days was shown to decrease rates of absenteeism. Egypt and Tunisia are on par with top-performing systems like Japan, Korea, and New Zealand that require teachers to work a relatively high number of hours teaching (above 1,500 hours per year) and a relatively high number of hours engaging in nonteaching activities. Across the OECD, the average class size is 21.3 students in primary education and 23.5 in lower-secondary education. Some top-performing systems like Singapore and Shanghai (China) opt for larger classes to free up teacher time for professional learning and self-improvement.	Ministry of education mandates the minimum number of working and teaching hours for each category of teachers and recommends minimum class sizes and ratios of teaching and nonteaching staff per student. Ministry of finance allocates adequate funding to employ enough teachers at competitive salaries. School-level authorities ensure efficient staffing and performance and allocate resources in accordance with recommended class sizes. Local and school-level authorities oversee teachers to ensure compliance and productive use of nonteaching time.

table continues next page

APPENDIX: OVERVIEW OF MENA POLICY RECOMMENDATIONS

TABLE A.1 Overview of MENA policy recommendations *(continued)*

Challenges	Policy directions	Examples	Responsible actors
Chapter 12: Strengthening skills by linking education to the labor market			
Provide more students the opportunity to gain work experience as part of their studies			
Curricula of the vocational track (at the upper-secondary level) is very theoretical, with limited practical content. Most students do not have the opportunity to gain work experience as part of their studies. The private sector is not consulted in the design of the curriculum, and there is little cooperation between the private sector and training institutions. The private sector does not see any value in providing training opportunities to students except for some ad hoc cases. Many students entering technical and vocational education and training tracks lack basic skills.	Coordinate and support dialogue between the private sector and training institutions in the form of platforms that allow exchange. Develop a strategic framework, which refers to advocacy, partnership, and coordination in relation to the objective of aligning training in critical economic sectors. Broaden public-private partnerships and ensure relevance of programs for the labor market. Strengthen and expand current efforts to put in place a quality assurance system (accreditation, standardization, and certification). Link secondary and tertiary vocational education and promote transferability. Formulate rigorous regulations and procedures for establishing and improving training programs, including updating and standardizing current regulations and procedures and assessing results of the training institutions' performance. Strengthen labor market information systems to improve outcomes and efficiency.	In Algeria, enrollment in vocational tracks is rising. The government has partnered with public and private companies to create suitable programs in construction, public works, electricity, agriculture, and tourism. In Saudi Arabia, several large private companies have developed industry-specific apprenticeship programs (ad hoc basis). Since 2011, the Tunisian Ministry of Education has been developing a reform plan, which will include restructuring its vocational education tracks. Other countries across the region have expressed an interest in making vocational education work better for students and for the labor market.	Ministry of education supports dialogue between training institutions and the private sector, adapts curriculum to match labor market needs with core elements of practical learning within the workplace, develops quality assurance mechanisms for training and accreditation mechanisms for training institutions, incentivizes the private sector, and informs the public about the benefits of apprenticeship schemes. Training institutions provide remedial education for students who lack basic skills, develop a system for matching students with companies and providing some elements of career guidance, and train teachers in the support of students while on practical training. Private sector representatives communicate skills needs and take on students to be trained within the company.
Chapter 13: Rethinking tertiary education: High-level skills and research			
Elaborate a vision that aligns tertiary education with skills and research for the future			
Many MENA tertiary education systems face an acute tension between the need to cope with fast-growing enrollments, while maintaining the quality and relevance of program offerings.	Produce a comprehensive vision and strategic plan for tertiary education development and reform to improve the quality and relevance of the tertiary system. Following international experience, adopt a reform process including the following four steps: (1) elaborate a comprehensive vision for the future, (2) define a set of interventions constituting the country's strategic plan, (3) launch the plan after adequate consensus building, and (4) consider factors of sustainability.	The California Higher Education Master Plan set the scene and the parameters for balanced growth and development of tertiary education in that state. China and New Zealand have elaborated long-term visions for development of their tertiary education systems.	Ministry of higher education, in close consultation with principal stakeholders (students, academics, university leaders, employers, and civil society), develops a comprehensive vision for the future development of the system, including defining the future size and shape of the system.

table continues next page

TABLE A.1 Overview of MENA policy recommendations *(continued)*

Challenges	Policy directions	Examples	Responsible actors
Chapter 13: Rethinking tertiary education: High-level skills and research *(continued)*			
Modernize governance for greater accountability			
Many tertiary education systems in MENA are constrained by centralized approaches. Lacking institutional autonomy, universities and other tertiary education institutions in the region do not have the flexibility needed to manage the rapid growth of enrollment and maintain high standards of quality and relevance.	Grant institutional autonomy to universities, which would allow them to manage their resources—human and financial—with more flexibility in order to strengthen performance.	Morocco and Saudi Arabia recently granted greater autonomy to their public universities, following the examples of Denmark and Finland, two countries that substantially improved the governance of their public universities in the past decade, allowing for more flexible management in all aspects (academic, organizational, human resources, and financial resources).	Ministry of higher education introduces the proper legal and regulatory changes needed to grant institutional autonomy. Greater autonomy goes hand in hand with greater accountability through appropriate means (accreditation, student engagement surveys, financial audits, and labor market information).
Put in place a sustainable financing model for long-term prosperity			
Lack of sufficient financial resources has been one of the main challenges facing universities in the MENA region. This lack of resources makes it extremely difficult to accommodate the rapidly growing demand for tertiary education, while improving or even only maintaining the quality and relevance of tertiary education programs.	Address the following questions about financial needs, funding sources, and resource allocation: *Strategic decisions that influence medium- and long-term financing needs.* What institutional configuration would allow for a balanced and affordable tertiary education system? What should be the balance of government support for public universities, short-duration institutions (community colleges or technical institutes), online education, and private institutions? *Resource mobilization options.* How can public and private funding sources be mobilized in the most effective manner? How can MENA governments rely on efficient and equitable student aid mechanisms (scholarships and loans) to maintain equality of opportunities? *Resource allocation approaches.* What performance-based mechanisms are appropriate for distributing public resources in a manner that encourages innovation and rewards good results?	Jordan and Lebanon have allowed private institutions to absorb a substantial share of enrollment, reducing pressure on the public budget. With its two open universities, Thailand has shown how online education can offer good educational opportunities to a large share of the student population. Denmark and the Netherlands rely on an objective and transparent funding formula to allocate public resources. Denmark also uses performance contracts to encourage innovation.	In each MENA country, ministry of finance and ministry of higher education work together to mobilize public resources, promote the development of private and online education, and design funding allocation mechanisms that encourage innovation and reward performance.

table continues next page

TABLE A.1 Overview of MENA policy recommendations *(continued)*

Challenges	Policy directions	Examples	Responsible actors
Chapter 14: Strengthening accountability for better learning outcomes			

Develop results-based monitoring and evaluation

Challenges	Policy directions	Examples	Responsible actors
Systems in most MENA countries focus on monitoring compliance rather than learning outcomes. Capacity is limited (1) for designing, implementing, and conducting monitoring and evaluation (M&E) of programs and (2) for generating information about what works based on evidence (for example, in most GCC countries). While data on learning are available, the information is often not used to improve learning; and the capacity to align all actors within the education system to improve teaching and learning (for example, in many GCC countries) is limited.	Shift to a results-driven culture, establish clear learning standards and targets, and strengthen education management information system (EMIS) capacity to provide reliable data on learning. Strengthen capacity in research, program design, implementation, and M&E functions of the education system. Focus more on communications to involve all stakeholders in decision making and establishment of goals.	Jordan uses benchmarks for achievement. Kuwait has established standards for supporting learning and implementation. Bahrain uses international test results to inform policy. Jordan's Center for Human Resources Development provides long-term monitoring of learning, with feedback loops to Ministry of Education. The health sector experience shows the potential of social and behavior change communications.	Ministry of education develops standards of learning, strengthens the EMIS, ensures use of data for decision making, and supports creation of research centers, which develop education research expertise. Ministry of finance provides funding for research functions.

Strengthen supervision and other support to schools

Challenges	Policy directions	Examples	Responsible actors
The inspection function focuses mainly on process and compliance with rules and standards, not on student learning results. There is a lack of support for disadvantaged geographic areas and for underperforming schools.	Change the role of inspector to providing instructional support for teachers with a focus on learning outcomes. Develop new models to monitor, evaluate, and support schools, such as focusing more on school self-evaluation. Have inspectors use results to work more effectively with schools. Target underperforming districts and schools with enhanced human and financial resources to improve learning.	Bahrain and Qatar have made efforts to shift supervision from compliance to instructional support. They have started implementing external school reviews combined with school self-reviews. Scotland's "How Good Is Our School?" framework can be adapted and used with school leaders, teachers, students, parents, and partners across the school community to support collaborative enquiry for self-evaluation. In the United States, the Boston public school system supports networks to improve learning, particularly for underperforming schools.	Ministry of education develops policies to reshape the role of inspectors and to shift resources to disadvantaged areas and schools.

table continues next page

TABLE A.1 Overview of MENA policy recommendations *(continued)*

Challenges	Policy directions	Examples	Responsible actors
Chapter 14: Strengthening accountability for better learning outcomes *(continued)*			
Shift to greater local and school-level autonomy for enhanced accountability			
Personnel functions and financial resource management are highly centralized in most MENA countries, and schools have little authority or responsibility for results. In cases where the devolution of authority and accountability to the school level has been piloted, this devolution is often not done systematically or systemwide (for example, in Egypt and Jordan). In cases where principals have greater autonomy, few incentives are given for performance, and system support for accountability is minimal (for example, in Lebanon, Qatar, and the United Arab Emirates).	Increase the role of district offices in supporting school leadership as a transitional step to strengthening school autonomy and pilot the devolution of authority and accountability to the school level. Build capacity at the ministry of education, district, and school levels to support local accountability and responsibility for results and establish financial management safeguards. Establish accountability mechanisms, provide opportunity for school-level input into hiring and firing of teachers, and consider student results in evaluation of principal's performance.	The Education Reform Program in Egypt piloted a model of resource allocation to schools in conjunction with the preparation of school improvement plans. Staff at the governorate and school levels received capacity building to improve their ability to carry out their roles. Lebanon, Qatar, and the United Arab Emirates provide greater autonomy to principals, which appears to affect learning results. Many OECD countries grant the school principal a substantial role in hiring and firing teachers.	Ministry of education provides training to district personnel to enable them to focus on improving school-level results and to develop policies, models, and capacity for decentralization, while building its own capacity to support local accountability. It ensures monitoring of results and establishes appropriate policy framework and safeguards for teacher personnel management. Ministry of finance provides financial resources for pilot programs and opportunities for devolving financial resource management to the school level.
Raise parents' expectation for learning			
Parents and students focus on credentials rather than actual learning outcomes.	Involve parents through communication strategies to increase the focus on actual learning outcomes.	The health sector has developed social and behavior change communications with a focus on the community.	Ministry of education establishes communications capacity and works closely with local structures.
Establish institutional arrangements for parents to support school accountability			
In some cases, data collection is limited and sharing is low, hampering the ability of parents and communities to pressure schools and teachers for school improvement (for example, in Jordan, Morocco, and the Republic of Yemen). Many systems have limited capacity to respond positively to pressure from parents or communities for improved accountability. Even in countries where parents participate and are engaged, local capacity is still too low to foster accountability and student learning (for example, in Qatar and the United Arab Emirates).	Create legal provisions for effective data collection, management, and sharing across schools, parents, and communities and disclose school data in user-friendly formats for parents and communities. Ensure that boards, councils, and school management committees (SMCs) have sufficient decision-making power that is adequately linked to resources and provide support for parents and communities to develop and implement school improvement plans.	Boston Public Schools in the United States provides parents with a detailed report card comparing their school's performance with that of other schools in the same district. Chile's new Local Education Services provide training and support to SMCs in several areas, including how to use data to improve school performance. In El Salvador, the Community-Managed Schools Program (EDUCO) strengthened the direct involvement and participation of parents and the community, which expanded rural schools and enrollments. Egypt's New Schools Program sought to engage community actors in school management by guiding the Board of Trustees in carrying out school self-assessments and improvement plans and in identifying gaps in learning, infrastructure, and school environment for community leaders to act on.	Ministry of education establishes data collection, management, and dissemination policies and sets up a technical department. It then establishes a body of facilitators to provide training and other support to parents, schools, and communities, working collaboratively with regional and local governments. Ministry of education and legislative branch of government create laws and regulations to establish SMCs involving parents and communities in school affairs. Ministry of education establishes a body of facilitators to develop and provide adequate training and support to boards, councils, and SMCs and promotes decentralized decision making. Ministry of finance budgets SMC operations and establishes mechanisms for timely transfers and financial decentralization.

table continues next page

TABLE A.1 Overview of MENA policy recommendations *(continued)*

Challenges	Policy directions	Examples	Responsible actors
Chapter 14: Strengthening accountability for better learning outcomes *(continued)*			
Provide a home environment that supports learning			
Children in MENA are less prepared for developing literacy than children in other regions, and they have less access to in-home materials for learning.	Use awareness campaigns and capacity-building efforts to inform parents of in-home approaches to support learning.	A study demonstrated the benefits of in-home exposure to literary Arabic and home reading.	Ministry of education communications units develop awareness campaigns to inform parents of in-home approaches such as home reading and storytelling to strengthen the literacy environment.
Use media and technology to support accountability systems			
Social media are not sufficiently exploited to strengthen accountability or to counter resistance to reforms.	Employ education dashboards and similar approaches to foster a move to open data- and evidence-based, transparent decision-making systems.	Egypt has leveraged modern technologies to promote accountability.	Ministry of education establishes information-sharing procedures using digital platforms and open communications through social media.

ECO-AUDIT
Environmental Benefits Statement

The World Bank Group is committed to reducing its environmental footprint. In support of this commitment, we leverage electronic publishing options and print-on-demand technology, which is located in regional hubs worldwide. Together, these initiatives enable print runs to be lowered and shipping distances decreased, resulting in reduced paper consumption, chemical use, greenhouse gas emissions, and waste.

We follow the recommended standards for paper use set by the Green Press Initiative. The majority of our books are printed on Forest Stewardship Council (FSC)–certified paper, with nearly all containing 50–100 percent recycled content. The recycled fiber in our book paper is either unbleached or bleached using totally chlorine-free (TCF), processed chlorine–free (PCF), or enhanced elemental chlorine–free (EECF) processes.

More information about the Bank's environmental philosophy can be found at http://www.worldbank.org/corporateresponsibility.

www.ingramcontent.com/pod-product-compliance
Lightning Source LLC
Chambersburg PA
CBHW041111070526
44584CB00002B/130